NOMENCLATURE 4.0
FOR MUSEUM CATALOGING

About the Series

The American Association for State and Local History Book Series publishes technical and professional information for those who practice and support history, and addresses issues critical to the field of state and local history. To submit a proposal or manuscript to the series, please request proposal guidelines from AASLH headquarters: AASLH Editorial Board, 1717 Church St., Nashville, Tennessee 37203. Telephone: (615) 320-3203. Website: www.aaslh.org.

About the Organization

The American Association for State and Local History (AASLH) is a national history organization headquartered in Nashville, Tennessee. AASLH provides leadership and support for its members who preserve and interpret state and local history in order to make the past more meaningful to all Americans. AASLH is a membership association representing history organizations and the professionals who work in them. AASLH members are leaders in preserving, researching, and interpreting traces of the American past to connect the people, thoughts, and events of yesterday with the creative memories and abiding concerns of people, communities, and our nation today. In addition to sponsorship of this book series, AASLH publishes *History News* magazine, a newsletter, technical leaflets and reports, and other materials; confers prizes and awards in recognition of outstanding achievement in the field; and supports a broad education program and other activities designed to help members work more effectively. To join AASLH, go to www.aaslh.org or contact Membership Services, AASLH, 1717 Church St., Nashville, TN 37203.

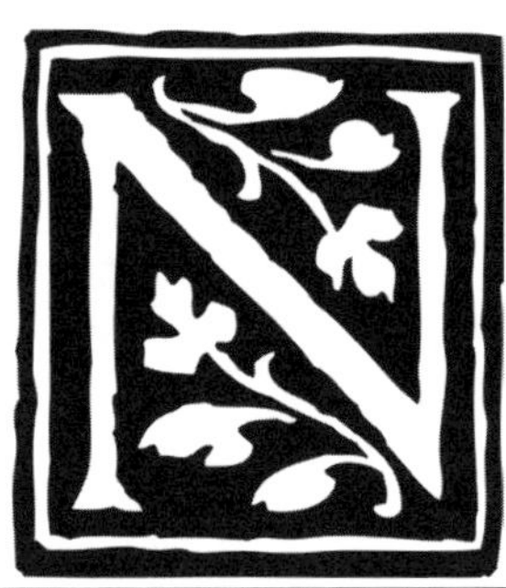

NOMENCLATURE 4.0
FOR MUSEUM CATALOGING

Fourth Edition
of Robert G. Chenhall's System
for Classifying Cultural Objects

Edited by
Paul Bourcier, Heather Dunn,
and the Nomenclature Task Force

ROWMAN & LITTLEFIELD
Lanham • Boulder • New York • London

Published by Rowman & Littlefield
A wholly owned subsidiary of The Rowman & Littlefield Publishing Group, Inc.
4501 Forbes Boulevard, Suite 200, Lanham, Maryland 20706
www.rowman.com

Unit A, Whitacre Mews, 26–34 Stannary Street, London SE11 4AB

ISBN: 978-1-4422-5098-7
e-ISBN: 978-1-4422-5099-4

∞™ The paper used in this publication meets the minimum requirements of American National Standard for Information Sciences—Permanence of Paper for Printed Library Materials, ANSI/NISO Z39.48-1992.

Printed in the United States of America

Contents at a Glance

Preface — vii
Acknowledgments — ix
An Introduction to Nomenclature 4.0 — xi
Nomenclature Users' Guide — xvii

CATEGORY 1: BUILT ENVIRONMENT OBJECTS — **1**
CATEGORY 2: FURNISHINGS — **43**
CATEGORY 3: PERSONAL OBJECTS — **81**
CATEGORY 4: TOOLS & EQUIPMENT FOR MATERIALS — **123**
CATEGORY 5: TOOLS & EQUIPMENT FOR SCIENCE & TECHNOLOGY — **261**
CATEGORY 6: TOOLS & EQUIPMENT FOR COMMUNICATION — **359**
CATEGORY 7: DISTRIBUTION & TRANSPORTATION OBJECTS — **409**
CATEGORY 8: COMMUNICATION OBJECTS — **449**
CATEGORY 9: RECREATIONAL OBJECTS — **501**
CATEGORY 10: UNCLASSIFIABLE OBJECTS — **527**

Alphabetical Index of Object Terms — 529

Preface

The American Association for State and Local History (AASLH) provides leadership and support for its members, who preserve and interpret state and local history in order to make the past more meaningful to all Americans. Publications are one way we support our members and the field at large in their work.

Since its first edition (published in 1978), *Nomenclature* has been one of our most important publications. In 1974 Robert Chenhall, then with what is now The Strong (née the Strong Museum), and a group of history museum professionals began work on a lexicon to address the need for consistency in naming and classifying collection objects as museums moved toward the computerization of their catalog records. The first edition was out of print by 1984. Instead of a second printing, the decision was made to revise and expand the 1978 version. The staff of The Strong led that effort, once again with the assistance of a committee from across North America. James Blackaby of the Bucks County Historical Society, Doylestown, Pennsylvania, revised the text and Patricia Greeno of The Strong edited the list of object terms. The second edition, *Revised Nomenclature*, was published in 1988.

More than a decade passed before work began on a third edition. In that time, many museums and historical societies converted from paper records to electronic databases and new standards of information management developed to meet the needs of the profession. In addition, a plethora of new objects, unaccounted for in earlier editions of *Nomenclature*, entered museum collections, requiring standardized cataloging terminology. *Nomenclature* had a lot of catching up to do.

Armed with survey work begun in 2000, Deb Arenz of the Nebraska Historical Society and another group of museum professionals set out to produce a new version of *Nomenclature* with improved utility and greater user-friendliness. The new committee agreed on an expanded lexicon hierarchy to include classifications, sub-classifications, and three levels of object terms within the existing ten *Nomenclature* categories. Under the direction of Ruby Rogers of the Cincinnati Museum Center, the team solicited and vetted new terms, reorganized terms into a new hierarchical structure, wrote a revamped introduction outlining new best practices, and made presentations of its progress at AASLH annual meetings. Paul Bourcier of the Wisconsin Historical Society assumed the task of editing the compiled content, and Alta Mira Press published *Nomenclature 3.0* in January 2010. The new volume contained 60 percent more terms than *Revised Nomenclature*.

The Nomenclature Committee (since redubbed the Nomenclature Task Force) did not disband as previous iterations of the group had done post-publication. While undergoing a series of membership changes, the committee, chaired by Paul Bourcier, worked with museum collections software vendors to adopt *Nomenclature 3.0* into their lexicons, produced and managed an online community resource on AASLH's website (http://community.aaslh.org/nomenclature/), and continued to solicit suggestions for additions and changes. For the first time, *Nomenclature* was an ongoing initiative. Recognizing that the standard needed to continually evolve to meet the profession's needs, the group resolved not to let another twenty years go by without an update. The Nomenclature Task Force began working on an update with Rowman & Littlefield Publishing Group in August 2013, and Heather Dunn of the Canadian Heritage Information Network was assigned to be co-editor in November 2014.

So here we are with the newest edition: *Nomenclature 4.0*, available in both book format and as an electronic file for use in collections management systems. And work is now in progress on a searchable, online version. On behalf of AASLH and the museum field, I want to express our thanks and appreciation to the Nomenclature Task Force members who have given countless hours to completing this vital project during the past several years, including the current members who compiled the latest edition:

Paul Bourcier, Editor
Wisconsin Historical Society, Madison, Wisconsin
Heather Dunn, Co-Editor
Canadian Heritage Information Network, Gatineau, Quebec
Kathleen Byrne
National Park Service, Harpers Ferry, West Virginia
Rosemary Campbell
Parks Canada / Independent Museum Professional, Ottawa, Ontario
John Hart, Jr.
Sullivan Museum and History Center, Norwich University, Northfield, Vermont
Sarah Kapellusch
Wisconsin Veterans Museum, Madison, Wisconsin
Ron Kley
Museum Research Associates, Hallowell, Maine
Jennifer Toelle
Smoky Hill Museum, Salina, Kansas

Jean-Luc Vincent
Parks Canada, Gatineau, Quebec
Geoffrey Woodcox
State Historical Society of North Dakota, Bismarck, North Dakota

And many thanks go out to past task force members who served from 2010–2013:

Joanne Avant
Texas Parks & Wildlife Dept., Austin, Texas
Laurie Baty
National Law Enforcement Museum, Washington, DC
Christopher Bensch
The Strong, Rochester, New York
Marie Demeroukas
Shiloh Museum of Ozark History, Springdale, Arkansas
Kristine Dobbins
Toy & Miniature Museum of Kansas City, Kansas City, Missouri
Trevor Jones
Kentucky Historical Society, Frankfort, Kentucky
Doug Kendall
New York State Historical Association, Cooperstown, New York
Vanya Scott
National Law Enforcement Museum, Washington, DC
Andy Stupperich
The Henry Ford, Dearborn, Michigan
Mick Woodcock
Sharlot Hall Museum, Prescott, Arizona

And one last thanks to each of you, striving to meet the highest standards in the profession as you serve your communities daily.

Bob Beatty
Chief Operating Officer
AASLH

ACKNOWLEDGMENTS

AASLH, the Nomenclature Task Force, and Rowman & Littlefield recognize the individuals and institutions that assisted in the creation of *Nomenclature 4.0* by submitting and reviewing suggestions for new terms and revisions, creating resources the Task Force used in its research, and in countless other ways. The geographical representation of the individuals and institutions listed below demonstrates how important *Nomenclature* is to museums across North America and beyond. We are indebted to the Wisconsin Historical Society, the Canadian Heritage Information Network, and the other institutions that have supported *Nomenclature* through the dedicated staff who have served on the Nomenclature Task Force over the years. We express our heartfelt thanks to the following for their assistance in this truly essential endeavor and their generous contribution to our field.

Individuals

Paul Adamthwaite	Naval Marine Archive: The Canadian Collection, Picton, ON
Jillian Allison	Denver Museum of Miniatures, Dolls, and Toys, Denver, CO
Ellen Anderson	Creative Spirit Art Centre, Toronto, ON
Deb Arenz	Nebraska Historical Society, Lincoln, NE
Erik R. Bauer	Peabody Institute Library, Peabody, MA
Susan J. Beates	Drake Well Museum, Titusville, PA
Ern Bieman	Canadian Heritage Information Network, Gatineau, QC
William Brewster	First Division Museum at Cantigny, Wheaton, IL
Elise Brunet	Law Society of Upper Canada, Toronto, ON
Laura Camilleri	Dufferin County Museum and Archives, Mulmur, ON
Alison Dingledine	Brockville Museum, Brockville, ON
Alice Donahue	National Electronics Museum, Baltimore, MD
Kiersten Frobom	Wisconsin Historical Society, Madison, WI
Ben Fuller	Penobscot Marine Museum, Searsport, ME
Art Goddart	Costa Mesa Historical Society, Costa Mesa, CA
Leah Griffiths	Shelburne County Museum, Shelburne, NS
Patricia Harpring	Getty Research Institute, Los Angeles, CA
Amy Heggemeyer	Spurlock Museum, University of Illinois at Urbana-Champaign, IL
Robert Henning	Campbell County Rockpile Museum, Gillette, WY
Kendra Hinkle	Andrew Johnson National Historic Site, Greeneville, TN
Micheal A. Hudson	American Printing House for the Blind, Louisville, KY
Andrea Hoffman	Wisconsin Veterans Museum, Madison, WI
Jeffery Kearney	Mountain View Museum & Archive, Olds, AB
Karin Kierstead	Association of Nova Scotia Museums, Halifax, NS
Dawnita Knight	Cheyenne River Sioux Tribe, Eagle Butte, SD
Madeleine Lafaille	Canadian Heritage Information Network, Gatineau, QC
Anne T. Lane	Mountain Heritage Center, Western Carolina University, Cullowhee, NC
Francis Lavoie	Canadian Heritage Information Network, Gatineau, QC
Janet Lundy	Valentine Richmond History Center, Richmond, VA
Adam MacPharlain	Cincinnati Art Museum, Cincinnati, OH
Julie Maio Kemper	Kentucky Historical Society and Thomas D. Clark Kentucky History Center, Frankfort, KY
Ian Mason	National Presbyterian Museum, Toronto, ON
Sharon McCullar	Lakeshore Museum Center, Muskegon, MI

Emma McDonald	Fort McMurray Historical Society, Fort McMurray, AB
Julie McVey	Mosaic Templars Cultural Center, Little Rock, AR
Corinne Midgett	High Point Museum, High Point, NC
Marven Moore	Maritime Museum of the Atlantic, Halifax, NS
Oralee O'Byrne	Age of Sail Heritage Center and Museum, Port Greville, NS
Anissa J. Paulsen	Maritime Museum of BC, Victoria, BC
Louise Pfotenhauer	Neville Public Museum, Green Bay, WI
Dianne Precosky	Fort Calgary National Historic Site, Calgary, AB
Lynn-Marie Richard	Maritime Museum of the Atlantic, Halifax, NS
Bill Roberts	Berkeley Historical Society, Berkeley, CA
Ruby Rogers	Cincinnati Museum Center, Cincinnati, OH
Ann Schempp	Moses Lake Museum & Art Center, Moses Lake, WA
Alain Simard	Canadian Museum of Immigration at Pier 21, Halifax, NS
Christopher Smith	Center for Sacramento History, Sacramento, CA
Maurice D Smith	Marine Museum of the Great Lakes at Kingston, Kingston, ON
Jennifer Spence	Kentucky Historical Society, Frankfort, KY
Wendy Thomas	Canadian Heritage Information Network, Gatineau, QC
Gwendolyn Waldorf	Tallahassee Museum, Tallahassee, FL
Patty Whan	Wellington County Museum & Archives, Fergus, ON

Institutions

Canadian Heritage Information Network/Réseau canadien d'information sur le patrimoine	Gatineau, QC
Cincinnati Museum Center	Cincinnati, OH
Collections Trust/Museum Documentation Association	London, England
English Heritage	London, England
Getty Research Institute	Los Angeles, CA
The Henry Ford	Dearborn, MI
Kentucky Historical Society	Frankfort, KY
Library of Congress	Washington, DC
Museum Research Associates	Hallowell, ME
National Law Enforcement Museum	Washington, DC
National Park Service	Washington, DC
Nebraska Historical Society	Lincoln, NE
Neville Public Museum	Green Bay, WI
New Bedford Whaling Museum	New Bedford, MA
New York State Historical Association	Cooperstown, NY
Parks Canada/Parcs Canada	Gatineau, QC
Sharlot Hall Museum	Prescott, AZ
Shiloh Museum of Ozark History	Springdale, AR
Smoky Hill Museum	Salina, KS
State Historical Society of North Dakota	Bismarck, ND
The Strong	Rochester, NY
Sullivan Museum & History Center	Norwich University, Northfield, VT
Texas Parks & Wildlife Dept.	Austin, TX
Toy & Miniature Museum of Kansas City	Kansas City, MO
Western Archaeological & Conservation Center	Tucson, AZ
Wisconsin Historical Society	Madison, WI
Wisconsin Veterans Museum	Madison, WI

An Introduction to Nomenclature 4.0

The Definition of *Nomenclature* xiii

What is *Nomenclature* and Why Should I Use It? xiii

What Does *Nomenclature* Do? xiii

The Format of *Nomenclature* Terms xiii

Inverted Word Order xiii

Singular Form xiv

The Structure of *Nomenclature 4.0* xiv

Alphabetical Listing of Terms xiv

Hierarchical Listing of Terms xiv

Categories, Classes, and Sub-Classes xiv

Three Hierarchical Levels of Object Terms xv

Organizational Principles xv

The Development of *Nomenclature* xvi

An Introduction to Nomenclature 4.0

The Definition of *Nomenclature*

What is *Nomenclature* and Why Should I Use It?

Nomenclature 4.0 for Museum Cataloging is a structured and controlled list of object terms organized in a classification system to provide a basis for indexing and cataloging collections of cultural objects. It was developed for people responsible for the creation and management of object records in human history collections within museums and other organizations, and focuses on objects relevant to North American history and culture. *Nomenclature* is based on three fundamental assumptions relating to the usefulness of catalog records for research, collection management, and exhibition planning:

(1) Catalog records are most useful if objects are named consistently;
(2) Creating functionally defined groupings of catalog records in a hierarchical format makes it easier to work with record groups; and
(3) Consistently cataloged records facilitate the sharing of data with researchers, other museums, and the public at large.

Standardized classification and controlled vocabularies greatly facilitate museums' ability to search, use, and share their collections data.

Nomenclature is built into the lexicons of many vendor-supported museum collections management systems, but it can also be a useful tool for museums with homemade databases and even for museums without computerized cataloging systems.

What Does *Nomenclature* Do?

Nomenclature 4.0 provides an extensive list of object terms based on the collections of many museums, and it relates each object term to others within a **hierarchical taxonomy based on the object's functional context**.

Nomenclature 4.0 includes thousands of terms. However, **it does not and should not include all possible names for all possible museum objects**. It is important to recognize that *Nomenclature* will not include all the terms any given museum needs, and that it will not be suitable for all purposes. Instead, *Nomenclature* provides a practical, flexible framework that has been used successfully by thousands of museums for more than three decades.

Because *Nomenclature* does not include all possible terms, some museums may need to expand the list of terms to express the finer points of distinction between similar but subtly different objects. *Nomenclature* is flexible, and the Nomenclature Task Force encourages museums having similar specialized collections to collaborate in compiling lists of specialized terms as the need arises. As long as new terms are added within the *Nomenclature* framework, reasons for adding the terms are documented, and additions are made only after careful consideration, *Nomenclature* will function as intended.

Bear in mind that ***Nomenclature* establishes a convention for object names only**. It is important to consider other standardized vocabularies for other useful pieces of data about museum objects and their characteristics, including materials, styles, design elements, geographic origins, manufacturing techniques, personal and corporate names, and related subjects and concepts. When considering new object terms, it is important to avoid using words that may belong in other fields of an object's catalog record such as "plastic," "wrought," "Civil War," or "suffrage." Computerized databases allow users to query multiple fields to narrow searches for objects that meet specific criteria.

Object terms in *Nomenclature* are indexing terms intended to facilitate data retrieval. They are not substitutes for fuller descriptions that may be useful for inventories, exhibition labels, catalog captions, or other applications. "Chair, Rocking" is a legitimate object term for *Nomenclature*, but "Chair, Victorian, walnut, with green needlework cushion" is not.

There are many useful books and online resources for learning more about data standards that apply to museum collections, including material developed and distributed by the Museum Computer Network, the Canadian Heritage Information Network, and the American Library Association (particularly its manual, *Cataloging Cultural Objects: A Guide to Describing Cultural Works and Their Images*).

The Format of *Nomenclature* Terms

Inverted Word Order

Anyone unfamiliar with *Nomenclature* may be puzzled by the book's extensive use of "inverted" terminology (e.g., "Chair, Rocking" or "License, Marriage," rather than "Rocking Chair" or "Marriage License"). Although this convention may seem awkward, *Nomenclature* was developed before

computers were in common usage, and at that time most cataloging systems were paper-based. Inverted word order served the valuable purpose of keeping similar objects together in alphabetical listings. It made more sense to have rocking chairs and folding chairs together under the "Chair" portion of an alphabetized object list than to have them scattered under "R" for rocking chairs and "F" for folding chairs. Although computers have made this practice less relevant, it still serves a valuable purpose in the alphabetical index of terms at the back of this book.

Exceptions to the inverted format do exist for terms for which inversion serves no practical purpose. Examples include "Certificate of Deposit," "Reward of Merit," and "Lazy Susan."

Singular Form

Most object terms are listed in singular form as it is more intuitive when cataloging objects individually, which is common practice in museums. When describing groupings of identical objects in a single catalog record, it is fine to continue to use the singular form (e.g., "Shoe" to indicate a pair of shoes). Doing so helps ensure consistency, which is important for computerized records. Remember that *Nomenclature* terms are indexing terms and that fuller descriptions (e.g., "Pair of shoes") may be made elsewhere in a catalog record.

Exceptions to the singular form do exist. Some object terms exist only in plural form, such as "Pants," "Scissors," or "Bars, Uneven." Other exceptions include broad terms for which singular forms are difficult; examples include "Jewelry," "Regalia," and various "Gear" terms under Sports Equipment.

The Structure of *Nomenclature 4.0*

Terms in *Nomenclature 4.0* are indexed in two ways—alphabetically and hierarchically according to object categories and classes.

Alphabetical Listing of Terms

Anyone interested in simply checking to see if a particular term is listed in *Nomenclature* should consult the alphabetical listing at the back of this book. The alphabetical index includes not only accepted, standardized object terms (preferred terms), but also alternate spellings and synonyms (non-preferred terms). This is done to facilitate reference, and for each non-preferred term, the alphabetical index notes the appropriate preferred term to use. Non-preferred terms are listed entirely in lower-case letters and do not appear in the hierarchical listing. The alphabetical index notes the sub-class (or class if there is no sub-class) in which each term is organized and the page number on which the term can be found in the hierarchical listing.

Hierarchical Listing of Terms

Categories, Classes, and Sub-Classes

Nomenclature's hierarchical listing, like those employed in scientific taxonomies, helps catalogers find the best term by grouping closely related objects together. *Nomenclature* organizes these groupings by function. Every human-made object has discoverable functions, ways in which the object was intended to mediate between people and their environment. There are three ways that objects mediate:

(1) they shelter us from the environment;
(2) they act on the environment; or
(3) they comment on the environment.

These functions define the ten major **categories** of the hierarchical listing in *Nomenclature 4.0*, which are conceptually unchanged from *The Revised Nomenclature for Museum Cataloging and Nomenclature 3.0*:

(1) Built Environment Objects (formerly Structures)
(2) Furnishings
(3) Personal Objects
(4) Tools & Equipment for Materials
(5) Tools & Equipment for Science & Technology
(6) Tools & Equipment for Communication
(7) Distribution & Transportation Objects
(8) Communication Objects
(9) Recreational Objects
(10) Unclassifiable Objects

The first nine categories are further divided into **classes**, the next hierarchical level that groups similar objects together by function. Many classes are further divided into **sub-classes**. Definitions are provided for all categories, classes, and sub-classes.

Categories, classes, and sub-classes appear consistently in the plural form to distinguish them from singular object terms. An outline of categories, classes, and sub-classes can be found on the inside front and back covers of this book. In the outline, "T&E" stands for "Tools & Equipment."

Those familiar with *Revised Nomenclature* or *Nomenclature 3.0* will notice that *Nomenclature 4.0* refers to "Category," "Class" and "Sub-Class," whereas previously the hierarchical levels were called "Category," "Classification," and "Sub-classification." This change was made because the noun forms, "Class" and "Sub-Class," are more appropriate labels than "Classification" (the action or process of classifying). This change also brings *Nomenclature* into line with the *Parks Canada Descriptive and Visual Dictionary of Objects,* which uses "Category" and "Class."

Revised Nomenclature and *Nomenclature 3.0* users will also notice that all references to "Artifacts," which used to appear in the names of some of the categories, classes, and sub-classes, have been replaced by "Objects" for the sake of consistency. This revision also harmonizes *Nomenclature* with the conventions used within the *Parks Canada Descriptive and Visual Dictionary of Objects.*

The changes to category names are as follows:

Built Environment Artifacts = Built Environment Objects
Personal Artifacts = Personal Objects
Distribution & Transportation Artifacts = Distribution & Transportation Objects
Communication Artifacts = Communication Objects
Recreational Artifacts = Recreational Objects
Unclassifiable Artifacts = Unclassifiable Objects

The changes to class and sub-class names are as follows:

Clothing Care Artifacts = Clothing Care Objects
Personal Assistive Artifacts = Personal Assistive Objects
Hair Care Artifacts = Hair Care Objects
Hygiene Artifacts = Hygiene Objects
Ceremonial Artifacts = Ceremonial Objects
Documentary Artifacts = Documentary Objects

Three Hierarchical Levels of Object Terms

Like *Nomenclature 3.0* before it, *Nomenclature 4.0* has a hierarchical arrangement of object terms *relative to one another* within each class or sub-class. This hierarchical arrangement of object terms is designed to help catalogers determine the best term rapidly and accurately and to speed the retrieval of information.

Nomenclature 4.0 presents the object term hierarchy in outline form, with one to three levels of terms, depending on the need for specificity. Within each class or sub-class, **primary object terms** are listed alphabetically in the left column of the outline. These are terms that have no broader term within the section. Indented under some primary object terms is an alphabetical list of narrower **secondary object terms**. These terms describe specific examples of the type of object noted by a primary term. Indented under some secondary object terms, in a third column, are even narrower **tertiary object terms**. Textbox 1.1 contains an example that shows the category, class, and sub-class, as well as the three-level term hierarchies in *Nomenclature 4.0.*

This hierarchical arrangement helps catalogers determine the most appropriate term for a given object and allows them to use a general term or one that is very specific. For example, a cataloger may know that an object is a carpenter's plane, but not necessarily what type of plane it is. The cataloger may elect to use the primary object term, "Plane," and stop there. But if he or she knows more about planes, the cataloger can instead use a narrower, secondary object term, such as "Plane, Grooving" or "Plane, Leveling." If the object is identified as a grooving plane, the secondary object term "Plane, Grooving" may be used, or the cataloger may wish to get even more specific and use an even narrower, tertiary object term, such as "Croze" or "Plane, Badger." The cataloger need use only one term, at whatever level of specificity is most useful or accurate.

When a cataloger enters a given term in an object name field, most museum collection software products automatically note that all the broader terms in the hierarchy apply to the object being cataloged. Some software products do this through the use of hierarchically organized lexicon records; others populate the object's catalog record with all the broader terms.

The hierarchical arrangement of object terms helps researchers. Object searches can be narrowed or broadened to include, for example:

(1) all items of furniture, or all support furniture, or only tables, or only some particular type of table;
(2) all musical instruments, or all keyboard instruments, or only pianos, or only spinets;
(3) all sports equipment, or all baseball gear, or only baseball gloves, or only catcher's mitts.

Organizational Principles

At the levels of categories, classes, and sub-classes, the general organizing principle of *Nomenclature* is functional context. Wherever possible, the object terms are also organized by functional context. However, it is often necessary to define object terms using other attributes, including:

(1) form (e.g., "Flask");
(2) location ("Chair, Patio");
(3) material ("Boater");
(4) context of use ("Pistol, Dueling");
(5) method of construction ("Bridge, Suspension");
(6) method of operation ("Clock, Mechanical");
(7) method of propulsion ("Sailboat"); or even
(8) fuel source ("Engine, Diesel").

It is sometimes impossible or impractical to differentiate on the basis of functional context because the functional context is common to all objects of a specific type, or because objects are used for multiple or unknown functions. In these cases, attributes other than functional context are used to group the terms to assist catalogers in determining the proper term and the level of specificity.

In general, *Nomenclature* avoids using terms that refer to attributes that belong in another field (such as materials, style, etc.). For example, *Nomenclature* does not include terms such as "Coat, Fur," because the term "Fur" belongs in a separate field for materials. There is, however, the occasional exception to that rule, such as "Hat, Straw," which serves to collocate

Textbox 1.1 Example of Hierarchical Structure in *Nomenclature 4.0*

Cabinet, Kitchen

Category 2: Furnishings
Furniture (Class)
Storage & Display Furniture (Sub-Class)
Cabinet (Primary Object Term)
Cabinet, Kitchen (Secondary Object Term)
Cabinet, Hoosier (Tertiary Object Term)

"Cabinet, Kitchen" is recognized not only as an example of furniture, but also as an example of a specific sub-class of furniture (storage and display furniture) and as an example of a cabinet. If a more precise term is required, the cataloger can use the tertiary-level term to indicate that a particular kitchen cabinet is more specifically a Hoosier cabinet.

more specific terms ("Boater," "Hat, Bergère," "Hat, Panama") and separate them from other hat terms.

The Development of *Nomenclature*

The Nomenclature Task Force has endeavored to create a product that is user-friendly, intuitive, comprehensive, and easy to use. That said, *Nomenclature* will always be a work in progress.

The *Nomenclature system*—including the first edition of Robert G. Chenhall in 1978, *Revised Nomenclature* in 1988, *Nomenclature 3.0* in 2010, and *Nomenclature 4.0* in 2015—has come about through voluntary contributions of terms and hierarchical structures by those institutions and individual professionals having sufficient interest, inclination, and expertise to make meaningful contributions. In each iteration, *Nomenclature* has expanded by inviting input from the museum community it serves.

Predictably, some individuals and institutions have invested more effort and energy than others. Just as predictably, some of the terms suggested for inclusion in the lexicon may represent personal, institutional, or regional preferences that do not reflect as broad a consensus as might be desired. Some areas of the *Nomenclature* hierarchy contain very specific terminology, whereas others have been developed only to a very general level. As contributions from multiple independent sources are merged, some inconsistencies and even contradictions are apt to be stirred into the mix, despite the best efforts of the Nomenclature Task Force and editors. However, *Nomenclature* continues to grow and improve, thanks to the dedication and expertise of hundreds of heritage institutions and individuals.

The Nomenclature Task Force invites those who have a specific interest and expertise within a given field to collaborate with colleagues in their discipline to develop terminology for the objects in their area of expertise and provide the Nomenclature Task Force with recommendations that they could endorse collectively.

As time goes on, *Nomenclature* will become a more flexible and versatile living medium whose further evolution lies squarely in the hands of its users. There are some exciting possibilities on the horizon. *Nomenclature* is being incorporated as a standard feature in an increasing number of commercial collections management software products. It is available as an electronic file for purchase by museums that wish to incorporate it within their own software products. The American Association for State and Local History (AASLH) and Parks Canada have agreed on the long-term goal of harmonizing their two standards, *Nomenclature* and the *Parks Canada Descriptive and Visual Dictionary of Objects*, which will promote standardized cataloging practices throughout the two countries. Furthermore, AASLH is pursuing the creation of a searchable, online database—*Nomenclature Online*. These initiatives will serve to increase the availability, usability, and adoption of *Nomenclature*.

We cannot predict how future technologies will affect the uses and usefulness of *Nomenclature*'s list of terms and classification structure, although we expect that new technologies will facilitate the sharing of data between museums on an unprecedented scale. The demands of the networked environment in the museum context are placing a new emphasis on the role and importance of museum documentation standards. Expectations of the public and professional user alike are increasing the pressure museums face to standardize and share their data at a local, national, or global level. Standards such as *Nomenclature* will allow museums to rise to that challenge.

Nomenclature Users' Guide

Using *Nomenclature 4.0* xix

Finding a Term xix

Unknown Objects xix

Adding Object Terms xx

Terms for Specialized Collections xx

Regional/Ethnic Terms xx

Terms for Natural History Collections xx

Terms for Archaeological and Ethnographic Collections xx

Terms for Raw Materials xx

Terms for Archival Lots xxi

Cross-Indexing xxi

Multi-Purpose Objects xxi

Combination Objects xxii

When Object Terms Are Not Mutually Exclusive xxii

Documentary Objects and Media xxii

Digital Objects xxii

"May Also Use" Notes xxiv

Object Sets xxiv

Object Components xxiv

Toys and Models xxv

Containers and Their Contents xxv

Product Packages xxv

Containers for Objects xxv

Containers for Consumable Products xxvi

Adopting *Nomenclature 4.0* xxvi

For First-Time Users of *Nomenclature* xxvi

For Users of Past Editions of *Nomenclature* xxvi

Changes From Previous Versions of Nomenclature xxvi

Vocabulary Upgrades for Collections Management Systems xxvii

Assistance for *Nomenclature* Users xxvii

NOMENCLATURE USERS' GUIDE

Using *Nomenclature 4.0*

The conventions suggested in this guide are intended to make recording, recovering, and sharing collection data easier and more consistent. All museums can benefit from data standardization, but the pragmatic needs and limitations of an institution also need to be considered. There is no single right answer for all circumstances. If a museum decides to depart from the recommended standard, the fact and the rationale of that decision should be well documented.

Finding a Term

Catalogers are advised to start by looking up likely terms in the alphabetical index at the back of the book. If a term is found, then go the page number indicated and find the term in the object term hierarchy. Look at broader and narrower terms and other terms grouped in the same part of the hierarchy to determine which term is most suitable.

Catalogers will notice that the alphabetical index includes multiple entries for certain terms. Sometimes different objects have identical names and spellings. Catalogers must differentiate between these homonyms by their hierarchical placement or by their qualifiers. For example, a cataloger trying to catalog a gun magazine might look up "Magazine" in the index and see the following entries:

Magazine	Other Documents
magazine, comic (use:	Book, Comic)
Magazine, Firearm	Armament Accessories
Magazine, Powder	Defense Structures
Magazine, Slide	Visual Communication Accessories

The term "Magazine" has multiple meanings and occurs multiple times in the index, but the various terms are differentiated either by qualifiers (the word after the comma), or by the hierarchy in which they are found (e.g., Defense Structures). When searching for a term for the gun magazine, the cataloger will note that the first entry for the term "Magazine" is part of the Other Documents sub-class, so it is not an appropriate term for the gun magazine. The cataloger would then scan down the list of terms in the index that begin with "Magazine" to see if an appropriate term exists with a qualifier. In this case, the cataloger would find and select the entry for "Magazine, Firearm."

Some non-preferred terms are listed more than once because catalogers have a choice of preferred terms to use. For example, the non-preferred term "microcomputer" is listed three times because a cataloger should select one of the preferred terms, "Computer, Desktop," "Computer, Handheld," or "Computer, Laptop." In cases of multiple index entries, choose the term that is most appropriate for the object.

If no likely terms for the object come to mind, catalogers are advised to look at the list of categories, classes, and subclasses inside the front and back covers. Select the likely category for the object based on its function, and then determine which class or sub-class is most appropriate for the object. Flip to the page for that class or sub-class and read the definition of the class or sub-class to confirm that it pertains to the object. Scan down the list of primary object terms. For any likely primary object term, check the list of narrower secondary and tertiary object terms to find the most appropriate term. Catalogers may use a broad or specific term, depending on their level of knowledge about the type of object being cataloged.

Nomenclature does not include definitions of object terms, and there is no single work containing authoritative definitions for every object listed in *Nomenclature.* It can help to keep a dictionary handy, along with a reference book or two relating to the kinds of objects that are being cataloged. Online dictionaries and other web-based references can offer a great deal of help. It can be useful to have an Internet browser open while cataloging. One online reference that is extremely helpful is the *Art & Architecture Thesaurus* (AAT) by the Getty Vocabulary Program. While the AAT does not cover every type of object included in *Nomenclature*, its coverage is far broader than the name implies. Another online resource that complements *Nomenclature* is the *Parks Canada Descriptive and Visual Dictionary of Objects*, which contains illustrations, definitions, French equivalents, and bibliographic references for many of the objects listed in *Nomenclature*.

Unknown Objects

The hierarchy of *Nomenclature* allows catalogers to assign a broad class to objects whose names or functions are unknown. If an object cannot be identified at all, catalogers can use "Object, Unidentified" from Unclassifiable Objects (Category 10).

Adding Object Terms

Terms for Specialized Collections

Some museums may find that the terms in *Nomenclature* are not adequate to provide meaningful distinctions among the objects in large, specialized collections. *Nomenclature* was never intended to incorporate *all* of the terms that might be appropriate for dealing with *all* collections. For example, *Nomenclature* includes the term "Sundial," but does not list any of the many different types of sundials; this level of specificity is sufficient for most museums. If a museum has a large collection of sundials and needs to differentiate among them, it may, after careful consideration, add its own terms to the lexicon and organize them as secondary object terms under "Sundial."

When deciding how to organize a new term hierarchically, be sure to refer to the definitions of *Nomenclature* classes and sub-classes and review existing object terms carefully to determine if any of them qualify as a broader term for your term. It is strongly recommended that museums check to see how other institutions have approached the same or similar objects. Develop a mutually acceptable set of object names to meet your needs and make your lexicon additions known to the Nomenclature Task Force, so that they may be considered for addition to future editions of *Nomenclature* for the benefit of others.

Regional/Ethnic Terms

Some museums are regionally or ethnically oriented. These museums may find it more appropriate to catalog their collections using regional/ethnic terms rather than "standard" *Nomenclature* terms that staff and visitors may find awkward and unfamiliar. While it is not necessarily wrong to use non-standard object names, doing so will make it more difficult to share data with other museums or outside researchers. Although it is not recommended, museums that choose to incorporate non-standard terminology into their object names should do so in a consistent fashion. A better solution is to use *Nomenclature*-approved terms and place the non-standard terms in an alternate name data field or descriptive field. Alternatively, regional and ethnic terms may be added as non-preferred terms for *Nomenclature* terms. It is much less time consuming to do initial classification using standardized terminology than it is to go back and reclassify later.

Terms for Natural History Collections

Although *Nomenclature* was created to deal with human-made objects, it can be used as a framework for broadly classifying natural history specimens as well. It is common for human history museums and historical associations to collect small numbers of these specimens, and *Nomenclature* accommodates this by including a few broad object terms that describe natural history specimens within the context of human activity. Examples include:

(1) "Biospecimen" and the narrower terms "Specimen, Animal" and "Specimen, Plant" under Biological T&E;
(2) "Geospecimen" under Geological T&E; and
(3) "Trophy, Game" under Achievement Symbols.

However, museums that need more specific terms for their specimens will require the use of naming conventions already established by the zoological, botanical, and geological sciences. It is recommended that catalogers use common (non-scientific) names for once-living things that are arranged according to a classification system (from broad kingdoms to narrow species). One lexicon authority that names and classifies living things is the online Integrated Taxonomic Information System. Other authorities exist for naming and classifying rocks and soils.

Catalogers may enter terms from these scientific classification authorities in a separate field or may enter them in the object name field and organize the standardized terms under "Specimen, Animal," "Specimen, Plant," or "Geospecimen" as appropriate. Software system limitations may prevent the organization of these natural history terms hierarchically, but this may not be important within the context of a history museum's needs. Using a lexicon authority for scientific specimens will not necessarily disturb or compromise the *Nomenclature* classification system.

Terms for Archaeological and Ethnographic Collections

Archaeological and ethnographic objects are objects that were created and used by human beings in the course of lives that involved conception, birth, beliefs, work, play, death, and other aspects of the human condition. But *Nomenclature* relies on determining the function of an object, and this can be challenging to determine for archaeological and ethnographic objects. For example, what might appear to be a weapon may in fact be a food preparation implement or a ceremonial object. Sometimes the object is so fragmented that it is impossible to determine function.

Despite this problem, archaeological and ethnographic objects nonetheless can be cataloged using the *Nomenclature* classification scheme; in fact, *Nomenclature 4.0* includes a large number of new terms for archaeological and ethnographic collections. If the function of the object is known, archaeological and ethnographic objects can be classified like any other. Some of the terms in Category 10 are useful for unidentified or fragmented objects.

Terms for Raw Materials

Many museums have examples of raw materials, such as a skein of wool, a sample of unworked pottery clay, or a piece of leather. In general, such objects should be classified along with the Tools & Equipment (T&E) category that would most probably be used in transforming that material into a finished product. Alternatively, such objects can be grouped with the T&E category that produced them as finished products. The same leather that is raw material to a shoemaker also can be viewed as a tanner's finished product, and the wool that is raw material for Textileworking T&E is a finished product of Agricultural T&E. The strengths and orientations of a

museum's collections may govern its choice of whether to regard a material such as leather as a finished product of one trade or as the raw material of another, or both.

That said, *Nomenclature* does include certain material genre terms. Several are listed under "Material, Animal" in Leather, Horn & Shellworking T&E and under "Stock, Metal" in Metalworking T&E, and "Bolt, Cloth" is listed under Needleworking Equipment. In many cases, a cataloger should use the term "Sample, Material" from Category 10 and enter the name of the material itself in a field dedicated to the materials of which objects are made. An appropriate term in a subject field may serve to associate the material with an activity.

Terms for Archival Lots

Nomenclature may be used to deal with batches of archival materials that may not be individually cataloged in the foreseeable future. Although *Nomenclature 4.0* includes such terms as "Archive" and "Fonds," catalogers may need to add other terms to the lexicon to assign an appropriately generic identity to such batches. Relating such batches to the classification structure of *Nomenclature* can be challenging. It may be possible to classify the entire collection as Government Records or Legal Documents, or the collection may consist of many types of records. And while a batch of archival materials may fit comfortably into the existing class of Documentary Objects, collections or accumulations of other types may pose classification challenges, especially if they were assembled with reference to criteria (e.g., material, shape, color, period, decorative motifs) independent of pragmatic function. In such instances, a cataloger may decide that a collection or assemblage of any sort represents a "documentation" of something, and thus can be classified under Other Documents. If a museum holds significant quantities of archival materials, archival description standards such as *Rules for Archival Description* (RAD) in Canada or *Describing Archives: A Content Standard* (DACS) in the United States should be consulted.

Cross-Indexing

No matter how any hierarchical taxonomy is structured, there are bound to be gaps and overlaps. Museum collections do not fall neatly into ten functional categories.

Nomenclature is a "monohierarchical" classification system. That means that every unique object term has one and only one position in the hierarchy; each term has one and only one immediate broader term (or parent term). The term "Dress, Wedding," for instance, is classified as a ceremonial object in Category 8, but it could have been classified as an article of clothing in Category 3. How can a cataloger ensure that such an object is cross-indexed in both categories? Rather than assign the same term to multiple places in the hierarchical system, **the recommended practice is to use more than one term to name the object**.

A single object can serve multiple functions or be named with terms that describe various characteristics of the object. Catalogers are strongly encouraged to use more than one term to describe a singular object if doing so will improve cross-referencing and make the object more accessible. Today's technology makes such cross-referencing easy. Some collections management software systems have multi-valued fields that allow the entry of multiple terms separated by delimiters such as vertical bars or semicolons. Other databases provide more than one field to accommodate multiple object terms.

Multi-Purpose Objects

An example of a multi-purpose object requiring more than one object term is a souvenir T-shirt. It is both an article of memorabilia (a documentary object) and a main garment (an article of clothing) and should be noted as both "Souvenir" and "T-Shirt." Countless types of objects can serve as souvenirs. It makes little sense to add to the lexicon hundreds of new terms with the word "souvenir" as a modifier (e.g., "T-Shirt, Souvenir") when the use of multiple existing terms serves to ensure proper cross-indexing.

Nomenclature 4.0 provides new ways of indexing multi-functional mobile devices. While *Nomenclature 3.0* included "Computer, Handheld," the new terms "Computer, Tablet," "Reader, Electronic," and "Smartphone" have now been added under the sub-class of Data Processing Devices, and it is advised that users cross-index by assigning more than one term to these objects. For example, while one purpose of smartphones is telecommunication, they are often used more for data processing, and so could be cross-indexed with both "Telephone, Cellular" from the Telecommunication Devices sub-class and "Smartphone" from the Data Processing Devices sub-class.

Textbox 1.2 notes several examples of cross-indexing multi-purpose objects.

When deciding which terms to include and where to place them, the Nomenclature Task Force considered how the use of multiple terms would enable catalogers to cross-index between categories, classes, and sub-classes.

Textbox 1.2 Cross-Indexing Multi-Purpose Objects

A ruler that serves as an advertisement for a business:
Use "Ruler" from Weights & Measures T&E *and* "Advertisement" from Advertising Media

A vase that is considered to be a work of art:
Use "Vase" from Horticultural Containers *and* "Artwork" from Art

A piano bench:
Use "Bench, Piano" from Musical Accessories *and* "Bench" from Seating Furniture

An egg timer:
Use "Timer, Egg" from Food Preparation Equipment *and* "Timer" from Timekeeping T&E

A chasuble:
Use "Chasuble" from Status Symbols *and* "Cloak" from Outerwear

A toy offered as a premium with a fast-food meal:
Use "Premium" from Advertising Media *and* a term from the "Toys" class

Combination Objects

Multiple terms should be used whenever an object consists of various components for which object terms exist. For example, a home entertainment center may be a piece of furniture with various built-in media players. A researcher will want to find the item whether he or she is searching specifically for furniture, sound communication equipment, or telecommunication equipment. The cataloger should use multiple terms to ensure such cross-indexing—"Cabinet, Entertainment" (from Display & Storage Furniture), "Phonograph" (from Sound Communication Devices), and "Radio" (from Telecommunication Devices). Textbox 1.3 notes several examples of combination objects. As many terms may be entered as software restrictions allow or as reason dictates.

Multiple terms may also be used to index objects that have been "recycled," such as a tire reused as a garden planter or a swing, or a guideboat fashioned into a bookcase.

Textbox 1.3 Cross-Indexing Combination Objects

A combination salt and pepper shaker:
Use "Saltshaker" *and* "Shaker, Pepper"

A flashlight key chain:
Use "Flashlight" *and* "Chain, Key"

A camera phone:
Use "Camera, Digital" *and* "Telephone, Cellular" *and/or* "Smartphone"

An alarm clock radio:
Use "Clock, Alarm" *and* "Radio, Table"

A bottle/can opener:
Use "Opener, Bottle" *and* "Opener, Can"

A pipe tomahawk that served as a presentation piece:
Use "Pipe" *and* "Tomahawk" *and* "Piece, Presentation"

A Swiss Army knife:
Use "Tool, Combination," *and* "Knife, Pocket," "Corkscrew," "Tweezers," etc.

When Object Terms Are Not Mutually Exclusive

Because object terms may be defined by many different attributes (e.g., function, form, location, material, context of use, method of construction, etc.), specific object terms listed in *Nomenclature* are not mutually exclusive. For this reason, one object may be described with more than one term *within* a given class or sub-class.

For example, a Noank sloop may be classified as both a sailboat (describing method of propulsion) and a commercial fishing vessel (describing context of use); both the term "Sloop, Noank" (a tertiary object term under the broader "Sloop, Fishing") and the generic term "Sloop" (a tertiary object term under the broader "Sailboat") should be used so that the Noank sloop may be found in a search for either boats or commercial fishing vessels. Textbox 1.4 notes several more examples of the use of multiple, non-exclusive terms.

Textbox 1.4 Cross-Indexing Objects with Multiple Terms within a Sub-Class

A self-propelled anti-tank gun:
Use "Gun, Self-Propelled" *and* "Gun, Anti-Tank"

An electric bass guitar:
Use "Guitar, Bass" *and* "Guitar, Electric"

A musical, mechanical, tall-case clock:
Use "Clock, Mechanical," "Clock, Musical," *and* "Clock, Tall-Case"

A purse seine:
Use "Net, Seine" *and* "Net, Purse"

A 35mm single lens reflex camera:
Use "Camera, Single Lens Reflex" *and* "Camera, 35mm"

A dining armchair:
Use "Armchair" *and* "Chair, Dining"

A saltbox parsonage:
Use "House, Saltbox" *and* "Parsonage"

An educational jigsaw puzzle:
Use "Puzzle, Jigsaw" *and* "Toy, Educational"

A serial dot matrix printer:
Use "Printer, Dot Matrix" *and* "Printer, Serial"

Documentary Objects and Media

Using multiple terms for singular items also comes in handy for cataloging certain documentary objects. *Nomenclature* distinguishes between objects that serve as media for recording information and objects that contain recorded information. The former are classified as Tools & Equipment for Communication (Category 6) and the latter as Documentary Objects (Category 8).

A cataloger should use more than one term for certain documentary objects to ensure proper cross-indexing with appropriate classes and sub-classes under Tools & Equipment for Communication. Textbox 1.5 notes several examples.

Digital Objects

Just as cross-indexing with *Nomenclature 4.0* allows museums to record information about both storage media (e.g., "Diskette") and intellectual content (e.g., "Report"), it also allows museums to record information about the format (e.g., "Document, Digital") for certain objects in the "Art," "Documentary Objects," and "Exchange Media" classes.

Museums have always been custodians of physical objects, responsible for their documentation and preservation. But now, an increasing proportion of the objects managed by museums are digital (for example, documents, artworks, photographs, and sound or video recordings in electronic format). Some of these materials are "born digital" and some are digitized from analog sources. Museums are increasingly consulting such controlled vocabularies as *Nomenclature* for guidance on naming these digital objects so they can be documented within their collections management systems.

Textbox 1.5 Cross-Indexing Documentary Objects and Supplies

A blank legal pad: *use* "Pad, Legal"
A legal pad on which notes are written: *use* "Pad, Legal" *and* "Note"

A blank postcard: *use* "Postcard"
A photographic postcard: *use* "Postcard, Picture" *and* "Print, Photomechanical"
A photographic postcard on which something is written: *use* "Postcard, Picture," "Print, Photomechanical," *and* "Correspondence"

A blank motion picture film: *use* "Film, Motion Picture"
A recorded motion picture film: *use* "Film, Motion Picture" *and* "Picture, Motion"

A blank audio cassette tape: *use* "Audiocassette"
A recorded audio cassette tape: *use* "Audiocassette" *and* "Recording, Audio"

A blank compact disc: *use* "Disc, Compact"
A compact disc containing browser software: *use* "Disc, Compact" *and* "Software, Browser"
A compact disc containing a sound recording: *use* "Disc, Compact" *and* "Recording, Audio"

Museums need to **ensure that only those digital objects that are actually a part of their collection are accessioned**. For example, museums should not accession digital images that only serve to document the physical objects in their collections—these digital images are part of the documentation of the physical collection, not part of the collection itself.

Museums do need to accession certain digital objects into their collections. This is normally the case when the digital object is a born-digital original, not a derivative. For example:

- Born-digital artworks
- Born-digital photographs
- Born-digital audio or video recordings (e.g., oral history recordings)
- Born-digital documents (e.g., e-mail correspondence)

In some unique cases, digital objects that are derivative (those created by converting from an analog source, e.g., scanning a photograph) may also be accessioned as part of the museum's formal collection. An example is a digital derivative that is the only copy available to the museum (in this case, the museum may have scanned a photo but does not hold the original format, or the original may have been lost or destroyed).

There is terminology in *Nomenclature's* Category 6: Tools and Equipment for Communication for describing the physical media used to store the digital file (e.g., "Diskette," "Drive, Flash," "Videodisc"). Category 6 also includes terminology to describe the applications that are used to create the digital objects (e.g., "Software, Word Processing," "Software, Email"). However, these terms are not sufficient to name and classify the digital file itself. In general, the digital object should be named just as a physical equivalent would be. For example: a digital photograph is still a photograph; a digital report is still a report; a digital ticket is still a ticket. So their object names should be "Photograph," "Report," and "Ticket."

However, the object's "digital" status should also be reflected in its object name (as a cross-reference) to make it possible for the museum to find all of its digital materials. Alternatively, the museum may choose to record the fact that the object is a digital object in a separate field. Textbox 1.6 provides some examples to illustrate the difference between cataloging three-dimensional objects, two-dimensional objects, and digital objects.

Nomenclature 4.0 includes new terms for digital objects within three different classes within the "Communication Objects" category—"Art," "Documentary Objects," and "Exchange Media." Textbox 1.7 outlines the new terms that have been added to *Nomenclature 4.0.*

Textbox 1.6 Cataloging Physical and Digital Objects

Physical 3D object (e.g., Ship):
Object name field—*use* "Ship"

Physical 2D objects (e.g., a painting or art photo depicting a ship):
Object name field—*use* "Painting" or "Photograph"
Subject field—*use* "Ship" (or term from an appropriate subject authority)

Digital objects (e.g., born-digital drawing or photograph depicting a ship):
Object name field—*use* "Drawing" or "Photograph"
Object name field—*also use* "Art, Digital" or "Document, Digital"
Subject field—*use* "Ship" (or term from an appropriate subject authority)
Although the primary name for this object is "Drawing" or "Photograph," the fact that it is a digital object should also be recorded. This can be done by adding a cross-reference in the object name field or recording the information in another field.

Textbox 1.7 New Terms for Digital Objects (New Terms in Bold)

PREFERRED TERMS
Category 8—Communication Objects

Art **Art, Digital**	May also use an appropriate term from Art to describe the type of work—e.g.: Drawing; Portrait; etc.
Documentary Objects Other Documents **Document, Digital** **Database** **Spreadsheet**	Use for digital documents *in addition to* an appropriate term from subclasses of Documentary Objects class to describe the function of the content
Exchange Media **Medium, Digital Exchange**	Use for digital exchange media *in addition to* an appropriate term from Exchange Media class, to describe the function of the content—e.g.: Money; Ticket; etc.

NON-PREFERRED TERMS (unique terms that are not just compounded from existing terms)
bitcoin [*use* "Medium, Digital Exchange" *and* "Money"]
cryptocurrency [*use* "Medium, Digital Exchange" *and* "Money"]
mail, electronic [*use* "Correspondence" *and* "Document, Digital"]

Like certain other terms in *Nomenclature* (such as "Recording, Audio" and "Recording, Video"), some of these terms for digital objects are not to be used alone, but are always used in combination (cross-indexed) with another object name to describe the content. Textbox 1.8 provides some examples of cross-indexing that can be used for digital objects.

Textbox 1.8 Cross-indexing Digital Objects

A diskette with a report on it: *use* "Diskette" *and* "Report" *and* "Document, Digital"

A CD with a digital audio file of a speech stored on it: *use* "Disc, Compact" *and* "Speech" *and* "Document, Digital"

A DVD with a digital video stored on it: *use* "Videodisc, Digital" *and* "Recording, Video" *and* "Document, Digital"

A diskette with a digital drawing stored on it: *use* "Diskette" *and* "Drawing" *and* "Art, Digital"

A flash drive containing a digital image used as an illustration: *use* "Drive, Flash" *and* "Illustration" *and* "Document, Digital"

"May Also Use" Notes

To aid catalogers in selecting appropriate additional terms for a given object, "may also use" notes are listed to the right of a number of object terms in the hierarchical listing of *Nomenclature 4.0*. These notes do not cover every possible instance in which an object may be cross-indexed with multiple terms; catalogers are encouraged to find additional terms for other objects as appropriate and useful. **"May also use" notes usually apply not only to the terms next to which they are listed, but also to all or most narrower terms**.

Object Sets

Nomenclature 4.0 includes a number of terms that describe sets of objects. Furniture sets are listed in a separate sub-class under Furniture. Other set terms may be found in Food Service T&E, Toilet Articles, Game Equipment, and Toys.

It is recommended that each object in a set is cataloged individually and that a separate catalog record is entered for the set. A descriptive field in the catalog record for the set should make reference to the specific pieces in the set and their catalog numbers.

If entire sets are cataloged in a single catalog record without separate records for the individual pieces, the set term should be used in addition to terms describing the objects in the set. For example, "Set, Sugar and Creamer," "Bowl, Sugar," and "Pitcher, Cream" all should be entered in the object name field(s) for the record. This practice ensures that all sugar bowls in a collection will be found in a query for "Bowl, Sugar," whether or not the bowls are parts of sets.

Catalogers may wish to add a set term to each of the catalog records for individual set pieces to indicate that each object is part of a set. For example:

(1) "Bed" and "Suite, Bedroom";
(2) "Dresser" and "Suite, Bedroom";
(3) "Highboy" and "Suite, Bedroom";
(4) "Table, Night" and "Suite, Bedroom"

In this case, a query for "Suite, Bedroom" will yield all objects in the collection that are parts of bedroom suites. The drawback to this practice is that, because each object is not itself a complete suite, the number of bedroom suites in the collection is falsely inflated.

Each institution should determine its own rules for cataloging sets based on what is practical. For example, it is impractical to catalog each chess piece in a chess set, but there may be merit in using the terms "Set, Chess," "Chessboard," and "Piece, Chess" in a single catalog record for the set.

Object Components

Nomenclature 4.0 features a number of terms to describe objects that serve as constituent parts of other objects. This is especially true of building components, electrical, power, and heating system components, transportation components, and game components. However, there are many thousands of terms that describe specialized parts of objects. It is impossible for *Nomenclature* to include them all. Catalogers are encouraged to determine what course of action to take to name and classify object parts not listed in *Nomenclature* and to be as consistent as is practical.

When cataloging object parts, some museums elect to use the term for the entire object. Thus, the term "Ax" would be entered in the object name field for the catalog record of an ax handle, and "Hamper" would be used for a hamper lid. This practice has the advantage of classifying the parts appropriately without glutting the lexicon with new terms. However, it gives a false impression because a handle is not an ax and a lid is not a hamper.

Some museums elect to add specific terms for components and organize the terms in the same classes or sub-classes as the term describing the entire object. In this practice, "Handle, Ax" would be added to the lexicon under Woodworking T&E (where "Ax" is) and "Lid, Hamper" would be added under Laundry Equipment (where "Hamper" is). This practice has the advantage of classifying the parts appropriately and labeling them accurately. However, because these terms are not included in *Nomenclature*, a museum would be responsible for ensuring the consistent and appropriate use of part terminology. It also may be difficult to find all axes and ax components in a single query. It is recommended that catalogers organize new part terms under an appropriate Accessories sub-class, if one exists. This practice would be consistent with the way a number of component terms are organized in *Nomenclature*.

The term "Fragment" in Category 10 is reserved for pieces that are not complete, constituent parts of other objects, but rather are portions of an object that have torn or broken off the whole item and do not necessarily have distinctive terms to describe them. If the identity of the whole object is known, the term for that object may also be entered, but again, use of

the whole object term in an object name field will be misleading. Catalogers should enter the term for the whole object in a subject field if appropriate.

Toys and Models

Most museums have miniature representations of objects. These items do not serve the practical purposes of the objects they depict, but rather are usually intended as toys, models, or works of art. Museums handle the naming and classification of such objects in different ways.

One solution is to use multiple terms for the object, e.g., "Cookstove" and "Toy" or "Ship" and "Model." The problem with this approach is that toys and models end up getting classified functionally with the objects they represent. A toy cookstove is not truly a cooking device nor is a model ship truly a watercraft. Any query for cooking devices or watercraft would result in inappropriate results and would require yet another query to find and eliminate all toys and models from the search results.

Another solution is to create compound terms for toys and models—e.g., "Cookstove, Toy" or "Ship, Model"—and organize them under the class "Toys" in Category 9 or as narrower terms under the primary object term "Model" under Other Documents in Category 8. One problem with this approach is that, because nearly any object may be represented by a toy or model, thousands of new object terms would end up appearing in Toys and Other Documents. Furthermore, these new terms would require a hierarchical structure of organization to enable the researcher to query for, say, all toy cooking devices or all model watercraft.

The best solution is to enter the term "Toy" or "Model" (or narrower term such as "Model, Patent" as appropriate) in the object name field and the term for the object that the toy or model represents in a separate subject field. After all, a three-dimensional representation is conceptually no different from a two-dimensional representation such as a drawing or painting. *Textbox 1.9* notes several examples of cataloging objects that depict or represent other objects.

However, one challenge in using *Nomenclature*'s hierarchy and terminology in a subject field is integrating them into a larger subject classification system, such as Library of Congress Subject Headings (LCSH), that includes topics other than object names. Usually, authorities such as LSCH have different organizing principles and different conventions (e.g., natural word order, use of plural nouns) than *Nomenclature*.

Textbox 1.9 Cataloging Objects that Depict Another Object

An advertising poster for a self-rake reaper:
Object name field—*use* "Poster"
Subject field—*use* "Reaper, Self-Rake" (or term from a subject authority)
A patent model of a self-rake reaper:
Object name field—*use* "Model, Patent"
Subject field—*use* "Reaper, Self-Rake"
A toy self-rake reaper:
Object name field—*use* "Toy"
Subject field—*use* "Reaper, Self-Rake"
A miniature art sculpture of a self-rake reaper:
Object name field—*use* "Miniature"
Subject field—*use* "Reaper, Self-Rake"
An actual self-rake reaper:
Object name field—*use* "Reaper, Self-Rake"

A query for "Reaper, Self-Rake" in the object field would yield all the self-rake reapers in a collection, but if someone were interested in the subject of self-rake reapers (perhaps for an exhibition, print article, or online feature), a query for "Reaper, Self-Rake" in the subject field would reap additional relevant collections.

Containers and Their Contents

Containers pose a special challenge in *Nomenclature*. On one hand, containers assume many forms, and unique terms exist to describe these forms, such as "Bag," "Bottle," "Box," "Can," and "Jar." On the other hand, many containers are specially made to hold specific objects and may be named and classified according to their intended contents.

Product Packages

Generic terms for container forms are listed in the Containers class in Category 7. Catalogers should use both "Package, Product" and a term from the Containers class to describe the container's form. Using two such terms cross-indexes the product package as both container and merchandising object. Catalogers should note the contents of a product package in a field other than the object name field.

Containers for Objects

Generally, *Nomenclature* classifies specialized containers for specific objects with the objects for which they were designed. Thus guitar cases are classified in Musical T&E with guitars (albeit in different sub-classes—Musical Accessories for the case and Musical Instruments for the guitar) and handkerchief boxes are classified in Personal Gear with handkerchiefs (albeit in different sub-classes—Personal Carrying & Storage Gear and Personal Assistive Objects, respectively). However, *Nomenclature* cannot include a term for every container designed to house a specific object.

A cataloger may add terms consisting of a generic container term such as "Case," modified with the *Nomenclature* term for the object for which the container is designed, such as "Clarinet," resulting in a new term, such as "Case, Clarinet." Such a term should be organized hierarchically under a broader *Nomenclature* term such as "Case, Musical Instrument." To accommodate the placement of such new terms, *Nomenclature* includes a number of broad object container terms such as "Case, Drafting Instrument," "Case, Medical Instrument," and "Case, Surveying Instrument." Many of these terms are organized in Accessories sub-classes in the classes that include the corresponding contained objects. Of course, a cataloger may

choose not to add a new term at all and just use the appropriate broader term from *Nomenclature*, such as "Case, Musical Instrument" for the clarinet case.

Containers for Consumable Products

While *Nomenclature* does include such terms as "Pillbox," "Bottle, Cologne," and "Can, Milk," it is beyond the scope of *Nomenclature* to name the many thousands of consumable products manufactured or processed by humans or to modify container terms to reflect the substances they contain or contained. The lexicon would be filled with terms such as "Bottle, Juice," "Can, Shaving Cream," and "Jar, Petroleum Jelly," and the task of organizing terms for such substances into a hierarchy would complicate matters considerably.

Catalogers should avoid including consumable product names in *Nomenclature* terms. Notation of consumable products is best left to a data field other than that designated for object names. This information may be entered as part of an object description or the product name may be entered in a subject field, especially if an appropriate lexicon authority is used to ensure consistency in data entry. In the latter case, a commercial mayonnaise jar would be entered thusly: "Package, Product" and "Jar" in the object name field; and "Mayonnaise" in the subject field. For many museums, including product names in a descriptive field is sufficient.

Adopting *Nomenclature 4.0*

For First-Time Users of *Nomenclature*

Some museums have never standardized their cataloging systems. They have records for virtually identical objects that have been called sofas, settees, love seats, couches, chesterfields, or davenports. Because these items have not been named consistently or grouped together using a rational classification system, the museum has to be sure to search for all the possible variations of all these different terms to find all the furniture of this type—and they can never be certain that all of them have been found. For these museums there is no easy way to convert their records to *Nomenclature* terminology and classification. It is much easier to avoid this sort of situation than to correct it after it occurs. There is hope, however. Here are three simple suggestions to get non-standardized records in order:

(1) Convert free-form object names to terms found in the *Nomenclature* lexicon. A staff person or a contractor familiar with *Nomenclature* should be able to do this quickly, but there's no magic conversion process that can do the job at the push of a button or click of a mouse.

(2) Move any descriptive information that has been intermixed with object names (like a "Victorian walnut turned-leg nightstand") to more appropriate data fields dealing with material, style, chronological period, etc. This will be time consuming, and there are no technological shortcuts.

(3) Relate the newly assigned object names to their respective categories in the *Nomenclature* classification system. Any one of the several computerized records management systems that incorporate *Nomenclature* will recognize valid object names as they are entered and will automatically assign them to the proper category, class, and sub-class, and even to broader object terms in the hierarchy.

For Users of Past Editions of *Nomenclature*

Changes From Previous Versions of Nomenclature

Since the publication of *Nomenclature 3.0* in 2010, more than 1,400 new terms have been added, based on suggestions from museums across Canada and the United States. The Nomenclature Task Force also consulted selected authoritative lexicons, particularly the Getty Vocabulary Program's *Art & Architecture Thesaurus* and the English Heritage *Archaeological Objects Thesaurus*, both available online.

Revised Nomenclature included about 8,500 preferred terms and about 1,500 non-preferred terms.
Nomenclature 3.0 included more than 13,700 preferred terms and nearly 1,800 non-preferred terms.
Nomenclature 4.0 includes more than 14,600 preferred object terms in the hierarchical listing and nearly 2,300 additional, non-preferred terms appear in the alphabetical listing in the back of the book.

A few terms from *Nomenclature 3.0* have been deleted because they were confusing, too specific, or too esoteric. Some terms have new spellings or new punctuation. Some terms have been moved between preferred and non-preferred status. A few terms were moved from one category or class to another, either to correct errors or to provide for a better fit. Substantial changes were made to the Water Transportation Equipment class, thanks to review and input from maritime field experts in both Canada and the United States. Small changes were made in the Art, Documentary Objects, and Exchange Media classes to accommodate the growing number of digital objects that are collected by museums. More than fifty coin terms were added to Exchange Media, and a number of terms in the Religious Objects sub-class were reorganized. *Nomenclature 4.0* has also been enhanced with terms for archaeological and ethnographic collections. Additionally, *Nomenclature 4.0* features corrections to nearly 100 typos and other small errors that appeared in *Nomenclature 3.0*.

Because there are thousands of collections and millions of objects that have been cataloged using previous *Nomenclature* editions, the Nomenclature Task Force resisted the temptation to eliminate inconsistencies whenever fixing them would require major changes to already cataloged records. However, because of the addition of hundreds of new terms and the alteration, deletion, and rearrangement of many existing terms, *Nomenclature* users will want to review existing data and make changes to be consistent with *Nomenclature 4.0*.

Vocabulary Upgrades for Collections Management Systems

The Nomenclature Task Force and Rowman & Littlefield have worked with the vendors of collections management software systems to upgrade built-in database lexicons and facilitate the migration of client data. Software upgrades are designed to modify or reorganize *Revised Nomenclature* or *Nomenclature 3.0* terms as appropriate and convert existing data in clients' catalog records accordingly.

Even after a conversion, museums will need to clean up some pre-existing data. First, museums will want to review all the local terms they added to their lexicons to determine if those terms are covered in some way by *Nomenclature 4.0*. If local terms are covered, then data will need to be changed to *Nomenclature 4.0* terminology. If they are not covered, museums will need to determine how to organize the local terms within the new hierarchical structure of *Nomenclature 4.0*.

Second, museums may want to review their records to determine if a better or more specific term from *Nomenclature 4.0* may now apply. For example, an object previously called a "Coin" may now be called a "Doubloon" or a "Quarter" and an object once called a "Record, Phonograph" may now be called a "Record, 33 1/3 RPM," a "Record, 45 RPM," or a "Record, 78 RPM."

Assistance for *Nomenclature* Users

The American Association for State and Local History (AASLH) has been the primary supporter of *Nomenclature* for more than 30 years, but its staff cannot respond to queries from *Nomenclature* users. There is, however, a web-based *Nomenclature Community* established by AASLH (http://community.aaslh.org/nomenclature/) specifically to facilitate contacts and mutual support among current and prospective users. Although there is no "official guru" available to provide authoritative answers to every question, there are people using this site who have decades of practical experience.

This web resource not only provides a forum for discussion and advice, it provides a way for *Nomenclature* users to submit proposals for additions and changes to *Nomenclature*. An ongoing Nomenclature Task Force will periodically review these proposals and make official updates to *Nomenclature*. These updates are expected to be incorporated into software lexicons and new publications (and/or an online resource) on a regular basis to avoid long delays which undermine the consistency that *Nomenclature* is intended to promote.

Contents

Preface vii
Acknowledgments ix
An Introduction to Nomenclature 4.0 xi
Nomenclature Users' Guide xvii

CATEGORY 1: BUILT ENVIRONMENT OBJECTS **1**
BUILDING COMPONENTS 1
Architectural Spaces 1
Barrier Elements 2
Construction Materials 3
Conveyance Devices 5
Door & Window Elements 6
Environmental Control Elements 8
Finish Hardware 10
Plumbing & Drainage Elements 12
Roof Elements 14
Stair Elements 15
Supporting Elements 16
Surface Elements 18
SITE FEATURES 20
STRUCTURES 23
Agricultural Structures 23
Ceremonial Structures 25
Civic & Social Structures 26
Commercial Structures 27
Cultural & Recreational Structures 29
Defense Structures 31
Dwellings 32
Hydraulic Structures 34
Industrial Structures 35
Institutional Structures 37
Outbuildings 38
Transportation Structures 39
Other Structures 41
CATEGORY 2: FURNISHINGS **43**
BEDDING 43
FLOOR COVERINGS 45
FURNITURE 46
Furniture Sets 46
Seating Furniture 47
Sleeping & Reclining Furniture 50
Storage & Display Furniture 52
Support Furniture 55
Other Furniture 58
HOUSEHOLD ACCESSORIES 59
Containers for Smoking & Tobacco 59
Decorative Furnishings 60
Furniture Coverings 61
Horticultural Containers 62
Storage & Display Accessories 63
Other Household Accessories 66
LIGHTING EQUIPMENT 68
Lighting Devices 68
Lighting Holders 71
Other Lighting Accessories 72
TEMPERATURE CONTROL EQUIPMENT 74
Firemaking Equipment 74
Heating & Cooling Equipment 75
Heating Equipment Accessories 76
WINDOW & DOOR COVERINGS 78
CATEGORY 3: PERSONAL OBJECTS **81**
ADORNMENT 81
Body Adornments 81
Hair Adornments 83
CLOTHING 84
Clothing Accessories 84
Dressingwear & Nightwear 88
Footwear 89
Headwear 91
Main Garments 95
Outerwear 100
Protective Wear 102
Underwear 103
PERSONAL GEAR 105
Clothing Care Objects 105
Personal Assistive Objects 107
Personal Carrying & Storage Gear 110
Smoking & Recreational Drug Equipment 114
TOILET ARTICLES 116
Beauty Supplies 116
Hair Care Objects 118
Hygiene Objects 120
CATEGORY 4: TOOLS & EQUIPMENT FOR MATERIALS **123**
AGRICULTURAL T&E 123
Cultivation Equipment 123
Feed Processing Equipment 126
Harvesting Equipment 127
Planting Equipment 132
Tending Equipment 133
ANIMAL HUSBANDRY T&E 134
Animal Care Equipment 134
Breeding Equipment 138
Farrier Equipment 139
Pet Supplies 141
Veterinary Equipment 142
FIBERWORKING T&E 144
FISHING & TRAPPING T&E 145
Fishing Equipment 145
Trapping Equipment 149
FOOD PROCESSING & PREPARATION T&E 150
Cooking Vessels 150
Food Preparation Accessories 152
Food Preparation Equipment 153
Food Processing Equipment 164
Food Storage Equipment 170
FOOD SERVICE T&E 173
Drinking Vessels 173
Eating Vessels 176
Eating & Drinking Utensils 178
Food Service Accessories 180
Food Service Sets 183
Serving Utensils 184
Serving Vessels 186
FORESTRY T&E 190
GLASS, PLASTICS & CLAYWORKING T&E 192
LEATHER, HORN & SHELLWORKING T&E 196
MASONRY & STONEWORKING T&E 203
METALWORKING T&E 207
MINING & MINERAL HARVESTING T&E 220
MULTIPLE USE T&E FOR MATERIALS 226
PAINTING T&E 229

PAPERMAKING T&E 232
TEXTILEWORKING T&E 234
Needleworking Equipment 234
Textile Manufacturing Equipment 239
WOODWORKING T&E 246
OTHER T&E FOR MATERIALS 260
CATEGORY 5: TOOLS & EQUIPMENT FOR SCIENCE & TECHNOLOGY 261
ACOUSTICAL T&E 261
ARMAMENTS 263
Ammunition 263
Armament Accessories 266
Artillery 274
Body Armor 275
Edged Weapons 277
Firearms 280
Percussive Weapons 283
ASTRONOMICAL T&E 284
BIOLOGICAL T&E 286
CHEMICAL T&E 289
Chemical Testing Devices 289
Labware 292
CONSTRUCTION T&E 295
ELECTRICAL & MAGNETIC T&E 297
Electrical & Magnetic Measurement Devices 297
Electrical Maintenance & Repair Equipment 299
Electrical System Components 300
ENERGY PRODUCTION T&E 303
Power Producing Equipment 303
Power Transmission Components 305
Other Energy Production T&E 306
GEOLOGICAL T&E 307
MAINTENANCE T&E 308
Dishwashing Equipment 308
Groundskeeping Equipment 309
Housekeeping Equipment 311
Laundry Equipment 313
MECHANICAL T&E 315
Mechanical Devices 315
Mechanical Measurement Equipment 318
MEDICAL & PSYCHOLOGICAL T&E 320
Dental Accessories 320
Dental Instruments 322
Medical Accessories 325
Medical Instruments 327
MERCHANDISING T&E 336
METEOROLOGICAL T&E 339
NUCLEAR PHYSICS T&E 341
OPTICAL T&E 343
REGULATIVE & PROTECTIVE T&E 345
Protective Devices 345
Regulative Devices 347
SURVEYING & NAVIGATIONAL T&E 349
Navigational Equipment 349
Surveying Equipment 352
THERMAL T&E 354
TIMEKEEPING T&E 355
WEIGHTS & MEASURES T&E 357
CATEGORY 6: TOOLS & EQUIPMENT FOR COMMUNICATION 359
DATA PROCESSING T&E 359
Data Processing Accessories 359
Data Processing Devices 361
Data Processing Media 363
Peripherals 364
DRAFTING T&E 366
MUSICAL T&E 368
Musical Accessories 368
Musical Instruments 370
PHOTOGRAPHIC T&E 376
Camera Equipment 376
Photographic Accessories 378
Photographic Media 380
Photoprocessing Equipment 381
PRINTING T&E 382
Bookbinding Equipment 382
Graphic Equipment 384
Printing Accessories 386
Replication Equipment 387
Typesetting Equipment 388
SOUND COMMUNICATION T&E 389
Sound Communication Accessories 389
Sound Communication Devices 391
Sound Communication Media 393
TELECOMMUNICATION T&E 394
Telecommunication Accessories 394
Telecommunication Devices 396
Telecommunication Media 398
VISUAL COMMUNICATION T&E 399
Visual Communication Accessories 399
Visual Communication Devices 400
WRITTEN COMMUNICATION T&E 402
Writing Accessories 402
Writing Devices 406
Writing Media 408
CATEGORY 7: DISTRIBUTION & TRANSPORTATION OBJECTS 409
AEROSPACE TRANSPORTATION T&E 409
Aerospace Transportation Accessories 409
Aircraft 411
Spacecraft 413
CONTAINERS 414
LAND TRANSPORTATION T&E 416
Land Transportation Accessories 416
Animal-Powered Vehicles 423
Human-Powered Vehicles 426
Motor Vehicles 428
RAIL TRANSPORTATION EQUIPMENT 431
Rail Transportation Accessories 431
Rail Vehicles 433
WATER TRANSPORTATION EQUIPMENT 436
Water Transportation Accessories 436
Watercraft 442
CATEGORY 8: COMMUNICATION OBJECTS 449
ADVERTISING MEDIA 449
ART 452
CEREMONIAL OBJECTS 456
Funerary Objects 456
Holiday Objects 458
Organizational Objects 459
Party Accessories 460
Religious Objects 461
Wedding Objects 466
DOCUMENTARY OBJECTS 467
Administrative Records 467
Declaratory Documents 468
Financial Records 469
Government Records 470
Graphic Documents 472
Instructional Documents 475
Legal Documents 476
Literary Works 477
Memorabilia 478
Other Documents 480
EXCHANGE MEDIA 487
PERSONAL SYMBOLS 491
Achievement Symbols 491
Belief Symbols 493
Personal Identification 495
Status Symbols 496
CATEGORY 9: RECREATIONAL OBJECTS 501
GAME EQUIPMENT 501
PUBLIC ENTERTAINMENT DEVICES 507
RECREATIONAL DEVICES 509
SPORTS EQUIPMENT 512
TOYS 520
CATEGORY 10: UNCLASSIFIABLE OBJECTS 527

Alphabetical Index of Object Terms 529

Category 1: BUILT ENVIRONMENT OBJECTS

Definition: **Objects originally created to define space for human activities or to be used as components of space-defining objects.**

Class:
BUILDING COMPONENTS

Definition: Objects originally created as part of a building's fabric. Although building components are distinct objects, they function as parts of larger structures rather than as independent units. Building components can be separate, distinct, and generally interchangeable structural, functional, or decorative parts of buildings such as beams, sinks, or architectural ornaments. This class also includes architectural samples integral to buildings, such as wall sections, staircases, or porches, as well as certain whole-structure building system components such as ventilators or furnaces. Excluded from this class are parts of buildings that are not integral parts of the structure, such as furnishings or lighting devices, which are included in the Furnishings category.

Sub-Class:
ARCHITECTURAL SPACES

Definition: Structures and other objects originally created to serve as space-defining internal or external architectural building components.

Primary Object Term	Secondary Term	Tertiary Term	Notes
Balcony			
Carport			
Catwalk			
Cellar			
	Cellar, Root		
	Cellar, Storm		
	Cellar, Wine		
Deck			
Gangway			
Loggia			
Platform			
Porch			
	Porch, Sleeping		
Porte-Cochère			
Portico			
Stage			
Stall, Shower			*Note:* For the plumbing fixture itself, use "Shower" from Plumbing & Drainage Elements
Stall, Toilet			
Stoop			
Tower, Church			
Turret			
Vault			

Sub-Class:
BARRIER ELEMENTS

Definition: Objects originally created to block passage, prohibit movement, shield dangerous situations, protect or cover openings, or otherwise serve as barriers in or on structures.

Primary Object Term	Secondary Term	Tertiary Term	Notes
Baluster			
Balustrade			
Case, Radiator			
Grate, Register			
Grille			
	Grille, Ventilator		
	Grille, Window		
Handrail			
Lattice			
Partition			
	Partition, Demountable		
	Partition, Folding		
Stanchion			
Wire, Barrier			
	Wire, Barbed		

Sub-Class:
CONSTRUCTION MATERIALS

Definition: Objects originally created for use in the construction of structures. This sub-class includes masonry units, such as bricks or stone, and ancillary materials such as plaster, flashing, or lath.

Primary Object Term	Secondary Term	Tertiary Term	Notes
Block, Construction			
	Block, Cinder		
	Block, Concrete		
	Block, Glass		
	Block, Mud		
Brick			
	Adobe		
	Brick, Air		
	Brick, Ashlar		
	Brick, Backing		
	Brick, Building		
	Brick, Capping		
	Brick, Face		
	Brick, Roman		
	Firebrick		
Concrete			
Lath			
Log, Timber			
Lumber			
	Board		
	Timber		
Mortar			
	Grout		
Nogging			
Pipe			
Plaster			
	Stucco		
Sealant			
	Caulk		
	Chinking		
	Daub		
	Flashing		
	Insulation		
	Oakum		
	Paper, Tar		
Stone, Building			
	Cornerstone		

Primary Object Term	Secondary Term	Tertiary Term	Notes
	Stone, Date		
	Stone, Dimension		
		Ashlar	
		Stone, Dressed	
	Stone, Quoin		
	Voussoir		
		Keystone	
		Springer	
Wattle			

Sub-Class:
CONVEYANCE DEVICES

Definition: Objects that are integral to structures and were originally created to transport humans, goods, or materials from one location in the structure to another. This sub-class also includes equipment and accessories that serve as parts of building conveyance systems.

Primary Object Term	Secondary Term	Tertiary Term	Notes
Chute			
	Chute, Coal		
	Chute, Deposit		
	Chute, Laundry		
	Chute, Mail		
	Chute, Refuse		
Dumbwaiter			
Elevator			
Escalator			
Firepole			
Indicator, Floor			
Lift, Stair			
Sidewalk, Moving			
Tube, Pneumatic			

Sub-Class:
DOOR & WINDOW ELEMENTS

Definition: Objects originally created to serve as doors, windows (whether fixed or movable), or components thereof, or to act as structural elements to complete openings. They may serve as coverings, operating mechanism components, or accessories for doors or windows. This sub-class does not include finish hardware such as knockers, kickplates, sash lifts, or shutterdogs.

Primary Object Term	Secondary Term	Tertiary Term	Notes
Awning			
Element, Door			
	Door		
		Door, Accordion	
		Door, Dutch	
		Door, French	
		Door, Garage	
		Door, Louver	
		Door, Pet	
		Door, Revolving	
		Door, Screen	
		Door, Sliding	
		Door, Storm	
	Doorbell		*Note:* May also use "Bell" from Sound Communication Devices
		Chime, Door	*Note:* May also use "Chime" from Sound Communication Devices
	Doorcap		
	Doorcase		
	Doorframe		
	Doorsill		
	Doorstone		
	Enframement, Door		*Note:* Use for the entire structure including case and frame and possibly other parts such as the door, fanlight, sidelight, etc.; may also use terms for each of the elements in the enframement
	Jamb, Door		
	Opener, Garage Door		
	Portcullis		
	Sweep, Door		
	Threshold		
	Track, Door		
	Weight, Door		
Element, Window			
	Box, Window		

Primary Object Term	Secondary Term	Tertiary Term	Notes
	Came		
	Cap, Window		
	Frame, Window		
	Jamb, Window		
	Pane		
	Sash, Window		
	Screen, Window		
	Seat, Window		*Note:* Use only for a built-in seat; for a free-standing bench, use "Bench, Window" from Seating Furniture
	Shutter, Exterior		
		Jalousie	
		Shutter, Louvered	
	Sill, Window		
	Stay, Casement		
	Ventilator, Window		
	Window		
		Fanlight	
		Sidelight	
		Window, Bay	
		Window, Casement	
		Window, Fixed	
		Window, Leaded	
		Window, Palladian	
		Window, Screen	
		Window, Sliding	
		Window, Storm	
		Window, Wheel	
Mullion			
Skylight			
Strip, Weather			
Transom			

Sub-Class:
ENVIRONMENTAL CONTROL ELEMENTS

Definition: Objects originally created to modify the environment of structures through mechanical means, whether as individual units or as a part of systems. Environmental control elements regulate heating, cooling, humidification, or ventilation. Portable equipment and equipment meant to heat or cool part of a structure are listed in Temperature Control Equipment.

Primary Object Term	Secondary Term	Tertiary Term	Notes
Blower			
Boiler, HVAC			
	Boiler, Hot Water		
	Boiler, Steam		
Cap, Vent			
Chiller			
Chimney			
	Smokestack		
Coil, HVAC			
Component, Chimney			
	Cap, Chimney		
	Door, Soot		
	Flue		
	Hood, Chimney		
	Lining, Flue		
	Pot, Chimney		
Component, Fireplace			
	Damper, Fireplace		
	Door, Fireplace		
	Fireback		
	Fireboard		
	Hearth		
		Hearth, Front	
		Hearthstone	
	Mantel		
Compressor, HVAC			
Condenser, HVAC			
Conditioner, Central Air			
Convector			
Damper, Ventilator			
Dehumidifier			
Duct, Air			

Primary Object Term	Secondary Term	Tertiary Term	Notes
Evaporator, HVAC			
Fan, Ventilation			
	Fan, Exhaust		
	Fan, Recirculating		
Filter, HVAC			
Fireplace			
Furnace			
	Furnace, Coal		
	Furnace, Electric		
	Furnace, Oil		
Heater, Convention			
Humidifier			
Panel, Solar Thermal			
Pump, Heat			
Radiator			
Thermostat			
Tower, Cooling			
Unit, Air Handling			
Unit, Baseboard			
Ventilator			

Sub-Class:
FINISH HARDWARE

Definition: Objects, usually made of metal, originally created to be visible, functional, and often decorative elements for the interior or exterior of buildings. This sub-class includes doorway accessories such as doorknobs or knockers, window accessories such as sash lifts or shutter dogs, and other objects such as brackets, strap hinges, or escutcheons.

Primary Object Term	Secondary Term	Tertiary Term	Notes
Bracket			
	Bracket, Flag		
	Bracket, Flowerpot		
	Bracket, Handrail		
	Bracket, Lamp		
	Bracket, Shelf		
	Bracket, Wall		
Device, Securing			*Note:* May also use "Device, Security" from Protective Devices, if appropriate
	Bolt, Chain		
	Bolt, Door		
	Bolt, Draw		
	Cleat, Awning		
	Fastener, Chain Bolt		
	Fitting, Keyhole		
	Hasp		
	Latch		
	Lock, Door		
	Lock, Window		
	Plate, Strike		
Escutcheon			
	Cover, Outlet		
	Plate, Key		
	Plate, Switch		
Hardware, Door			
	Bar, Pull		
	Bar, Push		
	Bumper, Door		
	Check, Door		
	Doorknob		
	Doorplate		
		Kickplate	
		Plate, Jamb	
		Pushplate	
		Rosette	

Primary Object Term	Secondary Term	Tertiary Term	Notes
	Handle, Door		
	Knocker		
	Ring, Door		
Hardware, Window			
	Bar, Shutter		
	Cord, Sash		
	Counterweight, Sash		
	Dog, Shutter		
	Lift, Sash		
Hinge			
	Hinge, Butt		
	Hinge, Strap		
Rail, Bar			
Rod, Stair			
Slot, Mail			
Valve			
	Valve, Pipe		

Sub-Class:
PLUMBING & DRAINAGE ELEMENTS

Definition: Objects originally created to serve as built-in receptacles for waste, as vessels or spaces for containing or dispensing water for sanitary needs, or as a means of dispensing water for drinking. Plumbing & Drainage Elements also treat water, facilitate or regulate the movement of water and sewage within structures, or transport unwanted water from one location to another, either through mechanical or gravitational means.

Primary Object Term	Secondary Term	Tertiary Term	Notes
Barrel, Rain			
Cistern			
Conditioner, Water			
Cover, Drain			
Disposer			
Downspout			
Drain			
Faucet			
Fitting, Pipe			
Fixture, Plumbing			
	Bathtub		
		Bath, Sitz	
		Footbath	
	Bidet		
	Fountain, Drinking		
	Fountain, Indoor		
	Shower		*Note:* Use only for the plumbing fixture itself; for the shower compartment, use "Stall, Shower" from Architectural Spaces
	Sink		
		Lavatory	
		Sink, Bathroom	
		Sink, Kitchen	
		Sink, Pedestal	
		Sink, Slop	
		Tub, Laundry	
		Washfountain	
	Toilet		
	Tub, Hot		
	Urinal		
Gutter			
Head, Shower			
Heater, Water			
Pipe, Plumbing			

Primary Object Term	Secondary Term	Tertiary Term	Notes
	Pipe, Drainage		
	Pipe, Riser		
	Pipe, Water Supply		
Pump, Plumbing			
	Pump, Sump		
	Pump, Water		
Scupper			
Spike, Gutter			
Sprayer, Sink			
Stand, Water Heater			
Stopper, Sink			
Tile, Drain			
Waterspout			
	Gargoyle		

Sub-Class:
ROOF ELEMENTS

Definition: Objects originally created as rooftop structures or structural elements or as architectural ornamentation for roofs.

Primary Object Term	Secondary Term	Tertiary Term	Notes
Antefix			
Bargeboard			
Belvedere			
Cap, Ridge			
Cote, Bell			
Cupola			
Dormer			
Finial			
Pendant, Architectural			
Rafter			
	Rafter, Show		
Rod, Lightning			
Roof			
Spire			
Steeple			
Walk, Widow's			

Sub-Class:
STAIR ELEMENTS

Definition: Objects originally created as structural or decorative components of staircases, whether rough and concealed or decorative and visible.

Primary Object Term	Secondary Term	Tertiary Term	Notes
Cap, Newel			
Newel			
Ramp			
	Ramp, Wheelchair		
Riser, Stair			
Staircase			
	Escape, Fire		
	Staircase, Spiral		
Stairstep			
Stringer			
Tread, Stair			

Sub-Class:
SUPPORTING ELEMENTS

Definition: Objects originally created to serve as structural elements for walls, ceilings, or floors. Some supporting elements may also serve as architectural ornamentation.

Primary Object Term	Secondary Term	Tertiary Term	Notes
Anchor, Architectural			
	Plate, Anchor		
	Tie, Anchor		
Bar			
	Bar, Reinforcing		
	Rod, Tie		
Beam			
	Beam, I		
	Beam, Truss		
	Crossbeam		
	Joist		
		Joist, Ceiling	
		Joist, Floor	
	Viga		
Brace			
Bracket, Pediment			
Buttress			
Capital			
Clip, Truss			
Column			
Corbel			
Entablature			
	Architrave		
	Cornice		
	Frieze		
		Metope	
		Triglyph	
Fishplate			
Foundation			
Girt			
Lintel			
Pedestal			
Pier, Supporting			
Pilaster			
Pillar			
Pin, Truss			

Primary Object Term	Secondary Term	Tertiary Term	Notes
Plate, Sill			
Plinth			
Pole, Tent			
Post			
	Puncheon		
Rib, Vault			
Rigging, Tent			
Shaft, Column			
Staddle			
Stake, Tent			
Stud			
Truss			
Wall			
	Parapet		

Sub-Class:
SURFACE ELEMENTS

Definition: Objects originally created as finishing elements in buildings, whether indoor or outdoor. Surface elements serve as permanent wall, floor, ceiling, or roof coverings, or as decorative trim.

Primary Object Term	Secondary Term	Tertiary Term	Notes
Covering, Wall			
	Backsplash		
	Baseboard		
	Block, Plinth		
	Brick, Decorative		
	Cresting		
	Frontispiece		
	Overmantel		
	Paneling		
	Pegboard		
	Rail, Wall		
		Rail, Chair	
		Rail, Peg	
		Rail, Picture	
		Rail, Plate	
	Siding		
		Siding, Asphalt	
		Siding, Board and Batten	
		Siding, Clapboard	
		Siding, Shiplap	
		Siding, Vinyl	
	Wainscoting		
	Wallpaper		
Enframement, Fireplace			
Flooring			
	Board, Floor		
	Flooring, Hardwood		
	Flooring, Puncheon		
	Flooring, Vinyl		
	Linoleum		
Molding			
	Block, Corner		
	Molding, Cap		
Mosaic			*Note:* May also use "Artwork" from Art
Ornament, Surface			

Primary Object Term	Secondary Term	Tertiary Term	Notes
	Ornament, Ceiling		
	Ornament, Fireplace		
	Ornament, Wall		
Panel			
	Panel, Fretwork		
Pediment			
Shingle			
	Shingle, Asphalt		
	Shingle, Fish Scale		
	Shingle, Shake		
Slate, Roofing			
Tessera			
Tile			
	Tile, Ceiling		
		Tile, Acoustical	
		Tile, Pressed Metal Ceiling	
	Tile, Decorative		
	Tile, Floor		*Note:* May also use "Flooring"
	Tile, Hearth		
	Tile, Hip		
	Tile, Ridge		
	Tile, Roof		
		Imbrex	
		Pantile	
	Tile, Wall		
Tympanum			

Class:
SITE FEATURES

Definition: Objects originally created as distinct elements associated with sites, buildings, or parts of larger structures. Rather than functioning simply as parts of larger structures, site features are independent entities that complement other structures. This class includes such objects as birdbaths, flagpoles, gates, and fences.

Primary Object Term	Secondary Term	Tertiary Term	Notes
Barrier, Site			
	Barrier, Road		
		Bollard, Road	
	Fence		
		Fence, Barbed Wire	
		Fence, Board	
		Fence, Chain Link	
		Fence, Electric	
		Fence, Picket	
		Fence, Rail	
		Fence, Snow	
	Gate		
	Gateway		
	Guardrail		
	Post, Fence		
	Post, Gate		
	Turnstile		
	Wall, Boundary		
Birdbath			
Birdhouse			
	Dovecote		
Cover, Manhole			
Cover, Well			
Doghouse			
Earthwork			
	Cairn		
	Geoglyph		
	Mound		
		Mound, Conical	
		Mound, Effigy	
		Mound, Linear	
		Mound, Platform	
	Trench		
Feature, Garden			
	Arbor		

Primary Object Term	Secondary Term	Tertiary Term	Notes
		Trellis	
	Bed, Planting		
	Exedra		
	Folly		
	Fountain, Water		
	Gazebo		
	Holder, Garden Sphere		
	Ornament, Garden		
		Sphere, Garden	
	Pavilion, Garden		
	Pedestal, Garden		
	Pergola		
	Planter, Garden		
	Urn, Garden		
Feeder, Wildlife			
	Feeder, Bird		
	Feeder, Deer		
	Feeder, Squirrel		
Firepit			
Flagpole			
Grate, Tree			
Lamppost			
Marker, Site			*Note:* May also use another term to describe the form of the marker, e.g., "Sign, Informational" from Visual Communication Devices or "Statue" from Art
	Marker, Boundary		
	Marker, Distance		
		Milestone	
	Monument		
		Cenotaph	
		Column, Memorial	
		Menhir	
		Obelisk	
		Stela	
		Stone, Commemorative	
		Stone, Rune	
Oven, Beehive			
Pavement			

Primary Object Term	Secondary Term	Tertiary Term	Notes
	Paver		
		Brick, Paving	
		Stone, Paving	
Petroform			
Sidewalk			
Stile			
Sweep, Well			
Wheel, Medicine			
Wheel, Well			
Windbreak			

Class:
STRUCTURES

Definition: Objects originally created to provide or define a space for human activities. Structures may be permanent, portable, climate-controlled, or open-air, and can be used for a variety of purposes including ceremonial, agricultural, recreational, commercial, cultural, civic, industrial, and social. Architectural samples integral to buildings such as wall sections, as well as separable, distinct, and interchangeable components, such as doorknobs or window sashes, are included in Building Components.

Sub-Class:
AGRICULTURAL STRUCTURES

Definition: Structures originally created for such agricultural purposes as housing animals, storing grains and farm implements, practicing animal husbandry, and processing plant and animal products. Structures used in the commercial processing of agricultural products are included in Industrial Structures. Agricultural Structures are not for public use or human habitation.

Primary Object Term	Secondary Term	Tertiary Term	Notes
Apiary			*Note:* May also use "Tool, Beekeeping" from Animal Care Equipment
	Beehive		
Barn			
	Barn, Cattle		
	Barn, Dairy		
	Barn, Hop		
	Barn, Horse		
	Barn, Tobacco		
Corncrib			
Elevator, Grain			
Granary			
Greenhouse			
House, Cow			
House, Fruit Drying			
House, Potato			
House, Poultry			
	Coop, Chicken		
	House, Broiler		
	House, Brooder		
House, Sugar			
House, Swine			
Malthouse			
Parlor, Milking			
Pigsty			
Shed, Livestock			

Primary Object Term	Secondary Term	Tertiary Term	Notes
	Shed, Cattle		
	Shed, Sheep		
Silo			
Stable			

Sub-Class:
CEREMONIAL STRUCTURES

Definition: Structures originally created for ceremonial activities such as conducting religious services or preparing or housing the remains of the dead. Such structures may also provide space for devotional activities, such as those associated with holy objects, or offer shelter for transformative practices or traditional rituals such as tea ceremonies. This sub-class does not include structures for human habitation or for ceremonial activities conducted by social organizations.

Primary Object Term	Secondary Term	Tertiary Term	Notes
Baldachin			
Maypole			
Structure, Funerary			
	Columbarium		
	Dolmen		
	Gravehouse		
	Home, Funeral		
	House, Charnel		
	Mausoleum		
	Tomb		
Structure, Religious			
	Chapel		
	Church		
		Cathedral	
	Kiva		
	Meetinghouse		
	Mosque		
	Pagoda		
	Shrine		
	Synagogue		
	Temple		
Teahouse			

Sub-Class:
CIVIC & SOCIAL STRUCTURES

Definition: Structures originally created to be used by governmental entities or community organizations for such purposes as governance activities, mail distribution, public safety, or social activities. This sub-class also includes structures used by trade, fraternal, professional, or special-interest groups or associations for such organizational purposes as conducting meetings or ceremonies or housing group-related objects such as regalia or records.

Primary Object Term	Secondary Term	Tertiary Term	Notes
Building, Public			
	Building, Public Safety		
		Station, Fire	
		Station, Police	
	Capitol		
	Courthouse		
	Hall, Town		
	Office, Post		
Building, Society			
Center, Community			
Customhouse			
Hall, Assembly			
	Clubhouse		
	Hall, Union		
	Lodge, Fraternal		
		Hall, Grange	
Library			

Sub-Class:
COMMERCIAL STRUCTURES

Definition: Structures originally created for the selling, exchanging, or housing of goods and services. This sub-class includes service industry-related structures, financial institutions, eating and drinking establishments, and mercantile buildings.

Primary Object Term	Secondary Term	Tertiary Term	Notes
Building, Financial			
	Bank		
	Exchange		
Center, Shopping			
	Mall, Shopping		
	Plaza, Shopping		
Facility, Lodging			
	Cabin, Tourist		
	Hotel		
	Inn		
	Lodge		
	Motel		
Restaurant			
	Café		
	Diner		
	Restaurant, Drive-In		
Saloon			
Shop			*Note:* Use for a building in which services are performed
	Barbershop		
	Laundry		
	Parlor, Beauty		
	Shop, Repair		
Stable, Livery			
Stand, Merchant's			
	Bookstall		
	Newsstand		
	Stand, Food		
		Stand, Produce	
Store			*Note:* Use for a building in which goods are sold
	Bakery		
	Bookstore		
	Confectionery		
	Pharmacy		
	Shop, Butcher		
	Shop, Florist		

Primary Object Term	Secondary Term	Tertiary Term	Notes
	Shop, Pet		
	Shop, Print		
	Store, Clothing		
	Store, General		
	Store, Grocery		
	Store, Hardware		
Tavern			
Warehouse			

Sub-Class:
CULTURAL & RECREATIONAL STRUCTURES

Definition: Structures originally created for cultural or recreational activities. Included in this sub-class are structures that provide exhibition space for music, fine arts, dance, drama, or collections of objects, flora, or fauna displayed for public benefit. Also included are structures that provide space for sporting or entertainment activities, usually for groups and occasionally for individuals.

Primary Object Term	Secondary Term	Tertiary Term	Notes
Building, Entertainment			
	Arcade		
	Casino		
	Funhouse		*Note:* May also use "Ride, Amusement" from Recreational Devices
	Hall, Bingo		
	Hall, Dance		
	Hall, Pool		
	Tunnel, Amusement		*Note:* May also use "Ride, Amusement" from Recreational Devices
Building, Exhibition			
	Aquarium, Public		
	Building, Fair		
	Building, Zoo		*Note:* May also use "Cage, Animal" from Animal Care Equipment if appropriate
	Museum		
	Planetarium		
Building, Performing Arts			
	Amphitheater		
	Bandstand		
	Hall, Concert		
	Nightclub		
	Shell, Band		
	Tent, Circus		*Note:* May also use "Tent" from Other Structures
	Theater		
		Cinema	
House, Tree			
Pavilion, Recreation			
Stand, Ticket			
Structure, Sports			
	Alley, Bowling		
	Arena		

Primary Object Term	Secondary Term	Tertiary Term	Notes
	Backstop		
	Bleacher		
	Cage, Batting		
	Goalpost		
	Grandstand		
	Gymnasium		
	Lodge, Sporting		
		Lodge, Fishing	
		Lodge, Hunting	
	Pool, Swimming		
	Rink, Skating		
	Scoreboard		
	Shack, Ice Fishing		
	Stadium		
	Stand, Deer		

Sub-Class:
DEFENSE STRUCTURES

Definition: Structures originally created for such defensive purposes as storing armaments and munitions, sheltering personnel, or providing fortified observational posts capable of facilitating or resisting attacks.

Primary Object Term	Secondary Term	Tertiary Term	Notes
Armory			
Arsenal			
Bastille			
Battlement			
Blockhouse			
Box, Sentry			
Bunker			
Cavalier			
Cheval de Frise			
Fortification			
	Barricade		
	Battery		
	Fort		
	Fortress		
	Palisade		
	Redoubt		
	Stockade		
Guardhouse			
Hall, Drill			
Magazine, Powder			
Mount, Panama			*Note:* May also use "Mount, Gun" from Armament Accessories
Outwork			
Post, Observation			
Shelter, Bomb			
Shelter, Gun			
Wall, Defensive			
	Breastwork		
	Rampart		

Sub-Class:
DWELLINGS

Definition: Residential structures originally created for long-term habitation rather than temporary housing. Dwellings are considered homes, places where domestic activities are conducted and personal effects are stored.

Primary Object Term	Secondary Term	Tertiary Term	Notes
Barrack			
Building, Apartment			
	Tenement		
Bunkhouse			
Castle			*Note:* May also use "Fortification" from Defense Structures
Condominium			
Dormitory			
Duplex			
Gatehouse			
House			
	A-Frame		
	Bungalow		
	Cabin		
		Cabin, Log	
	Chalet		
	Cottage		
	Farmhouse		
	Guesthouse		
	Hogan		
	Home, Mobile		
	House, Cape Cod		
	House, Clergy		
		Deanery	
		Parsonage	
		Rectory	
	House, Double-Pen		
	House, Foursquare		
	House, Fraternity		
	House, Garrison		
	House, Manor		
	House, Plantation		
	House, Ranch		
	House, Row		
	House, Saltbox		
	House, Shotgun		

Primary Object Term	Secondary Term	Tertiary Term	Notes
	House, Single-Pen		
	House, Sorority		
	House, Split-Level		
	Hut		
	Mansion		
	Quarters, Slave		
	Shack		
	Wickiup		
	Wigwam		
Longhouse			
Pueblo			

Sub-Class:
HYDRAULIC STRUCTURES

Definition: Structures originally created to collect, convey, regulate, or contain water for distribution, flood control, or power generation.

Primary Object Term	Secondary Term	Tertiary Term	Notes
Aqueduct			
Conduit			*Note:* Use for a building in which water is stored and distributed
Culvert			
Dam			
Floodgate			
Flume, Log			
Hydrant			
Lock			
Main, Water			
Millrace			
Penstock			
Pool			
Reservoir			
Sluice			
Spillway			
Tailrace			
Tower, Water			
Tunnel, Water			
Well, Water			

Sub-Class:
INDUSTRIAL STRUCTURES

Definition: Structures and complexes originally created for the extraction and processing of raw materials, the generation of power, the manufacture of goods, or the housing of industrial machinery.

Primary Object Term	Secondary Term	Tertiary Term	Notes
Building, Mine			
	Shafthouse		
Building, Utility			
	Plant, Power		
		Plant, Nuclear Power	
	Powerhouse		
Factory			
	Building, Sawmill		
	Factory, Metal		
		Foundry	
		Ironworks	
		Mill, Steel	
		Smelter	
		Tower, Shot	
	Mill, Paper		
	Mill, Powder		
	Mill, Pulp		
	Mill, Textile		
		Mill, Cotton	
		Mill, Woolen	
	Plant, Assembly		
	Plant, Beverage		
		Brewery	
		Distillery	
		Plant, Bottling	
		Winery	
	Plant, Chemical		
	Plant, Food		
		Cannery	
		Plant, Dairy	
		Plant, Packing	
		Refinery, Sugar	
	Pottery		*Note:* May also use “Workshop” if appropriate
	Tannery		
Mine, Industrial			
Pumphouse			

Primary Object Term	Secondary Term	Tertiary Term	Notes
Quarry			
Workshop			*Note:* Use for a building in which people engaged in crafts and trades make their products
	Shop, Cabinetmaking		
	Shop, Machine		
	Shop, Wheelwright		
	Smithy		

Sub-Class:
INSTITUTIONAL STRUCTURES

Definition: Buildings originally created for such institutional purposes as health and welfare services, educational instruction, or corrections.

Primary Object Term	Secondary Term	Tertiary Term	Notes
Center, Welfare			
	Almshouse		
	Asylum		
	House, Settlement		
	Orphanage		
	Shelter, Animal		
Facility, Correctional			
	Jail		
	Prison		
	Reformatory		
Facility, Health			
	Bath, Public		
	Clinic		
	Club, Health		
	Home, Nursing		
	Hospital		
	Infirmary		
	Sanatorium		
	Station, Comfort		
School			

Sub-Class:
OUTBUILDINGS

Definition: Buildings originally created for specific domestic activities such as baking or washing or for the storage of residential equipment and materials needed for domestic activities. Outbuildings are generally secondary structures adjacent to or near a dwelling or farm complex.

Primary Object Term	Secondary Term	Tertiary Term	Notes
Appentice			
Bakehouse			
Garage			
House, Carriage			
House, Kitchen			
Icehouse			
Outhouse			
Shed			
	Toolshed		
	Woodshed		
Smokehouse			
Springhouse			
Washhouse			
Wellhouse			
Workshop, Home			

Sub-Class:
TRANSPORTATION STRUCTURES

Definition: Structures and complexes originally created to facilitate the transportation of people and things. Such structures provide embarkation and debarkation points, allow passage from one point to another, house conveyance equipment, or serve as collection facilities for fares or tolls.

Primary Object Term	Secondary Term	Tertiary Term	Notes
Airport			*Note:* Use for the complex of landing field and associated buildings
Boathouse			
Bridge			
	Bridge, Covered		
	Bridge, Moveable		
		Bridge, Swing	
		Drawbridge	
	Bridge, Railroad		
	Bridge, Road		
	Bridge, Suspension		
	Bridge, Truss		
	Footbridge		
		Skybridge	
	Trestle		
Crane, Mail			*Note:* May also use "Crane" from Mechanical Devices
Depot			
	Depot, Bus		
	Depot, Railroad		
	Station, Subway		
Gantry, Signal			*Note:* May also use a signal term from Visual Communication Devices if appropriate
Hangar			
Landing, Marine			
	Dock		
	Pier		
	Wharf		
Lighthouse			
Meter, Parking			
Post, Hitching			
Pump, Gasoline			
Rack, Bicycle			
Ramp, Boat Launching			
Roundhouse			

Primary Object Term	Secondary Term	Tertiary Term	Notes
Shelter, Bus			
Slipway			
Snowshed			
Station, Railroad			*Note:* Use for the complex of depot and associated buildings
Station, Service			
Station, Weigh			
Structure, Toll			
	Machine, Toll Collection		
	Tollbooth		
	Tollgate		*Note:* May also use "Gate" from Site Features
	Tollhouse		
Terminal			
	Terminal, Airport		
	Terminal, Bus		
	Terminal, Marine		
	Terminal, Railroad		
	Terminal, Truck		
Tower, Control			
Tower, Signal			*Note:* May also use a signal term from Visual Communication Devices
Tunnel			
	Tunnel, Railroad		
Turntable, Railroad			

Sub-Class:
OTHER STRUCTURES

Definition: Structures that do not meet the definitions of this class's other sub-classes.

Primary Object Term	Secondary Term	Tertiary Term	Notes
Arch			
Building, Office			
Bulkhead			
Enclosure, Animal			
	Aviary		
	Kennel		
	Paddock		
	Stall, Animal		
Hut, Quonset			
Lean-To			
Sauna			
Station, Space			
Structure, Utility			
	Booth, Telephone		*Note:* May also use "Telephone" from Telecommunication Devices if the booth contains a telephone
	Office, Telegraph		
	Pole, Utility		
		Pole, Telephone	
Sukkah			
Tent			
	Tent, Camping		
	Tent, Canopy		
	Tipi		
Tower			
	Tower, Bell		
	Tower, Clock		
	Tower, Transmitting		
		Tower, Radio	
		Tower, Television	
	Watchtower		
		Tower, Fire	
Wanagan			

Category 2: FURNISHINGS

Definition: **Objects originally created to facilitate human activity and to provide for the physical needs of people, generally by offering comfort, convenience, or protection. Clothing is excluded from this category as it addresses only the needs of a specific individual. Furnishings are not objects used as active agents in other processes, such as objects used as tools or equipment; they passively enable human activity.**

Class:
BEDDING

Definition: Objects, usually soft furnishings, originally created to provide support for sleeping or to accessorize a bed. This class does not include beds and bed components, which are included in Furniture.

Primary Object Term	Secondary Term	Tertiary Term	Notes
Bag, Sleeping			
Bedcover			
	Bedspread		
	Comforter		
		Duvet	
	Coverlet		
	Quilt, Bed		*Note:* May also use "Quilt" from Art
		Quilt, Crib	
	Rug, Bed		
	Spread, Summer		
Bedsheet			
	Sheet, Blanket		
	Sheet, Fitted		
	Sheet, Flat		
Bedspring			*Note:* Use for a construction of springs and wire supports for a mattress
	Spring, Box		
Blanket			
	Blanket, Electric		
	Blanket, Trade		*Note:* May also use "Good, Trade" from Exchange Media
Bolster			
Canopy, Bed			
Casing, Bed			
	Cover, Bolster		
	Cover, Duvet		
	Cover, Mattress		
	Cover, Pillow		
Clip, Bedding			

Primary Object Term	Secondary Term	Tertiary Term	Notes
Cloth, Ground			
Hanging, Bed			
	Cloth, Tester		
	Curtain, Bed		
		Curtain, Case	
		Curtain, Foot	
		Curtain, Head	
	Headcloth, Bed		
	Net, Mosquito		
	Sparver		
	Tieback, Bed Curtain		
	Valance, Bed		
		Bedskirt	
		Valance, Double	
Headrest			
Mat, Bed			*Note:* Use for a woven mat placed between a feather mattress and the rope in a rope bed
Mat, Sleeping			
Mattress			
	Futon		
	Mattress, Air		
	Mattress, Feather		
	Mattress, Foam		
	Mattress, Horsehair		
	Mattress, Spring		
Pillow			
	Pillow, Air		
	Pillow, Body		
	Pillow, Feather		
	Pillow, Foam		
Pillowcase			
Sham			
	Sham, Bolster		
	Sham, Pillow		

Class:
FLOOR COVERINGS

Definition: Objects originally created as portable or temporary coverings for indoor or outdoor floors. This class includes rugs and carpeting but not permanently attached tile or linoleum, which are included in Building Components.

Primary Object Term	Secondary Term	Tertiary Term	Notes
Floorcloth			
	Crumbcloth		
	Drugget		
Mat			
	Doormat		
	Mat, Bath		
	Mat, Chair		
	Tatami		
Pad, Carpet			
Pad, Stove			
Rug			
	Carpet		
		Carpet, Broadloom	
		Tile, Carpet	
	Flatweave		
		Rug, Rag	
	Rug, Area		
	Rug, Hearth		
	Rug, Knotted		
	Rug, Linoleum		
	Rug, Loop		
	Rug, Oriental		
	Rug, Pelt		*Note:* The name of the animal may be entered in a subject field
	Rug, Pictorial		
	Rug, Shag		
	Rug, Stair		
	Rug, Throw		
Runner, Floor			
	Cover, Stair		
Turf, Artificial			

Class:
FURNITURE

Definition: Objects originally created to answer the physical requirements and comforts of people in their living and work spaces. This class includes desks, tables, beds, chairs, and outdoor furniture, but it excludes appliances and tools such as washing machines and ladders.

Sub-Class:
FURNITURE SETS

Definition: Matched groupings of objects originally created to meet the basic furniture needs of a specific area such as a nursery or bedroom. Note: Other terms also may be used to represent specific set components from other Furniture sub-classes, e.g., Seating Furniture, Support Furniture.

Primary Object Term	Secondary Term	Tertiary Term	Notes
Suite, Bedroom			
Suite, Dining			
Suite, Garden			
Suite, Hall			
Suite, Library			
Suite, Nursery			
Suite, Parlor			

Sub-Class:
SEATING FURNITURE

Definition: Objects originally created to allow one or more persons to sit upon or support a portion of their body, as in the case of footstools. Seating furniture includes both indoor and outdoor furniture and may be stationary pieces such as slipper chairs or allow for some movement such as rocking chairs. This class includes upright furniture that adjusts to a reclining position, but non-adjustable furniture that is designed for reclining is included in Sleeping & Reclining Furniture.

Primary Object Term	Secondary Term	Tertiary Term	Notes
Backrest			
Bench			
	Banquette		
	Bench, Bucket		
	Bench, Circular		
	Bench, Cradle		
	Bench, Deacon's		
	Bench, Folding		
	Bench, Garden		
	Bench, Park		
	Bench, Picnic		
	Bench, Window		*Note:* Use only for a free-standing bench; for a built-in seat, use "Seat, Window" from Door & Window Elements
	Board, Joggling		
	Booth, Restaurant		
	Pew		
	Settle		*Note:* May also use "Table" from Support Furniture
		Bench, Hooded	
		Table, Settle	
Chair			
	Armchair		
		Chair, Adirondack	
		Chair, Easy	
		Chair, Gondola	
		Chair, Great	
		Chair, Morris	
		Chair, Porter's	
		Chair, Tablet-Arm	
		Chair, Wing	
		Chair-Table	*Note:* May also use "Table" from Support Furniture

Primary Object Term	Secondary Term	Tertiary Term	Notes
	Chair, Ballroom		
	Chair, Barber's		
	Chair, Beanbag		
	Chair, Bed		
	Chair, Child's		
		Chair, Potty	
		Highchair	
	Chair, Commode		
	Chair, Corner		
	Chair, Dining		
	Chair, Fireplace		
	Chair, Folding		
		Chair, Beach	
		Chair, Camp	
		Chair, Director's	
	Chair, Garden		
	Chair, Hall		
	Chair, Hitchcock		
	Chair, Invalid		
		Chair, Bath	
	Chair, Kitchen		
	Chair, Massage		
	Chair, Office		
		Chair, Desk	
		Chair, Typing	
	Chair, Patio		
	Chair, Reclining		
	Chair, Rocking		
		Rocker, Platform	
	Chair, Shoeshine		
	Chair, Side		
	Chair, Slat-Back		
	Chair, Slipper		
	Chair, Smoking		
	Chair, Soda Fountain		
	Chair, Stacking		
	Chair, Step		
	Chair, Swivel		

Primary Object Term	Secondary Term	Tertiary Term	Notes
	Chair, Window		
	Chair, Windsor		
		Chair, Captain's	
	Klismos		
	Kubbestol		
	Seat, Theater		
Divan			
Glider, Porch			
Méridienne			
Pouffe			
Sofa			
	Bed, Sofa		
		Davenport	
	Seat, Love		
	Settee		*Note:* Use for a sofa that is all wood with an open or upholstered back
	Sofa, Chesterfield		
	Sofa, Conversational		*Note:* Use for a sofa seating two persons facing in opposite directions
	Sofa, Sectional		
	Veilleuse		
Stool			
	Barstool		
	Footstool		
		Hassock	
		Ottoman	
		Stool, Gout	
	Stool, Box		
		Stand, Bidet	
	Stool, Counter		
	Stool, Dressing		
	Stool, Folding		
		Stool, Camp	
	Stool, Kitchen		
	Stool, Milking		
	Stool, Stacking		
	Stool, Step		
	Taboret		
Swing, Porch			

Sub-Class:
SLEEPING & RECLINING FURNITURE

Definition: Objects originally created to allow one or more persons to lay down or recline. Component parts of beds such as headboards and footboards are also included in this sub-class.

Primary Object Term	Secondary Term	Tertiary Term	Notes
Bed			
	Bed, Bunk		
	Bed, Canopy		*Note:* May also use "Bed, Four-Poster" if appropriate
		Bed, Field	
	Bed, Child's		
		Bassinet	
		Cradle	
		Crib	
	Bed, Couch		
	Bed, Folding		
		Bed, Deception	
		Bed, Murphy	
	Bed, Four-Poster		
	Bed, Half-Tester		
	Bed, Hideaway		
	Bed, Hospital		
	Bed, Platform		
	Bed, Sleigh		
	Bed, Spool		
	Bed, Trundle		
	Bed, Water		
	Cot		
Chair, Deck			
Component, Bed			
	Bedpost		
	Footboard		
	Headboard		
	Siderail		
	Slat, Bed		
	Tester		
Couch			
	Recamier		

Primary Object Term	Secondary Term	Tertiary Term	Notes
Daybed			
Frame, Futon			
Hammock			
Lounge			*Note:* For an outdoor version of a lounge, use "Chair, Deck"
Table, Changing			
Table, Massage			

Sub-Class:
STORAGE & DISPLAY FURNITURE

Definition: Objects originally created to store, protect, and sometimes display items by means of an encasement with such features as shelves, drawers, cubbyholes, and doors. This sub-class does not include furniture created to store food, which is listed in Food Storage Equipment.

Primary Object Term	Secondary Term	Tertiary Term	Notes
Bookcase			*Note:* Use for a bookshelf with doors
Bookshelf			
Cabinet			
	Cabinet, Barber's		
	Cabinet, Card		
	Cabinet, China		
	Cabinet, Coin		
	Cabinet, Corner		
	Cabinet, Curio		*Note:* For a display cabinet made for commercial purposes, use "Cabinet, Display" from Merchandising T&E
	Cabinet, Entertainment		
		Cabinet, Media	
		Cabinet, Music	
		Cabinet, Phonograph	
		Cabinet, Radio	
		Cabinet, Record	
		Cabinet, Television	
	Cabinet, Filing		
	Cabinet, Hanging		
	Cabinet, Jewelry		
	Cabinet, Key		
	Cabinet, Kitchen		
		Cabinet, Hoosier	
	Cabinet, Liquor		
	Cabinet, Mail Sorting		
	Cabinet, Medicine		
	Cabinet, Office		
	Cabinet, Smoking		
	Cabinet, Thread		
	Cabinet, Utility		
	Cabinet, Weapon		
		Cabinet, Gun	
Canterbury			

Primary Object Term	Secondary Term	Tertiary Term	Notes
Chest			
	Cassone		
	Cellarette		
	Chest, Apothecary		
	Chest, Blanket		
	Chest, Campaign		
	Chest, Clothes		
	Chest, Hope		
	Chest, Sewing		
	Coffer		
Chest of Drawers			
	Chest on Chest		
	Chest on Frame		
	Chest, High		
	Chiffonier		
	Chifforobe		
	Commode		
	Desk, Butler's		
	Dresser		
	Highboy		
	Lowboy		*Note:* May also use "Table, Dressing" from Support Furniture
Counter			
	Bar, Serving		
	Island, Kitchen		
Cupboard			
	Cupboard, Corner		
	Cupboard, Hanging		
	Cupboard, Press		
		Press, Clothes	
		Press, Linen	
	Dresser, Kitchen		
	Sink, Dry		
Desk			
	Desk, Campaign		
	Desk, Computer		
	Desk, Drop-Front		
		Desk, Slant-Top	
		Vargueño	
	Desk, Kneehole		

Primary Object Term	Secondary Term	Tertiary Term	Notes
	Desk, Partner's		
	Desk, Quarter-Cylinder		
	Desk, Rolltop		
	Desk, School		
	Desk, Standing		
	Desk, Tambour		
	Desk, Writing		
	Secretary		
	Table, Writing		
		Table, Library	
Étagère			
Hutch			
Locker			
Safe			
	Safe, Gun		
Sideboard			
	Buffet		
	Credenza		
	Huntboard		
Unit, Shelving			
Wardrobe			
	Armoire		
	Kas		
	Shrank		

Sub-Class:
SUPPORT FURNITURE

Definition: Objects originally created to support and sometimes store or display items without encasement, to function as steps, or to serve as horizontal surfaces for such activities as working or dining.

Primary Object Term	Secondary Term	Tertiary Term	Notes
Easel			
Shelf			
	Shelf, Corner		
Stand, Floor			
	Bookstand		
	Hallstand		
	Lectern		
	Podium		
	Stand, Basket		
	Stand, Birdcage		
	Stand, Cabinet		
	Stand, Card		
	Stand, Dressing		
	Stand, Drinking		
	Stand, Globe		
	Stand, Hat		
	Stand, Map		
	Stand, Muffin		
	Stand, Pedestal		
	Stand, Plant		
	Stand, Portfolio		
	Stand, Printer		
	Stand, Shaving		
	Stand, Television		
	Stand, Tiered		
	Stand, Towel		
	Stand, Tray		
	Stand, Typewriter		
	Stand, Umbrella		
	Tree, Coat		
	Tripod		
	Valet		
	Washstand		
		Stand, Basin	
Step			
	Step, Bed		

Primary Object Term	Secondary Term	Tertiary Term	Notes
	Step, Library		
Table			
	Table, Breakfast		
	Table, Café		
	Table, Card		
	Table, Cart		
		Cart, Appliance	
		Cart, Computer	
		Cart, Media	
		Cart, Tea	*Note:* May also use "Cart, Food Service" from Food Service Accessories
	Table, Center		
	Table, Chart		
	Table, Cocktail		
	Table, Coffee		
	Table, Dining		
		Table, Extension Dining	
	Table, Dressing		
		Table, Commode	
	Table, Dropleaf		
		Table, Corner	
		Table, Gateleg	
	Table, Folding		
	Table, Game		*Note:* May also use a term from Game Equipment if appropriate
	Table, Garden		
	Table, Kitchen		
	Table, Manicure		
	Table, Mess		
	Table, Nesting		
	Table, Occasional		
	Table, Parlor		
	Table, Parsons		
	Table, Patio		
	Table, Pedestal		
	Table, Pembroke		
	Table, Picnic		
	Table, Rent		

Primary Object Term	Secondary Term	Tertiary Term	Notes
	Table, Restaurant		
	Table, Serving		
	Table, Side		
		Table, Console	
		Table, End	
		Table, Night	
		Table, Pier	
	Table, Snack		
	Table, Sofa		
	Table, Tea		
	Table, Tilt-Top		
	Table, Trestle		
	Table, Tripod		
	Table, Vesting		
	Table, Work		
		Table, Knitting	
		Table, Sewing	
	Workbench		

Sub-Class:
OTHER FURNITURE

Definition: Objects that do not meet the definitions of this class's other sub-classes. This sub-class includes such objects as mirrors or screens.

Primary Object Term	Secondary Term	Tertiary Term	Notes
Mirror			
	Mirror, Cheval		
		Glass, Dressing	
	Mirror, Curved		
	Mirror, Dresser		
	Mirror, Wall		
		Glass, Pier	
		Mirror, Architectural	
		Mirror, Girandole	
		Mirror, Hall	
		Mirror, Mantel	
Playpen			
Screen			
	Screen, Folding		
	Wall, Modular		

Class:
HOUSEHOLD ACCESSORIES

Definition: Objects originally created to be placed in or around a building for the convenience of people to enhance, complement, or facilitate the maintenance of their environment. This class includes: small furnishings, such as card receivers; non-furniture objects used for storage and display, such as boxes; and objects that protect furniture such as antimacassars. This class does not include furnishings intended primarily to communicate; they are classified as Art. Nor does this class include devices used in productive housekeeping activity such as cooking or maintenance. Curtains are included in Window & Door Coverings.

Sub-Class:
CONTAINERS FOR SMOKING & TOBACCO

Definition: Objects originally created to hold tobacco or smoking equipment or to serve as receptacles for tobacco-related waste such as ashes. Objects used by individuals to store smoking-related items on their persons are included in Personal Gear.

Primary Object Term	Secondary Term	Tertiary Term	Notes
Ashtray			
	Smoker		
	Stand, Smoking		*Note:* May also use "Stand, Floor" from Support Furniture
Box, Cigarette			
Container, Cigar			
	Box, Cigar		*Note:* Use for a storage accessory, not a product package
	Humidor		
Container, Spit			
	Box, Spit		
	Spittoon		
Holder, Pipe			
	Box, Pipe		
	Rack, Pipe		
	Stand, Pipe		
Holder, Pipe Cleaner			
Jar, Snuff			

Sub-Class:
DECORATIVE FURNISHINGS

Definition: Objects originally created primarily for decorative purposes. Decorative articles may have a secondary functional use, such as a plate, but their intended use is for display. Decorative ornaments used for special occasions are included in Holiday Objects and Party Accessories. Note: Terms from Art also may be used, as appropriate.

Primary Object Term	Secondary Term	Tertiary Term	Notes
Armor, Display			
Centerpiece			
Decoration			*Note:* Use this generic term for decoration that cannot be described with any of the other terms in this sub-class
Doll, Decorative			
	Doll, Boudoir		
Flora, Artificial			
	Flower, Artificial		
	Fruit, Artificial		
	Log, Artificial		
	Plant, Artificial		
Garniture, Clock			*Note:* May also use "Clock, Mantel" if appropriate
Hanging, Wall			*Note:* May also use a suitable term from Art, e.g., "Quilt," "Tapestry"
Knickknack			*Note:* Information about what the knickknack represents should be recorded in a subject field; this information may be entered according to the naming conventions and object terms used throughout *Nomenclature*, if appropriate
	Bowl, Decorative		
	Globe, Snow		
	Half-Figure		
	Mug, Decorative		
	Plate, Decorative		
Lamp, Lava			
Lithophane			
Mount, Taxidermy			
Ornament, Furniture			
Ornament, Window			
Screen, Table			
Towel, Show			
Trim, Furnishing			*Note:* For textile trim, use "Trim, Textile" from Needleworking Equipment
Urn, Decorative			

Sub-Class:
FURNITURE COVERINGS

Definition: Objects originally created as a protective and often decorative cover for furniture. This sub-class does not include bedcovers, which are included in Bedding, or tablecloths, which are included in Food Service Accessories.

Primary Object Term	Secondary Term	Tertiary Term	Notes
Antimacassar			
Cover, Furnishing			
	Carpet, Table		
	Cover, Chair Arm		
	Cover, Chair Seat		
	Cover, Cushion		
	Cover, Desk		
	Cover, Dust		
	Cover, Grill		
	Cover, Lamp		
	Cover, Stool		
	Cover, Throw Pillow		
	Cover, Toilet Seat		
	Slipcover		
Doily			
Lambrequin			*Note:* Use for a mantel cloth
Mat, Furniture			
	Mat, Table		
Runner, Furniture			
	Runner, Table		
Scarf, Furniture			
	Scarf, Bureau		
	Scarf, Piano		
	Scarf, Table		
Throw			
	Afghan		
	Throw, Chair		
	Throw, Sofa		
	Throw, Table		

Sub-Class:
HORTICULTURAL CONTAINERS

Definition: Objects originally created to hold living plants, cut specimens, or bulbs in the home. Horticultural containers can be purely functional or serve in a decorative capacity, either as the original container or as a vessel used to conceal the original container.

Primary Object Term	Secondary Term	Tertiary Term	Notes
Basket, Flower			
Bell, Garden			
Bowl, Bulb			
Bowl, Flower			
Cachepot			
Case, Wardian			
Frog, Flower			
Planter			
	Flowerpot		
		Flowerpot, Hanging	
	Jar, Strawberry		
	Jardinière		
Saucer, Flowerpot			
Vase			
	Vase, Bud		
	Vase, Flower		
	Vase, Wall		

Sub-Class:
STORAGE & DISPLAY ACCESSORIES

Definition: Objects, too small to be considered furniture, originally created to store or display such items as small furnishings, articles of clothing, works of art, and household linens either on walls, floors, or horizontal surfaces such as tables. Large or more substantial storage and display pieces are included in Storage & Display Furniture. Other storage objects are included in Food Preparation Accessories, Toilet Articles, and other classes featuring the objects they contain.

Primary Object Term	Secondary Term	Tertiary Term	Notes
Basket, Household			
	Basket, Hanging		
Board, Key			
Box, Household			
	Box, Bible		
	Box, Candle		
	Box, Dresser		
	Box, Incense		
	Box, Letter		
	Box, Missal		
	Box, Presentation		
	Box, Recipe		
	Box, Wall		
	Chest, Medicine		
	Chest, Silver		
	Strongbox		
Caddy, Drawer			
Case, Curio			
	Box, Shadow		
Cozy, Toilet Paper			
Frame			
	Frame, Mirror		
	Frame, Picture		*Note:* May also use "Holder, Photograph" from Photographic Accessories if appropriate
Hanger			
	Hanger, Picture		
	Hanger, Plant		
	Hanger, Plate		
Holder			
	Bar, Towel		
	Holder, Bottle		
	Holder, Match		
	Holder, Scarf		

Primary Object Term	Secondary Term	Tertiary Term	Notes
	Holder, Shoe		*Note:* Use for a hanging container with multiple pockets
	Holder, Spill		
	Holder, Toilet Paper		
	Holder, Watch		
	Stacker, Diaper		
Hook, Household			
	Hook, Ceiling		
	Hook, Wall		
		Hook, Coat	
		Hook, Picture	
		Hook, Towel	
		Hook, Wardrobe	
Jar, Bell			
Jar, Watch			
Jar, Water			
	Hydria		
Magnet, Refrigerator			*Note:* May also use "Advertisement" from Advertising Media or "Decoration" from Decorative Furnishings if appropriate
Nail, Picture			
Pocket, Crib			
Pocket, Wall			
Rack			
	Coatrack		*Note:* Use for a wall-mounted rack; for a floor-standing object, use "Tree, Coat" from Support Furniture
	Rack, Book		
	Rack, Boot		
	Rack, Firewood		
	Rack, Gun		
	Rack, Hat		*Note:* Use for a wall-mounted rack; for a floor-standing object, use "Stand, Hat" from Support Furniture
	Rack, Key		
	Rack, Magazine		
	Rack, Media		
		Rack, Record	
	Rack, Music		
	Rack, Newspaper		

Primary Object Term	Secondary Term	Tertiary Term	Notes
	Rack, Plant		
	Rack, Plate		
	Rack, Spoon		
	Rack, Tie		
	Rack, Tool		
	Rack, Towel		*Note:* Use for a wall-mounted rack designed for many towels; for a smaller object, use "Bar, Towel;" for a floor-standing object, use "Stand, Towel" from Support Furniture
Rod, Closet			
Roller, Towel			
Safe, Candle			
Safe, Match			*Note:* Use for a wall-mounted container
Stand			*Note:* Use for a small stand designed for tables or shelves; for floor stands, use "Stand, Floor" from Support Furniture
	Easel, Picture		
	Stand, Flower		
	Stand, Mucilage		
	Stand, Plate		
	Stand, Watch		
Tray, Household			
	Receiver, Card		
	Tray, Candlesnuffer		
	Tray, Dresser		

Sub-Class:
OTHER HOUSEHOLD ACCESSORIES

Definition: Household accessories that do not meet the definitions of this class's other sub-classes. This sub-class includes objects used to control pests, dispense fragrance, and facilitate certain activities in the home such as tightening rope beds. This sub-class does not include objects listed in such classes and sub-classes as Toilet Articles, Maintenance T&E, Regulative & Protective T&E, Art, and Holiday Objects.

Primary Object Term	Secondary Term	Tertiary Term	Notes
Bedkey			
Bellpull			
Bookend			
Bootjack			
Castor			
Catcher, Water			
Cover, Air Conditioner			
Cover, Ash			
Cover, Flue			
Cup, Caster			
Curtain, Shower			
Cushion			
	Pad, Chair		
Device, Pest Control			
	Flywhisk		
	Swatter, Fly		
	Trap, Insect		
		Catcher, Fly	
		Flypaper	
		Flytrap	
		Trap, Roach	
	Trap, Rodent		
		Mousetrap	
		Rattrap	
	Zapper, Bug		
Dispenser, Fragrance			
	Bowl, Potpourri		
	Burner, Incense		*Note:* For a ceremonial incense burner, use "Censer" from Religious Objects
	Cassolette		
	Freshener, Air		
	Jar, Potpourri		

Primary Object Term	Secondary Term	Tertiary Term	Notes
Doorstop			*Note:* May also use "Hardware, Door" from Finish Hardware if appropriate
Gate, Safety			
Glass, Picture Frame			
Ladder			
	Stepladder		
Material, Fragrance			
	Incense		
		Stick, Incense	
	Potpourri		
Pad, Furniture			
Pillow, Throw			
Plug, Drain			
Pole, Sash			
Pot, Paste			
Purifier, Air			
Rail, Safety			
	Bar, Grab		
	Rail, Toilet Safety		
Ring, Shower Curtain			
Scraper, Boot			
Screen, Candle			
Seat, Toilet			
Trellis, Plant			
Warmer, Bed			

Class:
LIGHTING EQUIPMENT

Definition: Objects originally created to provide illumination. This class includes lighting accessories such as candlesnuffers and wick trimmers, general purpose portable lighting devices such as kerosene lanterns, and specialized fixtures such as streetlamps and theater lighting devices.

Sub-Class:
LIGHTING DEVICES

Definition: Objects originally created to shield and protect a burning substance such as oil, or that are connected to an energy source such as electricity. Lighting devices may be free-standing, portable, or fixed in place. Exposed forms of illumination are included in Lighting Holders.

Primary Object Term	Secondary Term	Tertiary Term	Notes
Corona			
Droplight			
Fixture, Lighting			
	Fixture, Ceiling		
		Chandelier	
		Light, Pendant	
		Light, Recessed	
		Light, Track	
	Fixture, Combination		
	Fixture, Electric		
	Fixture, Gas		*Note:* May also use "Chandelier" for a gasolier
	Fixture, Wall		
		Sconce	
Flashlight			
Floodlight			
Jacklight			*Note:* May also use "Lure" from Fishing Equipment if appropriate
Lamp			
	Lamp, Burning Fluid		
	Lamp, Camphene		
	Lamp, Candle		
		Lamp, Fairy	
	Lamp, Carbide		
	Lamp, Desk		
	Lamp, Electric		
		Lamp, Battery Operated	
	Lamp, Floor		
	Lamp, Gas		
	Lamp, Gasoline		

Primary Object Term	Secondary Term	Tertiary Term	Notes
	Lamp, Kerosene		
		Lamp, Banquet	
	Lamp, Mantel		
	Lamp, Oil		*Note:* Use for a lamp designed to burn whale oil, seal oil, colza oil, or rosin oil
		Lamp, Argand	
		Lamp, Astral	
		Lamp, Carcel	
		Lamp, Hitchcock	
		Lamp, Moderator	
		Lamp, Rumford	
		Lamp, Wanzer	
	Lamp, Pole		
	Lamp, Reflector		
	Lamp, Safety		
		Lamp, Davy	
		Lamp, Stephenson	
	Lamp, Semiliquid		
		Lamp, Betty	
		Lamp, Crusie	
		Lamp, Grease	
		Lamp, Lard	
	Lamp, Spark		
	Lamp, Spirit		
	Lamp, Spout		
	Lamp, Student		
	Lamp, Table		
	Lampion		
Lantern			
	Lantern, Candle		
	Lantern, Carbide		
	Lantern, Dark		
	Lantern, Electric		
	Lantern, Gasoline		
	Lantern, Kerosene		
	Lantern, Oil		
Light, Emergency			
Light, Night			
Light, Outdoor			

Primary Object Term	Secondary Term	Tertiary Term	Notes
	Light, Bollard		
	Light, Solar		
	Streetlamp		
Light, Rope			
Light, String			*Note:* May also use "Light, Holiday" or "Light, Christmas Tree" from Holiday Objects if appropriate
Light, Strobe			
Projector, Light			
Searchlight			
Spotlight			
Striplight			
	Borderlight		
	Footlight		

Sub-Class:
LIGHTING HOLDERS

Definition: Objects originally created to hold or support an unshielded exposed flame. Shielded forms of illumination are included in Lighting Devices.

Primary Object Term	Secondary Term	Tertiary Term	Notes
Candleholder			
	Bracket, Candle		
	Candelabrum		
	Candlestand		*Note:* May also use "Stand, Floor" from Support Furniture
		Torchère	
	Candlestick		
		Candlestick, Hogscraper	
		Candlestick, Miner's	
		Chamberstick	
	Girandole		
	Holder, Taper		
		Jack, Wax	
Cresset			
Holder, Lamp			
Holder, Rushlight			
Holder, Splint			
Holder, Torch			
Torch			
	Flambeau		
	Torch, Tiki		

Sub-Class:
OTHER LIGHTING ACCESSORIES

Definition: Lighting objects that do not meet the definitions of this class's other sub-classes. This sub-class includes objects originally created: as functional or decorative components of lamps or fixtures; as controls for illumination sources, either through mechanical means or through the ignition or extinguishing of burning substances; or to service lamps or fixtures. This sub-class also includes objects originally created to be burned as a source of illumination or to produce artificial light in a lighting device.

Primary Object Term	Secondary Term	Tertiary Term	Notes
Bobeche			
Bulb, Light			
	Bulb, Black Light		
	Bulb, Fluorescent		
	Bulb, Halogen		
	Bulb, Incandescent		
	Bulb, Neon		
	Bulb, Ultraviolet		
	Diode, Light-Emitting		
	Tube, Fluorescent		
Burner, Lamp			
Candle			
	Candle, Pillar		
	Taper		
Candlelighter			
Candlesnuffer			
Changer, Bulb			
Chimney, Lamp			
Console, Lighting			
Counterweight, Lamp			
Dimmer			
Douter			
Extinguisher, Candle			
Filler, Lamp			
Finial, Lamp			
Follower, Candle			
Glass, Hurricane			
Globe, Lamp			
Grisett			
Harp, Lamp			
Lightstick			

Primary Object Term	Secondary Term	Tertiary Term	Notes
Luster			
Mantle, Lamp			
Pick, Wick			
Pole, Lamplighter			*Note:* Use for a long pole with attached wick used by gas lamplighters
Prism			
Reflector			
Rushlight			
Shade, Lighting			
	Lampshade		
		Lantern, Paper	
	Shade, Candle		
	Shade, Smoke		
Splint, Lighting			
Timer, Light			
Trimmer, Wick			
Wick			

Class:
TEMPERATURE CONTROL EQUIPMENT

Definition: Objects originally created to enable people to control the temperature of their immediate environment according to their needs. This class does not include devices to control temperature for purposes other than human comfort, as is the case with bake ovens and kilns. Nor does it include relatively permanent structural parts of a building, such as fireplaces or flues or whole-structure systems for environmental control; such items are included in Building Components.

Sub-Class:
FIREMAKING EQUIPMENT

Definition: Objects originally created to produce or assist in producing fire, or to serve as a source of fuel. This sub-class includes matchbooks, charcoal, and tinderpistols. It does not include lighters, which are included in Smoking & Recreational Drug Equipment.

Primary Object Term	Secondary Term	Tertiary Term	Notes
Block, Firemaking			
Bow, Fire			
Drill, Firemaking			
Firesteel			
Flint			
Igniter, Portable			
Kindling			
	Charcoal		
	Wood, Kindling		
Match			
Matchbook			
Matchbox			
Spill			
Strike-a-Light			
Striker, Match			
Tinder			
	Punk		
Tinderpistol			

Sub-Class:
HEATING & COOLING EQUIPMENT

Definition: Objects originally created to heat or cool individual spaces by burning substances, by connection to an energy source such as electricity, or by hand-operated devices. Whole-structure heating and cooling systems and humidity control devices are included in Environmental Control Elements.

Primary Object Term	Secondary Term	Tertiary Term	Notes
Conditioner, Air			*Note:* For large-scale air conditioners, use "Conditioner, Central Air" from Environmental Control Elements
Fan, Electric			
	Fan, Ceiling		
Heater			
	Heater, Alcohol		
	Heater, Coal		
	Heater, Electric		
		Heater, Fan	
		Heater, Lamp	
	Heater, Gas		
	Heater, Kerosene		
	Heater, Oil		
	Heater, Radiant		
	Heater, Wood		
Lamp, Heat			
Punkah			
Stove, Heating			
	Stove, Charcoal Heating		
	Stove, Coal Heating		
	Stove, Oil Heating		
	Stove, Pellet		
	Stove, Wood Heating		

Sub-Class:
HEATING EQUIPMENT ACCESSORIES

Definition: Objects originally created to assist in the management of fire within a stove or fireplace, including tools and their associated holders, protective screens and doors, supports, and radiant surfaces. This sub-class also includes functional components of stoves (whether heating stoves or cookstoves) as well as objects originally created to store supplies of fuel or tinder or contain burning substances for use in igniting fires. Structural components of fireplaces such as flues and chimney hoods are included in Environmental Control Elements.

Primary Object Term	Secondary Term	Tertiary Term	Notes
Accessory, Fireplace			
	Andiron		
	Bracket, Fireset		
	Broom, Fireplace		
	Carrier, Ember		
	Curfew		
	Fender		
	Fireset		
	Fork, Fireplace		
	Grate, Fireplace		
	Insert, Fireplace		
	Rake, Fireplace		
	Screen, Fire		
		Screen, Pole	
	Shovel, Fireplace		
	Stand, Fireset		
	Tongs, Fireplace		
Bellows			
Carrier, Log			
Cleaner, Furnace			
Component, Stove			
	Board, Stove		
	Damper, Stovepipe		
	Grate, Stove		
	Hood, Stove		
	Lid, Stove		
	Plate, Stove		
	Stovepipe		
	Support, Stove		
Container, Fuel			

Primary Object Term	Secondary Term	Tertiary Term	Notes
	Bin, Coal		
	Hod, Coal		
	Tank, Oil		
	Tinderbox		
	Woodbin		
Fan, Fire			
Pick, Coal			
Poker			
Scraper, Ash			
Shovel, Coal			
Stand, Bellows			
Tool, Stove			
	Lifter, Stove		
	Scraper, Stove		
	Shaker, Grate		
	Shovel, Stove		

Class:
WINDOW & DOOR COVERINGS

Definition: Objects originally created to cover or adorn a window, door, or doorway. This class does not include relatively permanent structural parts of buildings such as canopies, exterior shutters, and window sashes. These items are included in Door & Window Elements.

Primary Object Term	Secondary Term	Tertiary Term	Notes
Blind			
	Blind, Venetian		
	Blind, Vertical		
	Miniblind		
Bracket, Rod			
Curtain			
	Curtain, Doorway		
		Curtain, Beaded	
		Portiere	
	Curtain, Window		
		Curtain, Café	
		Curtain, Cottage	
		Curtain, Dress	
		Curtain, Festoon	
		Curtain, Priscilla	
		Curtain, Sheer	
		Drapery	
		Undercurtain	
Fastener, Curtain			
	Hook, Curtain		
	Ring, Curtain		
	Tieback		
		Hook, Tieback	
		Knob, Tieback	
		Loop, Tieback	
Finial, Curtain Rod			
Fitting, Blind			
Pull, Shade			
Rod, Curtain			
Shade			
	Shade, Accordion		
	Shade, Austrian		

Primary Object Term	Secondary Term	Tertiary Term	Notes
	Shade, Balloon		
	Shade, Roller		
	Shade, Roman		
Shutter, Interior			
Swag			
Valance			
Weight, Curtain			

Category 3:
PERSONAL OBJECTS

Definition: **Objects originally created to serve the personal needs of an individual as clothing, adornment, body protection, or an aid in grooming.**

Class:
ADORNMENT

Definition: Objects originally created to be worn on the human body for ornamentation. Adornment lacks the communicative aspect of objects listed in the Personal Symbols class and is more decorative than those listed in the Personal Gear class. This class does not include objects created to adorn clothing, which are listed in Clothing Accessories.

Sub-Class:
BODY ADORNMENTS

Definition: Objects originally created as ornaments for parts of the body other than hair.

Primary Object Term	Secondary Term	Tertiary Term	Notes
Jewelry			
	Anklet		
	Armlet		
	Bracelet		
		Bangle	
		Bracelet, Charm	
	Gorget, Ornamental		
	Labret		
	Locket		
	Necklace		
		Choker	
		Esclavage	
		Rivière	
		Sautoir	
		Torque	
	Ornament, Ear		
		Earring	
		Earspool	
	Ornament, Nose		
		Plug, Nose	
		Ring, Nose	
		Stud, Nose	
	Pendant		
		Breloque	
		Lavaliere	*Note:* May also use "Necklace"
		Pendant, Charm	
	Ring, Finger		
		Ring, Eternity	

Primary Object Term	Secondary Term	Tertiary Term	Notes
		Ring, Gimmel	
	Ring, Nipple		
	Ring, Toe		
	Set, Jewelry		*Note:* May also use terms to represent the individual items in the set
	Stud, Tongue		
Pasty			
Tattoo, Temporary			

Sub-Class:
HAIR ADORNMENTS

Definition: Objects originally created as ornaments for hair, as implements for securing a hairstyle, or as artificial substitutes for hair.

Primary Object Term	Secondary Term	Tertiary Term	Notes
Hairpiece			
	Extension, Hair		
	Rat, Hair		
	Toupee		
Ornament, Hair			
	Aigrette		
	Barrette		
	Bow, Hair		
	Clip, Hair		
	Comb, Ornamental		
		Comb, Side	
		Comb, Tuck	
	Hairbag		
	Hairband		
	Hairpin		
		Bodkin, Hair	
		Pin, Bobby	
	Hairstick		
	Tie, Hair		
		Ribbon, Hair	
		Scrunchie	
Wig			
	Bagwig		
	Peruke		
	Wig, Bob		
	Wig, Tie		

Class:
CLOTHING

Definition: Objects originally created as coverings for the human body. This class includes all forms of garments and also accessories such as belts or cuff links.

Sub-Class:
CLOTHING ACCESSORIES

Definition: Articles of clothing worn on the hands, arms, or neck, and objects originally created for the securement, protection, or adornment of clothing. This sub-class does not include objects used for the minor care of clothing, which are listed under Clothing Care Objects.

Primary Object Term	Secondary Term	Tertiary Term	Notes
Armband			
Belt			
	Belt, Cinch		
	Belt, Girdle		
	Belt, Web		
Boutonniere			
Bow, Clothing			
Bretelle			
Buckle, Clothing			
	Buckle, Belt		
	Buckle, Knee		
	Buckle, Shoe		
Canion			
Chatelaine			
Clasp, Clothing			
	Guard, Lingerie		
	Holder, Cuff		
Clip, Clothing			*Note:* May also use "Jewelry" from Body Adornments, if appropriate
	Clip, Collar		
	Clip, Dress		
	Clip, Glove		
	Clip, Scarf		
	Clip, Shirt		
	Clip, Shoe		
	Clip, Sweater		
	Clip, Tie		
Collar			
	Bertha		
	Ruff		
Concho			
Corsage			

Primary Object Term	Secondary Term	Tertiary Term	Notes
	Corsage, Wrist		
Cover, Headwear			
	Cover, Bonnet		
	Cover, Hat		
Cover, Shoe			
Cuff			
Cushion, Helmet			
Dickey			
Garter			
	Garter, Sock		
Glove			
	Gauntlet		
	Glove, Disposable		
	Glove, Driving		
	Glove, Evening		
	Glove, Work		
Guard, Pant			
Holder, Sash			
Insole			
Jabot			
Lace, Corset			
Lifter, Skirt			
Lining, Garment			
Link, Cuff			*Note:* May also use "Jewelry" from Body Adornments
Mitt			
Mitten			
Modesty			
Muff			
Neckcloth			
	Ascot		
	Cravat		
	Neckerchief		
	Stock		
Neckpiece			
	Boa		
Necktie			
	Tie, Bolo		
	Tie, Bow		
	Tie, String		

Primary Object Term	Secondary Term	Tertiary Term	Notes
Ornament, Footwear			
	Ornament, Shoe		
		Bow, Shoe	
Ornament, Headwear			
	Hatband		
	Holder, Plume		
	Lappet		
	Plume, Hat		
	Ribbon, Hat		
Pad, Nursing			
Pin, Clothing			*Note:* May also use "Jewelry" from Body Adornments, if appropriate
	Brooch		
	Hatpin		
	Pin, Bar		
	Pin, Collar		
	Pin, Diaper		
	Pin, Lapel		
	Pin, Scatter		
	Pin, Skirt		
	Pin, Watch		
	Stickpin		
	Tack, Tie		
Plate, Heel			
Protector, Pocket			
Sash			*Note:* May also use "Regalia" from Status Symbols, if appropriate
	Cummerbund		
	Obi		
Scarf			
	Fichu		
	Scarf, Neck		
		Muffler	
Shield, Dress			
Shoelace			
Sleeve			
	Manchette		
	Oversleeve		

Primary Object Term	Secondary Term	Tertiary Term	Notes
	Undersleeve		
Slide, Bolo			
Slide, Scarf			*Note:* May also use "Jewelry" from Body Adornments, if appropriate
Spreader, Collar			*Note:* May also use "Jewelry" from Body Adornments, if appropriate
Stay, Collar			
Stay, Corset			
Stomacher			
Stud, Clothing			
	Button, Collar		
	Stud, Cuff		
	Stud, Shirt		
Suspenders			
Tinkler			
Tippet			
Train, Dress			
Tucker			
Vestee			
Waistband			
Weight, Skirt			
Wristlet			
Yoke, Clothing			

Sub-Class:
DRESSINGWEAR & NIGHTWEAR

Definition: Articles of clothing worn for sleeping, convalescing, bathing, or during dressing when partially dressed or without clothing underneath. This sub-class includes garments intended for private wear at home.

Primary Object Term	Secondary Term	Tertiary Term	Notes
Bathrobe			
Cape, Dressing			
Gown, Dressing			
Gown, Hospital			
Housecoat			
Jacket, Bed			
Jacket, Dressing			
Negligee			
Nightgown			
Nightshirt			
Pajamas			
	Pajamas, Baby Doll		
	Sleeper		
Peignoir			

Sub-Class:
FOOTWEAR

Definition: Articles of clothing worn on the feet and/or lower legs for protection or cover. This sub-class includes boots, shoes, and hosiery that may cover more than the feet or lower legs.

Primary Object Term	Secondary Term	Tertiary Term	Notes
Blucher			*Note:* May also use "Boot" or "Shoe" as appropriate
Boot			
	Boot, Balmoral		
	Boot, Carriage		
	Boot, Cowboy		
	Boot, Diving		
	Boot, Hiking		
	Boot, Hip		
	Boot, Riding		
	Boot, Ski		
	Boot, Snow		
	Boot, Thigh		
	Boot, Wellington		
	Botte Sauvage		
	Jackboot		
	Mukluk		
	Pac		
Bootee			*Note:* Use for sock-like footwear worn by infants
Bootie			*Note:* Use for soft, ankle-high footwear worn by girls and women
Calf, Downy			
Crakow			*Note:* May also use "Boot" or "Shoe" as appropriate
Gaiter			
	Spat		
Hosiery			
	Pantyhose		
	Sock		
		Sock, Ankle	
		Sock, Knee	
		Sock, Sport	
		Sock, Water	
		Tabi	
	Stocking		
	Tights		
	Warmer, Knee		

Primary Object Term	Secondary Term	Tertiary Term	Notes
	Warmer, Leg		
Liner, Boot			
Overshoe			
	Galosh		
	Patten		
	Rubber		
Puttee			
Sandal			
	Flip-Flop		
	Huarache		
Shoe			
	Brogue		
	Chopine		
	Clog		
		Geta	
	Espadrille		
	Ghillie		
	Loafer		
	Moccasin		
	Mule		
	Oxford		
	Sabot		
	Shoe, Bathing		
	Shoe, Brogan		
	Shoe, Clown		
	Shoe, Deck		
	Shoe, Platform		
	Shoe, Pump		
		Slingback	
	Shoe, Saddle		
	Shoe, Sport		*Note:* May be used in addition to specific sport shoe terms listed in Sports Equipment
	Shoe, Tap		
	Slipper		
		Slipper, Bathing	
		Slipper, Bedroom	
	Slipper, Ballet		
		Shoe, Toe	
	Sneaker		

Sub-Class:
HEADWEAR

Definition: Articles of clothing worn on the head for protection or cover.

Primary Object Term	Secondary Term	Tertiary Term	Notes
Barbette			
Bonnet, Indoor			*Note:* May also use "Cap" or "Bonnet" as appropriate
Cap			
	Balmoral		
	Beret		
	Biggin		
	Busby		
	Cap, Aviator's		
	Cap, Baby		
	Cap, Bathing		
	Cap, Boudoir		
	Cap, Breakfast		
	Cap, Deerstalker		
	Cap, Military		
		Cap, Bearskin	
		Cap, Forage	
		Cap, Garrison	
		Cap, Sailor	
		Cap, Service	
		Cap, Watch	
		Kepi	
		Shako	
	Cap, Miner's		
	Cap, Nurse's		
	Cap, Round-Eared		
	Cap, Scottish		
		Glengarry	
		Tam-o'-Shanter	
	Cap, Smoking		
	Cap, Sport		
		Cap, Baseball	*Note:* May also use "Gear, Baseball" from Sports Equipment if appropriate
		Cap, Golf	*Note:* May also use "Gear, Golf" from Sports Equipment if appropriate
		Cap, Jockey	
		Cap, Riding	
		Cap, Yachting	

Primary Object Term	Secondary Term	Tertiary Term	Notes
	Cap, Stocking		
		Tuque	
	Caul		
	Dormeuse		
	Fez		
	Flatcap		
	Mobcap		
	Mutch		
	Nightcap		
	Pinner		
	Skullcap		
		Beanie	
	Taj		
	Toque		
Chaperon			
Chaplet			
Cornette			
Earmuff			
Hairnet			
	Snood		
Hat			
	Bonnet		
		Bonnet, Baby	
		Bonnet, Poke	
		Bonnet, Rain	
		Fanchon	
		Sunbonnet	
	Cloche		
	Derby		
	Fedora		
	Hat, Alpine		
	Hat, Campaign		
	Hat, Castor		
	Hat, Cocked		
		Bicorn	
		Tricorn	
	Hat, Conductor		
	Hat, Cowboy		
	Hat, Jungle		
	Hat, Mushroom		

Primary Object Term	Secondary Term	Tertiary Term	Notes
	Hat, Picture		
	Hat, Pillbox		
	Hat, Pork Pie		
	Hat, Rain		
	Hat, Shovel		
	Hat, Slouch		
	Hat, Snap-Brim		
	Hat, Straw		
		Boater	
		Hat, Bergère	
		Hat, Panama	
	Hat, Sun		
	Hat, Top		
		Gibus	
	Homberg		
	Montera		
	Sombrero		
	Tholia		
Hat, Beekeper's			
Headband			
	Agal		
	Bandeau		
	Ferronière		*Note:* May also use "Jewelry" from Body Adornments
	Frontlet		*Note:* May also use "Jewelry" from Body Adornments
		Cloth, Forehead	
		Sweatband	
Headcloth			
	Do-Rag		
	Fascinator		
	Havelock		
	Headscarf		
	Headtie		
	Kerchief		
		Babushka	
		Kaffiyeh	
	Stayband		
	Veil		
		Hijab	

Primary Object Term	Secondary Term	Tertiary Term	Notes
		Khimar	
		Mantilla	
		Niqab	
		Veil, Hat	
		Yashmak	
	Wimple		
Headpiece			*Note:* Use for an item of headwear that lacks another descriptive or generic term
Helmet			
	Hat, Hard		
	Helmet, Aviator's		
	Helmet, Crash		
	Helmet, Firefighter's		
	Helmet, Flight		
	Helmet, Military		
	Helmet, Miner's		
	Helmet, Pith		
Hennin			
Hood			
	Balaclava		
	Calash		
Mask, Cold Weather			
Net, Head			
Turban			
Visor			
	Eyeshade		
Wreath, Hair			*Note:* Use for a wreath intended to be worn in the hair; for a wreath made of hair, use "Wreath, Hairwork" from Memorabilia

Sub-Class:
MAIN GARMENTS

Definition: Articles of clothing worn as normal indoor or temperate outdoor public wear to cover parts of the body, exclusive of accessories, footwear, and headwear.

Primary Object Term	Secondary Term	Tertiary Term	Notes
Bodice			
Burka			
Caftan			
Chemisette			
Coat			*Note:* For a coat worn over main garments for warmth or weather protection, use "Overcoat" from Outerwear
	Coat, Cutaway		
	Coat, Frock		
	Coat, Morning		
	Coat, Sack		
	Coat, Suit		
	Coat, Tail		
	Coatee		
	Jacket, Dinner		
	Sportcoat		
Codpiece			
Doublet			
Dress			
	Coatdress		
	Dress, Ballet		
	Dress, Chemise		
	Dress, Cocktail		
	Dress, Day		
	Dress, House		
	Dress, Lingerie		
	Dress, Maternity		
	Dress, Maxi		
	Dress, Midi		
	Dress, Mini		
	Dress, Redingote		
	Dress, Sheath		
	Dress, Skating		
	Dress, Sweater		
	Dress, Wrap		
	Gown		
		Gown, Open	

Primary Object Term	Secondary Term	Tertiary Term	Notes
		Gown, Round	
	Gown, Evening		
	Gown, Tea		
	Jumper		
	Muumuu		
	Overdress		
		Polonaise	
	Sack		
	Sundress		
Ensemble			*Note:* May also use other terms to represent individual items in the grouping
Garment, Combination			*Note:* Use for a main garment that covers the body above and below the waist and is bifurcated; for a similar undergarment, use "Combination" from Underwear
	Bodysuit		
	Catsuit		
	Creeper		
	Jumpsuit		
	Leotard		
	Overalls		*Note:* For a similar garment worn over clothes, use "Coveralls" from Protective Wear
	Playsuit		
	Romper		
	Singlet, Wrestling		
	Sunsuit		
	Unitard		
Jacket			*Note:* For a jacket worn over main garments for warmth or weather protection, use "Overcoat" or a more specific term under it from Outerwear
	Basquine		
	Blazer		
	Bolero		
	Caraco		
	Jacket, Battle		
	Jacket, Hunting		
	Jacket, Jean		
	Jacket, Mess		
	Jacket, Nehru		
	Jacket, Norfolk		

Primary Object Term	Secondary Term	Tertiary Term	Notes
	Jacket, Riding		
	Jacket, Shirt		
	Jacket, Smoking		
	Jacket, Spencer		
	Jacket, Waiter's		
	Jerkin		
Kimono			
Loincloth			
Mantua			
Pants			
	Bombachas		
	Breeches		
		Breeches, Trunk	
		Knickers	
		Lederhosen	
	Breeches, Riding		
	Chalwar		
	Culottes		
	Gauchos		
	Hiphuggers		
	Jeans		
	Jodhpur		
	Legging		
	Pantaloons		
	Pants, Capri		
	Pants, Palazzo		
	Pants, Toreador		
	Pushers, Pedal		
	Slacks		
	Sweatpants		
	Trousers, Bell-Bottom		
Plaid			
Pullover			*Note:* May also use a "Shirt" or "Sweater" term as appropriate
	Jersey		
Robe			
Sari			
Sarong			
Sheath, Penis			
Shirt			

Primary Object Term	Secondary Term	Tertiary Term	Notes
	Blouse		
		Blouse, Middy	
		Choli	
		Overblouse	
		Shirtwaist	
	Shirt, Aloha		
	Shirt, Dress		
	Shirt, Maternity		
	Shirt, Polo		
	Shirt, Shell		
	Shirt, Shooter's		
	Sweatshirt		
	Top, Tank		
	T-Shirt		
Shorts			
	Shorts, Athletic		
	Shorts, Bermuda		
	Shorts, Short		
		Pants, Hot	
	Trunks		
Shrug			*Note:* May also use "Jacket" or "Sweater" as appropriate
Skirt			
	Dirndl		
	Kilt		
	Maxiskirt		
	Miniskirt		
	Overskirt		
	Skirt, Bell		
	Skirt, Bubble		
	Skirt, Circular		
	Skirt, Harem		
	Skirt, Hobble		
	Skirt, Hoop		
	Skirt, Hula		
	Skirt, Peg-Top		
	Skirt, Pencil		
	Skirt, Poodle		
	Skirt, Riding		
	Skirt, Trumpet		

Primary Object Term	Secondary Term	Tertiary Term	Notes
	Skirt, Umbrella		
	Skirt, Walking		
	Skirt, Wrap		
	Tutu		
Suit			*Note:* May also use other terms to represent individual items in the grouping
	Habit, Riding		
	Pantsuit		
	Suit, Bathing		
		Bikini	
		Suit, Tank	
	Suit, Buster		
	Suit, Bicycle		
	Suit, Evening		
		Tuxedo	
	Suit, Exercise		
	Suit, Gym		
	Suit, Hiking		
	Suit, Leisure		
	Suit, Norfolk		
	Suit, Sailor		
	Suit, Skeleton		
	Suit, Walking		
	Sweatsuit		
Sweater			
	Cardigan		
	Guernsey		
	Turtleneck		
Thawb			
Toga			
Top, Halter			
Top, Tube			
Tunic			
Vest			
Waistcoat			

Sub-Class:
OUTERWEAR

Definition: Articles of clothing worn as outer layers over main garments, usually for warmth or weather protection. This sub-class does not include articles of clothing worn for protection against extreme environmental conditions, dangerous conditions, food, or dust. This sub-class does not include footwear or headwear.

Primary Object Term	Secondary Term	Tertiary Term	Notes
Aba			
Anorak			
Barrowcoat			
Blanket, Wearing			
	Sarape		
	Shawl, Maiden		
Cape			
	Cape, Tippet		
	Capelet		
	Cardinal		
	Mantle		
		Mantelet	
	Pelerine		
Capote			*Note:* May also use "Cloak" or Overcoat" as appropriate
Cloak			
	Burnous		
	Capuchin		
	Pelisse		
Dashiki			
Overcoat			
	Amautik		
	Chesterfield		
	Coat, Blanket		
	Coat, Car		
	Coat, Duffle		
	Coat, Evening		
	Coat, Riding		
	Coat, Vest		
	Greatcoat		
		Surtout	
	Inverness		
	Jacket, Bush		
	Jacket, Dolman		
	Jacket, Flight		

Primary Object Term	Secondary Term	Tertiary Term	Notes
	Jacket, Pea		
	Jacket, Shooting		
	Jacket, Ski		
	Mackinaw		
	Parka		
	Raincoat		
		Coat, Trench	
		Mackintosh	
		Slicker	
	Redingote		
	Windbreaker		
Paletot			
Pants, Ski			
Pants, Snow			
Poncho			
Shawl			
Snowsuit			
Stole			
Suit, Ski			
Tabard			*Note:* May also use "Regalia" from Status Symbols if appropriate

Sub-Class:
PROTECTIVE WEAR

Definition: Articles of clothing worn over main garments or in place of main garments for protection from extreme environmental conditions, dangerous conditions, or substances such as food or dust. This sub-class does not include footwear, headwear, body armor, or sports equipment.

Primary Object Term	Secondary Term	Tertiary Term	Notes
Apron			
	Apron, Cocktail		
	Apron, Cooking		
	Apron, Occupational		*Note:* Specific occupations may be noted in a subject field; "Apron, Blacksmith's" is grandfathered from *Revised Nomenclature*
		Apron, Blacksmith's	
	Apron, Sewing		
	Apron, Tea		
Bib			
Cape, Hairdressing			
Chaps			
Coat, Dust			
Coat, Laboratory			
Coveralls			
Gear, Turnout			
	Coat, Turnout		
	Pants, Turnout		
	Suit, Proximity		
Oilskin			
Pad, Knee			
Pinafore			
Protector, Sleeve			
Scrub			
	Gown, Scrub		
	Pants, Scrub		
	Shirt, Scrub		
Smock			
Suit, Diver's			
	Drysuit		
	Wetsuit		
Suit, Pressure			
	Suit, Flier's		
	Suit, Space		
Vest, Safety			

Sub-Class:
UNDERWEAR

Definition: Articles of clothing worn beneath main garments or protective wear to protect clothing from the body or the body from clothing or to shape or support parts of the body. Underwear is the layer of clothing that is closest to the skin.

Primary Object Term	Secondary Term	Tertiary Term	Notes
Belt, Garter			
Binder			
Chemise			
Combination			
	Bodystocking		
	Camiknickers		
	Suit, Union		
	Teddy		
Cover, Diaper			
Diaper			
Garment, Foundation			
	Brassiere		
		Brassiere, Nursing	
	Busk		
	Bustle		
	Corselet		
	Corset		
		Bustier	
	Crinoline		
		Crinoline, Cage	
	Farthingale		
	Friend, Bosom		
	Girdle		
		Cincher, Waist	
		Girdle, Panty	
	Hoop, Skirt		
	Improver, Bust		
		Falsie	
	Pad, Bustle		
	Pad, Garment Shoulder		
	Pannier		
	Panties, Control		
	Reducer, Bust		
	Shaper, Body		
G-String			

Primary Object Term	Secondary Term	Tertiary Term	Notes
Slip			
	Slip, Full		
	Slip, Half		
Supporter			
	Jockstrap		
Underbodice			
	Camisole		
	Cover, Corset		
	Jump		
Underdress			
Underpants			
	Briefs		
		Briefs, Bikini	
		Shorts, Jockey	
	Drawers		
		Bloomers	
		Pantalettes	
	Panties		
	Pants, Tap		
	Pants, Training		
	Shorts, Boxer		
	Underpants, Bikini		
	Underpants, Long		
	Underpants, Maternity		
	Underpants, Protective		
Undershirt			
	Singlet		
Underskirt			
	Petticoat		
Underwear, Long			
Underwear, Thong			
Waist, Corset			

Class:
PERSONAL GEAR

Definition: Objects originally created to be used by individuals as clothing care tools such as glove stretchers, as personal carrying or storage gear such as wallets or backpacks, as protective equipment such as umbrellas or goggles, as personal or physical aids such as canes or eyeglasses, or as personal smoking or drug equipment such as pipes.

Sub-Class:
CLOTHING CARE OBJECTS

Definition: Tools, equipment, and supplies originally created to assist in the minor care or routine maintenance of clothing. This sub-class does not include laundry objects, which are listed in Maintenance T&E.

Primary Object Term	Secondary Term	Tertiary Term	Notes
Applicator, Shoe Polish			
Board, Button Polishing			
Brush, Garment			
	Brush, Clothes		
		Brush, Hat	
		Brush, Lint	
	Brush, Shoe		
	Brush, Suede		
Buffer, Shoe			
Guard, Hanger			*Note:* Use for protective strips designed for use on clothes hangers
Guard, Pants			*Note:* Use for bands designed to protect pants legs during activities such as cycling
Hanger, Clothes			
	Coathanger		
	Hanger, Pants		
	Hanger, Skirt		
Kit, Hosiery Mending			*Note:* May also use terms from Needleworking Equipment to represent the individual items in the kit
Kit, Shoeshine			*Note:* May also use terms to represent the individual items in the kit
Roller, Lint			
Sachet			
Stretcher, Glove			
Stretcher, Hat			
Stretcher, Shoe			
Stretcher, Tie			

Primary Object Term	Secondary Term	Tertiary Term	Notes
Tree, Footwear			
	Tree, Boot		
	Tree, Shoe		
Wax, Shoe			

Sub-Class:
PERSONAL ASSISTIVE OBJECTS

Definition: Tools, equipment, and supplies originally created to help individuals in performing day-to-day activities or to keep them safe or comfortable. This sub-class includes devices that enhance personal vision, hearing, or mobility. It does not include clothing or tools and equipment designed for specific activities.

Primary Object Term	Secondary Term	Tertiary Term	Notes
Apparatus, Breathing			*Note:* Use for a protective breathing device; for a device that treats respiratory medical conditions, use "Device, Respiratory Treatment" from Medical Instruments
	Hookah		
	Mask, Cup		
	Mask, Respirator		
	Regulator, Breathing		
	Tank, Breathing		
Blindfold			
	Mask, Sleep		
Bottle, Smelling			
	Vinaigrette		
Brace, Orthopedic			
	Brace, Leg		
	Brace, Neck		
Buttonhook			
Chain, Shoe			
Cooler, Hand			
Cover, Parasol			
Creeper, Ice			
Crutch			
Cushion, Body			
	Cushion, Air		
	Cushion, Neck		
	Headring		
Device, Hearing			
	Aid, Hearing		
	Trumpet, Ear		
Device, Massage			
	Brush, Massage		
	Massager, Scalp		
	Vibrator		
Device, Vision			
	Eyeglasses		
		Glasses, Safety	

Primary Object Term	Secondary Term	Tertiary Term	Notes
		Lorgnette	
		Monocle	
		Pince-Nez	
		Spectacles	
		Sunglasses	
	Glass, Opera		*Note:* May also use "Binoculars" from Optical T&E
	Goggles		
		Goggles, Aviator's	
		Goggles, Driving	
		Goggles, Night Vision	
		Goggles, Snow	
		Goggles, Welder's	
	Lens, Contact		
Dildo			
Earplug			
Fan, Hand			
	Fan, Brisé		
	Fan, Cockade		
	Fan, Fixed		
Guard, Fingernail			
Guard, Hand			*Note:* May also use "Protector, Body" from Sports Equipment if appropriate
Handkerchief			
	Bandana		
Hook, Boot			
Hook, Shoelace			
Knife, Pocket			
	Jackknife		
	Knife, Clasp		
	Penknife		
Noseplug			
Pacifier			
Pad, Bunion			
Pillow, Neck			
Pomander			
Prosthesis			
	Implant, Breast		
	Limb, Artificial		
		Arm, Artificial	

Primary Object Term	Secondary Term	Tertiary Term	Notes
		Hand, Artificial	
		Leg, Artificial	
	Prosthesis, Dental		
		Denture	
Pump, Breast			
Ring, Teething			
Scratcher, Back			
Shoehorn			
Sling, Arm			
Splitter, Pill			
Stick, Walking			
	Cane		
	Staff, Walking		
Strip, Nasal			
Umbrella			
	Parasol		
Walker			
	Walker, Baby		
	Walker, Invalid		
		Rollator	
Warmer, Body			
	Bottle, Hot Water		
	Pad, Heating		
	Warmer, Foot		
	Warmer, Hand		
Wheelchair			*Note:* May also use "Chair, Invalid" from Seating Furniture
	Wheelchair, Motorized		

Sub-Class:
PERSONAL CARRYING & STORAGE GEAR

Definition: Objects originally created to assist individuals in housing or transporting personal items such as clothing, adornment, or personal accessories. This sub-class includes handheld containers such as luggage and containers that are worn such as bandolier bags or tool belts. It also includes clips, chains, and beads that are worn or carried to hold items. This sub-class does not include containers that are listed in other classes with the specific objects for which they were made.

Primary Object Term	Secondary Term	Tertiary Term	Notes
Apron, Tool			
Bag, Carrying			
	Backpack		
	Bag, Bandolier		
	Bag, Barrack		
	Bag, Chatelaine		
	Bag, Collar		
	Bag, Diaper		
	Bag, Ditty		
	Bag, Doctor's		
	Bag, Duffel		
	Bag, Garment		
	Bag, Kit		
	Bag, Lingerie		
	Bag, Mail Carrier's		
	Bag, Messenger		
	Bag, Newspaper Carrier's		
	Bag, Pajama		
	Bag, School		
	Bag, Shoe		
	Bag, Shoulder		
		Bag, Sling	
	Bag, Sport		
	Bag, Toiletry		
	Bag, Tote		
	Bindle		
	Carpetbag		
	Haversack		
	Pack, Fanny		
	Parfleche		
	Pouch, Carrying		
		Pocket	

Primary Object Term	Secondary Term	Tertiary Term	Notes
		Sporran	
	Purse		
		Bag, Clutch	
		Bag, Evening	
		Purse, Change	
	Reticule		
	Sabratache		
	Satchel		
Basket, Carrying			
	Basket, Burden		
	Basket, Pack		
Basket, Trinket			
Belt, Storage			
	Belt, Money		
	Belt, Tool		
Box, Accessory			
	Bandbox		*Note:* Use for a cylindrical wood or pasteboard container for such articles as collars
	Box, Collar		
	Box, Glove		
	Box, Handkerchief		
	Box, Jewelry		
	Box, Shoe		*Note:* May also use "Package, Product" from Merchandising T&E if appropriate
	Box, Trinket		
		Box, Bride's	*Note:* Use for an oval container made of wood splint
	Hatbox		
Caddy, Belt			
Carrier, Luggage			*Note:* Use for a carrying device, not a vehicle
Case, Personal			
	Briefcase		
	Case, Attaché		
	Case, Card		
	Case, Contact Lens		
	Case, Coupon		
	Case, Denture		
	Case, Dressing		
	Case, Epaulet		

Primary Object Term	Secondary Term	Tertiary Term	Notes
	Case, Eyeglass		
	Case, Jewelry		
	Case, Key		
	Case, Match		
	Case, Medicine		
	Case, Necktie		
	Case, Slipper		*Note:* Use for a pouch-like case into which contents slip
	Case, Stamp		
	Case, Stud		
	Case, Traveling		
		Kit, Toilet	*Note:* Use for a case designed to hold cosmetics, hair care items, and hygiene objects
	Case, Wig		
	Etui		
	Pillbox		
		Timer, Pill	
	Suitcase		
	Wallet		
Chain, Eyeglass			
	Chain, Lorgnette		
Chain, Key			
Chain, Watch			
Cleaner, Eyeglass			
Clip, Key			
Clip, Money			
Clip, Pacifier			
Container, Hairpin			
	Box, Hairpin		
	Case, Hairpin		
	Receiver, Hairpin		
Cover, Checkbook			
Dish, Ring			
Flask, Pocket			
Fob			*Note:* May also use "Jewelry" from Body Adornments
	Fob, Key		
	Fob, Watch		
Frame, Pack			

Primary Object Term	Secondary Term	Tertiary Term	Notes
Guard, Key			
Holder, Bouquet			
	Holder, Nosegay		
Holder, Coin			
	Folder, Coin		
Holder, Handkerchief			
Holder, Hatpin			
Lanyard			
Mocock			
Netsuke			*Note:* May also use "Sculpture" from Art or "Jewelry" from Body Adornments as appropriate
Ojime			
Ring, Key			
Sagemono			
	Inro		
Stand, Wig			
Strap, Carrying			
	Tumpline		
Trunk			
	Chest, Liquor		
	Chest, Sea		
	Footlocker		

Sub-Class:
SMOKING & RECREATIONAL DRUG EQUIPMENT

Definition: Tools, equipment, and supplies originally created for the preparation, consumption, or personal storage of tobacco products or non-pharmaceutical drugs. This sub-class does not include equipment used for the manufacture of tobacco products, which is listed in Other T&E for Materials. It does not include household receptacles for tobacco, tobacco equipment, or tobacco waste that are listed in Containers for Smoking & Tobacco.

Primary Object Term	Secondary Term	Tertiary Term	Notes
Bag, Pipe			*Note:* May also use "Bag, Carrying" from Personal Carrying & Storage Gear
Board, Tobacco Cutting			
Bowl, Pipe			
Box, Tobacco			
Case, Cigar			
Case, Cigarette			
Case, Pipe			*Note:* May also use "Case, Personal" from Personal Carrying & Storage Gear
Cigar			
Cigarette			
Cleaner, Pipe			
Clip, Roach			
Container, Snuff			
	Bottle, Snuff		
	Snuffbox		
Cutter, Cigar			
Dispenser, Cigarette Paper			
Grater, Tobacco			
Holder, Cigar			*Note:* Use for a tube that holds a cigar for smoking
Holder, Cigarette			*Note:* Use for a tube that holds a cigarette for smoking
Kit, Cocaine			
Knife, Pipe			
Lamp, Opium			
Lighter			
Paper, Rolling			
Pipe, Smoking			
	Pipe, Opium		
	Pipe, Water		
		Hookah, Smoking	

Primary Object Term	Secondary Term	Tertiary Term	Notes
Pouch, Tobacco			*Note:* May also use "Pouch, Carrying" from Personal Carrying & Storage Gear
Spoon, Cocaine			
Spoon, Snuff			
Stem, Pipe			
Stick, Snuff			
Stopper, Pipe			
Tobacco			
	Snuff		
	Tobacco, Chewing		
Tongs, Pipe			

Class:
TOILET ARTICLES

Definition: Tools, equipment, and supplies originally created to be used for grooming, hygiene, personal sanitation, or for enhancing one's appearance.

Sub-Class:
BEAUTY SUPPLIES

Definition: Objects used to enhance or care for the appearance of skin, nails, or eyelashes. This sub-class includes cosmetics, manicure and pedicure tools, tattooing and skin piercing tools, and associated containers and accessories. It does not include tools or supplies used for cleaning skin.

Primary Object Term	Secondary Term	Tertiary Term	Notes
Applicator, Cosmetic			*Note:* Use for an applicator that is independent of the cosmetic it applies
	Brush, Cosmetic		
		Brush, Lipstick	
		Brush, Nail	
	Puff, Powder		
	Sponge, Cosmetic		
Blotter, Cosmetic			
Buffer, Skin			
	Stone, Pumice		
Case, Manicure			*Note:* May also use "Case, Personal" from Personal Carrying & Storage Gear; may also use terms to represent individual items in the case, if present
Container, Cosmetic			
	Bag, Cosmetic		*Note:* May also use "Bag, Carrying" from Personal Carrying & Storage Gear
	Box, Puff		
	Case, Cosmetic		*Note:* May also use "Case, Personal" from Personal Carrying & Storage Gear
	Compact		
	Jar, Cosmetic		
	Purse, Cosmetic		*Note:* May also use "Purse" from Personal Carrying & Storage Gear
	Shaker, Powder		
Cosmetic			
	Blush		
	Eyelash, False		
	Eyeliner		
	Eyeshadow		
	Fingernail, Artificial		
	Foundation, Cosmetic		

Primary Object Term	Secondary Term	Tertiary Term	Notes
	Lipstick		
	Mascara		
	Pencil, Eyebrow		
	Polish, Nail		
Curler, Eyelash			
Device, Tanning			
	Bed, Tanning		
	Booth, Tanning		
	Lamp, Tanning		
Dispenser, Lotion			
Gun, Piercing			
Kit, Cosmetic			*Note:* May also use terms to represent individual items in the kit
Knife, Callus			
Machine, Tattoo			
Mirror, Hand			
Stand, Mirror			
Tool, Manicure			
	Buffer, Nail		
	Cleaner, Nail		
	Clipper, Nail		
	File, Nail		
		Board, Emery	
	Knife, Cuticle		
	Scissors, Manicure		
	Separator, Toe		
	Set, Manicure		*Note:* May also use terms to represent individual items in the set
	Stick, Cuticle		
Tool, Scarification			

Sub-Class:
HAIR CARE OBJECTS

Definition: Tools, equipment, and supplies originally created to be used for the care, grooming, or removal of hair on the body, head, or face, except for eyelashes.

Primary Object Term	Secondary Term	Tertiary Term	Notes
Applicator, Hair Dye			
Brush, Razor			
Brush, Scalp			
Comb, Hair			
	Comb, Eyebrow		
	Comb, Hot		
	Comb, Lice		
	Comb, Mustache		
	Pick, Hair		
Container, Comb			
	Case, Comb		*Note:* May also use "Case, Personal" from Personal Carrying & Storage Gear
	Dish, Comb		
Cutter, Hair			
	Clipper, Hair		
		Trimmer, Beard	
		Trimmer, Nose Hair	
	Scissors, Hair		
		Shears, Thinning	
Dryer, Hair			
	Dryer, Portable Hair		
	Dryer, Standing Hair		
Dye, Hair			
Hairbrush			
Heater, Curling Iron			
Iron, Hair			
	Iron, Crimping		
	Iron, Curling		
	Iron, Straightening		
Machine, Permanent Wave			
Product, Shaving			
	Blade, Razor		
	Bowl, Shaving		
	Box, Shaving		
	Brush, Shaving		

Primary Object Term	Secondary Term	Tertiary Term	Notes
	Case, Razor		*Note:* May also use "Case, Personal" from Personal Carrying & Storage Gear
	Case, Shaving Brush		*Note:* May also use "Case, Personal" from Personal Carrying & Storage Gear
	Dispenser, Shaving Cream		
	Holder, Shaving Paper		
	Kit, Shaving		*Note:* May also use "Case, Traveling" from Personal Carrying & Storage Gear
	Machine, Shaving Lather		
	Mirror, Shaving		
	Mug, Shaving		
	Paper, Shaving		
	Pencil, Styptic		
	Razor		
		Razor, Disposable	
		Razor, Electric	
		Razor, Safety	
		Razor, Straight	
	Set, Shaving		
	Sharpener, Razor		
		Hone, Razor	
		Strop	
	Stick, Shaving		
Receiver, Hair			
Remover, Hair			
	Epilator		
	Tweezers, Hair		
	Wand, Hair Removal		
Roller, Hair			
Set, Hair Care			*Note:* May also use terms to represent individual items in the set
	Set, Barber's		
	Set, Dresser		
Stand, Hair Care			
	Stand, Curling Iron		

Sub-Class:
HYGIENE OBJECTS

Definition: Tools, equipment, and supplies originally created to assist people with personal sanitation and health preservation activities such as bathing, routine oral care, or birth control. This sub-class does not include furniture or plumbing and drainage elements such as toilets or bathtubs.

Primary Object Term	Secondary Term	Tertiary Term	Notes
Bottle, Toilet			
	Bottle, Barber		
	Bottle, Cologne		
	Bottle, Perfume		
		Atomizer, Perfume	
Box, Pouncet			
Brush, Bath			
Caddy, Bath			
Case, Toilet Bottle			
Case, Toothbrush			
Container, Soap			
	Case, Soap		
	Dish, Soap		
	Dispenser, Soap		
Dispenser, Hand Towel			
Dryer, Hand			
Eyecup			
Eyedropper			
Holder, Tissue			
Holder, Toothbrush			
Hose, Bath			
Liner, Commode			
Liner, Toilet Seat			
Mitt, Bath			
Paper, Toilet			
Pitcher, Wash			
Product, Feminine Hygiene			
	Applicator, Tampon		
	Belt, Sanitary		
	Douche		
	Napkin, Sanitary		
	Pan, Douche		
	Tampon		
Product, Oral Care			

Primary Object Term	Secondary Term	Tertiary Term	Notes
	Floss, Dental		
	Pick, Water		
	Scraper, Tongue		
	Toothbrush		
		Brush, Denture	
		Toothbrush, Electric	
	Toothpick		
Prophylactic			
	Condom		
	Diaphragm		
	Sponge, Contraceptive		
Receptacle, Human Waste			
	Bedpan		
	Pan, Stool		
	Pot, Chamber		
	Urinal, Portable		
		Flask, Urinal	
Set, Toilet			*Note:* May also use terms to represent individual items in the set, e.g., "Pitcher, Wash," "Washbasin"
Shaker, Soap			
Soap			
Sponge, Bath			
Spoon, Ear Wax			
Strigil			
Tissue			
Towel			
	Towel, Bath		
	Towel, Beach		
	Towel, Face		
	Towel, Fingertip		
	Towel, Hand		
	Towelette		
	Washcloth		
Washbasin			

Category 4:
TOOLS & EQUIPMENT FOR MATERIALS

Definition: **Tools, equipment, and supplies originally created to manage, oversee, capture, harvest, or collect resources or to transform or modify particular materials, either raw or processed. These objects are normally created in response to problems inherent in the materials themselves; for example, wood requires certain kinds of cutting devices, fish require certain lures, and food requires certain serving utensils.**

Class:
AGRICULTURAL T&E

Definition: Tools, equipment, and supplies originally created for farming or gardening. This class includes implements used in planting, tending, harvesting, and storing crops and in processing food for animals but not food for humans. This class does not include tools and equipment used in caring for animals, in working with forest products, or in preparing fibers for textiles or other products from agricultural products. It does not include agricultural structures, groundskeeping equipment, or objects that serve primarily as vehicles.

Sub-Class:
CULTIVATION EQUIPMENT

Definition: Tools, equipment, and supplies originally created for the preparation of land for planting or sowing. This sub-class includes objects used in clearing, grading, digging, loosening, turning, or weeding soil. These items may be used prior to planting or sowing or during the growing process.

Primary Object Term	Secondary Term	Tertiary Term	Notes
Chopper, Drum			
Cultivator			
	Cultivator, Field		*Note:* Use for a cultivator used for field preparation
	Cultivator, Garden		*Note:* Use for a cultivator pushed by hand
	Cultivator, Hand		*Note:* Use for a hand tool employed in garden cultivation
	Cultivator, Rotary		*Note:* Use for a machine used for weed control or shallow mulching
	Cultivator, Row Crop		
	Cultivator, Straddle-Row		
	Cultivator, Walking		*Note:* Use for an animal-drawn cultivator behind which the operator walks
Cutter, Root			
Cutter, Stalk			
Drag, Smoothing			
Fork, Cultivating			
	Fork, Spading		
Grinder, Soil			
Harrow			
	Harrow, Acme		

Primary Object Term	Secondary Term	Tertiary Term	Notes
	Harrow, Disk		
	Harrow, Spading		
	Harrow, Spike-Tooth		
	Harrow, Spring-Tooth		
	Harrow, Tine-Tooth		
Hoe			
	Hoe, Celery		
	Hoe, Corn		
	Hoe, Cotton		
	Hoe, Garden		
		Hoe, Scuffle	
	Hoe, Grape		
	Hoe, Grub		
	Hoe, Hop		
	Hoe, Mattock		
	Hoe, Meadow		
	Hoe, Nursery		
	Hoe, Sugar Beet		
	Hoe, Tobacco		
	Hoe, Turnip		
	Hoe, Warren		
Hook, Grub			
Hook, Manure			
Leveler, Land			
Machine, Ditching			
Mattock			
Mulcher			
Picker, Stone			
Plow			
	Plow, Bog		
	Plow, Disk		
	Plow, Gang		
	Plow, Garden		
	Plow, Moldboard		
		Middlebuster	
		Plow, Breaking	
		Plow, Hillside	
		Plow, Ridging	

Primary Object Term	Secondary Term	Tertiary Term	Notes
		Plow, Shovel	
		Plow, Stubble	
		Plow, Two-Way	
	Plow, Scratch		
	Plow, Subsoil		
	Plow, Wheel		
		Plow, Sulky	
Puller, Stump			
Pulper, Root			
Rake, Garden			
Roller, Land			
	Cultipacker		
Sifter, Soil			
Spade			
	Spade, Ditching		
	Spade, Drain		
	Spade, Garden		
	Spade, Peat		
Stick, Digging			
Stoneboat			*Note:* May also use "Sledge" from Animal-Powered Vehicles
Tiller, Rotary			
	Tiller, Garden Rotary		
Trowel, Garden			
Weeder			
	Chisel, Weeding		
	Cutter, Weed		
	Fork, Weeding		
	Hoe, Weeding		
	Hook, Weeding		
	Scythe, Weed		
	Spud, Weeding		
	Weeder, Flame		
	Weeder, Rod		
	Weeder, Spring-Tooth		

Sub-Class:
FEED PROCESSING EQUIPMENT

Definition: Tools, equipment, and supplies originally created for treating or preparing food for animals. This sub-class does not include objects used for serving food to animals, which are listed in Animal Care Equipment or Pet Supplies. It does not include feed structures such as silos, which are listed in Agricultural Structures.

Primary Object Term	Secondary Term	Tertiary Term	Notes
Bag, Silage			
Blower, Ensilage			
Chopper, Feed			
Cooker, Feed			
Cutter, Ensilage			
Fork, Ensilage			
Grinder, Feed			
	Crusher, Corn		
	Grinder, Alfalfa		
	Grinder, Bone		
Mixer, Feed			
Wagon, Feeder			

Sub-Class:
HARVESTING EQUIPMENT

Definition: Tools, equipment, and supplies originally created for gathering or handling crops or other agricultural products. This sub-class includes objects for picking, reaping, threshing, sifting, drying, bunching, binding, and loading crops. Note: For a piece of equipment made for a specific crop, the name of the crop may be entered in a subject field, whether or not the crop is noted in the object term.

Primary Object Term	Secondary Term	Tertiary Term	Notes
Ax, Tobacco			
Bagger, Grain			
Baler			
	Baler, Cotton		
	Baler, Hay		
	Baler, Tobacco		
Barrow, Apple			*Note:* May also use "Wheelbarrow" from Human-Powered Vehicles
Bearder, Barley			
Beater, Seed			
Belt, Binder			
Binder, Grain			
	Binder, Corn		
	Binder, Twine		
	Binder, Wire		
Brake, Hemp			
Cap, Grain			
Card, Picker's			*Note:* May also use "Tally" from Financial Records
Cleaner, Cottonseed			
Conditioner, Hay			
Container, Crop			
	Bag, Harvesting		
		Bag, Fruit Picking	
	Basket, Gathering		
		Basket, Cotton	
		Basket, Egg Gathering	
		Basket, Fruit Picking	
	Bin, Grain		
		Bin, Chaser	*Note:* May also use "Trailer, Farm" from Motor Vehicles
		Bin, Corn	
		Bin, Rice	

Primary Object Term	Secondary Term	Tertiary Term	Notes
	Bowl, Gathering		
	Box, Field		
	Chute, Grain		
	Hopper, Grain		
Conveyor, Crop			
	Derrick, Grain		*Note:* May also use "Derrick" from Mechanical Devices
	Elevator, Crop		
		Elevator, Auger	
		Elevator, Bale	
Cornhusker			
	Cornhusker, Hand		
	Husker-Shredder, Corn		
Crook, Hay			
Cuber, Hay			
Dryer, Crop			
	Dryer, Grain		
Flail, Threshing			
Fork, Harvesting			
	Fork, Alfalfa		
	Fork, Barley		
	Fork, Beet		
	Fork, Cabbage		
	Fork, Potato		
	Fork, Vegetable Scoop		
Fork, Hay Lifting			
	Fork, Grapple		
	Fork, Harpoon		
Gauge, Fruit			
Harvester			
	Combine		
		Combine, Corn	
		Combine, Green Pea	
		Combine, Hillside	
		Combine, Peanut	
		Combine, Pull-Type	
		Combine, Self-Propelled	
	Harvester, Bean		
	Harvester, Carrot		

Primary Object Term	Secondary Term	Tertiary Term	Notes
	Harvester, Corn		
	Harvester, Forage		
	Harvester, Onion		
	Harvester, Potato		
		Digger, Potato	
	Harvester, Sugar Beet		
	Harvester, Sugarcane		
	Harvester, Tomato		
	Header, Grain		
	Picker, Crop		
		Picker, Corn	
		Picker, Cotton	
		Picker, Fruit	
	Reaper		
		Reaper, Hand-Rake	
		Reaper, Self-Rake	
	Snapper, Corn		
	Stripper, Crop		
		Stripper, Cotton	
		Stripper, Grain	
		Stripper, Sugarcane	
Hayfork			
	Fork, Header		
Hoe, Potato			
Hook, Hay Bale			
Hook, Reaping			
	Hook, Corn		
	Hook, Drill		
	Hook, Potato		
	Sickle		
Knife, Band-Cutter			
Knife, Harvesting			
	Cutter, Potato Seed		
	Knife, Beet-Topping		
	Knife, Corn		
	Knife, Grain-Heading		
	Knife, Hay		
		Spade, Hay	
	Knife, Mescal		

Primary Object Term	Secondary Term	Tertiary Term	Notes
	Knife, Sugarcane		
	Knife, Tobacco		
	Machete		
Ladder, Orchard			
Loader, Crop			
	Loader, Corn Shock		
	Loader, Hay		
		Loader, Bale Hay	
		Stacker, Hay	
Mower			
	Mower, Horse-Drawn		
	Mower, Tractor-Drawn		
	Windrower		
Net, Harvesting			
Plane, Pulping			
Press, Tobacco			
Rack, Tobacco			
Rake			
	Rake, Blueberry		
	Rake, Clover		
	Rake, Cranberry		
	Rake, Grain Binder's		
	Rake, Hay		
		Rake, Common Hay	
		Rake, Dump	
		Rake, Hand Hay	
		Rake, Revolving Hay	
		Rake, Side Delivery	
		Rake, Sweep	
		Tedder	
	Rake, Onion		
	Rake, Reaper Platform		
Scabbard, Machete			
Scissors, Vine			
Scraper, Cotton			
Scythe			
	Scythe, Cradle		
	Scythe, Flemish		
Shaker, Tree			

Primary Object Term	Secondary Term	Tertiary Term	Notes
Shears, Band Cutter			
Sheller			
	Sheller, Bean		
	Sheller, Corn		
Shocker, Grain			
	Shocker, Corn		
Shovel, Grain			
Shredder, Flail			
Slicer, Ear Corn			
Sling, Hay			*Note:* May also use "Hoist" from Mechanical Devices
Spear, Tobacco			
Stick, Harvesting			
	Stick, Ricing		
Thresher			
	Thresher, Groundhog		
	Thresher, Peanut		
	Thresher, Portable		
	Thresher, Simple		
	Thresher, Stationary		
	Thresher-Separator		
Tier, Corn Shock			
Viner, Pea			
Winnower			
	Basket, Winnowing		
	Mill, Fanning		
	Riddle, Grain		
	Screen, Winnowing		
	Tray, Winnowing		
Wire, Baling			

Sub-Class:
PLANTING EQUIPMENT

Definition: Tools, equipment, and supplies originally created for setting or sowing plants or seeds for crops.

Primary Object Term	Secondary Term	Tertiary Term	Notes
Broadcaster			
	Seeder, Centrifugal		
		Seeder, Hand Centrifugal	*Note:* Use for a hand-powered centrifugal seeder
	Seeder, Seedbox		
		Seeder, Hand Seedbox	*Note:* Use for a hand-carried or hand-pushed seedbox seeder
Container, Seed			
	Bag, Seed		
	Box, Grain		
	Jar, Seed		
	Packet, Seed		*Note:* May also use "Package, Product" from Merchandising T&E if appropriate
	Tape, Seed		
Dibble			
Drill, Seed			
	Drill, Disk		
		Drill, Double Disk	
		Drill, Single Disk	
	Drill, Hoe		
	Drill, Press		
	Drill, Shoe		
Germinator			
Machine, Dibbling			
Planter, Seed			
	Planter, Corn		
	Planter, Garden Seed		
	Planter, Hand		
	Planter, Lister		
	Planter, Potato		
	Planter, Precision		
	Planter, Walking		*Note:* Use for an animal-drawn planter behind which the operator walks
Setter, Seedling			
Transplanter			
	Machine, Transplanting		
	Transplanter, Hand		

Sub-Class:
TENDING EQUIPMENT

Definition: Tools, equipment, and supplies originally created for managing or caring for crops, including objects used for fertilization, irrigation, pest control, or grafting. This sub-class does not include weeding tools, which are listed in Cultivation Equipment.

Primary Object Term	Secondary Term	Tertiary Term	Notes
Cover, Crop			
Fertilizer			
Fork, Manure			
Heater, Orchard			
Kit, Soil Testing			
Sifter, Compost			
Sprayer			
	Duster, Powder		
	Sprayer, Hand		
		Sprayer, Bucket	
		Sprayer, Knapsack	
		Sprayer, Wheelbarrow	
	Sprayer, Power		
Spreader, Mineral			
	Spreader, Manure		*Note:* Use for an animal- or machine-drawn spreader
	Spreader, Wheelbarrow		*Note:* Use for a hand-pushed spreader
Thinner, Fruit			
Tool, Fertilizing			
	Bucket, Manure		
	Distributor, Fertilizer		
	Feeder, Root		
	Injector, Fertilizer		
Tool, Grafting			
	Chisel, Grafting		
	Clip, Grafting		
	Iron, Grafting		
	Knife, Grafting		
	Mallet, Grafting		
Tool, Irrigation			
	Hose, Irrigation		
	Pipe, Irrigation		
	Sprinkler, Irrigation		

Class:
ANIMAL HUSBANDRY T&E

Definition: Tools, equipment, and supplies originally created for the care, breeding, or study of animals. This class includes instruments used in the practice of veterinary medicine, in the psychological study of animals, and in the care of animals, such as the tools a farrier uses to shoe animals. This class does not include equipment used in processing animal products for human use (see Food Processing T&E or Leather, Horn, Shellworking T&E). Also excluded are structures for housing animals and the tools of trades related to animal husbandry that are not used directly with animals, such as a farrier's metal-working tools.

Sub-Class:
ANIMAL CARE EQUIPMENT

Definition: Tools, equipment, and supplies originally created for the routine maintenance of animals. This sub-class includes objects for feeding, grooming, identifying, training, or controlling animals. It does not include objects used for the care of household pets or objects used for animal medical treatment.

Primary Object Term	Secondary Term	Tertiary Term	Notes
Bell, Animal			*Note:* May also use "Bell" from Sound Communication Devices; the name of the animal may be noted in a subject field
	Bell, Horse		
	Cowbell		
Cage, Animal			*Note:* The name of the animal may be noted in a subject field
	Cage, Bird		
	Cage, Insect		
Carrier, Litter			
Coop, Poultry Shipping			
Covering, Animal			
	Blanket, Animal		*Note:* The name of the animal may be noted in a subject field
	Cap, Horse		
	Hood, Sweat		
	Net, Fly		
Cutter, Snout			
Feeder, Animal			
	Box, Feed		
	Bucket, Slop		
	Bunk, Feed		
	Carrier, Feed		
	Dispenser, Powder		
	Feedbag		

Primary Object Term	Secondary Term	Tertiary Term	Notes
	Feeder, Livestock		
		Trough, Feeding	
	Feeder, Poultry		
	Nipple, Nursing		
	Scoop, Feed		
	Weaner, Calf		
Oiler, Hog			
Perch			
Pin, Picket			
Restraint, Animal			
	Bit, Training		
	Catcher, Hog		
	Catcher, Poultry		
	Halter, Show		
	Harness, Casting		
	Hobble		
	Holder, Cow Tail		
	Holder, Hog		
	Kick-Stop		
	Lariat		
	Leader, Livestock		
		Leader, Cattle	
	Leash		
	Muzzle		
	Net, Animal		
	Poke		
	Restraint, Bird		
		Brail	
		Hood, Falconry	
		Jess	
	Ring, Animal Nose		
	Ringer, Animal Nose		
	Tackle, Breaking		
	Tie, Cattle		
	Tongs, Hog		
	Twister, Nose		
	Vervel		
	Weight, Horn		
Scale, Animal			
	Scale, Livestock		

Primary Object Term	Secondary Term	Tertiary Term	Notes
Switch, Fly			
Swivel, Lariat			
Tool, Animal Grooming			
	Brush, Animal		
	Clipper, Animal		
		Trimmer, Ear	
	Comb, Animal		
		Currycomb	
	Pick, Hoof		
	Scraper, Sweat		
	Shears, Animal		
		Shears, Fetlock	
		Shears, Horse	
		Shears, Sheep	
Tool, Animal Identification			
	Brand, Animal		
		Brand, Freeze	
		Brand, Horn	
	Gun, Animal Marking		
	Gun, Livestock Tattoo		
	Punch, Poultry		
	Set, Livestock Tattoo		
	Tag, Animal		*Note:* May also use "Tag, Identification" from Other Documents
		Band, Leg	
	Tool, Ear Marking		
		Notcher, Ear	
		Pattern, Ear	
		Punch, Ear Tag	
Tool, Beekeeping			
	Box, Bee		
	Excluder, Queen		
	Gum, Bee		
	Knife, Decapping		
	Skep, Bee		
	Smoker, Bee		
Tool, Herding			
	Bullhook		

Primary Object Term	Secondary Term	Tertiary Term	Notes
	Crook, Shepherd's		
	Prod, Stock		
		Prod, Cattle	
	Slapper, Livestock		
	Stick, Show		
Waterer, Animal			
	Trough, Watering		
	Waterer, Livestock		
	Waterer, Poultry		
Whip, Animal			
	Whip, Training		

Sub-Class:
BREEDING EQUIPMENT

Definition: Tools, equipment, and supplies originally created to promote the propagation of animals.

Primary Object Term	Secondary Term	Tertiary Term	Notes
Box, Nesting			
Brooder, Poultry			
Crate, Breeding			
	Crate, Hog Breeding		
Detector, Heatmount			
Egg, Nest			
Harness, Marking			
Hatcher, Poultry			
Incubator			
	Incubator, Fish		
	Incubator, Poultry		
Kit, Insemination			
Pipette, Intrauterine			
Thermometer, Incubator			

Sub-Class:
FARRIER EQUIPMENT

Definition: Tools, equipment, and supplies originally created to support the shoeing of horses and other animals. This sub-class does not include general blacksmithing tools, which are listed in Metalworking T&E.

Primary Object Term	Secondary Term	Tertiary Term	Notes
Bench, Farrier's			
Block, Clinching			
Box, Farrier's			
	Box, Farrier's Nail		
	Box, Shoeing		
Calk, Horseshoe			
Cover, Horseshoe			
	Boot, Lawn		
Cropper, Shoe			
Frame, Ox-Shoeing			
Groover, Hoof			
Hammer, Farrier's			
	Hammer, Driving		
	Hammer, Fitting		
Knife, Farrier's			
	Knife, Sole		
	Knife, Toe		
Knocker, Snow			
Nail, Shoeing			
	Nail, Horseshoe		
Pad, Horseshoe			
Pincers, Farrier's			
Rack, Horseshoeing			
Shoe, Animal			
	Guard, Hoof		
	Horseshoe		
	Muleshoe		
	Oxshoe		
Stalljack			
Stand, Shoeing			
Tongs, Farrier's			
	Tongs, Clinching		
	Tongs, Shoe-Spreading		
Tool, Calk			
	Driver, Calk		
	Extractor, Calk		

Primary Object Term	Secondary Term	Tertiary Term	Notes
	Wrench, Calk		
Tool, Hoof			
	Buffer, Hoof		
	Chisel, Hoof		
	Gauge, Hoof		
	Iron, Hoof-Searing		
	Knife, Hoof		
	Leveler, Hoof		
	Parer, Hoof		
	Protractor, Hoof		
	Rasp, Hoof		
	Trimmer, Hoof		
Weight, Toe			

Sub-Class:
PET SUPPLIES

Definition: Objects originally created for the care and maintenance of household pets.

Primary Object Term	Secondary Term	Tertiary Term	Notes
Bowl, Pet			
Box, Litter			
Brush, Pet			
Carrier, Pet			
Collar, Pet			
	Collar, Bark Training		
	Collar, Bell		
	Collar, Choke		
	Collar, Flea		
Dish, Pet			
Feeder, Pet			
Gag, Canine			
Garment, Pet			
Gate, Pet			
Habitat, Pet			
	Aquarium		
	Cage, Pet		
		Birdcage	
	Fishbowl		
	Terrarium		
Leash, Pet			
Muzzle, Pet			
Nipper, Toenail			
Pin, Stake			
Post, Scratching			
Scale, Pet			
Scoop, Pet Waste			
	Pooper-Scooper		
	Scoop, Litter		
Toy, Pet			

Sub-Class:
VETERINARY EQUIPMENT

Definition: Tools, equipment, and supplies originally created for the medical examination, diagnosis, or treatment of animals. This sub-class includes objects used by animal doctors or others responsible for the care of animals.

Primary Object Term	Secondary Term	Tertiary Term	Notes
Adapter, Enema			
Aid, Pill			
	Forceps, Pill		
	Gun, Balling		
Barrel, Syringe			
Chest, Veterinary			
Cutter, Molar			
Debeaker			
Dehorner			
	Knife, Dehorning		
	Saw, Dehorning		
Docker, Tail			
Drencher			
Fecalyzer			
Feeder, Esophageal			
Float, Dental			
Iron, Balling			
Iron, Cauterizing			
Knife, Teat			
Lancet, Animal			
Lift, Cow			
Needlepin, Inoculating			
Pin, Bandage			
Pin, Prolapse			
Ring, Rectal			
Shears, Dental			
Slitter, Teat			
Speculum, Animal			
Syringe, Dose			
Tester, Hoof			
Tool, Animal Obstetrical			
	Chain, Obstetrical		
	Extractor, Fetal		
		Puller, Calf	

Primary Object Term	Secondary Term	Tertiary Term	Notes
Tool, Castration			
	Band, Elastrator		
	Emasculator		
	Knife, Castrating		
	Pliers, Elastrator		
Tube, Enema			
Tube, Tracheotomy			

Class:
FIBERWORKING T&E

Definition: Tools, equipment, and supplies originally created to fabricate objects out of minimally processed, fibrous plant material, including grass, straw, reeds, bark, splints, and twigs, or from fibrous animal material, including bristles and hair. This class includes tools used for basket-making, broom-making, brush-making, thatching, and wigmaking. It also includes tools, equipment, and supplies used for crafting similar products from synthetic fibers. This class does not include tools used for working with textiles or processed wood.

Primary Object Term	Secondary Term	Tertiary Term	Notes
Beater, Straw			
Bodkin, Basketmaker's			
	Bodkin, Hollow		
	Bodkin, Solid		
Brake, Peeling			
Cleave			
Comb, Broomcorn			
Fork, Thatching			
Gauge, Splint			
Hammer, Broom Maker's			
Hatchel, Wigmaker's			
Horse, Broom			
Iron, Rapping			
Knife, Picking			
Knife, Willow			
Lapboard, Basketmaker's			
Machine, Broom			
Mold, Basket Weaving			
Needle, Thatching			
Poker, Bond			
Press, Straw			
Shave, Basket			
Shave, Upright			
Shears, Basketmaker's			
Splitter, Bond			
Tool, Fiber Plaiting			
Tool, Wigmaking			

Class:
FISHING & TRAPPING T&E

Definition: Tools, equipment, and supplies originally created for capturing aquatic and terrestrial animals by any means other than weaponry. This class does not include hunting and fishing weapons, which are listed in such Armament sub-classes as Armament Accessories, Edged Weapons, and Firearms.

Sub-Class:
FISHING EQUIPMENT

Definition: Tools, equipment, and supplies originally created for capturing aquatic animals by any means other than weaponry. This sub-class includes objects used in the commercial or recreational catching or harvesting of fish, shellfish, or marine mammals such as whales.

Primary Object Term	Secondary Term	Tertiary Term	Notes
Anchor, Net			
Board, Fish Measuring			*Note:* May also use "Ruler" from Weights & Measures T&E
Bridle, Net			
Buoy, Fishing			
	Buoy, Lobster		
	Buoy, Net		
Club, Fish			*Note:* May also use "Club" from Percussive Weapons
Container, Fishing			
	Bag, Whaling		
	Basket, Oyster		
	Car, Lobster		
	Case, Fishing Gear		*Note:* Use for any container specifically designed for protecting and/or transporting fishing gear; if a case is designed specifically for a given tool, a new term may be created with the *Nomenclature* term for that tool as a modifier; that term may be organized under "Case, Fishing Gear," as the three items are below
		Box, Net	
		Box, Tackle	
		Case, Fishing Rod	
	Container, Bait		
		Basket, Bait	
		Box, Bait	
		Bucket, Bait	
	Creel, Fishing		
	Holder, Fishing Gear		
		Holder, Fishhook	

Primary Object Term	Secondary Term	Tertiary Term	Notes
		Holder, Fishing Line	
		Holder, Fishing Rod	
Gaff, Fish			
	Gaff, Sealing		
	Hook, Lobster		
Gauge, Lobster			
Grabber, Fish			
Gurdy			*Note:* May also use "Winch" from Mechanical Devices
Hoe, Clamming			
Kite, Fishing			
Net, Fishing			
	Net, Crab		
	Net, Drift		
		Net, Bottom-Set	
		Net, Gill	
	Net, Lift		
		Net, Blanket	
	Net, Reef		
	Net, Scoop		
		Net, Brail	
		Net, Dip	
		Net, Landing	
	Net, Surrounding		
		Net, Casting	
		Net, Dredge	
		Net, Purse	
		Net, Seine	
		Net, Trawl	
	Net, Trap		
		Net, Fyke	
		Net, Hoop	
		Net, Pound	
Peg, Lobster			
Rake, Fishing			
	Rake, Herring		
	Rake, Shellfish		
		Rake, Clam	
Scoop, Limpet			
Scoop, Turtle			

Primary Object Term	Secondary Term	Tertiary Term	Notes
Shears, Fishing			
Strainer, Ice			
Tackle, Fishing			
	Disgorger		
	Fishhook		
		Hook, Circle	
	Gorge, Fish		
	Indicator, Bite		
		Bell, Fishing	
		Float, Fishing	
	Line, Fishing		
	Lure		
		Decoy, Fish	
		Fly, Artificial	
		Jig, Fishing	
		Lure, Plug	
		Lure, Soft	
		Lure, Spoon	
		Lure, Surface	
		Spinnerbait	
		Swimbait	
	Reel, Fishing		
		Reel, Bait Casting	
		Reel, Fly	
		Reel, Spin Cast	
		Reel, Spinning	
	Rig, Fishing		
		Longline	
		Rig, Trolling	
	Rod, Fishing		
		Rod, Casting	
		Rod, Fly	
		Rod, Sea	
		Rod, Spinning	
		Rod, Trolling	
	Stick, Jigging		
	Weight, Fishing		
		Sinker	
		Weight, Net	

Primary Object Term	Secondary Term	Tertiary Term	Notes
Tongs, Fishing			
	Tongs, Clam		
	Tongs, Oyster		
Tool, Fly Tying			
Tool, Whale Blubber			
	Dipper, Whale Oil		
	Fork, Blubber		
	Hook, Blubber		
	Knife, Blubber		
		Knife, Boarding	
		Knife, Leaning	
		Knife, Mincing	
	Pot, Try		
	Skimmer, Whale Oil		
	Spade, Whaling		
		Spade, Blubber	
		Spade, Boat	
		Spade, Bone	
		Spade, Gouge	
		Spade, Head	
	Tool, Flensing		
Trap, Fish			
	Eelpot		
	Pot, Crab		
	Pot, Fish		
	Pot, Lobster		
	Weir		
	Wheel, Fish		

Sub-Class:
TRAPPING EQUIPMENT

Definition: Tools, equipment, and supplies originally created for capturing terrestrial animals by any means other than weaponry. This sub-class does not include objects used for the trapping of household pests.

Primary Object Term	Secondary Term	Tertiary Term	Notes
Setter, Trap			
Stone, Tethering			
Trap, Animal			
	Snare		
	Trap, Cage		
	Trap, Foothold		
		Trap, Bear	
		Trap, Beaver	

Class:
FOOD PROCESSING & PREPARATION T&E

Definition: Tools, equipment, and supplies originally created for the processing, storage, and preparation of food or beverages for human consumption. This class does not include tools for gathering, production, or management of food materials that are listed in Agricultural T&E or Animal Husbandry T&E.

Sub-Class:
COOKING VESSELS

Definition: Objects originally created to serve as containers for baking, roasting, braising, broiling, steaming, boiling, or warming food. This sub-class does not include devices that heat food, such as stoves, rice cookers, and waffle irons, which are listed in Food Preparation Equipment.

Primary Object Term	Secondary Term	Tertiary Term	Notes
Bakeware			*Note:* This term may be used to describe a bakeware set if the specific pieces are not identified individually
	Cover, Bakeware		
	Dish, Baking		
		Casserole	
		Dish, Quiche	
		Dish, Soufflé	
		Ramekin	
		Terrine	
	Pan, Baking		
		Pan, Bread	
		Pan, Breadstick	
		Pan, Bundt	
		Pan, Cake	
		Pan, Cornstick	
		Pan, Dripping	
		Pan, Jelly Roll	
		Pan, Madeleine	
		Pan, Muffin	
		Pan, Patty	
		Pan, Pie	
		Pan, Popover	
		Pan, Pudding	
		Pan, Sheet	
		Pan, Springform	
		Pan, Taco Shell	
		Pan, Tart	
		Pan, Tube	
		Sheet, Cookie	

Primary Object Term	Secondary Term	Tertiary Term	Notes
	Pot, Baking		
		Beanpot	
Cookware			*Note:* This term may be used to describe a cookware set if the specific pieces are not identified individually
	Bain-Marie		
	Basket, Cooking		
		Basket, Steaming	
	Basket, Fry		
	Boiler, Asparagus		
	Boiler, Double		
	Cauldron		
	Cover, Cookware		
	Kettle		
		Kettle, Fish	
		Kettle, Frying	
		Kettle, Preserving	
		Oven, Dutch	
		Teakettle	
	Pan, Broiler		
	Pan, Crepe		
	Pan, Ebelskiver		
	Pan, Frying		
		Spider	
	Pan, Jam		
	Pan, Omelet		
	Pan, Paella		
	Pan, Roasting		
	Pan, Stew		
	Pipkin		
	Poacher		
		Poacher, Egg	
		Poacher, Fish	
	Posnet		
	Saucepan		
	Steamer		
	Stockpot		
	Tagine		
	Tin, Mess		
	Wok		

Sub-Class:
FOOD PREPARATION ACCESSORIES

Definition: Objects that facilitate the preparation of food or beverages but do not play an active role in food preparation. This sub-class includes objects used specifically for the handling, maintenance, or storage of kitchenware.

Primary Object Term	Secondary Term	Tertiary Term	Notes
Auger, Food			
	Auger, Fruit		
	Auger, Sugar		
Box, Camp			
Box, Knife			*Note:* Use for a container that stores kitchen knives; for containers that store serving knives, use "Case, Food Service" from Food Service Accessories
Cover, Food			
	Screen, Food		*Note:* Use for a screened cover meant to keep insects away
Cover, Rolling Pin			
Holder, Skewer			
Knifeboard			
Lifter, Plate			
Lifter, Pot			
Mender, Pot			
Mitt, Oven			
Potholder			
Rack, Kitchenware			
	Rack, Pot		
		Rack, Saucepan	
	Rack, Spit		
	Rack, Utensil		
		Rack, Knife	
Rest, Spoon			
Screen, Splatter			
Sheath, Kitchen Knife			
Stand, Rolling Pin			
Steel, Carving			*Note:* May also use "Steel" from Metalworking T&E
Trivet			
	Pad, Hot		
Warmer, Plate			
	Warmer, Electric Plate		
Warmer, Spoon			

Sub-Class:
FOOD PREPARATION EQUIPMENT

Definition: Tools, equipment, and supplies originally created for mixing, chopping, grinding, decorating, separating, shaping, extracting, or measuring food or beverages. This sub-class also includes hearth equipment, devices for cooking and drying, and other miscellaneous tools. It does not include cooking vessels, food storage equipment, or equipment for processing plants or animals into food products.

Primary Object Term	Secondary Term	Tertiary Term	Notes
Bag, Cooking			
	Bag, Oven		
	Bag, Pudding		
Bakestone			
Baster			
Block, Chopping			
Board, Food Preparation			
	Board, Candy		
	Board, Cutting		
		Breadboard	
	Board, Pastry		
Brush, Food			
	Brush, Pastry		
Cleaner, Shrimp			
Container, Food Preparation			
	Basket, Dough		
	Bowl, Batter		
	Bowl, Chopping		
	Bowl, Mixing		
	Freezer, Ice Cream		
	Keeler		
	Pan, Comfit		
	Pitcher, Batter		
	Shaker, Beverage		
		Shaker, Cocktail	
	Tray, Chopping		
	Tray, Ice Cube		
	Trough, Dough		
	Tub, Salting		
Device, Cooking			
	Brazier, Cooking		
		Hibachi	

Primary Object Term	Secondary Term	Tertiary Term	Notes
	Broiler		
	Burner, Spirit		
	Coddler		
	Cooker, Pressure		
	Cooker, Steam		
		Cooker, Rice	
	Cookstove		
		Cookstove, Alcohol	
		Cookstove, Coal	
		Cookstove, Electric	
		Cookstove, Gas	
		Cookstove, Kerosene	
		Cookstove, Portable	
		Cookstove, Wood	
	Crockpot		
	Fryer, Deep		
	Griddle		
		Comal	
	Grill		
		Grill, Charcoal	
		Grill, Electric	
		Grill, Gas	
		Stone, Cooking	
	Incubator, Yogurt		
	Iron, Cooking		
		Iron, Mulling	
		Iron, Rosette	
		Iron, Wafer	
		Iron, Waffle	
	Maker, Bread		*Note:* Use for a bread mixer that bakes bread
	Maker, Coffee		
		Boiler, Coffee	
		Machine, Cappuccino	
		Machine, Espresso	
		Percolator	
		Press, Coffee	
	Oven		
		Oven, Bake	

Primary Object Term	Secondary Term	Tertiary Term	Notes
		Oven, Convection	
		Oven, Electric	
		Oven, Microwave	
		Oven, Solar	
		Oven, Toaster	
		Oven, Warming	
	Pan, Electric Frying		
	Plate, Hot		
	Popper, Corn		
		Machine, Popcorn	
		Popper, Electric	
		Popper, Stovetop	
	Pot, Fondue		
	Roaster, Coffee		
		Machine, Coffee Roasting	
	Rotisserie		
	Slab, Cooking		
	Toaster		
Dowel, Cake			
Dryer, Food			
	Dehydrator, Food		
	Dryer, Corn		
	Dryer, Fruit		
	Dryer, Herb		
		Rack, Herb Drying	
	Tray, Drying		
Filter, Coffee			
Filter, Water			
Foil, Cooking			
Fuel, Canned			
Funnel, Kitchen			
Funnel, Pie			
Funnel, Wine			
Greaser, Pan			
Infuser, Tea			
	Ball, Tea		
Injector, Marinade			
Machine, Cotton Candy			

Primary Object Term	Secondary Term	Tertiary Term	Notes
Machine, Sno-Cone			
Machine, Taffy Pulling			
Maker, Pasta			
Masher			
	Masher, Kraut		
	Masher, Potato		
	Maul, Meat		
Measure, Culinary			
	Cup, Measuring		
	Glass, Measuring		
	Jigger, Measuring		
	Pitcher, Measuring		
	Spoon, Measuring		
Needle, Larding			
Needle, Trussing			
Opener, Food Container			
	Extractor, Cork		
		Corkscrew	
	Key, Church		
	Opener, Bottle		
	Opener, Can		
		Opener, Electric Can	
	Opener, Jar		
Pin, Rolling			
Press, Culinary			
	Press, Candy		
	Press, Cookie		
	Press, Garlic		
	Press, Oil		
	Press, Ravioli		
	Press, Tortilla		
	Press, Wafer		
	Ricer		
Press, Meat			
Processor, Food			
Punch, Egg			
Rack, Cooling			
Rack, Meat			

Primary Object Term	Secondary Term	Tertiary Term	Notes
Salamander			
Scale, Kitchen			*Note:* May also use "Scale" from Weights & Measures T&E
	Scale, Meat		
	Scale, Nutritional		
	Scale, Spice		
Scaler, Fish			
Shaper, Food			
	Baller, Melon		
	Curler, Butter		
	Dropper, Funnel		
	Hand, Scotch		
	Mold, Food		*Note:* May also use "Bakeware" from Cooking Vessels if appropriate
		Mold, Butter	
		Mold, Cake	
		Mold, Candy	
		Mold, Chocolate	
		Mold, Cookie	
		Mold, Cutlet	
		Mold, Doughnut	
		Mold, Gelatin	
		Mold, Ice Cream	
		Mold, Jelly	
		Mold, Pastry	
		Mold, Pudding	
		Mold, Rice	
		Mold, Ring	
		Mold, Sugar	
		Timbale	
Skewer			
Slab, Candy Making			
Smoker, Food			
	Smoker, Fish		
	Smoker, Meat		
Spinner, Salad			
Spoon, Basting			
Sterilizer, Bottle			
Stuffer, Sausage			
Table, Kneading			

Primary Object Term	Secondary Term	Tertiary Term	Notes
Tester, Cake			
Thermometer, Culinary			*Note:* May also use "Thermometer" from Thermal T&E
	Thermometer, Candy		
	Thermometer, Deep Frying		
	Thermometer, Meat		
	Thermometer, Oven		
Timer, Kitchen			*Note:* May also use "Timer" from Timekeeping T&E
	Timer, Egg		
Tool, Food Cutting			
	Chopper, Food		
		Box, Chopping	
		Chopper, Meat	
	Corer, Fruit		
	Crusher, Ice		
	Cutter, Biscuit		
	Cutter, Butter		
	Cutter, Cookie		
	Cutter, Dough		
		Blender, Pastry	
		Cutter, Doughnut	
		Scraper, Dough	
	Cutter, French Fry		
	Cutter, Julienne		
	Cutter, Pasta		
		Cutter, Noodle	
	Cutter, Pizza		
	Cutter, Sugar		
	Cutter, Vegetable		
		Cutter, Cabbage	
	Grater		
		Grater, Bread	*Note:* Use for a tool that makes breadcrumbs
		Grater, Cheese	
		Grater, Spice	
		Rasp, Bread	*Note:* Use for a tool that removes the crust of singed bread
	Hatchet, Candy		
	Knife, Kitchen		

Primary Object Term	Secondary Term	Tertiary Term	Notes
		Cleaver	
		Knife, Boning	
		Knife, Butcher	
		Knife, Chef's	
		Knife, Chopping	
		Knife, Fillet	
		Knife, Grapefruit	
		Knife, Ham	
		Knife, Orange	
		Knife, Oyster	
		Knife, Paring	
		Knife, Pastry	
		Knife, Santoku	
	Mezzaluna		
	Peeler		
		Peeler, Fruit	
		Peeler, Vegetable	
	Pick, Ice		
	Scraper, Corn		
	Shave, Ice		
	Shears, Poultry		
	Slicer, Food		
		Slicer, Cheese	
		Slicer, Egg	
		Slicer, Fruit	
		Slicer, Mandoline	
		Slicer, Meat	
		Slicer, Vegetable	
	Snip, Pineapple		
	Topper, Egg		
	Wheel, Jagging		
Tool, Food Decorating			
	Bag, Pastry		
	Press, Butter		
	Roller, Springerle		
	Stencil, Cake Decorating		
	Syringe, Icing		
	Tip, Cake Decorating		
Tool, Food Extracting			

Primary Object Term	Secondary Term	Tertiary Term	Notes
	Deveiner, Shrimp		
	Huller, Strawberry		
	Juicer		
		Press, Fruit	
		Press, Wine	
		Reamer, Juice	
		Squeezer, Fruit	
	Nutcracker		
	Nutpick		
	Pitter, Fruit		
		Seeder, Raisin	
		Stoner, Cherry	
		Stoner, Peach	
	Sheller, Nut		
	Squeezer, Lard		
Tool, Food Grinding			
	Basket, Mortar		
	Grinder, Food		
		Grinder, Meat	
	Mano		
	Mill, Culinary		
		Grinder, Herb	
		Mill, Coffee	
		Mill, Food	
		Mill, Nut	
		Mill, Spice	
		Quern	
	Mortar, Food		
	Pestle, Food		
		Stone, Nutting	
	Pounder, Poi		
Tool, Food Handling			
	Fork, Cooking		
		Fork, Barbecue	
		Fork, Meat	
	Ladle, Kitchen		
		Ladle, Wok	
	Lifter, Pie		
	Lifter, Roast		

Primary Object Term	Secondary Term	Tertiary Term	Notes
	Peel		
		Peel, Bread	
		Peel, Pizza	
	Scoop, Food		
		Scoop, Coffee	
		Scoop, Flour	
		Scoop, Ice	
	Skimmer, Wok		
	Spatula, Kitchen		
		Spatula, Offset	
		Spatula, Wok	
	Tamp, Butter		
	Tongs, Kitchen		
		Tongs, Toast	
	Turner, Cake		
Tool, Food Mixing			
	Beater, Food		
		Beater, Batter	
		Eggbeater	
	Blender		
		Blender, Countertop	
		Blender, Stick	
	Hook, Dough		
	Mixer, Food		
		Mixer, Cake	
		Mixer, Drink	
		Mixer, Dough	
		Mixer, Electric Hand	
		Mixer, Electric Stand	
		Mixer, Ice Cream	*Note:* Use for a device that stirs malts, shakes, and frappes
		Mixer, Mayonnaise	
		Mixer, Meat	
	Paddle, Food		
		Paddle, Apple Butter	
	Spoon, Mixing		
	Stick, Mixing		
	Stirrer		
		Barspoon	
		Molinet	

Primary Object Term	Secondary Term	Tertiary Term	Notes
		Muddler	
		Spurtle	
		Stick, Swizzle	
		Stick, Toddy	
		Stirrer, Apple Butter	
		Stirrer, Scrapple	
		Twirler	
	Whip, Cream		
	Whisk		
Tool, Food Separating			
	Boultel		
	Colander		
	Mazarine		
	Separator, Egg		
	Separator, Gravy		
	Sieve		
		Cap, China	
		Chinois	
		Riddle	
		Sieve, Hair	
	Sifter		
		Basket, Sifter	
		Sifter, Flour	
	Skimmer, Kitchen		
	Strainer, Kitchen		
		Spoon, Strainer	
		Strainer, Beverage	
		Strainer, Gravy	
		Strainer, Grease	
		Strainer, Jelly	
		Strainer, Punch	
		Strainer, Tea	
Tool, Hearth Cooking			*Note:* May also be used for an item known to have been used in a hearth (e.g., skewer), but which are listed elsewhere in this sub-class
	Board, Bannock		
	Broiler, Hearth		*Note:* Use for a gridded plate with a handle
		Broiler, Oyster	
	Crane, Fireplace		

Primary Object Term	Secondary Term	Tertiary Term	Notes
	Fork, Toasting		
	Gridiron		
	Jack, Roasting		
		Engine, Spit	
		Jack, Bottle	
		Smokejack	
	Oven, Reflector		
		Kitchen, Tin	
		Roaster, Apple	
		Roaster, Bird	
		Screen, Meat	
		Toaster, Cheese	
	Pothook		
		Trammel	
	Rake, Potato		
	Roaster, Chestnut		
	Roaster, Fish		*Note:* Use for a pronged utensil that holds fish by a fire
	Spit		
		Spit, Basket	
		Spit, Bird	
		Spit, Dangle	
	Tripod, Hearth		
Warmer, Food			
	Dish, Chafing		
	Lamp, Food Heat		
	Plate, Warming		
	Table, Steam		
	Warmer, Beverage		
	Warmer, Bottle		
	Warmer, Brandy		
Washer, Salad			
Wrap, Food			

Sub-Class:
FOOD PROCESSING EQUIPMENT

Definition: Objects originally created to manufacture food products from animals, animal products, grains, vegetables, fruits, or other plant materials. This sub-class includes tools, equipment, and supplies used in such activities as milling, butchering, cheesemaking, and rendering which are often, but not always, handled outside of the home kitchen.

Primary Object Term	Secondary Term	Tertiary Term	Notes
Bag, Grain			
Chink, Iron			
Container, Food Processing			
	Tank, Food Processing		
		Trough, Meat Salting	
	Vat, Food Processing		
		Vat, Cooling	
Crusher, Seed			
Extractor, Honey			
Huller			
	Huller, Nut		
	Huller, Pea		
	Huller, Seed		
Knife, Produce			
Knife, Uncapping			
Machine, Brush			*Note:* Use for a machine that rubs rice grains smooth
Magnet, Drum			
Mill, Cane			
Pan, Salt			
Sample, Food			*Note:* The specific type of food may be entered in a subject field
Skimmer, Molasses			
Sorter, Food			
	Sorter, Apple		
	Sorter, Bean		
	Sorter, Cranberry		
	Sorter, Potato		
Still			
Still, Solar			
Tester, Alcohol			
	Oenometer		*Note:* May also use "Alcoholometer" from Chemical Testing Devices
	Thief, Wine		
	Zymosismeter		

Primary Object Term	Secondary Term	Tertiary Term	Notes
Tool, Butchering			
	Ax, Slaughtering		
	Bar, Meat Hanging		
		Gambrel	
	Bench, Slaughtering		
	Cutter, Bone		
	Deflesher		
	Hammer, Slaughtering		
	Hoist, Dressing		
	Hook, Meat		
	Knife, Poultry Killing		
	Knife, Skinning		
	Knife, Sticking		
	Saw, Meat		
	Scalder, Hog		
	Scraper, Casing		
	Scraper, Hog		
	Skewer, Butchering		
	Table, Meat Cutting		*Note:* May also use "Table" from Support Furniture
Tool, Canning			
	Autoclave, Canning		
	Canner		
	Funnel, Canning		
	Jar, Preserving		
	Lifter, Jar		
	Rack, Canning		
	Retort, Canning		
	Seal, Jar Lid		
	Wrench, Jar		
Tool, Cider Making			
	Cutter, Cider Cheese		
	Mill, Apple		
	Press, Cider		
	Rake, Pomace		
Tool, Dairy			
	Aerator, Milk		
	Bowl, Butter-Working		
	Bowl, Skimming		
	Can, Dairy		

Primary Object Term	Secondary Term	Tertiary Term	Notes
		Can, Cream	
		Can, Milk	
		Can, Settling	
	Carrier, Cheese		
	Carrier, Milk Bottle		
	Cheesecloth		
	Churn		
	Condenser, Milk		
	Cooler, Dairy		
		Cooler, Milk	
		Tank, Cooling	
	Cutter, Curd		
		Knife, Cheese	*Note:* Use for a large spatula for breaking up curd
		Knife, Curd	
		Mill, Curd	
	Dasher, Churn		
	Evaporator, Milk		
	Fork, Butter		
	Fork, Curd		
	Heater, Milk		
	Homogenizer, Milk		
	Machine, Milking		
		Milker, Surge	
	Mold, Cheese		
	Packer, Butter		
	Paddle, Butter		
	Pail, Milking		
		Piggin, Milking	
	Pan, Milk		
	Pasteurizer, Milk		
	Press, Cheese		
	Pump, Milk		
	Rake, Curd		
	Sampler, Milk		
	Saw, Cheese		
	Scale, Dairy		*Note:* May also use "Scale" from Weights & Measures T&E
		Scale, Butter	
		Scale, Milk	

Primary Object Term	Secondary Term	Tertiary Term	Notes
	Scoop, Butter		
	Scoop, Curd		
	Separator, Cream		
	Sink, Curd		
	Skimmer, Cream		
	Squeezer, Curd		
	Stand, Churn		
	Stirrer, Curd		
	Stirrer, Milk		
	Strainer, Milk		
	Strainer, Whey		
	Tester, Cheese		
		Tester, Acidity	
		Trier, Cheese	
	Tester, Milk		
		Butyrometer	
		Galactometer	
		Lactobutyrometer	
		Lactometer	
		Milkometer	
		Pioscope	
		Tester, Babcock	
		Tester, Milk Sediment	
		Thermometer, Milk	
	Tester, Overrun		
	Trier, Butter		
	Tub, Butter		
	Tube, Milk		
	Vat, Cheese		
	Washer, Milk Bottle		
	Washer, Milk Can		
	Whip, Curd		
	Worker, Butter		
Tool, Egg Processing			
	Candler, Egg		
	Carrier, Egg		
	Grader, Egg		*Note:* May also use "Scale" from Weights & Measures T&E
	Washer, Egg		

Primary Object Term	Secondary Term	Tertiary Term	Notes
Tool, Food Packaging			
	Cap, Bottle		
	Capper, Bottle		
	Corker, Bottle		
	Filler, Bottle		
	Machine, Bag Closing		
		Machine, Bag Sewing	
		Machine, Bag Tying	
	Machine, Bottling		
	Machine, Can Capping		
	Machine, Cork		
	Machine, Food Packing		
	Machine, Packaging		
		Machine, Cartoning	
		Machine, Wrapping	
	Packer, Barrel		
	Sealer, Vacuum		
Tool, Fruit Processing			
	Grader, Fruit		
Tool, Grain Processing			
	Agitator, Flour-Bleaching		
	Aleurometer		
	Blender, Flour		
	Cleaner, Grain		
		Scourer, Grain	
		Screen, Rolling	
		Smutter	
	Conditioner, Grain		
		Conditioner, Wheat	
	Duster, Bran		
	Electrifier, Flour-Bleaching		
	Feeder, Blending		
	Feeder, Flour-Bleaching		
	Feeder, Roll		
	Grinder, Bran		
	Handstone		
	Holder, Grain Bag		
	Mill, Grain		

Primary Object Term	Secondary Term	Tertiary Term	Notes
		Mill, Buhr	
		Mill, Corn	
		Mill, Flour	
		Mill, Hammer	
		Mill, Middlings	
		Mill, Roller	
		Mill, Sorghum	
	Millstone		
	Mortar, Grain		
		Metate	
		Mortar, Stamp	
	Purifier, Middlings		
	Scale, Grain		*Note:* May also use "Scale" from Weights & Measures T&E
	Separator, Grain		
		Bolter, Sieve	
		Plansifter	
		Separator, Disk	
		Separator, Grading	
		Separator, Milling	
		Separator, Receiving	
	Washer, Grain		
		Washer, Wheat	
Tool, Lard Processing			
	Cooler, Lard		
	Kettle, Lard Rendering		
	Paddle, Lard		
	Press, Lard		
	Press, Tankage		
	Roll, Lard		
	Stirrer, Lard		
	Tank, Lard Settling		
Tool, Maple Sugaring			
	Bucket, Sap		
	Dipper, Syrup		
	Evaporator, Sugar		
	Mold, Maple Sugar		
	Pan, Sap		
	Skimmer, Syrup		
	Spout, Sap		

Sub-Class:
FOOD STORAGE EQUIPMENT

Definition: Objects originally created specifically to keep food or beverages, either as pieces of furniture such as cabinets, as appliances such as refrigerators, or as containers such as casks and tea caddies. This sub-class also includes container accessories such as bungs, stoppers, and stands. It does not include shipping containers, product packages, general cabinetry, or storage items used for kitchenware or the serving of food.

Primary Object Term	Secondary Term	Tertiary Term	Notes
Bag, Food Storage			
	Bag, Freezer		
Basket, Food Storage			
	Basket, Ring		
Bin, Food Storage			
	Bin, Flour		
	Bin, Vegetable		
Bowl, Food Storage			
Box, Food Storage			
	Box, Biscuit		
	Box, Bread		
	Box, Cake		
	Box, Cheese		
	Box, Chuck		
	Box, Pantry		
	Box, Porch		
	Box, Salt		
	Box, Spice		
Bucket, Food Storage			
	Bucket, Flour		
Bung			
Cabinet, Food Storage			*Note:* May also use "Cabinet" from Storage & Display Furniture
	Cabinet, Spice		
Caddy, Food			
	Caddy, Tea		
Can, Food Storage			
	Can, Grease		
	Can, Lard		
Canister, Food Storage			
	Canister, Coffee		
	Canister, Flour		
	Canister, Sugar		

Primary Object Term	Secondary Term	Tertiary Term	Notes
	Canister, Tea		
Cask, Food			
	Cask, Bread		
	Cask, Rum		
	Cask, Water		
	Cask, Whiskey		
	Cask, Wine		
Chest, Food Storage			*Note:* May also use "Chest" from Storage & Display Furniture
	Chest, Spice		
	Chest, Tea		
Cover, Food Storage			
Crock, Food Storage			
	Crock, Butter		
Cupboard, Food Storage			*Note:* May also use "Cupboard" from Storage & Display Furniture
	Cupboard, Jelly		
	Cupboard, Spice		
	Safe, Kitchen		
Dredger			
	Shaker, Flour		
Firkin			
Freezer			
	Freezer, Chest		
	Freezer, Upright		
	Freezer, Walk-In		
Jar, Food Storage			
	Jar, Cookie		
	Jar, Ginger		
Jug, Food Storage			
	Jug, Syrup		
	Jug, Whiskey		
Keeper, Oil			
Keg, Food Storage			
	Keg, Beer		
Pan, Freezer			
Rack, Food Storage			*Note:* May also use "Rack" from Storage & Display Accessories
	Rack, Bottle Storage		
		Rack, Wine	

Primary Object Term	Secondary Term	Tertiary Term	Notes
	Rack, Spice		
Refrigerator			
	Icebox		
	Refrigerator, Portable		
	Refrigerator, Window		
Stand, Cask			
Stopper			
Tank, Food Storage			
Tantalus			
Tub, Food Storage			
Vat, Food Storage			
Wineskin			

Class:
FOOD SERVICE T&E

Definition: Tools, equipment, and supplies originally created for the presentation, serving, or consumption of food or beverages by humans.

Sub-Class:
DRINKING VESSELS

Definition: Objects originally created as receptacles from which beverages are directly consumed. This sub-class includes containers intended for individual place settings. It does not include eating vessels or vessels designed for the presentation and serving of beverages, which are listed in Serving Vessels.

Primary Object Term	Secondary Term	Tertiary Term	Notes
Beaker, Drinking			
	Passglas		
Biberon			
Bottle, Drinking			
	Bottle, Nursing		
	Bottle, Water		
Bowl, Drinking			
	Bowl, Brandy		
	Bowl, Tea		
	Mazer		
	Mether		
Canteen			
Cantir			
Cover, Drinking Vessel			
Cup			
	Cann		
	Charka		
	Cup, Canteen		
	Cup, Caudle		
	Cup, Chocolate		
	Cup, Coffee		
		Cup, Demitasse	
	Cup, Collapsible		
	Cup, Covered		
	Cup, Disposable		
	Cup, Dram		
	Cup, Fuddling		
	Cup, Invalid		
	Cup, Mustache		
	Cup, Nursing		
	Cup, Punch		

Primary Object Term	Secondary Term	Tertiary Term	Notes
	Cup, Saki		
	Cup, Spout		
	Cup, Standing		
	Cup, Straw		
	Cup, Traveling		
	Cup, Wine		
	Taster, Wine		
	Tazza		
	Teacup		
Cup, Stirrup			
Glass, Drinking			
	Glass, Cider		
	Glass, Cocktail		
	Glass, Cordial		
	Glass, Dram		
	Glass, Flip		
	Glass, Gin		
	Glass, Juice		
	Glass, Lemonade		
	Glass, Malt Beverage		
	Glass, Mead		
	Glass, Shot		
	Glass, Soda Fountain		
	Glass, Syllabub		
	Glass, Trick		
	Glass, Water		
	Glass, Whiskey		
	Glass, Wine		
		Glass, Champagne	
		Glass, Flute	
		Roemer	
	Goblet		
		Pokal	
	Rummer		
	Snifter		
	Tumbler		
Hen, Tappit			
Horn, Drinking			
Jack, Leather			

Primary Object Term	Secondary Term	Tertiary Term	Notes
Jug, Puzzle			
Lid, Drinking Vessel			
Mug			
	Mug, Coffee		
	Mug, Travel		
	Stein		
	Tankard		
	Tyg		
Pannikin			
Porro			
Pot, Posset			
Stoup			

Sub-Class:
EATING VESSELS

Definition: Objects originally created as receptacles from which food is directly consumed. This sub-class includes containers intended for individual place settings. It does not include drinking vessels or vessels designed for the presentation and serving of food, which are listed in Serving Vessels.

Primary Object Term	Secondary Term	Tertiary Term	Notes
Bowl, Eating			
	Bowl, Cereal		
	Bowl, Dessert		
		Bowl, Ice Cream	
	Bowl, Salad		
	Bowl, Soup		
		Bowl, Bouillon	
Cup, Favor			
Cup, Soup			
Dish, Eating			
	Chip, Butter		
	Cup, Custard		*Note:* Use for a cup that serves as an eating vessel; for a baking cup, use "Ramekin" from Cooking Vessels
	Cup, Orange		
	Dish, Corn		
	Dish, Dessert		
		Coupe	
		Dish, Banana Split	
		Dish, Berry	
		Dish, Pudding	
		Dish, Sherbet	
		Dish, Sundae	
	Dish, Sauce		
	Eggcup		
	Glass, Dessert		
		Glass, Custard	
		Glass, Jelly	
		Glass, Sweetmeat	
	Plate, Food		
		Plate, Butter	
		Plate, Cup	
		Plate, Dessert	
		Plate, Dinner	
		Plate, Luncheon	
		Plate, Place	

Primary Object Term	Secondary Term	Tertiary Term	Notes
		Plate, Salad	
		Plate, Soup	
		Plate, Tea	
		Twiffler	
	Porringer		
	Saucer		
		Saucer, Berry	
		Saucer, Bouillon Cup	
		Saucer, Demitasse	
Feeder, Invalid			
Papboat			
Tray, Frozen Dinner			
Tray, Mess			

Sub-Class:
EATING & DRINKING UTENSILS

Definition: Objects originally created as implements for consuming food or beverages. This sub-class includes tools intended for individual place settings. It does not include utensils designed for the serving of food or beverages, which are listed in Serving Utensils.

Primary Object Term	Secondary Term	Tertiary Term	Notes
Chopstick			
Fork, Eating			
	Fork, Berry		
	Fork, Cake		
	Fork, Dessert		
		Fork, Ice Cream	
		Fork, Pastry	
	Fork, Dinner		
	Fork, Fish		
	Fork, Folding		
	Fork, Hors d'Oeuvre		
	Fork, Lobster		
	Fork, Luncheon		
	Fork, Oyster		
	Fork, Salad		
Holder, Corn			
Knife, Eating			
	Knife, Dessert		
	Knife, Dinner		
	Knife, Fish		
	Knife, Fruit		
	Knife, Luncheon		
	Knife, Steak		
	Spreader, Butter		
Knork			
Pick, Eating			
	Pick, Hors d'Oeuvre		
	Pick, Seafood		
Scoop, Marrow			
Spife			
Spoon, Eating			
	Spoon, Cereal		
	Spoon, Chocolate		
	Spoon, Coffee		
		Spoon, Demitasse	

Primary Object Term	Secondary Term	Tertiary Term	Notes
	Spoon, Cream		
	Spoon, Dessert		
		Spoon, Ice Cream	
		Spoon, Sherbet	
	Spoon, Egg		
	Spoon, Folding		
	Spoon, Fruit		
		Spoon, Grapefruit	
		Spoon, Orange	
	Spoon, Iced Tea		
	Spoon, Lemonade		
	Spoon, Marrow		
	Spoon, Soda		
	Spoon, Soup		
		Spoon, Bouillon	
	Teaspoon		
Spork			
	Fork, Sucket		
Straw			
	Bombilla		
Utensil, Infant			
	Pusher, Food		
	Spoon, Baby		
	Spoon, Feeding		
	Spoon, Pap		

Sub-Class:
FOOD SERVICE ACCESSORIES

Definition: Tools, equipment, and supplies originally created to facilitate the use of food service vessels, utensils, or related articles. This sub-class includes food waste containers, dining table coverings, and containers for food service objects.

Primary Object Term	Secondary Term	Tertiary Term	Notes
Basket, Wine Bottle			
Bowl, Finger			
Bucket, Ice			
Caddinet			
Carrier, Food			
	Bag, Lunch		
	Basket, Lunch		
	Basket, Picnic		
		Hamper, Picnic	
	Bottle, Vacuum		
	Lunchbox		
		Box, Bento	
		Pail, Dinner	
Cart, Food Service			
	Cart, Beverage		
	Cart, Dish		
	Cart, Tray		
Case, Food Service			*Note:* Use for any container specifically designed for protecting and/or transporting food service objects; if a case is designed specifically for a given object, a new term may be created with the *Nomenclature* term for that object as a modifier; that term may be organized under "Case, Food Service," as the six terms are below
	Case, Eating Utensil		
		Case, Chopstick	
		Case, Flatware	
	Case, Napkin		
	Case, Serving Utensil		
	Cover, Canteen		
Charm, Beverage			
Chest, Mess			
Coaster			
	Coaster, Wine		
Collar, Wine			

Primary Object Term	Secondary Term	Tertiary Term	Notes
Container, Food Waste			*Note:* Use only for a waste container intended for table use
	Bowl, Waste		
	Dish, Bone		
	Dish, Tea Bag		
	Dish, Waste		
Cooler			
	Cooler, Beer		
	Cooler, Wine		
	Cooler, Wine Glass		
Cozy			
	Cozy, Tea		
Cross, Dish			
Dispenser, Food Service			
	Dispenser, Cup		
	Dispenser, Napkin		
	Dispenser, Plate		
	Dispenser, Straw		
	Dispenser, Toothpick		
Holder, Beverage			
	Holder, Cup		
	Holder, Insulated Beverage		
Holder, Casserole			
Holder, Coaster			
Holder, Menu			
Holder, Napkin			
Holder, Placecard			
Holder, Toothpick			
Label, Decanter			
Linen, Table			*Note:* In this context, "linen" may refer to items made from non-textile materials such as paper or plastic
	Napkin		
		Napkin, Bread Basket	
	Pad, Table		
	Placemat		
	Tablecloth		
		Cloth, Tea	

Primary Object Term	Secondary Term	Tertiary Term	Notes
Liner, Platter			
Monteith			
Plateau			
Rack, Bottle Serving			
Rack, Pie			
Rack, Tray			
Rest, Knife			
Ring, Dish			
Ring, Napkin			
Spigot			
Spooner			
Stand, Carafe			
Stopper, Bottle			
Tap, Beer			
Tilter, Platter			
Tray, Food Service			*Note:* Use for a tray created to store or transport food service objects; for a tray used to present or serve food, use "Tray, Serving" from Serving Vessels
	Lazy Susan		
	Tray, Bed		
	Tray, Butler's		
	Tray, Cafeteria		*Note:* Use for a tray designed to hold food service utensils and vessels; for a compartmentalized tray designed to hold food, use "Tray, Mess" from Eating Vessels
	Tray, Flatware		

Sub-Class:
FOOD SERVICE SETS

Definition: Groupings of objects originally created for the presentation, serving, or consumption of food or beverages. Note: Other terms also may be used to represent specific set components from other Food Service T&E sub-classes.

Primary Object Term	Secondary Term	Tertiary Term	Notes
Kit, Mess			
Service, Coffee			
Service, Dessert			
Service, Tea			
Set, Beverage			*Note:* Use for a set comprising a pitcher and matching glasses
Set, Carving			
Set, Condiment			
Set, Cup and Saucer			
Set, Decanter			
Set, Flatware			
Set, Luncheon			*Note:* Use for a matching set of placemats, coasters, centerpiece, etc., or for a relatively small tablecloth and matching napkins
Set, Mayonnaise			
Set, Salt and Pepper			
Set, Spoon and Salt			
Set, Sugar and Creamer			
Set, Tablecloth			*Note:* Use for a matching set of napkins and tablecloth
Set, Tableware			*Note:* Use for any matched set of cups, saucers, plates, etc.

Sub-Class:
SERVING UTENSILS

Definition: Objects originally created as implements for the serving of food or beverages. This sub-class does not include tools used for food preparation or consumption.

Primary Object Term	Secondary Term	Tertiary Term	Notes
Dipper, Honey			
Fork, Serving			
	Fork, Asparagus		
	Fork, Carving		
	Fork, Cold-Meat		
	Fork, Fish Serving		
	Fork, Fondue		
	Fork, Lemon		
	Fork, Olive		
	Fork, Pickle		
	Fork, Sardine		
Hammer, Sugar			
Knife, Serving			
	Knife, Bread		
	Knife, Butter		
	Knife, Cake		
	Knife, Carving		
	Knife, Cheese Serving		
	Knife, Ice Cream		
	Knife, Jelly		
Ladle, Serving			
	Dipper		
	Ladle, Cream		
	Ladle, Gravy		
	Ladle, Mayonnaise		
	Ladle, Punch		
	Ladle, Sauce		
	Ladle, Soup		
	Ladle, Toddy		
Scoop, Serving			
	Scoop, Cheese		
	Scoop, Ice Cream		
	Scoop, Nut		
	Scoop, Salt		
	Scoop, Sugar		

Primary Object Term	Secondary Term	Tertiary Term	Notes
Server			
	Server, Cake		
	Server, Cheese		
	Server, Ice Cream		
	Server, Lemon		
	Server, Pie		
	Server, Salad		
	Server, Tomato		
	Slice, Fish		
Shears, Grape			
Spoon, Serving			
	Spoon, Berry		
	Spoon, Bonbon		
	Spoon, Caddy		
	Spoon, Claret		
	Spoon, Jam		
	Spoon, Mustard		
	Spoon, Olive		
	Spoon, Salt		
	Spoon, Sugar		
	Tablespoon		
Tongs, Serving			
	Tongs, Asparagus		
	Tongs, Ice		
	Tongs, Salad		
	Tongs, Sandwich		
	Tongs, Spaghetti		
	Tongs, Sugar		

Sub-Class:
SERVING VESSELS

Definition: Objects originally created as containers in or on which food or beverage is presented or from which food or beverage is served but not directly consumed.

Primary Object Term	Secondary Term	Tertiary Term	Notes
Argyle			
Basin, Serving			
Basket, Food			
	Basket, Bread		
	Basket, Cake		
	Basket, Fruit		
Bowl, Serving			
	Bowl, Berry		
	Bowl, Bride's		
	Bowl, Covered		
	Bowl, Fruit		
	Bowl, Jelly		
	Bowl, Mayonnaise		
	Bowl, Nut		
	Bowl, Salad Serving		
	Bowl, Sugar		
	Bowl, Whipped Cream		
	Compote		
	Nappy		
Box, Serving			
	Box, Comfit		
	Box, Sardine		
	Box, Sugar		
Cover, Serving Vessel			
Dish, Serving			
	Cooler, Butter		
	Dish, Butter		
	Dish, Candy		
		Dish, Bonbon	
	Dish, Celery		
	Dish, Cheese		
	Dish, Honey		
	Dish, Jelly		
	Dish, Nut		
	Dish, Relish		
	Dish, Sweetmeat		
	Dish, Vegetable		

Primary Object Term	Secondary Term	Tertiary Term	Notes
	Plate, Serving		
		Plate, Cake	
		Plate, Fruit	
		Plate, Mayonnaise Bowl	
		Plate, Oyster	
		Plate, Sauceboat	
		Plate, Spice	
		Plate, Toddy	
		Plate, Vegetable	
	Platter		
		Charger	
		Platter, Well	
		Trencher	
	Sauceboat		
Dome, Food			
	Dome, Cheese		
Lid, Dish			
Rack, Toast			
Salver			
Stand, Serving			
	Epergne		
	Pyramid, Dessert		
	Stand, Cake		
	Stand, Cruet		
	Stand, Egg		
	Stand, Ham		
	Stand, Spoon		
	Stand, Sweetmeat		
	Stand, Teapot		
	Tilter, Pot		
Tray, Serving			*Note:* Use for a tray created to present or serve food; for a tray used to store or transport food service objects, use "Tray, Food Service" from Food Service Accessories
	Cheeseboard		
	Tray, Bread		
	Tray, Butter		
	Tray, Cracker		
	Tray, Fruit		
	Tray, Ice Cream		

Primary Object Term	Secondary Term	Tertiary Term	Notes
	Tray, Relish		
	Tray, Sauceboat		
	Tray, Tea		
	Tray, Tureen		
Tureen			
	Pot, Ollio		
	Tureen, Soup		
	Tureen, Sauce		
Vase, Celery			
Vessel, Condiment			
	Bottle, Condiment		
	Caster		
		Caster, Mustard	
		Caster, Pepper	
		Caster, Sugar	
		Muffineer	
	Caster, Pickle		
	Cruet		
	Dish, Salt		
		Salt, Standing	
		Saltcellar	
	Jar, Condiment		
		Jar, Honey	
		Jar, Pickle	
		Pot, Jam	
		Pot, Mustard	
	Mill, Pepper		
	Saltshaker		
	Shaker, Pepper		
	Shaker, Sugar		
Vessel, Drink Serving			
	Bottle, Serving		
		Bottle, Decanter	
		Bottle, Milk	*Note:* May also use "Package, Product" from Merchandising T&E
		Bottle, Seltzer	
		Bottle, Wine	*Note:* May also use "Package, Product" from Merchandising T&E
	Bowl, Punch		
	Carafe		

Primary Object Term	Secondary Term	Tertiary Term	Notes
	Coffeepot		
		Biggin, Coffee	
	Cooler, Water		
	Decanter		
		Decanter, Bar	
		Decanter, Ship's	
		Jug, Claret	
	Dispenser, Beverage		
		Fountain, Soda	
	Flagon		
	Jug, Serving		
		Growler, Beer	
		Jug, Bunghole	
		Jug, Milk	
		Jug, Monkey	
		Jug, Toby	
	Lifter, Toddy		
	Pitcher		
		Ewer	
		Pitcher, Beer	
		Pitcher, Cream	
		Pitcher, Hot Water	
		Pitcher, Ice Water	
		Pitcher, Milk	
		Pitcher, Syrup	
		Pitcher, Water	
	Pot, Chocolate		
	Teapot		
	Urn, Beverage		
		Samovar	
		Urn, Coffee	
		Urn, Hot Water	
		Urn, Tea	
Warmer, Egg			*Note:* May also use "Warmer, Food" from Food Preparation Equipment

Class:
FORESTRY T&E

Definition: Tools, equipment, and supplies originally created for the management and harvesting of forests. This class includes objects used for cutting, handling, or processing timber or for harvesting non-food forest crops such as bark or rubber. This class does not include equipment for cartage, which is classified under Distribution & Transportation Objects, or equipment for manufacturing products from wood, which is classified under Woodworking T&E or Papermaking T&E.

Primary Object Term	Secondary Term	Tertiary Term	Notes
Adz, Marking			
Auger, Raft			
Ax, Timber			
	Ax, Barking		
	Ax, Double-Bitted		
	Ax, Felling		
	Ax, Lopping		
	Ax, Marking		
	Ax, Split		
	Ax, Turpentine		
Caliper, Timber			
Chain, Brake			
Chain, Log			
Cup, Turpentine			
Dendrometer			
Dipper, Turpentine			
Dolly, Timber			
Hack, Turpentine			
Hammer, Marking			
Hook, Logging			
	Carrier, Timber		
	Dog, Log		
	Dog, Raft		
	Dog, Span		
	Hook, Cant		
		Dog, Ring	
	Hook, Grappling		
	Hook, Pulp		
	Hook, Raft		
	Hook, Swamp		
	Hookaroon		
	Peavy		
	Pickaroon		

Primary Object Term	Secondary Term	Tertiary Term	Notes
	Tongs, Skidding		
Knife, Brush			
Knife, Shearing			
Maul, Grab			
Mill, Bark			
Pike, Pole			
	Pike, Jam		
Pin, Boom			
Ring, Snub			
Rule, Log			
Saw, Timber			
	Bucksaw		
	Saw, Chain		
	Saw, Crosscut		
		Saw, One-Handed Crosscut	
		Saw, Two-Handed Crosscut	
	Trimmer, Log		
Scale, Timber			
Scraper, Tree			
Scraper, Turpentine			
Scribe, Timber			
Shackle, Raft			
Shredder, Bark			
Spade, Tree			
Spike, Tree Climbing			
Tool, Barking			
	Chisel, Barking		
	Iron, Barking		
Torch, Drip			
Trough, Sap			
Wedge, Felling			
Wheel, Log			

Class:
GLASS, PLASTICS & CLAYWORKING T&E

Definition: Tools, equipment, and supplies originally created for fabricating objects from homogenous, complex compounds, such as glass, clay, rubber, synthetic resins, plastics, or waxes. This class also includes the tools, equipment, and supplies used for producing such homogenous, complex compounds. These compounds differ from other materials because they generally require elaborate processing at some point during their use. As compounds, they differ from other processed materials such as leather because they are not discrete units; they differ from aggregate materials such as masonry because of their homogeneity and their need for elaborate processing.

Primary Object Term	Secondary Term	Tertiary Term	Notes
Armature			
Battledore			
Bench, Glassmaker's			
Block, Forming			
Block, Glassblower's			
Blowpipe			
Blunger			
Boss			
Box, Wax			
Brick, Kiln			*Note:* May also use "Firebrick" from Construction Materials
Brush, Glazing			
Bucket, Water			
Buffer, Glass			
Caliper, Glassmaker's			
Caliper, Potter's			
Cart, Batch			
Case, Snap			
Clamp, Glassworking			
Coggle			
Compass, Potter's			
Cone, Pyrometric			
Crimper, Glass			
Cutter, Glass			
Cutter, Toggle			
Dod			
Drill, Flexible-Shaft			
Extruder			
	Mill, Pug		
File, Glass			
Fork, Carrying-In			

Primary Object Term	Secondary Term	Tertiary Term	Notes
Funnel, Wax			
Furnace, Glass			
	Lehr		
Furniture, Kiln			
	Sagger		
	Spacer, Kiln		
Glaze			
Heater, Strip			
Heater, Thermoforming			
	Heater, Calrod		
Hook, Glassworker's			
Iron, Gathering			
Kidney			
Kiln			
	Kiln, Mold		
	Kiln, Pot		
	Oven, Curing		
Knife, Chest			
Knife, Fettling			
Knife, Stopping			
Ladle, Melting			
	Ladle, Wax		
Lathe			
Machine, Blowing			
Machine, Clay Coating			
Machine, Engraving			
Machine, Filament Winding			
Machine, Foam			
Machine, Foam Cutting			
Machine, Metering			
Machine, Molding			
Machine, Plastic Forming			
Machine, Preform			
Machine, Pumping			
Machine, Stamping			
Machine, Vulcanizing			

Primary Object Term	Secondary Term	Tertiary Term	Notes
Marver			
Mask, Lip			
Mask, Plug			
Mill, Glaze			
Mold			*Note:* Information about what the mold produces should be recorded in a subject field; this information may be entered according to the naming conventions and object terms used throughout *Nomenclature*
	Mold, Candle		
	Mold, Glass		
	Mold, Piece		
	Mold, Plate		
	Mold, Pottery		
Opener, Lead			
Pan, Drip			
Pig			
Pincers			
Pliers, Glass			
Point, Glazier's			
Pontil			
Pot, Melting			
Press, Mold			
Press, Vacuum			
Pucella			
Rack, Blowpipe			
Rake, Kiln			
Reamer			
Reel, Candle Dipping			
Rod, Tungsten			
Roller, Impregnating			
Roller, Potter's			
Roulette, Potter's			
Shears, Glass			
Slab, Graphite			
Spatula, Kiln			
Stand, Sculpting			
Stick, Steam			
Stilt, Kiln			
Stone, Polishing			

Primary Object Term	Secondary Term	Tertiary Term	Notes
Stylus, Clay			
Test, Oven			
Tongs, Pottery			
	Tongs, Dipping		
	Tongs, Raku		
Tool, Finishing			
Tool, Flaring			
Tool, Foam Cutting			
Tool, Forming			
Tool, Incising			
Tool, Modeling			
	Rib, Potter's		
	Scraper		
	Tool, Loop		
	Tool, Turning		
Tool, Needle			
Tool, Pot-Setting			
Tracer			
Trailer, Slip			
	Cup, Slip-Trailing		
	Syringe, Slip-Trailing		
Tub, Iron Cooling			
Tweezers, Glassworking			
V-Block			
Wheel, Glassworking			
	Wheel, Cutting		
	Wheel, Grinding		
		Wheel, Lapping	
	Wheel, Polishing		
Wheel, Potter's			
	Wheel, Banding		
	Wheel, Bench		
	Wheel, Kick		

Class:
LEATHER, HORN & SHELLWORKING T&E

Definition: Tools, equipment, and supplies originally created for processing materials that are animal in origin. This class includes tools and equipment for processing furs or hides, for preparing leather, for fabricating leather products, for working shell, horn, bone, or ivory, and for making things from quills or feathers. This class also includes objects for processing materials that are the products of insects or bacteria.

Primary Object Term	Secondary Term	Tertiary Term	Notes
Anvil, Shoemaker's			
Awl, Leather			
	Awl, Closing		
	Awl, Collar		
	Awl, Drawing		
	Awl, Garnish		
	Awl, Harness		
	Awl, Peg		
	Awl, Saddler's		
	Awl, Scratch		
	Awl, Seat		
	Awl, Sewing		
	Awl, Stabbing		
	Awl, Stitching		
Beam, Currier's			
Beam, Tanner's			
Bench, Leatherworker's			
	Bench, Cobbler's		
	Bench, Harness Maker's		
Board, Drying			
Board, Graining			
Bristle, Sewing			
Brush, Polish			
Burnisher			
Cage, Drying			
Case, Punch			
Channeler, Leather			
Chisel, Thonging			
Clamp, Leatherworking			
	Clamp, Boot		
	Clamp, Last		
	Clamp, Saddler's		

Primary Object Term	Secondary Term	Tertiary Term	Notes
	Clamp, Stretching		
Compass, Scratch			
Creaser			
	Creaser, Double		
	Creaser, Edge		
	Creaser, Screw		
	Creaser, Single		
Crimper, Leather			
Cutter, Leather			
	Beveler		
		Beveler, Edge	
		Beveler, Safety	
	Cutter, Rotary Leather		
	Edger, Leather		
	Knife, Leather		
		Knife, Currier's	
		Knife, Draw	
		Knife, Feathering	
		Knife, Head	
		Knife, Skiving	
		Knife, Square Point	
		Knife, Stretching	
		Knife, Welt	
	Shave, Leather		
		Shave, Edge	
		Shave, Heel	
		Shave, Skirt	
		Spokeshave, Leather	
	Shears, Leather		
	Trimmer, Leather		
		Trimmer, Edge	
		Trimmer, Welt	
Dish, Nail			
Divider, Stitch			
Drum, Sawdust			
Fastener, Button			
Fid, Leatherworking			
File, Saddler's			
Fingerstall			

Primary Object Term	Secondary Term	Tertiary Term	Notes
Fork, Straining			
Frame, Toggling			
Gauge, Leather			
	Gauge, Draw		
	Gauge, Plough		
Glazer			
Gouge, Leather			
	Gouge, Adjustable		
	Gouge, Channel		
	Gouge, V		
	Groover, Stitching		
Haft, Sewing			
Hammer, Leatherworking			
	Hammer, Cobbler's		
	Hammer, Heel		
	Hammer, Saddler's		
	Hammer, Shoemaker's		
	Hammer, Turn-Shoe		
Hook, Last			
Iron, Pinking			
Iron, Seat			
Jack, Glazing			
Jack, Last			
Kicker			
Knife, Fleshing			
Knife, Unhairing			
Lapstone			
Last			
	Last, Boot		
	Last, Saddle		
	Last, Shoe		
Machine, Beating			
Machine, Leatherworking			
	Machine, Beaming		
	Machine, Deburring		
	Machine, Dehairing		
	Machine, Drying		
	Machine, Eyelet		

Primary Object Term	Secondary Term	Tertiary Term	Notes
	Machine, Fleshing		
	Machine, Leather Brushing		
	Machine, Leather Buffing		
	Machine, Leather Carding		
	Machine, Leather Creasing		
	Machine, Leather Ironing		
	Machine, Leather Sewing		
	Machine, Leather Shearing		
	Machine, Leather Stretching		
	Machine, Riveting		
	Machine, Shoemaking		
	Machine, Skiving		
	Machine, Splitting		
	Press, Clicker		
Machine, Pulling			
Mallet, Leatherworking			
Material, Animal			
	Blank, Horn		
	Blank, Ivory		
	Blank, Tortoise		
	Hide		
	Horn, Buffalo		
	Pelt		
Maul, Rawhide			
Nail, Cobbler's			
	Hobnail		
Needle, Leatherworking			
	Needle, Glover's		
	Needle, Harness		
	Needle, Lacing		
Nipper			
Palm			

Primary Object Term	Secondary Term	Tertiary Term	Notes
Peg, Shoe			
Pincers, Lasting			
Pliers, Leatherworking			
	Pliers, Lacing		
	Pliers, Pad Screw		
Pony, Lacing			
Press, Fur			
Punch, Leather			
	Punch, Arch		
	Punch, Belt		
	Punch, Button Hole		
	Punch, Drive		
	Punch, Eyelet		
	Punch, Hand		
	Punch, Hole		
	Punch, Line		
	Punch, Oblong		
	Punch, Piercing		
	Punch, Revolving		
	Punch, Saddler's		
	Punch, Scalloping		
	Punch, Strap End		
Rasp, Shoemaker's			
Rivet, Leather			
Rod, Stuffing			
Rounder			
Scraper, Hide			
	Scraper, End		
	Scraper, Side		
	Scraper, Thumbnail		
Setter			
	Setter, Grommet		
	Setter, Rivet		
Slicker, Edge			
Smoother			
Stamp, Leather			
Stand, Awl			
Stand, Cobbler's			
Steel, Finger			

Primary Object Term	Secondary Term	Tertiary Term	Notes
Steel, Turning			
Stick, Size			
Stretcher, Pelt			
Stretcher, Web			
Template, Leather			
	Pattern, Leather		
		Pattern, Sole	
	Stencil, Leather		
Tongs, Tanner's			
Tool, Hornworker's			
	Bar, Hornworker's		
	Bench, Hornworker's		
	Carlet		
	Clamp, Hornworker's		
	Die, Hornworker's		
	Drawknife, Hornworker's		
	File, Hornworker's		
		Graille	
	Horse, Hornworker's		
	Kettle, Hornworker's		
	Machine, Hornworker's		
		Machine, Twinning	
	Mandrel, Hornworker's		
	Press, Hornworker's		
	Quarnet, Hornworker's		
	Reamer, Hornworker's		
	Tongs, Hornworker's		
	Topper, Hornworker's		
Tray, Peg			
Turner, Seam			
Vat, Leather Processing			
	Vat, Leather Bleaching		
	Vat, Leather Dyeing		
	Vat, Leather Pickling		
Vise, Leatherworking			
	Vise, Harness Maker's		
Wheel, Leatherworking			

Primary Object Term	Secondary Term	Tertiary Term	Notes
	Wheel, Embossing		
	Wheel, Finishing		
	Wheel, Polishing/ Sanding		
	Wheel, Pricking		
Wringer, Leather			

Class:
MASONRY & STONEWORKING T&E

Definition: Tools, equipment, and supplies originally created for working with natural stone or with aggregate materials such as concrete, mortar, brick, or plaster. These aggregate materials can be of natural or manufactured origin. They differ from materials related to Glass, Plastics & Clayworking T&E because they lack homogeneity and the need for complex processing.

Primary Object Term	Secondary Term	Tertiary Term	Notes
Anvil, Slater's			
Ax, Brick			
Ax, Mason's			
	Ax, Tooth		
	Cavil		
Badger			
Bench, Banker			
Bit, Masonry			
	Bit, Scutch		
	Point		
Blade, Cleaving			
Block, Polishing			
Brush, Mason's			
Chisel, Brick			
Chisel, Stone			
	Boaster		
	Chisel, Blocking		
	Chisel, Cutting		
	Chisel, Octagonal		
	Chisel, Pitching		
	Chisel, Plugging		
	Chisel, Point		
	Chisel, Splitting		
	Chisel, Straight		
	Chisel, Tooth		
Chute, Drop			
Drill, Stone			
	Drill, Octagonal		
	Drill, Round		
	Drill, Star		
Edger, Masonry			
Feather			
Float, Hand			
	Float, Angle		

Primary Object Term	Secondary Term	Tertiary Term	Notes
	Float, Bull		
	Float, Long		
	Float, Texture		
Floatstone			
Graver, Stone			
	Burin, Stone		
Groover			
Hammer, Stone			
	Bushhammer		
	Hammer, Ax		
	Hammer, Brick		
	Hammer, Crandall		
	Hammer, Face		
	Hammer, Knapping		
	Hammer, Mason's		
	Hammer, Patent		
	Hammer, Slater's		
		Zax	
	Hammer, Spalling		
Hammerstone			
Jointer, Masonry			
Kiln, Brick			
Kiln, Cement			
Kiln, Lime			
Knife, Slate Trimming			
Level, Mason's			
Lewis			
Machine, Brick			
Machine, Concrete Finishing			
Machine, Gunite			
Mallet, Stone			
	Dummy		
	Mallet, Mason's		
	Mallet, Stonecarver's		
Marker, Mason's			
Mixer, Masonry			
	Batcher		
	Mixer, Concrete		
	Mixer, Jiffler		

Primary Object Term	Secondary Term	Tertiary Term	Notes
Mold, Brick			
Nipper, Tile			
Pattern, Masonry			
Pick, Stone			
	Pick, Flinting		
	Pick, Mason's		
	Pick, Mill		
	Pick, Slate		
Pin, Line			
Plug, Masonry			
Poker, Kiln			
Profile, Bricklaying			
Puller, Slate			
Pump, Concrete			
Punch, Slater's			
Raker			
Rasp, Stone			
Ripper, Slater's			
Rule, Jointing			
Saw, Brick			
Saw, Stone			
	Saw, Grub		
	Saw, Mason's		
Scotch			
Scraper, Block			
Screed			
Scutch			
Spatula, Plasterer's			
Spoon, Mud			
Spreader, Concrete			
Square, Mason's			
Stake, Slater's			
Tie, Wall			
Tongs, Brick			
Tool, Plastering			
	Hawk		
	Hod		
	Knife, Elastic		
	Knife, Plaster		

Primary Object Term	Secondary Term	Tertiary Term	Notes
	Machine, Plastering		
	Paddle, Angle		
	Plane, Angle		
	Plow, Angle		
	Rab		
	Rule, Featheredge		
	Tool, Radius		
	Tool, Scratch		
		Comb, Cock's	
		Drag	
		Float, Devil	
		Scarifier, Plaster	
Trough, Mixing			
Trowel			
	Trowel, Brick		
	Trowel, Buttering		
	Trowel, Corner		
	Trowel, Grouting		
	Trowel, Margin		
	Trowel, Mechanical		
	Trowel, Pointing		
	Trowel, Smoothing		
Tube, Grouting			

Class:
METALWORKING T&E

Definition: Tools, equipment, and supplies originally created for casting, forging, machining, or fabricating metals or metal products. This class does not include tools, equipment, and supplies used in mining or preliminary processing of ores, which are listed in Mining & Mineral Harvesting T&E.

Primary Object Term	Secondary Term	Tertiary Term	Notes
Anvil			
	Anvil, Concave		
	Anvil, Filecutter's		
	Anvil, Nailmaker's		
	Anvil, Scythe Sharpening		
	Anvil, Stake		
		Stake, Beakhorn	
		Stake, Blowhorn	
		Stake, Candlemold	
		Stake, Creasing	
		Stake, Double-Creasing	
		Stake, Hatchet	
		Stake, Hollow Mandrel	
		Stake, Needle Case	
		Stake, Planishing	
		Stake, Seaming	
		Stake, Square	
	Beakiron		
	Horse, Anvil		
Arrastra			
Awl, Metalworking			
Barrel, Amalgamating			
Bender, Metal			
	Bender, Flange		
	Bender, Pipe		
	Bender, Tire		
	Brake, Bending		
	Fork, Bending		
	Tool, Angle-Bending		
Bit, Metal Cutting			*Note:* May also use "Bit, Drill" from Multiple Use T&E for Materials
	Bit, Flat		
Block, Metalworking			

Primary Object Term	Secondary Term	Tertiary Term	Notes
	Block, Dapping		
	Block, Filing		
	Block, Holding		
	Block, Striking		
Blower, Metalworking			
	Bellows, Blacksmith's		
	Bellows, Foundry		
	Blower, Blacksmith's		
	Engine, Blowing		
Blowtorch			
	Torch, Alcohol		
	Torch, Gas		
		Torch, Acetylene	
		Torch, Oxyacetylene	
		Torch, Oxyhydrogen	
		Torch, Propane	
	Torch, Gasoline		
	Torch, Kerosene		
Bolt, Fastener			
Boss, Filecutter's			
Box, Charging			
Box, Core			
Box, Drill Bit			
Brazier			
Broach, Metalworking			
Brush, File			
Burnisher, Metal			
Caliper, Machining			
Car, Slag			
Chisel, Metalworking			
	Chisel, Cold		
		Chisel, Cape	
		Chisel, Flat	
		Chisel, Diamond-Point	
		Chisel, Half Round Nose	
	Chisel, Hot		
Chuck, Tap			
Concentrator			

Primary Object Term	Secondary Term	Tertiary Term	Notes
	Concentrator, Cyclone		
	Concentrator, Electromagnetic		
	Concentrator, Flotation		
	Concentrator, Jig		
	Concentrator, Shaking Table		
Crucible, Metal			
	Cupel		
Cup, Grinder			
Cup, Oil			
Cushion, Lead			
Cutter, Metal			
	Cutter, Bar		
	Cutter, Clinch		
	Cutter, Milling		
	Cutter, Pinion		
	Cutter, Pipe		
	Cutter, Rivet		
	Cutter, Sprue		
	Cutter, Washer		
	Cutter, Wire		
	Nibbler		
	Shears, Metal		
		Cutter, Bolt	
		Shears, Bench	
		Shears, Circle	
		Shears, Lever	
		Shears, Squaring	
		Snip, Sheet Metal	
		Snip, Tin	
Cutter, Thread			
	Chaser		
	Die, Thread Cutting		
		Die, Screw	
	Plate, Screw		
	Set, Tap and Die		
	Tap		
		Tap, Bottom	
		Tap, Plug	

Primary Object Term	Secondary Term	Tertiary Term	Notes
		Tap, Taper	
Die, Coin			
Die, Wire Drawing			
Diestock			
Dog, Lathe			
Dolly, Metalworking			
Dresser, Grinding Wheel			
Drift, Cutting			
Drill, Metalworking			
	Centerdrill		
	Counterbore		
	Countersink		
	Drill, Post		
Embosser, Metal			
	Graphotype		
Engraver, Metal			
Expander, Metal			
Extender, Handle			
Extruder, Metal			
Fastener, Metal			
	Pin, Cotter		
	Rivet, Metal		
		Rivet, Tong	
File, Metalworking			
	File, Flat		
	File, Half Round		
	File, Joint		
	File, Machine		
	File, Mill		
	File, Needle		
	File, Round		
	File, Saw		
	File, Square		
	File, Triangular		
Flask, Molding			
	Flask, Snap		
Forge			
	Forge, Blacksmith's		
Fuller			

Primary Object Term	Secondary Term	Tertiary Term	Notes
	Fuller, Bottom		
	Fuller, Top		
Furnace, Metal			
	Bloomery		
	Furnace, Annealing		
	Furnace, Blast		
	Furnace, Converter		
	Furnace, Cupola		
	Furnace, Hearth		
	Furnace, Muffle		
	Furnace, Reverberatory		
	Oven, Coke		
Gate, Casting			
Gauge, Metalworking			
	Gauge, Center		
	Gauge, Drill		
	Gauge, Screw Pitch		
	Gauge, Thread		
	Gauge, Wire		
Graver, Metal			
Grinder, Metal			
	Grinder, Cylindrical		
	Grinder, Mower Knife		
	Grinder, Planer Knife		
	Grinder, Surface		
	Grinder, Tool		
	Grinder, Valve		
	Grindstone		
Groover, Hand			
Guide, Sharpening			
Gun, Soldering			
Hammer, Metalworking			
	Flatter		
	Hammer, Ball-Peen		
	Hammer, Blast		
	Hammer, Chipping		
	Hammer, Cross-Peen		
	Hammer, Drop		
		Hammer, Board	

Primary Object Term	Secondary Term	Tertiary Term	Notes
	Hammer, File-Cutting		
	Hammer, Foot-Powered		
	Hammer, Forging		
	Hammer, Helve		
		Hammer, Tilt	
	Hammer, Ironing		
	Hammer, Jeweler's		
	Hammer, Pewterer's		
	Hammer, Planishing		
	Hammer, Plow		
	Hammer, Raising		
	Hammer, Riveting		
	Hammer, Set		
	Hammer, Setting		
	Hammer, Sharpening		
	Hammer, Steam		
	Hammer, Straight-Peen		
	Hammer, Swage		
	Hammer, Turning		
	Hammer, Welding		
	Maul, Spike		
	Sledgehammer		
		Sledge, Cross-Peen	
		Sledge, Double-Face	
		Sledge, Shoe-Turning	
		Sledge, Straight-Peen	
Hardy			*Note:* May also use "Chisel, Metalworking," "Fuller," "Swage," or other appropriate term to describe the hardy's function
	Hardy, Half Round		
	Hardy, Side Cut		
	Hardy, Straight		
Heater, Branding Iron			
Holder, Metalworking Tool			
	Holder, Die		
	Holder, Scythe Sharpener		

Primary Object Term	Secondary Term	Tertiary Term	Notes
	Holder, Soldering Iron		
	Holder, Tire Bolt		
Hook, Forge			
Impactor			
Iron, Metalworking			
	Iron, Snarling		
	Iron, Soldering		
Jig, Metalworking			
	Hand, Helping		
Ladle, Foundry			
	Ladle, Cinder		
	Ladle, Hot Metal		
	Ladle, Slag		
Lamp, Soldering			
Lathe, Metalworking			
	Lathe, Engine		*Note:* Use for a lathe with a slide rest and a power feed on the carriage
	Lathe, Foot		*Note:* Use for a lathe operated by a treadle
	Lathe, Hand		*Note:* Use for a lathe in which the lathe tool is hand-held
	Lathe, Turret		*Note:* Use for a multi-tooled lathe
		Machine, Screw Cutting	
Lifter, Sand			
Lighter, Friction			
Liner, Cylinder			
Machine, Metalworking			
	Machine, Beading		
	Machine, Bolt Heading		
	Machine, Brading		
	Machine, Broaching		
	Machine, Burring		
	Machine, Charging		
	Machine, Cone		
	Machine, Die Cutting		
	Machine, Double Seaming		
	Machine, Gear Cutting		
	Machine, Grooving		
	Machine, Key Cutting		

Primary Object Term	Secondary Term	Tertiary Term	Notes
	Machine, Metal Boring		
	Machine, Metal Buffing		
	Machine, Metal Creasing		
	Machine, Metal Crimping		
	Machine, Metal Folding		
	Machine, Metal Forming		
	Machine, Metal Shearing		
	Machine, Milling		
	Machine, Nail Cutting		
	Machine, Pipe Threading		
	Machine, Polishing		
	Machine, Rifling		
	Machine, Rivet Making		
	Machine, Saw Sharpening		
	Machine, Setting Down		
	Machine, Sintering		
	Machine, Soldering		
	Machine, Straightening		
	Machine, Tapping		
	Machine, Tire Bending		
	Machine, Turning		
	Machine, Wiring		
	Mill, Rail		
	Mill, Rolling		
		Mill, Tube	
	Mill, Sampling		
	Mill, Slitting		
	Mill, Stamping		
	Mill, Wire		
Mandrel			
Mask, Welder's			
Mold, Casting			
Nipper, Metal			
	Nipper, Nail		
	Nipper, Pulling		
	Nipper, Sheet		
Oilcan			
Pan, Amalgamating			

Primary Object Term	Secondary Term	Tertiary Term	Notes
Pan, Soldering			
Pincers, Wire			
Pipe, Coupling			
Planer, Metal			
Plate, Bench			
Pliers, Metalworking			
	Pliers, Gas		
	Pliers, Setting		
	Puller, Wire		
Poker, Blacksmith's			
Pot, Soldering			
Press, Metal			
	Press, Drill		
	Press, Punch		
	Press, Stamping		
Punch, Metal			
	Counterpunch		
	Pritchel		
	Punch, Backing-Out		
	Punch, Center		
	Punch, Dapping		
	Punch, Drift		
	Punch, Fore		
	Punch, Hollow		
	Punch, Oval		
	Punch, Prick		
	Punch, Round		
	Punch, Square		
Rabble			
Rake, Blacksmith's			
Rammer, Sand			
Ratchet, Thread			
Reamer, Metalworking			
Retort, Amalgam			
Riddle, Foundry			
Ring, Clinch			
Ring, Forge			
Ring, Tong			
Roaster, Ore			

Primary Object Term	Secondary Term	Tertiary Term	Notes
Roller, Metal			
Saw, Metalworking			
	Hacksaw		
	Saw, Piercing		
Saw-Set			
	Wrest, Saw		
Scraper, Metal			
	Scraper, Flat		
	Scraper, Half-Round		
	Scraper, Hook		
	Scraper, Three-Cornered		
Screw, Metalworking			
	Bolt, Eye		
	Screw, Machine		
	Screw, Riggers		
	Screw, Sheet Metal		
Scribe, Metal			
Seamer, Metal			
Separator, Metal			
Shaper, Metal			
Sharpener, Metal			
	Block, Stropping		
	Sharpener, Tool		
		Sharpener, Knife	
		Sharpener, Scissors	
	Steel		
	Whetstone		
		Oilstone	
		Stone, Scythe Sharpening	
Shovel, Blacksmith's			
Skimmer			
Socket			
Spoon, Blacksmith's			
Sprinkler, Blacksmith's			
Stamp, Metal			
	Stamp, Die		
Stand, Blacksmith's			
Stand, Crucible			

Primary Object Term	Secondary Term	Tertiary Term	Notes
Stock, Metal			
	Bar, Metal		
	Billet		
	Blank, Metal		
		Blank, Coin	
		Blank, Key	
		Blank, Knife	
	Bloom		
	Ingot		
Swage			
	Swage, Anvil		
	Swage, Bolt Heading		
	Swage, Bottom		
	Swage, Creasing		
	Swage, Forming		
	Swage, Half-Round Top		
	Swage, Hatchet		
	Swage, Mandrel		
	Swage, Necking		
	Swage, Nut		
	Swage, Spring		
	Swage, Top		
	Swage, V-Shaped		
Table, Metalworking			
	Table, Amalgamating		
	Table, Welding		
Template, Metalworking			
	Pattern, Metalworking		
		Pattern, Casting	
		Pattern, Tracing	
	Stencil, Metal		
Tongs, Metalworking			
	Tongs, Bending		
	Tongs, Box		
		Tongs, Double Box	
	Tongs, Brazing		
	Tongs, Drawing		
	Tongs, Flat		
		Tongs, Clip	

Primary Object Term	Secondary Term	Tertiary Term	Notes
	Tongs, Gad		
	Tongs, Half-Round		
	Tongs, Hammer		
		Tongs, Box Hammer	
	Tongs, Hollow-Bit		
		Tongs, Bolt	
		Tongs, Round-Lip	
	Tongs, Hoop		
	Tongs, Link		
	Tongs, Nail		
	Tongs, Pickup		
	Tongs, Pincer		
	Tongs, Plow		
	Tongs, Roofing		
	Tongs, Shoe		
	Tongs, Side		
		Tongs, Crook-Bit	
	Tongs, Sliding		
	Tongs, Swivel Jaw		
	Tongs, Tire		
Tool, Boring			
Tool, Heading			
	Header, Bolt		
	Header, Nail		
Tool, Knurling			
Traveler			
Trowel, Molder's			
Tub, Slack			
Tuyere			
Twister, Wire			
Upsetter, Tire			
Vessel, Parting			
Vise, Metalworking			
	Vise, Bench		
	Vise, Blacksmith's		
	Vise, Hand		
	Vise, Leg		
	Vise, Machine		
	Vise, Pipe		

Primary Object Term	Secondary Term	Tertiary Term	Notes
	Vise, Wire		
Welder, Electric			
Winder, Spring			
Wrench			
	Wrench, Allen		
	Wrench, Alligator		
	Wrench, Axle Cap		
	Wrench, Box		
	Wrench, Box-End		
	Wrench, Carriage Nut		
	Wrench, Closed End		
	Wrench, Combination		
	Wrench, Crescent		
	Wrench, Impact		
	Wrench, Key		
	Wrench, Monkey		
	Wrench, Open-End		
	Wrench, Pipe		
		Tongs, Chain	
	Wrench, Saw		
	Wrench, Socket		
	Wrench, Spud		
	Wrench, T		
	Wrench, Tap		
	Wrench, Torque		

Class:
MINING & MINERAL HARVESTING T&E

Definition: Tools, equipment, and supplies originally created for extracting materials in solid, liquid, or gaseous state from the natural environment. This class includes equipment used for underground and surface mines, quarries, oil and water wells, for prospecting, and for supplemental processing operations such as breaking, milling, washing, cleaning, or grading. It also includes tools used for ice harvesting and salt harvesting.

Primary Object Term	Secondary Term	Tertiary Term	Notes
Apparatus, Assay			
Bag, Tamping			
Bailer, Well			
Balance, Assay			
Balance, Water			
Bar, Boring			
Bar, Busting			
Bar, Claying			
Bar, Miner's			
Bar, Quarry			
Bar, Rigging			
Bar, Stretcher			
Bar, Tamping			
	Stemmer		
Bar, Wagon Pinch			
Bender, Rail			
Bit, Mining			
	Bit, Core		
	Bit, Percussion		
	Bit, Reamer		
	Bit, Rotary		
	Bit, Spudding		
Bob, Balance			
Bogie			
Boiler, Mining			
Bolt, Mining			
	Bolt, Lewis		
	Bolt, Rag		
	Bolt, Roof		
Bottle, Sample			
Box, Stuffing			
Bucket, Mining			

Primary Object Term	Secondary Term	Tertiary Term	Notes
	Bucket, Dredge		
	Bucket, Rock		
	Kibble		
Bucketline			
Cadger			
Cage, Mining			
	Cage, Man		
Can, Blasting			
Can, Carbide			
Cap, Blasting			
Car, Mining			*Note:* May also use "Car, Railroad" from Rail Vehicles
	Car, Man		
	Car, Mine Ambulance		
	Car, Ore		
	Tram, Mine		
Carriage, Tunnel			
Casing			
Cell, Flotation			
Changkol			
Channeler, Rock			
Classifier			
Concentrator, Mineral			
Container, Ore			
	Bag, Ore		
	Basket, Ore		
	Bin, Ore		
	Tray, Ore		
Crib, Cribbing			
Crimper, Blasting Cap			
Crusher, Mineral			
	Crusher, Ball		
	Crusher, Cone		
	Crusher, Gyratory		
	Crusher, Hammer		
	Crusher, Jaw		
	Crusher, Roller		
	Crusher, Stamp		
		Mill, Quartz	
Cutter, Coal			

Primary Object Term	Secondary Term	Tertiary Term	Notes
Dart, Spring			
Detector, Firedamp			*Note:* May also use "Detector, Gas" from Protective Devices
Detonator			
Dial, Miner's			*Note:* May also use "Compass, Surveyor's" from Surveying Equipment
Dredge, Mining			
	Dredge, Bucketline		
	Dredge, Suction		
Drill, Mining			
	Drill, Churn		
		Drill, Pole	
	Drill, Core		
		Drill, Diamond	
		Drill, Shot	
	Drill, Gang		
	Drill, Hurdy Gurdy		
	Drill, Jumper		
	Drill, Percussive Mining		
		Drill, Drifter	
		Drill, Jetting	
		Drill, Sinker	
	Drill, Placer		
	Drill, Rotary		
	Drill, Stopper		
	Drill, Turbo		
	Hammer, Hand		
	Handsteel		
Elevator, Drilling			
	Elevator, Casing		
	Elevator, Rod		
	Elevator, Tubing		
Engine, Man			
Fork, Sluice			
Fuse, Detonating			
Gad			
	Moil		
Gadder			
Galvanometer, Blasting			

Primary Object Term	Secondary Term	Tertiary Term	Notes
Governor, Mine Hoist			
Grapnel			
Hammer, Pick			
Head, Casing			
Hoist, Mining			
	Hoist, Mine		
	Hoist, Quarry		
Hook, Grab			
Indicator, Borehole Drift			*Note:* May also use "Instrument, Surveying" from Surveying Equipment
Injector, Cement			
Iron, Bucking			
Jumbo			
Leg, Air			
Lift, Drawing			
Locomotive, Mine			*Note:* May also use a "Locomotive" term from Rail Vehicles
Log, Lithology			
	Log, Neutron		
Machine, Cutting			
Machine, Loading			
	Machine, Mucking		
Machine, Pressing			
Machine, Quarrying			
Mill, Flint			
Miner, Continuous			
Monitor, Hydraulic			
Needle, Dipping			*Note:* May also use "Magnetometer" from Surveying Equipment
Nozzle, Hydraulic			
Pan, Miner's			
	Dulang		
Phanarogrisonmeter			
Photoclinometer			*Note:* May also use "Inclinometer" from Surveying Equipment
Pick, Mining			
	Pick, Double-Pointed		
	Pick, Drifting		
	Pick, Driving		
	Pick, Poll		

Primary Object Term	Secondary Term	Tertiary Term	Notes
	Pick, Undercutting		
Plate, Snatch			
Point, Steam Thawing			
Pole, Spring			
Pricker			
Riffle			
Rod, Divining			
Rod, Sucker			
Sampler, Sidewall			
Scraper, Hoe			
Separator, Mineral			
	Box, Dip		
	Box, Sluice		
	Grizzly		
	Rocker, Ore		
	Screen, Trommel		
	Separator, Cradle		
	Separator, Electromagnetic		
	Separator, Electrostatic		
	Separator, Frame		
	Separator, Jig		
	Separator, Washer		
	Splitter, Sample		
	Tom, Long		
	Vanner		
	Washer, Dry		
	Washer, Ore		
Shield, Mining			
Shovel, Mining			
Skip			
Slusher			
Snore			
Socket, Rope			
Spade, Grafting			
Spoon, Miner's			
	Horn, Miner's		
Spud			
Squib			
Stem, Drill			

Primary Object Term	Secondary Term	Tertiary Term	Notes
Strake, Blanket			
Support, Mine			*Note:* May also use a term from Supporting Elements if appropriate
	Support, Powered		
	Timber, Mine		
		Cap, Timber	
		Sprag	
		Stull	
Tester, Casing			
Tester, Tubing			
Tool, Ice Harvesting			
	Adz, Ice		
	Ax, Ice		
	Chisel, Ice		
	Cutter, Ice		
	Gauge, Ice		
	Hook, Ice		
	Marker, Ice		
	Plow, Ice		
	Saw, Ice		
	Tongs, Block Ice		
Tool, Well Fishing			
Torpedo, Well			
Tripod, Mining			
Undercurrent			
Valve, Well Pump			
	Valve, Standing		
	Valve, Working		
Vat, Cyanidation			
Wedge, Deflection			
Worm, Spiral			
Wrench, Sucker Rod			

Class:
MULTIPLE USE T&E FOR MATERIALS

Definition: Objects originally created to transform or modify materials in ways that extend beyond the range of one class. This class includes terms for multi-purpose tools and tools that work with a variety of materials as well as generic terms that may be used if the particular context of use is unknown.

Primary Object Term	Secondary Term	Tertiary Term	Notes
Abrader			
Awl			
Bit, Drill			
	Bit, Straight-Fluted		
	Bit, Twist		
Borer			
Brush			
Cable			
	Guy		
Celt			
Chain			
Chisel			
Chopper			
Chuck			
	Chuck, Drill		
	Chuck, Lathe		
Cloth, Emery			
Container, Tool			
	Board, Tool		
	Chest, Tool		
	Kit, Tool		
	Rest, Tool		
	Sheath, Tool		
	Toolbox		
Cord			
	Cord, Elastic		
	Rope		
	String		
		Twine	
Die, Forming			
Dispenser, Tape			
Drill			
	Drill, Bow		
	Drill, Electric		
	Drill, Hand		

Primary Object Term	Secondary Term	Tertiary Term	Notes
Fastener			
	Band, Elastic		
	Batten		
	Bolt		
		Bolt, Molly	
	Buckle		
	Clasp		
	Clip		
	Fastener, Anchor		
	Link, Snap		
	Nut		
		Locknut	
		Nut, Adjusting	
		Nut, Back	
		Nut, Wing	
	Screw		
		Setscrew	
	Spike		
	Strap		
		Strap, Reinforcing	
	Tack		
	Tie, Fastener		
	Tie, Twist		
	Washer		
Ferrule			
File			
Flaker			
Flange			
Funnel			
Gasket			
Gun, Calking			
Gun, Staple			
Horn, Grease			
Hose			
	Hose, Air		
Jig			
Kit, Repair			
Knife			
	Knife, Utility		
	Ulu		

Primary Object Term	Secondary Term	Tertiary Term	Notes
Palstave			
Pliers			
	Pliers, Combination		
	Pliers, Needlenose		
Printer, 3D			
Punch			
Saw			
Scissors			
Scoop			
	Scoop, Digging		
Screwdriver			
	Screwdriver, Offset		
	Screwdriver, Ratchet		
Slab, Grinding			
Stencil			
Syringe			
Tape, Adhesive			
	Tape, Duct		
	Tape, Masking		
	Tape, Packaging		
	Tape, Transparent		
Tarpaulin			
Tool, Combination			*Note:* May also use terms to represent the individual tools featured
Tool, Pyrography			
	Pen, Pyrography		
	Point, Pyrography		
Tweezers			

Class:
PAINTING T&E

Definition: Tools, equipment, and supplies originally created for working with materials that mask surfaces by depositing a residual film such as a paint film, or by using adhesives to attach a thin covering such as wallpaper or gold leaf to a surface. This class includes tools, equipment, and supplies used in decorative, artistic, and protective applications. Excluded from this class are tools and equipment that are used with thicker coatings, such as wood veneers or plastic laminates, and tools and equipment used for metal plating. Also excluded are tools and equipment associated with printing processes, such as printing blocks and silkscreens.

Primary Object Term	Secondary Term	Tertiary Term	Notes
Airbrush			
Box, Artist's			
	Box, Paint		
Brush, Artist's			*Note:* Use for a small precision brush
	Brush, Lettering		
	Brush, Stencilling		
Brush, Paint			*Note:* Use for a larger brush for applying paint as a coating
	Brush, Graining		
Can, Paint			
Cloth, Drop			
Comb, Graining			
Crayon			
Cup, Palette			
Cushion, Gilder's			
Cutter, Mat			
Driver, Point			
Easel, Studio			
Figure, Lay			
Grinder, Paint			
Gun, Spray			
Holder, Brush			
Keg, Paint			
Key, Paint Can			
Knife, Gilder's			
Knife, Graining			
Knife, Mat			
Knife, Painting			
Knife, Palette			
Knife, Putty			
Leaf, Metal			

Primary Object Term	Secondary Term	Tertiary Term	Notes
Maulstick			
Mill, Ball			
Pad, Paint			
Paint			
Palette			
	Palette, Arm		
Paper, Art			
Paper, Stencil			
Pencil, Art			
	Pencil, Coloring		
	Pencil, Paint		
Pestle, Paint			
	Muller		
Pigment, Paint			
Pliers, Stretching			
Powder, Bronze			
Roller, Graining			
Roller, Paint			
Saucer, Nest			
Scraper, Wall			
Set, Drawing			
Set, Paint			
	Set, Paint By Numbers		
Shaker, Paint			
Sketchbook			
Spatula, Artist's			
	Cauterium		
	Cestrum		
Sponge, Paint			
Stencil, Paint			
Stretcher, Canvas			
Stirrer, Paint			
Stone, Paint			
Stump			
	Tortillon		
Tape, Painter's			
Tip, Gilder's			
Tool, Wallpapering			
	Brush, Wallpaper		

Primary Object Term	Secondary Term	Tertiary Term	Notes
		Brush, Wallpaper Paste	
		Brush, Wallpaper Smoothing	
	Cutter, Wallpaper		
		Cutter, Base	
		Cutter, Edge	
		Knife, Wallpaper	
		Scissors, Wallpaper	
	Roller, Wallpaper		
		Roller, Seam	
	Smoother, Wallpaper		
	Steamer, Wallpaper		
	Table, Pasting		
Tray, Paint			
Washer, Brush			

Class:
PAPERMAKING T&E

Definition: Tools, equipment, and supplies originally created for the manufacture of materials formed from the residue of suspensions or in the fabrication of products made of such materials. Paper (whether made from wood pulp, textile fibers, or plastic fibers) is the principal product that falls in this class. Particles mixed with liquids form suspensions. Although felt is made of materials that are matted like paper, tools for felting are listed in Textileworking T&E because felt is not formed from a suspension.

Primary Object Term	Secondary Term	Tertiary Term	Notes
Barker			
Blender, Stock			
Box, Suction			
Calender, Paper			
Cell, Bleaching			
Chipper			
Deckle			
Digester			
Dryer, Paper			
Finisher, Paper			
	Finisher, Flint-Glazing		
	Finisher, Pebbling		
Machine, Bag Forming			
Machine, Paper			
	Machine, Cylinder		
	Machine, Fourdrinier		
	Machine, Yankee		
Machine, Paper Coating			
Machine, Paper Cutting			
	Machine, Paper Trimming		
	Slitter, Paper		
Machine, Paper Packing			
Machine, Pulp Washing			
Machine, Scoring			
Marker, Ream			
Mold, Papermaking			
Press, Smoothing			
Pulper			

Primary Object Term	Secondary Term	Tertiary Term	Notes
	Beater, Hollander		
	Beater, Jordan		
	Trip-Hammer		
Rewinder			
Roll, Dandy			
Runner, Edge			
Save-All			
Skid			
Supercalender			
Tester, Paper			
	Glarimeter		
	Opacimeter		
	Tester, Mullen		
	Tester, Paper Moisture		
	Tester, Schopper		
Vat, Pulp			

Class:
TEXTILEWORKING T&E

Definition: Tools, equipment, and supplies originally created for the preparation of materials made from fibers and the preparation of woven fabrics. Also included in this class are tools, equipment, and supplies used for manufacturing objects from fibers or cloth. This class includes tools specific to the preparation of fibers, such as hatchels and cotton gins, but excludes tools, such as sheep shears and cotton balers, that are related to sources of fibers.

Sub-Class:
NEEDLEWORKING EQUIPMENT

Definition: Tools, equipment, and supplies originally created for processes and techniques involving needle and thread, including appliqué, beading, sewing, quilting, and embroidery. This sub-class includes objects used in gathering, hooking, and pleating. It includes objects used by dressmakers, tailors, hatters, and sailmakers.

Primary Object Term	Secondary Term	Tertiary Term	Notes
Bench, Rigger's			*Note:* May also use "Bench" from Seating Furniture
Bench, Sailmaker's			*Note:* May also use "Bench" from Seating Furniture
Bench-Hook, Sailmaker's			
Block, Hat			
Block, Quilt			
Board, Darning			
Board, Fabric Cutting			
Bobbin, Sewing			
Bolt, Cloth			
Breaker, Button			
Canvas, Needlework			
Clamp, Needlework			
	Clamp, Quilting Frame		
	Clamp, Rigger's		
	Clamp, Sewing		
	Clamp, Winding		
Container, Needlework			*Note:* Use for an object created to contain needlework tools and supplies
	Bag, Needlework		
	Basket, Needlework		
	Box, Needlework		
		Box, Pin	
	Case, Needlework		
		Case, Bodkin	
		Case, Needle	

Primary Object Term	Secondary Term	Tertiary Term	Notes
		Case, Pin	
		Case, Scissors	
		Case, Spool	
		Case, Thimble	
		Case, Thread	
	Holder, Needlework		
		Holder, Needle	
		Holder, Spool	
		Holder, Tape	
		Holder, Thimble	
		Holder, Thread	
		Pincushion	
	Housewife		
	Rack, Needlework		
		Rack, Safety Pin	
		Rack, Spool	
	Tray, Needlework		
		Tray, Pin	
Cushion, Emery			
Cutter, Fabric			
	Knife, Carpet		
	Knife, Sailmaker's		
	Scissors, Fabric		
	Shears, Fabric		
		Shears, Dressmaker's	
		Shears, Fuller's	
		Shears, Pinking	
Egg, Darning			
Fid			
Form, Dress			
Guide, Buttonhole			
Guide, Seam			
Ham, Tailor's			
Heaver, Stitch			
Kit, Needlework			
	Kit, Sailmaker's		
	Kit, Sewing		
Machine, Needlework			
	Machine, Embroidery		

Primary Object Term	Secondary Term	Tertiary Term	Notes
	Machine, Knitting Sewing		
	Machine, Quilting		
	Machine, Sewing		
		Machine, Hemstitching	
Marker, Fabric			
	Chalk, Tailor's		
	Marker, Hem		
	Marker, Pattern		
	Wheel, Tracing		
Marlinespike			
Notion			*Note:* Use for an object that is applied to textiles for embellishment, reinforcement, or securement
	Bead		
	Binding		
		Tape, Bias	
		Tape, Twill	
	Fastener, Textile		
		Button	
		Button, Stud	
		Fastener, Hook and Eye	
		Fastener, Hook and Loop	
		Frog	
		Grommet	
		Pin, Safety	
		Pin, Straight	
		Snap	
		Tack, Upholstery	
		Toggle	
		Zipper	
	Patch, Textile		
	Pompon		
	Ruche		
	Tape, Mending		
	Thread		
	Trim, Textile		
		Braid	

Primary Object Term	Secondary Term	Tertiary Term	Notes
		Fringe	
		Lace	*Note:* May also use "Needlework" from Art
		Piping	
		Ribbon, Textile	
		Sequin	
		Tassel	
Palm, Sailmaker's			
Paper, Pattern Tracing			
Pattern			
	Pattern, Clothes		
	Pattern, Needlework		
		Pattern, Quilt	
Pricker, Sailmaker's			
Ripper, Stitch			
Rubber, Sailmaker's			
Sharpener, Needle			
Sheath, Marlinespike			
Snapsetter			
Spool, Sewing			
Square, Tailor's			
Stapler, Upholstery			
Stretcher, Needlework			
	Frame, Needlework		
		Frame, Embroidery	
		Frame, Quilting	
	Hoop, Needlework		
		Hoop, Embroidery	
		Hoop, Quilting	
Thimble			
Threader			
Tool, Fabric Piercing			
	Awl, Cloth		
	Bodkin		
	Hook, Tambour		
	Needle, Sewing		
		Needle, Carpet	
		Needle, Darning	
		Needle, Embroidery	
		Needle, Sailmaker's	

Primary Object Term	Secondary Term	Tertiary Term	Notes
		Needle, Upholsterer's	
	Punch, Fabric		
		Punch, Embroidery	
		Punch, Grommet	
		Punch, Sailmaker's	
	Stiletto		
Winder, Thread			
	Winder, Bobbin		
	Winder, Spool		

Sub-Class:
TEXTILE MANUFACTURING EQUIPMENT

Definition: Tools, equipment, and supplies originally created to assist in the processing of natural fibers into thread and yarn or in the processing of thread and yarn into finished textiles such as lace, cloth, or cordage. Processes include spinning, weaving, knitting, knotting, twining, and finishing.

Primary Object Term	Secondary Term	Tertiary Term	Notes
Bar, Warping			
Batten, Weaving			
Beam, Cloth			
Beam, Warp			
Beamer			
Bench, Carding			
Bench, Weaver's			
Billy, Slubbing			
Board, Macrame			
Board, Scutching			
Bobbin			
	Bobbin, Knitting		
	Bobbin, Lace		
	Bobbin, Weaving		
Bowl, Scouring			
Box, Gill			
Box, Loom			
Box, Stuffer			
Braider			
Breaker, Bale			
Breaker, Flax			
Calender, Embossing			
Card, Hand			
Card, Jacquard			
Case, Textilemaking Tool			
	Case, Crochet Hook		
	Case, Knitting Needle		
Comb, Textile			
	Comb, Carding		
	Comb, Hand		
	Comb, Weaving		
	Hatchel		
	Ripple		
Condenser			
	Condenser, Cotton		

Primary Object Term	Secondary Term	Tertiary Term	Notes
	Condenser, Goulding		
	Condenser, Rub-Apron		
	Condenser, Rub-Roll		
	Condenser, Tape		
Cone, Braiding			
Converter, Pacific			
Counter, Thread			
Creel, Bobbin			
Cross, Teasel			
Cushion, Lacemaker's			
Distaff			
Dresser, Warp			
Dryer, Textile			
	Dryer, Loop		
	Dryer, Reel		
	Dryer, Yarn		
Finger, Wool			
Frame, Drawing			
Frame, Lace			
Frame, Roving			
Frame, Slubbing			
Frame, Spinning			
	Frame, Ring		
Frame, Tenter			
Frame, Throstle			
Frame, Twisting			
Frame, Warping			
Gauge, Knitting Needle			
Gauge, Net			
Gig, Napping			
Gin, Cotton			
Globe, Lace			
Grinder, Card			
Harbick			
Heddle			
Holder, Flax			
Holder, Stitch			
Hook, Crochet			
Hook, Reed			

Primary Object Term	Secondary Term	Tertiary Term	Notes
Hook, Rug			
Jack, Spinning			
Jenny, Spinning			
Kettle, Dyeing			
Knife, Scutching			
Knotter			
Loom			
	Loom, Backstrap		
	Loom, Broad		
	Loom, Cam		
	Loom, Carpet		
	Loom, Counterbalance		
	Loom, Countermarch		
	Loom, Dobby		
	Loom, Hand		
		Loom, Bead	
		Loom, Belt	
		Loom, Bow	
		Loom, Draw	
		Loom, Frame	
		Loom, Ground	
		Loom, Inkle	
		Loom, Table	
		Loom, Tablet	
		Loom, Treadle	
		Loom, Warp-Weighted	
	Loom, Jack		
	Loom, Jacquard		
	Loom, Lace		
	Loom, Leno		
	Loom, Needlepoint		
	Loom, Pile Fabric		
	Loom, Rigid Heddle		
	Loom, Shuttleless		
		Loom, Rapier	
		Loom, Water-Jet	
	Loom, Swivel		
	Loom, Tape		
	Powerloom		

Primary Object Term	Secondary Term	Tertiary Term	Notes
Loomweight			
Lucet			
Machine, Textile			
	Machine, Backfilling		
	Machine, Batt Making		
	Machine, Beetle		
	Machine, Bleaching		
	Machine, Blending		
		Blender, Feeder	
		Blender, Sandwich	
	Machine, Bonding		
	Machine, Braiding		
	Machine, Bulking		
	Machine, Burling		
	Machine, Card Clothing		
	Machine, Card Punching		
	Machine, Chinchilla		
	Machine, Crabbing		
	Machine, Crocheting		
	Machine, Decating		
	Machine, Drawing-In		
	Machine, Dyeing		
	Machine, Felting		
	Machine, Float Cutting		
	Machine, Flocking		
	Machine, Fulling		
	Machine, Garnett		
	Machine, Gigging		
	Machine, Heat Setting		
	Machine, Knitting		
	Machine, Looping		
	Machine, Mercerizing		
	Machine, Package Changing		
	Machine, Pad		
	Machine, Perlock		
	Machine, Pinking		
	Machine, Pleating		
	Machine, Ropemaking		
	Machine, Shrinking		

Primary Object Term	Secondary Term	Tertiary Term	Notes
	Machine, Simplex		
	Machine, Stuffing		
		Machine, Pillow	
	Machine, Sueding		
	Machine, Textile Brushing		
	Machine, Textile Carding		
	Machine, Textile Coating		
	Machine, Textile Crimping		
	Machine, Textile Folding		
	Machine, Textile Shearing		
	Machine, Textile Stretching		
	Machine, Texturing		
	Machine, Throwing		
	Machine, Tufting		
	Machine, Tying-In		
	Machine, Waste		
Mallet, Serving			
Mill, Fulling			
Mill, Warping			
Mold, Hat			
Napper			
Needle, Textile Making			
	Needle, Knitting		
		Needle, Finishing	
	Needle, Netmaking		
Picker, Fiber			
Press, Cloth			
Pulley, Heddle			
Reed, Textile			
Remover, Burr			
Rod, Heddle			
Roller, Felting			
Sheath, Knitting			
Shuttle			
	Shuttle, Netting		
	Shuttle, Tatting		

Primary Object Term	Secondary Term	Tertiary Term	Notes
	Shuttle, Weaving		
Slasher			
Smoother, Linen			
Spindle			
	Spindle, Ropemaking		
Spinneret			
Straightener, Cloth			
Stretcher, Cloth			
Tablet, Weaving			
Temple, Weaving Machine			
Tenterhook			
Tester, Fabric			
	Fadeometer		
	Prover, Linen		
	Tester, Burst		
	Tester, Crimp		
	Tester, Fiber Fineness		
	Tester, Fire Resistance		
	Tester, Nep		
	Tester, Scorch		
	Tester, Shrinkage		
	Tester, Sliver		
	Tester, Tear		
	Tester, Twist		
	Tester, Washfastness		
	Tintometer		
Train, Scouring			
Twister			
Vat, Fulling			
Vat, Textile Dyeing			
Weight, Loom			
Wheel, Hand			
Wheel, Lace			
Wheel, Spinning			
Wheel, Stretching			
Whorl, Spindle			
Winder, Yarn			
	Baller		
	Niddy-Noddy		

Primary Object Term	Secondary Term	Tertiary Term	Notes
	Quiller		
	Reel, Clock		
	Reel, Warping		
	Reel, Yarn		
	Skeiner		
	Spooler		
	Swift		
		Swift, Umbrella	
	Wheel, Quilling		
	Winder, Cone		
Yarn			

Class:
WOODWORKING T&E

Definition: Tools, equipment, and supplies originally created for the fabrication of objects from wood. This class includes objects used with and to create physically modified wood by-products such as plywood, chipboard, and masonite. This class excludes tools and equipment for making objects out of chemically modified wood by-products such as paper, rayon, or rubber. Note: Various woodworking trades, such as carpentry, coopering, shipbuilding, or wheelwrighting, may be noted in a subject field.

Primary Object Term	Secondary Term	Tertiary Term	Notes
Adz			
	Adz, Bunging		
	Adz, Carpenter's		
	Adz, Cleaving		
	Adz, Cooper's		
	Adz, Guttering		
	Adz, Hollowing		
	Adz, Lipped		
	Adz, Railroad		
	Adz, Shipwright's		
	Adz, Trussing		
	Adz, Wheelwright's		
Attachment, Lathe			
	Center, Lathe		
Auger			
	Auger, Breast		
	Auger, Burn		
	Auger, Cylinder		
	Auger, Hollow		
	Auger, Pipe		
	Auger, Pod		
	Auger, Pump		
	Auger, Shell		
	Auger, Snail		
	Auger, Spiral		
	Auger, Spoon		
	Auger, Taper		
Awl, Woodworking			
	Awl, Burning		
	Awl, Marking		
	Awl, Square		
	Bradawl		

Primary Object Term	Secondary Term	Tertiary Term	Notes
Ax			
	Ax, Cooper's		
	Ax, Cratemaker's		
	Ax, Fitting		
	Ax, Mast		
	Ax, Mortising		
		Twibil	
	Ax, Shipwright's		
	Ax, Side		
	Broadax		
	Hatchet		
		Hatchet, Claw	
		Hatchet, Hewing	
		Hatchet, Lathing	
		Hatchet, Shingling	
Bellows, Cooper's			
Bench, Woodworking			
	Bench, Basketmaker's		
	Bench, Box Making		
	Bench, Carpenter's		
	Bench, Caulker's		
	Bench, Cooper's		
	Bench, Shingle		
	Bench, Wheelwright's		
	Horse, Froe		
	Horse, Saw-Sharpening		
	Horse, Shaving		
Bit, Woodworking			*Note:* May also use "Bit, Drill" from Multiple Use T&E for Materials
	Bit, Annular		
	Bit, Center		
	Bit, Countersink		
	Bit, Dowel Point		
	Bit, Expansion		
	Bit, Gimlet		
	Bit, Hollow		
	Bit, Mortise		
	Bit, Nose		
	Bit, Shell		
	Bit, Spiral		

Primary Object Term	Secondary Term	Tertiary Term	Notes
	Bit, Spoke Trimmer		
	Bit, Spoon		
	Bit, Taper		
	Bit, Tenon-Cutting		
	Cutter, Plug		
Blank, Wood			
Block, Woodworking			
	Block, Bevel		
	Block, Framing		
	Block, Miter		
	Block, Sanding		
	Block, Shaving		
	Jack, Miter		
Board, Shooting			
Borer, Cork			
Box, Miter			
Box, Molding			
Box, Screw			*Note:* Use for a tool used to cut threads on wood screws or pegs
Box, Shipwright's Caulking			
Box, Shipwright's Oil			
Brace, Woodworking			
	Brace, Extension		
	Brace, Ratchet		
	Brace, Spofford		
	Brace, Wimble		
Breastplate			
Brush, Seam			
Chalk, Woodworking			
	Chalk, Lumber		
	Line, Chalk		
	Reel, Chalk		
Chisel, Woodworking			
	Chisel, Bench		
		Chisel, Butt	
		Chisel, Corner	
		Chisel, Firmer	
		Chisel, Mortise	
		Chisel, Paring	

Primary Object Term	Secondary Term	Tertiary Term	Notes
		Slick	
	Chisel, Bent		
	Chisel, Boatbuilder's		
	Chisel, Carving		
	Chisel, Fishtail		
	Chisel, Floor		
	Chisel, Gooseneck		
	Chisel, Hinge		
	Chisel, Parting		
	Chisel, Ripping		
	Chisel, Sash		
	Chisel, Skew		
	Chisel, Socket		
	Chisel, Turning		
	Veiner		
Clamp, Woodworking			
	Clamp, Bar		
	Clamp, Bench		
	Clamp, C		
	Clamp, Collar and Screw		
	Clamp, Corner		
	Clamp, Flooring		
	Clamp, Furniture		
	Clamp, Joiner's		
	Clamp, Panel		
	Clamp, Saw		
	Clamp, Screw		
	Clamp, Slat-Bending		
	Clamp, Spring		
	Clamp, Universal		
	Clamp, Web		
Compass, Woodworking			
Cradle, Hub			
Crayon, Lumber			
Cresset, Cooper's			
Cutter, Wood			
	Cutter, Dovetail		
	Cutter, Miter		
	Cutter, Peg		

Primary Object Term	Secondary Term	Tertiary Term	Notes
	Cutter, Set		
	Cutter, Shingle		
Dividers, Carpenter's			
Dog			
	Dog, Bench		
	Dog, Hooping		
	Dog, Joiner's		
	Dog, Spoke		
Drift, Drill			
Drill, Woodworking			
	Drill, Breast		
	Drill, Pump		
	Drill, Push		
Driver, Hoop			
Extractor, Bung			
Fastener, Wood			
	Brad		
	Dowel		
	Driftbolt		
	Nail		
	Peg		
	Screw, Wood		
	Spike, Barge		
	Staple, Wood		
	Treenail		
File, Woodworking			
	File, Cabinet		
	File, Float		
	File, Knife		
	File, Riffler		
	Rasp		
		Rasp, Cabinet	
		Rasp, Riffler	
Fingerstall, Shipwright's			
Float, Woodworking			
Frame, Wheel			
Froe			
	Froe, Cooper's		
	Froe, Knife		

Primary Object Term	Secondary Term	Tertiary Term	Notes
	Froe, Lathmaker's		
Gauge, Woodworking			
	Gauge, Bevel		
	Gauge, Boring		
	Gauge, Clapboard		
	Gauge, Combination		
	Gauge, Cutting		
	Gauge, Dovetail		
	Gauge, Marking		
		Gauge, Butt	
		Gauge, Mortise	
		Gauge, Panel	
		Gauge, Thumb	
	Gauge, Monkey		
	Gauge, Rabbet		
	Gauge, Saw		
	Gauge, Stave		
	Gauge, Turner's		
	Gauge, Wheelwright's		
Gimlet			
Gluepot			
Gouge, Woodworking			
	Gouge, Bent		
	Gouge, Bowl		
	Gouge, Carving		
	Gouge, Firmer		
	Gouge, Fishtail		
	Gouge, Fluting		
	Gouge, Paring		
	Gouge, Parting		
	Gouge, Turning		
	Gouge, Wheelwright's		
Hammer			*Note:* Use for a general-purpose hammer
	Hammer, Claw		
	Hammer, Clench		
	Hammer, Cooper's		
	Hammer, Framing		
	Hammer, Joiner's		
	Hammer, Patternmaker's		

Primary Object Term	Secondary Term	Tertiary Term	Notes
	Hammer, Tack		
	Hammer, Top Maul		
	Hammer, Trimmer's		
	Hammer, Veneer		
Header, Barrel			
Holder, Drill Bit			
Holder, Nail			
Holdfast			
Hook, Bench			
Hook, Caulking			
Hoop, Barrel			
Iron, Woodworking			
	Iron, Caulking		
		Iron, Horsing	
		Iron, Making	
		Iron, Shipwright's Caulking	
	Iron, Cooper's Burning		
	Iron, Flagging		
	Iron, Marking		
	Iron, Raising		
	Iron, Shipwright's Meaking		
	Iron, Veneering		
	Iron, Wheelwright's Burning		
Jig, Woodworking			
Key, Chuck			
Knife, Woodworking			
	Drawknife		
		Downshave, Cooper's	
		Drawknife, Backing	
		Drawknife, Barking	
		Drawknife, Carpenter's	
		Drawknife, Chamfering	
		Drawknife, Cooper's	
		Drawknife, Handlemaker's	

Primary Object Term	Secondary Term	Tertiary Term	Notes
		Drawknife, Heading	
		Drawknife, Hollowing	
		Drawknife, Mast	
		Drawknife, Wheelwright's	
		Jigger	
		Spokeshave	
	Knife, Bench		
	Knife, Block		
	Knife, Crooked		
	Knife, Finger		
	Knife, Hoop-Notching		
	Knife, Marking		
	Knife, Shaving		
	Knife, Woodcarving		
Ladle, Shipwright's Caulking			
Lathe, Woodworking			
	Lathe, Boring		
	Lathe, Duplicating		
	Lathe, Pole		
	Lathe, Spoke		
	Lathe, Wheel		
Level, Carpenter's			
	Level, Plumb		
	Level, Spirit		
Machine, Woodworking			
	Jointer		
	Jointer-Planer		
	Machine, Bedding		
	Machine, Dovetailing		
	Machine, Mitering		
	Machine, Mortising		
	Machine, Profiling		
	Machine, Shaving		
	Machine, Spotting		
	Machine, Tenoning		
	Machine, Tongue and Groove		

Primary Object Term	Secondary Term	Tertiary Term	Notes
	Machine, Treenailing		
	Machine, Trimming		
	Machine, Wheel Making		
	Machine, Wood Bending		
	Machine, Wood Boring		
	Mortiser		
	Moulder		
	Planer, Wood		
	Shaper, Wood		
Mallet			
	Beetle		
	Bungstart		
	Club, Froe		
	Mallet, Carpenter's		
	Mallet, Carver's		
	Mallet, Caulking		
	Mallet, Dead-Blow		
	Mallet, Shipwright's		
	Mallet, Wood Carver's		
Marker, Clapboard			
Maul			
	Maul, Chime		
	Maul, Post		
Mop, Pitch			
Pencil, Carpenter's			*Note:* May also use "Pencil" from Writing Devices
Pin, Draw Bore			
Pincers, Woodworking			
Plane			
	Plane, Coach		
	Plane, Combination		
	Plane, Drawer		
	Plane, Grooving		
		Croze	
		Plane, Badger	
		Plane, Banding	
		Plane, Bullnose	
		Plane, Dado	
		Plane, Edge	
		Plane, Fillister	

Primary Object Term	Secondary Term	Tertiary Term	Notes
		Plane, Miter	
		Plane, Plow	
		Plane, Rabbet	
		Plane, Router	
		Plane, Sash	
		Plane, Shoulder	
		Plane, Side Rabbet	
		Plane, Tongue and Groove	
		Plane, Tonguing	
	Plane, Leveling		
		Plane, Block	
		Plane, Compass	
		Plane, Cooper's Stoup	
		Plane, Finger	
		Plane, Floor	
		Plane, Fore	
		Plane, Howell	
		Plane, Jack	
		Plane, Jointer	
		Plane, Panel	
		Plane, Smoothing	
		Plane, Sun	
		Plane, Toothing	
		Plane, Trying	
	Plane, Modeling		
	Plane, Molding		
		Plane, Astragal	
		Plane, Centerboard	
		Plane, Cornice	
		Plane, Cove	
		Plane, Guttering	
		Plane, Handrail	
		Plane, Hollow	
		Plane, Nosing	
		Plane, Ogee	
		Plane, Ovolo	
		Plane, Round	
		Plane, Stairbuilder's	

Primary Object Term	Secondary Term	Tertiary Term	Notes
	Plane, Raising		
	Plane, Roughing		
	Plane, Rounder		
	Plane, Scoopmaker		
	Plane, Splint		
	Plane, Spoke		
	Plane, Thumb		
	Plane, Violinmaker's		
Plate, Glue			
Pointer, Picket			
Pointer, Spoke			
Pouch, Nail			
Press, Cork			
Press, Veneer			
Puller, Fastener			
	Puller, Nail		
	Puller, Staple		
	Puller, Tack		
Punch, Wood			
	Punch, Carver's		
	Punch, Cooper's		
	Punch, Handrail		
	Punch, Marking		
	Punch, Nail		
	Punch, Shingle		
	Punch, Starting		
	Punch, Veneer		
Reamer, Woodworking			
	Reamer, Broach		
	Reamer, Hooked		
Rod, Gauge			
Router			
Rule, Woodworking			*Note:* May also use a "Rule, Retractable" or "Ruler" term from Weights & Measures T&E if appropriate
	Rule, Bench		
	Rule, Board		
	Rule, Caliper		
	Rule, Carpenter's		

Primary Object Term	Secondary Term	Tertiary Term	Notes
	Rule, Patternmaker's		
	Rule, Protractor		
Sander			
	Sander, Belt		
	Sander, Contour		
	Sander, Disk		
	Sander, Spindle		
Sandpaper			
Saw, Woodworking			
	Backsaw		
		Saw, Bead	
		Saw, Blitz	
		Saw, Carcass	
		Saw, Dovetail	
		Saw, Miter-Box	
		Saw, Rabbet	
		Saw, Stairbuilder's	
		Saw, Tenon	
		Saw, Veneer	
	Jigsaw		
	Ripsaw		
	Saw, Band		
	Saw, Cabinet		
	Saw, Circular		
		Saw, Bench	
		Saw, Drunken	
		Saw, Electric Portable	
		Saw, Radial Arm	
		Saw, Table	
	Saw, Compass		
		Locksaw	
		Saw, Keyhole	
		Saw, Square Hole	
	Saw, Crown		
	Saw, Frame		
		Fretsaw	
		Saw, Bow	
		Saw, Coping	
		Saw, Felloe	

Primary Object Term	Secondary Term	Tertiary Term	Notes
		Saw, Framed Veneer	
		Saw, Pit	
		Saw, Scroll	
	Saw, Hand		
		Saw, Flooring	
	Saw, Heading		
	Saw, Open Pit		
	Saw, Panel		
	Saw, Patternmaker's		
	Saw, Saber		
	Saw, Treadle		
	Saw, Vellum		
Sawmill			*Note:* Use for the machine; for the structure in which a sawmill is housed, use "Building, Sawmill" from Industrial Structures
	Sawmill, Band		
	Sawmill, Circular		
	Sawmill, Gang		
	Sawmill, Gate-Type		
	Sawmill, Muley		
	Sawmill, Up-and-Down		
Scorper			
	Scorper, Closed		
	Scorper, Open		
Scraper, Wood			
	Scraper, Box		
	Scraper, Cabinet		
Scribe, Wood			
Sheath, Ax			
Square			
	Square, Bevel		
	Square, Carpenter's		
	Square, Drill Point		
	Square, Miter		
	Square, Set		
	Square, Sliding		
	Square, Try		
Stand, Saw			
	Prop, Sawyer's		

Primary Object Term	Secondary Term	Tertiary Term	Notes
	Sawbuck		
	Sawhorse		
	Tackle, Sawing		
Stand, Shaft			
Stave			
Stool, Caulker's			
Stop, Bench			
Tap, Screw			
Template, Woodworking			
	Pattern, Woodworking		
Topper, Barrel			
Vise, Woodworking			
	Vise, Box		
	Vise, Carving		
	Vise, Chair		
Wedge, Splitting			
Wheel, Caulking			

Class:
OTHER T&E FOR MATERIALS

Definition: Tools, equipment, and supplies that do not meet the definitions of this category's other classes. This class includes specialized tools originally created to transform raw materials into specific finished products such as cigars, gems, and soap.

Primary Object Term	Secondary Term	Tertiary Term	Notes
Cauldron, Potash			
Knife, Snow			
Mold, Jewelry			
Tool, Cigar Making			
	Block, Booking		
	Board, Cigar		
	Box, Cigar Drying		
	Box, Cigar Packer's		
	Clamp, Cigar		
	Cutter, Tuck		
	Knife, Cigar		
		Chaveta	
	Machine, Tobacco		
	Mold, Cigar		
		Mold, Revolving	
	Packer, Cigar		
	Press, Cigar		
		Press, Cigar Mold	
		Press, Cigar Packer's	
	Rack, Cigar Bundling		
	Roller, Tobacco		
		Roller, Cigar	
		Roller, Cigarette	
	Sprinkler, Tobacco		
	Stick, Tobacco		
Tool, Lapidary			
	Cadran, Gemologist's		
	Cutter, Gem		
	Wheel, Buffing		
Tool, Sinew			
	Knife, Sinew		
	Stone, Sinew		
Tool, Soapmaking			
	Mold, Soap		
	Stick, Soap		
	Strainer, Lye		

Category 5: TOOLS & EQUIPMENT FOR SCIENCE & TECHNOLOGY

Definition: **Tools, equipment, and supplies used for the observation of natural phenomena or to apply knowledge gained from such observation. Tools in this category tend to be made to enlarge or record our understanding of the world or to help express such understanding. The classes in this category are related by virtue of the fact that they include objects created to employ a particular body of knowledge. The classes are based on knowledge rather than materials.**

Class:
ACOUSTICAL T&E

Definition: Tools, equipment, and supplies originally created for the study of sound and its effect on hearing. Objects listed in this class may be used for generating, detecting, observing, testing, modifying, and/or measuring sound. They differ from objects in Sound Communication T&E in that their function is to study sound, not to transmit or receive it. They differ from some related items in Medical & Psychological T&E in that the function of items in Acoustical T&E is to examine the nature and effects of sound, not to diagnose or treat medical conditions.

Primary Object Term	Secondary Term	Tertiary Term	Notes
Amplifier, Sound			
	Horn, Funnel		
Analyzer, Clang			
Analyzer, Sound			
Apparatus, Tone Difference			
Audiometer			
Cage, Sound			
Controller, Sound			
Fork, Tuning			
Generator, Sound			
	Measurer, Sound		*Note:* Use for a sound generator with scales
Harmonometer			
Logograph			
Masker, Audio			
Opeidoscope			
Organ, Laboratory			
Oscillator, Audio			
Pendulum, Sound			
Perimeter, Sound			
Phonelescope			
Phonodeik			
Phonometer			
Phono-Projectoscope			
Phonorganon			
Phonoscope			

Primary Object Term	Secondary Term	Tertiary Term	Notes
Photophone			
Pseudophone			
Receiver, Sound			
Recorder, Sound			
Reproducer, Sound			
Resonator			
Reverberator			
Sonometer			
Spectrogram, Sound			
Spectrograph, Sound			
Stimulator, Sound			
Strobilion			*Note:* Use for an instrument that records vibrational patterns
Tonometer, Acoustical			
Tonoscope			
Topophone			
Transmitter, Sound			
Tube, Quincke's			
Variator, Stern			
Vibroscope			
Wheel, Savart			
Whistle, Galton			

Class:
ARMAMENTS

Definition: Tools, equipment, and supplies originally created to be used for hunting, target-shooting, warfare, or self-protection. This class includes firearms, artillery, bladed weapons, and striking weapons. It does not include structures designed for housing troops or supplies and objects designed for transporting troops or supplies.

Sub-Class:
AMMUNITION

Definition: Ammunition for armament, whether intended for particular weapons, such as BBs and cartridges, or intended to be deployed alone, such as grenades, missiles, or bombs. This sub-class includes ammunition casings, such as sabots, and planted explosive weapons, such as mines or petards.

Primary Object Term	Secondary Term	Tertiary Term	Notes
Bomb			
	Bomb, Air-to-Air		
	Bomb, Air-to-Surface		
	Bomb, Air-to-Underwater		
	Bomb, Incendiary		
	Charge, Depth		
Bullet			
	Ball, Musket		
	Ball, Pistol		
	Bullet, Armor-Piercing		
	Bullet, Controlled Expansion		
	Bullet, Expanding		
	Bullet, Incendiary		
	Bullet, Minie		
	Bullet, Sling		
	Bullet, Tracer		
Cannonball			
Cartridge			
	Cartridge, Blank		
	Cartridge, Caseless		
	Cartridge, Center-Fire		
	Cartridge, Dummy		
	Cartridge, Linen		
	Cartridge, Paper		
	Cartridge, Pinfire		
	Cartridge, Rimfire		
		Cap, BB	

Primary Object Term	Secondary Term	Tertiary Term	Notes
Grenade			
	Grenade, Antipersonnel		
	Grenade, Antitank		
	Grenade, Hand		
	Grenade, Incendiary		
	Grenade, Rifle		
	Grenade, Smoke		
	Grenade, Tear Gas		
Gunpowder			
Mine			
	Mine, Aerial		
	Mine, Land		
	Mine, Underwater		
Missile			
	Missile, Air-to-Air		
	Missile, Air-to-Surface		
	Missile, Air-to-Underwater		
	Missile, Air-to-Water		
	Missile, Antimissile		
	Missile, Ballistic		
	Missile, Guided		
	Missile, Surface-to-Air		
	Missile, Surface-to-Surface		
	Missile, Underwater-to-Surface		
	Torpedo		
Petard			
Primer, Detonation			
	Fuze		
	Primer, Friction		
Sabot, Ammunition			
Shell, Armament			
	Shell, Artillery		
		Carcass	
		Shell, Mortar	
	Shell, Shotgun		
Shot			
	Grapeshot		

Primary Object Term	Secondary Term	Tertiary Term	Notes
	Shot, Bar		
	Shot, Case		
	Shot, Chain		
	Shot, Solid		
		Shot, BB	
Shrapnel			
Wad, Gun			

Sub-Class:
ARMAMENT ACCESSORIES

Definition: Objects used as accessories for hunting, target-shooting, warfare, or self-protection. This sub-class includes weapon components and objects used for weapon care or storage.

Primary Object Term	Secondary Term	Tertiary Term	Notes
Adapter, Weapon			
	Adapter, Barrel		
	Adapter, Grip		
Auger, Fuze			
Baldric			*Note:* May also use "Sash" or "Belt" from Clothing Accessories
Bandolier, Ammunition			*Note:* May also use "Belt, Shoulder"
Bar, Elevating			
Barrel, Firearm			
Belt, Armament			*Note:* May also use "Belt" from Clothing Accessories
	Belt, Accessory		
	Belt, Ammunition		
		Belt, Cartridge	
		Belt, Cartridge Box	
	Belt, Link		
	Belt, Sam Browne		
	Belt, Shoulder		
	Belt, Sword		
Bowstring			
Brake, Muzzle			
Brush, Bore			
Bucket, Grease			
Bucket, Tar			
Buffer, Recoil			
Buttplate			
Caliper, Artillery			
	Caliper, Gunner's		
	Caliper, Shell		
Call, Game			
Caltrop			
Cap, Muzzle			
Cap, Percussion			
	Cap, Musket		
Cap, Snap			

Primary Object Term	Secondary Term	Tertiary Term	Notes
Charger, Nipple			
Clip, Cartridge			
	Clip, Stripper		
Container, Armament			*Note:* Use for any container specifically designed for protecting and/or transporting armaments; if a case is designed specifically for a given weapon, ammunition, or accessory, a new term may be created with the *Nomenclature* term for that armament as a modifier (e.g., "Case, Pistol"); that term may be organized under "Bag, Armament," "Box, Armament," "Case, Armament," "Chest, Armament," etc., as appropriate; cabinets for storing and displaying weapons are included in Storage & Display Furniture
	Bag, Armament		
		Bag, Hunting	
		Bag, Powder	
		Bag, Shot	
	Box, Armament		
		Box, Ammunition	
		Box, Cap	
		Box, Cartridge	
		Box, Patch	
		Box, Percussion Cap	
	Bucket, Artillery		
	Case, Armament		
		Case, Artillery Shell	
		Case, Bow	
		Case, Cartridge	
		Case, Gun	
		Case, Powder Box	
		Case, Sword	
	Chest, Armament		
		Chest, Ammunition	
	Cover, Cartridge Box		
	Flask, Ammunition		
		Flask, Powder	
		Flask, Priming	
		Flask, Shot	
		Horn, Powder	

Primary Object Term	Secondary Term	Tertiary Term	Notes
	Garland, Shot		*Note:* May also use "Component, Watercraft" from Water Transportation Accessories
	Holder, Ammunition		
		Holder, Cartridge	
		Holder, Clip	
		Holder, Shell	
	Holster		
	Keg, Powder		
	Locker, Arms		
	Pouch, Arms		
		Pouch, Cap	
		Pouch, Cartridge	
		Pouch, Gunner's	
		Pouch, Primer	
		Pouch, Shot	
	Quiver		
	Rack, Arms		
		Rack, Bomb	
	Scabbard		
		Scabbard, Bayonet	
		Scabbard, Carbine	
		Scabbard, Dagger	
		Scabbard, Sword	
	Sheath		
	Tray, Ammunition		
Cover, Vent			
Cradle, Cannon			
Crimper, Cap			
Cutter, Cake			
Cutter, Fuze			
Cutter, Wad			
Decapper/Recapper			
Decoy			*Note:* The name of the animal represented by the decoy may be entered in a subject field; "Decoy, Fish" is included in Fishing Equipment
Detector, Mine			
Die, Loading			
Disk, Sight			
Dispenser, Cap			

Primary Object Term	Secondary Term	Tertiary Term	Notes
Extension, Sight			
Extractor, Fuze			
Extractor, Headless Shell			
Flag, Wind			
Flint, Gun			
Fork, Hot Shot			
Frog, Weapon			
Gauge, Armament			
	Gauge, Artillery		
		Gauge, Cannonball	
	Gauge, Barrel		
	Gauge, Bullet		
	Gauge, Powder		
	Gauge, Vent		
Gimlet, Artillery			
	Gimlet, Fuze		
	Gimlet, Gunner's		
Glove, Target Shooter's			
Gouge, Fuze			
Grate, Hot Shot			
Guard, Weapon			
	Guard, Arm		
	Guard, Knuckle		
	Guard, Sword		
	Guard, Trigger		
	Guard, Wrist		
Gunflint			
Handspike, Gunner's			
Haversack, Gunner's			*Note:* May also use "Haversack" from Personal Carrying & Storage Gear
Hook, Shell			
Jacket, Target Shooter's			
Jag, Cleaning			
Keeper, Sling			
Kit, Gun Cleaning			
Kit, Gun Loading			
Knife, Patch			

Primary Object Term	Secondary Term	Tertiary Term	Notes
Ladle, Hot Shot			
Lanyard, Weapon			
Launcher, Target			
Level, Gunner's			
Light, Aiming Post			*Note:* May also use "Lamp, Electric" from Lighting Devices
Limber, Artillery			
Linstock			
Loader, Ammunition			
	Loader, Ammunition Belt		
	Loader, Shell		
Lock, Cannon			
Lubricator-Sizer			
Magazine, Firearm			
Mallet, Fuze			
Measure, Powder			
Mitten, Target Shooter's			
Mold, Ammunition			
	Mold, Ball		
	Mold, Bullet		
	Mold, Wad		
Mount, Gun			
	Rest, Firearm		
		Rest, Machine	
		Rest, Musket	
	Stick, Shooting		
		Bipod, Shooting	
		Monopod, Shooting	
		Tripod, Shooting	
	Turret, Machine Gun		
Mount, Sight			
Muzzle, False			
Pants, Bazooka			
Patch, Gun Cleaning			
Pendulum, Ballistic			
Pin, Priming			
Pincers, Gunner's			
Post, Aiming			

Primary Object Term	Secondary Term	Tertiary Term	Notes
Press, Priming			
Pricker, Military			
Primer, Nipple			
Protector, Throat			
Puller, Bullet			
Punch, Vent			
Quadrant, Gunner's			
Quoin, Artillery			
Rake, Hot Shot			
Ramrod			
Reamer, Chamber			
Reamer, Fuze Plug			
Release, Bomb			
Remover, Case			
Rod, Gun Cleaning			
Rod, Knockout			
Rule, Trunnion			
Safety, Grip			
Saw, Fuze			
Scraper, Armament			
	Scraper, Band		
	Scraper, Gun Barrel		
	Scraper, Mortar		
	Scraper, Shell		
Searcher, Vent			
Seater, Bullet			
Set, Loading Tool			
Setter, Fuze			
Shears, Portfire			
Shoe, Trigger			
Sight			
	Sight, Globe		
	Sight, Micrometer		
	Sight, Military		
	Sight, Tang		
	Sight, Telescope		
	Sight, Vernier		
	Sight, Windgauge		
Silencer			

Primary Object Term	Secondary Term	Tertiary Term	Notes
Sled, Artillery			
Sleeve, Gunner's			
Spike, Cannon			
Sponge, Artillery			
Stabilizer, Armament			
Starter, Bullet			
Stock, Portfire			
Stopper, Muzzle			
Straightener, Arrow			
Suppressor, Flash			
Tab, Archery			
Target			
	Target, Archery		
	Target, Skeet		
Telescope, Spotting			
Tester, Powder			
Testudo			
Thumbstall			
Tinderbox, Pocket			
Tompion			
Tongs, Rocket			
Tool, Tong			
Trap, Bullet			
Trap, Hand			
Trap, Skeet			
Trunnion			
Tube, Percussion			
Vise, Armament			
	Vise, Breeching		
	Vise, Hammer Spring		
	Vise, Lock Spring		
	Vise, Shell		
Weight, Atlatl			
	Bannerstone		
	Birdstone		
	Boatstone		
Wire, Priming			
Worm			
Wrench, Armament			

Primary Object Term	Secondary Term	Tertiary Term	Notes
	Wrench, Breeching		
	Wrench, Cock		
	Wrench, Cock and Hammer		
	Wrench, Front Sight		
	Wrench, Fuze		
	Wrench, Gun Carriage		
	Wrench, Muzzle		
	Wrench, Nipple		
	Wrench, Pin		

Sub-Class:
ARTILLERY

Definition: Heavy weapons that employ combustion or explosion to fire a projectile. Artillery may be portable and may be employed by one person, but typically it is fired from a more or less stationary position.

Primary Object Term	Secondary Term	Tertiary Term	Notes
Artillery, Breech-Loading			
Artillery, Muzzle-Loading			
Cannon			
	Cannon, Serpentine		
	Carronade		
	Culverin		
		Demi-Culverin	
		Minion	
		Robinet	
		Saker	
	Demi-Cannon		
	Falcon		
	Falconet		
	Perrier		
Gun, Antiaircraft			
Gun, Antitank			
	Destroyer, Tank		
Gun, Field			
Gun, Garrison			
Gun, Naval			
Gun, Railway			
Gun, Recoilless			
Gun, Sea-Coast			
Gun, Siege			
Gun, Self-Propelled			
Gun, Swivel			
Gun, Volley			
Howitzer			
Launcher, Rocket			
	Bazooka		
Mortar, Artillery			
	Mortar, Proving		
Rifle, Field			
Rifle, Recoilless			
Rifle, Spotting			

Sub-Class:
BODY ARMOR

Definition: Clothing worn as defensive armament, including formal parts of a suit of armor and protective devices used in combat.

Primary Object Term	Secondary Term	Tertiary Term	Notes
Armor			*Note:* Use only for an entire suit of armor
	Armor, Parade		
Backplate			
Breastplate, Armor			
Brigandine			
Coat, Buff			
Cover, Helmet			
	Net, Helmet		
Cuirass			
Cuisse			
Culet			
Fauld			
Gauntlet, Plate			
Gorget			
Greave			
Hauberk			
Helmet, Plate			
	Armet		
	Bascinet		
	Burgonet		
		Zischagge	
	Cabasset		
	Hat, Kettle		
	Heaume		
	Helm		
	Morion		
	Sallet		
Legharness			
Liner, Helmet			
Mail			
Pauldron			
	Spaudler		
Plate, Armor			
Poleyn			
Sabaton			
Shield			
	Adargas		
	Buckler		
	Pavis		

Primary Object Term	Secondary Term	Tertiary Term	Notes
	Targe		
Shirt of Mail			
Tasset			
Tonlet			
Vambrace			
Vest, Bulletproof			
Vest, Flak			

Sub-Class:
EDGED WEAPONS

Definition: Weapons that cut or pierce by cutting. This sub-class includes edged weapons such as bayonets that are accessories to firearms and tools such as crossbows that launch edged weapons.

Primary Object Term	Secondary Term	Tertiary Term	Notes
Arrow			
	Bolt, Crossbow		
Atlatl			
Barb, Lance			
Bayonet			
	Bayonet, Knife		
	Bayonet, Plug		
	Bayonet, Socket		
	Bayonet, Sword		
	Bayonet, Triangular		
Blowgun			
Bow			
	Crossbow		
	Longbow		
Dagger			
	Baselard		
	Dagger, Stiletto		
	Dirk		
	Knife, Trench		
	Kris		
	Poniard		
Dart			
Glaive			
	Fauchard		
Harpoon			
	Harpoon, Two Flue		
	Harpoon, Single Flue		
	Harpoon, Toggling		
	Iron, Lily		
	Lance, Bomb		
Knife, Weapon			
	Bolo		
	Knife, Bleeding		
	Knife, Hunting		
		Knife, Bowie	
	Knife, Sheath		

Primary Object Term	Secondary Term	Tertiary Term	Notes
	Knife, Switchblade		
	Knife, Throwing		
	Misericorde		
Point, Projectile			
	Arrowhead		
	Point, Spear		
Pole-Arm			
	Bill		
	Brandistock		
	Gisarme		
	Halberd		
	Partisan		
	Poleax		
		Bardiche	
	Staff, Leading		
		Spontoon	
Spear			
	Javelin		
		Angon	
	Lance		
		Lance, Whale	
	Pike		
		Pike, Awl	
		Pike, Boarding	
	Spear, Fish		
		Spear, Eel	
		Spear, Squid	
	Spear, Hunting		
		Spear, Muskrat	
	Trident		
Sword			
	Backsword		
	Broadsword		
		Claymore	
	Cane, Sword		
	Cutlass		
	Gladius		
	Rapier		
	Saber		

Primary Object Term	Secondary Term	Tertiary Term	Notes
		Scimitar	
	Saber, Short		
	Smallsword		
	Sword, Artillery		
	Sword, Hanger		
		Cuttoe	
	Sword, Hunting		
Weapon, Ax			
	Ax, Belt		
	Ax, Boarding		
	Battle-Ax		
		Ax, Throwing	
	Tomahawk		

Sub-Class:
FIREARMS

Definition: Projectile-firing weapons that can be deployed easily by one person and, in most cases, use explosive propellant. This sub-class does not include ammunition, firearm accessories, or crew-served heavy armament. Note: For combination and conversion pieces, use multiple terms, e.g., "Pistol" and "Carbine" for a pistol carbine, and "Musket, Flintlock" and "Musket, Percussion" for a musket converted from flintlock to percussion.

Primary Object Term	Secondary Term	Tertiary Term	Notes
Caliver			
Cannon, Hand			
Carbine			
Flamethrower			
Gun, Air			
	Gun, Bellows		
	Gun, Pellet		
	Gun, Pump-Up		
	Gun, Spring Air		
		Gun, BB	
Gun, Bomb			
Gun, Cane			
Gun, Combination			
Gun, Dart			
	Gun, Tranquilizer		
Gun, Folding			
Gun, Hunting			
Gun, Machine			
	Gun, Gatling		
Gun, Riot			
Gun, Spear			
	Gun, Harpoon		
Gun, Stun			
Gun, Submachine			
Gun, Tear Gas			
Gyrojet			*Note:* May also use "Pistol," "Carbine," or "Rifle"
Harquebus			
Launcher, Grenade			
Musket			
	Gun, Wall		
	Musket, Cartridge		
	Musket, Flintlock		

Primary Object Term	Secondary Term	Tertiary Term	Notes
		Fusil	
	Musket, Matchlock		
	Musket, Percussion		
	Musket, Wheelock		
	Musketoon		
Petronel			
Pistol			
	Pepperbox		
	Pistol, Automatic		
	Pistol, Blank		
	Pistol, Blunderbuss		
	Pistol, Cartridge		
	Pistol, Dueling		
	Pistol, Flintlock		
	Pistol, Holster		
	Pistol, Matchlock		
	Pistol, Percussion		
	Pistol, Pocket		
		Derringer	
		Pistol, Belt	
		Pistol, Palm	
	Pistol, Saddle		
	Pistol, Semi-Automatic		
	Pistol, Target		
	Pistol, Wheelock		
Revolver			
	Revolver, Cartridge		
	Revolver, Percussion		
Rifle			
	Rifle, Assault		
	Rifle, Cartridge		
	Rifle, Flintlock		
		Rifle, Long	
	Rifle, Half Stock		
	Rifle, Hunting		
		Rifle, Jaeger	
	Rifle, Matchlock		
	Rifle, Military		
	Rifle, Over and Under		*Note:* May also use "Gun, Combination" and "Shotgun" if appropriate

Primary Object Term	Secondary Term	Tertiary Term	Notes
	Rifle, Percussion		
		Rifle, Plains	
	Rifle, Repeating		
	Rifle, Target		
		Rifle, Schuetzen	
	Rifle, Training		
	Rifle, Wheelock		
Shotgun			
	Blunderbuss		
	Fowler		
		Gun, Punt	
	Shotgun, Cartridge		
	Shotgun, Double-Barrel		
	Shotgun, Flintlock		
	Shotgun, Multi-Barrel		
	Shotgun, Percussion		
	Shotgun, Repeating		
	Shotgun, Single-Barrel		
	Shotgun, Skeet		
	Shotgun, Trap		

Sub-Class:
PERCUSSIVE WEAPONS

Definition: Armaments designed to batter or crush by weight or momentum, including weapons that propel non-explosive or non-penetrating missiles.

Primary Object Term	Secondary Term	Tertiary Term	Notes
Ballista			
Biffa			
Blackjack			
Bola			
Catapult			
	Mangonel		
Club			
	Mace		
	Nightstick		
	Pogamoggan		
	Shillelagh		
Flail			
Hammer, War			
Knuckles, Brass			
Quarterstaff			
Ram, Battering			
Sling			
Slingshot			
Stick, Throwing			
	Boomerang		
Switch			
Trebucket			

Class:
ASTRONOMICAL T&E

Definition: Tools, equipment, and supplies originally created to observe, measure, or document objects and events outside of the earth's atmosphere. Objects listed in this class differ from those in Optical T&E in that they are specifically associated with astronomy. They differ from those in Surveying & Navigational T&E in that they are concerned with observation rather than with the practical uses for such observation.

Primary Object Term	Secondary Term	Tertiary Term	Notes
Astrodicticum			
Astrolabe			
Astrometer			
Astropatrotometer			
Astroscope			
Case, Astronomical Instrument			*Note:* Use for any container specifically designed for protecting and/or transporting astronomical instruments; if a case is designed specifically for a given instrument, a new term may be created with the *Nomenclature* term for that instrument as a modifier; that term may be organized under "Case, Astronomical Instrument"
Circle, Meridian			
Clock, Astronomical			*Note:* May also use "Clock" from Timekeeping T&E
	Clock, Sidereal		
Coronograph			
Cosmolabe			
Cyanometer			
Dipleidoscope			
Eclipsareon			
Globe, Celestial			*Note:* May also use "Globe" from Graphic Documents
	Cosmosphere		
	Geodescope		
	Sphere, Armillary		
Heliometer			
Helioscope			
Instrument, Astronomical			*Note:* Use for an astronomical instrument that lacks another descriptive or generic name or if the specific name of the instrument is unknown
Instrument, Azimuth			
Interferometer, Radio			

Primary Object Term	Secondary Term	Tertiary Term	Notes
Magnetograph			
Meteoroscope			
Mirror, Astronomical			
Orrery			*Note:* May also use "Model" from Other Documents
Photometer, Photoelectric			
Planisphere			
Prism, Objective			
Projector, Planetarium			*Note:* May also use "Projector" from Visual Communication Devices
Pyrheliometer			
Quadrant, Astronomical			
Selenotrope			
Siderostat			
	Heliostat		
Spectroheliograph			
Spheroscope			
Telengiscope			
Telepolariscope			*Note:* May also use "Polariscope" from Optical T&E
Telescope, Astronomical			*Note:* May also use "Telescope" from Optical T&E
	Camera, Schmidt		
	Photoheliograph		
	Telescope, Equatorial		
	Telescope, Orbiting		
	Telescope, Radio		
	Telescope, Reflecting		
		Chromatoscope	
		Telescope, Cassegrain	
	Telescope, Refracting		
		Telescope, Achromatic	
		Telescope, Galilean	
	Telescope, Solar		
Telespectroscope			

Class:
BIOLOGICAL T&E

Definition: Tools, equipment, and supplies originally created to observe, measure, or document physiological or anatomical aspects of organisms for purposes other than diagnosis or treatment. Tools for diagnosis and treatment of people are included in Medical & Psychological T&E; those for animals are in Veterinary Equipment.

Primary Object Term	Secondary Term	Tertiary Term	Notes
Aeroscope			
Apparatus, Ammonia Absorption			
Apparatus, Counting			
Apparatus, Culture			
Apparatus, Kahn Test			
Apparatus, Metabolism			
Apparatus, Shaking			
Apparatus, Staining			
Apparatus, Van Slyke			
Auxanometer			
Bacterioscope			
Bath			
	Bath, Dehydrating		
	Bath, Embedding		
Biospecimen			*Note:* The name of the specimen may be entered in a subject field
	Specimen, Animal		
	Specimen, Plant		
Blowpipe, Anatomical			
Board, Spreading			
Box, Germination			
Case, Biological Instrument			*Note:* Use for any container specifically designed for protecting and/or transporting biological instruments; if a case is designed specifically for a given instrument, a new term may be created with the *Nomenclature* term for that instrument as a modifier; that term may be organized under "Case, Biological Instrument"
Centrifuge, Human			
Chamber, Heliotropic			
Clinostat			

Primary Object Term	Secondary Term	Tertiary Term	Notes
Coagulometer			
Conchometer			
Container, Biological Specimen			
	Mount, Specimen		
	Vasculum		
Craniometer			
	Conformateur		
Cutter, Microscopic Section			
	Microtome		
Esthesiometer			
Filter, Specimen			
	Filter, Seitz		
	Filter, Serum		
Granometer			
Hemocytometer			*Note:* May also use "Device, Blood Testing" from Medical Instruments if appropriate
Hemoglobinometer			
Incubator, Biological			
Instrument, Biological			*Note:* Use for a biological instrument that lacks another descriptive or generic name or if the specific name of the instrument is unknown
Kit, Dissecting			
Loop, Bacteriology			
Lysimeter			
Needle, Inoculating			
Osmoscope			
Paper, Filter			
Pencil, Skin Marking			
Photosynthometer			
Posturometer			
Potometer			
Press, Plant			
Respirometer			
Sample, Tissue			
Set, Dissecting			*Note:* May also use "Tool, Dissecting" or narrower terms
Slide, Microscope			

Primary Object Term	Secondary Term	Tertiary Term	Notes
Stethogoniometer			
Tool, Dissecting			
	Forceps, Dissecting		
	Needle, Dissecting		
	Scissors, Dissecting		

Class:
CHEMICAL T&E

Definition: Tools, equipment, and supplies originally created for the study or manufacture of substances based upon their molecular composition, structure, and properties. Objects used for the study of atomic and subatomic particles are included in Nuclear Physics T&E, and objects used for the study of the interaction of physical objects are in Mechanical Measurement Equipment.

Sub-Class:
CHEMICAL TESTING DEVICES

Definition: Tools, equipment, and supplies originally created for the sampling, observation, measurement, or recording of specific chemical properties in specialized applications.

Primary Object Term	Secondary Term	Tertiary Term	Notes
Actinograph			
Actinometer			
Alkalimeter			
Analyzer, Gas			
Anthrocometer			
Apophorometer, Chemical			
Apparatus, Catalytic			
Apparatus, Distilling			
	Alembic		
	Receiver, Distilling		
	Retort		
Apparatus, Float Test			
Apparatus, Hot Extraction			
Apparatus, Micro Combustion			
Aquameter			
Atmolyser			
Blanchimeter			
Calcimeter			
Carbolimeter			
Carbonometer			
Carburometer			
Case, Chemical Instrument			*Note:* Use for any container specifically designed for protecting and/or transporting chemical instruments; if a case is designed specifically for a given instrument, a new term may be created with the *Nomenclature* term for that instrument as a modifier; that term may be organized under "Case, Chemical Instrument"

Primary Object Term	Secondary Term	Tertiary Term	Notes
Cathetometer, Laboratory			
Chyometer			
Colorimeter			
Comparator, Laboratory			
	Comparator, High Phosphate Slide		
	Comparator, Hydrogenation		
	Comparator, Nessler Tube		
Condenser, Laboratory			
Cone, Imhoff			
Densimeter			
	Dasymeter		
	Hydrometer		
		Acidimeter	
		Alcoholometer	
		Ammoniameter	
		Argentometer	
		Litrameter	
		Oleometer	
		Salimeter	
	Pycnometer		
	Sclerometer		
Densitometer			
Diffusiometer			
Dilatometer			
Durometer			
Elacometer			
Furnace, Test			
Goniometer			
Halometer			
Hydrophore			
Indicator, Volume Change			
Indicator, Water Stability			
Indigometer			

Primary Object Term	Secondary Term	Tertiary Term	Notes
Instrument, Chemical			*Note:* Use for a chemical instrument that lacks another descriptive or generic name or if the specific name of the instrument is unknown
Kit, Chemical Test			
	Kit, Water Analysis		
Logometer			
Manometer			
	Micromanometer		
Melanoscope			
Needle, Gillmore			
Nitrometer			
Osmometer			
Penetrometer			
Phosphoroscope			
Refractometer			
Saccharimeter			
Sampler, Effluent			
Spinthariscope			
Support, Imhoff Cone			
Table, Flow			
Tester, Fineness			
Tester, Sediment			
Tester, Soundness			
Tithonometer			
Titrometer			
Trough, Pneumatic			
Vaporimeter			

Sub-Class:
LABWARE

Definition: Glassware and other general equipment used in different types of laboratories.

Primary Object Term	Secondary Term	Tertiary Term	Notes
Adapter, Tubing			
Bath, Water			
Brush, Laboratory			
	Brush, Burette		
	Brush, Pipette		
Burner, Laboratory			
	Burner, Alcohol		
	Burner, Argand		
	Burner, Bunsen		
Centrifuge, Laboratory			
	Centrifuge, Chemical		
	Centrifuge, Clinical		
Clamp, Laboratory			
	Clamp, Hosecock		
	Clamp, Stopcock		
	Clamp, Suspension		
Container, Laboratory			
	Basin, Laboratory		
		Basin, Flushing	
		Basin, Rinsing	
	Beaker		
		Beaker, Berzelius	
		Beaker, Griffen	
		Beaker, Phillips	
	Bottle, Laboratory		
		Bottle, Aspirator	
		Bottle, Centrifuge	
		Bottle, Gas Washing	
		Bottle, Reagent	
		Bottle, Wash	
	Bulb, Laboratory		
		Bulb, Absorption	
		Bulb, Connecting	
	Burette		
		Burette, Geissler	
		Burette, Mohr	

Primary Object Term	Secondary Term	Tertiary Term	Notes
		Burette, Stopcock	
		Burette, Titration	
	Crucible, Laboratory		
	Dish, Laboratory		
		Dish, Culture	
		Dish, Dissolving	
		Dish, Evaporating	
		Dish, Petri	
	Dispenser, Laboratory		
	Flask, Laboratory		
		Flask, Boiling	
		Flask, Culture	
		Flask, Distilling	*Note:* May also use "Apparatus, Distilling" from Chemical Testing Devices
		Flask, Erlenmeyer	
		Flask, Filtering	
	Graduate		
	Tube, Laboratory		
		Tube, Barometer	
		Tube, Boiling	
		Tube, Capillary	
		Tube, Centrifuge	
		Tube, Combustion	
		Tube, Test	
Desiccator			
Dye, Laboratory			
Extractor, Laboratory			
Filter, Laboratory			
Flask, Vacuum			
Frame, Heating			
Funnel, Laboratory			
	Funnel, Filter		
	Pipe, Draught		
Glass, Watch			
Holder, Retort			
Mortar, Laboratory			
Paper, Litmus			
Percolator, Laboratory			
Pestle, Laboratory			

Primary Object Term	Secondary Term	Tertiary Term	Notes
Pipette			
	Pipette, Absorption		
	Pipette, Volumetric		
Rack, Laboratory			
	Rack, Test Tube		
Ring, Burner			
Separator, Laboratory			
Shaker, Laboratory			
	Shaker, Pipette		
	Shaker, Water Bath		
Siphon			
Spider, Burner			
Stand, Laboratory			
	Tripod, Laboratory		
Stirrer, Laboratory			
Stopcock			
Stopper, Laboratory			
Titrator			
Tongs, Laboratory			
	Tongs, Beaker		
	Tongs, Flask		
	Tongs, Mercury		
Tubing, Laboratory			
Washer, Glassware			

Class:
CONSTRUCTION T&E

Definition: Tools, equipment, and supplies originally created for moving earth or building structures. This class includes paving machines and equipment that modify by demolition, such as wrecking balls or jack hammers. It also includes tools such as pile drivers used for the construction of highways or structural facilities. This class does not include specialized tools listed in other classes or used in the construction industries, such as cranes, hammers, or cement mixers.

Primary Object Term	Secondary Term	Tertiary Term	Notes
Ball, Wrecking			
Bob, Plumb			
Bucket, Mechanical			
	Bucket, Clamshell		
	Bucket, Dipper		
	Bucket, Dragline		
Compactor			
	Roller		
		Steamroller	
	Tamper		
		Rammer, Paver's	
Digger, Post Hole			
	Auger, Post Hole		
Drill, Percussive			
	Jackhammer		
Driver, Pile			
Driver, Stud			
	Gun, Stud		
Earthmover			
	Bulldozer		
	Excavator		
		Backhoe	
		Machine, Trenching	
	Grader		
	Loader, Front End		
	Loader, Skid		
	Ripper		
	Scarifier		
	Scraper, Earth		
	Shovel, Power		
		Shovel, Steam	
	Tractor, Crawler		

Primary Object Term	Secondary Term	Tertiary Term	Notes
Falsework			
Finder, Stud			
Formwork			
Machine, Tiering			
Pick			
Picker, Cherry			
Platform, Working			
	Gantry		
	Platform, Roofing		
	Scaffold		
Pole, Pick			
Puller, Pole			
Puller, Stake			
Rake, Grading			
Saw, Concrete			
Shovel			
Spreader, Paving			
	Spreader, Asphalt		
Tool, Entrenching			
Tool, Fence			
	Pliers, Fence		
	Staple, Fence		
	Stretcher, Fence Wire		
	Stringer, Fence Wire		

Class:
ELECTRICAL & MAGNETIC T&E

Definition: Tools, equipment, and supplies originally created to control, distribute, modify, observe, measure, or document electricity or magnetism. This class includes tools, equipment, and components used in the manufacture, installation, maintenance, or repair of electrical and electronic devices as well as those used in the delivery of electricity or electrical power. This class does not include electrical or electronic devices created to serve other specific purposes, such as sound communication or data processing, nor does it include electrical motors and generators, which are listed in Power Producing Equipment.

Sub-Class:
ELECTRICAL & MAGNETIC MEASUREMENT DEVICES

Definition: Tools, equipment, and supplies originally created to observe, measure, or document electrical or magnetic activity.

Primary Object Term	Secondary Term	Tertiary Term	Notes
Instrument, Electrical			
	Ammeter		
		Milliammeter	
		Thermoammeter	
	Bridge, Wheatstone		
	Electrometer		
	Electroscope		
	Galvanometer		
	Galvanoscope		
	Generator, Electrostatic		
		Generator, Van de Graaf	
	Indicator, Strain		
	Inductometer		
	Megger		
	Meter, Electric		
	Meter, Phase		
	Multimeter		
	Ohmeter		
	Oscillograph		
	Oscilloscope		
	Platymeter		
	Potentiometer		
	Radiometer		
	Rheoscope		
	Voltmeter		

Primary Object Term	Secondary Term	Tertiary Term	Notes
		Millivoltmeter	
	Wattmeter		
	Wavemeter		
Instrument, Magnetic			
	Declinometer		
	Fluxmeter		
	Magnet		
	Shield, Magnetic		
	Sideroscope		

Sub-Class:
ELECTRICAL MAINTENANCE & REPAIR EQUIPMENT

Definition: Objects originally created to maintain or repair electrical monitoring equipment or install or repair electrical delivery systems.

Primary Object Term	Secondary Term	Tertiary Term	Notes
Growler			
Locator, Cable Fault			
Pliers, Electrician's			
Puller, Fuse			
Sorter, Wire			
Stripper, Wire			
Tape, Electrical			
Tester, Electrical			
	Tester, Battery		
	Tester, Circuit		
	Tester, Magneto and Coil		
	Tester, Tube		

Sub-Class:
ELECTRICAL SYSTEM COMPONENTS

Definition: Objects originally created to serve as part of an electricity delivery system.

Primary Object Term	Secondary Term	Tertiary Term	Notes
Actuator			
Adapter, Electrical			
	Adapter, Battery		
	Adapter, Battery Charger		
	Adapter, Plug		
Amplifier			
	Amplifier, Carrier		
	Amplifier, Direct Current		
Arrester, Spark			
Block, Fuse			
Board, Circuit			
Box, Electrical			
	Box, Control		
	Box, Decade		
	Box, Fuse		
	Box, Junction		
	Box, Outlet		
	Box, Resistance		
	Box, Utility		
Breaker, Circuit			
Cable, Electric			
	Cord, Extension		
	Cord, Power		
Capacitor			
	Capacitor, Electrolytic		
	Capacitor, Variable		
Choke, Electrical			
Circuit			
Conduit, Electric			
Converter, AC-DC			
Cover, Socket			
Electrode			
	Anode		
	Cathode		
Insulator			

Primary Object Term	Secondary Term	Tertiary Term	Notes
Jar, Battery			
Line, Power			
Modulator, Electrical			
	Modulator, Single Side Band		
Multiplier, Voltage			
Nut, Wire			
Oscillator			
Outlet, Electrical			
Plug, Electrical			
	Plug, Receptacle		
	Plug, Socket		
Post, Binding			
Regulator, Voltage			
Relay			
Resistor			
	Rheostat		
Rheotome			
Sensor, Occupancy			
Shunt, Electrical			
Socket, Tube			
Solenoid			
Switch, Electrical			
	Switch, Dimmer		
	Switch, Knife		
	Switch, Solenoid		
	Switch, Time		
	Switch, Transfer		
Terminal, Electrical			
	Clip, Alligator		
Transformer			
	Coil, Induction		
	Transformer, Impedance		
	Transformer, Resonant		
		Coil, Tesla	
Transistor			
Tube, Electrical			
	Tube, Ballast		

Primary Object Term	Secondary Term	Tertiary Term	Notes
	Tube, Electron		
		Diode	
	Tube, Vacuum		
		Magnetron	
Wire, Electric			

Class:
ENERGY PRODUCTION T&E

Definition: Tools, equipment, and supplies originally created to generate, convert, or distribute energy or power. This class does not include objects listed in Electrical System Components.

Sub-Class:
POWER PRODUCING EQUIPMENT

Definition: Objects originally created to generate power.

Primary Object Term	Secondary Term	Tertiary Term	Notes
Battery, Electrical			
	Battery, Dry-Cell		
	Battery, Gravity		
	Battery, Solar		
	Battery, Wet-Cell		
Boiler, Power			
	Boiler, Steam Power		
Carburetor			
Charger, Battery			
Compressor			
	Compressor, Blowing Engine		
	Compressor, Duplex Air		
	Compressor, Rotary		
	Compressor, Sullivan Angle		
	Compressor, Turbo		
Dynamotor			
Engine			*Note:* May also use "Engine, Aircraft" from Aerospace Transportation Accessories or "Engine, Automotive" from Land Transportation Accessories if appropriate
	Engine, Diesel		
	Engine, Gas		
	Engine, Gasoline		
	Engine, Hot Air		
	Engine, Liquid Fuel		
	Engine, Oil Traction		
	Engine, Radial		
	Engine, Reciprocating		
	Engine, Steam		
		Engine, Walking Beam	
	Engine, Steam Gas		

Primary Object Term	Secondary Term	Tertiary Term	Notes
	Engine, Steam Traction		
Exciter			
Furnace, Solar			
Generator			
	Generator, Gasoline		
	Generator, Steam		
	Generator, Thermoelectric		
	Generator, Water		
	Generator, Wind		
	Magneto		
Motor			
	Motor, Electric		
	Motor, Hydraulic		
	Motor, Pneumatic		
Panel, Solar			
Reactor, Nuclear			
Sweep			
	Sweep, Animal-Powered		
	Sweep, Human-Powered		
Transducer			
Treadle			
Treadmill			
	Treadmill, Animal		
	Treadmill, Human		
Turbine			
	Turbine, Gas		
	Turbine, Hydraulic		
	Turbine, Impulse		
		Wheel, Pelton	
	Turbine, Internal Combustion		
	Turbine, Steam		
Waterwheel			
	Waterwheel, Breast		
	Waterwheel, Overshot		
	Waterwheel, Tub		
	Waterwheel, Undershot		
Windmill			

Sub-Class:
POWER TRANSMISSION COMPONENTS

Definition: Objects originally created to assist in the transmission or regulation of power, particularly mechanical power in power-producing equipment or other machines.

Primary Object Term	Secondary Term	Tertiary Term	Notes
Bearing			
Belt, Power Transmission			
Block, Bearing			
Box, Journal			
Coupling, Shaft			
Crank			
Differential			
Driveline			
Filter, Engine			
Fitting, Grease			
Gear			
Governor			
Hanger, Shaft			
Housing, Clutch			
Idler			
Indicator, Horsepower			
Joint, Universal			
Manifold			
Mount, Engine			
Pipe, Exhaust			
Piston			
Pump, Fuel			
Rod, Connecting			
Rod, Nuclear Control			
Rotor			
Shaft			
	Jackshaft		
	Lineshaft		
Sparkplug			
Valve, Steam			
Weight, Safety Blow Off			
Weight, Windmill			

Sub-Class:
OTHER ENERGY PRODUCTION T&E

Definition: Objects related to energy production that do not meet the definitions of this class's other sub-classes.

Primary Object Term	Secondary Term	Tertiary Term	Notes
Reflector, Solar			
Shield, Solar			

Class:
GEOLOGICAL T&E

Definition: Tools, equipment, and supplies originally created to observe, measure, or document geological phenomena. This class includes geologists' picks and seismic measuring devices, but it excludes tools used for harvesting or mining rock or mineral materials.

Primary Object Term	Secondary Term	Tertiary Term	Notes
Geophone			
Geospecimen			*Note:* The name of the specimen may be entered in a subject field
Microscope, Petrographic			*Note:* May also use "Microscope" from Optical T&E
Pick, Paleontologist's			
Seismograph			
Seismophone			
Tromometer			

Class:
MAINTENANCE T&E

Definition: Tools, equipment, and supplies originally created for cleaning, laundering, or groundskeeping activities performed in and around a home or a public building, whether performed occasionally or as a business.

Sub-Class:
DISHWASHING EQUIPMENT

Definition: Tools, equipment, and supplies originally created to wash or assist in the washing of food service or food preparation items.

Primary Object Term	Secondary Term	Tertiary Term	Notes
Brush, Bottle			
Cleaner, Knife			
Dishcloth			
Dishpan			
Dishwasher			
Drainboard			
Drainer, Dish			
Pad, Scouring			
Rack, Dish			
Saver, Soap			
Scrubber, Pot			
Sponge, Dish			
Strainer, Sink			
Towel, Dish			

Sub-Class:
GROUNDSKEEPING EQUIPMENT

Definition: Tools, equipment, and supplies originally created for the care or maintenance of areas around structures such as lawns, flower beds, or sidewalks, or for larger landscaped areas such as athletic fields or golf courses. This sub-class does not include objects used to prepare land specifically for the cultivation of crops.

Primary Object Term	Secondary Term	Tertiary Term	Notes
Barrier, Weed			
Bin, Compost			
Blower, Leaf			
Can, Watering			
Cart, Street Sweeping			*Note:* May also use "Handcart" from Human-Powered Vehicles
Catcher, Grass			
Clipper, Flower			
Composter			
Cutter, Brush			
Cutter, Sod			
Edger, Lawn			
Edging, Landscape			
Grinder, Stump			
Hook, Brush			
Hook, Grass			
Hose, Garden			
Lifter, Sod			
Mower, Lawn			
	Mower, Power		
		Mower, Riding	
	Mower, Reel		
		Mower, Gang Reel	
Nozzle, Garden Hose			
Protector, Tree Trunk			
Rake, Lawn			
Reel, Garden Hose			
Roller, Garden			
Scythe, Brush			
Scythe, Grass			
Sealer, Tree			
Seeder, Grass			
Shears, Grass			
Shears, Hedge			
Shovel, Snow			

Primary Object Term	Secondary Term	Tertiary Term	Notes
Snowblower			
Spreader, Lawn			
Sprinkler, Lawn			
Stick, Litter			
Sweeper, Lawn			
Timer, Watering			
Tool, Pruning			
	Chisel, Pruning		
	Hook, Pruning		
		Billhook	
	Knife, Pruning		
	Pruner, Tree		
	Saw, Pruning		
	Shears, Pruning		
	Stilt, Pruning		
Tractor, Garden			*Note:* May also use "Tractor" from Motor Vehicles
Trimmer, Hedge			
	Hook, Hedge		
Trimmer, String			

Sub-Class:
HOUSEKEEPING EQUIPMENT

Definition: Tools, equipment, and supplies originally created for the cleaning or tidying of furnishings, buildings, or building spaces.

Primary Object Term	Secondary Term	Tertiary Term	Notes
Ashpan			
Attachment, Vacuum Cleaner			
Bag, Litter			
Bag, Trash			
Beater, Rug			
Bottle, Spray			
Broom			
	Broom, Electric		
	Broom, Push		
	Broom, Whisk		
Brush, Cleaning			
	Brush, Chimney		
		Brush, Flue	
	Brush, Dusting		
	Brush, Scrub		
	Brush, Toilet		
	Brush, Window		
Butler, Silent			
Cake, Urinal			
Can, Kerosene			
Can, Trash			
Cart, Janitorial			*Note:* May also use “Handcart” from Human-Powered Vehicles
Changer, Light Bulb			
Cleaner, Carpet			
	Shampooer, Carpet		
	Steamer, Carpet		
Cleaner, Lamp Chimney			
Cleaner, Vacuum			
	Vacuum, Canister		
	Vacuum, Handheld		
	Vacuum, Upright		
	Vacuum, Wet		
	Vacuum, Wet/Dry		
Cloth, Cleaning			
Cloth, Polishing			
Compactor, Trash			

Primary Object Term	Secondary Term	Tertiary Term	Notes
Container, Recycling			
	Bin, Recycling		
	Rack, Recycling		
Crumber			
Duster			
Dustpan			
Holder, Housekeeping Equipment			
	Holder, Broom		
		Holder, Whisk Broom	
	Holder, Cleaning Brush		
	Holder, Duster		
	Holder, Paper Towel		
Holystone			
Incinerator			
Jar, Slop			
Mop			
	Mop, Sponge		
	Mop, String		
Pail			
Paper, Shelf			
Plate, Tarnish Remover			
Plunger			
Polisher, Floor			
Rake, Carpet			
Scraper, Floor			
Scrubber			
Sifter, Ash			
Smoother, Bed			
Sponge			
Squeegee			
Stretcher, Carpet			
Sweeper, Carpet			
Tack, Carpet			
Tacker, Carpet			
Towel, Paper			
Washer, Power			
Wastebasket			
Wringer, Mop			

Sub-Class:
LAUNDRY EQUIPMENT

Definition: Tools, equipment, and supplies originally created for the cleaning, drying, or pressing of clothing and linens.

Primary Object Term	Secondary Term	Tertiary Term	Notes
Agitator, Laundry			
	Dolly, Wash		
Bag, Blueing			
Bench, Laundry			
Board, Ironing			
	Board, Sleeve		
	Table, Ironing		
Boiler, Laundry			
Cloth, Pressing			
Clothesline			
Clothespin			
Container, Laundry			
	Bag, Laundry		
	Basket, Laundry		
	Hamper		
Cover, Ironing Board			
Dispenser, Fabric Softener			
Dryer, Clothes			
Dryer, Glove			
Fork, Laundry			
Form, Collar			
Grater, Soap			
Hanger, Hosiery			
Heater, Iron			
Holder, Clothespin			
Horse, Clothes			*Note:* May also use “Rack” from Storage & Display Accessories
Iron			
	Flatiron		
	Iron, Electric		
	Iron, Fluting		
	Iron, Tailor’s		
	Sadiron		
Machine, Dry Cleaning			
Pail, Diaper			
Press, Laundry			

Primary Object Term	Secondary Term	Tertiary Term	Notes
	Mangle		
	Press, Hot-Head		
	Press, Pants		
Rack, Drying			
Reel, Clothesline			
Rest, Iron			
	Trivet, Ironing		
Sheet, Dryer			
Soap, Laundry			
Sprinkler, Laundry			
Stick, Laundry			
Stove, Laundry			
Stretcher, Clothes			*Note:* Use only for a stretcher associated with laundry; stretchers associated with non-laundry maintenance are listed in Personal Assistive Objects
	Stretcher, Sock		
Stretcher, Curtain			
Tongs, Laundry			
Washboard			
Washer, Clothes			
Wash-Pounder			
Washtub			
Waxer, Iron			
Wringer, Clothes			

Class:
MECHANICAL T&E

Definition: Tools, equipment, and supplies originally created for the study, measurement, or utilization of the static or dynamic properties of solids, liquids and gasses. This class includes general-purpose mechanical devices, such as wedges or hoists, and specialized devices, such as tensiometers or pressure gauges, used to measure mechanical properties.

Sub-Class:
MECHANICAL DEVICES

Definition: Objects that utilize the static or dynamic properties of solids, liquids, and gasses, including general-purpose mechanical devices and objects used specifically for the maintenance of mechanical devices.

Primary Object Term	Secondary Term	Tertiary Term	Notes
Absorber, Shock			
Apparatus, Hoisting			
	Crane		
	Derrick		
		Pole, Gin	
	Hoist		
		Block and Tackle	
		Come-Along	
		Gin	
		Winch	
		Windlass	
		Windlass, Hand	
Block, Snatch			
Clamp			
Clevis			
Conveyor			
	Conveyor, Belt		
	Conveyor, Bucket		
Coupling			
Ejector			
Fairlead			
Flywheel			
Grapple			
Gripper			
Heaver			
Hook			
	Hook, Cargo		
	Hook, Chain		
	Hook, Sister		
	Hook, Swivel		

Primary Object Term	Secondary Term	Tertiary Term	Notes
Jack			
	Jack, Hoisting		
	Jack, Lifting		
		Jack, Fence	*Note:* May also use "Tool, Fence" from Construction T&E
		Jack, Furniture	
	Jack, Pulling		
Lagging			
Lever			
	Bar, Tommy		
	Crowbar		
		Bar, Claw	
		Pinchbar	
	Handspike		
Lift, Hydraulic			
Machine, Fall			
Parbuckle			
Pendulum			
Plane, Inclined			
Puller, Gear			
Pulley			
	Pulley, Crown		
Pump			
	Pump, Barrel		
	Pump, Centrifugal		
	Pump, Diver's		
	Pump, Double-Action		
	Pump, Hydrostatic Test		
	Pump, Piston		
	Pump, Plunger		
	Pump, Single-Action		
	Pump, Submersible		
	Pumpjack		
Ram, Hydraulic			
Ratchet			
Reel			
Regulator, Gas			
Screw, Archimedean			
Sheave, Winding			
Sling, Hoist			

Primary Object Term	Secondary Term	Tertiary Term	Notes
Spreader, Hydraulic			
Spreader, Load			
Spring			
	Spring, Indicator		
	Spring, Pressure		
	Spring, Spiral		
Swivel			
Table, Oscillating			
Tool, Lubrication			
	Can, Oil		
	Cup, Grease		
	Fitting, Oil		
	Lubricator, Pressure		
Turnbuckle			
Vise			
Wedge			
	Chock		
Wheel			
Wheel, Bull			

Sub-Class:
MECHANICAL MEASUREMENT EQUIPMENT

Definition: Objects used for the study or measurement of the static or dynamic properties of solids, liquids, or gasses, including force, motion, pressure, flow, tension, friction, ductility, torque, velocity, and viscosity.

Primary Object Term	Secondary Term	Tertiary Term	Notes
Accelerometer			
	Gravimeter		
Apparatus, Cement Vicat			
Apparatus, Permeability			
Batoreometer			
Brake, Band			
Ductilometer			
Dynamometer			
Gauge, Pressure			
	Gauge, Air Pressure		
	Gauge, Steam Pressure		
	Gauge, Vacuum		
Gyroscope			
	Gyrostat		
Hydrodynamometer			
Jar, Vacuum			
Kymograph			
Meter, Gas			
Meter, Water			
Operameter			
Piezometer			
Rheometer			
Speedometer			*Note:* May also use "Component, Vehicle" from Land Transportation Accessories or "Component, Watercraft" from Water Transportation Accessories if appropriate
Stalagmometer			
Stroboscope			
Tachometer			*Note:* May also use "Component, Aircraft" from Aerospace Transportation Accessories, "Component, Vehicle" from Land Transportation Accessories or "Component, Watercraft" from Water Transportation Accessories if appropriate
Tasimeter			
Tensiometer			

Primary Object Term	Secondary Term	Tertiary Term	Notes
Tensometer			
Tester, Torsion			
Tonometer			
Tribometer			
Tunnel, Wind			
Turbidimeter			
Velocimeter			
	Gun, Radar		
Viscosimeter			
Voluminometer			
	Stereometer		

Class:
MEDICAL & PSYCHOLOGICAL T&E

Definition: Tools, equipment, and supplies originally created for the examination, testing, diagnosis, or treatment of humans. This class includes dental tools, objects used for sight and hearing, and objects used for psychological testing or treatment. It does not include objects used to study physical phenomena (see Acoustical T&E, Biological T&E, Chemical T&E, and Optical T&E) or tools for veterinary medicine, which are included in Animal Husbandry T&E.

Sub-Class:
DENTAL ACCESSORIES

Definition: Tools, equipment, and supplies intended to facilitate dental examination, testing, diagnosis, or treatment but that do not play a direct or essential role in these activities.

Primary Object Term	Secondary Term	Tertiary Term	Notes
Amalgamator			
Annealer			
Bellows, Dentist's			
Bib, Dental			
Bowl, Dental Mixing			
Cabinet, Dental			*Note:* May also use "Cabinet" from Storage & Display Furniture
Carrier, Amalgam			
Carrier, Gold Foil			
Case, Dental			
Cast, Dental			
Chair, Dentist's			*Note:* May also use "Chair" from Seating Furniture
Compound, Impression			
Compressor, Dental			
Condenser, Amalgam			
Cup, Dental			
	Cup, Amalgam		
	Cup, Dental Waste		
	Cup, Impression		
	Cup, Prophylaxis		
Dehydrator, Dental			
Disk, Abrasive Dental			
Dispenser, Dental			
Duplicator, Denture			
Engine, Dental			
Flask, Denture Curing			
Former, Bite Rim			

Primary Object Term	Secondary Term	Tertiary Term	Notes
Gauge, Crown			
Holder, Dental Equipment			
	Holder, Broach		
	Holder, Dental Bur		
	Holder, Dental Film		
	Holder, Dental Instrument		
	Holder, Rubber Dam		
Light, Dental Curing			
Machine, Metal Casting			
Mill, Gold Rolling			
Mixer, Dental Casting			
Mold, Dental Casting			
Pliers, Contouring			
Plugger, Dental			
Press, Crown			
Slab, Dental Mixing			
Table, Dental Instrument			
Template, Dental			
Tray, Dental Accessory			
Tray, Impression			
Tweezers, Soldering			
Unit, Denture Curing			
Unit, Prophylaxis			
Vibrator, Dental			
Vulcanizer, Dental			
Wax, Dental			

Sub-Class:
DENTAL INSTRUMENTS

Definition: Tools and equipment originally created for the examination, testing, diagnosis, or treatment of the human mouth and teeth.

Primary Object Term	Secondary Term	Tertiary Term	Notes
Anchor, Tooth			
Anvil, Dental			
Appliance, Orthodontic			
	Band, Dental		
	Brace, Dental		
	Bridge, Dental		
	Crown, Dental		
	Expander, Palatal		
	Headgear, Orthodontic		
	Retainer, Orthodontic		
	Wire, Orthodontic		
Applicator, Dental			
Articulator, Dental			
Blade, Dental			
Block, Bite			
Bracket, Dental			
Broach, Dental			
Bur, Dental			
Burnisher, Dental			
Carver, Dental			
Chisel, Dental			
Clamp, Dental			
Curette, Periodontal			
Dam, Dental			
Dentimeter			
Drill, Dental			
Elevator, Dental			
	Elevator, Root		
Evacuator, Dental			
Excavator, Dental			
Extractor, Dental			
	Extractor, Root		
	Extractor, Tooth		
	Forceps, Dental		
	Pelican		

Primary Object Term	Secondary Term	Tertiary Term	Notes
	Pliers, Dental		
	Toothkey		
Face-Bow			
File, Dental			
Hammer, Dental			
Handle, Dental			
Handpiece, Dental			
Hatchet, Dental			
Hoe, Periodontal			
Irrigator, Dental			
Kit, Dental Filling			
Lamp, Teeth Whitening			
Lathe, Dental			
Light, Plaque			
Mallet, Dental			
	Mallet, Oral Surgery		
Mandrel, Dental			
Mirror, Mouth			
Mouthpiece, Saliva Ejector			
Needle, Dental			
Paper, Articulating			
Pick, Dental			
Plate, Bite			
Plate, Tracing			
Pliers, Dressing			
Point, Dental			
Polisher, Dental			
	Polisher, Porte		
Post, Dental			
Probe, Dental			
	Explorer, Dental		
	Probe, Periodontal		
Punch, Rubber Dam			
Reamer, Endodontic			
Retainer, Matrix			
Saw, Dental			
Scaler, Dental			
Scalpel, Dental			

Primary Object Term	Secondary Term	Tertiary Term	Notes
Scissors, Dental			
Scraper, Dental			
Separator, Teeth			
Slitter, Crown			
Spatula, Dental			
Spreader, Jaw			
Stimulator, Gum			
Syringe, Dental			
Tester, Dental Pulp			
Trimmer, Dental			
Wedge, Dental			
Weight, Rubber Dam			

Sub-Class:
MEDICAL ACCESSORIES

Definition: Tools, equipment, and supplies intended to facilitate human medical examination, testing, diagnosis, or treatment but that do not play a direct or essential role in these activities.

Primary Object Term	Secondary Term	Tertiary Term	Notes
Ampul			
Basin, Medical			
Cabinet, Autoclave			*Note:* May also use "Cabinet" from Storage & Display Furniture
Cabinet, X-Ray			*Note:* May also use "Cabinet" from Storage & Display Furniture
Capsule, Pharmaceutical			
Case, Medical Instrument			*Note:* Use for any container specifically designed for protecting and/or transporting medical instruments; if a case is designed specifically for a given instrument, a new term may be created with the *Nomenclature* term for that instrument as a modifier; that term may be organized under "Case, Medical Instrument," as the two terms are below
	Case, Lancet		
	Case, Medical Thermometer		
Chair, Medical			*Note:* May also use "Chair" from Seating Furniture
	Chair, Chiropody		
	Chair, Examining		
	Chair, Treatment		
Container, Medicine			
	Bottle, Medicine		
		Bottle, Serum	
		Bottle, Vaccine	
	Gallipot		
	Jar, Ointment		
Container, Specimen			
	Bottle, Specimen		
	Jar, Specimen		
Cutter, Cast			
Duplicator, X-Ray			
Filler, Capsule			
Holder, Medical Supply			
	Holder, Ampul		

Primary Object Term	Secondary Term	Tertiary Term	Notes
	Holder, X-Ray		
	Jar, Syringe		
Mask, Surgical			
Measure, Pharmaceutical			
	Cup, Pharmaceutical Measuring		
	Spoon, Pharmaceutical Measuring		
Mixer, Pharmaceutical			
Model, Anatomical			*Note:* May also use "Model" from Other Documents
Mold, Suppository			
Roller, Bandage			
Shears, Medical			
	Scissors, Bandage		
Shield, X-Ray			
Spoon, Medical			
Sterilizer			
	Autoclave		
Swab			
Table, Medical			*Note:* May also use "Table" from Supporting Furniture
	Table, Embalming		
	Table, Examination		
	Table, Operating		
Tape, Medical			
	Tape, Umbilical		
Tool, Pharmaceutical			
	Ladle, Apothecary		
	Machine, Pill		
		Roller, Pill	
	Mill, Drug		
	Mortar, Pharmaceutical		
	Pestle, Pharmaceutical		
	Rounder, Pill		
	Silverer, Pill		
	Tile, Pill		
Tray, Organ			
Warmer, Frame			

Sub-Class:
MEDICAL INSTRUMENTS

Definition: Tools and equipment used for human medical examination, testing, diagnosis, or treatment that are not specifically designed for dental purposes.

Primary Object Term	Secondary Term	Tertiary Term	Notes
Applicator, Medical			
Instrument, Anesthetic			
	Mask, Anesthesia		
Instrument, Diagnostic			
	Albuminometer		
	Apparatus, Urea		
	Barostat		
	Biometer		
	Caliper, Medical		
	Cardiograph		
		Electrocardiograph	
	Cephalometer		
	Chamber, Counting		
	Cheilvangroscope		
	Climatometer		
	Device, Blood Pressure		
		Kymoscope	
		Sphygmomanometer	
	Device, Blood Testing		
		Counter, Blood	
		Globulimeter	
		Hemoscope	
		Needle, Blood Collecting	
		Scale, Hemoglobin	
		Set, Blood Collecting	
		Tube, Blood Collecting	
	Device, Respiratory Testing		
		Meter, Peak Flow	
		Spirograph	
		Spirometer	
		Stethometer	
	Diascope		
	Echoscope		

Primary Object Term	Secondary Term	Tertiary Term	Notes
	Endoscope		
		Bronchoscope	
		Gastroscope	
	Faciometer		
	Glucometer		
	Goniometer, Medical		
	Hammer, Medical		
		Hammer, Reflex	
		Percussor	
	Kit, Pregnancy Test		
	Machine, Medical X-Ray		
		Fluoroscope	
	Mydynamometer		
	Myograph		
	Oncometer		
	Pelvimeter		
	Phrenograph		
	Plethysmograph		
	Polygraph		
	Probe		
	Punch, Biopsy		
	Set, Biopsy		
	Sound		
	Speculum		
	Stethoscope		
	Tetanometer		
	Thermometer, Medical		*Note:* May also use "Thermometer" from Thermal T&E
	Transilluminator		
	Viewer, X-Ray		
	Visiometer		
Instrument, Ear			
	Audiphone		
	Otacoustic		
	Otoscope		*Note:* May also use "Endoscope"
	Speculum, Ear		
	Spout, Ear		
Instrument, Embalming			

Primary Object Term	Secondary Term	Tertiary Term	Notes
	Pump, Embalming		
Instrument, Eye			
	Anomaloscope		
	Campimeter		
	Chart, Visual Acuity		
	Chromatometer		
	Cone, Adjusting		
	Gonioscope		
	Lencoscope		
	Lens, Stenopaic		
	Manoptoscope		
	Mirror, Eye Observation		
	Occluder, Eye		
	Ophthalmometer		
	Ophthalmoscope		
	Optometer		
	Orthoscope		
	Pachymeter		
	Patch, Eye		
	Perimeter		
	Perspectoscope		
	Pseudoscope, Lenticular		
	Pupilometer		
	Retinoscope		
	Set, Lens		
	Spud, Eye		
	Stereogram		
	Stereoscope, Medical		
		Amblyoscope	
		Tropostereoscope	
	Strabismometer		
	Test, Color Perception		
	Tester, Color Sense		
	Tonometer, Ocular		
	Wash, Eye		
Instrument, Gynecological			
	Carrier, Ligature		

Primary Object Term	Secondary Term	Tertiary Term	Notes
	Irrigator, Uterine		
	Metroscope		*Note:* May also use "Endoscope"
	Probe, Uterine		
	Repositor, Uterine		
	Speculum, Vaginal		*Note:* May also use "Speculum"
Instrument, Nasal			
	Douche, Nasal		
	Rhinoscope		*Note:* May also use "Endoscope"
	Speculum, Nasal		
Instrument, Obstetrical			
	Cephalotribe		
	Forceps, Obstetrical		
		Cranioclast	
	Handle, Traction		
	Hook, Blunt		
	Perforator, Obstetrical		
Instrument, Oral			
	Depressor, Tongue		
	Laryngoscope		*Note:* May also use "Endoscope"
	Stomatoscope		
Instrument, Rectal			
	Anoscope		
	Colonoscope		*Note:* May also use "Endoscope"
	Hose, Enema		
	Proctoscope		*Note:* May also use "Endoscope"
Instrument, Surgical			
	Adenotome		
	Aspirator		
	Button, Intestinal		
	Cauterizer		
	Chisel, Surgical		
		Chisel, Trephining	
	Clamp, Surgical		
		Clamp, Bone	
		Clamp, Bowel	
		Clamp, Cervical	
		Clamp, Rectal	
	Curette		
		Curette, Adenoid	

Primary Object Term	Secondary Term	Tertiary Term	Notes
		Curette, Alveolar	
		Curette, Bone	
	Cutter, Medical Bone		
	Dermatome		
	Dilator		
		Dilator, Cervical	
		Dilator, Uterine	
	Drill, Bone		
	Electrotome		
	Elevator, Surgical		
		Elevator, Malar	
		Elevator, Periosteal	
		Elevator, Trephining	
	Forceps		
		Forceps, Bone Cutting	
		Forceps, Catch	
		Forceps, Trephining	
		Serrefine	
	Hemostat		
	Holder, Surgical Needle		
	Hook, Surgical		
		Hook, Tendon	
	Hyfrecator		
	Kit, Surgical		
	Kit, Thermo-Cautery		
	Knife, Surgical		
		Bistoury	
		Keratome	
		Knife, Amputation	
		Knife, Cartilage	
		Knife, Circumcision	
		Lancet	
		Scalpel	
	Ligature		
	Mallet, Surgical		
	Needle, Surgical		
		Needle, Ligating	
		Needle, Suturing	

Primary Object Term	Secondary Term	Tertiary Term	Notes
	Passer, Catheter		
	Perforator, Surgical		
	Photocoagulator		
	Pin, Surgical		
	Plate, Circumcision		
	Point, Cautery		
	Probang		
	Probe, Bullet		
	Remover, Blade		
	Retractor		
	Rongeur		
	Saw, Surgical		
		Saw, Amputation	
	Scissors, Surgical		
		Scissors, Circumcision	
	Shears, Rib		
	Snare, Surgical		
		Ecraseur	
	Spatula, Surgical		
	Sponge, Surgical		
	Stripper, Rib		
	Stripper, Vein		
	Suture		
	Tenaculum		
	Tonsillotome		
	Trephine		
	Trocar		
	Tube, Tracheostomy		
	Tweezers, Surgical		
Instrument, Therapeutic			
	Atomizer		
	Bag, Ice		
	Bandage		
	Binder, Medical		
		Binder, Abdominal	
		Binder, Obstetrical	
	Cast, Medical		
	Corset, Surgical		

Primary Object Term	Secondary Term	Tertiary Term	Notes
	Cotton, Dressing		
	Cuirass, Medical		
	Cup, Medicine		
	Defibrillator		
	Device, Bloodletting		
		Bowl, Bleeding	
		Cup, Bleeding	
		Fleam	
		Kit, Cupping	
		Scarificator	
		Set, Bleeding	
	Device, Respiratory Treatment		*Note:* Use for a device created for treating a medical condition; for a protective breathing device, use "Apparatus, Breathing" from Personal Assistive Objects
		Apparatus, Pneumothorax	
		Inhalator	
		Inhaler	
		Lung, Iron	
		Machine, Oxygen	
		Mask, Oxygen	
		Nebulizer	
		Respirator	
		Resuscitator	
		Tent, Oxygen	
		Vaporizer	
		Ventilator, Medical	
	Dressing		
		Compress	
		Pledget	
	Dropper, Medicine		
	Irrigator		
	Kit, Medical		*Note:* May also use other terms to indicate contents
		Kit, First Aid	
		Kit, Medicine	
		Kit, Midwife	
		Kit, Suction	
	Lancet, Vaccine		

Primary Object Term	Secondary Term	Tertiary Term	Notes
	Machine, Diathermy		
	Machine, Electrotherapy		
	Maker, Dimple		
	Osteophone		
	Pacemaker		
	Pessary		
	Pillow, Medicinal		
	Plaster, Cough		
	Splint		
		Splint, Jaw	
		Splint, Thomas	
	Table, Inversion		
	Tourniquet		
	Truss, Hernia		
Instrument, Urological			
	Lithotrite		
	Resectoscope		*Note:* May also use "Endoscope"
	Ureometer		
	Urethroscope		*Note:* May also use "Endoscope"
	Urethrotome		*Note:* May also use "Instrument, Surgical"
	Uricometer		
	Urinometer		
Needle, Injection			
	Needle, Hypodermic		
	Needle, Spinal		
Pump, Infusion			
Pump, Perfusion			
Set, Inoculating			
Set, Intravenous			
Shunt, Medical			
Syringe, Medical			
	Syringe, Bulb		
	Syringe, Piston		
Tube, Medical			
	Bougie		
	Cannula		
	Catheter		

Primary Object Term	Secondary Term	Tertiary Term	Notes
		Airway, Nasopharyngeal	
		Airway, Oropharyngeal	
	Tube, Stomach		
	Tube, Sucking		

Class:
MERCHANDISING T&E

Definition: Tools, equipment, and supplies originally created to facilitate or enable the exchange of money, goods, or services. This class includes those objects used to present goods, such as counters, as well as product packages and labels.

Primary Object Term	Secondary Term	Tertiary Term	Notes
Case, Sales Sample			
Changer, Money			
	Changer, Belt Coin		
	Machine, Change		
Container, Apothecary			
	Bottle, Apothecary		*Note:* May also use "Bottle, Medicine" from Medical Accessories
	Jar, Apothecary		
Container, Money			
	Bag, Money		
		Bag, Deposit	
	Box, Money		
		Box, Donation	*Note:* Use for non-religious contexts
		Cashbox	
	Dispenser, Coin		
	Drawer, Cash		
	Envelope, Money		
	Tray, Money		
Container, Shopping			
	Bag, Shopping		
	Basket, Shopping		
	Cart, Shopping		*Note:* May also use "Handcart" from Human-Powered Vehicles
Counter, Sales			*Note:* May also use "Counter" from Storage & Display Furniture
Cutter, Tobacco			
Dispenser, Ticket			
Dispenser, Token			
Fixture, Store Display			
	Bin, Display		
	Cabinet, Display		*Note:* For a non-commercial display cabinet, use "Cabinet, Curio" from Storage & Display Furniture
	Case, Display		*Note:* For a non-commercial display case, use "Case, Curio" from Storage & Display Furniture

Primary Object Term	Secondary Term	Tertiary Term	Notes
	Fixture, Wall Display		
	Jar, Display		
		Jar, Confectionery	
	Manikin, Display		
	Rack, Display		
		Rack, Garment	
	Shelf, Display		
	Stand, Display		
	Table, Display		
	Tray, Display		
	Unit, Gondola Shelving		
Gun, Price Label			*Note:* May also use "Printer, Label" from Writing Devices
Gun, Tagging			
Holder, Bag			
Holder, String			
Label, Product			*Note:* Use for a paper label, bottle cap, jar lid, or other component of product packaging that identifies products and/or manufacturers; may also use "Label, Identification" from Other Documents and any other appropriate term, such as "Cap, Bottle" from Food Processing Equipment
	Band, Cigar		
Machine, Automatic Teller			
Machine, Credit Card			
	Imprinter, Credit Card		*Note:* May also use "Imprinter" from Writing Devices
	Reader, Credit Card		*Note:* May also use "Reader, Card" from Peripherals
Machine, Ticket Punch			
Machine, Vending			
Mat, Counter			
Package, Product			*Note:* May also use terms from Containers to describe the form that the product package takes, e.g., "Box," "Can," "Pack," "Tube"; the contents for which the package was made may be noted in a subject field
Paper, Wrapping			*Note:* For gift wrap, use "Wrap, Gift" from Party Accessories
Punch, Ticket			

Primary Object Term	Secondary Term	Tertiary Term	Notes
Register, Cash			
Sample, Sales			
	Book, Sample		
	Card, Sample		
	Kit, Sales Sample		
	Swatch		
Scale, Market			*Note:* May also use "Scale" from Weights & Measures T&E
Scanner, Price			*Note:* May also use "Scanner, Barcode" from Peripherals
Sealer, Heat			
Tape, Register			
Tongs, Shelf			
Tray, Vending			

Class:
METEOROLOGICAL T&E

Definition: Tools, equipment, and supplies originally created to observe, measure, or document atmospheric phenomena.

Primary Object Term	Secondary Term	Tertiary Term	Notes
Aerometer			
Aethrioscope			
Balloon, Weather			
Barometer			
	Barograph		
	Barometer, Aneroid		
		Aneroidograph	
	Barometer, Mercury		
	Sympiesometer		
Ceilometer			
Diaphanometer			
Disdrometer			
Drosometer			
Evaporimeter			
Gauge, Precipitation			
	Gauge, Snow		
	Ombrometer		
	Pluviometer		
		Pluviograph	
	Udometer		
Gauge, Wind			
	Anemometer		
		Anemograph	
		Meter, Air	
	Anemoscope		
	Sock, Wind		
	Weathervane		
Hygrometer			
	Hygrograph		
	Psychrometer		
Hygrothermograph			
Instrument, Meteorological			*Note:* Use for a meteorological instrument that lacks another descriptive or generic name or if the specific name of the instrument is unknown
Koniscope			
Meteorometer			

Primary Object Term	Secondary Term	Tertiary Term	Notes
	Meteorograph		
Nephoscope			
	Mirror, Cloud		
Ozonometer			
Pagoscope			
Poise, Air			
Radiosonde			
	Rawinsonde		
Recorder, Sunshine			
Thermometer, Meteorological			*Note:* May also use "Thermometer" from Thermal T&E

Class:
NUCLEAR PHYSICS T&E

Definition: Tools, equipment, and supplies originally created to study atomic structure and elementary particles as well as the physical properties of the universe.

Primary Object Term	Secondary Term	Tertiary Term	Notes
Accelerator, Particle			
	Accelerator, Linear		
	Cyclotron		
		Betatron	
		Cyclotron, AVF	
		Cyclotron, Isochronous	
		Synchrocyclotron	
	Machine, Tandem		
	Synchrotron		
		Synchrotron, Alternating Gradient	
		Synchrotron, Constant Gradient	
		Synchrotron, Proton	
		Synchrotron, Zero Gradient	
Collimator			
Condenser, Rotating			
Damper, Vibration			
Deflector, Flow			
Desiccator, Balance			
Detector, Radiation			
	Chamber, Particle Detection		
		Chamber, Bubble	
		Chamber, Cloud	
		Chamber, Vacuum	
	Counter, Geiger		
	Detector, Neutron		
	Dosimeter		
	Ratemeter		
	Scaler, Nuclear		
Eliminator, Nuclear Static			
Generator, Cockcroft-Walton			*Note:* May also use "Multiplier, Voltage" from Electrical System Components

Primary Object Term	Secondary Term	Tertiary Term	Notes
Klystron			*Note:* May also use "Tube, Electron" from Electrical System Components
Magnet, Accelerator			
	Magnet, Bending		
	Magnet, Quadruple		
	Magnet, Sextuple		
Separator, Beam			
Spectroscope, Mass			
	Spectrograph, Mass		
	Spectrometer, Mass		

Class:
OPTICAL T&E

Definition: Tools, equipment, and supplies originally created to observe, measure, or record light. This class includes commonly used equipment, such as binoculars and microscopes. It excludes specialized objects created for other scientific observation, such as visual acuity charts or telescopes that are used particularly for astronomy.

Primary Object Term	Secondary Term	Tertiary Term	Notes
Absorptiometer			
Apertometer			
Astrometeoroscope			
Axometer			
Binoculars			
	Glasses, Field		
	Polemoscope		
Borescope			
Case, Optical Instrument			*Note:* Use for any container specifically designed for protecting and/or transporting optical instruments; if a case is designed specifically for a given instrument, a new term may be created with the *Nomenclature* term for that instrument as a modifier; that term may be organized under "Case, Optical Instrument," as the three terms are below
	Case, Binoculars		
	Case, Microscope		
	Case, Telescope		
Catopter			
Chromascope			
Chromatrope			
Collimator, Optical			
Condenser, Optical			
Dichroscope			
Dynactinometer			
Dynameter			
Eikonometer			
Focometer			
Holophote			
Instrument, Optical			*Note:* Use for an optical instrument that lacks another descriptive or generic name or if the specific name of the instrument is unknown
Interferometer, Optical			

Primary Object Term	Secondary Term	Tertiary Term	Notes
Lens			
	Glass, Magnifying		
		Loupe	
	Glass, Reducing		
	Lens, Anastigmatic		
	Lens, Water		
Metrochrome			
Microscope			
	Engiscope		
	Microscope, Binocular		
	Microscope, Confocal		
	Microscope, Electron		
		Microscope, Scanning Electron	
		Microscope, Transmission Electron	
	Microscope, Fluorescence		
	Microscope, Phase Contrast		
Microspectroscope			
Otheoscope			
Periscope			
Phoneidoscope			
Photodrome			
Photometer			
	Goniophotometer		
	Luminometer		
	Photometer, Polarizing		
	Spectrophotometer		
Polariscope			
	Polarimeter		
Pseudoscope			
Scotoscope			
Spectroscope			
	Spectrograph		
	Spectrometer		
Stauroscope			
Teinoscope			
Telescope			

Class:
REGULATIVE & PROTECTIVE T&E

Definition: Tools, equipment, and supplies originally created for controlling the behavior of people or for providing security or protection for property.

Sub-Class:
PROTECTIVE DEVICES

Definition: Tools, equipment, and supplies originally created to provide security or protection for property.

Primary Object Term	Secondary Term	Tertiary Term	Notes
Alarm			*Note:* May also use "Device, Sound Signaling" or narrower term from Sound Communication Devices if appropriate
	Alarm, Burglar		
	Alarm, Fire		
		Box, Fire Alarm	
		System, Fire Alarm	
	Alarm, Gas		
	Alarm, Smoke		
Carrier, Gas Mask			
Detector, Gas			
Device, Fire Protection			
	Adapter, Fire Hose		
	Ax, Fire		
	Blanket, Fire		
	Bucket, Fire		
	Extinguisher, Fire		
	Holder, Fire Extinguisher		
	Hook, Fire		
	Hose, Fire		
	Jacket, Fire Hose		
	Ladder, Fire		
	Nozzle, Fire Hose		
	Pulaski		
	Pump, Backpack		
	Rack, Fire Bucket		
	Rack, Fire Hose		
	Reel, Fire Hose		
	Sprinkler, Fire		
	Wrench, Fire Plug		
Device, Security			
	Card, Key		
	Key		

Primary Object Term	Secondary Term	Tertiary Term	Notes
	Keypad, Security		
	Lock, Security		
		Padlock	
	Reader, Security Card		
	Scanner, Security		
		Scanner, X-Ray Security	
Mask, Gas			
Sandbag			

Sub-Class:
REGULATIVE DEVICES

Definition: Tools, equipment, and supplies originally created to control the behavior of people. This sub-class includes objects used for restraint, prosecution, punishment, torture, and execution.

Primary Object Term	Secondary Term	Tertiary Term	Notes
Bag, Evidence			
Device, Execution			
	Block, Executioner's		
	Chair, Electric		
	Gallows		
	Guillotine		
	Noose, Hangman's		
	Stake, Impalement		
Device, Punishment			
	Bridle, Scold's		
	Cap, Dunce		
	Headband, Tightening		
	Horse, Punishment		
	Paddle		
	Pillory		
	Rack, Torture		
	Stocks		
	Stool, Ducking		
Device, Torture			
	Cradle with Spikes		
	Daughter, Scavenger's		
	Post, Whipping		
	Thumbscrew		
	Whip		
		Cat-o'-Nine-Tails	
		Knout	
Enclosure, Prisoner			
	Cell, Detention		
	Cell, Jail		
	Dock, Prisoner's		
Hood, Gallows			
Key, Handcuff			
Key, Jail			
Restraint			
	Ball and Chain		
	Band, Swaddling		
	Belt, Chastity		

Primary Object Term	Secondary Term	Tertiary Term	Notes
	Belt, Safety		
	Bilbo		
	Cangue		
	Chain, Restraining		
	Collar, Slave		
	Gag		
	Harness, Safety		
	Leash, Child		
	Shackle		
		Handcuff	
		Shackle, Leg	
	Straitjacket		
	Strap, Restraining		

Class:
SURVEYING & NAVIGATIONAL T&E

Definition: Tools, equipment, and supplies originally created to determine the position of an observer relative to known reference points or to indicate the form and extent of a region, such as land surface.

Sub-Class:
NAVIGATIONAL EQUIPMENT

Definition: Tools, equipment, and supplies originally created to determine the position or course of an observer relative to known reference points.

Primary Object Term	Secondary Term	Tertiary Term	Notes
Altimeter			
Antenna, Radar			
Astrolabe, Mariner's			
Backstaff			
Bathometer			
Board, Navigator's			
Card, Compass			
	Pelorus		
Case, Navigational Instrument			*Note:* Use for any container specifically designed for protecting and/or transporting navigational instruments; if a case is designed specifically for a given instrument, a new term may be created with the *Nomenclature* term for that instrument as a modifier; that term may be organized under "Case, Navigational Instrument," as "Case, Octant" and "Case, Sextant" are below
	Case, Octant		
	Case, Sextant		
Chronometer			*Note:* May also use "Timepiece" from Timekeeping T&E
Circle, Reflecting			
Compass			
	Compass, Telltale		
	Compass, Wrist		
	Gyrocompass		
Compass, Radio			
Corrector, Course			
Device, Sounding			
	Lead, Sounding		
	Machine, Sounding		
	Sondograph		
	Tube, Sounding		
Driftsight			

Primary Object Term	Secondary Term	Tertiary Term	Notes
Echometer			
Finder, Depth			
Finder, Direction			
	Finder, Radio Direction		
Finder, Distance			
Finder, Star			*Note:* May also use "Globe, Celestial" from Astronomical T&E if appropriate
Gauge, Depth			
Gimbal, Compass			
Indicator, Position			
	Indicator, Height-Range		
Instrument, Navigational			*Note:* Use for a navigational instrument that lacks another descriptive or generic name or if the specific name of the instrument is unknown
Marker, Navigational			
	Beacon		
		Beacon, Aircraft	
		Beacon, Lighthouse	
		Light, Channel	
	Buoy, Navigational		
	Foghorn		*Note:* May also use "Horn" from Sound Communication Devices
Meter, Yaw			
Nocturnal			
Octant			
Opisometer			
Oscillometer			
Palinurus			
Pointer, Station			
Quadrant			
Receiver, Tracking			
	Receiver, Beacon		
	Receiver, Global Positioning		
	Receiver, Loran		
	Receiver, Radar		
Recorder, Sceptre			
Reel, Log			
Ruler, Parallel			

Primary Object Term	Secondary Term	Tertiary Term	Notes
Scale, Navigational			
Sextant			
Shade, Sextant			
	Shade, Horizon Glass		
	Shade, Index		
Spherograph			
Telescope, Navigational			*Note:* May also use "Telescope" from Optical T&E
	Telescope, Quadrant		
	Telescope, Sextant		
Zenometer			

Sub-Class:
SURVEYING EQUIPMENT

Definition: Tools, equipment, and supplies originally created to indicate the form or extent of a region such as a land surface.

Primary Object Term	Secondary Term	Tertiary Term	Notes
Alidade			
Apomecometer			
Case, Surveying Instrument			*Note:* Use for any container specifically designed for protecting and/or transporting surveying instruments; if a case is designed specifically for a given instrument, a new term may be created with the *Nomenclature* term for that instrument as a modifier; that term may be organized under "Case, Surveying Instrument," as "Case, Surveyor's Compass" is below
	Case, Surveyor's Compass		
Cathetometer			
Chain, Surveyor's			
	Chain, Engineer's		
Chorograph			
Circle, Azimuth			
Circle, Repeating			
Circumferentor			
Clinograph			
Clinometer			
Compass, Surveyor's			
	Compass, Borehole		
	Compass, Dip		
	Compass, Drycard		
	Compass, Solar		
Compensator			
Cross-Staff			
	Groma		
Geodolite			
Gradiometer			
Graphometer			
Heliotrope			
Inclinometer			
Instrument, Surveying			*Note:* Use for a surveying instrument that lacks another descriptive or generic name or if the specific name of the instrument is unknown
Level, Surveyor's			

Primary Object Term	Secondary Term	Tertiary Term	Notes
	Level, Automatic		
	Level, Dumpy		
	Level, Wye		
Magnetometer			*Note:* May also use "Instrument, Magnetic" from Electrical & Magnetic Measurement Devices
	Detector, Metal		*Note:* May also use "Scanner, Security" from Protective Devices if appropriate
Marker, Survey			*Note:* May also use "Marker, Site" from Site Features
	Blaze, Tree		
	Marker, Concrete		
	Stake, Survey		
Meter, Angle			
Orograph			
Pantometer			
Pin, Chaining			
Platometer			
Pole, Picket			
Rangefinder			
	Rangefinder, Laser		
	Rangefinder, Radio		
Rod, Boning			
Rod, Leveling			
Rod, Stadia			
Scale, Surveyor's			
Semicircumferentor			
Square, Optical			
Stadimeter			
Staff, Station			
Stand, Surveyor's			
	Staff, Jacob's		
	Tripod, Surveyor's		
Table, Plane			
Tape, Surveyor's			
Tellurometer			
Theodolite			
	Omnimeter		
	Transit		
Vertimeter			
Wheel, Surveyor's			

Class:
THERMAL T&E

Definition: Tools, equipment, and supplies originally created to observe, measure, or document heat and its effects. Excluded from this class are specialized objects created to serve specific purposes, such as a meteorological thermometer.

Primary Object Term	Secondary Term	Tertiary Term	Notes
Bolometer			
Calorimeter			
Case, Thermal Instrument			*Note:* Use for any container specifically designed for protecting and/or transporting thermal instruments; if a case is designed specifically for a given instrument, a new term may be created with the *Nomenclature* term for that instrument as a modifier; that term may be organized under "Case, Thermal Instrument," as "Case, Thermometer" is below
	Case, Thermometer		
Cryophorus			
Ebullioscope			
Gauge, Temperature			*Note:* May also use "Component, Vehicle" from Land Transportation Accessories or "Component, Watercraft" from Water Transportation Accessories if appropriate
Hypsometer			
Instrument, Thermal			*Note:* Use for a thermal instrument that lacks another descriptive or generic name or if the specific name of the instrument is unknown
Stick, Tempil			
Thermocouple			
Thermohydrometer			
Thermometer			
	Chronothermometer		
	Cryometer		
	Galvanothermometer		
	Geothermometer		
	Pyrometer		
	Thermograph		
	Thermoscope		
Thermomultiplier			

Class:
TIMEKEEPING T&E

Definition: Tools, equipment, and supplies originally created for recording or measuring time. This class does not include timekeeping objects created for specialized purposes, such as chronometers.

Primary Object Term	Secondary Term	Tertiary Term	Notes
Ball, Time			
Case, Timepiece			*Note:* Use for any container specifically designed for protecting and/or transporting timepieces; if a case is designed specifically for a given instrument, a new term may be created with the *Nomenclature* term for that instrument as a modifier; that term may be organized under "Case, Timepiece," as "Case, Watch" is below
	Case, Watch		
Chronograph			
Chronoscope			
Clock			
	Clock, Alarm		
	Clock, Bracket		
	Clock, Calendar		
	Clock, Carriage		
	Clock, Electronic		
		Clock, Digital	
		Clock, Quartz	
	Clock, Floor		
		Clock, Dwarf Tall	
		Clock, Tall Case	
	Clock, Mantel		
	Clock, Mechanical		
	Clock, Musical		
	Clock, Pedestal		
	Clock, Regulator		
	Clock, Self-Winding		
	Clock, Shelf		
	Clock, Ship's		*Note:* May also use "Component, Watercraft" from Water Transportation Accessories
	Clock, Table		
	Clock, Time Recording		
		Watchclock	
	Clock, Travel		

Primary Object Term	Secondary Term	Tertiary Term	Notes
	Clock, Turret		
	Clock, Wall		
		Clock, Cuckoo	
	Clock, Water		
Component, Timepiece			
	Gnomon		
	Key, Timepiece		
		Key, Clock	
		Key, Watch	
Horometer			
Jack, Clock			
Moondial			
Sandglass			
	Hourglass		
Sundial			
Synchronizer			
Timepiece			*Note:* Use for a timepiece that lacks another descriptive or generic name or if the specific name of the timepiece is unknown
Timer			
Watch			
	Stopwatch		
	Watch, Calendar		
	Watch, Clock		
	Watch, Electronic		
		Watch, Digital	
		Watch, Quartz	
	Watch, Mechanical		
	Watch, Pendant		
	Watch, Pocket		
	Watch, Self-Winding		
	Wristwatch		

Class:
WEIGHTS & MEASURES T&E

Definition: Tools, equipment, and supplies originally created to observe, record, or measure mass (weight) or physical dimensions such as length, area, or volume. This class includes general-purpose measuring devices such as precision balances or folding rules. It excludes objects created to measure time and to measure particular scientific data. Also excluded are specialized measuring devices and gauges such as sextants or carpenter's squares.

Primary Object Term	Secondary Term	Tertiary Term	Notes
Angleometer			
Caliper			
	Caliper, Double		
	Caliper, Hermaphrodite		
	Caliper, Inside		
	Caliper, Outside		
	Caliper, Vernier		
Case, Measuring Instrument			*Note:* Use for any container specifically designed for protecting and/or transporting measuring instruments; if a case is designed specifically for a given instrument, a new term may be created with the *Nomenclature* term for that instrument as a modifier; that term may be organized under "Case, Measuring Instrument," as "Case, Scale" is below
	Case, Scale		
Comparator, Length			
Component, Scale			
	Scoop, Scale		
	Weight, Balance		
		Weight, Coin	
Dipstick			*Note:* May also use "Component, Vehicle" from Land Transportation Accessories if appropriate
Eriometer			
Extensometer			
Gauge			*Note:* Use this generic term when the function of a gauge is unknown
Gauge, Feeler			
Gauge, Ring			
Gauge, Water			
Holometer			
Measure, Dry			
Measure, Liquid			

Primary Object Term	Secondary Term	Tertiary Term	Notes
Measure, Spring			
Micrometer			
Odometer			*Note:* May also use "Component, Vehicle" from Land Transportation Accessories if appropriate
Rod, Wantage			
Rule, Retractable			
	Measure, Tape		
		Tape, Steel	
Ruler			
	Meterstick		
	Rule, Extension		
	Rule, Folding		
	Rule, Foot		
	Yardstick		
Scale			
	Balance		
		Balance, Analytical	
		Balance, Beranger	
		Balance, Demonstration	
		Balance, Gram Chain	
		Balance, Roberval	
		Balance, Specific Gravity	
		Balance, Torsion	
	Scale, Apothecary		
	Scale, Bathroom		
	Scale, Computing		
	Scale, Cylinder		
	Scale, Hopper		
	Scale, Lever		
	Scale, Platform		
	Scale, Postal		
	Scale, Spring		
	Scale, Triangular		
	Scale, Truck		
Spherometer			

Category 6: TOOLS & EQUIPMENT FOR COMMUNICATION

Definition: **Tools, equipment, and supplies used to enable communication. This category includes those classes for literal and abstract communication—Printing T&E and Musical T&E. This category does not include things produced as communication, such as works of art or documents. These are the objects created by the tools in this category, and they are listed in Communication Objects.**

Class:
DATA PROCESSING T&E

Definition: Tools, equipment, and supplies originally created for processing information by manual, mechanical, or electronic means, and in a manner subject to human intervention (e.g., by physical manipulation of beads in an abacus, or by varying the parameters incorporated into computer software). Single-purpose devices, such as a digital watch or a digital thermometer, whose functions involve only the conversion of physical input (e.g., temperature, pressure, etc.) into visual, audible, or mechanical output, are not included here, but are classified according to their specific function (e.g., Timekeeping T&E or Thermal T&E).

Sub-Class:
DATA PROCESSING ACCESSORIES

Definition: Tools, equipment, and supplies that facilitate the processing of information, but that do not themselves process information.

Primary Object Term	Secondary Term	Tertiary Term	Notes
Burster			
Case, Computer Equipment			*Note:* Use for any container specifically designed for protecting and/or transporting computer equipment and supplies; if a case is designed specifically for a given item, a new term may be created with the *Nomenclature* term for that instrument as a modifier; that term may be organized under "Case, Computer Equipment," as the four terms are below
	Case, Compact Disc		
	Case, Digital Videodisc		
	Case, Diskette		
	Case, Laptop Computer		
Chad			
Connector, Data			
	Cable, Data		
		Cable, Network	
		Cable, Parallel	
		Cable, Power	
		Cable, Serial	

Primary Object Term	Secondary Term	Tertiary Term	Notes
		Cable, USB	
	Coupler, Acoustic		
	Multiplexer		
	Panel, Data Patch		
	Router, Data		
Pad, Mouse			
Pinboard			
Sleeve, Disk			
Software			
	Software, Browser		
	Software, Database		
	Software, Diagnostic		
	Software, Email		
	Software, Gaming		
	Software, Graphics		
	Software, Multifunction System		
	Software, Operating System		
	Software, Security		
	Software, Specialty		
	Software, Spreadsheet		
	Software, Utility		
	Software, Word Processing		
Sorter, Card			
Template, Keyboard			

Sub-Class:
DATA PROCESSING DEVICES

Definition: Tools and equipment originally created for processing information by manual, mechanical, or electronic means.

Primary Object Term	Secondary Term	Tertiary Term	Notes
Analyzer, Network			
Automaton			
Computer, Hybrid			
Converter, Data			
	Converter, Card-to-Tape		
	Converter, Digital-to-Analog		
	Decoder		
	Digitizer		
	Encoder		
Counter, Tally			
	Stick, Tally		
Device, Test Scoring			
Machine, Teaching			
Processor, Analog Data			
	Abacus		
	Comparator		
	Computer, Analog		
		Analyzer, Differential	
		Analyzer, Harmonic	
	Integrator		
		Planimeter	
	Machine, Calculating		
		Engine, Difference	
		Machine, Adding	
		Machine, Billing	
		Machine, Bookkeeping	
		Machine, Tabulating	
	Nomogram		
	Rod, Calculating		
	Rule, Slide		
Processor, Digital Data			
	Calculator		
		Calculator, Desktop	
		Calculator, Pocket	

Primary Object Term	Secondary Term	Tertiary Term	Notes
	Computer, Digital		
		Computer, Desktop	
		Computer, Handheld	*Note:* Use for a device such as a mobile computer, personal digital assistant (PDA), or portable media player; global positioning devices are included in Navigational Equipment, handheld electronic games are included in Game Equipment, and electronic readers are included in Visual Communication Devices
		Computer, Laptop	
		Computer, Mainframe	
		Computer, Tablet	*Note:* May also use "Reader, Electronic" from Visual Communication Devices if appropriate
		Minicomputer	
		Server, Network	
		Smartphone	*Note:* May also use "Telephone, Cellular" from Telecommunication Devices
Punch, Data			
	Punch, Gang		
	Punch, Keyboard		
	Punch, Spot		
	Punch, Summary		
Reader, Tape			
Reproducer, Data			
	Reproducer, Card		
	Reproducer, Tape		
Robot			*Note:* Should also use another term to describe the robot's specific function
	Robot, Industrial		
Simulator			
Typewriter, Encoding			
	Typewriter, Magnetic Card		
	Typewriter, Magnetic Disk		
	Typewriter, Magnetic Tape		
	Typewriter, Paper Tape		
Verifier			

Sub-Class:
DATA PROCESSING MEDIA

Definition: Storage devices for processed information. Note: "Recording" from Other Documents also may be used for media containing recorded music and video, and "Software" or a narrower term from Data Processing Accessories also may be used for media containing computer programs.

Primary Object Term	Secondary Term	Tertiary Term	Notes
Card, Data			
	Card, Edge-Notched		
	Card, Punched		
Disk, Magnetic			
	Diskette		
Disk, Optical			
	Disc, Compact		
	Videodisc, Digital		
Drive, Flash			
Drum, Magnetic			
Tape, Magnetic			
Tape, Paper			

Sub-Class:
PERIPHERALS

Definition: Tools and equipment specifically created to facilitate data processing by accomplishing input, storage, or output of data, but that do not have independent data processing capabilities.

Primary Object Term	Secondary Term	Tertiary Term	Notes
Console, Computer			
Device, Input			
	Glove, Data		
	Joystick		
	Keyboard, Computer		
	Mouse		
	Pen, Light		
	Reader		
		Reader, Card	
		Reader, Character	
		Reader, Magnetic Tape	
		Reader, Punched Tape	
	Scanner, Optical		
		Orthoscanner	
		Scanner, Barcode	
		Scanner, Flatbed	
		Scanner, Handheld	
	Tablet, Graphics		
	Touchpad		
	Touchscreen		*Note:* May use with "Monitor, Computer"
	Trackball		
	Tracker, Head		*Note:* May use with "Display, Head-Mounted"
Device, Output			
	Display, Head-Mounted		
	Glasses, Data		
	Monitor, Computer		
	Plotter		
	Printer		
		Printer, Character Impact	
		Printer, Daisywheel	
		Printer, Dot Matrix	
		Printer, Inkjet	
		Printer, Laser	
		Printer, Line	

Primary Object Term	Secondary Term	Tertiary Term	Notes
		Printer, On-the-Fly	
		Printer, Serial	
		Printer, Thermal	
	Recorder, Film		
	Unit, Audio Response		
Drive, Data			
	Drive, Disk		
	Drive, Hard		
	Drive, Tape		
Modem			
Printer, Keyboard			
Processor, Card			
Terminal, Computer			
	Terminal, CRT		
	Terminal, Magnetic Tape		
	Terminal, Typewriter		
Unit, Peripheral Control			

Class:
DRAFTING T&E

Definition: Tools, equipment, and supplies originally created to be used for the creation of precision drawings, such as architectural plans, mechanical designs, maps, or charts. This class does not include general purpose writing, drawing, and lettering tools.

Primary Object Term	Secondary Term	Tertiary Term	Notes
Board, Drawing			
Case, Drafting Instrument			*Note:* Use for any container specifically designed for protecting and/or transporting a drafting instrument
Instrument, Drafting			
	Arcograph		
	Campylometer		
	Centrolinead		
	Chartometer		
	Compass, Drafting		
		Compass, Beam	
		Compass, Bow	
		Compass, Napier	
		Compass, Pencil	
		Compass, Pillar	
		Compass, Proportional	
		Compass, Wing	
	Conograph		
	Curve		
		Curve, Brook's	
		Curve, Flexible	
		Curve, French	
	Cycloidograph		
	Cymograph		
	Divider		
	Eccentrolinead		
	Ellipsograph		
	Engine, Dividing		
	Engine, Ruling		
	Graduator		
	Helicograph		
	Hyalograph		
	Isograph		
	Machine, Drafting		
	Micrograph		
	Odontograph		

Primary Object Term	Secondary Term	Tertiary Term	Notes
	Pantograph		
	Pen, Drafting		
		Pen, Ruling	
		Stylograph	
		Wheel, Drafting	
	Perspectograph		
	Protractor		
	Rhumboscope		
	Rule, Parallel		
	Scale, Architect's		
	Sectograph		
	Set, Drafting		*Note:* May also use terms for individual drafting instruments as appropriate
	Straightedge		
	Stylus, Drawing		
	Template, Drafting		
		Template, Lettering	
	Triangle, Drafting		
		Triangle, 30-60-90	
		Triangle, 45-45-90	
		Triangle, Adjustable	
	T-Square		
Machine, Blueprint			
Model, Geometric			*Note:* May also use "Model" from Other Documents
Shield, Erasing			
Table, Drafting			*Note:* May also use "Table" from Support Furniture
Tape, Drafting			

Class:
MUSICAL T&E

Definition: Tools, equipment, and supplies originally created to produce musical sounds or to be audibly incorporated into musical performances. This class does not include devices that amplify, transmit, or record musical sound, or devices intended for other purposes whose sound may, on occasion, be integrated into a musical performance (e.g., cannons or church bells to accompany the *1812 Overture*).

Sub-Class:
MUSICAL ACCESSORIES

Definition: Tools, equipment, and supplies that facilitate the production of musical sound by manual or mechanical/electronic means, but do not themselves generate such sound. Included in this subclass are musical instrument components.

Primary Object Term	Secondary Term	Tertiary Term	Notes
Baton, Conductor's			
Beater, Percussion			
	Brush, Percussion		
		Brush, Wire	
	Clapper, Musical		
	Drumstick		
	Hammer, Percussion		*Note:* If a hammer is designed specifically for a given instrument, a new term may be created with the *Nomenclature* term for that instrument as a modifier; that term may be organized under "Hammer, Percussion," as "Hammer, Xylophone" is below
		Hammer, Xylophone	
Bow, Instrument			*Note:* If a bow is designed specifically for a given instrument, a new term may be created with the *Nomenclature* term for that instrument as a modifier; that term may be organized under "Bow, Instrument," as "Bow, Violin" is below
	Bow, Violin		
Case, Musical Instrument			*Note:* Use for any container specifically designed for protecting and/or transporting a musical instrument; if a case is designed specifically for a given instrument, a new term may be created with the *Nomenclature* term for that instrument as a modifier (e.g., "Case, Banjo"); that term may be organized under "Case, Musical Instrument," as the four terms are below
	Case, Clarinet		
	Case, Fife		
	Case, Guitar		

Primary Object Term	Secondary Term	Tertiary Term	Notes
	Case, Violin		
Clip, Music			
Component, Musical Instrument			
	Capo		
	Mouthpiece		
	Pipe, Organ		
	String, Instrument		
	Whistle, Calliope		
Cone, Tuning			
Cylinder, Music Box			
Disk, Music Box			
Metronome			
Mute			
Pick, Instrument			
Pickup, Acoustic			
Pipe, Pitch			
Rest, Musical Instrument			
	Rest, Chin		
	Rest, Shoulder		
Roll, Music			
Rosin, Bowstring			
Seat, Music			
	Bench, Music		*Note:* May also use "Bench" from Seating Furniture
		Bench, Organ	
		Bench, Piano	
	Chair, Music		*Note:* May also use "Chair, Side" from Seating Furniture
	Stool, Music		*Note:* May also use "Stool" from Seating Furniture
		Stool, Piano	
Slide, Guitar			
Stand, Drum			
Stand, Music			
Strap, Instrument			

Sub-Class:
MUSICAL INSTRUMENTS

Definition: Objects created to produce musical sounds.

Primary Object Term	Secondary Term	Tertiary Term	Notes
Instrument, Brass			*Note:* Despite the name, instruments listed under this term are not necessarily made of brass
	Bugle		
		Bugle, Key	
		Bugle, Valve	
	Cornet		
		Cornet, Valve	
		Horn, Alto	
		Horn, Tenor	
	Flugelhorn		
	Horn, Baritone		
	Horn, French		
	Inventionshorn		
	Mellophone		
	Serpent		
		Horn, Bass	
		Bassoon, Russian	
	Trombone		
		Sackbut	
		Trombone, Slide	
		Trombone, Valve	
	Trumpet		
		Alpenhorn	
		Buccin	
		Clavicor	
		Trumpet, Key	
		Trumpet, Slide	
		Trumpet, Valve	
	Tuba		
		Euphonium	
		Helicon	
		Sousaphone	
		Tuba, Wagner	
Instrument, Electronic			*Note:* May be used in addition to another musical instrument term, such as "Drum," "Guitar, Electric, "Organ," or "Piano"

Primary Object Term	Secondary Term	Tertiary Term	Notes
	Device, Electronic Effects		
		Pedal, Effects	
	Sampler, Music		
	Synthesizer		
	Theremin		
Instrument, Friction			
	Drum, Friction		
	Harmonica, Glass		
	Harp, Friction		
Instrument, Keyboard			
	Carillon		
	Celesta		
	Clavichord		
	Concertina		
	Harpsichord		
		Virginal	
	Keyboard, Electronic		*Note:* Use for an electronic keyboard that may not be described as either a piano or an organ; may also use "Instrument, Electronic"
		Mellotron	
	Organ		
		Accordion	
		Calliope	
		Melodeon	
		Orchestrion	
		Organ, Barrel	
		Organ, Chamber	
		Organ, Parlor	
		Organ, Pipe	
		Organ, Reed	
	Piano		
		Piano, Baby Grand	
		Piano, Grand	
		Piano, Square	
		Piano, Upright	
		Spinet	
Instrument, Mechanical			
	Box, Music		

Primary Object Term	Secondary Term	Tertiary Term	Notes
		Organette	
	Hurdy-Gurdy		*Note:* May also use "Fiddle"
	Organ, Band		*Note:* May also use "Organ, Pipe"
	Piano, Player		*Note:* May also use "Piano"
Instrument, Percussion			
	Anvil, Musical		
	Bell, Musical		
		Cowbell, Musical	
		Handbell	
	Bones		
	Castanet		
	Chime, Musical		
		Chime, Wind	*Note:* May also use "Assemblage" from Art
	Clave		
	Cymbal		
	Drum		
		Drum, Bass	
		Drum, Bongo	
		Drum, Side	
		Drum, Slit	
		Drum, Snare	
		Drum, Steel	
		Drum, Tenor	
		Tabor	
		Timpanum	
		Tomtom	
	Glockenspiel		
	Gong, Musical		
		Tam-Tam	
	Harp, Jaw		
	Marimba		
	Rattle, Musical		
		Bell, Kiva	
		Jingle	
		Maraca	
	Saw, Musical		
	Scraper, Musical		
	Stick, Clapper		

Primary Object Term	Secondary Term	Tertiary Term	Notes
	Stone, Ringing		
	Tambourine		
	Triangle, Musical		
	Vibraphone		
	Wheel, Scraped		
	Whip, Musical		
	Woodblock		
	Xylophone		
Instrument, Stringed			
	Autoharp		
	Balalaika		
	Banjo		
	Banjolele		
	Cittern		
	Dulcimer		
		Cimbalom	
		Dulcimer, Hammered	
	Dulcimer, Appalachian		
	Fiddle		*Note:* Use for a stringed instrument with a soundbox and played with a bow
		Bass, Double	
		Cello	
		Fiddle, Hardanger	
		Husle	
		Kit	
		Viol	
		Viola	
		Viola d'Amore	
		Violin	
		Violoncello	
	Guitar		
		Guitar, Bass	
		Guitar, Electric	
		Guitar, Resonator	
		Guitar, Steel	
		Guitar, Tenor	
		Guitar, 12-String	
		Lyre-Guitar	
		Ukulele	
	Harp		

Primary Object Term	Secondary Term	Tertiary Term	Notes
		Harp, Aeolian	
		Harp, Celtic	
		Harp, Pedal	
	Lute		
	Lyre		
		Crwth	
		Lyra	
	Mandolin		
		Mandocello	
		Mandore	
	Psaltery		
	Rebec		
	Sitar		
	Solophone		
	Tambouritza		
	Theorobo		
	Tiple		
	Trumpet, Marine		
	Ukelin		
	Zither		
Instrument, Woodwind			
	Bagpipe		
		Bagpipe, Highland	
		Bagpipe, Irish	
	Bassoon		
		Bassoon, Double	
	Chanter, Practice		
	Clarinet		
		Chalumeau	
		Horn, Basset	
	Crumhorn		
	Didgeridoo		
	Dulcian		
	Flageolet		
		Flageolet, Double	
		Flageolet, Triple	
	Flute		
		Fife	
		Flute, Courting	

Primary Object Term	Secondary Term	Tertiary Term	Notes
		Ocarina	
		Panpipe	
		Piccolo	
		Pipe, Tabor	
	Harmonica		
	Kazoo		
	Oboe		
		Horn, English	
		Oboe d'Amore	
	Octavin		
	Racket		
	Recorder		
	Reedpipe		
	Sarrusophone		
	Saxophone		
		Saxophone, Alto	
		Saxophone, Baritone	
		Saxophone, Soprano	
		Saxophone, Tenor	
	Shawm		
	Tarogato		
	Tenoroon		
	Whistle, Musical		

Class:
PHOTOGRAPHIC T&E

Definition: Tools, equipment, and supplies originally created to capture a visual image by optical, chemical, or digital means, such as cameras, film, or darkroom equipment.

Sub-Class:
CAMERA EQUIPMENT

Definition: Cameras and equipment attached to cameras for the purpose of capturing a visual image. Included in this sub-class are camera parts, lenses, filters, lighting attachments, and camera supports.

Primary Object Term	Secondary Term	Tertiary Term	Notes
Camera			
	Camera, 35 mm		
	Camera, Box		
	Camera, Detective		
	Camera, Digital		
	Camera, Disposable		
	Camera, Folding		
	Camera, Instant		
	Camera, Kinescope		
	Camera, Motion Picture		
	Camera, Panoramic		
	Camera, Pinhole		
	Camera, Press		
	Camera, Process		
	Camera, Rangefinder		
	Camera, Reflex		
		Camera, Single Lens Reflex	
		Camera, Twin Lens Reflex	
	Camera, Stereoscopic		
	Camera, Video		
		Camcorder	
	Camera, View		
Cap, Lens			
Card, Camera			*Note:* May also use "Drive, Flash" from Data Processing Media
Cord, Sync			
Device, Flash			
	Attachment, Flash		
	Flash, Handheld		
	Flash, Stroboscopic		

Primary Object Term	Secondary Term	Tertiary Term	Notes
	Flashbulb		
	Flashgun		
	Trigger, Flash		
Dolly, Camera			
Filter, Camera			
	Filter, Cloud		
	Filter, Color Correcting		
	Filter, Daylight		
	Filter, Polarizing		
Holder, Film			
	Holder, Cut Film		
	Holder, Photographic Plate		
	Holder, Roll Film		
	Holder, Sheet Film		
Holder, Flash Powder			
Hood, Focusing			
Hood, Lens			
Lamp, Photoflood			
Lens, Camera			
	Lens, Fisheye		
	Lens, Macro		
	Lens, Telephoto		
	Lens, Wide Angle		
	Lens, Zoom		
Matte			
Monopod, Camera			
	Stick, Selfie		
Release, Cable			
Shutter, Camera			
Tripod, Camera			
Viewfinder			

Sub-Class:
PHOTOGRAPHIC ACCESSORIES

Definition: Tools, equipment, and supplies that play an ancillary or facilitating role in the production of photographic images and are not used directly with cameras or photoprocessing equipment. Included in this sub-class are maintenance gear and ancillary studio equipment.

Primary Object Term	Secondary Term	Tertiary Term	Notes
Back, Film			
Back, Focusing			
Backdrop, Photographic			
Bag, Film Changing			
Booth, Photo			
Brush, Lens			
Case, Photographic Equipment			*Note:* Use for any container specifically designed for protecting and/or transporting one or more than one article of photographic equipment. If a case is designed specifically for a given object, a new term may be created with the *Nomenclature* term for that object as a modifier; that term may be organized under "Case, Photographic Equipment," as the two terms are below
	Case, Camera		
	Case, Camera Battery		
Clip, Print			
Container, Film			
	Can, Film		
	Canister, Film		
Drive, Motorized Film			
Editor, Film			
Headrest, Photographer's			
Holder, Photograph			*Note:* May also use "Frame, Picture" from Storage & Display Accessories if appropriate
	Case, Photograph		
		Case, Daguerreotype	
	Mat, Picture		
Knife, Film			
Loupe, Focusing			
Meter, Light			*Note:* May also use "Photometer" from Optical T&E

Primary Object Term	Secondary Term	Tertiary Term	Notes
	Densitometer, Photographic		
	Meter, Exposure		
Reflector, Studio			
Ring, Adapter			
Splicer, Film			
Tissue, Lens			

Sub-Class:
PHOTOGRAPHIC MEDIA

Definition: Paper, film, and tape created to capture and present images.

Primary Object Term	Secondary Term	Tertiary Term	Notes
Film, Photographic			
	Film, Magazine		
	Film, Motion Picture		
	Film, Roll		
	Film, Self-Developing		
	Film, Sheet		
Paper, Photographic			
Plate, Photographic			
	Plate, Dry		
	Plate, Wet		
Videodisc			
Videotape			

Sub-Class:
PHOTOPROCESSING EQUIPMENT

Definition: Tools, equipment, and supplies used in transforming a latent image, as captured by light-sensitive chemicals on film, into a visible negative or positive image.

Primary Object Term	Secondary Term	Tertiary Term	Notes
Board, Lens			
Brush, Bromoil			
Developer			
Dodger			
Dryer, Film			
Dryer, Print			
Easel, Darkroom			*Note:* May also use "Easel" from Support Furniture
Enlarger			
Fixer			
Frame, Contact Printing			
Hanger, Film			
Iron, Tacking			
Mask, Photographic			
Plate, Ferrotype			
Powder, Developing			
Printer, Contact			
Rod, Stirring			
Roller, Print			
Safelight			
Tank, Developing			
Thermometer, Darkroom			*Note:* May also use "Thermometer" from Thermal T&E
Timer, Darkroom			*Note:* May also use "Timer" from Timekeeping T&E
Tongs, Darkroom			
Tray, Darkroom			
Trimmer, Photograph			
Washer, Film			
Washer, Print			

Class:
PRINTING T&E

Definition: Tools, equipment, and supplies originally created to reproduce written, photographic, or artistic material, whether in very limited quantities (as in the case of artistic engravings or lithographs) or in quantities required for widespread distribution. This class includes specialized tools such as handpresses, engraver's blocks, or photocopiers, that are used for bookbinding, engraving, etching, lithography, or screen printing.

Sub-Class:
BOOKBINDING EQUIPMENT

Definition: Tools and equipment used to assemble sheets of printed material into collated and/or bound volumes.

Primary Object Term	Secondary Term	Tertiary Term	Notes
Bandstick			
Board, Binding			
Board, Tying-Up			
Bodkin, Bookbinder's			
Clamp, Bookbinding			
Cutter, Board			
Die, Binder			
Frame, Sewing			
Goffer			
Hammer, Backing			
Iron, Knocking-Down			
Iron, Polishing			
Machine, Backstripping			
Machine, Batcher-Jogger			
Machine, Binding			
Machine, Book Smashing			
Machine, Book Stitching			
Machine, Book Trimming			
Machine, Casemaking			
Machine, Casing-In			
Machine, Collating			
Machine, Gluing			
Machine, Round Cornering			
Machine, Ruling			
Machine, Stitching			
Machine, Tipping			

Primary Object Term	Secondary Term	Tertiary Term	Notes
Needle, Binding			
Nipper, Band			
Pallet, Bookbinding			
Plow, Bookbinding			
Press, Bookbinding			
	Press, Blocking		
	Press, Cutting		
	Press, Finishing		
	Press, Lying		
	Press, Nipping		
	Press, Standing		
Stove, Finishing			
Table, Bindery			*Note:* May also use "Table" from Support Furniture
Tin, Pressing			
Trindle			

Sub-Class:
GRAPHIC EQUIPMENT

Definition: Tools, equipment, and supplies used in conjunction with replication equipment to reproduce quantities of graphic material.

Primary Object Term	Secondary Term	Tertiary Term	Notes
Blanket, Offset			
Burin			
	Tool, Tint		
Burnisher, Printmaking			
Crayon, Lithographic			
Frisket			
Gauge, Plate			
Levigator			
Knife, Etching			
Mallet, Printer's			
Mattoir			
Needle, Etching			
	Echoppe		
Planer, Printer's			
Point, Lithographic			
Rocker			
Roulette			
Scraper, Press			
Sheet, Plate Backing			
Silkscreen			
Squeegee, Silkscreen			
Stencil, Film			
Surface, Printing			
	Block, Printing		
		Block, Engraving	
		Block, Fabric	
		Block, Linoleum	
		Block, Wallpaper	
		Block, Wood	
	Plate, Printing		
		Plate, Electrotype	
		Plate, Embossing	
		Plate, Lithograph	
		Plate, Offset	
		Plate, Stereotype	
	Stone, Lithograph		
Table, Etching			

Primary Object Term	Secondary Term	Tertiary Term	Notes
Table, Imposing			
Tool, Inking			
	Dabber		
	Inkball		
	Roller, Ink		
		Brayer	

Sub-Class:
PRINTING ACCESSORIES

Definition: Tools, equipment, and supplies that play an ancillary or facilitating role in the printing process, but do not by themselves generate multiple copies of original written, graphic, or photographic material.

Primary Object Term	Secondary Term	Tertiary Term	Notes
Acid, Lithographic			
Cartridge, Toner			
Cutter, Slug			
Folder, Bone			
Guillotine, Paper			
	Knife, Sheeter		
	Knife, Trimmer		
Ink, Printer's			
Inkstone			
Knife, Folding			
Machine, Banding			
Machine, Numbering			
Machine, Paper Folding			
Machine, Stock Compressing			
Machine, Tab Cutting			
Peel, Printer's			
Perforator, Printing			
Pot, Glue			
Stencil, Printing			
Table, Stripping			
Toner			
Tube, Ink			
Wax, Lithographic			

Sub-Class:
REPLICATION EQUIPMENT

Definition: Tools and equipment that replicate written or graphic/photographic material through the application of ink or other pigment to the surface of paper or other media.

Primary Object Term	Secondary Term	Tertiary Term	Notes
Duplicator			
	Hectograph		
	Machine, Ditto		
	Mimeograph		
Letterpress			
Machine, Addressing			
Photocopier			
Press, Printing			
	Handpress		
	Press, Book		
	Press, Cylinder		
	Press, Embossing		
	Press, Lithographic		
	Press, Newspaper		
	Press, Rolling		
	Press, Rotary		
		Press, Offset	
	Press, Toggle		
Stamp, Embroidery			

Sub-Class:
TYPESETTING EQUIPMENT

Definition: Tools and equipment used to assemble physical or virtual alphanumeric printing elements or "type" into assemblages (words, lines, paragraphs, etc.) in preparation for reproduction by replication equipment.

Primary Object Term	Secondary Term	Tertiary Term	Notes
Cabinet, Type Case			*Note:* May also use "Cabinet" from Storage & Display Furniture
Case, Type			
Chase			
Fillet			
Galley			
Gauge, Composing Stick			
Key, Quoin			
Machine, Type Casting			
Quad			
Quoin			
Rule, Composing			
	Gauge, Line		
	Gauge, Type		
	Ruler, Pica		
Rule, Makeup			
Slug, Type			
Stick, Composing			
Stick, Foot			
Stick, Printer's Shooting			
Type			
Typesetter			
	Phototypesetter		
	Typesetter, Computer		
	Typesetter, Keyboard		

Class:
SOUND COMMUNICATION T&E

Definition: Tools, equipment, and supplies, other than musical instruments, originally created to generate, amplify, reproduce, or store music, spoken words, or other sounds that are useful for human communication.

Sub-Class:
SOUND COMMUNICATION ACCESSORIES

Definition: Tools, equipment, and supplies that facilitate, but do not actually perform, the generation, amplification, reproduction, or storage of sounds for communication.

Primary Object Term	Secondary Term	Tertiary Term	Notes
Adapter, Record			
Album, Audio Recording			*Note:* Use only for a bound collection of sleeves or other compartments for the storage of sound recordings
	Album, Audiotape		
	Album, Record		
Board, Sounding			
Cartridge, Phonograph			
Case, Audio Equipment			*Note:* Use for any container specifically designed for protecting and/or transporting a piece of audio equipment; if a case is designed specifically for a given item, a new term may be created with the *Nomenclature* term for that item as a modifier; that term may be organized under "Case, Audio Equipment," as "Case, Phonograph" is below
	Case, Phonograph		
Case, Audio Recording			
	Case, Audiotape		
	Case, Record		
Cleaner, Record			
	Brush, Record		
	Preener, Record		
Cover, Record			
	Jacket, Record		
	Sleeve, Record		
Cutter, Phonograph Needle			
Eraser, Audio Tape			
Foil, Phonograph			
Mandrel, Phonograph			
Needle, Phonograph			

Primary Object Term	Secondary Term	Tertiary Term	Notes
Reel, Tape			
Shaver, Dictating Machine			
Stand, Microphone			
Turntable, Phonograph			
Winder, Phonograph			
	Crank, Phonograph		
	Key, Phonograph		

Sub-Class:
SOUND COMMUNICATION DEVICES

Definition: Tools and equipment that play an active role in the generation, amplification, or reproduction of sounds for communication.

Primary Object Term	Secondary Term	Tertiary Term	Notes
Amplifier, Audio			
Button, Call			
Clapper			
Device, Sound Signaling			
	Bell		
		Bell, Annunciator	
		Bell, Church	
		Bell, Dinner	
		Bell, Factory	
		Bell, School	
		Bell, Service	
		Chime	
	Buzzer		
	Horn		
		Horn, Coach	
		Horn, Dinner	
		Horn, Hunting	
		Horn, Post	
		Vuvuzela	
	Pistol, Starter		
	Rattle		
	Rattle, Ratchet		
	Siren		
	Trumpet, Hailing		
	Whistle		
		Pipe, Boatswain's	
		Whistle, Factory	
		Whistle, Steam	
Gong			
Headphone			
	Earphone		
Horn, Phonograph			
Intercom			
Jukebox			
Mallet, Gong			
Megaphone			

Primary Object Term	Secondary Term	Tertiary Term	Notes
	Bullhorn		
	Trumpet, Speaking		
		Trumpet, Fire	
Microphone			
	Microphone, Clip		
Mixer, Audio			
Optophone			
Phonograph			
	Gramophone		
	Phonograph, Console		
	Phonograph, Cylinder		
	Phonograph, Portable		
	Player, Record		
Player, Audio			
	Player, Compact Disc		
	Player, Digital Audio		
	Player, Tape		
		Player, Audiocassette	
		Player, Eight-Track	
		Player, Reel-to-Reel Tape	
Recorder, Audio			
	Machine, Dictating		
	Recorder, Audio Disk		
	Recorder, Audio Tape		
		Recorder, Audiocassette	
		Recorder, Reel-to-Reel Tape	
	Recorder, Audio Wire		
Simulator, Sound Effect			
Speaker			
	Speaker, Jukebox		
Tube, Speaking			

Sub-Class:
SOUND COMMUNICATION MEDIA

Definition: Objects originally created as repositories for the storage of sounds reproduced by a sound communication device. This sub-class does not include digital media for sound, which are listed in Data Processing Media. Note: If content is on the medium, "Recording" from Other Documents also may be used.

Primary Object Term	Secondary Term	Tertiary Term	Notes
Audiotape			
	Audiocassette		
		Microcassette	
		Minicassette	
		Tape, Eight-Track	
	Tape, Audio Reel		
Belt, Dictation			
Cylinder, Audio			
	Cylinder, Dictation		
	Cylinder, Phonograph		
Record, Phonograph			
	Record, 33 1/3 RPM		
	Record, 45 RPM		
	Record, 78 RPM		
Wire, Audio Recording			

Class:
TELECOMMUNICATION T&E

Definition: Tools, equipment, and supplies intended to facilitate communication at a distance by electrical or electronic means. This class includes telegraph, telephone, radio, and television equipment.

Sub-Class:
TELECOMMUNICATION ACCESSORIES

Definition: Tools, equipment, and supplies that facilitate telecommunication but do not play a direct role in the transmission or reception of telecommunication messages.

Primary Object Term	Secondary Term	Tertiary Term	Notes
Amplifier, Radio Frequency			
Box, Call			
Case, Telecommunication Equipment			*Note:* Use for any container specifically designed for protecting and/or transporting a piece of telecommunication equipment; if a case is designed specifically for a given item, a new term may be created with the *Nomenclature* term for that item as a modifier; that term may be organized under "Case, Telecommunication Equipment," as "Case, Telephone" is below
	Case, Telephone		
Connector, Cable			
Converter, Television			
	Converter, Cable		
	Converter, Color		
	Converter, UHF		
Descrambler			
Device, Morse Code Instruction			
	Instructograph		
	Natrometer		
	Omnigraph		
Doubler, Telephone Line			
Headset, Radio			
Insulator, Communication			
	Insulator, Antenna		
	Insulator, Telegraph Wire		
	Insulator, Telephone Wire		

Primary Object Term	Secondary Term	Tertiary Term	Notes
Jack, Telephone			
Rod, Grounding			
Rotor, Antenna			
Scrambler			
Splitter, Signal			
Tuner, Television			

Sub-Class:
TELECOMMUNICATION DEVICES

Definition: Tools and equipment that play a direct role in the generation or reception of telecommunication messages.

Primary Object Term	Secondary Term	Tertiary Term	Notes
Antenna			
	Antenna, Parabolic		
		Dish, Satellite	
	Antenna, Radio		
	Antenna, Rooftop		
	Antenna, Set-Top		
	Antenna, Television		
Camera, Television			
Coherer			
Control, Remote			
	Servo, Remote		
Headset			
Machine, Answering			
Machine, Ticker Tape			
	Ticker, Stock		
Monitor, Video			
Pager			
Radio			
	Radio, Car		
	Radio, Console		
	Radio, Crystal		
	Radio, Portable		
		Radio, Transistor	
	Radio, Table		
	Scanner, Radio		
	Tuner, Radio		
Switchboard, Telephone			
Telegraph			
	Key, Telegraph		
	Printer, Telegraph		
	Sounder, Telegraph		
Telemeter			
Telephone			
	Telephone, Cellular		*Note:* May also use “Smartphone” from Data Processing Devices if appropriate
	Telephone, Coin-Operated		

Primary Object Term	Secondary Term	Tertiary Term	Notes
	Telephone, Cordless		
	Telephone, Desk		
	Telephone, Field		
	Telephone, Magneto		
	Telephone, Satellite		
	Telephone, Wall		
Teletype			
	Teleprinter		
	Teletypewriter		
		TDD	
Television			
	Television, Console		
	Television, Portable		
Transceiver			
	Radio, CB		
	Radiophone		
		Walkie-Talkie	
Transmitter			
	Transmitter, Radio		
	Transmitter, Television		
Transponder			
Varioplex			

Sub-Class:
TELECOMMUNICATION MEDIA

Definition: Objects that function as carriers of telecommunication messages.

Primary Object Term	Secondary Term	Tertiary Term	Notes
Cable, Telecommunication			
	Cable, Antenna Lead		
	Cable, Coaxial		
	Cable, Submarine		
	Cable, Telephone		
Tape, Ticker			
Wire, Telecommunication			
	Wire, Antenna		
	Wire, Telegraph		
	Wire, Telephone		

Class:
VISUAL COMMUNICATION T&E

Definition: Tools, equipment, and supplies originally created to facilitate communication by means of symbols, patterns, colors, text, or pictures that are directly observable by and intelligible to the recipient. Included in this class are signs, visual signals, and devices that project images.

Sub-Class:
VISUAL COMMUNICATION ACCESSORIES

Definition: Tools, equipment, and supplies that facilitate visual communication but do not play a direct role in the generation or display of visual content.

Primary Object Term	Secondary Term	Tertiary Term	Notes
Adapter, Media			
	Adapter, Filmstrip		
	Adapter, Slide		
Cart, Projector			
Case, Visual Communication Equipment			*Note:* Use for any container specifically designed for protecting and/or transporting a piece of visual communication equipment; if a case is designed specifically for a given item, a new term may be created with the *Nomenclature* term for that item as a modifier; that term may be organized under "Case, Visual Communication Equipment," as "Case, Projector" is below
	Case, Projector		
	Locker, Flag		
Eyeglasses, 3D			
Holder, Sign			
Holder, Slide			
	Magazine, Slide		
	Tray, Slide		
Magazine, Film			
Ornament, Transfer			
Press, Dry Mount			
Reel, Film			
Screen, Projection			
	Screen, Rear Projection		
Table, Light			
Tissue, Dry Mount			
Viewer, Filmstrip			
Viewer, Slide			

Sub-Class:
VISUAL COMMUNICATION DEVICES

Definition: Tools, equipment, and supplies that play a direct role in the generation or display of visual symbols.

Primary Object Term	Secondary Term	Tertiary Term	Notes
Device, Visual Signaling			
	Card, Signal		
	Flag, Signal		
		Flag, Semaphore	
	Flare, Signal		
	Gun, Flare		
	Heliograph		
	Lamp, Signal		*Note:* May also use "Lamp" from Lighting Devices
		Lamp, Alarm	
		Lamp, Aldis	
		Lamp, Semaphore	
	Lantern, Signal		*Note:* May also use "Lantern" from Lighting Devices
		Lantern, Railroad	
	Mirror, Signaling		
	Pointer		
		Pointer, Laser	
		Stick, Pointer	
	Rocket, Signal		
	Signal, Railroad		
		Semaphore, Railroad	
	Signal, Traffic		
Graphoscope			
Kinetoscope			
	Kinetophone		
Megalethoscope			
Panel, Aerial Marker			
Player, Digital Videodisc			
Pot, Smudge			
Projector			
	Camera Lucida		
	Camera Obscura		
	Projector, Filmstrip		
	Projector, Lantern Slide		
		Sciopticon	

Primary Object Term	Secondary Term	Tertiary Term	Notes
	Projector, Motion Picture		
	Projector, Opaque		
		Projector, Postcard	
	Projector, Overhead		
	Projector, Slide		
Reader, Electronic			*Note:* May also use "Computer, Handheld" or "Computer, Tablet" from Data Processing Devices if appropriate
Reader, Microform			
	Reader, Microfiche		
	Reader, Microfilm		
Recorder, Videotape			
Sign			
	Sign, Directional		
		Guidepost	
	Sign, Identification		
		Signboard	
	Sign, Informational		*Note:* May also use "Marker, Site" from Site Features if appropriate
	Sign, Instructional		
	Sign, Regulatory		
	Sign, Traffic		*Note:* May use with another sign term, depending on the sign's message
Stereoscope			*Note:* Use for a card-type stereoscopic viewer
Stereoviewer			*Note:* Use for a wheel-type stereoscopic viewer; may also use "Toy" from Toys if appropriate
Tachistoscope			

Class:
WRITTEN COMMUNICATION T&E

Definition: Tools, equipment, and supplies originally created to facilitate the preparation and maintenance of written documents. This class does not include the documents themselves or equipment and supplies relating to the replication or electronic transmission of documents. This class includes objects relating to the sending and receipt of postal communication, but not to the actual processing, transportation, or delivery of mail by postal agencies or other delivery services.

Sub-Class:
WRITING ACCESSORIES

Definition: Tools, equipment, and supplies intended to facilitate written communication but that do not play a direct or essential role in the creation or transmission of written messages.

Primary Object Term	Secondary Term	Tertiary Term	Notes
Affixer, Stamp			
Blotter, Desk			
Board, Bulletin			
Board, Writing			
	Clipboard		
	Lapboard		
Bookmark			
Brush, Erasure			
Card, Divider			
Cartridge, Ink			
Clip, Pencil			
Container, Document			
	Binder, Loose-Leaf		
		Binder, Clip	
		Binder, Post	
		Binder, Ring	
	Book, Letter		
	Box, File		
	Box, Index Card		
	Case, Document		
		Case, Parchment	
	Envelope		*Note:* May also use "Stationery" from Writing Media if appropriate
	File, Portable		
	Folder, File		
	Holder, Card File		
		Holder, Rotary Card File	*Note:* Use for the object commonly known by the brand name, Rolodex
	Holder, Label		

Primary Object Term	Secondary Term	Tertiary Term	Notes
	Holder, Letter		
	Organizer, File		
	Portfolio		
	Slipcase		
	Solander		
	Tray, Paper		
	Trunk, Document		
	Tube, Document		
Container, Postage Stamp			
	Box, Stamp		
	Dispenser, Stamp		
Container, Writing Equipment			
	Bottle, Ink		
	Box, Pounce		
	Case, Writing Equipment		*Note:* Use for any container specifically designed for protecting and/or transporting writing equipment and supplies; if a case is designed specifically for a given item, a new term may be created with the *Nomenclature* term for that instrument as a modifier; that term may be organized under "Case, Writing Equipment," as the five terms are below
		Case, Pen	
		Case, Pencil	
		Case, Pencil Lead	
		Case, Typewriter	
		Case, Writing	
	Holder, Writing Equipment		
		Holder, Chalk	
		Holder, Marking Stamp	
		Holder, Paper Clip	
		Holder, Pen	
		Holder, Pencil	
		Organizer, Desk	
	Inkstand		
	Inkwell		
	Liner, Inkwell		

Primary Object Term	Secondary Term	Tertiary Term	Notes
	Tray, Writing Equipment		
		Tray, Desk	
		Tray, Pen	
Cover, Typewriter			
Cutter, Paper			*Note:* Use for a desktop paper cutter; for a handheld device, use "Trimmer, Paper"
Cutter, Quill			
Desk, Portable			*Note:* May also use "Desk" from Storage & Display Furniture
Divider, File			
	Divider, Chart		
Eraser			
Fastener, Paper			
	Clip, Paper		
		Clip, Binder	
	Pushpin		
	Staple		
	Thumbtack		
Fitting, Book			
Guide, Lettering			
Holder, Page			
Ink			
Inkpad			
Laminator			
Lead, Pencil			
Machine, Mailing			
	Meter, Postage		
	Sorter, Mail		
Machine, Receipt			
Machine, Stencil			
Moistener			
Opener, Letter			
Pad, Desk			
Paperweight			
Perforator			
Powder, Ink			
Protector, Sheet			
Punch, Paper			
Remover, Staple			

Primary Object Term	Secondary Term	Tertiary Term	Notes
Ribbon, Adding Machine			
Ribbon, Typewriter			
Set, Desk			*Note:* May also use terms to describe the components of the set
Shaker, Sand			
Sharpener, Pencil			
Shredder, Paper			
Spindle, Paper			
Stapler, Paper			
Stencil, Letter			
Sticker, Seal			
Suspender, File			
Tab, Index			
Trimmer, Paper			*Note:* Use for a handheld paper cutting tool; for a desktop device, use "Cutter, Paper"
Wax, Sealing			
Wiper, Pen			

Sub-Class:
WRITING DEVICES

Definition: Tools, equipment, and supplies that play a direct and essential role in the creation or transmission of written messages, such as writing implements or typewriters. This sub-class does not include computer printers, which are included in Peripherals.

Primary Object Term	Secondary Term	Tertiary Term	Notes
Bag, Pounce			
Brush, Writing			
Chalk			
Crayon, Marking			
Embosser			
	Embosser, Braille		
	Embosser, Check		
	Embosser, Label		
	Press, Seal		
Imprinter			
Iron, Branding			*Note:* Use "Brand, Animal" from Animal Care Equipment if appropriate
Machine, Cipher			
Machine, Signature			
Nib, Pen			
Pen			
	Brush, Calligraphic		
	Pen, Dip		
		Pen, Lettering	
		Pen, Metal Nib	
		Pen, Quill	
		Pen, Reed	
	Pen, Reservoir		
		Pen, Ballpoint	
		Pen, Fountain	
		Pen, Gel	
		Pen, Marker	
Pencil			
	Pencil, Colored		
	Pencil, Grease		
	Pencil, Mechanical		
	Pencil, Slate		
Printer, Label			
	Printer, Barcode		
Set, Scribe			
Slate, Braille			

Primary Object Term	Secondary Term	Tertiary Term	Notes
Stamp, Marking			
	Stamp, Address		
	Stamp, Cancellation		
	Stamp, Date		
	Stamp, Message		
	Stamp, Name		
	Stamp, Notary		
	Stamp, Numbering		
	Stamp, Postmark		
Typewriter			
	Typewriter, Electric		
	Typewriter, Manual		

Sub-Class:
WRITING MEDIA

Definition: Paper and other materials intended for the recording of written and printed communications. Note: if any items listed in the sub-class have contents, terms from Documentary Objects also may be used to describe the contents, e.g., "Label, Identification" for a label, "Tag, Identification" for a tag, "Letter" for a sheet of letterhead, "Note" for a notecard, and "Correspondence" and "Print, Photographic" for a postcard.

Primary Object Term	Secondary Term	Tertiary Term	Notes
Book, Writing			
	Blankbook		
		Book, Composition	
		Notebook	
	Notepad		*Note:* Use for a writing book with a top binding
		Notepad, Adhesive	
		Pad, Flip Chart	
		Pad, Legal	
Card, Index			
Label			*Note:* Use for a blank label
	Tag		*Note:* Use for a blank tag
Notecard			
Paper			
	Paper, Adhesive Note		
	Paper, Carbon		
	Paper, Copy		
	Paper, Onionskin		
	Paper, Staff		
	Paper, Typing		
	Paper, Writing		
	Stationery		*Note:* May also use "Envelope" from Writing Accessories if appropriate
Postcard			
	Postcard, Picture		*Note:* May also use a suitable term from Graphic Documents
Tablet, Writing			*Note:* Use for a non-paper flat surface intended for written communications
	Chalkboard		
	Slate, Writing		
	Whiteboard		

Category 7:
DISTRIBUTION & TRANSPORTATION OBJECTS

Definition: **Objects originally created to transport or distribute animate and inanimate things. This category also includes objects originally created to facilitate such transportation or as an adjunct to such transportation. This category includes propelled vehicles such as automobiles or wheelbarrows as well as containers that facilitate distribution. Also included are parts of aircraft, spacecraft, land vehicles, rail vehicles, and watercraft.**

Class:
AEROSPACE TRANSPORTATION T&E

Definition: Objects originally created to transport people or goods above the surface of the earth.

Sub-Class:
AEROSPACE TRANSPORTATION ACCESSORIES

Definition: Objects originally created as accessories used in the transportation of people or goods above the face of the earth. Included are objects created to be parts of aircraft or spacecraft.

Primary Object Term	Secondary Term	Tertiary Term	Notes
Booster			
Component, Aircraft			*Note:* This generic term may be used for a part not listed here or may be used in addition to terms from other sub-classes, such as Navigational Equipment
	Airframe		
	Cone, Nose		
	Engine, Aircraft		*Note:* May also use an "Engine" term from Power Producing Equipment
		Engine, Ramjet	
		Engine, Turbojet	
		Engine, Turboprop	
	Fuselage		
	Gear, Landing		
	Instrument, Flight		
		Altimeter, Aircraft	*Note:* May also use "Altimeter" from Navigational Equipment
		Compass, Aircraft	*Note:* May also use "Compass" from Navigational Equipment
		Gyrocompass, Aircraft	*Note:* May also use "Gyrocompass" from Navigational Equipment
		Horizon, Artificial	
		Indicator, Airspeed	
		Indicator, Drift	
		Indicator, Rate-of-Climb	
		Indicator, Turn and Bank	
	Lamp, Aircraft		*Note:* May also use a suitable "Lamp" term from Lighting Devices

Primary Object Term	Secondary Term	Tertiary Term	Notes
		Lamp, Landing	
		Lamp, Position	
		Light, Aircraft Running	
	Module, Airlock		
	Propeller, Aircraft		
		Propeller, Adjustable-Pitch	
		Propeller, Fixed-Pitch	
	Rotor, Aircraft		
	Seat, Aircraft		
		Seat, Ejection	
	Shackle, Bomb		
	Shield, Heat		
	Ski, Aircraft		
	Stick, Aircraft Control		
	Windshield, Aircraft		
	Wire, Aircraft		
		Wire, Antidrag	
		Wire, Antiflutter	
		Wire, Fairing	
		Wire, Stagger	
	Yoke, Flight		
Launcher, Kite			
Line, Aircraft Mooring			
Parachute			
	Parachute, Cargo		
	Parachute, Drogue		
	Parachute, Personnel		
Pot, Blow			
Recorder, Flight			
Reel, Kite			
Simulator, Flight			
	Simulator, Air Flight		
	Simulator, Space Flight		

Sub-Class:
AIRCRAFT

Definition: Objects originally created to transport people or goods above the surface of the earth but within the confines of earth's atmosphere.

Primary Object Term	Secondary Term	Tertiary Term	Notes
Aerostat			
	Airship		
		Airship, Pressure-Rigid	
		Airship, Rigid	
		Airship, Semi-Rigid	
		Blimp	
	Balloon		
		Balloon, Barrage	
		Balloon, Captive	
		Balloon, Free	
		Balloon, Hot-Air	
Airplane			
	Airplane, Drone		
	Airplane, Jet		
	Airplane, Military		
		Airplane, Reconnaissance	
		Bomber	
		Fighter	
		Torpedo, Aerial	
	Biplane		
	Monoplane		
	Plane, Cargo		
	Plane, Passenger		
		Airliner	
	Seaplane		
		Boat, Flying	
		Plane, Float	
Belt, Rocket			
Drone			*Note:* May also use another aircraft term as appropriate
Glider			
	Glider, Hang		
	Paraglider		
	Sailplane		

Primary Object Term	Secondary Term	Tertiary Term	Notes
Hovercraft			
Kite			*Note:* Use for a heavier-than-air aircraft propelled by a towline
Ornithopter			
Rotorplane			
	Autogyro		
	Helicopter		

Sub-Class:
SPACECRAFT

Definition: Objects originally created to transport people or equipment outside the confines of earth's atmosphere.

Primary Object Term	Secondary Term	Tertiary Term	Notes
Spacecraft, Manned			
	Module, Command		
	Module, Lunar		
	Orbiter		
	Shuttle, Space		
Spacecraft, Unmanned			
	Satellite		
		Biosatellite	
		Observatory, Orbiting Solar	
		Satellite, Communications	
		Satellite, Datasphere	
		Satellite, Meteorological	
	Spaceprobe		

Class:
CONTAINERS

Definition: Objects originally created to transport or distribute objects or substances. Included in this class are terms to describe generic forms used to store or ship any variety of materials. The term "Package, Product" from Merchandising T&E should be used in addition to a term from the Container class to describe containers used for the marketing and merchandising of specific products; the products themselves may be noted in a subject field. Containers made for the personal storage or transport of specific objects are listed in Storage & Display Accessories, Personal Carrying & Storage Gear, or other classes with the objects for which they were made.

Primary Object Term	Secondary Term	Tertiary Term	Notes
Bag			
	Sack, Gunny		
Bale			
Barrel			
Basket			*Note:* May also use a term to describe form, e.g., "Bowl," "Tray"
Bin			*Note:* For display bins, use "Bin, Display" in Merchandising T&E
	Bin, Sorting		
	Bin, Storage		
Blanket, Moving			
Box			
	Box, Packing		
	Box, Storage		
Caddy			
Can			
	Tin		
Canister			
Carton			
Case			
Cask			
Container, Mail			
	Mailbag		*Note:* Use for a large sack intended for bulk mail; "Bag, Mail Carrier's" is listed in Personal Carrying & Storage Gear
	Mailbox		
		Box, Mail Collection	
		Box, Post Office	
Container, Shipping			*Note:* Use for a cargo transport unit
Crate			

Primary Object Term	Secondary Term	Tertiary Term	Notes
	Crate, Shipping		
	Crate, Storage		
Drum, Storage			
Envelope, Shipping			*Note:* Use only for an envelope used in the transportation of goods; for a stationery envelope, use "Envelope" from Writing Accessories
Keg			
Pack			
Packet			
Pouch			
Spool			
Tank			
Tray			*Note:* Use only for a shipping or storage tray
Tub			
Tube			
Vat, Storage			
Vessel			
	Basin		
	Bottle		
		Bottle, Gemel	
		Carboy	
		Demijohn	
		Flask	
	Bowl		
	Bucket		
	Crock		
	Jar		
	Jug		
		Jug, Bartmann	
	Vial		
Wrapper			

Class:
LAND TRANSPORTATION T&E

Definition: Objects originally created to transport people or goods on land without restriction to a fixed route determined by a track or other guidance device.

Sub-Class:
LAND TRANSPORTATION ACCESSORIES

Definition: Objects originally created as accessories used in the transportation of people or goods on land without restriction to a fixed route determined by a track or other guidance device. Included are objects created to be parts of land vehicles.

Primary Object Term	Secondary Term	Tertiary Term	Notes
Apron, Carriage			
Bar, Load			
Bell, Bicycle			*Note:* May also use "Bell" from Sound Communication Devices
Bell, Crotal			*Note:* May also use "Rattle" from Sound Communication Devices
	Bell, Sleigh		
Blade, Snow			
Blanket, Carriage			
Block, Mounting			
Brush, Snow			
Cable, Jumper			
Can, Gasoline			
Carrier, Cargo			
	Bag, Bicycle		*Note:* Use for a bicycle saddlebag
	Bag, Water		
	Basket, Bicycle		
	Net, Luggage		
	Pannier, Motorcycle		*Note:* Use for a motorcycle saddlebag
	Rack, Luggage		
	Saddlebag		*Note:* Use for a saddlebag used on animals
		Mochila	
Chain, Tire			
Chock, Wheel			*Note:* May also use "Chock" from Mechanical Devices
Component, Vehicle			*Note:* This generic term may be used for a part not listed here or may be used in addition to terms from other classes
	Axle		
	Belt, Fan		
	Body, Vehicle		
	Bow, Wagon		
	Brake, Vehicle		

Primary Object Term	Secondary Term	Tertiary Term	Notes
	Cap, Gas		
	Chain, Cycle		
		Chain, Bicycle	
		Chain, Motorcycle	
	Door, Vehicle		
	Engine, Automotive		*Note:* May also use an "Engine" term from Power Producing Equipment
	Fender, Vehicle		
	Frame, Vehicle		
	Hardware, Vehicle		
	Heater, Vehicle		*Note:* May also use "Heater" from Heating & Cooling Equipment
		Heater, Block	
	Hub, Wheel		
	Hubcap		
	Lamp, Vehicle		*Note:* May also use a suitable "Lamp" term from Lighting Devices or "Bulb, Light" term from Other Lighting Accessories
		Headlamp	
		Lamp, Bicycle	
		Lamp, Carriage	
		Light, Vehicle Running	
		Taillamp	
	Linchpin		
	Muffler, Automotive		
	Ornament, Vehicle		
		Ornament, Hood	
	Radiator, Automotive		
	Reflector, Vehicle		
	Runner, Vehicle		
		Runner, Gig	
		Runner, Sleigh	
	Seat, Vehicle		
		Seat, Automotive	
		Seat, Bicycle	
		Seat, Folding	
		Seat, Wagon	
	Shaft, Drive		

Primary Object Term	Secondary Term	Tertiary Term	Notes
	Spring, Vehicle		*Note:* May also use "Spring" from Mechanical Devices
		Spring, Leaf	
	Step, Vehicle		
	Tailgate		
	Tire		
	Tongue, Vehicle		
	Wheel, Vehicle		
		Wheel, Bicycle	
		Wheel, Carriage	
		Wheel, Wagon	
	Wheel, Vehicle Steering		
	Windshield, Vehicle		
Container, Tack			
	Box, Tack		
	Rack, Tack		*Note:* May also use "Rack" from Storage & Display Accessories
		Mount, Bridle	
		Rack, Harness	
		Rack, Saddle	
Cover, Automotive			
	Cover, Seat		
	Cover, Steering Wheel		
	Cover, Tire		
	Cover, Truck Bed		
	Cover, Vehicle		
Cover, Saddle			
Cushion, Vehicle Seat			
Defroster, Windshield			
Footrest, Vehicle			
Gauge, Tire Pressure			
Gauge, Tire Tread			
Hitch, Trailer			
Holder, Whip			
Horn, Vehicle			*Note:* May also use "Horn" from Sound Communication Devices
	Horn, Bicycle		
Jack, Vehicle			*Note:* May also use "Jack" from Mechanical Devices

Primary Object Term	Secondary Term	Tertiary Term	Notes
	Jack, Automotive		
	Jack, Stagecoach		
	Jack, Wagon		
Key, Ignition			
Mat, Vehicle Floor			
Mudflap			
Parasol, Carriage			
Patch, Tire			
Plate, License			*Note:* May also use "Plate, Identification" from Other Documents
Pump, Tire			
Robe, Lap			
Scraper, Ice			
Seat, Child Safety			*Note:* May also use "Restraint" from Regulative Devices
Stand, Bicycle			
Stand, Truing			
Tack, Animal			
	Armor, Horse		
	Bar, Draught		
		Doubletree	
		Evener, Horse	
		Singletree	
		Tripletree	
	Bit, Bridle		
	Blanket, Saddle		
	Blinder		
	Boot, Horse Ankle		
	Bridle		
		Bridle, Single	
		Bridle, Team	
	Caparison		
	Chain, Curb		
	Chain, Draught		
	Collar, Breast		
	Collar, Horse		
	Crop, Riding		*Note:* May also use "Gear, Animal Racing" from Sports Equipment if appropriate
	Hackamore		
	Halter		

Primary Object Term	Secondary Term	Tertiary Term	Notes
	Hame		
		Hame, Covered	
		Hame, Plated	
	Hardware, Harness		
		Buckle, Tack	
	Harness, Animal		
		Harness, Buggy	
		Harness, Dog	
		Harness, Donkey	
		Harness, Express	
		Harness, Farm	
		Harness, Horse	
		Harness, Ox	
		Harness, Pony	
		Harness, Runabout	
		Harness, Track	
	Headstall		
	Ornament, Tack		
		Ornament, Bridle	
		Ornament, Harness	
	Pad, Animal		
		Pad, Buckle	
		Pad, Collar	
		Pad, Horse Knee	
		Pad, Saddle	
		Pad, Withers	
	Rein		
		Rein, Check	
		Rein, Driving	
	Ring, Cinch		
	Ring, Harness		
	Roll, Bucking		
	Saddle		
		Howdah	
		Saddle, Pack	
		Saddle, Pad	
		Saddle, Racing	
		Saddle, Riding	
		Saddle, Stock	

Primary Object Term	Secondary Term	Tertiary Term	Notes
		Sidesaddle	
	Spur		
		Spur, Box	
		Spur, Prick	
		Spur, Rowel	
	Stirrup		
	Strap, Harness		
		Bellyband	
		Britching	
		Crupper	
		Girth	
		Martingale	
		Surcingle	
	Strap, Spur		
	Tapadera		
	Terret		
	Trace		
	Tree, Saddle		
	Tug, Shaft		
	Whip, Driving		*Note:* May also use "Whip, Animal" from Animal Care Equipment
		Whip, Buggy	
		Whip, Coach	
	Whip, Riding		*Note:* May also use "Whip, Animal" from Animal Care Equipment
		Quirt	
	Yoke, Animal		
		Yoke, Head	
		Yoke, Neck	
		Yoke, Withers	
Tarpot			
Taximeter			
Tightener, Chain			
Tool, Vehicle			
	Gun, Grease		
	Iron, Tire		
	Kit, Automotive Tool		
	Kit, Bicycle Tool		
	Spreader, Tire		

Primary Object Term	Secondary Term	Tertiary Term	Notes
	Wrench, Lug		*Note:* May also use "Wrench, Socket" from Metalworking T&E
	Wrench, Wagon		
Topper, Antenna			
Towline, Vehicle			
Vase, Automobile			
Weight, Hitching			
Weight, Wheel			
Yoke, Human			

Sub-Class:
ANIMAL-POWERED VEHICLES

Definition: Objects, powered by animal energy, originally created to transport people or goods on land without restriction to a fixed route determined by a track or guidance device.

Primary Object Term	Secondary Term	Tertiary Term	Notes
Carriage			
	Ambulance, Horse-Drawn		
	Barouche		
	Break		
		Break, Skeleton	
		Break, Wagonette	
	Buckboard		
	Cab, Hansom		
	Cabriolet		
	Carriage, Runabout		
	Chaise		
		Caleche	
		Whisky	
	Chaise, Post		
	Chariot		
	Coach		
		Brougham	
		Coach, Berlin	
		Coach, Concord	
		Coach, Road	
		Coach, State	
		Coachee	
		Drag, Park	
		Hack	
		Stagecoach	
	Curricle		
	Droshky		
	Gig		
		Stanhope	
		Tilbury	
	Hearse, Horse-Drawn		
	Landau		
	Landaulet		
	Phaeton		
		Buggy	

Primary Object Term	Secondary Term	Tertiary Term	Notes
	Rockaway		
	Sociable		
	Sulky		
	Surrey		
	Trap		
	Victoria		
	Vis-à-Vis		
Carriage, Artillery			
	Caisson		
	Carriage, Cannon		
Cart			
	Cart, Dog		
	Cart, Governess		
	Cart, Irish Jaunting		
	Cart, Lumber		
	Cart, Mail		
	Oxcart		
	Tumbrel		
Dray			
Omnibus			
Roller, Snow			
Sledge			
	Dogsled		
	Sled, Log		
Sleigh			
	Booby		
	Carriole		
	Cutter		
		Cutter, Albany	
		Cutter, Country	
		Cutter, Portland	
	Pung		
	Sleigh, Runabout		
	Sleigh, Surrey		
Snowplow, Horse-Drawn			
Travois			
Van, Gypsy			
Wagon			
	Bandwagon		

Primary Object Term	Secondary Term	Tertiary Term	Notes
	Chuckwagon		
	Wagon, Baggage		
	Wagon, Battery		
	Wagon, Chemical		
	Wagon, Circus		
	Wagon, Covered		
		Schooner, Prairie	
		Wagon, Conestoga	
	Wagon, Delivery		
	Wagon, Farm		
		Wagon, Hay	
	Wagon, Fire		
		Pumper, Horse-Drawn Hand	
		Pumper, Horse-Drawn Steam	
		Reel, Horse-Drawn Hose	
		Wagon, Hook and Ladder	
		Wagon, Hose	
	Wagon, Ice		
	Wagon, Log		
	Wagon, Market		
	Wagon, Mortar		
	Wagon, Mountain		
	Wagon, Patrol		
	Wagon, Peddler's		
	Wagon, Sheep		
	Wagon, Thoroughbrace		
	Wagon, Tray		

Sub-Class:
HUMAN-POWERED VEHICLES

Definition: Objects, powered by human energy alone, originally created to transport people or goods on land without restriction to a fixed route determined by a track or guidance device.

Primary Object Term	Secondary Term	Tertiary Term	Notes
Carrier, Child			
	Cradle, Basket		
	Cradle, Slat		
	Cradleboard		
	Sling, Infant		
Chair, Sedan			
Chair, Touring			
Cycle			
	Bicycle		
		Bicycle, Ordinary	
		Bicycle, Safety	
		Bicycle, Side-By-Side	
		Bicycle, Tandem	
	Draisine		
	Quadricycle		
	Tricycle		*Note:* May also use "Toy, Riding" from Toys to describe a toy tricycle
		Tricycle, Side-By-Side	
		Tricycle, Tandem	
		Tricycle, Two-Track	
	Unicycle		
	Velocipede		
Dolly			
Gurney			
Handcart			
	Bookcart		
	Cart, Firehose		
	Cart, Luggage		
		Cart, Hotel Luggage	
		Cart, Portable Luggage	
	Cart, Panel		
	Cart, Service		
	Cart, Utility		
	Pushcart		

Primary Object Term	Secondary Term	Tertiary Term	Notes
		Wheelbarrow	
	Truck, Garment		
	Truck, Hand		
Jack, Pallet			
Litter			
	Palanquin		
Pumper, Hand-Drawn Fire			
	Pumper, Hand-Drawn Hand		
	Pumper, Hand-Drawn Steam		
Rickshaw			
Snowshoe			
Stretcher			
Trailer, Bicycle			*Note:* May also use "Vehicle, Child Transport" if the trailer is designed for children
Vehicle, Child Transport			
	Carriage, Baby		
	Stroller		

Sub-Class:
MOTOR VEHICLES

Definition: Objects, powered by some kind of self-acting mechanism such as a motor, originally created to transport people or goods on land without restriction to a fixed route determined by a track or other guidance device. Included are wheeled vehicles towed by motor vehicles.

Primary Object Term	Secondary Term	Tertiary Term	Notes
Automobile			
	Ambulance, Motor		
	Car, Police		
	Car, Racing		
		Car, Midget	
		Car, Stock Race	
	Convertible		
	Hatchback		
	Hearse, Motor		
	Limousine		
	Minivan		
	Roadster		
	Sedan		
	Taxicab		
	Vehicle, Sport Utility		
	Wagon, Station		
Bus			
	Bus, School		
	Trolleybus		
Jeep			
Motorcycle			
	Bike, Dirt		
	Moped		
	Motorbike		
	Scooter, Motor		
	Tricycle, Gasoline		
Sidecar, Motorcycle			
Tractor			
	Tractor, Farm		
Trailer			
	Camper		
	Semitrailer		
	Trailer, Animal		
		Trailer, Horse	

Primary Object Term	Secondary Term	Tertiary Term	Notes
	Trailer, Boat		
	Trailer, Farm		
	Trailer, House		
	Trailer, Snowmobile		
	Trailer, Travel		
Transporter, Personal			
Truck			
	Dolly, Motorized		
	Forklift		
	Tractor, Truck		
	Truck, Baggage		
	Truck, Boom		
	Truck, Crash		
	Truck, Delivery		
		Car, Armored	
		Truck, Mail	
		Truck, Milk	
		Truck, Panel	
	Truck, Dump		
	Truck, Fire		
		Truck, Aerial Ladder	
		Truck, Hook and Ladder	
		Truck, Pumper	
		Truck, Pumper Ladder	
		Truck, Pumper/ Aerial Ladder	
	Truck, Flatbed		
	Truck, Lighting		
	Truck, Lumber		
	Truck, Maintenance		
		Snowplow	*Note:* For the plow attachment alone, use "Blade, Snow" from Land Transportation Accessories
		Sweeper, Street	
	Truck, Pickup		
	Truck, Stake		
	Truck, Tank		
	Truck, Tow		
	Van		

Primary Object Term	Secondary Term	Tertiary Term	Notes
	Wrecker		
Vehicle, Lunar			
Vehicle, Military			
	Carrier, Ammunition		
	Carrier, Personnel		
	Tank, Military		
	Tractor, Artillery		
	Truck, Ordnance Workshop		
	Truck, Troop		
Vehicle, Recreational			
	Buggy, Dune		
	Cart, Golf		*Note:* May also use "Gear, Golf" from Sports Equipment
	Motorhome		
	Snowmobile		
	Vehicle, All Terrain		
Vehicle, Steam			
	Bicycle, Steam		
	Car, Steam		
	Tricycle, Steam		

Class:
RAIL TRANSPORTATION EQUIPMENT

Definition: Objects originally created to transport people or goods on or along a fixed route determined by a track, rail, cable, or similar device.

Sub-Class:
RAIL TRANSPORTATION ACCESSORIES

Definition: Objects originally created as accessories used in the transportation of people or goods on or along a fixed route determined by a track, rail, cable, or similar device. Included are objects created to be parts of rail vehicles.

Primary Object Term	Secondary Term	Tertiary Term	Notes
Cable, Railway			
Component, Rail Vehicle			*Note:* This generic term may be used for a part not listed here or may be used in addition to terms from other classes
	Bell, Locomotive		*Note:* May also use "Bell" from Sound Communication Devices
	Brake, Railway		
		Brake, Emergency	
		Brake, Service	
	Coupler, Car		
		Coupler, Knuckle	
		Coupler, Link and Pin	
	Device, Flashing Rear-End		
	Handle, Controller		
	Headlamp, Locomotive		
	Horn, Locomotive		*Note:* May also use "Horn" from Sound Communication Devices
	Iron, Grab		
	Lever, Throttle		
	Pantograph, Rail		
	Pilot, Locomotive		
	Pin, Coupling		
	Sandbox, Locomotive		
	Seal, Railcar		
	Seat, Railway		
	Shoe, Third Rail		
	Stoker, Locomotive		
	Whistle, Locomotive		*Note:* May also use "Whistle" from Sound Communication Devices
Component, Track			

Primary Object Term	Secondary Term	Tertiary Term	Notes
	Anticreeper		
	Crosstie		
	Fishplate, Rail		
	Pan, Track		
	Rail		
	Spike, Rail		
	Switch, Railroad		
	Track		
	Treadle, Railway		
Hook, Pullman Porter's			
Hoop, Train Order			
Iron, Switch			
Key, Switch			
Machine, Interlocking			
Panel, Dispatcher's			
Pole, Push			
Recorder, Train Event			
Scraper, Snow			
Tool, Track			
	Bar, Jack		
	Fork, Ballast		
	Gauge, Railway		
	Hammer, Railroad Spike		
	Jack, Track		
	Level, Track		
	Puller, Crosstie		
	Puller, Rail Spike		
	Wrench, Track		*Note:* May also use "Wrench" from Metalworking T&E
Wrench, Locomotive			*Note:* May also use "Wrench" from Metalworking T&E

Sub-Class:
RAIL VEHICLES

Definition: Objects originally created to transport people or goods on or along a fixed route determined by a track, rail, cable, or similar device.

Primary Object Term	Secondary Term	Tertiary Term	Notes
Car, Railroad			
	Car, Freight		
		Boxcar	
		Caboose	
		Car, Coal	
		Car, Container	
		Car, Dump	
		Car, Gondola	
		Car, Hopper	
		Car, Piggyback	
		Car, Rack	
		Car, Refrigerator	
		Car, Stock	
		Car, Tank	
		Flatcar	
		Tender	
	Car, Passenger		
		Car, Baggage	
		Car, Business	*Note:* Use for a car created for use by an executive or official
		Car, Bilevel	
		Car, Crew	
		Car, Dining	
		Car, Dome	
		Car, Express	
		Car, Lounge	
		Car, Self-Propelled Train	
		Car, Sleeping	
		Coach, Rail	
		Office, Railway Post	
	Car, Service		
		Car, Clearance	
		Car, Dynamometer	
		Car, Instructional	
		Car, Scale Test	
		Car, Snowplow	

Primary Object Term	Secondary Term	Tertiary Term	Notes
		Car, Tower	
		Car, Track Geometry	
		Cleaner, Ballast	
		Comboliner	
		Handcar	
		Mover, Rail Car	
		Railgrinder	
		Speeder	
		Spiker, Railway	
		Tamper, Ballast	
Chair, Rail			
Locomotive			
	Locomotive, Diesel-Electric		
	Locomotive, Diesel-Hydraulic		
	Locomotive, Electric		
	Locomotive, Gasoline		
	Locomotive, Gasoline-Electric		
	Locomotive, Gear		
	Locomotive, Steam		
		Locomotive, Articulated	
		Locomotive, Geared	
		Locomotive, Tank	
	Locomotive, Turbine		
Sled, Rocket			
Train			*Note:* Use only when cataloging a complete unit of locomotive(s) and cars; may also use terms for individual units
	Train, Freight		
	Train, Passenger		
Vehicle, Transit Railway			
	Car, Funicular		
	Car, Monorail		
	Car, Subway		
	Lift, Chair		
	Lift, Gondola		
	Streetcar		

Primary Object Term	Secondary Term	Tertiary Term	Notes
		Car, Cable	
		Horsecar	
		Trolley	
	Telpher		

Class:
WATER TRANSPORTATION EQUIPMENT

Definition: Objects originally created to transport people or goods on or under water.

Sub-Class:
WATER TRANSPORTATION ACCESSORIES

Definition: Objects originally created as accessories for the transportation of people or goods on or under water. Included are objects created to be parts of watercraft.

Primary Object Term	Secondary Term	Tertiary Term	Notes
Bag, Buoyancy			
Bailer, Boat			
Board, Tally			*Note:* Use for the board with printed instructions employed during rescue operations; the term does not refer to tallying cargo
Bollard			
Box, Faking			
Box, Ship's Log			
Bucket, Deck			
Buoy, Mooring			
Cable, Marine			
Cask, Harness			
Chain, Marine			
	Chain, Anchor		
Chair, Boatswain's			
Component, Watercraft			*Note:* This generic term may be used for a structural part or integral piece of gear not listed here or may be used in addition to terms from other sub-classes, such as Navigational Equipment
	Anchor		
	Beakhead		
	Bell, Nautical		*Note:* May also use "Bell" from Sound Communication Devices
		Bell, Ship's	
	Bimini		
	Binnacle		
	Bitt		
	Board, Bunk		
	Bowgrace		
	Bracket, Ship's Bell		
	Breasthook		
	Bridge, Ship's		
	Bulwark		

Primary Object Term	Secondary Term	Tertiary Term	Notes
	Bung, Boat		
	Capstan		
	Carving, Marine		*Note:* May also use "Carving" from Art
		Billethead	
		Board, Gangway	*Note:* Use for the carved board that flanks a gangplank
		Carving, Cathead	
		Carving, Paddlebox	
		Carving, Stern	
		Carving, Taffrail	
		Figurehead	
		Trailboard	
	Centerboard		
	Clamp, Beam		
	Cleat		
	Coaming		
	Compass, Ship's		*Note:* May also use "Compass" from Navigational Equipment
		Compass, Binnacle	
		Compass, Box	
	Cover, Hatch		
	Cover, Hawse		
	Crow's-Nest		
	Crutch, Boom		
	Daggerboard		
	Davit		*Note:* May also use "Crane" from Mechanical Devices
		Davit, Anchor	
		Davit, Boat	
	Decking, Watercraft		
	Dodger, Boat		
	Engine, Watercraft		*Note:* May also use an "Engine" term from Power Producing Equipment
	Euphroe		
	Fantail		
	Fender, Watercraft		
	Flagstaff, Watercraft		
		Jackstaff	
		Staff, Ensign	
	Forecastle		

Primary Object Term	Secondary Term	Tertiary Term	Notes
	Frame, Transom		
	Frame, Watercraft		
	Horse, Sheet		
	House, Pilot		
	Hull		
	Keel		
	Keelson		
	Knee, Watercraft		
	Knighthead		
	Lamp, Watercraft		*Note:* May also use a suitable "Lamp" term from Lighting Devices
		Lamp, Anchor	
		Lamp, Binnacle	
		Lamp, Stern	
		Lantern, Battle	
		Light, Masthead	
		Light, Navigation	
		Light, Overtaking	
		Light, Watercraft Running	
	Leeboard		
	Oarlock		
		Pin, Thole	
	Ornament, Watercraft		
		Ornament, Masthead	
		Ornament, Pilothouse	
		Ornament, Yacht	
	Outrigger		
	Pedestal, Wheel		
	Pin, Belaying		
	Pinrail		
	Pipe, Scupper		
	Prism, Deck		
	Propeller, Watercraft		
	Rack, Life Ring		
	Rack, Signal Flag		
	Rail, Watercraft		
		Rail, Fife	

Primary Object Term	Secondary Term	Tertiary Term	Notes
	Rib, Watercraft		
	Rigging		*Note:* Terms for hoists and pulleys are listed under Mechanical Devices
		Bead, Parrel	
		Bullseye	
		Chock, Mast	
		Deadeye	
		Fitting, Boom	
		Halyard	
		Hank, Jib	
		Hoop, Mast	
		Iron, Clew	
		Line, Tack	
		Parrel	
		Screw, Rigging	
		Sheet	*Note:* Use for a line used to control the clew of a sail
		Shroud	
		Spreader	
		Stay	
	Rode, Anchor		
	Rudder		
	Sail		
		Foresail	
		Genoa	
		Headsail	
		Jib	
		Mainsail	
		Mizzen	
		Sail, Fore-and-Aft	
		Sail, Square	
		Spanker	
		Spinnaker	
		Staysail	
		Topsail	
	Scuttle, Deadlight		
	Scuttle, Deck		
	Seacock		
	Seat, Watercraft		
	Shutter, Deadlight		

Primary Object Term	Secondary Term	Tertiary Term	Notes
	Sign, Nautical		*Note:* May also use "Sign" from Visual Communication Devices
		Board, Name	
		Quarterboard	
	Spar		
		Boom	
		Bowsprit	
		Gaff	
		Jibboom	
		Mast	
		Pole, Spinnaker	
		Sprit	
		Yard	
	Stanchion, Watercraft		
	Sternpost		
	Taffrail		
	Telegraph, Ship's		
	Tiller		
	Unit, Hydrostatic Release		
	Wheel, Watercraft Steering		
		Wheel, Ship's	
	Wheelbox		
	Whistle, Watercraft		*Note:* May also use "Whistle" from Sound Communication Devices
		Whistle, Boat	
		Whistle, Ship	
	Windlass, Ship's		*Note:* May also use "Windlass" from Mechanical Devices
	Window, Watercraft		
		Porthole	
Container, Chart			
	Case, Chart		
	Chest, Chart		
Cordage, Marine			*Note:* Use for rope or other line used in an unspecified marine context
Cover, Boat			
Cover, Motor			
Cradle, Boat			

Primary Object Term	Secondary Term	Tertiary Term	Notes
Gangplank			
Gun, Line-Throwing			
	Gun, Lyle		
Hawser			
Hook, Boat			
Ladder, Watercraft			
	Ladder, Jacob's		
	Ladder, Ship's		
Lantern, Ship's			*Note:* May also use "Lantern" from Lighting Devices
Log, Nautical			*Note:* Use for an instrument that measures a ship's speed; for a ship's record book, use "Log, Ship's" from Other Documents
	Log, Impeller		
	Log, Pit		
	Log, Taffrail		
Motor, Outboard			*Note:* May also use "Motor" from Power Producing Equipment
Net, Torpedo			
Oar			
	Oar, Sculling		
		Yuloh	
	Oar, Steering		
	Oar, Sweep		
Paddle, Boat			
	Paddle, Canoe		
	Paddle, Double-Bladed		
Pistol, Line Throwing			
Preserver, Life			
	Buoy, Breeches		
	Float, Life		
	Jacket, Life		
	Ring, Life		
Pump, Bilge			*Note:* May also use "Pump" from Mechanical Devices
Quant			
Stone, Ballast			
Telltale			
Weight, Heaving Line			

Sub-Class:
WATERCRAFT

Definition: Objects originally created to transport people or goods on or under water. Watercraft terms are generally organized by functional context; watercraft that may be used in multiple contexts are organized by size (boat, ship) or positional use (semisubmersible, subsurface), and organization at more specific levels take other properties, such as shape and power source, into account. Catalogers are encouraged to use multiple terms to cross-index as needed (e.g., "Ship, Clipper" and "Ship, Sailing;" "Whaleboat" and "Boat"); some cross-referencing suggestions are made in notes below.

Primary Object Term	Secondary Term	Tertiary Term	Notes
Boat			*Note:* Small vessels with no specific purpose or multiple purposes are organized under this term, which itself may be used in addition to functional vessel terms as appropriate
	Bateau		
	Boat, Beach		
	Boat, Durham		
	Boat, Gunning		
		Boat, Bushwack	
		Duckboat	
		Skiff, Rail	
		Sneakbox	
	Boat, Inflatable		*Note:* May also use a term to describe the boat's function (e.g., "Lifeboat")
	Boat, Skin		
		Boat, Bull	
		Coracle	
		Umiak	
	Canoe		
		Canoe, Bark	
		Canoe, Decked	
		Canoe, Dugout	
		Canoe, Outrigger	
		Canoe, Sailing	
		Canoe, War	
		Kayak	*Note:* May also use "Boat, Skin" if appropriate
	Gondola		
	Guideboat		
		Boat, Rangely	
		Guideboat, Adirondack	

Primary Object Term	Secondary Term	Tertiary Term	Notes
	Johnboat		
	Motorboat		
		Launch, Diesel	
		Launch, Gasoline	
		Launch, Naphtha	
		Launch, Steam	
		Outboard	
		Speedboat	
	Motorsailer		
	Multihull		
		Catamaran	
		Trimaran	
	Peapod		
	Pram		
	Punt		
	Rowboat		
		Wherry	
		Whitehall	
	Sailboat		
		Bugeye	
		Catboat	
		Cutter, Sailing	
		Daysailer	*Note:* May also use "Classboat" if appropriate
		Dhow	
		Dinghy, Abaco	
		Dinghy, Bermuda	
		Felucca	
		Iceboat	
		Ketch	
		Knockabout	
		Pink	
		Pram, Sailing	
		Sandbagger	
		Sharpie	
		Sloop	
		Yawl	
	Sampan		
	Skiff		
		Skiff, Flatiron	

Primary Object Term	Secondary Term	Tertiary Term	Notes
		Skiff, St. Lawrence River	
Craft, Competition			
	Classboat		*Note:* May also use "Sailboat"
	Raceboat		
	Shell		
Craft, Pleasure			*Note:* May also use "Motorboat," "Sailboat," or other watercraft terms as appropriate with this term and narrower terms
	Boat, Pedal		
	Boat, Pontoon		
	Boat, Sport Fishing		
		Bassboat	*Note:* May also use "Outboard"
		Sportfisherman	*Note:* May also use "Speedboat"
	Cruiser, Cabin		*Note:* May also use "Motorboat"
	Dinghy, Sailing		
	Houseboat		
	Runabout		*Note:* May also use "Motorboat"
	Ski, Jet		
	Yacht		
Raft			
Semisubmersible			
Ship			*Note:* Large vessels with no specific purpose or multiple purposes are organized under this term, which itself may be used in addition to functional vessel terms as appropriate
	Ship, Sailing		
		Bark	
		Bark, Jackass	
		Barkentine	
		Brig	
		Brig, Hermaphrodite	
		Brigantine	
		Carrack	
		Clipper, Baltimore	
		Galleon	
		Junk	
		Pinky	
		Schooner	
	Ship, Training		*Note:* May also use "Vessel, Naval" if appropriate

Primary Object Term	Secondary Term	Tertiary Term	Notes
	Steamship		
Steamboat			
	Steamer, Paddle		
Vessel, Commercial Fishing			
	Banker		
	Boat, Buoy		
	Boat, Hampton		
	Boat, Tonging		
	Dory		
		Dory, Banks	
		Dory, Swampscott	
	Garvey		
	Ship, Factory		
	Sloop, Fishing		*Note:* May also use "Sloop"
		Sloop, Friendship	*Note:* May also use "Yacht" if appropriate
		Sloop, Noank	
	Vessel, Dredging		*Note:* For dredging vessels not used for fishing, use "Dredge" instead
		Skipjack	*Note:* May also use "Ship, Sailing"
	Vessel, Line Fishing		
		Longliner	
		Schooner, Fishing	
		Skiff, Crabbing	*Note:* May also use "Skiff"
		Vessel, Handlining	
	Vessel, Net Fishing		
		Dragger	
		Driveboat	*Note:* May also use "Rowboat"
		Gillnetter	
		Seiner	
		Steamer, Menhaden	*Note:* May also use "Steamboat"
		Trawler	
	Vessel, Trapping		
		Crabber	
		Lobsterboat	
	Whaler		
		Catcher, Whale	
		Whaleboat	
		Whaleship	
	Whaler, Tancook		*Note:* May also use "Schooner"

Primary Object Term	Secondary Term	Tertiary Term	Notes
	Wherry, Salmon		
Vessel, Emergency			
	Fireboat		
	Lifeboat		*Note:* May also use "Boat, Ship's"
		Lifeboat, Rescue	
		Lifeboat, Ship's	
		Lifecar	
		Raft, Life	*Note:* May also use "Raft"
		Surfboat	
Vessel, Merchant			
	Ferry		
		Ferry, Car	
	Motorship		
	Ship, Clipper		
	Ship, Packet		
	Slaver		
	Vessel, Cargo		
		Barge	
		Boat, Canal	
		Collier	
		Freighter, Bulk	
		Gundalow	
		Lighter, Marine	
		Raft, Lumber	
		Scow	
		Ship, Container	
		Tanker	
		Vessel, Refrigerator	
	Vessel, Passenger		
		Boat, Excursion	
		Liner, Ocean	
		Riverboat	
		Ship, Cruise	
		Submarine, Commercial	*Note:* May also use "Submarine"
		Taxi, Water	
Vessel, Naval			
	Barge, Admiral's		
	Galley, Row		
	Oiler		

Primary Object Term	Secondary Term	Tertiary Term	Notes
	Ship, Hospital		
	Submarine, Naval		*Note:* May also use "Submarine"
		Submarine, Attack	
		Submarine, Ballistic Missile	
	Transport, Naval		
	Warship		
		Battleship	
		Boat, Patrol	
		Boat, Torpedo	
		Carrier, Aircraft	
		Chaser, Submarine	
		Corvette	
		Craft, Landing	
		Cruiser, Guided Missile	
		Cruiser, Heavy	
		Cruiser, Light	
		David	*Note:* May also use "Semisubmersible"
		Destroyer	
		Frigate	
		Gunboat, Patrol	
		Minelayer	
		Minesweeper	
		Privateer	
		Ram	
		Sloop-of-War	
		Tender, Submarine	
		Vessel, Bomb	
Vessel, Planing			*Note:* Use only for vessels designed for planing, not for ordinary motorboats that plane
	Hydrofoil		
	Hydroplane		
Vessel, Remotely Operated			*Note:* May also use "Vessel, Naval," "Vessel, Research," or other appropriate term
Vessel, Research			
	Submarine, Research		*Note:* May also use "Submarine"
	Vessel, Survey		
Vessel, Service			

Primary Object Term	Secondary Term	Tertiary Term	Notes
	Barge, Training		
	Boat, Pilot		
	Boat, Ship's		
		Boat, Jolly	
		Dinghy	
		Launch	
		Longboat	
		Pinnace	
		Yawlboat	
	Cutter, Coast Guard		
	Cutter, Revenue		
	Dredge		
	Dry-Dock, Floating		
	Icebreaker		
	Lightship		
	Pontoon		
	Tender, Buoy		
	Tender, Yacht		*Note:* May also use "Boat, Ship's" if appropriate
	Tugboat		*Note:* Use for a vessel that tows ships and barges
		Towboat	*Note:* Use for a vessel limited to pushing barges
	Vessel, Petroleum Service		
Watercraft, Subsurface			
	Submarine		
	Submersible		
		Bathyscaphe	*Note:* May also use "Vessel, Research" if appropriate
		Bathysphere	*Note:* May also use "Vessel, Research" if appropriate
		Mesoscaphe	

Category 8:
COMMUNICATION OBJECTS

Definition: **Objects originally created as expressions of human thought. Communication objects comment on, interpret, or enhance people's environments. Communication objects can function symbolically or literally. This category excludes the tools and equipment that are used to create communication objects.**

Class:
ADVERTISING MEDIA

Definition: Objects originally created to call public attention to a product, service, or event and to elicit a specific response in regard to a product, service, or event. Generally, the intended response is to urge people to acquire, use, or participate in the product, service, or event that is being advertised. Note: Subjects and themes of advertisements may be indicated in a separate subject field.

Primary Object Term	Secondary Term	Tertiary Term	Notes
Ad, Print			
	Ad, Magazine		
	Ad, Newspaper		
Advertisement			*Note:* Use this generic term in addition to terms from other classes to index advertising objects that may serve other functions as well, e.g., "T-Shirt" from Main Garments, "Sticker, Bumper" from Other Documents
Balloon, Promotional			
	Balloon, Political		
Banner, Promotional			
Broadside			
Brochure			
Button, Promotional			*Note:* Use for a button designed to promote a non-political cause, belief, organization, product, service, or event; may also use "Symbol, Social" from Belief Symbols for a button that communicates personal allegiance to the promoted subject
Card, Advertising			
	Card, Political		
	Card, Show		
	Card, Tobacco		
	Card, Trade		
Catalog, Sales			
	Catalog, Auction		
	Catalog, Mail Order		
	Catalog, Trade		
Flag, Promotional			

Primary Object Term	Secondary Term	Tertiary Term	Notes
	Pennant, Promotional		
Flier			
	Circular		
	Flier, Political		*Note:* May be used in addition to "Circular" or "Handbill"
	Flier, Trade		*Note:* May be used in addition to "Circular" or "Handbill"
	Handbill		
		Hanger, Door	
Model, Product			*Note:* May also use "Model" from Other Documents; information about what the model represents should be recorded in a subject field
Novelty, Promotional			
Piece, Display			
Pin, Promotional			*Note:* Use for a pin designed to promote a non-political cause, belief, organization, product, service, or event; may also use "Symbol, Social" from Belief Symbols for a pin that communicates personal allegiance to the promoted subject
Placard			
	Sign, Picket		
Poster			
	Poster, Music		
	Poster, Political		
	Poster, Theater		
		Card, Lobby	
Premium			*Note:* May also use terms from other classes for premiums that serve other functions as well
	Premium, Tobacco		
		Flannel, Tobacco	
		Ribbon, Cigar	
		Silk, Tobacco	
Ribbon, Promotional			*Note:* Use for a ribbon designed to promote a non-political cause, belief, organization, product, service, or event; may also use "Symbol, Social" from Belief Symbols for a ribbon that communicates personal allegiance to the promoted subject
Sign, Advertising			*Note:* May also use "Sign" from Visual Communication Devices

Primary Object Term	Secondary Term	Tertiary Term	Notes
	Billboard		
	Board, Sandwich		
	Marquee		
	Sign, Trade		
	Sign, Yard		
Symbol, Trade			
	Figure, Tobacconist's		
	Pole, Barber		

Class:
ART

Definition: Objects originally created for the expression and communication of ideas, values, or attitudes through images, symbols, or abstractions. Art often reflects aesthetic pleasure or demonstrates creative skills and dexterity. Art can be uniquely created or it can be produced in a medium that allows many duplicates to be made. Terms from this class, whether the generic "Artwork" term or more specific terms, may be used in addition to terms from other classes that index objects by other, practical functions (e.g., "Vase" and "Artwork," "Pillow" and "Embroidery," "Mocock" and "Quillwork," "Moccasin" and "Beadwork").

Primary Object Term	Secondary Term	Tertiary Term	Notes
Art, Digital			*Note:* May also use an appropriate term from Art to describe the type of work, e.g., "Drawing," "Portrait"
Art, Trench			
Artwork			*Note:* Use this generic term for art that cannot be described with any of the other terms in this class
Beadwork			
Calligraphy			
Collage			
Decoupage			
Drawing			
Featherwork			
Fretwork			
Hairwork			
Knot, Ornamental			
Montage			
Mural			
Needlework			
	Appliqué		
		Mola	
	Cloth, Flower		*Note:* May also use "Appliqué" or "Embroidery" as appropriate
		Cloth, Story	*Note:* May also use "Picture, History"
	Crochet		
	Embroidery		
		Arpillera	
		Crewelwork	
		Cross-Stitch	
		Embroidery, Punched Paper	

Primary Object Term	Secondary Term	Tertiary Term	Notes
		Needlepoint	
		Sampler	
	Knitwork		
	Quilt		*Note:* May also use "Quilt, Bed" from Bedding or "Hanging, Wall" from Decorative Furnishings to indicate function, if known
Painting			
	Painting, Bark		
	Painting, Ceiling		
	Painting, Miniature		
	Painting, Panel		
	Painting, Wall		
Pastel			
Picture			*Note:* This generic term and all terms organized under it should be used in addition to a term describing form or medium (e.g., "Drawing," "Painting," "Sculpture," "Needlework") and may also be used with Graphic Document terms such as "Photograph"
	Cityscape		
	Landscape		
	Petrograph		
		Petroglyph	*Note:* May also use "Engraving" from Graphic Documents
	Picture, Animal		
	Picture, Genre		
	Picture, History		
	Portrait		
	Seascape		
	Still-Life		
	Townscape		
Picture, Woven			
	Stevengraph		
Piece, Floral			
	Bouquet, Floral		
	Flora, Pressed		
	Picture, Flora		
		Picture, Leaf	
		Picture, Seed	

Primary Object Term	Secondary Term	Tertiary Term	Notes
	Wreath, Floral		
Plaque, Decorative			
Quillwork			
Ribbonwork			
Sculpture			
	Bust		
	Carving		
		Pole, Totem	
		Scrimshaw	
		Whimsey	
	Casting		
		Mask, Life	
	Construction		
		Assemblage	
		Bottle, Impossible	
	Intaglio		
	Jug, Face		
	Maquette		
	Miniature		*Note:* May also use “Model” from Other Documents or “Toy” from Toys if appropriate; information about what the miniature represents should be recorded in a subject field; this information may be entered according to the naming conventions and object terms used throughout *Nomenclature*
	Mobile		
	Relief		
		Bas-Relief	
		Cameo	*Note:* May also use a term from Adornment if appropriate
		Relief, High	
	Sculpture, Origami		
	Statue		
		Figurine	*Note:* For more specific figurines, e.g., “Figurine, Animal,” “Figurine, Bird,” and “Figurine, Group,” use the term “Figurine” and enter the subject depicted in a subject field
		Statue, Garden	
Shellwork			
	Valentine, Sailor’s		

Primary Object Term	Secondary Term	Tertiary Term	Notes
Silhouette			
Sketch			
Tapestry			*Note:* May also use "Hanging, Wall" from Decorative Furnishings
Work, Cut Paper			

Class:
CEREMONIAL OBJECTS

Definition: Objects originally created for carrying on governmental, fraternal, religious, or other organized and sanctioned societal activities. Such objects are intended to evoke, symbolize, or express certain aspects of the traditions or heritage of a community or group of people. Usually, they are associated with rituals or ceremonies. This class includes: (1) any religious object, such as communion cups and altar pieces; note that personal devotional objects (such as religious medals or talismans) and religious symbols of office (such as vestments or crosiers) are classified under Personal Symbols; (2) any object used specifically in a ceremony concerned with a major personal event or crisis, such as birth, puberty, sickness, or death, or concerned with a community event or crisis, such as a harvest festival or the need for rain; and (3) any object, except for personal symbols, used in the ceremonial activities of a fraternity, lodge, club, governmental, or military organization, such as the pennant of a Girl Scout troop.

Sub-Class:
FUNERARY OBJECTS

Definition: Objects intended for use in funerals, burials, mourning, or other death rites, independent of formal religious worship. This sub-class does not include structures, vehicles, memorabilia, or official records of death or burial.

Primary Object Term	Secondary Term	Tertiary Term	Notes
Armband, Mourning			*Note:* May also use "Armband" from Clothing Accessories
Badge, Mourning			
Bottle, Tear			
Card, Mourning			
Cloth, Mourning			
Container, Funerary			
	Case, Mummy		
	Casket		
	Coffin		
	Jar, Canopic		
	Ossuary		
	Sarcophagus		
	Urn, Cremation		
	Vault, Burial		
Disk, Pi			
Dress, Mourning			*Note:* May also use "Dress" from Main Garments
Good, Grave			
Hearse, Candle			*Note:* May also use "Candleholder" from Lighting Holders
Mask, Burial			

Primary Object Term	Secondary Term	Tertiary Term	Notes
Ornament, Mourning			*Note:* Use for a piece of mourning jewelry in addition to an appropriate term from Adornment or Clothing Accessories, e.g., "Earring," "Pin"
	Ring, Mourning		*Note:* May also use "Ring" from Body Adornments
Pall, Funeral			
Pillow, Coffin			
Plate, Coffin			
Quilt, Mourning			*Note:* May also use "Quilt" from Art
Sculpture, Funerary			*Note:* May also use "Sculpture" from Art
	Effigy		
	Shawabti		
Shroud, Burial			
	Kittel		
Slab, Tomb			
Stand, Funerary			
	Bier		
	Catafalque		
Tombstone			
	Footstone		
	Headstone		
	Marker, Grave		*Note:* Use for a flat stone set into the ground
Veil, Mourning			*Note:* May also use "Veil" from Headwear

Sub-Class:
HOLIDAY OBJECTS

Definition: Objects intended for use in the celebration of religious or secular holidays, independent of formal religious worship or general partying and gift-giving.

Primary Object Term	Secondary Term	Tertiary Term	Notes
Bag, Afikomen			
Basket, Easter			
Box, Etrog			
Container, Trick or Treat			
	Bag, Trick or Treat		
Costume, Holiday			*Note:* May also use appropriate terms from Clothing
Cover, Matzah			
Decoration, Holiday			*Note:* Terms under this broad term may be used in addition to the generic term "Decoration" from Decorative Furnishings, especially for handcrafted items
	Garland		
	Holder, Stocking		
	Hook, Ornament		
	Light, Holiday		*Note:* May also use "Light, String" from Lighting Devices
		Light, Christmas Tree	
	Ornament, Holiday		
		Ornament, Christmas Tree	
	Stocking, Christmas		
	Tinsel		
	Tree, Holiday		
		Tree, Christmas	
	Wreath, Holiday		
Egg, Easter			
Holder, Tree			
Mask, Holiday			

Sub-Class:
ORGANIZATIONAL OBJECTS

Definition: Objects routinely used by organizations, businesses, governments, or other corporate bodies in codified formal proceedings or ritual events. These objects sometimes serve to symbolize civic or corporate identities. This sub-class does not include objects used to associate individuals with corporate bodies; these are organized under Personal Symbols.

Primary Object Term	Secondary Term	Tertiary Term	Notes
Belt, Flag			*Note:* Use for a belt or harness that supports a flag while it is carried
Block, Gavel			
Bottle, Christening			
Bunting			
Calumet			*Note:* May also use "Pipe, Smoking" from Smoking & Recreational Drug Equipment
Device, Voting			
	Booth, Voting		
	Container, Ballot		
		Bag, Ballot	
		Box, Ballot	
	Machine, Voting		
	Marble, Voting		
Flag			
	Guidon		
	Pennant		
		Pennon	
Gavel			
Holder, Flagpole			
Medal, Peace			
Plaque			
Standard			
Stick, Talking			
Torch, Campaign			*Note:* May also use "Lamp" from Lighting Devices
Wheel, Jury			

Sub-Class:
PARTY ACCESSORIES

Definition: Objects intended for use at parties or on gift-giving or other special occasions, but not exclusively for weddings.

Primary Object Term	Secondary Term	Tertiary Term	Notes
Bag, Gift			
Balloon, Toy			*Note:* May also use "Toy" from Toys
Blower, Party			
Bow, Gift			
Box, Gift			
Candle, Cake			*Note:* May also use "Candle" from Other Lighting Accessories
Confetti			
Decoration, Cake			
Favor			
Hat, Party			*Note:* May also use "Hat" from Headwear
Ornament, Party			
Pick, Floral			
Ribbon, Gift Wrap			
Streamer			
Tag, Gift			
Wrap, Gift			

Sub-Class:
RELIGIOUS OBJECTS

Definition: Objects intended for use in public religious worship or spiritual ceremonies.

Primary Object Term	Secondary Term	Tertiary Term	Notes
Altar			
Aspergillum			
Ball, Crystal			
Bell, Altar			
Bema			
Board, Hymn			
Board, Mass			
Board, Spirit			*Note:* A similar object, intended as a toy, is listed as "Set, Ouija" in Toys
Bull-Roarer			
Butsudan			
Candle, Votive			*Note:* May also use "Candle" from Other Lighting Accessories
Candlestick, Religious			*Note:* May also use "Candlestick" from Lighting Holders
	Chanukiah		
	Kinara		
	Menorah		
Chair, Altar			*Note:* May also use "Chair" from Seating Furniture
	Cathedra		
Confessional			
Container, Offering			
	Bag, Offering		
	Basket, Offering		
	Bowl, Offering		
	Box, Alms		
	Dish, Offering		
	Plate, Offering		
	Tray, Offering		
Container, Ritual			*Note:* May also use an appropriate generic term from Containers
	Ampulla		
	Ark, Torah		
	Bag, Medicine		
	Boat, Incense		
	Bottle, Witch		
	Burse		
	Case, Chalice		

Primary Object Term	Secondary Term	Tertiary Term	Notes
	Case, Ciborium		
	Case, Mezuzah		
	Case, Monstrance		
	Censer		
	Chrismatory		
	Ciborium		
	Cup, Kiddush		*Note:* May also use "Cup, Wine" from Drinking Vessels
	Cup, Washing		
	Monstrance		
	Navette		
	Paten		
	Phiale		
	Plate, Seder		*Note:* May also use "Plate, Food" from Eating Vessels
	Pyx		
	Reliquary		
	Tabernacle		
	Vase, Altar		*Note:* May also use "Vase, Flower" from Horticultural Containers
	Vase, Temple		
	Vessel, Baptismal		
		Bowl, Baptismal	
		Cup, Baptismal	
		Dish, Baptismal	
		Font, Baptismal	
	Vessel, Communion		
		Chalice	*Note:* May also use "Cup, Wine" from Drinking Vessels
		Cruet, Altar	
		Cup, Communion	*Note:* May also use "Cup" from Drinking Vessels
		Pitcher, Communion	
		Plate, Communion	
		Set, Communion	
		Spoon, Communion	
	Vessel, Holy Water		
		Bottle, Holy Water	
		Font, Holy Water	
	Vessel, Libation		
		Bowl, Libation	

Primary Object Term	Secondary Term	Tertiary Term	Notes
		Cup, Libation	
		Jug, Libation	
		Tank, Libation	
		Vase, Libation	
Covering, Altar			
	Cloth, Credence		
	Cloth, Fair Linen		
	Corporal		
	Dossal		
	Frontal		
	Purificator		
	Superfrontal		
	Veil, Chalice		
	Veil, Ciborium		
	Veil, Tabernacle		
Credence			*Note:* May also use "Table" from Support Furniture
Doll, Voodoo			
Dress, Confirmation			*Note:* May also use "Dress" from Main Garments
Dress, Jingle			*Note:* May also use "Dress" from Main Garments
Dressing, Torah			
Flabellum			
Flail, Ritual			*Note:* May also use "Flail" from Percussive Weapons
Garment, Baptismal			
	Gown, Baptismal		*Note:* May also use "Dress" from Main Garments
	Jacket, Baptismal		*Note:* May also use "Jacket" from Main Garments
Grager			*Note:* May also use "Rattle" from Sound Communication Devices
Host			
Hymnal			
Kneeler			
	Prie-Dieu		*Note:* May also use "Chair" from Seating Furniture or "Desk" from Storage & Display Furniture depending on the nature of the prie-dieu
Knife, Sacrificial			*Note:* May also use "Knife, Weapon" from Edged Weapons

Primary Object Term	Secondary Term	Tertiary Term	Notes
Lamp, Religious			*Note:* May also use “Lamp” from Lighting Devices
	Lamp, Hanukkah		
	Lamp, Mosque		
	Lamp, Sabbath		
	Lamp, Sanctuary		
	Lamp, Votive		
Lavabo			*Note:* May also use “Sink” from Plumbing & Drainage Elements
Manuterge			*Note:* May also use “Towel” from Hygiene Objects
Mask, Ritual			
Object, Divination			*Note:* Use for bones, stones, figures, dice, etc., that are cast and then interpreted to predict the future. Also use for the casting surface or container for such objects, e.g., divination tray, bowl, or box
Plaque, Religious			
Pulpit			
Rattle, Ceremonial			*Note:* May also use “Rattle” from Sound Communication Devices
Relic, Religious			
Robe, Séance			*Note:* May also use “Robe” from Main Garments
Rug, Prayer			*Note:* May also use “Rug” from Floor Coverings
Shofar			
Staff, Dance			
Stand, Missal			*Note:* May also use “Stand” from Storage & Display Accessories
Stick, Prayer			
	Paho		
Stone, Lightning			
Symbol, Religious			
	Altarpiece		
		Diptych	
		Retable	
		Triptych	
	Creche		
	Cross		*Note:* May also use “Sculpture” from Art or “Pendant, Religious” from Belief Symbols, as appropriate

Primary Object Term	Secondary Term	Tertiary Term	Notes
		Crucifix	
	Figure, Religious		
	Icon		
	Idol		
	Kachina		
	Pax		
	Standard, Religious		*Note:* Use for a flag or object depicting a symbolic representation carried as part of a religious ceremony
	Station of the Cross		
	Tiki		
Table, Communion			*Note:* May also use "Table" from Support Furniture
Text, Religious			*Note:* May also use "Book" or other suitable term from Documentary Objects
	Bible		
	Book, Prayer		
	Breviary		
	Card, Altar		
	Card, Devotional		
	Card, Prayer		
	Koran		
	Mezuzah		
	Missal		
	Scroll, Prayer		
	Tanakh		
	Torah, Sepher		
Tool, Incense			
	Shovel, Incense		
	Spoon, Incense		
	Tongs, Incense		
Wheel, Prayer			
Yad			

Sub-Class:
WEDDING OBJECTS

Definition: Objects intended for use in weddings, independent of formal religious worship or general partying and gift-giving.

Primary Object Term	Secondary Term	Tertiary Term	Notes
Bouquet, Wedding			
Bowl, Marriage			
Cup, Bride's			
Dress, Bridesmaid			*Note:* May also use "Dress" from Main Garments
Dress, Wedding			*Note:* May also use "Dress" from Main Garments
Glass, Toasting			*Note:* May also use "Glass, Wine" from Drinking Vessels
Huppah			
Pillow, Ring			
Ring, Wedding			*Note:* May also use "Ring, Finger" from Body Adornments
Veil, Wedding			*Note:* May also use "Veil" from Headwear
Wreath, Wedding			*Note:* May also use "Wreath, Hair" from Headwear

Class:
DOCUMENTARY OBJECTS

Definition: Objects originally created to communicate information to people. Unlike Advertising Media, a Documentary Object is not generally intended to elicit a specific response in regards to products, services, or events. Instead, it presents a point of view, an image, or a set of ideas, often with the aim of enlightening or swaying the attitude of people. This class includes printed documents on paper and also non-print, non-paper objects that serve a documentary purpose.

Sub-Class:
ADMINISTRATIVE RECORDS

Definition: Records that document organizational functions or business operations.

Primary Object Term	Secondary Term	Tertiary Term	Notes
Agenda			
Ballot			
Book, Record			
Bylaws			
Constitution			
Minutes			
Order, Work			
Prospectus			
Record, Personnel			
	Application, Job		
	Resume		
Record, Shipping			
	Bill of Lading		
	Manifest		
	Slip, Packing		
	Waybill		
Report			
	Proceedings		
	Report, Administrative		
		Report, Annual	
		Report, Quarterly	
	Report, Technical		
Resolution			
Rules			

Sub-Class:
DECLARATORY DOCUMENTS

Definition: Public notices intended to be posted or distributed, the primary purpose of which is not advertising.

Primary Object Term	Secondary Term	Tertiary Term	Notes
Announcement			
	Announcement, Anniversary		
	Announcement, Award		
	Announcement, Birth		
	Announcement, Business		
	Announcement, Funeral		
	Announcement, Graduation		
	Announcement, Meeting		
	Announcement, Moving		
	Announcement, Wedding		
	Notice, Legal		
	Obituary		
	Release, News		
Banner			
	Flag, Service		
Declaration			
Decree			
Editorial			
Kit, Press			
Manifesto			
Proclamation			
Testimonial			

Sub-Class:
FINANCIAL RECORDS

Definition: Records that document the exchange or management of money or other items of value.

Primary Object Term	Secondary Term	Tertiary Term	Notes
Appraisal			
Bankbook			
Budget			
Certificate of Deposit			
Certificate, Stock			
Checkbook			*Note:* May also use "Check, Bank" from Exchange Media
Estimate			
Mortgage			
Receipt			
	Book, Receipt		
Record, Bookkeeping			
	Blotter		
	Book, Account		
		Ledger	
	Cashbook		
	Daybook		
	Record, Payroll		
		Book, Time	
		Paybook	
		Payroll	
		Timecard	
		Timesheet	
Record, Insurance			
	Policy, Insurance		
Record, Sales			
	Bill of Sale		
	Invoice		
	Order, Purchase		
		Requisition	
	Voucher		
Return, Tax			
Statement, Financial			
	Statement, Bank		
Tally			

Sub-Class:
GOVERNMENT RECORDS

Definition: Records created or maintained by a government agency. Included in this sub-class are legislative, judicial, trade, immigration, patent, military, census, and vital records.

Primary Object Term	Secondary Term	Tertiary Term	Notes
Record, Executive			
	Certificate, Citizenship		
	Lettre de Cachet		
	Pardon		
	Patent		
	Patent, Letters		
	Record, Census		
	Record, Customs		
		Declaration, Customs	
	Record, Immigration		
	Record, Military		
		Discharge, Military	
		Document, Surrender	
		Orders, Military	
		Record, Service	
		Roll, Muster	
	Regulation		
	Roll, Tax		
Record, Judicial			
	Docket		
	Judgment		
	Probate		
	Subpoena		
	Summons		
	Warrant		
	Writ		
Record, Legislative			
	Act		
		Statute	
	Bill, Legislative		
Record, Vital			
	Record, Birth		
		Certificate, Birth	
		Register, Birth	
	Record, Death		
		Certificate, Death	
		Record, Burial	

Primary Object Term	Secondary Term	Tertiary Term	Notes
		Register, Death	
	Record, Marriage		
		Certificate, Marriage	
		License, Marriage	
		Record, Divorce	
		Register, Marriage	

Sub-Class:
GRAPHIC DOCUMENTS

Definition: Documents that provide primarily non-textual visual information. Included in this sub-class are maps, charts, graphs, diagrams, and pictorial works produced through photographic, photomechanical, electronic, printing, or other processes. Terms in this sub-class may be used in addition to terms from Art to index graphic documents that are also works of art.

Primary Object Term	Secondary Term	Tertiary Term	Notes
Book, Flip			
Cartograph			
	Atlas		
		Book, Plat	
	Globe		
	Map		
		Chart, Plotting	
		Map, Road	
		Plat	
		Survey, Land	
Cartoon			
Chart			
	Chart, Color		
	Chart, Flow		
	Chart, Navigational		
	Chart, Organizational		
	Chart, Seating		
	Tree, Family		*Note:* Use for a genealogical chart; for a textual genealogy, use "Book" from Other Documents and indicate genealogy in a subject field
Comic			
	Book, Comic		
	Novel, Graphic		
	Strip, Comic		
Graph			
Photograph			*Note:* Use for a pictorial work produced by the chemical action of radiation on a sensitive surface, or by the capture of an image using electronic photodetectors; for photographs in digital form, also use "Document, Digital" from Other Documents
	Hologram		
	Negative		
		Calotype	

Primary Object Term	Secondary Term	Tertiary Term	Notes
		Negative, Glass Plate	
		Negative, Roll Film	
		Negative, Sheet Film	
	Photograph, Black-and-White		
	Photograph, Color		
	Positive, Direct		
		Ambrotype	
		Daguerreotype	
		Tintype	
	Print, Photographic		
		Anaglyph	
		Carte-de-visite	
		Cyanotype	
		Photograph, Cabinet	
		Print, Albumen	
		Print, Digital	
		Print, Platinum	
		Print, Salted Paper	
		Snapshot	
		Stereograph	
		Stereoview	
	Radiogram		
	Transparency		
		Transparency, Lantern Slide	
		Transparency, Roll Film	
		Transparency, Slide	
Pictograph			
Print			*Note:* Use for a pictorial work produced through a printing process
	Print, Embossed		
	Print, Intaglio		
		Engraving	
		Etching	
	Print, Photomechanical		
		Collotype	
		Photoengraving	
		Photogravure	

Primary Object Term	Secondary Term	Tertiary Term	Notes
		Photolithograph	
		Print, Dye Transfer	
	Print, Planographic		
		Lithograph	
		Monotype	
	Print, Relief		
		Engraving, Wood	
		Etching, Relief	
		Linocut	
		Metalcut	
		Vinylcut	
		Woodcut	
	Print, Screen		*Note:* Use for a print made from screen printing, not printing from a computer screen
Projection			
	Drawing, Architectural		
	Drawing, Technical		
	Elevation		
	Plan		
		Plan, Floor	
		Plan, Site	
	Section		
Rubbing			
Storyboard			
Strip, Zoetrope			

Sub-Class:
INSTRUCTIONAL DOCUMENTS

Definition: Prints or non-print items created to impart, test, or demonstrate knowledge or skill, either in the context of formal teaching and training or in more informal contexts.

Primary Object Term	Secondary Term	Tertiary Term	Notes
Aid, Visual			
Book, Instruction			
Card, Instruction			
	Card, Flash		
Catechism			
Chart, Instructional			
Copybook			
Examination			
Exercise, School			
Grammar			
Guidebook			
Kit, Learning			
Manikin, Teaching			
Manual			
	Manual, Employee		
	Manual, Training		
Pamphlet, Instruction			
Poster, Instructional			
Primer			
	Hornbook		
Recipe			
	Card, Recipe		
	Cookbook		*Note:* May also use "Book" from Other Documents
Sheet, Instruction			
Syllabus			
Textbook			*Note:* May also use "Book" from Other Documents
Workbook			*Note:* May also use "Book" from Other Documents
Worksheet			

Sub-Class:
LEGAL DOCUMENTS

Definition: Documents that pertain to legal actions and rights.

Primary Object Term	Secondary Term	Tertiary Term	Notes
Affidavit			
Agreement			
	Bond, Legal		
	Contract		
		Lease	
	Guaranty		
		Warranty	
	Treaty		
Article of Incorporation			
Award, Contract			
Brief			
Charter			
Claim			
Discharge			
Indenture			
Indictment			
Muniment			
	Deed		
Power of Attorney			
Testimony			
	Deposition		
	Oath		
Ticket, Traffic			
Will			

Sub-Class:
LITERARY WORKS

Definition: Written or printed items that express creative works intended to be read, heard, or performed. Such works include fictional and non-fictional literature, oral presentations, music, and theatrical productions.

Primary Object Term	Secondary Term	Tertiary Term	Notes
Abstract			
Anthology			
Article			
Biography			
Composition, Musical			
	Book, Music		
		Songbook	
	Music, Sheet		
	Score		
	Sheet, Song		
Essay			
History			
Memoir			
Monograph			
Narrative			
Novel			
Play			
Poem			
Prayer			
Reminiscence			
Review			
Script			
Speech			
	Eulogy		
	Lecture		
	Sermon		
Thesis			
	Dissertation		
Transcript			
Travelogue			
Treatise			
	Tract		

Sub-Class:
MEMORABILIA

Definition: Tokens of remembrance or commemoration of a person, place, event, or experience. This sub-class includes objects created to contain or display such tokens.

Primary Object Term	Secondary Term	Tertiary Term	Notes
Album			
	Album, Autograph		*Note:* May also use "Book, Writing" from Writing Media
	Album, Card		
	Album, Photograph		
	Album, Postcard		
	Album, Stamp		
	Book, Baby		
	Book, Bridal		
	Scrapbook		
Capsule, Time			
Case, Commemorative			
Commemorative			*Note:* This generic term may be used in addition to terms from other classes to index commemorative objects that serve other functions as well
	Card, Commemorative		
	Certificate, Commemorative		
	Coin, Commemorative		
	Cover, First Day		
	Key, Commemorative		
	Medal, Commemorative		
	Plate, Commemorative		
	Ribbon, Commemorative		
	Token, Commemorative		
Mask, Death			*Note:* May also use "Casting" from Art
Quilt, Memory			*Note:* May also use "Quilt" from Art
Relic, Historic			
Souvenir			*Note:* This generic term may be used in addition to terms from other classes to index souvenir objects that serve other functions as well
	Card, Souvenir		
	Crown, Death		

Primary Object Term	Secondary Term	Tertiary Term	Notes
	Fairing		*Note:* May also use "Figurine" or other appropriate term from Art and/ or "Knickknack" from Decorative Furnishings if appropriate
	Spoon, Souvenir		
Wreath, Hairwork			*Note:* May also use "Hairwork" from Art

Sub-Class:
OTHER DOCUMENTS

Definition: Documentary objects that routinely may be classified in none or more than one of the other sub-classes. These include objects that are defined more by form than by function or context. Many terms may be used in addition to other terms for cross-referencing purposes.

Primary Object Term	Secondary Term	Tertiary Term	Notes
Acknowledgment			
Archive			*Note:* Use for a collection of historical records and primary source materials in cases in which contents are not cataloged individually
	Fonds		*Note:* Use for an archive of material from one source
Book			*Note:* Use for a bound volume containing printed or written content; may be used in addition to many other terms, including literary works and religious texts; some types of books are listed elsewhere—see alphabetical index
	Book, Address		
	Book, Appointment		
	Book, Pattern		
	Dictionary		
		Gazetteer	
	Directory		
		Directory, Business	
		Directory, City	
		Directory, County	
		Directory, Membership	
		Directory, Telephone	
	Encyclopedia		
	Journal		*Note:* Use for a bound account of activities and events, not for a periodical
		Book, Commonplace	
		Diary	
	Thesaurus		
Calendar			
	Calendar, Perpetual		
Card, Documentary			*Note:* Some types of cards are listed elsewhere—see alphabetical index
	Card, Attendance		
	Card, Autograph		
	Card, Catalog		

Primary Object Term	Secondary Term	Tertiary Term	Notes
	Card, Collecting		*Note:* For a collecting card other than a baseball card, use this generic term and a descriptor in a subject field
		Card, Baseball	
	Card, Escort		
	Card, Inspirational		
	Card, Insurance		
	Card, QSL		
	Card, Report		
	Placecard		
Catalog			
Certificate			
	Certificate, Attendance		
	Certificate, Church		
		Certificate, Baptismal	
		Certificate, Confirmation	
		Certificate, First Communion	
	Certificate, Membership		
Clipping			
	Clipping, Magazine		
	Clipping, Newspaper		
Copy, Reprographic			*Note:* May use this term or narrower terms in addition to a term that describes the content of the original item from which the copy was made, e.g., "Blueprint" with "Drawing, Architectural" from Graphic Documents
	Blueprint		
	Photocopy		
	Reprint		
Correspondence			
	Card, Greeting		
		Card, Congratulatory	*Note:* The occasion for congratulations may be noted in a subject field
		Card, Courting	
		Card, Get Well	
		Card, Holiday	*Note:* The holiday may be noted in a subject field
		Card, Sympathy	

Primary Object Term	Secondary Term	Tertiary Term	Notes
		Valentine	
	Dispatch		
	Letter		
		Letter, Form	
		Letter, Recommendation	
		Letter, Referral	
	Mail, Electronic		
	Memorandum		
	Telegram		
	V-Mail		
Cover, Document			
	Cover, Map		
	Jacket, Book		
	Slipcase, Book		
Decal			
Display			
Document, Digital			*Note:* May also use an appropriate term from the Documentary Objects class to describe the function of the content, e.g., "Map," "Photograph," "Composition, Musical," "Report," "Novel," "Correspondence"
	Database		
	Spreadsheet		
Document, Scoring			
	Scorebook		
	Scorecard		
Document, Travel			
	Itinerary		
	Passport		
	Visa		
Draft			
	Layout		
	Proof, Printing		
File, Document			*Note:* Use for an organized grouping of documents; may also use terms to indicate specific contents
Form			
	Application		
		Application, Financial	

Primary Object Term	Secondary Term	Tertiary Term	Notes
		Application, License	
		Application, Membership	
		Application, Registration	
	Form, Order		
	Slip, Call		
Label, Identification			
	Bookplate		
	Label, Address		
	Label, Shipping		
	Tag, Identification		
		Tag, Carcass	
		Tag, Inventory	
		Tag, Luggage	
		Tag, Merchandise	
		Tag, Shipping	
Leaf			*Note:* May use this term or narrower terms in addition to a term indicating the source of the leaf
	Folio		
	Page		
	Tearsheet		
Leaflet			
List			*Note:* May use this term or narrower terms in addition to "Book" whenever appropriate
	Bibliography		
	Checklist		
	Guestbook		
	Index		
	Inventory		
	List, Attendance		
	List, Mailing		
	List, Membership		
	List, Passenger		
	List, Subscription		
	List, Voters'		
	Menu		
	Pricelist		
	Register		
		Register, Family	

Primary Object Term	Secondary Term	Tertiary Term	Notes
	Roster		
Log			
	Log, Flight		
	Log, Ship's		
Manuscript			*Note:* Use for handwritten documents; may be used in addition to many other terms
	Autograph		
Microform			
	Microfiche		
	Microfilm		
Model			*Note:* May also use "Miniature" from Art or "Toy" from Toys if appropriate; information about what the model represents should be recorded in a subject field; this information may be entered according to the naming conventions and object terms used throughout *Nomenclature*
	Diorama		
		Diorama, Automata	
	Model, Architect's		
	Model, Half		
	Model, Instructional		*Note:* May also use "Aid, Visual" from Instructional Documents
	Model, Patent		
	Model, Topographic		
	Room, Miniature		
Note			
	Note, Field		
Pamphlet			
Permission			
	Commission		
	License		
		License, Animal	
		License, Occupational	
		License, Sporting	*Note:* The sport may be noted in a subject field
		License, Transportation	*Note:* May also use "Card, Identification" from Personal Identification
		Registration	
	Permit		

Primary Object Term	Secondary Term	Tertiary Term	Notes
		Permit, Building	
		Permit, Business	
		Permit, Interment	
	Prescription		
Plate, Identification			
	Mark, Fire		
	Nameplate		
	Plaque, Date		
	Plate, Builder's		
	Plate, Number		
Pledge			
	Card, Pledge		
	Sheet, Pledge		
Program			
	Program, Concert		
	Program, Dance		
	Program, Theater		
Questionnaire			
Rebus			
Record, Medical			
Record, Student			
Recording			*Note:* Use for recorded audio and video material in addition to an appropriate term from Data Processing Media, Photographic Media, or Sound Communication Media to describe the format, e.g., "Disc, Compact," "Disc, Digital Video," "Film, Motion Picture," "Videotape," "Cassette, Audio Tape," "Record, Phonograph"; the four specific terms below assume recorded content
	Filmstrip		
	Picture, Motion		
	Recording, Audio		
	Recording, Video		
Reproduction			
	Facsimile		
	Replica		
Request			
	Invitation		
	Petition		

Primary Object Term	Secondary Term	Tertiary Term	Notes
Schedule			
	Schedule, Fee		
	Timetable		
Scroll			
Serial			
	Almanac		
	Bulletin		
	Gazette		
	Newsletter		
	Newspaper		
	Periodical		
		Digest	
		Magazine	
		Supplement, Newspaper	
	Yearbook		
Specification			
Sticker			
	Sticker, Bumper		
Tablet			*Note:* Use for a slab bearing pictures and/or inscriptions
Typescript			*Note:* May be used in addition to many other terms

Class:
EXCHANGE MEDIA

Definition: Objects originally created to be used as media of exchange, such as currency, or as a means of obtaining specific goods and services, such as admission tickets, coupons, postage stamps, or tokens.

Primary Object Term	Secondary Term	Tertiary Term	Notes
Card, Money			
	Card, Credit		
	Card, Debit		
Certificate, Gift			
Check, Rain			
Coupon			
	Book, Coupon		
	Coupon, Ration		
		Book, Ration	
Forgery			*Note:* May also use a term representing what the forgery is imitating
	Counterfeit		
		Slug	
Good, Trade			*Note:* This generic term may be used in addition to terms from other classes to index trade goods that serve other functions as well
Medium, Digital Exchange			*Note:* May also use another appropriate Exchange Media term to describe the function of the content, e.g., "Money," "Ticket"
Money			
	Bead, Trade		
		Wampum	
	Coin		
		Cent, Half	
		Centavo	
		Centime	
		Cob	
		Coin, Crown	
		Coin, Pagoda	
		Coin, Two-Dollar	
		Croat	
		Crown, Half	
		Denier	
		Dime	
		Dime, Half	

Primary Object Term	Secondary Term	Tertiary Term	Notes
		Dinar	
		Dollar	*Note:* Use for coin only
		Dollar, Half	
		Doubloon	
		Ducat	
		Eagle	
		Eagle, Double	
		Eagle, Half	
		Eagle, Quarter	
		Écu	
		Escudo	
		Euro	
		Farthing	
		Franc	
		Goschen	
		Guinea	
		Halfpenny	
		Heller	
		Koban	
		Kopek	
		Lira	
		Louis d'Or	
		Mark	
		Nickel	
		Oban	
		Penny	
		Penny, English	
		Penny, New	
		Peso	
		Pfennig	
		Piece of Eight	
		Piece, Three-Cent	
		Pound	
		Quarter	
		Real	
		Schilling	
		Shilling	
		Sixpence	
		Sous Marqué	

Primary Object Term	Secondary Term	Tertiary Term	Notes
		Sovereign	
		Taler	
		Testone	
	Money, Paper		
		Certificate, Gold	
		Certificate, Silver	
		Currency, Continental	
		Currency, Fractional	
		Note, Confederate	
		Note, Federal Reserve	*Note:* This term describes today's federally issued United States paper money
		Note, Private Bank	
		Note, United States	
		Scrip	
	Money, Shell		
Order, Pay			
	Bill of Exchange		
	Bond		
		Bond, War	
	Check, Bank		*Note:* May also use "Checkbook" from Financial Records if appropriate
		Check, Certified	
		Check, Traveler's	
	Draft, Bank		
	Letter of Credit		
	Note, Promissory		
	Order, Money		
	Warrant, Dividend		
Slip, Bank			
	Slip, Deposit		
	Slip, Withdrawal		
Stamp			
	Book, Stamp		
	Stamp, Postage		
	Stamp, Ration		
	Stamp, Tax		
	Stamp, Telegraph		
	Stamp, Trading		
Ticket			
	Book, Ticket		

Primary Object Term	Secondary Term	Tertiary Term	Notes
	Card, Admittance		
	Pass		
		Pass, Boarding	
	Ticket, Admission		
	Ticket, Meal		
	Ticket, Transportation		*Note:* The method of transportation may be noted in a subject field
		Ticket, Transfer	
	Wristband, Admission		
Token			
	Card, Store		*Note:* Use for a card exchanged for goods or services at a specific business
	Token, Communion		
	Token, Ration		
	Token, Store		
	Token, Tax		
	Token, Transportation		

Class:
PERSONAL SYMBOLS

Definition: Objects originally created to communicate a particular personal belief, opinion, achievement, status, rank, occupation, membership, office, or identity. This class includes articles of adornment or clothing worn primarily for their symbolism; these objects may be assigned additional terms from Personal Objects to ensure appropriate cross-indexing. A personal symbol differs from a ceremonial object in that it expresses individual ideas, not the ideas of a group, or it communicates the relationship of individuals to a group.

Sub-Class:
ACHIEVEMENT SYMBOLS

Definition: Objects that convey social recognition of achievements by individuals or groups of people.

Primary Object Term	Secondary Term	Tertiary Term	Notes
Award			*Note:* Use for an object that communicates an honor bestowed or conferred on an individual or corporate entity
	Badge, Merit		
	Certificate, Achievement		*Note:* May also use "Certificate" from Other Documents
		Diploma	
		Reward of Merit	
	Decoration of Honor		*Note:* Indicate context in a subject field
		Bar, Ribbon	
		Medal	
		Stripe, Service	
	Piece, Presentation		*Note:* May be used in addition to terms from other classes for objects that serve other functions as well, e.g., "Bowl, Punch" from Serving Vessels, "Sword" from Edged Weapons
	Pin, Award		
	Plaque, Award		
Cup, Loving			*Note:* May also use "Award" or "Prize" as appropriate
Prize			*Note:* Use for an object won by chance or competition or claimed as a spoil of victory in sport or war; this generic term may be used in addition to terms from other classes for objects that serve other functions as well
	Belt, Prize		
	Medal, Prize		
	Ribbon, Prize		
	Scalp		
	Stick, Coup		

Primary Object Term	Secondary Term	Tertiary Term	Notes
	Trophy		*Note:* May also use a term from another class for an object that serves another function as well, e.g., "Football" from Sports Equipment for a game ball trophy
		Trophy, Game	*Note:* Use for an animal trophy; may also use "Mount, Taxidermy" from Decorative Furnishings; animal and sport names may be entered in a subject field

Sub-Class:
BELIEF SYMBOLS

Definition: Personal objects, usually worn or carried, that express an individual's thoughts, opinions, convictions, allegiances, interests, or attitudes.

Primary Object Term	Secondary Term	Tertiary Term	Notes
Symbol, Political			*Note:* Use for an object that is worn to communicate opinions about political causes, issues, or candidates for office; may be used in addition to "Advertisement" from Advertising Media and/or terms from other classes for a political symbol that serves other functions as well
	Armband, Political		*Note:* May also use "Armband" from Clothing Accessories
	Badge, Political		
		Badge, Campaign	
	Button, Political		
		Button, Campaign	
	Medal, Political		
	Pin, Political		
		Pin, Campaign	
	Ribbon, Political		
		Ribbon, Campaign	
Symbol, Social			*Note:* Use for an item that is worn as a non-political social statement of greeting, opinion, or support; may be used in addition to "Button, Promotional," "Pin, Promotional," or "Ribbon, Promotional," all from Advertising Media, and/or terms from other classes for an object that serves other functions as well
Symbol, Spiritual			*Note:* Use for an object that is worn or used to express individual or clan spiritual beliefs or religious devotion; may be used in addition to other terms for an object that serves other functions as well
	Bundle, Medicine		
	Charm		
		Amulet	
		Talisman	
	Object, Devotional		
		Agnus Dei	
		Bead, Prayer	
		Dominical	*Note:* May also use "Veil" from Headwear

Primary Object Term	Secondary Term	Tertiary Term	Notes
		Pendant, Religious	*Note:* May also use "Pendant" from Body Adornments
		Rosary	
		Tallith	*Note:* May also use "Shawl" from Outerwear
		Tefillin	
		Yarmulke	*Note:* May also use "Skullcap" from Headwear
	Pin, Inspirational		
	Stone, Spirit		
	Totem		*Note:* "Pole, Totem" is organized under Art

Sub-Class:
PERSONAL IDENTIFICATION

Definition: Objects that note individual identity.

Primary Object Term	Secondary Term	Tertiary Term	Notes
Badge, Identification			
Bracelet, Identification			*Note:* May also use "Bracelet" from Body Adornments
Card, Identification			
	Card, Business		
	Card, Calling		
	Card, Draft		
	Card, Membership		
		Card, Library	
		Card, Union	
	Card, Social Security		
Nametag			
	Tag, Dog		
Seal			
	Ring, Signet		*Note:* May also use "Ring, Finger" from Body Adornments
	Wafer		

Sub-Class:
STATUS SYMBOLS

Definition: Articles of adornment, clothing, accessories, and personal gear, the primary purpose of which is to communicate a particular status, rank, occupation, membership, or office. Such an article serves to associate individuals with social roles and relationships, either generally or under certain circumstances.

Primary Object Term	Secondary Term	Tertiary Term	Notes
Insignia			*Note:* Use for an item of personal gear or an accessory that is routinely worn or displayed to identify a person as belonging to a given group, organization, rank, or status
	Badge, Insignia		
		Badge, Cap	
		Badge, Fire	
		Badge, Law Enforcement	
		Badge, Membership	
		Badge, Military	
	Brassard		*Note:* May also use "Armband" from Clothing Accessories
	Button, Insignia		*Note:* May also use "Button" from Needleworking Equipment
		Button, Fraternal	
		Button, Law Enforcement	
		Button, Membership	
		Button, Military	
		Stud, Fraternal	*Note:* May also use "Stud, Clothing" from Clothing Accessories
	Coat of Arms		*Note:* May also use other insignia terms to note form, e.g., "Ring, Insignia," "Plaque, Insignia," "Shield, Insignia"
	Cockade		
	Hat, Fraternal		*Note:* May also use "Hat" from Headwear
	Insignia, Shoulder		
		Aiguillette	
		Bandolier	
		Board, Shoulder	
		Epaulet	
		Fourragère	
		Knot, Shoulder	
		Loop, Shoulder	
		Strap, Shoulder	

Primary Object Term	Secondary Term	Tertiary Term	Notes
	Knot, Sword		
	Mug, Fraternal		
	Paddle, Fraternal		
	Patch, Insignia		
		Chevron	
		Patch, Fire	
		Patch, Fraternal	
		Patch, Law Enforcement	
		Patch, Membership	
		Patch, Military	
	Pendant, Insignia		*Note:* May also use "Pendant" from Body Adornments
		Pendant, Fraternal	
		Pendant, Gorget	
	Pin, Insignia		
		Pin, Fire	
		Pin, Fraternal	
		Pin, Law Enforcement	
		Pin, Membership	
		Pin, Military	
		Pin, Occupational	
		Pin, Sororital	
	Plaque, Insignia		
	Plate, Insignia		
		Plate, Belt	
		Plate, Helmet	
	Plume		
	Ribbon, Insignia		
		Ribbon, Fraternal	
		Ribbon, Membership	
	Ring, Insignia		*Note:* May also use "Ring, Finger" from Body Adornments
		Ring, Class	
		Ring, Fraternal	
	Shield, Insignia		
	Trowel, Fraternal		

Primary Object Term	Secondary Term	Tertiary Term	Notes
Regalia			*Note:* Use for an item of personal attire, gear, or paraphernalia, the primary purpose of which is to symbolize office or status, especially during ceremonies or other special events; often used by clergy, title holders, heads of state, or other officials
	Apron, Fraternal		*Note:* May also use "Apron" from Protective Wear
	Armilla		*Note:* May also use "Armlet" or "Bracelet" from Body Adornments, or "Stole" from Outerwear to indicate form
	Baton		
		Mace, Ceremonial	
	Blanket, Button		*Note:* May also use "Blanket, Wearing" from Outerwear
	Blanket, Nobility		*Note:* May also use "Blanket, Wearing" from Outerwear
	Bustle, Ceremonial		
		Bustle, Dance	
	Chain of Office		
	Costume, Academic		
		Gown, Academic	*Note:* May also use "Robe" from Main Garments
		Hood, Academic	*Note:* May also use "Hood" from Headwear
		Mortarboard	*Note:* May also use "Cap" from Headwear
		Tassel, Academic	
	Costume, Legal		
		Gown, Barrister's	*Note:* May also use "Robe" from Main Garments
		Robe, Judicial	*Note:* May also use "Robe" from Main Garments
		Tab, Barrister's	*Note:* May also use "Collar" from Clothing Accessories
		Wig, Barrister's	*Note:* May also use "Wig" from Hair Adornments
	Cowl		*Note:* May also use "Cloak" from Outerwear
	Crosier		
	Crown		*Note:* May also use "Headpiece" from Headwear
		Coronet	
	Diadem		*Note:* May also use "Headband" from Headwear
	Habit		

Primary Object Term	Secondary Term	Tertiary Term	Notes
		Habit, Monk's	
		Habit, Nun's	
	Headdress		*Note:* May also use "Headpiece" from Headwear
		Bonnet, War	
		Headdress, Roach	
		Tablita	
	Orb		
	Pschent		
	Ring, Pastoral		*Note:* May also use "Ring, Finger" from Body Adornments
	Scepter		
	Stick, Swagger		
	Tiara		*Note:* May also use "Headpiece" from Headwear
	Vestment		
		Alb	*Note:* May also use "Tunic" from Main Garments
		Amice	*Note:* May also use "Hood" from Headwear
		Biretta	*Note:* May also use "Cap" from Headwear
		Buskin	*Note:* May also use "Stocking" from Footwear
		Cassock	*Note:* May also use "Robe" from Main Garments
		Chasuble	*Note:* May also use "Cloak" from Outerwear
		Chimere	*Note:* May also use "Robe" from Main Garments
		Cincture	*Note:* May also use "Belt, Cinch" from Clothing Accessories
		Collar, Clerical	*Note:* May also use "Collar" from Clothing Accessories
		Cope	*Note:* May also use "Cloak" from Outerwear
		Cotta	*Note:* May also use "Robe" from Main Garments
		Dalmatic	*Note:* May also use "Tunic" from Main Garments
		Gown, Geneva	*Note:* May also use "Robe" from Main Garments
		Hat, Ecclesiastical	*Note:* May also use "Hat" from Headwear
		Kamelaukion	*Note:* May also use "Cap" from Headwear
		Maniple	*Note:* May also use "Armband" from Clothing Accessories

Primary Object Term	Secondary Term	Tertiary Term	Notes
		Mantle, Ecclesiastical	*Note:* May also use "Mantle" from Outerwear
		Miter	*Note:* May also use "Hat" from Headwear
		Morse	*Note:* May also use "Clasp, Clothing" from Clothing Accessories
		Mozzetta	*Note:* May also use "Cape" from Outerwear
		Rochet	*Note:* May also use "Tunic" from Main Garments
		Scapular	*Note:* May also use "Cloak" from Outerwear
		Stole, Ecclesiastical	*Note:* May also use "Stole" from Outerwear
		Surplice	*Note:* May also use "Robe" from Main Garments
		Veil, Humeral	*Note:* May also use "Stole" from Outerwear
		Zuccheto	*Note:* May also use "Skullcap" from Headwear
Uniform			*Note:* Use for a garment routinely worn by a member of a given profession or organization; may be used with terms from Clothing to denote specific articles of clothing; specific occupations, organizations, military branches, sports, etc. may be entered in a subject field
	Uniform, Fire		
	Uniform, Law Enforcement		
	Uniform, Military		
		Fatigues	
		Uniform, Military Dress	
	Uniform, Occupational		
	Uniform, Organizational		
	Uniform, Sports		

Category 9: RECREATIONAL OBJECTS

Definition: **Objects created to be used as toys or to carry on the activities of games, sports, gambling, or public entertainment.**

Class:
GAME EQUIPMENT

Definition: Objects originally created for competitive activities based on chance, problem-solving, manual dexterity, or calculation, rather than strenuous physical effort, and conducted according to stated rules. This class also includes all forms of gambling devices.

Primary Object Term	Secondary Term	Tertiary Term	Notes
Case, Game			
Component, Game			*Note:* Use for an individual object that, when used in conjunction with other objects, constitutes a game; game component terms may be used with terms under "Game" as appropriate
	Card, Game		
	Component, Billiard		
		Ball, Billiard	
		Bridge, Billiard	
		Chalk, Billiard	
		Cue, Billiard	
		Rack, Billiard Ball	
	Component, Video Game		
		Console, Video Game	
		Controller, Video Game	*Note:* Use for a gamepad, joystick, paddle, light gun, and other input device for a video game; may also use a suitable term under "Device, Input" from Peripherals in Data Processing T&E
	Cup, Dice		
	Dart, Game		
		Dart, Lawn	
	Dartboard		
	Gameboard		
		Board, Cribbage	
		Checkerboard	
		Chessboard	
	Gear, Croquet		
		Ball, Croquet	
		Mallet, Croquet	
		Post, Croquet	
		Stand, Croquet	

Primary Object Term	Secondary Term	Tertiary Term	Notes
		Wicket, Croquet	
	Gear, Shuffleboard		
		Cue, Shuffleboard	
		Disk, Shuffleboard	
	Mat, Game		
		Felt, Game	
	Money, Play		
	Piece, Game		*Note:* Use for a small, individual piece from a board, card, and table game that is manipulated by players; may use this generic term for a game piece that is suitable for multiple games or for an unidentified game
		Checker	
		Counter, Game	
		Die	
		Jack, Toy	
		Marker, Game	
		Piece, Chess	
		Tile, Game	
	Spinner, Game		
	Target, Gallery		
	Timer, Game		*Note:* May also use "Timer" from Timekeeping T&E
Container, Game			*Note:* Use for any container designed specifically for storing, protecting, or transporting games or game equipment; may also use "Package, Product" from Merchandising T&E if appropriate
	Bag, Marble		
	Holder, Card		
		Box, Card	
		Shoe, Card	
		Shuffler, Card	
	Rack, Cue		
Device, Gambling			
	Board, Roulette		
	Chip, Gambling		
		Chip, Poker	
	Cup, Wager		
	Device, Bingo		
		Ball, Bingo	

Primary Object Term	Secondary Term	Tertiary Term	Notes
		Card, Bingo	
		Tumbler, Bingo	
	Device, Lottery		
		Ball, Lottery	
		Dispenser, Lottery Ball	
		Ticket, Lottery	
	Machine, Slot		
	Paddle, Croupier's		
	Punchboard		
	Rack, Poker Chip		
	Stick, Gaming		
	Table, Gaming		*Note:* Use for a table designed specifically for a casino-style game; may also use "Table" from Support Furniture
	Tray, Gambling		
	Wheel, Roulette		
	Wheel of Fortune		
Game			*Note:* May also use "Component, Game" or narrower terms if appropriate; the titles of proprietary games may be entered in another field
	Game, Arcade		*Note:* For a video arcade game, also use "Game, Video"
		Gallery, Shooting	
		Game, Skee-Ball	
		Machine, Pachinko	
		Machine, Pinball	
	Game, Bingo		*Note:* May also use "Device, Gambling" if the object was used in a gambling context
	Game, Board		*Note:* Use for any game with a proprietary title played on a horizontal printed, painted, or molded board; use a more specific term for the non-proprietary games listed here
		Set, Backgammon	
		Set, Checkers	*Note:* Use for a complete or partial checkers set; may also use "Checker" and/or "Checkerboard"
		Set, Chess	*Note:* Use for a complete or partial chess set; may also use "Piece, Chess" and/or "Chessboard"

Primary Object Term	Secondary Term	Tertiary Term	Notes
		Set, Chinese Checkers	
		Set, Halma	
		Set, Mancala	
		Set, Parcheesi	
	Game, Bowling		
		Set, Carpet Bowls	
		Set, Ninepins	
		Set, Tenpins	
	Game, Card		*Note:* Use for a game that primarily utilizes printed cards
		Card, Playing	*Note:* Use for a standard playing card or a deck of such cards, including bridge and pinochle cards
		Card, Tarot	
		Set, Cribbage	*Note:* Use for a complete or partial cribbage set; may also use "Board, Cribbage"
	Game, Dart		*Note:* Use for a complete or partial dart set; may also use "Dart, Game" and/or "Dartboard"
	Game, Dexterity		*Note:* Use for a game that features manual dexterity, not played on a special table or in an arcade
		Cup, Stacking	
		Marble	*Note:* Use for a single marble or a set
		Set, Jacks	*Note:* Use for a complete or partial jacks set; may also use "Jack, Toy"
		Set, Tiddlywinks	*Note:* Use for a complete or partial tiddlywinks set
		Stick, Pick-Up	*Note:* Use for a single stick or a set
	Game, Dice		*Note:* Use for a non-gambling game that primarily uses dice; may also use "Die" and/or "Cup, Dice"
	Game, Educational		*Note:* Use for a game intended primarily to test or impart knowledge, skills, or abilities
		Game, Memory	
		Game, Trivia	
	Game, Electronic		*Note:* For an electronic video game, use "Game, Video"
		Game, Audio	
		Game, Handheld Electronic	

Primary Object Term	Secondary Term	Tertiary Term	Notes
		Game, Tabletop Electronic	
		Game, Teletype	
	Game, Lotto		
	Game, Mechanical		
	Game, Outdoor		
		Ball, Bocce	
		Ball, Kick	
		Horseshoe, Pitching	
		Quoit	
		Sack, Hacky	
		Set, Croquet	
		Set, Hopscotch	
		Set, Lawn Dart	
		Set, Shuffleboard	
		Tetherball	
	Game, Paddle Ball		
	Game, Party		
		Piñata	
		Set, Pin the Tail on the Donkey	
		Stick, Piñata	
	Game, Ring Toss		
	Game, Role-Playing		
	Game, Table		
		Game, Air Hockey	
		Game, Bagatelle	
		Game, Carrom	
		Game, Crokinole	
		Game, Foosball	
		Set, Skittle	
		Set, Table Croquet	
		Table, Billiard	*Note:* May also use “Table” from Support Furniture
		Table, Pool	*Note:* May also use “Table” from Support Furniture
	Game, Tile		*Note:* Use for a game that primarily utilizes tiles
		Domino	*Note:* Use for a single domino or a set
		Set, Mah-Jongg	
	Game, Tivoli		

Primary Object Term	Secondary Term	Tertiary Term	Notes
	Game, Video		*Note:* Also use "Game, Arcade" for a video arcade game
		Game, Computer	*Note:* Use for a game designed to be played on a personal computer; may also use a term from Data Processing Media to describe the format in which the game program is stored
		Game, Console	*Note:* Use for a game designed to be played through a game console; may also use a term from Data Processing Media to describe the format in which the game program is stored
	Game, Word		
		Puzzle, Crossword	
	Tic-Tac-Toe		

Class:
PUBLIC ENTERTAINMENT DEVICES

Definition: Objects originally created for the presentation of non-competitive spectator entertainment.

Primary Object Term	Secondary Term	Tertiary Term	Notes
Backdrop, Stage			
	Drop, Flat		
	Drop, Roll		
	Drop, Scrim		
Ball, Mirror			
Basket, Snake			
Board, Balance			
	Rola Bola		
	Teeterboard		
Case, Public Entertainment			*Note:* Use for any container specifically designed for protecting and/or transporting a public entertainment device; if a case is designed specifically for a given device, a new term may be created with the *Nomenclature* term for that device as a modifier; that term may be organized under "Case, Public Entertainment," as the three terms are below
	Case, Firework		
	Case, Prop		
	Case, Puppet		
Costume, Performance			*Note:* May also use appropriate terms from Clothing
	Costume, Dance		
	Costume, Theater		
Curtain, Stage			
Firework			
	Firecracker		
	Sparkler		
Globe, Rolling			
Launcher, Fireworks			
Mask, Theatrical			
Prop			
	Prop, Aerialist's		
		Bicycle, High Wire	
		Harness, Foot	
		Mouthpiece, Iron Jaw	
		Net, Safety	
		Pole, Balancing	

Primary Object Term	Secondary Term	Tertiary Term	Notes
		Rigging, Aerial	
		Trapeze	
		Wire, High	
	Prop, Juggler's		
		Ball, Juggling	
		Club, Juggling	
		Pin, Juggling	
		Plate, Juggling	
		Plate, Spinning	
		Ring, Juggling	
		Torch, Juggling	
	Prop, Magician's		
		Board, Levitation	
		Coin, Disappearing	
		Hat, Magic	
		Knife, Magician's	
		Lift, Levitation	
		Trunk, Escape	
		Wand, Magic	
	Prop, Theatrical		*Note:* May also use another term to describe the object
Puppet			*Note:* May also use "Toy" from Toys if appropriate
	Dummy, Ventriloquist		
	Marionette		
	Puppet, Finger		
	Puppet, Hand		
	Puppet, Rod		
	Puppet, Shadow		
Set, Stage			
Stage, Puppet			
Stand, Animal			

Class:
RECREATIONAL DEVICES

Definition: Objects originally created for participatory, usually non-competitive, recreational activities other than athletic games. This class includes equipment for entertainment, such as a carousel, a pinball machine, a swing, or a slide, whether such equipment is publicly or privately owned and whether or not a charge is associated with its use.

Primary Object Term	Secondary Term	Tertiary Term	Notes
Board, Rocking			
Board, Walking			
Car, Coaster			
Coaster, Snow			
	Saucer, Snow		
	Sled		
	Toboggan		
Device, Fitness			
	Ball, Exercise		
		Ball, Medicine	
	Bar, Chin-Up		
	Bar, Stall		
	Belt, Weight		
	Bench, Weight Training		
	Club, Indian		
	Developer, Wrist		
	Gripper, Hand		
	Machine, Exercise		
		Bicycle, Stationary	
		Gym, Home	
		Machine, Elliptical	
		Machine, Rowing	
		Machine, Ski	
		Machine, Step	
		Machine, Weight	
		Pulley, Exercise	
		Treadmill, Exercise	
	Massager, Belt		
	Mat, Exercise		
	Pedometer		
	Rack, Weight		
	Ring, Exercise		
	Rope, Gym		
	Step, Aerobics		

Primary Object Term	Secondary Term	Tertiary Term	Notes
	Weight, Exercise		
		Barbell	
		Dumbbell	
Device, Playground			
	Backhoe, Sandbox		
	Climber		
		Junglegym	
		Ladder, Horizontal	
		Net, Climbing	
	Gate, Swinging		
	Glider, Playground		
	Ladder, Rope		
	Merry-Go-Round		*Note:* Use for a non-motorized spinning piece of playground equipment
	Pit, Ball		
	Pole, Sliding		
	Rider, Spring		
	Sandbox		
	Seesaw		
		Seesaw, Spring	
	Slide		
	Swing		
		Swing, Circle	
	Trapeze, Playground		
	Wall, Climbing		
Device, Water Recreation			
	Aquaplane		
	Board, Diving		
	Bodyboard		
	Fin, Swim		
	Flag, Water Ski		
	Goggles, Swim		*Note:* May also use "Goggles" from Personal Assistive Objects
	Helmet, Diver's		*Note:* May also use "Helmet" from Headwear
	Kickboard		
	Knife, Scuba		
	Mask, Diving		
	Mask, Swim		

Primary Object Term	Secondary Term	Tertiary Term	Notes
	Pool, Wading		
	Raft, Pool		
	Regulator, Scuba		*Note:* May also use "Regulator, Breathing" from Personal Assistive Objects
	Sailboard		
	Shoe, Diving		
	Ski, Water		
	Sled, Water		
	Slide, Water		
	Snorkel		
	Sprinkler		
	Surfboard		
	Tank, Scuba		*Note:* May also use "Tank, Breathing" from Personal Assistive Objects
	Towline, Water Ski		
	Tube, Pool		
	Tube, Ski		
	Weightbelt		
	Wing, Water		
Ride, Amusement			
	Animal, Carousel		
	Bull, Mechanical		
	Carousel		
	Coaster, Roller		
	Vehicle, Amusement Ride		
		Car, Bumper	
	Wheel, Ferris		
	Whirl		

Class:
SPORTS EQUIPMENT

Definition: Objects originally created for physical activities that are often competitive. This class includes equipment used in all forms of athletic games, including individual and team sports. Sports and their specialized equipment have proliferated over the years. Object groupings in this class focus on the most popular sports while not attempting to be encyclopedic. Object terms seek to cover the forms that are most familiar and most likely to be part of museum collections. If a specific term is not listed, consider using the broader "Gear" term. Terms covering practice, warm-up, and exercise equipment can be found in Recreational Devices. Note: The word "Gear," employed in many of the primary object terms below, suggests a plural connotation even though *Nomenclature* object terms are in the singular. The use of "Gear" as an object term (rather than as a sub-class) provides the cataloger with terms that allow the indexing of an unlisted object or an object whose term is listed elsewhere with its associated sport.

Primary Object Term	Secondary Term	Tertiary Term	Notes
Ball, Chalk			*Note:* May be used with a generic "Gear" term (e.g., "Gear, Climbing") if the chalk ball is for a specific sport
Cleat, Shoe			*Note:* May be used with a generic "Gear" term (e.g., "Gear, Cycling") if the cleat is for a specific sport
Gear, Animal Racing			
	Lure, Dog Track		
	Sled, Dog Racing		
Gear, Badminton			
	Net, Badminton		
	Racket, Badminton		
	Shuttlecock		
Gear, Baseball			
	Bag, Rosin		
	Base		
	Baseball		
		Baseball, Training	
	Bat, Baseball		
	Bat, Softball		
	Glove, Baseball		
		Glove, Batting	
		Glove, Fielder's	
		Mitt, Catcher's	
		Mitt, First Baseman's	
	Glove, Softball		

Primary Object Term	Secondary Term	Tertiary Term	Notes
	Guard, Batting Helmet		
	Guard, Leg		
	Guard, Neck		
	Helmet, Baseball		*Note:* May also use "Helmet" from Headwear
		Helmet, Batter's	
		Helmet, Catcher's	
	Mask, Catcher's		
	Rag, Pine Tar		
	Shell, Bat		
	Shoe, Baseball		*Note:* May also use "Shoe, Sport" from Footwear
	Shorts, Sliding		
	Softball		
	Tape, Bat Grip		
	Tee, Batting		
	Weight, Bat		
Gear, Basketball			
	Backboard, Basketball		
	Basketball		
	Hoop, Basketball		
	Net, Basketball		
	Pole, Basketball		
	Shoe, Basketball		*Note:* May also use "Shoe, Sport" from Footwear
Gear, Bowling			
	Alley, Portable Bowling		
	Bag, Bowling Ball		
	Ball, Bowling		
	Console, Bowling Scoring		
	Glove, Bowling		
	Pin, Bowling		
		Candlepin	
		Duckpin	
	Pinsetter		
	Return, Bowling Ball		
	Shoe, Bowling		*Note:* May also use "Shoe, Sport" from Footwear

Primary Object Term	Secondary Term	Tertiary Term	Notes
	Towel, Bowling		*Note:* May also use "Towel" from Hygiene Objects
Gear, Boxing			
	Bag, Punching		
	Glove, Boxing		
	Ring, Boxing		
Gear, Bullfighting			
	Banderilla		*Note:* May also use "Dart" from Edged Weapons
	Estoque		*Note:* May also use "Rapier" from Edged Weapons
	Muleta		
	Rejon		*Note:* May also use "Spear" from Edged Weapons
Gear, Climbing			
	Alpenstock		
	Ax, Ice Climbing		
	Carabiner		
	Crampon		
	Harness, Climbing		
	Piton		
	Quickdraw		
	Rope, Climbing		
	Spur, Climbing		
Gear, Cockfighting			
	Gaff, Cockfighting		
	Spur, Cockfighting		
Gear, Cricket			
	Ball, Cricket		
	Bat, Cricket		
	Glove, Wicket Keeping		
	Helmet, Cricket		*Note:* May also use "Helmet" from Headwear
Gear, Curling			
	Broom, Curling		
	Stone, Curling		
Gear, Cycling			
	Helmet, Cycling		*Note:* May also use "Helmet" from Headwear
Gear, Fencing			

Primary Object Term	Secondary Term	Tertiary Term	Notes
	Glove, Fencing		
	Helmet, Fencing		*Note:* May also use "Helmet" from Headwear
	Mask, Fencing		
	Plastron		
	Sword, Fencing		*Note:* May also use "Sword" from Edged Weapons
		Épée	*Note:* May also use "Sword" from Edged Weapons
		Foil	*Note:* May also use "Sword" from Edged Weapons
		Saber, Fencing	*Note:* May also use "Saber" from Edged Weapons
Gear, Field Hockey			
	Ball, Field Hockey		
	Glove, Field Hockey		
	Goal, Field Hockey		
	Goggles, Field Hockey		*Note:* May also use "Goggles" from Personal Assistive Objects
	Helmet, Field Hockey		*Note:* May also use "Helmet" from Headwear
	Stick, Field Hockey		
Gear, Football			
	Dummy, Football		
		Dummy, Blocking	
		Dummy, Tackling	
	Flag, Football		
	Football		
	Helmet, Football		*Note:* May also use "Helmet" from Headwear
	Shoe, Football		*Note:* May also use "Shoe, Sport" from Footwear
	Tee, Football		
Gear, Golf			
	Bag, Golf		
	Ball, Golf		
	Club, Golf		
		Driver	
		Putter	
	Cover, Golf Club Head		
	Cup, Putting		

Primary Object Term	Secondary Term	Tertiary Term	Notes
	Flag, Golf		
	Glove, Golf		
	Marker, Golf Ball		
	Set, Golf		*Note:* May also use specific terms for items in the set
	Shoe, Golf		*Note:* May also use "Shoe, Sport" from Footwear
	Tee, Golf		
Gear, Gymnastics			
	Bar, Horizontal		
	Bars, Parallel		
	Bars, Uneven		
	Baton, Twirling		
	Beam, Balance		
	Horse, Pommel		
	Horse, Side		
	Horse, Vaulting		
	Mat, Gymnastics		
	Ring, Gymnastics		
	Springboard		
	Trampoline		
Gear, Handball			
	Handball		
Gear, Hockey			
	Glove, Hockey		
		Blocker	
	Goal, Ice Hockey		
	Helmet, Ice Hockey		*Note:* May also use "Helmet" from Headwear
	Mask, Goalie		
	Puck, Hockey		
	Shorts, Hockey		*Note:* May also use "Shorts" from Main Garments
	Stick, Hockey		
		Stick, Goalie	
Gear, Jai Alai			
	Ball, Jai Alai		
	Basket, Jai Alai		
Gear, Lacrosse			
	Ball, Lacrosse		

Primary Object Term	Secondary Term	Tertiary Term	Notes
	Glove, Lacrosse		
	Helmet, Lacrosse		*Note:* May also use "Helmet" from Headwear
	Stick, Lacrosse		
Gear, Polo			
	Ball, Polo		
	Helmet, Polo		*Note:* May also use "Helmet" from Headwear
	Stick, Polo		
Gear, Racquetball			
	Ball, Racquetball		
	Racket, Racquetball		
Gear, Rugby			
	Ball, Rugby		
Gear, Skating			
	Bag, Skate		
	Goggles, Skating		
	Guard, Skate		
	Key, Skate		
	Ramp, Skateboard		
	Skate, Ice		
	Skate, Roller		
		Skate, Inline	
	Skateboard		
	Suit, Speedskating		
Gear, Skiing			
	Basket, Ski Pole		
	Binding, Ski		
	Gate, Ski		
	Glove, Ski		
	Helmet, Ski		*Note:* May also use "Helmet" from Headwear
	Pole, Ski		
	Ski, Snow		
		Ski, Cross-Country	
		Ski, Downhill	
	Wax, Ski		
Gear, Sled Racing			
	Bobsled		
	Luge		

Primary Object Term	Secondary Term	Tertiary Term	Notes
	Sled, Skeleton		
Gear, Snowboarding			
	Snowboard		
Gear, Soccer			
	Ball, Soccer		
	Glove, Soccer Goalie		
	Goal, Soccer		
Gear, Squash			
	Ball, Squash		
	Racket, Squash		
Gear, Stickball			
	Ball, Stickball		
	Stick, Stickball		
Gear, Table Tennis			
	Ball, Table Tennis		
	Net, Table Tennis		
	Paddle, Table Tennis		
	Set, Table Tennis		*Note:* May also use specific terms for items in the set
	Table, Table Tennis		*Note:* May also "Table, Game" from Support Furniture
Gear, Tennis			
	Ball, Paddle Tennis		
	Ball, Tennis		
	Net, Tennis		
	Paddle, Tennis		
	Post, Tennis		
	Press, Tennis Racket		
	Racket, Tennis		
	Ring, Deck Tennis		
	Shoe, Tennis		*Note:* May also use "Shoe, Sport" from Footwear
Gear, Track and Field			
	Block, Starting		
	Caber		
	Discus		
	Gear, Pole Vault		
		Crossbar, Pole Vault	
		Pole, Vaulting	
		Standard, Pole Vault	

Primary Object Term	Secondary Term	Tertiary Term	Notes
	Hammer, Throwing		
	Hurdle		
	Javelin, Track and Field		
	Shoe, Track		*Note:* May also use "Shoe, Sport" from Footwear
	Shotput		
Gear, Volleyball			
	Net, Volleyball		
	Volleyball		
Gear, Water Polo			
	Ball, Water Polo		
	Goal, Water Polo		
Gear, Wrestling			
	Cage, Wrestling		
	Mat, Wrestling		
Protector, Body			*Note:* This term and narrower terms describe protective gear that is not necessarily restricted to one sport; these terms may be used with a generic "Gear" term (e.g., "Gear, Football") if a specific sport is known
	Guard, Chest		
	Guard, Ear		
	Guard, Eye		
	Guard, Foot		
	Guard, Shin		
	Mouthguard		
	Pad, Hip		
	Pad, Leg		
	Pad, Rib		
	Pad, Shoulder		
	Protector, Chest		

Class:
TOYS

Definition: Objects originally created as playthings. Toys often represent functional objects, such as toy teapots or toy ships, or living things, such as baby dolls or stuffed animals. Toys also include objects developed primarily for play, such as balls, tops, or kites. Note: Toys that are small representations of objects normally used in human activity should be given the object name "Toy." The cataloger may also use "Model" from Other Documents or "Miniature" from Art if appropriate. Information about what the toy represents should be recorded in a subject field; this information may be entered according to the naming conventions and object terms used throughout *Nomenclature*.

Primary Object Term	Secondary Term	Tertiary Term	Notes
Accessory, Doll			
	Carriage, Doll		
	Chest, Doll		
	Clothing, Doll		
	Cradle, Doll		
	Furniture, Doll		
	Stand, Doll		
	Stroller, Doll		
	Trunk, Doll		
Ark, Noah's			
Ball, Toy			
	Ball, Nesting		
Bank, Toy			
	Bank, Mechanical		
	Bank, Semi-Mechanical		
	Bank, Still		
Bead, Toy			
	Bead, Sliding		
	Bead, Stringing		
Beanbag			
Block, Toy			
	Block, Alphabet		
	Block, Building		
	Block, Nesting		
	Block, Parquetry		
	Block, Picture		
	Block, Telescopic		
Book, Activity			
	Book, Coloring		
	Book, Sticker		

Primary Object Term	Secondary Term	Tertiary Term	Notes
Bouncer, Baby			
Card, Activity			
	Card, Sewing		
Costume, Dress-Up			*Note:* May also use "Costume, Holiday" from Holiday Objects if appropriate
Disk, Flying			
	Frisbee		
Doll			
	Doll, Mechanical		*Note:* May also use "Toy, Mechanical"
	Doll, Nesting		
	Doll, Paper		
	Head, Doll		
Dollhouse			
Engine, Toy Steam			
Exploder, Cap			
Figure, Toy			
	Animal, Toy		
	Figure, Action		
	Figure, Mechanical		*Note:* May also use "Toy, Mechanical"
		Animal, Mechanical	*Note:* May also use "Animal, Toy"
	Jack, Jumping		
	Jack-in-the-Box		
	Marotte		
	Soldier, Toy		
	Tumbler, Toy		
		Rolly-Doll	
Furnishing, Dollhouse			
Gun, Toy			
	Gun, Cap		
	Gun, Laser Tag		
	Gun, Toy Air		
		Gun, Paintball	
		Popgun	
	Gun, Toy Dart		
	Gun, Water		
Hoop, Toy			
	Hoop, Hula		
	Hoop, Rolling		
Kit, Toy			
	Kit, Model		

Primary Object Term	Secondary Term	Tertiary Term	Notes
	Kit, Science		
		Set, Chemistry	
Kite, Toy			
Mobile, Toy			
Pail, Toy			
Puzzle			
	Block, Puzzle		
	Puzzle, Dexterity		
	Puzzle, Jigsaw		
	Puzzle, Mental		
	Puzzle, Number		
	Puzzle, Slide		
	Puzzle, Word		
Rattle, Baby			
	Rattle, Combination		
Rope, Jump			
Set, Activity			
Set, Construction			
Set, Magic			
Set, Magnet			
Set, Play			*Note:* Use for a toy with a number of pieces typically unified by a topic or setting, such as a toy farm set with barn and animals or a toy doctor's bag with stethoscope; information about what the toy represents should be recorded in a subject field; this information may be entered according to the naming conventions and object terms used throughout *Nomenclature*
	Garden, Play		
	Kitchen, Play		
	Set, Racetrack		
	Set, Train		
	Village, Toy		
	Zoo, Toy		
Shovel, Toy			
Stick, Hoop			
Stilt			
Stomper, Romper			
Structure, Play			
	Playhouse		

Primary Object Term	Secondary Term	Tertiary Term	Notes
	Tent, Play		
	Tunnel, Play		
Toy			*Note:* Use for a toy that lacks another descriptive or generic term
Toy, Balance			
Toy, Bath			
Toy, Bell			
Toy, Bubble			
	Blower, Bubble		
		Pipe, Bubble	
	Wand, Bubble		
Toy, Car			*Note:* Use for an infant toy that fits on or around a car seat
Toy, Craft			
	Paper, Craft		
		Paper, Construction	
		Paper, Origami	
	Set, Arts and Crafts		*Note:* May also use terms from Painting T&E or Written Communication T&E to describe set contents, e.g., "Brush, Artist's," "Crayon," "Chalk," "Stamp, Marking"
		Set, Pyrography	
	Toy, Pegboard		
Toy, Crib			
Toy, Dexterity			
	Toy, Cup and Ball		
Toy, Drawing			
Toy, Educational			
Toy, Fortune Telling			
	Ball, Fortune		
	Set, Ouija		*Note:* A similar object, not intended as a toy, is listed as "Board, Spirit" in Religious Objects
Toy, Inflatable			
Toy, Magnetic			
Toy, Mechanical			
Toy, Musical			
Toy, Optical			
	Anorthoscope		
	Kaleidoscope		

Primary Object Term	Secondary Term	Tertiary Term	Notes
	Panorama, Toy		
		Myriopticon	
	Peepshow		
		Mutascope	
	Phenakistoscope		
	Praxinoscope		
	Thaumatrope		
	Zoetrope		
	Zoopraxinoscope		
Toy, Penny			
Toy, Pounding			
Toy, Pull			
Toy, Push			
Toy, Riding			
	Ball, Hop		
	Car, Kiddie		
		Car, Pedal	
	Hobbyhorse		
	Horse, Rocking		
	Mail, Irish		
	Scooter		
	Stick, Pogo		
	Wagon, Child's		
Toy, Sand			
Toy, Scissor			
Toy, Sculpting			
	Clay, Modeling		
	Putty, Play		
	Tool, Toy Sculpting		
Toy, Sound			
	Noisemaker		
	Squeaker		
	Whistle, Toy		
Toy, Spring			
	Slinky		
Toy, Stacking			
Toy, Stuffed			
	Animal, Stuffed		*Note:* May also use "Animal, Toy"
		Bear, Teddy	

Primary Object Term	Secondary Term	Tertiary Term	Notes
Toy, Teething			
Whirligig			
	Diabolo		
	Pinwheel		
	Top		
		Dreidel	
		Top, Bowstring	
		Top, Gyroscope	
		Top, Magnetic	
		Top, Peg	
		Top, Whip	
	Yo-Yo		

Category 10:
UNCLASSIFIABLE OBJECTS

Definition: **Objects originally created to serve a purpose that cannot be identified at the time the object is cataloged.**

Primary Object Term	Secondary Term	Tertiary Term	Definitions & Notes
Fragment			*Note:* May also use a term that represents the entire object if known and if institutional protocol allows
	Scrap		
	Sherd		
		Potsherd	
		Sherd, Base	
		Sherd, Body	
		Sherd, Rim	
Hoard			
Material, Worked			*Note:* Material may be noted in a separate field
	Biface		
	Blank		
		Mood	
	Core		
	Debitage		
	Flake		
		Flake, Modified	
		Flake, Primary	
		Flake, Secondary	
		Flake, Tertiary	
		Spall	
	Preform		
	Shatter		
	Uniface		
Object, Unidentified			
Sample, Material			*Note:* Material may be noted in a separate field
	Ecofact		
	Quid		

Index

Aba Outerwear 100
Abacus Data Processing Devices 361
Abrader Multiple Use T&E for Materials 226
Absorber, Shock Mechanical Devices 315
Absorptiometer Optical T&E 343
Abstract Literary Works 477
Accelerator, Linear Nuclear Physics T&E 341
Accelerator, Particle Nuclear Physics T&E 341
Accelerometer Mechanical Measurement Equipment 318
Accessory, Doll Toys 520
Accessory, Fireplace Heating Equipment Accessories 76
Accordion Musical Instruments 371
Acid, Lithographic Printing Accessories 386
Acidimeter Chemical Testing Devices 290
Acknowledgment Other Documents 480
Act Government Records 470
Actinograph Chemical Testing Devices 289
Actinometer Chemical Testing Devices 289
Actuator Electrical System Components 300
Ad, Magazine Advertising Media 449
Ad, Newspaper Advertising Media 449
Ad, Print Advertising Media 449
Adapter, Barrel Armament Accessories 266
Adapter, Battery Electrical System Components 300
Adapter, Battery Charger Electrical System Components 300
Adapter, Electrical Electrical System Components 300
Adapter, Enema Veterinary Equipment 142
Adapter, Filmstrip Visual Communication Accessories 399
Adapter, Fire Hose Protective Devices 345
Adapter, Grip Armament Accessories 266
Adapter, Media Visual Communication Accessories 399
Adapter, Plug Electrical System Components 300
Adapter, Record Sound Communication Accessories 389
Adapter, Slide Visual Communication Accessories 399
Adapter, Tubing Labware 292
Adapter, Weapon Armament Accessories 266
Adargas Body Armor 275
Adenotome Medical Instruments 330
Adobe Construction Materials 3
Advertisement Advertising Media 449
Adz Woodworking T&E 246
Adz, Bunging Woodworking T&E 246
Adz, Carpenter's Woodworking T&E 246
Adz, Cleaving Woodworking T&E 246
Adz, Cooper's Woodworking T&E 246
Adz, Guttering Woodworking T&E 246
Adz, Hollowing Woodworking T&E 246
Adz, Ice Mining & Mineral Harvesting T&E 225
Adz, Lipped Woodworking T&E 246
Adz, Marking Forestry T&E 190
Adz, Railroad Woodworking T&E 246
Adz, Shipwright's Woodworking T&E 246
Adz, Trussing Woodworking T&E 246
Adz, Wheelwright's Woodworking T&E 246
Aerator, Milk Food Processing Equipment 165
Aerometer Meteorological T&E 339
Aeroscope Biological T&E 286
Aerostat Aircraft 411
Aethrioscope Meteorological T&E 339
Affidavit Legal Documents 476
Affixer, Stamp Writing Accessories 402
Afghan Furniture Coverings 61
A-Frame Dwellings 32
Agal Headwear 93
Agenda Administrative Records 467
Agitator, Flour-Bleaching Food Processing Equipment 168
Agitator, Laundry Laundry Equipment 313
Agnus Dei Belief Symbols 493
Agreement Legal Documents 476
Aid, Hearing Personal Assistive Objects 107
Aid, Pill Veterinary Equipment 142
Aid, Visual Instructional Documents 475
Aigrette Hair Adornments 83
Aiguillette Status Symbols 496
Airbrush Painting T&E 229
Airframe Aerospace Transportation Accessories 409
Airliner Aircraft 411
Airplane Aircraft 411
Airplane, Drone Aircraft 411
Airplane, Jet Aircraft 411
Airplane, Military Aircraft 411
Airplane, Reconnaissance Aircraft 411
Airport Transportation Structures 39
Airship Aircraft 411
Airship, Pressure-Rigid Aircraft 411
Airship, Rigid Aircraft 411
Airship, Semi-Rigid Aircraft 411
Airway, Nasopharyngeal Medical Instruments 335
Airway, Oropharyngeal Medical Instruments 335
Alarm Protective Devices 345
Alarm, Burglar Protective Devices 345
Alarm, Fire Protective Devices 345

Term	Category	Page
Alarm, Gas	Protective Devices	345
Alarm, Smoke	Protective Devices	345
Alb	Status Symbols	499
Album	Memorabilia	478
Album, Audio Recording	Sound Communication Accessories	389
Album, Audiotape	Sound Communication Accessories	389
Album, Autograph	Memorabilia	478
Album, Card	Memorabilia	478
Album, Photograph	Memorabilia	478
Album, Postcard	Memorabilia	478
Album, Record	Sound Communication Accessories	389
Album, Stamp	Memorabilia	478
Albuminometer	Medical Instruments	327
Alcoholometer	Chemical Testing Devices	290
Alembic	Chemical Testing Devices	289
Aleurometer	Food Processing Equipment	168
Alidade	Surveying Equipment	352
Alkalimeter	Chemical Testing Devices	289
Alley, Bowling	Cultural & Recreational Structures	29
Alley, Portable Bowling	Sports Equipment	513
Almanac	Other Documents	486
Almshouse	Institutional Structures	37
Alpenhorn	Musical Instruments	370
Alpenstock	Sports Equipment	514
Altar	Religious Objects	461
Altarpiece	Religious Objects	464
Altimeter	Navigational Equipment	349
Altimeter, Aircraft	Aerospace Transportation Accessories	409
Amalgamator	Dental Accessories	320
Amautik	Outerwear	100
Amblyoscope	Medical Instruments	329
Ambrotype	Graphic Documents	473
Ambulance, Horse-Drawn	Animal-Powered Vehicles	423
Ambulance, Motor	Motor Vehicles	428
Amice	Status Symbols	499
Ammeter	Electrical & Magnetic Measurement Devices	297
Ammoniameter	Chemical Testing Devices	290
Amphitheater	Cultural & Recreational Structures	29
Amplifier	Electrical System Components	300
Amplifier, Audio	Sound Communication Devices	391
Amplifier, Carrier	Electrical System Components	300
Amplifier, Direct Current	Electrical System Components	300
Amplifier, Radio Frequency	Telecommunication Accessories	394
Amplifier, Sound	Acoustical T&E	261
Ampul	Medical Accessories	325
Ampulla	Religious Objects	461
Amulet	Belief Symbols	493
Anaglyph	Graphic Documents	473
Analyzer, Clang	Acoustical T&E	261
Analyzer, Differential	Data Processing Devices	361
Analyzer, Gas	Chemical Testing Devices	289
Analyzer, Harmonic	Data Processing Devices	361
Analyzer, Network	Data Processing Devices	361
Analyzer, Sound	Acoustical T&E	261
Anchor	Water Transportation Accessories	436
Anchor, Architectural	Supporting Elements	16
Anchor, Net	Fishing Equipment	145
Anchor, Tooth	Dental Instruments	322
Andiron	Heating Equipment Accessories	76
Anemograph	Meteorological T&E	339
Anemometer	Meteorological T&E	339
Anemoscope	Meteorological T&E	339
Aneroidograph	Meteorological T&E	339
Angleometer	Weights & Measures T&E	357
Angon	Edged Weapons	278
Animal, Carousel	Recreational Devices	511
Animal, Mechanical	Toys	521
Animal, Stuffed	Toys	524
Animal, Toy	Toys	521
Anklet	Body Adornments	81
Annealer	Dental Accessories	320
Announcement	Declaratory Documents	468
Announcement, Anniversary	Declaratory Documents	468
Announcement, Award	Declaratory Documents	468
Announcement, Birth	Declaratory Documents	468
Announcement, Business	Declaratory Documents	468
Announcement, Funeral	Declaratory Documents	468
Announcement, Graduation	Declaratory Documents	468
Announcement, Meeting	Declaratory Documents	468
Announcement, Moving	Declaratory Documents	468
Announcement, Wedding	Declaratory Documents	468
Anode	Electrical System Components	300
Anomaloscope	Medical Instruments	329
Anorak	Outerwear	100
Anorthoscope	Toys	523
Anoscope	Medical Instruments	330
Antefix	Roof Elements	14
Antenna	Telecommunication Devices	396
Antenna, Parabolic	Telecommunication Devices	396
Antenna, Radar	Navigational Equipment	349
Antenna, Radio	Telecommunication Devices	396
Antenna, Rooftop	Telecommunication Devices	396
Antenna, Set-Top	Telecommunication Devices	396
Antenna, Television	Telecommunication Devices	396
Anthology	Literary Works	477
Anthrocometer	Chemical Testing Devices	289
Anticreeper	Rail Transportation Accessories	432

Term	Category	Page
Antimacassar	Furniture Coverings	61
Anvil	Metalworking T&E	207
Anvil, Concave	Metalworking T&E	207
Anvil, Dental	Dental Instruments	322
Anvil, Filecutter's	Metalworking T&E	207
Anvil, Musical	Musical Instruments	372
Anvil, Nailmaker's	Metalworking T&E	207
Anvil, Scythe Sharpening	Metalworking T&E	207
Anvil, Shoemaker's	Leather, Horn & Shellworking T&E	196
Anvil, Slater's	Masonry & Stoneworking T&E	203
Anvil, Stake	Metalworking T&E	207
Apertometer	Optical T&E	343
Apiary	Agricultural Structures	23
Apomecometer	Surveying Equipment	352
Apophorometer, Chemical	Chemical Testing Devices	289
Apparatus, Ammonia Absorption	Biological T&E	286
Apparatus, Assay	Mining & Mineral Harvesting T&E	220
Apparatus, Breathing	Personal Assistive Objects	107
Apparatus, Catalytic	Chemical Testing Devices	289
Apparatus, Cement Vicat	Mechanical Measurement Equipment	318
Apparatus, Counting	Biological T&E	286
Apparatus, Culture	Biological T&E	286
Apparatus, Distilling	Chemical Testing Devices	289
Apparatus, Float Test	Chemical Testing Devices	289
Apparatus, Hoisting	Mechanical Devices	315
Apparatus, Hot Extraction	Chemical Testing Devices	289
Apparatus, Kahn Test	Biological T&E	286
Apparatus, Metabolism	Biological T&E	286
Apparatus, Micro Combustion	Chemical Testing Devices	289
Apparatus, Permeability	Mechanical Measurement Equipment	318
Apparatus, Pneumothorax	Medical Instruments	333
Apparatus, Shaking	Biological T&E	286
Apparatus, Staining	Biological T&E	286
Apparatus, Tone Difference	Acoustical T&E	261
Apparatus, Urea	Medical Instruments	327
Apparatus, Van Slyke	Biological T&E	286
Appentice	Outbuildings	38
Appliance, Orthodontic	Dental Instruments	322
Application	Other Documents	482
Application, Financial	Other Documents	482
Application, Job	Administrative Records	467
Application, License	Other Documents	483
Application, Membership	Other Documents	483
Application, Registration	Other Documents	483
Applicator, Cosmetic	Beauty Supplies	116
Applicator, Dental	Dental Instruments	322
Applicator, Hair Dye	Hair Care Objects	118
Applicator, Medical	Medical Instruments	327
Applicator, Shoe Polish	Clothing Care Objects	105
Applicator, Tampon	Hygiene Objects	120
Appliqué	Art	452
Appraisal	Financial Records	469
Apron	Protective Wear	102
Apron, Blacksmith's	Protective Wear	102
Apron, Carriage	Land Transportation Accessories	416
Apron, Cocktail	Protective Wear	102
Apron, Cooking	Protective Wear	102
Apron, Fraternal	Status Symbols	498
Apron, Occupational	Protective Wear	102
Apron, Sewing	Protective Wear	102
Apron, Tea	Protective Wear	102
Apron, Tool	Personal Carrying & Storage Gear	110
Aquameter	Chemical Testing Devices	289
Aquaplane	Recreational Devices	510
Aquarium	Pet Supplies	141
Aquarium, Public	Cultural & Recreational Structures	29
Aqueduct	Hydraulic Structures	34
Arbor	Site Features	20
Arcade	Cultural & Recreational Structures	29
Arch	Other Structures	41
Architrave	Supporting Elements	16
Archive	Other Documents	480
Arcograph	Drafting T&E	366
Arena	Cultural & Recreational Structures	29
Argentometer	Chemical Testing Devices	290
Argyle	Serving Vessels	186
Ark, Noah's	Toys	520
Ark, Torah	Religious Objects	461
Arm, Artificial	Personal Assistive Objects	108
Armature	Glass, Plastics & Clayworking T&E	192
Armband	Clothing Accessories	84
Armband, Mourning	Funerary Objects	456
Armband, Political	Belief Symbols	493
Armchair	Seating Furniture	47
Armet	Body Armor	275
Armilla	Status Symbols	498
Armlet	Body Adornments	81
Armoire	Storage & Display Furniture	54
Armor	Body Armor	275
Armor, Display	Decorative Furnishings	60
Armor, Horse	Land Transportation Accessories	419
Armor, Parade	Body Armor	275
Armory	Defense Structures	31
Arpillera	Art	452
Arrastra	Metalworking T&E	207
Arrester, Spark	Electrical System Components	300
Arrow	Edged Weapons	277

Term	Category	Page
Arrowhead	Edged Weapons	278
Arsenal	Defense Structures	31
Art, Digital	Art	452
Art, Trench	Art	452
Article	Literary Works	477
Article of Incorporation	Legal Documents	476
Articulator, Dental	Dental Instruments	322
Artillery, Breech-Loading	Artillery	274
Artillery, Muzzle-Loading	Artillery	274
Artwork	Art	452
Ascot	Clothing Accessories	85
Ashlar	Construction Materials	4
Ashpan	Housekeeping Equipment	311
Ashtray	Containers for Smoking & Tobacco	59
Aspergillum	Religious Objects	461
Aspirator	Medical Instruments	330
Assemblage	Art	454
Astrodicticum	Astronomical T&E	284
Astrolabe	Astronomical T&E	284
Astrolabe, Mariner's	Navigational Equipment	349
Astrometeoroscope	Optical T&E	343
Astrometer	Astronomical T&E	284
Astropatrotometer	Astronomical T&E	284
Astroscope	Astronomical T&E	284
Asylum	Institutional Structures	37
Atlas	Graphic Documents	472
Atlatl	Edged Weapons	277
Atmolyser	Chemical Testing Devices	289
Atomizer	Medical Instruments	332
Atomizer, Perfume	Hygiene Objects	120
Attachment, Flash	Camera Equipment	376
Attachment, Lathe	Woodworking T&E	246
Attachment, Vacuum Cleaner	Housekeeping Equipment	311
Audiocassette	Sound Communication Media	393
Audiometer	Acoustical T&E	261
Audiotape	Sound Communication Media	393
Audiphone	Medical Instruments	328
Auger	Woodworking T&E	246
Auger, Breast	Woodworking T&E	246
Auger, Burn	Woodworking T&E	246
Auger, Cylinder	Woodworking T&E	246
Auger, Food	Food Preparation Accessories	152
Auger, Fruit	Food Preparation Accessories	152
Auger, Fuze	Armament Accessories	266
Auger, Hollow	Woodworking T&E	246
Auger, Pipe	Woodworking T&E	246
Auger, Pod	Woodworking T&E	246
Auger, Post Hole	Construction T&E	295
Auger, Pump	Woodworking T&E	246
Auger, Raft	Forestry T&E	190

Term	Category	Page
auger, screw (*use:* Auger, Spiral)	Woodworking T&E	246
Auger, Shell	Woodworking T&E	246
Auger, Snail	Woodworking T&E	246
Auger, Spiral	Woodworking T&E	246
Auger, Spoon	Woodworking T&E	246
Auger, Sugar	Food Preparation Accessories	152
auger, tap (*use:* Auger, Taper)	Woodworking T&E	246
Auger, Taper	Woodworking T&E	246
auger, twist (*use:* Auger, Spiral)	Woodworking T&E	246
auriscope (*use:* Otoscope)	Medical Instruments	328
Autoclave	Medical Accessories	326
Autoclave, Canning	Food Processing Equipment	165
Autograph	Other Documents	484
Autogyro	Aircraft	412
Autoharp	Musical Instruments	373
Automaton	Data Processing Devices	361
automaton, toy (*use:* Toy, Mechanical)	Toys	523
Automobile	Motor Vehicles	428
autopen (*use:* Machine, Signature)	Writing Devices	406
Auxanometer	Biological T&E	286
Aviary	Other Structures	41
Award	Achievement Symbols	491
Award, Contract	Legal Documents	476
Awl	Multiple Use T&E for Materials	226
awl, brad (*use:* Bradawl)	Woodworking T&E	246
awl, bridle (*use:* Awl, Harness)	Leather, Horn & Shellworking T&E	196
Awl, Burning	Woodworking T&E	246
Awl, Closing	Leather, Horn & Shellworking T&E	196
Awl, Cloth	Needleworking Equipment	237
Awl, Collar	Leather, Horn & Shellworking T&E	196
Awl, Drawing	Leather, Horn & Shellworking T&E	196
awl, flooring (*use:* Bradawl)	Woodworking T&E	246
Awl, Garnish	Leather, Horn & Shellworking T&E	196
Awl, Harness	Leather, Horn & Shellworking T&E	196
Awl, Leather	Leather, Horn & Shellworking T&E	196
Awl, Marking	Woodworking T&E	246
Awl, Metalworking	Metalworking T&E	207
Awl, Peg	Leather, Horn & Shellworking T&E	196
Awl, Saddler's	Leather, Horn & Shellworking T&E	196

Term	Category	Page
Awl, Scratch	Leather, Horn & Shellworking T&E	196
awl, scratch (*use:* Awl, Marking)	Woodworking T&E	246
awl, scribe (*use:* Awl, Marking)	Woodworking T&E	246
Awl, Seat	Leather, Horn & Shellworking T&E	196
Awl, Sewing	Leather, Horn & Shellworking T&E	196
Awl, Square	Woodworking T&E	246
Awl, Stabbing	Leather, Horn & Shellworking T&E	196
Awl, Stitching	Leather, Horn & Shellworking T&E	196
Awl, Woodworking	Woodworking T&E	246
Awning	Door & Window Elements	6
ax (*use:* Weapon, Ax)	Edged Weapons	279
Ax	Woodworking T&E	247
Ax, Barking	Forestry T&E	190
ax, battle (*use:* Battle-Ax)	Edged Weapons	279
ax, beginning (*use:* Ax, Fitting)	Woodworking T&E	247
Ax, Belt	Edged Weapons	279
Ax, Boarding	Edged Weapons	279
Ax, Brick	Masonry & Stoneworking T&E	203
ax, broad (*use:* Broadax)	Woodworking T&E	247
Ax, Cooper's	Woodworking T&E	247
Ax, Cratemaker's	Woodworking T&E	247
Ax, Double-Bitted	Forestry T&E	190
Ax, Felling	Forestry T&E	190
Ax, Fire	Protective Devices	345
Ax, Fitting	Woodworking T&E	247
ax, goosewing (*use:* Broadax)	Woodworking T&E	247
ax, hand (*use:* Biface)	Unclassifiable Objects	527
ax, hewing (*use:* Broadax)	Woodworking T&E	247
Ax, Ice	Mining & Mineral Harvesting T&E	225
Ax, Ice Climbing	Sports Equipment	514
ax, killing (*use:* Ax, Slaughtering)	Food Processing Equipment	165
Ax, Lopping	Forestry T&E	190
Ax, Marking	Forestry T&E	190
Ax, Mason's	Masonry & Stoneworking T&E	203
Ax, Mast	Woodworking T&E	247
Ax, Mortising	Woodworking T&E	247
Ax, Shipwright's	Woodworking T&E	247
Ax, Side	Woodworking T&E	247
Ax, Slaughtering	Food Processing Equipment	165
Ax, Split	Forestry T&E	190
ax, stone (*use:* Ax, Mason's)	Masonry & Stoneworking T&E	203
Ax, Throwing	Edged Weapons	279
Ax, Timber	Forestry T&E	190
Ax, Tobacco	Harvesting Equipment	127
Ax, Tooth	Masonry & Stoneworking T&E	203
Ax, Turpentine	Forestry T&E	190
Axle	Land Transportation Accessories	416
Axometer	Optical T&E	343
azotometer (*use:* Nitrometer)	Chemical Testing Devices	291
Babushka	Headwear	93
Back, Film	Photographic Accessories	378
Back, Focusing	Photographic Accessories	378
Backboard, Basketball	Sports Equipment	513
Backdrop, Photographic	Photographic Accessories	378
Backdrop, Stage	Public Entertainment Devices	507
backgammon (*use:* Set, Backgammon)	Game Equipment	503
Backhoe	Construction T&E	295
Backhoe, Sandbox	Recreational Devices	510
Backpack	Personal Carrying & Storage Gear	110
Backplate	Body Armor	275
backplate (*use:* Fireback)	Environmental Control Elements	8
Backrest	Seating Furniture	47
Backsaw	Woodworking T&E	257
Backsplash	Surface Elements	18
Backstaff	Navigational Equipment	349
Backstop	Cultural & Recreational Structures	30
Backsword	Edged Weapons	278
Bacterioscope	Biological T&E	286
Badge, Campaign	Belief Symbols	493
Badge, Cap	Status Symbols	496
Badge, Fire	Status Symbols	496
Badge, Identification	Personal Identification	495
Badge, Insignia	Status Symbols	496
Badge, Law Enforcement	Status Symbols	496
Badge, Membership	Status Symbols	496
Badge, Merit	Achievement Symbols	491
Badge, Military	Status Symbols	496
Badge, Mourning	Funerary Objects	456
badge, name (*use:* Nametag)	Personal Identification	495
badge, police (*use:* Badge, Law Enforcement)	Status Symbols	496
Badge, Political	Belief Symbols	493
Badger	Masonry & Stoneworking T&E	203
Bag	Containers	414
Bag, Afikomen	Holiday Objects	458
Bag, Armament	Armament Accessories	267
Bag, Ballot	Organizational Objects	459
Bag, Bandolier	Personal Carrying & Storage Gear	110
Bag, Barrack	Personal Carrying & Storage Gear	110

Term	Category	Page
Bag, Bicycle	Land Transportation Accessories	416
Bag, Blueing	Laundry Equipment	313
bag, book (*use:* Satchel)	Personal Carrying & Storage Gear	111
Bag, Bowling Ball	Sports Equipment	513
Bag, Buoyancy	Water Transportation Accessories	436
bag, burial (*use:* Shroud, Burial)	Funerary Objects	457
bag, carpet (*use:* Carpetbag)	Personal Carrying & Storage Gear	110
Bag, Carrying	Personal Carrying & Storage Gear	110
Bag, Chatelaine	Personal Carrying & Storage Gear	110
Bag, Clutch	Personal Carrying & Storage Gear	111
Bag, Collar	Personal Carrying & Storage Gear	110
bag, collection (*use:* Bag, Offering)	Religious Objects	461
Bag, Cooking	Food Preparation Equipment	153
Bag, Cosmetic	Beauty Supplies	116
bag, courier (*use:* Bag, Messenger)	Personal Carrying & Storage Gear	110
Bag, Deposit	Merchandising T&E	336
Bag, Diaper	Personal Carrying & Storage Gear	110
Bag, Ditty	Personal Carrying & Storage Gear	110
Bag, Doctor's	Personal Carrying & Storage Gear	110
Bag, Duffel	Personal Carrying & Storage Gear	110
bag, emery (*use:* Cushion, Emery)	Needleworking Equipment	235
Bag, Evening	Personal Carrying & Storage Gear	111
Bag, Evidence	Regulative Devices	347
bag, feed (*use:* Feedbag)	Animal Care Equipment	134
Bag, Film Changing	Photographic Accessories	378
Bag, Food Storage	Food Storage Equipment	170
Bag, Freezer	Food Storage Equipment	170
Bag, Fruit Picking	Harvesting Equipment	127
Bag, Garment	Personal Carrying & Storage Gear	110
Bag, Gift	Party Accessories	460
Bag, Golf	Sports Equipment	515
Bag, Grain	Food Processing Equipment	164
bag, hand (*use:* Purse)	Personal Carrying & Storage Gear	111
Bag, Harvesting	Harvesting Equipment	127
Bag, Hunting	Armament Accessories	267
Bag, Ice	Medical Instruments	332
Bag, Kit	Personal Carrying & Storage Gear	110
Bag, Laundry	Laundry Equipment	313
Bag, Lingerie	Personal Carrying & Storage Gear	110
Bag, Litter	Housekeeping Equipment	311
Bag, Lunch	Food Service Accessories	180
Bag, Mail Carrier's	Personal Carrying & Storage Gear	110
Bag, Marble	Game Equipment	502
Bag, Medicine	Religious Objects	461
Bag, Messenger	Personal Carrying & Storage Gear	110
Bag, Money	Merchandising T&E	336
bag, musette (*use:* Haversack)	Personal Carrying & Storage Gear	110
Bag, Needlework	Needleworking Equipment	234
Bag, Newspaper Carrier's	Personal Carrying & Storage Gear	110
Bag, Offering	Religious Objects	461
Bag, Ore	Mining & Mineral Harvesting T&E	221
Bag, Oven	Food Preparation Equipment	153
Bag, Pajama	Personal Carrying & Storage Gear	110
Bag, Pastry	Food Preparation Equipment	159
Bag, Pipe	Smoking & Recreational Drug Equipment	114
Bag, Pounce	Writing Devices	406
Bag, Powder	Armament Accessories	267
Bag, Pudding	Food Preparation Equipment	153
Bag, Punching	Sports Equipment	514
bag, roasting (*use:* Bag, Oven)	Food Preparation Equipment	153
Bag, Rosin	Sports Equipment	512
bag, sand (*use:* Sandbag)	Protective Devices	346
Bag, School	Personal Carrying & Storage Gear	110
Bag, Seed	Planting Equipment	132
Bag, Shoe	Personal Carrying & Storage Gear	110
Bag, Shopping	Merchandising T&E	336
Bag, Shot	Armament Accessories	267
Bag, Shoulder	Personal Carrying & Storage Gear	110
Bag, Silage	Feed Processing Equipment	126
Bag, Skate	Sports Equipment	517
Bag, Sleeping	Bedding	43
Bag, Sling	Personal Carrying & Storage Gear	110
Bag, Sport	Personal Carrying & Storage Gear	110
Bag, Tamping	Mining & Mineral Harvesting T&E	220

Term	Category	Page
bag, tobacco (*use:* Pouch, Tobacco)	Smoking & Recreational Drug Equipment	115
Bag, Toiletry	Personal Carrying & Storage Gear	110
Bag, Tote	Personal Carrying & Storage Gear	110
Bag, Trash	Housekeeping Equipment	311
Bag, Trick or Treat	Holiday Objects	458
Bag, Water	Land Transportation Accessories	416
Bag, Whaling	Fishing Equipment	145
bag, wig (*use:* Hairbag)	Hair Adornments	83
bagatelle (*use:* Game, Bagatelle)	Game Equipment	505
Bagger, Grain	Harvesting Equipment	127
Bagpipe	Musical Instruments	374
Bagpipe, Highland	Musical Instruments	374
Bagpipe, Irish	Musical Instruments	374
Bagwig	Hair Adornments	83
Bailer, Boat	Water Transportation Accessories	436
Bailer, Well	Mining & Mineral Harvesting T&E	220
Bain-Marie	Cooking Vessels	151
Bakehouse	Outbuildings	38
Bakery	Commercial Structures	27
Bakestone	Food Preparation Equipment	153
Bakeware	Cooking Vessels	150
Balaclava	Headwear	94
Balalaika	Musical Instruments	373
Balance	Weights & Measures T&E	358
Balance, Analytical	Weights & Measures T&E	358
Balance, Assay	Mining & Mineral Harvesting T&E	220
Balance, Beranger	Weights & Measures T&E	358
Balance, Demonstration	Weights & Measures T&E	358
Balance, Gram Chain	Weights & Measures T&E	358
Balance, Roberval	Weights & Measures T&E	358
Balance, Specific Gravity	Weights & Measures T&E	358
Balance, Torsion	Weights & Measures T&E	358
Balance, Water	Mining & Mineral Harvesting T&E	220
Balcony	Architectural Spaces	1
Baldachin	Ceremonial Structures	25
Baldric	Armament Accessories	266
Bale	Containers	414
Baler	Harvesting Equipment	127
Baler, Cotton	Harvesting Equipment	127
Baler, Hay	Harvesting Equipment	127
Baler, Tobacco	Harvesting Equipment	127
Ball and Chain	Regulative Devices	347
ball, antenna (*use:* Topper, Antenna)	Land Transportation Accessories	422
Ball, Billiard	Game Equipment	501
Ball, Bingo	Game Equipment	502
Ball, Bocce	Game Equipment	505
Ball, Bowling	Sports Equipment	513
Ball, Chalk	Sports Equipment	512
Ball, Cricket	Sports Equipment	514
Ball, Croquet	Game Equipment	501
Ball, Crystal	Religious Objects	461
Ball, Exercise	Recreational Devices	509
Ball, Field Hockey	Sports Equipment	515
Ball, Fortune	Toys	523
ball, gazing (*use:* Sphere, Garden)	Site Features	21
Ball, Golf	Sports Equipment	515
ball, headache (*use:* Ball, Wrecking)	Construction T&E	295
Ball, Hop	Toys	524
Ball, Jai Alai	Sports Equipment	516
Ball, Juggling	Public Entertainment Devices	508
Ball, Kick	Game Equipment	505
Ball, Lacrosse	Sports Equipment	516
Ball, Lottery	Game Equipment	503
Ball, Medicine	Recreational Devices	509
ball, minie (*use:* Bullet, Minie)	Ammunition	263
Ball, Mirror	Public Entertainment Devices	507
Ball, Musket	Ammunition	263
Ball, Nesting	Toys	520
Ball, Paddle Tennis	Sports Equipment	518
ball, ping pong (*use:* Ball, Table Tennis)	Sports Equipment	518
Ball, Pistol	Ammunition	263
Ball, Polo	Sports Equipment	517
Ball, Racquetball	Sports Equipment	517
Ball, Rugby	Sports Equipment	517
Ball, Soccer	Sports Equipment	518
Ball, Squash	Sports Equipment	518
Ball, Stickball	Sports Equipment	518
Ball, Table Tennis	Sports Equipment	518
Ball, Tea	Food Preparation Equipment	155
Ball, Tennis	Sports Equipment	518
Ball, Time	Timekeeping T&E	355
Ball, Toy	Toys	520
Ball, Water Polo	Sports Equipment	519
Ball, Wrecking	Construction T&E	295
Baller	Textile Manufacturing Equipment	244
Baller, Melon	Food Preparation Equipment	157
Ballista	Percussive Weapons	283
Balloon	Aircraft	411
Balloon, Barrage	Aircraft	411
Balloon, Captive	Aircraft	411
Balloon, Free	Aircraft	411
Balloon, Hot-Air	Aircraft	411
Balloon, Political	Advertising Media	449
Balloon, Promotional	Advertising Media	449

Balloon, Toy | Party Accessories | 460
Balloon, Weather | Meteorological T&E | 339
Ballot | Administrative Records | 467
Balmoral | Headwear | 91
Baluster | Barrier Elements | 2
Balustrade | Barrier Elements | 2
band, barrister's (*use:* Tab, Barrister's) | Status Symbols | 498
band, belly (*use:* Bellyband) | Land Transportation Accessories | 421
Band, Cigar | Merchandising T&E | 337
Band, Dental | Dental Instruments | 322
band, ear (*use:* Headband) | Headwear | 93
Band, Elastic | Multiple Use T&E for Materials | 227
Band, Elastrator | Veterinary Equipment | 143
Band, Leg | Animal Care Equipment | 136
band, rubber (*use:* Band, Elastic) | Multiple Use T&E for Materials | 227
band, rubber (*use:* Band, Elastic) | Multiple Use T&E for Materials | 227
Band, Swaddling | Regulative Devices | 347
Bandage | Medical Instruments | 332
Bandana | Personal Assistive Objects | 108
Bandbox | Personal Carrying & Storage Gear | 111
Bandeau | Headwear | 93
Banderilla | Sports Equipment | 514
bandolier (*use:* Bag, Bandolier) | Personal Carrying & Storage Gear | 110
Bandolier | Status Symbols | 496
Bandolier, Ammunition | Armament Accessories | 266
Bandstand | Cultural & Recreational Structures | 29
Bandstick | Bookbinding Equipment | 382
Bandwagon | Animal-Powered Vehicles | 424
Bangle | Body Adornments | 81
banister (*use:* Baluster) | Barrier Elements | 2
banister (*use:* Handrail) | Barrier Elements | 2
Banjo | Musical Instruments | 373
Banjolele | Musical Instruments | 373
Bank | Commercial Structures | 27
Bank, Mechanical | Toys | 520
Bank, Semi-Mechanical | Toys | 520
Bank, Still | Toys | 520
Bank, Toy | Toys | 520
Bankbook | Financial Records | 469
banker (*use:* Bench, Banker) | Masonry & Stoneworking T&E | 203
Banker | Watercraft | 445
Banner | Declaratory Documents | 468
Banner, Promotional | Advertising Media | 449
Bannerstone | Armament Accessories | 272
Banquette | Seating Furniture | 47
Bar | Supporting Elements | 16
Bar, Boring | Mining & Mineral Harvesting T&E | 220
Bar, Busting | Mining & Mineral Harvesting T&E | 220
bar, cargo (*use:* Bar, Load) | Land Transportation Accessories | 416
Bar, Chin-Up | Recreational Devices | 509
Bar, Claw | Mechanical Devices | 316
Bar, Claying | Mining & Mineral Harvesting T&E | 220
Bar, Draught | Land Transportation Accessories | 419
Bar, Elevating | Armament Accessories | 266
Bar, Grab | Other Household Accessories | 67
Bar, Horizontal | Sports Equipment | 516
Bar, Hornworker's | Leather, Horn & Shellworking T&E | 201
bar, jack (*use:* Bar, Load) | Land Transportation Accessories | 416
Bar, Jack | Rail Transportation Accessories | 432
Bar, Load | Land Transportation Accessories | 416
Bar, Meat Hanging | Food Processing Equipment | 165
Bar, Metal | Metalworking T&E | 217
Bar, Miner's | Mining & Mineral Harvesting T&E | 220
bar, pinch (*use:* Pinchbar) | Mechanical Devices | 316
bar, planting (*use:* Dibble) | Planting Equipment | 132
bar, pry (*use:* Crowbar) | Mechanical Devices | 316
Bar, Pull | Finish Hardware | 10
Bar, Push | Finish Hardware | 10
Bar, Quarry | Mining & Mineral Harvesting T&E | 220
Bar, Reinforcing | Supporting Elements | 16
Bar, Ribbon | Achievement Symbols | 491
Bar, Rigging | Mining & Mineral Harvesting T&E | 220
Bar, Serving | Storage & Display Furniture | 53
Bar, Shutter | Finish Hardware | 11
Bar, Stall | Recreational Devices | 509
Bar, Stretcher | Mining & Mineral Harvesting T&E | 220
Bar, Tamping | Mining & Mineral Harvesting T&E | 220
bar, tie (*use:* Rod, Tie) | Supporting Elements | 16
Bar, Tommy | Mechanical Devices | 316
Bar, Towel | Storage & Display Accessories | 63
Bar, Wagon Pinch | Mining & Mineral Harvesting T&E | 220
Bar, Warping | Textile Manufacturing Equipment | 239
bar, wrecking (*use:* Pinchbar) | Mechanical Devices | 316
Barb, Lance | Edged Weapons | 277

Barbell	Recreational Devices	510
Barbershop	Commercial Structures	27
Barbette	Headwear	91
Bardiche	Edged Weapons	278
Barge	Watercraft	446
Barge, Admiral's	Watercraft	446
Barge, Training	Watercraft	448
Bargeboard	Roof Elements	14
Bark	Watercraft	444
Bark, Jackass	Watercraft	444
Barkentine	Watercraft	444
Barker	Papermaking T&E	232
Barn	Agricultural Structures	23
Barn, Cattle	Agricultural Structures	23
Barn, Dairy	Agricultural Structures	23
Barn, Hop	Agricultural Structures	23
Barn, Horse	Agricultural Structures	23
Barn, Tobacco	Agricultural Structures	23
Barograph	Meteorological T&E	339
Barometer	Meteorological T&E	339
Barometer, Aneroid	Meteorological T&E	339
Barometer, Mercury	Meteorological T&E	339
Barostat	Medical Instruments	327
Barouche	Animal-Powered Vehicles	423
barque (*use:* Bark)	Watercraft	444
barquentine (*use:* Barkentine)	Watercraft	444
Barrack	Dwellings	32
Barrel	Containers	414
Barrel, Amalgamating	Metalworking T&E	207
Barrel, Firearm	Armament Accessories	266
Barrel, Rain	Plumbing & Drainage Elements	12
Barrel, Syringe	Veterinary Equipment	142
Barrette	Hair Adornments	83
Barricade	Defense Structures	31
Barrier, Road	Site Features	20
Barrier, Site	Site Features	20
Barrier, Weed	Groundskeeping Equipment	309
barrow (*use:* Pushcart)	Human-Powered Vehicles	426
Barrow, Apple	Harvesting Equipment	127
Barrowcoat	Outerwear	100
bars, monkey (*use:* Junglegym)	Recreational Devices	510
Bars, Parallel	Sports Equipment	516
Bars, Uneven	Sports Equipment	516
Barspoon	Food Preparation Equipment	161
Barstool	Seating Furniture	49
baryton (*use:* Viol)	Musical Instruments	373
Bascinet	Body Armor	275
Base	Sports Equipment	512
Baseball	Sports Equipment	512
Baseball, Training	Sports Equipment	512
Baseboard	Surface Elements	18
Baselard	Edged Weapons	277
Basin	Containers	415
Basin, Flushing	Labware	292
Basin, Laboratory	Labware	292
Basin, Medical	Medical Accessories	325
Basin, Rinsing	Labware	292
Basin, Serving	Serving Vessels	186
basin, shaving (*use:* Bowl, Shaving)	Hair Care Objects	118
basin, wash (*use:* Washbasin)	Hygiene Objects	121
Basket	Containers	414
Basket, Bait	Fishing Equipment	145
basket, berry (*use:* Basket, Fruit Picking)	Harvesting Equipment	127
Basket, Bicycle	Land Transportation Accessories	416
Basket, Bread	Serving Vessels	186
Basket, Burden	Personal Carrying & Storage Gear	111
Basket, Cake	Serving Vessels	186
Basket, Carrying	Personal Carrying & Storage Gear	111
basket, cheese (*use:* Strainer, Whey)	Food Processing Equipment	167
Basket, Cooking	Cooking Vessels	151
Basket, Cotton	Harvesting Equipment	127
Basket, Dough	Food Preparation Equipment	153
Basket, Easter	Holiday Objects	458
Basket, Egg Gathering	Harvesting Equipment	127
basket, fire (*use:* Cresset)	Lighting Holders	71
basket, fishing (*use:* Creel, Fishing)	Fishing Equipment	145
Basket, Flower	Horticultural Containers	62
Basket, Food	Serving Vessels	186
Basket, Food Storage	Food Storage Equipment	170
Basket, Fruit	Serving Vessels	186
Basket, Fruit Picking	Harvesting Equipment	127
Basket, Fry	Cooking Vessels	151
Basket, Gathering	Harvesting Equipment	127
Basket, Hanging	Storage & Display Accessories	63
Basket, Household	Storage & Display Accessories	63
Basket, Jai Alai	Sports Equipment	516
Basket, Laundry	Laundry Equipment	313
Basket, Lunch	Food Service Accessories	180
basket, market (*use:* Basket, Shopping)	Merchandising T&E	336
basket, milk bottle (*use:* Carrier, Milk Bottle)	Food Processing Equipment	166
Basket, Mortar	Food Preparation Equipment	160
Basket, Needlework	Needleworking Equipment	234
Basket, Offering	Religious Objects	461
Basket, Ore	Mining & Mineral Harvesting T&E	221

Basket, Oyster	Fishing Equipment	145
Basket, Pack	Personal Carrying & Storage Gear	111
Basket, Picnic	Food Service Accessories	180
basket, plaque (*use:* Plaque, Decorative)	Art	454
Basket, Ring	Food Storage Equipment	170
basket, ritual (*use:* Container, Ritual)	Religious Objects	461
basket, sewing (*use:* Basket, Needlework)	Needleworking Equipment	234
Basket, Shopping	Merchandising T&E	336
Basket, Sifter	Food Preparation Equipment	162
Basket, Ski Pole	Sports Equipment	517
Basket, Snake	Public Entertainment Devices	507
Basket, Steaming	Cooking Vessels	151
Basket, Trinket	Personal Carrying & Storage Gear	111
Basket, Wine Bottle	Food Service Accessories	180
Basket, Winnowing	Harvesting Equipment	131
Basketball	Sports Equipment	513
basnet (*use:* Bascinet)	Body Armor	275
Basquine	Main Garments	96
Bas-Relief	Art	454
Bass, Double	Musical Instruments	373
Bassboat	Watercraft	444
Bassinet	Sleeping & Reclining Furniture	50
Bassoon	Musical Instruments	374
Bassoon, Double	Musical Instruments	373
Bassoon, Russian	Musical Instruments	370
Baster	Food Preparation Equipment	153
Bastille	Defense Structures	31
Bat, Baseball	Sports Equipment	512
Bat, Cricket	Sports Equipment	514
Bat, Softball	Sports Equipment	512
Batcher	Masonry & Stoneworking T&E	204
Bateau	Watercraft	442
bateau, V-bottomed (*use:* Skipjack)	Watercraft	445
Bath	Biological T&E	286
Bath, Dehydrating	Biological T&E	286
Bath, Embedding	Biological T&E	286
bath, eye (*use:* Wash, Eye)	Medical Instruments	329
bath, hip (*use:* Bath, Sitz)	Plumbing & Drainage Elements	12
Bath, Public	Institutional Structures	37
Bath, Sitz	Plumbing & Drainage Elements	12
Bath, Water	Labware	292
Bathometer	Navigational Equipment	349
Bathrobe	Dressingwear & Nightwear	88
Bathtub	Plumbing & Drainage Elements	12
Bathyscaphe	Watercraft	448
Bathysphere	Watercraft	448
Baton	Status Symbols	498
Baton, Conductor's	Musical Accessories	368
Baton, Twirling	Sports Equipment	516
Batoreometer	Mechanical Measurement Equipment	318
Batten	Multiple Use T&E for Materials	227
Batten, Weaving	Textile Manufacturing Equipment	239
Battery	Defense Structures	31
Battery, Dry-Cell	Power Producing Equipment	303
Battery, Electrical	Power Producing Equipment	303
Battery, Gravity	Power Producing Equipment	303
Battery, Solar	Power Producing Equipment	303
Battery, Wet-Cell	Power Producing Equipment	303
Battle-Ax	Edged Weapons	279
Battledore	Glass, Plastics & Clayworking T&E	192
battledore (*use:* Racket, Badminton)	Sports Equipment	512
Battlement	Defense Structures	31
Battleship	Watercraft	447
Bayonet	Edged Weapons	277
Bayonet, Knife	Edged Weapons	277
Bayonet, Plug	Edged Weapons	277
Bayonet, Socket	Edged Weapons	277
Bayonet, Sword	Edged Weapons	277
Bayonet, Triangular	Edged Weapons	277
Bazooka	Artillery	274
BB (*use:* Shot, BB)	Ammunition	265
Beacon	Navigational Equipment	350
Beacon, Aircraft	Navigational Equipment	350
Beacon, Lighthouse	Navigational Equipment	350
Bead	Needleworking Equipment	236
Bead, Parrel	Water Transportation Accessories	439
Bead, Prayer	Belief Symbols	493
Bead, Sliding	Toys	520
Bead, Stringing	Toys	520
bead, toggle (*use:* Netsuke)	Personal Carrying & Storage Gear	113
Bead, Toy	Toys	520
Bead, Trade	Exchange Media	487
beads, rosary (*use:* Rosary)	Belief Symbols	494
Beadwork	Art	452
Beaker	Labware	292
Beaker, Berzelius	Labware	292

Beaker, Drinking — Drinking Vessels 173
Beaker, Griffen — Labware 292
Beaker, Phillips — Labware 292
Beakhead — Water Transportation Accessories 436
Beakiron — Metalworking T&E 207
Beam — Supporting Elements 16
Beam, Balance — Sports Equipment 516
Beam, Cloth — Textile Manufacturing Equipment 239
Beam, Currier's — Leather, Horn & Shellworking T&E 196
Beam, I — Supporting Elements 16
Beam, Tanner's — Leather, Horn & Shellworking T&E 196
Beam, Truss — Supporting Elements 16
Beam, Warp — Textile Manufacturing Equipment 239
Beamer — Textile Manufacturing Equipment 239
Beanbag — Toys 520
Beanie — Headwear 92
Beanpot — Cooking Vessels 151
Bear, Teddy — Toys 524
Bearder, Barley — Harvesting Equipment 127
Bearing — Power Transmission Components 305
Beater, Batter — Food Preparation Equipment 161
beater, cake (*use:* Mixer, Cake) — Food Preparation Equipment 161
Beater, Food — Food Preparation Equipment 161
Beater, Hollander — Papermaking T&E 233
Beater, Jordan — Papermaking T&E 233
Beater, Percussion — Musical Accessories 368
Beater, Rug — Housekeeping Equipment 311
Beater, Seed — Harvesting Equipment 127
Beater, Straw — Fiberworking T&E 144
beater, weaving (*use:* Comb, Weaving) — Textile Manufacturing Equipment 239
beater, weft (*use:* Picker, Fiber) — Textile Manufacturing Equipment 243
Bed — Sleeping & Reclining Furniture 50
bed, bookcase (*use:* Bed, Deception) — Sleeping & Reclining Furniture 50
Bed, Bunk — Sleeping & Reclining Furniture 50
Bed, Canopy — Sleeping & Reclining Furniture 50
Bed, Child's — Sleeping & Reclining Furniture 50
Bed, Couch — Sleeping & Reclining Furniture 50
Bed, Deception — Sleeping & Reclining Furniture 50
Bed, Field — Sleeping & Reclining Furniture 50
Bed, Folding — Sleeping & Reclining Furniture 50
Bed, Four-Poster — Sleeping & Reclining Furniture 50
Bed, Half-Tester — Sleeping & Reclining Furniture 50
Bed, Hideaway — Sleeping & Reclining Furniture 50
bed, high-post (*use:* Bed, Four-Poster) — Sleeping & Reclining Furniture 50
Bed, Hospital — Sleeping & Reclining Furniture 50
bed, Jenny Lind (*use:* Bed, Spool) — Sleeping & Reclining Furniture 50
Bed, Murphy — Sleeping & Reclining Furniture 50
bed, plantation (*use:* Bed, Canopy) — Sleeping & Reclining Furniture 50
Bed, Planting — Site Features 21
Bed, Platform — Sleeping & Reclining Furniture 50
Bed, Sleigh — Sleeping & Reclining Furniture 50
Bed, Sofa — Seating Furniture 49
Bed, Spool — Sleeping & Reclining Furniture 50
Bed, Tanning — Beauty Supplies 117
bed, tester (*use:* Bed, Canopy) — Sleeping & Reclining Furniture 50
Bed, Trundle — Sleeping & Reclining Furniture 50
Bed, Water — Sleeping & Reclining Furniture 50
Bedcover — Bedding 43
Bedkey — Other Household Accessories 66
Bedpan — Hygiene Objects 121
Bedpost — Sleeping & Reclining Furniture 50
Bedsheet — Bedding 43
Bedskirt — Bedding 44
Bedspread — Bedding 43
Bedspring — Bedding 43
Beehive — Agricultural Structures 23
beeper (*use:* Pager — Telecommunication Devices)
beetle (*use:* Machine, Beetle) — Textile Manufacturing Equipment 242
Beetle — Woodworking T&E 254
belfry (*use:* Tower, Bell) — Other Structures 41
Bell — Sound Communication Devices 391
Bell, Altar — Religious Objects 461
Bell, Animal — Animal Care Equipment 134
Bell, Annunciator — Sound Communication Devices 391

Term	Category	Page
Bell, Bicycle	Land Transportation Accessories	416
Bell, Church	Sound Communication Devices	391
bell, cow (*use:* Cowbell)	Animal Care Equipment	134
Bell, Crotal	Land Transportation Accessories	416
Bell, Dinner	Sound Communication Devices	391
Bell, Factory	Sound Communication Devices	391
bell, fire (*use:* Alarm, Fire)	Protective Devices	345
Bell, Fishing	Fishing Equipment	147
Bell, Garden	Horticultural Containers	62
Bell, Horse	Animal Care Equipment	134
bell, jingle (*use:* Bell, Crotal)	Land Transportation Accessories	416
bell, jingle (*use:* Jingle)	Musical Instruments	372
Bell, Kiva	Musical Instruments	372
Bell, Locomotive	Rail Transportation Accessories	431
Bell, Musical	Musical Instruments	372
Bell, Nautical	Water Transportation Accessories	436
bell, rumble (*use:* Bell, Crotal)	Land Transportation Accessories	416
Bell, School	Sound Communication Devices	391
Bell, Service	Sound Communication Devices	391
Bell, Ship's	Water Transportation Accessories	436
Bell, Sleigh	Land Transportation Accessories	416
bell, wind (*use:* Chime, Wind)	Musical Instruments	372
Bellows	Heating Equipment Accessories	76
Bellows, Blacksmith's	Metalworking T&E	208
Bellows, Cooper's	Woodworking T&E	247
Bellows, Dentist's	Dental Accessories	320
Bellows, Foundry	Metalworking T&E	208
Bellpull	Other Household Accessories	66
Bellyband	Land Transportation Accessories	421
Belt	Clothing Accessories	84
Belt, Accessory	Armament Accessories	266
Belt, Ammunition	Armament Accessories	266
Belt, Armament	Armament Accessories	266
Belt, Binder	Harvesting Equipment	127
Belt, Cartridge	Armament Accessories	266
Belt, Cartridge Box	Armament Accessories	266
Belt, Chastity	Regulative Devices	347
Belt, Cinch	Clothing Accessories	84
Belt, Dictation	Sound Communication Media	393
belt, drive (*use:* Belt, Power Transmission)	Power Transmission Components	305
Belt, Fan	Land Transportation Accessories	416
Belt, Flag	Organizational Objects	459
Belt, Garter	Underwear	103
Belt, Girdle	Clothing Accessories	84
Belt, Link	Armament Accessories	266
Belt, Money	Personal Carrying & Storage Gear	111
Belt, Power Transmission	Power Transmission Components	305
Belt, Prize	Achievement Symbols	491
Belt, Rocket	Aircraft	411
Belt, Safety	Regulative Devices	348
Belt, Sam Browne	Armament Accessories	266
Belt, Sanitary	Hygiene Objects	120
Belt, Shoulder	Armament Accessories	266
Belt, Storage	Personal Carrying & Storage Gear	111
Belt, Sword	Armament Accessories	266
Belt, Tool	Personal Carrying & Storage Gear	111
Belt, Web	Clothing Accessories	84
Belt, Weight	Recreational Devices	509
Belvedere	Roof Elements	14
Bema	Religious Objects	461
Bench	Seating Furniture	47
Bench, Banker	Masonry & Stoneworking T&E	203
Bench, Basketmaker's	Woodworking T&E	247
Bench, Box Making	Woodworking T&E	247
Bench, Bucket	Seating Furniture	47
Bench, Carding	Textile Manufacturing Equipment	239
Bench, Carpenter's	Woodworking T&E	247
Bench, Caulker's	Woodworking T&E	247
Bench, Circular	Seating Furniture	47
Bench, Cobbler's	Leather, Horn & Shellworking T&E	196
Bench, Cooper's	Woodworking T&E	247
Bench, Cradle	Seating Furniture	47
Bench, Deacon's	Seating Furniture	47
Bench, Farrier's	Farrier Equipment	139
Bench, Folding	Seating Furniture	47
Bench, Garden	Seating Furniture	47
Bench, Glassmaker's	Glass, Plastics & Clayworking T&E	192
Bench, Harness Maker's	Leather, Horn & Shellworking T&E	196
Bench, Hooded	Seating Furniture	47
Bench, Hornworker's	Leather, Horn & Shellworking T&E	201
bench, joggling (*use:* Board, Joggling)	Seating Furniture	47

Term	Category	Page
Bench, Laundry	Laundry Equipment	313
Bench, Leatherworker's	Leather, Horn & Shellworking T&E	196
bench, mammy (*use:* Bench, Cradle)	Seating Furniture	47
Bench, Music	Musical Accessories	369
Bench, Organ	Musical Accessories	369
Bench, Park	Seating Furniture	47
Bench, Piano	Musical Accessories	369
Bench, Picnic	Seating Furniture	47
Bench, Rigger's	Needleworking Equipment	234
Bench, Sailmaker's	Needleworking Equipment	234
bench, saw-sharpening (*use:* Horse, Saw-Sharpening)	Woodworking T&E	247
Bench, Shingle	Woodworking T&E	247
Bench, Slaughtering	Food Processing Equipment	165
Bench, Weaver's	Textile Manufacturing Equipment	239
Bench, Weight Training	Recreational Devices	509
Bench, Wheelwright's	Woodworking T&E	247
Bench, Window	Seating Furniture	47
Bench, Woodworking	Woodworking T&E	247
Bench-Hook, Sailmaker's	Needleworking Equipment	234
Bender, Flange	Metalworking T&E	207
Bender, Metal	Metalworking T&E	207
Bender, Pipe	Metalworking T&E	207
Bender, Rail	Mining & Mineral Harvesting T&E	220
Bender, Tire	Metalworking T&E	207
Beret	Headwear	91
berth, building (*use:* Slipway)	Transportation Structures	40
Bertha	Clothing Accessories	84
Betatron	Nuclear Physics T&E	341
bevel (*use:* Square, Bevel	Woodworking T&E)	
Beveler	Leather, Horn & Shellworking T&E	197
Beveler, Edge	Leather, Horn & Shellworking T&E	197
Beveler, Safety	Leather, Horn & Shellworking T&E	197
Bib	Protective Wear	102
Bib, Dental	Dental Accessories	320
Biberon	Drinking Vessels	173
Bible	Religious Objects	465
Bibliography	Other Documents	483
bickern (*use:* Beakiron)	Metalworking T&E	207
Bicorn	Headwear	92
Bicycle	Human-Powered Vehicles	426
bicycle, gasoline (*use:* Motorbike)	Motor Vehicles	428
Bicycle, High Wire	Public Entertainment Devices	507
Bicycle, Ordinary	Human-Powered Vehicles	426
Bicycle, Safety	Human-Powered Vehicles	426
Bicycle, Side-By-Side	Human-Powered Vehicles	426
Bicycle, Stationary	Recreational Devices	509
Bicycle, Steam	Motor Vehicles	430
Bicycle, Tandem	Human-Powered Vehicles	426
Bidet	Plumbing & Drainage Elements	12
Bier	Funerary Objects	457
Biface	Unclassifiable Objects	527
Biffa	Percussive Weapons	283
Biggin	Headwear	91
Biggin, Coffee	Serving Vessels	189
Bike, Dirt	Motor Vehicles	428
Bikini	Main Garments	99
Bilbo	Regulative Devices	348
bilboquet (*use:* Toy, Cup and Ball)	Toys	523
Bill	Edged Weapons	278
Bill of Exchange	Exchange Media	489
Bill of Lading	Administrative Records	467
Bill of Sale	Financial Records	469
Bill, Legislative	Government Records	470
Billboard	Advertising Media	451
Billet	Metalworking T&E	217
Billethead	Water Transportation Accessories	437
billfold (*use:* Wallet)	Personal Carrying & Storage Gear	112
Billhook	Groundskeeping Equipment	310
Billy, Slubbing	Textile Manufacturing Equipment	239
bima (*use:* Bema)	Religious Objects	461
Bimini	Water Transportation Accessories	436
Bin	Containers	414
Bin, Chaser	Harvesting Equipment	127
Bin, Coal	Heating Equipment Accessories	77
Bin, Compost	Groundskeeping Equipment	309
Bin, Corn	Harvesting Equipment	127
Bin, Display	Merchandising T&E	336
bin, filing (*use:* Tray, Paper)	Writing Accessories	403
Bin, Flour	Food Storage Equipment	170
Bin, Food Storage	Food Storage Equipment	170
Bin, Grain	Harvesting Equipment	127
Bin, Ore	Mining & Mineral Harvesting T&E	221
Bin, Recycling	Housekeeping Equipment	312
Bin, Rice	Harvesting Equipment	127
Bin, Sorting	Containers	414
Bin, Storage	Containers	414
Bin, Vegetable	Food Storage Equipment	170
Binder	Underwear	103
Binder, Abdominal	Medical Instruments	332
Binder, Clip	Writing Accessories	402
Binder, Corn	Harvesting Equipment	127
Binder, Grain	Harvesting Equipment	127
Binder, Loose-Leaf	Writing Accessories	402

Binder, Medical	Medical Instruments	332
Binder, Obstetrical	Medical Instruments	332
Binder, Post	Writing Accessories	402
Binder, Ring	Writing Accessories	402
binder, row (*use:* Binder, Corn)	Harvesting Equipment	127
Binder, Twine	Harvesting Equipment	127
Binder, Wire	Harvesting Equipment	127
Binding	Needleworking Equipment	236
Binding, Ski	Sports Equipment	517
Bindle	Personal Carrying & Storage Gear	110
bingo (*use:* Game, Bingo)	Game Equipment	503
Binnacle	Water Transportation Accessories	436
Binoculars	Optical T&E	343
biofact (*use:* Ecofact)	Unclassifiable Objects	527
Biography	Literary Works	477
Biometer	Medical Instruments	327
Biosatellite	Spacecraft	413
bioscope (*use:* Projector, Motion Picture)	Visual Communication Devices	401
Biospecimen	Biological T&E	286
Biplane	Aircraft	411
Bipod, Shooting	Armament Accessories	270
bird, clay (*use:* Target, Skeet)	Armament Accessories	272
bird, pie (*use:* Funnel, Pie)	Food Preparation Equipment	155
bird, sewing (*use:* Clamp, Sewing)	Needleworking Equipment	234
Birdbath	Site Features	20
Birdcage	Pet Supplies	141
Birdhouse	Site Features	20
Birdstone	Armament Accessories	272
Biretta	Status Symbols	499
Bistoury	Medical Instruments	331
Bit, Annular	Woodworking T&E	247
Bit, Bridle	Land Transportation Accessories	419
Bit, Center	Woodworking T&E	247
Bit, Core	Mining & Mineral Harvesting T&E	220
Bit, Countersink	Woodworking T&E	247
Bit, Dowel Point	Woodworking T&E	247
Bit, Drill	Multiple Use T&E for Materials	226
Bit, Expansion	Woodworking T&E	247
Bit, Flat	Metalworking T&E	207
Bit, Gimlet	Woodworking T&E	247
Bit, Hollow	Woodworking T&E	247
Bit, Masonry	Masonry & Stoneworking T&E	203
Bit, Metal Cutting	Metalworking T&E	207
Bit, Mining	Mining & Mineral Harvesting T&E	220
Bit, Mortise	Woodworking T&E	247
Bit, Nose	Woodworking T&E	247
Bit, Percussion	Mining & Mineral Harvesting T&E	220
bit, pivot (*use:* Bit, Tenon-Cutting)	Woodworking T&E	248
Bit, Reamer	Mining & Mineral Harvesting T&E	220
Bit, Rotary	Mining & Mineral Harvesting T&E	220
Bit, Scutch	Masonry & Stoneworking T&E	203
Bit, Shell	Woodworking T&E	247
Bit, Spiral	Woodworking T&E	247
Bit, Spoke Trimmer	Woodworking T&E	248
Bit, Spoon	Woodworking T&E	248
Bit, Spudding	Mining & Mineral Harvesting T&E	220
Bit, Straight-Fluted	Multiple Use T&E for Materials	226
Bit, Taper	Woodworking T&E	248
Bit, Tenon-Cutting	Woodworking T&E	248
Bit, Training	Animal Care Equipment	135
Bit, Twist	Multiple Use T&E for Materials	226
Bit, Woodworking	Woodworking T&E	247
bitcoin (*use:* Medium, Digital Exchange)	Exchange Media	487
bitstock (*use:* Brace, Woodworking)	Woodworking T&E	248
Bitt	Water Transportation Accessories	436
blackboard (*use:* Chalkboard)	Writing Media	408
blackjack (*use:* Jack, Leather)	Drinking Vessels	174
Blackjack	Percussive Weapons	283
blade (*use:* Grader)	Construction T&E	295
Blade, Cleaving	Masonry & Stoneworking T&E	203
Blade, Dental	Dental Instruments	322
Blade, Razor	Hair Care Objects	118
Blade, Snow	Land Transportation Accessories	416
Blanchimeter	Chemical Testing Devices	289
Blank	Unclassifiable Objects	527
Blank, Coin	Metalworking T&E	217
Blank, Horn	Leather, Horn & Shellworking T&E	199
Blank, Ivory	Leather, Horn & Shellworking T&E	199
Blank, Key	Metalworking T&E	217
Blank, Knife	Metalworking T&E	217
Blank, Metal	Metalworking T&E	217
Blank, Tortoise	Leather, Horn & Shellworking T&E	199
Blank, Wood	Woodworking T&E	248
Blankbook	Writing Media	408

Blanket	Bedding	43
Blanket, Animal	Animal Care Equipment	134
Blanket, Button	Status Symbols	498
Blanket, Carriage	Land Transportation Accessories	416
Blanket, Electric	Bedding	43
Blanket, Fire	Protective Devices	345
Blanket, Moving	Containers	414
Blanket, Nobility	Status Symbols	498
Blanket, Offset	Graphic Equipment	384
Blanket, Saddle	Land Transportation Accessories	419
blanket, sheet (*use:* Sheet, Blanket)	Bedding	43
Blanket, Trade	Bedding	43
Blanket, Wearing	Outerwear	100
blaster (*use:* Detonator)	Mining & Mineral Harvesting T&E	222
Blaze, Tree	Surveying Equipment	353
Blazer	Main Garments	96
Bleacher	Cultural & Recreational Structures	30
Blender	Food Preparation Equipment	161
blender, bread (*use:* Mixer, Dough)	Food Preparation Equipment	161
Blender, Countertop	Food Preparation Equipment	161
Blender, Feeder	Textile Manufacturing Equipment	242
Blender, Flour	Food Processing Equipment	168
Blender, Pastry	Food Preparation Equipment	158
Blender, Sandwich	Textile Manufacturing Equipment	242
Blender, Stick	Food Preparation Equipment	161
Blender, Stock	Papermaking T&E	232
Blimp	Aircraft	411
Blind	Window & Door Coverings	78
blind, mini (*use:* Miniblind)	Window & Door Coverings	78
Blind, Venetian	Window & Door Coverings	78
Blind, Vertical	Window & Door Coverings	78
Blinder	Land Transportation Accessories	419
Blindfold	Personal Assistive Objects	107
Block and Tackle	Mechanical Devices	315
Block, Alphabet	Toys	520
Block, Bearing	Power Transmission Components	305
Block, Bevel	Woodworking T&E	248
Block, Bite	Dental Instruments	322
Block, Booking	Other T&E for Materials	260
Block, Building	Toys	520
block, butcher (*use:* Block, Chopping)	Food Preparation Equipment	153
Block, Chopping	Food Preparation Equipment	153
Block, Cinder	Construction Materials	3
Block, Clinching	Farrier Equipment	139
Block, Concrete	Construction Materials	3
Block, Construction	Construction Materials	3
Block, Corner	Surface Elements	18
Block, Dapping	Metalworking T&E	208
Block, Engraving	Graphic Equipment	384
Block, Executioner's	Regulative Devices	347
Block, Fabric	Graphic Equipment	384
Block, Filing	Metalworking T&E	208
Block, Firemaking	Firemaking Equipment	74
Block, Forming	Glass, Plastics & Clayworking T&E	192
	Woodworking T&E	248
Block, Framing	Electrical System Components	300
Block, Fuse		
Block, Gavel	Organizational Objects	459
Block, Glass	Construction Materials	3
Block, Glassblower's	Glass, Plastics & Clayworking T&E	192
Block, Hat	Needleworking Equipment	234
Block, Holding	Metalworking T&E	208
Block, Linoleum	Graphic Equipment	384
Block, Metalworking	Metalworking T&E	207
Block, Miter	Woodworking T&E	248
block, miter-shooting (*use:* Jack, Miter)	Woodworking T&E	248
Block, Mounting	Land Transportation Accessories	416
Block, Mud	Construction Materials	3
Block, Nesting	Toys	520
Block, Parquetry	Toys	520
Block, Picture	Toys	520
block, pillow (*use:* Block, Bearing)	Power Transmission Components	305
Block, Plinth	Surface Elements	18
block, plummer (*use:* Block, Bearing)	Power Transmission Components	305
Block, Polishing	Masonry & Stoneworking T&E	203
Block, Printing	Graphic Equipment	384
Block, Puzzle	Toys	522
Block, Quilt	Needleworking Equipment	234
Block, Sanding	Woodworking T&E	248
Block, Shaving	Woodworking T&E	248
Block, Snatch	Mechanical Devices	315
Block, Starting	Sports Equipment	518
Block, Striking	Metalworking T&E	208
Block, Stropping	Metalworking T&E	216
Block, Telescopic	Toys	520
Block, Toy	Toys	520
Block, Wallpaper	Graphic Equipment	384
Block, Wood	Graphic Equipment	384
Block, Woodworking	Woodworking T&E	248
Blocker	Sports Equipment	516

Blockhouse — Defense Structures 31
Bloom — Metalworking T&E 217
Bloomers — Underwear 104
Bloomery — Metalworking T&E 211
Blotter — Financial Records 469
Blotter, Cosmetic — Beauty Supplies 116
Blotter, Desk — Writing Accessories 402
Blouse — Main Garments 98
blouse, battle dress (*use:* Jacket, Battle) — Main Garments 96
Blouse, Middy — Main Garments 98
Blower — Environmental Control Elements 8
Blower, Blacksmith's — Metalworking T&E 208
Blower, Bubble — Toys 523
Blower, Ensilage — Feed Processing Equipment 126
blower, forage (*use:* Blower, Ensilage) — Feed Processing Equipment 126
blower, impeller (*use:* Blower, Ensilage) — Feed Processing Equipment 126
Blower, Leaf — Groundskeeping Equipment 309
Blower, Metalworking — Metalworking T&E 208
Blower, Party — Party Accessories 460
blower, silage (*use:* Blower, Ensilage) — Feed Processing Equipment 126
blower, silo (*use:* Blower, Ensilage) — Feed Processing Equipment 126
blower, snow (*use:* Snowblower) — Groundskeeping Equipment 310
Blowgun — Edged Weapons 277
blowiron (*use:* Blowpipe) — Glass, Plastics & Clayworking T&E 192
blowpipe (*use:* Blowgun) — Edged Weapons 277
Blowpipe — Glass, Plastics & Clayworking T&E 192
Blowpipe, Anatomical — Biological T&E 286
Blowtorch — Metalworking T&E 208
Blucher — Footwear 89
bludgeon (*use:* Club) — Percussive Weapons 283
Blueprint — Other Documents 481
Blunderbuss — Firearms 282
Blunger — Glass, Plastics & Clayworking T&E 192
Blush — Beauty Supplies 116
Boa — Clothing Accessories 85
Board — Construction Materials 3
Board, Balance — Public Entertainment Devices 507
Board, Bannock — Food Preparation Equipment 162
board, bed (*use:* Component, Bed) — Sleeping & Reclining Furniture 50
Board, Binding — Bookbinding Equipment 382
board, bread (*use:* Breadboard) — Food Preparation Equipment 153
Board, Bulletin — Writing Accessories 402
Board, Bunk — Water Transportation Accessories 436
Board, Button Polishing — Clothing Care Objects 105
Board, Candy — Food Preparation Equipment 153
board, checker (*use:* Checkerboard) — Game Equipment 501
board, cheese (*use:* Cheeseboard) — Serving Vessels 187
Board, Cigar — Other T&E for Materials 260
Board, Circuit — Electrical System Components 300
Board, Cribbage — Game Equipment 501
Board, Cutting — Food Preparation Equipment 153
Board, Darning — Needleworking Equipment 234
board, dibble (*use:* Dibble) — Planting Equipment 132
board, distribution (*use:* Box, Fuse) — Electrical System Components 300
Board, Diving — Recreational Devices 510
Board, Drawing — Drafting T&E 366
Board, Drying — Leather, Horn & Shellworking T&E 196
Board, Emery — Beauty Supplies 117
Board, Fabric Cutting — Needleworking Equipment 234
Board, Fish Measuring — Fishing Equipment 145
Board, Floor — Surface Elements 18
Board, Food Preparation — Food Preparation Equipment 153
board, fuse (*use:* Box, Fuse) — Electrical System Components 300
Board, Gangway — Water Transportation Accessories 437
Board, Graining — Leather, Horn & Shellworking T&E 196
board, hunt (*use:* Huntboard) — Storage & Display Furniture 54
Board, Hymn — Religious Objects 461
Board, Ironing — Laundry Equipment 313
Board, Joggling — Seating Furniture 47
Board, Key — Storage & Display Accessories 63
Board, Lens — Photoprocessing Equipment 381
Board, Levitation — Public Entertainment Devices 508
Board, Macrame — Textile Manufacturing Equipment 239
board, mangle (*use:* Mangle) — Laundry Equipment 314
Board, Mass — Religious Objects 461
board, message (*use:* Board, Bulletin) — Writing Accessories 402
Board, Name — Water Transportation Accessories 440
Board, Navigator's — Navigational Equipment 349

Board, Pastry	Food Preparation Equipment	153
board, quarter (*use:* Quarterboard)	Water Transportation Accessories	440
board, raising (*use:* Board, Graining)	Leather, Horn & Shellworking T&E	196
Board, Rocking	Recreational Devices	509
Board, Roulette	Game Equipment	502
Board, Sandwich	Advertising Media	451
Board, Scutching	Textile Manufacturing Equipment	239
Board, Shooting	Woodworking T&E	248
Board, Shoulder	Status Symbols	496
Board, Sleeve	Laundry Equipment	313
Board, Sounding	Sound Communication Accessories	389
Board, Spirit	Religious Objects	461
board, spotting (*use:* Dibble)	Planting Equipment	132
Board, Spreading	Biological T&E	286
Board, Stove	Heating Equipment Accessories	76
board, tally (*use:* Board, Fish Measuring)	Fishing Equipment	145
Board, Tally	Water Transportation Accessories	436
board, throwing (*use:* Atlatl)	Edged Weapons	277
Board, Tobacco Cutting	Smoking & Recreational Drug Equipment	114
Board, Tool	Multiple Use T&E for Materials	226
board, trail (*use:* Trailboard)	Water Transportation Accessories	437
Board, Tying-Up	Bookbinding Equipment	382
Board, Walking	Recreational Devices	509
Board, Writing	Writing Accessories	402
Boaster	Masonry & Stoneworking T&E	203
Boat	Watercraft	442
boat, Albemarle Sound (*use:* Seiner)	Watercraft	445
Boat, Beach	Watercraft	442
Boat, Bull	Watercraft	442
Boat, Buoy	Watercraft	445
Boat, Bushwack	Watercraft	442
Boat, Canal	Watercraft	446
boat, class (*use:* Classboat)	Watercraft	444
boat, dredge (*use:* Dragger)	Watercraft	445
boat, dredge (*use:* Dredge)	Watercraft	448
Boat, Durham	Watercraft	442
Boat, Excursion	Watercraft	446
boat, feeding (*use:* Feeder, Invalid)	Eating Vessels	177
Boat, Flying	Aircraft	411
boat, gravy (*use:* Sauceboat)	Serving Vessels	187
Boat, Gunning	Watercraft	442
Boat, Hampton	Watercraft	445
boat, incense (*use:* Navette)	Religious Objects	462
Boat, Incense	Religious Objects	461
Boat, Inflatable	Watercraft	442
Boat, Jolly	Watercraft	448
boat, jon (*use:* Johnboat)	Watercraft	443
boat, lobster (*use:* Lobsterboat)	Watercraft	445
boat, motor torpedo (*use:* Boat, Torpedo)	Watercraft	447
boat, Newport (*use:* Catboat)	Watercraft	443
boat, oyster (*use:* Boat, Tonging)	Watercraft	445
boat, oyster (*use:* Vessel, Dredging)	Watercraft	445
boat, packet (*use:* Ship, Packet)	Watercraft	446
boat, paddle (*use:* Steamer, Paddle)	Watercraft	445
boat, pap (*use:* Papboat)	Eating Vessels	177
Boat, Patrol	Watercraft	447
Boat, Pedal	Watercraft	444
boat, picket (*use:* Boat, Patrol)	Watercraft	447
Boat, Pilot	Watercraft	448
Boat, Pontoon	Watercraft	444
boat, PT (*use:* Boat, Torpedo)	Watercraft	447
boat, pulling (*use:* Rowboat)	Watercraft	443
boat, race (*use:* Raceboat)	Watercraft	444
Boat, Rangely	Watercraft	442
boat, seine (*use:* Seiner)	Watercraft	445
Boat, Ship's	Watercraft	448
Boat, Skin	Watercraft	442
Boat, Sport Fishing	Watercraft	444
boat, stone (*use:* Stoneboat)	Cultivation Equipment	125
boat, striker (*use:* Driveboat)	Watercraft	445
Boat, Tonging	Watercraft	445
Boat, Torpedo	Watercraft	447
boat, waterfowl (*use:* Boat, Gunning)	Watercraft	442
boat, yawl (*use:* Yawlboat)	Watercraft	448
Boater	Headwear	93
Boathouse	Transportation Structures	39
Boatstone	Armament Accessories	272
Bob, Balance	Mining & Mineral Harvesting T&E	220
Bob, Plumb	Construction T&E	295

Term	Category	Page
bobber (*use:* Float, Fishing)	Fishing Equipment	147
Bobbin	Textile Manufacturing Equipment	239
Bobbin, Knitting	Textile Manufacturing Equipment	239
Bobbin, Lace	Textile Manufacturing Equipment	239
Bobbin, Sewing	Needleworking Equipment	234
Bobbin, Weaving	Textile Manufacturing Equipment	239
Bobeche	Other Lighting Accessories	72
Bobsled	Sports Equipment	517
Bodice	Main Garments	95
Bodkin	Needleworking Equipment	237
Bodkin, Basketmaker's	Fiberworking T&E	144
Bodkin, Bookbinder's	Bookbinding Equipment	382
Bodkin, Hair	Hair Adornments	83
Bodkin, Hollow	Fiberworking T&E	144
Bodkin, Solid	Fiberworking T&E	144
Body, Vehicle	Land Transportation Accessories	416
Bodyboard	Recreational Devices	510
Bodystocking	Underwear	103
Bodysuit	Main Garments	96
Bogie	Mining & Mineral Harvesting T&E	220
Boiler, Asparagus	Cooking Vessels	151
Boiler, Coffee	Food Preparation Equipment	154
Boiler, Double	Cooking Vessels	151
boiler, feed (*use:* Cooker, Feed)	Feed Processing Equipment	126
Boiler, Hot Water	Environmental Control Elements	8
Boiler, HVAC	Environmental Control Elements	8
Boiler, Laundry	Laundry Equipment	313
Boiler, Mining	Mining & Mineral Harvesting T&E	220
Boiler, Power	Power Producing Equipment	303
Boiler, Steam	Environmental Control Elements	8
Boiler, Steam Power	Power Producing Equipment	303
boiler, wash (*use:* Boiler, Laundry)	Laundry Equipment	313
Bola	Percussive Weapons	283
Bolero	Main Garments	96
Bollard	Water Transportation Accessories	436
Bollard, Road	Site Features	20
Bolo	Edged Weapons	277
Bolometer	Thermal T&E	354
Bolster	Bedding	43
Bolt	Multiple Use T&E for Materials	227
Bolt, Chain	Finish Hardware	10
Bolt, Cloth	Needleworking Equipment	234
Bolt, Crossbow	Edged Weapons	277
Bolt, Door	Finish Hardware	10
Bolt, Draw	Finish Hardware	10
bolt, drift (*use:* Driftbolt)	Woodworking T&E	250
Bolt, Eye	Metalworking T&E	216
Bolt, Fastener	Metalworking T&E	208
Bolt, Lewis	Mining & Mineral Harvesting T&E	220
Bolt, Mining	Mining & Mineral Harvesting T&E	220
Bolt, Molly	Multiple Use T&E for Materials	227
Bolt, Rag	Mining & Mineral Harvesting T&E	220
Bolt, Roof	Mining & Mineral Harvesting T&E	220
bolter, cloth (*use:* Bolter, Sieve)	Food Processing Equipment	169
Bolter, Sieve	Food Processing Equipment	169
Bomb	Ammunition	263
Bomb, Air-to-Air	Ammunition	263
Bomb, Air-to-Surface	Ammunition	263
Bomb, Air-to-Underwater	Ammunition	263
bomb, antiaircraft (*use:* Bomb, Air-to-Air)	Ammunition	263
Bomb, Incendiary	Ammunition	263
Bombachas	Main Garments	97
bombardon (*use:* Tuba)	Musical Instruments	370
Bomber	Aircraft	411
Bombilla	Eating & Drinking Utensils	179
bombship (*use:* Vessel, Bomb)	Watercraft	447
bonbonniere (*use:* Dish, Bonbon)	Serving Vessels	186
Bond	Exchange Media	489
Bond, Legal	Legal Documents	476
Bond, War	Exchange Media	489
Bones	Musical Instruments	372
boneshaker (*use:* Velocipede)	Human-Powered Vehicles	426
Bonnet	Headwear	92
Bonnet, Baby	Headwear	92
Bonnet, Indoor	Headwear	91
Bonnet, Poke	Headwear	92
Bonnet, Rain	Headwear	92
Bonnet, War	Status Symbols	499
Booby	Animal-Powered Vehicles	424
Book	Other Documents	480
Book, Account	Financial Records	469
Book, Activity	Toys	520
Book, Address	Other Documents	480
Book, Appointment	Other Documents	480
Book, Baby	Memorabilia	478
Book, Bridal	Memorabilia	478

Term	Category	Page
Book, Coloring	Toys	520
Book, Comic	Graphic Documents	472
Book, Commonplace	Other Documents	480
Book, Composition	Writing Media	408
book, copy (*use:* Copybook)	Instructional Documents	475
Book, Coupon	Exchange Media	487
Book, Flip	Graphic Documents	472
book, guest (*use:* Guestbook)	Other Documents	483
book, hymn (*use:* Hymnal)	Religious Objects	463
Book, Instruction	Instructional Documents	475
Book, Letter	Writing Accessories	402
book, log (*use:* Log)	Other Documents	484
book, match (*use:* Matchbook)	Firemaking Equipment	74
Book, Music	Literary Works	477
Book, Pattern	Other Documents	480
Book, Plat	Graphic Documents	472
book, poll (*use:* List, Voters')	Other Documents	483
Book, Prayer	Religious Objects	465
Book, Ration	Exchange Media	487
Book, Receipt	Financial Records	469
book, recipe (*use:* Cookbook)	Instructional Documents	475
Book, Record	Administrative Records	467
Book, Sample	Merchandising T&E	338
Book, Stamp	Exchange Media	489
Book, Sticker	Toys	520
book, telephone (*use:* Directory, Telephone)	Other Documents	480
Book, Ticket	Exchange Media	489
Book, Time	Financial Records	469
book, visitor's (*use:* Guestbook)	Other Documents	483
Book, Writing	Writing Media	408
Bookcart	Human-Powered Vehicles	426
Bookcase	Storage & Display Furniture	52
Bookend	Other Household Accessories	66
booklet (*use:* Pamphlet)	Other Documents	484
booklet, instruction (*use:* Pamphlet, Instruction)	Instructional Documents	475
booklet, recipe (*use:* Cookbook)	Instructional Documents	475
Bookmark	Writing Accessories	402
Bookplate	Other Documents	483
Bookshelf	Storage & Display Furniture	52
Bookstall	Commercial Structures	27
Bookstand	Support Furniture	55
Bookstore	Commercial Structures	27
Boom	Water Transportation Accessories	440
boom, jib (*use:* Jibboom)	Water Transportation Accessories	440
Boomerang	Percussive Weapons	283
Booster	Aerospace Transportation Accessories	409
Boot	Footwear	89
Boot, Balmoral	Footwear	89
Boot, Carriage	Footwear	89
Boot, Cowboy	Footwear	89
Boot, Diving	Footwear	89
boot, diving (*use:* Shoe, Diving)	Recreational Devices	511
Boot, Hiking	Footwear	89
Boot, Hip	Footwear	89
Boot, Horse Ankle	Land Transportation Accessories	419
Boot, Lawn	Farrier Equipment	139
Boot, Riding	Footwear	89
Boot, Ski	Footwear	89
Boot, Snow	Footwear	89
Boot, Thigh	Footwear	89
Boot, Wellington	Footwear	89
Bootee	Footwear	89
Booth, Photo	Photographic Accessories	378
Booth, Restaurant	Seating Furniture	47
Booth, Tanning	Beauty Supplies	117
Booth, Telephone	Other Structures	41
booth, ticket (*use:* Stand, Ticket)	Cultural & Recreational Structures	29
booth, toll (*use:* Tollbooth)	Transportation Structures	40
Booth, Voting	Organizational Objects	459
Bootie	Footwear	89
Bootjack	Other Household Accessories	66
Borderlight	Lighting Devices	70
Borer	Multiple Use T&E for Materials	226
Borer, Cork	Woodworking T&E	248
Borescope	Optical T&E	343
Boss	Glass, Plastics & Clayworking T&E	192
Boss, Filecutter's	Metalworking T&E	208
Botte Sauvage	Footwear	89
Bottle	Containers	415
Bottle, Apothecary	Merchandising T&E	336
Bottle, Aspirator	Labware	292
Bottle, Barber	Hygiene Objects	120
Bottle, Centrifuge	Labware	292
Bottle, Christening	Organizational Objects	459
Bottle, Cologne	Hygiene Objects	120
Bottle, Condiment	Serving Vessels	188
Bottle, Decanter	Serving Vessels	188
Bottle, Drinking	Drinking Vessels	173
bottle, drug (*use:* Bottle, Medicine)	Medical Accessories	325
Bottle, Gas Washing	Labware	292

Term	Category	Page
Bottle, Gemel	Containers	415
Bottle, Holy Water	Religious Objects	462
Bottle, Hot Water	Personal Assistive Objects	109
Bottle, Impossible	Art	454
Bottle, Ink	Writing Accessories	403
Bottle, Laboratory	Labware	292
Bottle, Medicine	Medical Accessories	325
Bottle, Milk	Serving Vessels	188
Bottle, Nursing	Drinking Vessels	173
Bottle, Perfume	Hygiene Objects	120
Bottle, Reagent	Labware	292
Bottle, Sample	Mining & Mineral Harvesting T&E	220
Bottle, Seltzer	Serving Vessels	188
Bottle, Serum	Medical Accessories	325
Bottle, Serving	Serving Vessels	188
Bottle, Smelling	Personal Assistive Objects	107
Bottle, Snuff	Smoking & Recreational Drug Equipment	114
Bottle, Specimen	Medical Accessories	325
Bottle, Spray	Housekeeping Equipment	311
Bottle, Tear	Funerary Objects	456
bottle, thermos (*use:* Bottle, Vacuum)	Food Service Accessories	180
Bottle, Toilet	Hygiene Objects	120
Bottle, Vaccine	Medical Accessories	325
Bottle, Vacuum	Food Service Accessories	180
Bottle, Wash	Labware	292
Bottle, Water	Drinking Vessels	173
Bottle, Wine	Serving Vessels	188
Bottle, Witch	Religious Objects	461
bottlescrew (*use:* Screw, Rigging)	Water Transportation Accessories	439
Bougie	Medical Instruments	334
Boultel	Food Preparation Equipment	162
Bouncer, Baby	Toys	521
Bouquet, Floral	Art	453
Bouquet, Wedding	Wedding Objects	466
Boutonniere	Clothing Accessories	84
Bow	Edged Weapons	277
Bow, Clothing	Clothing Accessories	84
Bow, Fire	Firemaking Equipment	74
Bow, Gift	Party Accessories	460
Bow, Hair	Hair Adornments	83
bow, horse (*use:* Yoke, Animal)	Land Transportation Accessories	421
Bow, Instrument	Musical Accessories	368
Bow, Shoe	Clothing Accessories	86
bow, spring (*use:* Compass, Bow)	Drafting T&E	366
Bow, Violin	Musical Accessories	368
Bow, Wagon	Land Transportation Accessories	416
Bowgrace	Water Transportation Accessories	436
Bowl	Containers	415
Bowl, Baptismal	Religious Objects	462
bowl, barber (*use:* Bowl, Shaving)	Hair Care Objects	118
Bowl, Batter	Food Preparation Equipment	153
Bowl, Berry	Serving Vessels	186
Bowl, Bleeding	Medical Instruments	333
Bowl, Bouillon	Eating Vessels	176
Bowl, Brandy	Drinking Vessels	173
Bowl, Bride's	Serving Vessels	186
Bowl, Bulb	Horticultural Containers	62
Bowl, Butter-Working	Food Processing Equipment	165
Bowl, Cereal	Eating Vessels	176
Bowl, Chopping	Food Preparation Equipment	153
Bowl, Covered	Serving Vessels	186
Bowl, Decorative	Decorative Furnishings	60
Bowl, Dental Mixing	Dental Accessories	320
Bowl, Dessert	Eating Vessels	176
bowl, dough (*use:* Trough, Dough)	Food Preparation Equipment	153
Bowl, Drinking	Drinking Vessels	173
Bowl, Eating	Eating Vessels	176
Bowl, Finger	Food Service Accessories	180
bowl, fish (*use:* Fishbowl)	Pet Supplies	141
Bowl, Flower	Horticultural Containers	62
Bowl, Food Storage	Food Storage Equipment	170
Bowl, Fruit	Serving Vessels	186
Bowl, Gathering	Harvesting Equipment	128
Bowl, Ice Cream	Eating Vessels	176
bowl, incense (*use:* Censer)	Religious Objects	462
Bowl, Jelly	Serving Vessels	186
Bowl, Libation	Religious Objects	462
Bowl, Marriage	Wedding Objects	466
Bowl, Mayonnaise	Serving Vessels	186
Bowl, Mixing	Food Preparation Equipment	153
Bowl, Nut	Serving Vessels	186
Bowl, Offering	Religious Objects	461
Bowl, Pet	Pet Supplies	141
Bowl, Pipe	Smoking & Recreational Drug Equipment	114
Bowl, Potpourri	Other Household Accessories	66
Bowl, Punch	Serving Vessels	188
bowl, rose (*use:* Bowl, Flower)	Horticultural Containers	62
Bowl, Salad	Eating Vessels	176
Bowl, Salad Serving	Serving Vessels	186
Bowl, Scouring	Textile Manufacturing Equipment	239
Bowl, Serving	Serving Vessels	186
Bowl, Shaving	Hair Care Objects	118
Bowl, Skimming	Food Processing Equipment	165
bowl, slop (*use:* Bowl, Waste)	Food Service Accessories	181

Bowl, Soup	Eating Vessels	176
Bowl, Sugar	Serving Vessels	186
Bowl, Tea	Drinking Vessels	173
bowl, wash (*use:* Washbasin)	Hygiene Objects	121
Bowl, Waste	Food Service Accessories	181
Bowl, Whipped Cream	Serving Vessels	186
bowler (*use:* Derby)	Headwear	93
Bowsprit	Water Transportation Accessories	440
Bowstring	Armament Accessories	266
Box	Containers	414
Box, Accessory	Personal Carrying & Storage Gear	111
Box, Alms	Religious Objects	461
Box, Ammunition	Armament Accessories	267
Box, Armament	Armament Accessories	267
Box, Artist's	Painting T&E	229
Box, Bait	Fishing Equipment	145
box, baling (*use:* Bailer, Well)	Mining & Mineral Harvesting T&E	220
Box, Ballot	Organizational Objects	459
box, band (*use:* Bandbox)	Personal Carrying & Storage Gear	111
Box, Bee	Animal Care Equipment	136
Box, Bento	Food Service Accessories	180
Box, Bible	Storage & Display Accessories	63
Box, Biscuit	Food Storage Equipment	170
Box, Bread	Food Storage Equipment	170
Box, Bride's	Personal Carrying & Storage Gear	111
box, cable converter (*use:* Converter, Cable)	Telecommunication Accessories	394
Box, Cake	Food Storage Equipment	170
Box, Call	Telecommunication Accessories	394
Box, Camp	Food Preparation Accessories	152
Box, Candle	Storage & Display Accessories	63
Box, Cap	Armament Accessories	267
Box, Card	Game Equipment	502
Box, Cartridge	Armament Accessories	267
box, casting (*use:* Mold, Casting)	Metalworking T&E	214
Box, Charging	Metalworking T&E	208
Box, Cheese	Food Storage Equipment	170
Box, Chopping	Food Preparation Equipment	158
box, chuck (*use:* Box, Camp)	Food Preparation Accessories	152
Box, Chuck	Food Storage Equipment	170
Box, Cigar	Containers for Smoking & Tobacco	59
Box, Cigar Drying	Other T&E for Materials	260
Box, Cigar Packer's	Other T&E for Materials	260
Box, Cigarette	Containers for Smoking & Tobacco	59
Box, Collar	Personal Carrying & Storage Gear	111
box, collection (*use:* Box, Alms)	Religious Objects	461
Box, Comfit	Serving Vessels	186
Box, Control	Electrical System Components	300
Box, Core	Metalworking T&E	208
box, dealing (*use:* Shoe, Card)	Game Equipment	502
Box, Decade	Electrical System Components	300
Box, Dip	Mining & Mineral Harvesting T&E	224
box, document (*use:* Box, File)	Writing Accessories	402
Box, Donation	Merchandising T&E	336
box, dough (*use:* Trough, Dough)	Food Preparation Equipment	153
box, dowry (*use:* Chest, Hope)	Storage & Display Furniture	53
box, dresser (*use:* Box, Jewelry)	Personal Carrying & Storage Gear	111
Box, Dresser	Storage & Display Accessories	63
Box, Drill Bit	Metalworking T&E	208
Box, Electrical	Electrical System Components	300
Box, Etrog	Holiday Objects	458
Box, Faking	Water Transportation Accessories	436
Box, Farrier's	Farrier Equipment	139
Box, Farrier's Nail	Farrier Equipment	139
Box, Feed	Animal Care Equipment	134
Box, Field	Harvesting Equipment	128
Box, File	Writing Accessories	402
Box, Fire Alarm	Protective Devices	345
box, flatware (*use:* Tray, Flatware)	Food Service Accessories	182
Box, Food Storage	Food Storage Equipment	170
Box, Fuse	Electrical System Components	300
Box, Germination	Biological T&E	286
Box, Gift	Party Accessories	460
Box, Gill	Textile Manufacturing Equipment	239
Box, Glove	Personal Carrying & Storage Gear	111
Box, Grain	Planting Equipment	132
Box, Hairpin	Personal Carrying & Storage Gear	112
Box, Handkerchief	Personal Carrying & Storage Gear	111
Box, Household	Storage & Display Accessories	63

box, incense (*use:* Navette) Religious Objects 462
Box, Incense Storage & Display Accessories 63
Box, Index Card Writing Accessories 402
Box, Jewelry Personal Carrying & Storage Gear 111
Box, Journal Power Transmission Components 305
Box, Junction Electrical System Components 300
Box, Knife Food Preparation Accessories 152
box, knife (*use:* Tray, Flatware) Food Service Accessories 182
box, knife and fork (*use:* Tray, Flatware) Food Service Accessories 182
Box, Letter Storage & Display Accessories 63
Box, Litter Pet Supplies 141
Box, Loom Textile Manufacturing Equipment 239
box, lunch (*use:* Lunchbox) Food Service Accessories 180
Box, Mail Collection Containers 414
box, match (*use:* Matchbox) Firemaking Equipment 74
Box, Missal Storage & Display Accessories 63
box, mite (*use:* Box, Alms) Religious Objects 461
Box, Miter Woodworking T&E 248
Box, Molding Woodworking T&E 248
Box, Money Merchandising T&E 336
box, moving (*use:* Box, Packing) Containers 414
Box, Music Musical Instruments 371
Box, Needlework Needleworking Equipment 234
Box, Nesting Breeding Equipment 138
Box, Net Fishing Equipment 145
box, offering (*use:* Box, Alms) Religious Objects 461
box, offering (*use:* Box, Alms) Religious Objects 461
Box, Outlet Electrical System Components 300
Box, Packing Containers 414
Box, Paint Painting T&E 229
Box, Pantry Food Storage Equipment 170
Box, Patch Armament Accessories 267
Box, Percussion Cap Armament Accessories 267
box, picnic (*use:* Hamper, Picnic) Food Service Accessories 180
box, pill (*use:* Pillbox) Personal Carrying & Storage Gear 112
Box, Pin Needleworking Equipment 234
Box, Pipe Containers for Smoking & Tobacco 59
Box, Porch Food Storage Equipment 170
Box, Post Office Containers 414
Box, Pounce Writing Accessories 403
Box, Pouncet Hygiene Objects 120
box, powder (*use:* Box, Puff) Beauty Supplies 116
Box, Presentation Storage & Display Accessories 63
Box, Puff Beauty Supplies 116
Box, Recipe Storage & Display Accessories 63
Box, Resistance Electrical System Components 300
Box, Salt Food Storage Equipment 170
Box, Sardine Serving Vessels 186
Box, Screw Woodworking T&E 248
Box, Sentry Defense Structures 31
Box, Serving Serving Vessels 186
box, sewing (*use:* Box, Needlework) Needleworking Equipment 234
Box, Shadow Storage & Display Accessories 63
Box, Shaving Hair Care Objects 118
Box, Ship's Log Water Transportation Accessories 436
Box, Shipwright's Caulking Woodworking T&E 248
Box, Shipwright's Oil Woodworking T&E 248
Box, Shoe Personal Carrying & Storage Gear 111
Box, Shoeing Farrier Equipment 139
Box, Sluice Mining & Mineral Harvesting T&E 224
box, sneak (*use:* Sneakbox) Watercraft 442
box, snuff (*use:* Snuffbox) Smoking & Recreational Drug Equipment 114
Box, Spice Food Storage Equipment 170
Box, Spit Containers for Smoking & Tobacco 59
box, spoon (*use:* Tray, Flatware) Food Service Accessories 182
Box, Stamp Writing Accessories 403
box, stomp (*use:* Pedal, Effects) Musical Instruments 371
Box, Storage Containers 414
box, strong (*use:* Strongbox) Storage & Display Accessories 63
Box, Stuffer Textile Manufacturing Equipment 239
Box, Stuffing Mining & Mineral Harvesting T&E 220
Box, Suction Papermaking T&E 232
Box, Sugar Serving Vessels 186

box, surprise (*use:* Jack-in-the-Box) Toys 521
Box, Tack Land Transportation Accessories 418
Box, Tackle Fishing Equipment 145
Box, Tobacco Smoking & Recreational Drug Equipment 114
box, tool (*use:* Toolbox) Multiple Use T&E for Materials 226
Box, Trinket Personal Carrying & Storage Gear 111
box, turning (*use:* Box, Molding) Woodworking T&E 248
Box, Utility Electrical System Components 300
box, voting (*use:* Box, Ballot) Organizational Objects 459
Box, Wall Storage & Display Accessories 63
Box, Wax Glass, Plastics & Clayworking T&E 192
Box, Window Door & Window Elements 6
box, wood (*use:* Woodbin) Heating Equipment Accessories 77
Boxcar Rail Vehicles 433
boxers (*use:* Shorts, Boxer) Underwear 104
Brace Supporting Elements 16
Brace, Dental Dental Instruments 322
brace, engineer's ratchet (*use:* Brace, Ratchet) Woodworking T&E 248
Brace, Extension Woodworking T&E 248
Brace, Leg Personal Assistive Objects 107
Brace, Neck Personal Assistive Objects 107
Brace, Orthopedic Personal Assistive Objects 107
Brace, Ratchet Woodworking T&E 248
Brace, Spofford Woodworking T&E 248
Brace, Wimble Woodworking T&E 248
Brace, Woodworking Woodworking T&E 248
Bracelet Body Adornments 81
Bracelet, Charm Body Adornments 81
Bracelet, Identification Personal Identification 495
bracer (*use:* Guard, Arm) Armament Accessories 269
Bracket Finish Hardware 10
Bracket, Candle Lighting Holders 71
Bracket, Dental Dental Instruments 322
Bracket, Fireset Heating Equipment Accessories 76
Bracket, Flag Finish Hardware 10
Bracket, Flowerpot Finish Hardware 10
Bracket, Handrail Finish Hardware 10
Bracket, Lamp Finish Hardware 10
bracket, lamp (*use:* Holder, Lamp) Lighting Holders 71
Bracket, Pediment Supporting Elements 16
bracket, plant (*use:* Bracket, Flowerpot) Finish Hardware 10
Bracket, Rod Window & Door Coverings 78
Bracket, Shelf Finish Hardware 10
Bracket, Ship's Bell Water Transportation Accessories 436
Bracket, Wall Finish Hardware 10
Brad Woodworking T&E 250
Bradawl Woodworking T&E 246
Braid Needleworking Equipment 236
Braider Textile Manufacturing Equipment 239
Brail Animal Care Equipment 135
braillewriter (*use:* Embosser, Braille) Writing Devices 406
brake (*use:* Break) Animal-Powered Vehicles 423
Brake, Band Mechanical Measurement Equipment 318
Brake, Bending Metalworking T&E 207
brake, cleaving (*use:* Horse, Froe) Woodworking T&E 247
Brake, Emergency Rail Transportation Accessories 431
Brake, Hemp Harvesting Equipment 127
Brake, Muzzle Armament Accessories 266
Brake, Peeling Fiberworking T&E 144
Brake, Railway Rail Transportation Accessories 431
Brake, Service Rail Transportation Accessories 431
Brake, Vehicle Land Transportation Accessories 416
Brand, Animal Animal Care Equipment 136
Brand, Freeze Animal Care Equipment 136
Brand, Horn Animal Care Equipment 136
brander, freezing (*use:* Brand, Freeze) Animal Care Equipment 136
brander, horn (*use:* Brand, Horn) Animal Care Equipment 136
Brandistock Edged Weapons 278
Brassard Status Symbols 496
Brassiere Underwear 103
Brassiere, Nursing Underwear 103
Brayer Graphic Equipment 385
Brazier Metalworking T&E 208
Brazier, Cooking Food Preparation Equipment 153
Breadboard Food Preparation Equipment 153
Break Animal-Powered Vehicles 423
break, flax (*use:* Breaker, Flax) Textile Manufacturing Equipment 239
break, peg (*use:* Rasp, Shoemaker's) Leather, Horn & Shellworking T&E 200
Break, Skeleton Animal-Powered Vehicles 423
Break, Wagonette Animal-Powered Vehicles 423
Breaker, Bale Textile Manufacturing Equipment 239
Breaker, Button Needleworking Equipment 234

Term	Category	Page
Breaker, Circuit	Electrical System Components	300
Breaker, Flax	Textile Manufacturing Equipment	239
Breasthook	Water Transportation Accessories	436
Breastplate	Woodworking T&E	248
Breastplate, Armor	Body Armor	275
Breastwork	Defense Structures	31
breechcloth (*use:* Loincloth)	Main Garments	97
Breeches	Main Garments	97
breeches, jodhpur (*use:* Jodhpur)	Main Garments	97
Breeches, Riding	Main Garments	97
Breeches, Trunk	Main Garments	97
Breloque	Body Adornments	81
Bretelle	Clothing Accessories	84
Breviary	Religious Objects	465
Brewery	Industrial Structures	35
bric-a-brac (*use:* Knickknack)	Decorative Furnishings	60
Brick	Construction Materials	3
Brick, Air	Construction Materials	3
Brick, Ashlar	Construction Materials	3
Brick, Backing	Construction Materials	3
Brick, Building	Construction Materials	3
Brick, Capping	Construction Materials	3
Brick, Decorative	Surface Elements	18
Brick, Face	Construction Materials	3
Brick, Kiln	Glass, Plastics & Clayworking T&E	192
Brick, Paving	Site Features	22
Brick, Roman	Construction Materials	3
Bridge	Transportation Structures	39
Bridge, Billiard	Game Equipment	501
Bridge, Covered	Transportation Structures	39
Bridge, Dental	Dental Instruments	322
Bridge, Moveable	Transportation Structures	39
Bridge, Railroad	Transportation Structures	39
Bridge, Road	Transportation Structures	39
Bridge, Ship's	Water Transportation Accessories	436
Bridge, Suspension	Transportation Structures	39
Bridge, Swing	Transportation Structures	39
Bridge, Truss	Transportation Structures	39
Bridge, Wheatstone	Electrical & Magnetic Measurement Devices	297
Bridle	Land Transportation Accessories	419
bridle, brank's (*use:* Bridle, Scold's)	Regulative Devices	347
Bridle, Net	Fishing Equipment	145
Bridle, Scold's	Regulative Devices	347
Bridle, Single	Land Transportation Accessories	419
Bridle, Team	Land Transportation Accessories	419
Brief	Legal Documents	476
Briefcase	Personal Carrying & Storage Gear	111
Briefs	Underwear	104
Briefs, Bikini	Underwear	104
Brig	Watercraft	444
brig, half (*use:* Brig, Hermaphrodite)	Watercraft	444
Brig, Hermaphrodite	Watercraft	444
Brigandine	Body Armor	275
Brigantine	Watercraft	444
Bristle, Sewing	Leather, Horn & Shellworking T&E	196
Britching	Land Transportation Accessories	421
broach (*use:* Reamer, Broach)	Woodworking T&E	256
Broach, Dental	Dental Instruments	322
Broach, Metalworking	Metalworking T&E	208
Broadax	Woodworking T&E	247
Broadcaster	Planting Equipment	132
Broadside	Advertising Media	449
Broadsword	Edged Weapons	278
Brochure	Advertising Media	449
brogan (*use:* Boat, Tonging)	Watercraft	445
Brogue	Footwear	90
Broiler	Food Preparation Equipment	154
Broiler, Hearth	Food Preparation Equipment	162
Broiler, Oyster	Food Preparation Equipment	162
Bronchoscope	Medical Instruments	328
Brooch	Clothing Accessories	86
Brooder, Poultry	Breeding Equipment	138
Broom	Housekeeping Equipment	311
Broom, Curling	Sports Equipment	514
Broom, Electric	Housekeeping Equipment	311
Broom, Fireplace	Heating Equipment Accessories	76
Broom, Push	Housekeeping Equipment	311
Broom, Whisk	Housekeeping Equipment	311
Brougham	Animal-Powered Vehicles	423
Brush	Multiple Use T&E for Materials	226
Brush, Animal	Animal Care Equipment	136
Brush, Artist's	Painting T&E	229
Brush, Bath	Hygiene Objects	120
Brush, Bore	Armament Accessories	266
Brush, Bottle	Dishwashing Equipment	308
Brush, Bromoil	Photoprocessing Equipment	381
Brush, Burette	Labware	292
Brush, Calligraphic	Writing Devices	406
Brush, Chimney	Housekeeping Equipment	311

Brush, Cleaning	Housekeeping Equipment	311
Brush, Clothes	Clothing Care Objects	105
Brush, Cosmetic	Beauty Supplies	116
Brush, Denture	Hygiene Objects	121
Brush, Dusting	Housekeeping Equipment	311
Brush, Erasure	Writing Accessories	402
Brush, File	Metalworking T&E	208
Brush, Flue	Housekeeping Equipment	311
Brush, Food	Food Preparation Equipment	153
Brush, Garment	Clothing Care Objects	105
Brush, Glazing	Glass, Plastics & Clayworking T&E	192
Brush, Graining	Painting T&E	229
Brush, Hat	Clothing Care Objects	105
Brush, Laboratory	Labware	292
Brush, Lens	Photographic Accessories	378
Brush, Lettering	Painting T&E	229
Brush, Lint	Clothing Care Objects	105
Brush, Lipstick	Beauty Supplies	116
Brush, Mason's	Masonry & Stoneworking T&E	203
Brush, Massage	Personal Assistive Objects	107
Brush, Nail	Beauty Supplies	116
Brush, Paint	Painting T&E	229
Brush, Pastry	Food Preparation Equipment	153
Brush, Percussion	Musical Accessories	368
Brush, Pet	Pet Supplies	141
Brush, Pipette	Labware	292
Brush, Polish	Leather, Horn & Shellworking T&E	196
Brush, Razor	Hair Care Objects	118
Brush, Record	Sound Communication Accessories	389
Brush, Scalp	Hair Care Objects	118
Brush, Scrub	Housekeeping Equipment	311
Brush, Seam	Woodworking T&E	248
Brush, Shaving	Hair Care Objects	118
Brush, Shoe	Clothing Care Objects	105
Brush, Snow	Land Transportation Accessories	416
brush, snuff (*use:* Stick, Snuff)	Smoking & Recreational Drug Equipment	115
Brush, Stencilling	Painting T&E	229
Brush, Suede	Clothing Care Objects	105
Brush, Toilet	Housekeeping Equipment	311
Brush, Wallpaper	Painting T&E	230
Brush, Wallpaper Paste	Painting T&E	231
Brush, Wallpaper Smoothing	Painting T&E	231
Brush, Window	Housekeeping Equipment	311
Brush, Wire	Musical Accessories	368
Brush, Writing	Writing Devices	406
Buccin	Musical Instruments	370
buck-a-bout (*use:* Seesaw, Spring)	Recreational Devices	510
Buckboard	Animal-Powered Vehicles	423
Bucket	Containers	415
bucket (*use:* Pail)	Housekeeping Equipment	312
Bucket, Artillery	Armament Accessories	267
bucket, bailing (*use:* Bailer, Well)	Mining & Mineral Harvesting T&E	220
Bucket, Bait	Fishing Equipment	145
bucket, butter (*use:* Tub, Butter)	Food Processing Equipment	167
Bucket, Clamshell	Construction T&E	295
Bucket, Deck	Water Transportation Accessories	436
Bucket, Dipper	Construction T&E	295
Bucket, Dragline	Construction T&E	295
Bucket, Dredge	Mining & Mineral Harvesting T&E	221
Bucket, Fire	Protective Devices	345
Bucket, Flour	Food Storage Equipment	170
Bucket, Food Storage	Food Storage Equipment	170
Bucket, Grease	Armament Accessories	266
Bucket, Ice	Food Service Accessories	180
Bucket, Manure	Tending Equipment	133
Bucket, Mechanical	Construction T&E	295
Bucket, Mining	Mining & Mineral Harvesting T&E	220
bucket, minnow (*use:* Bucket, Bait)	Fishing Equipment	145
Bucket, Rock	Mining & Mineral Harvesting T&E	221
Bucket, Sap	Food Processing Equipment	169
bucket, sinking (*use:* Kibble)	Mining & Mineral Harvesting T&E	221
Bucket, Slop	Animal Care Equipment	134
bucket, slop (*use:* Jar, Slop)	Housekeeping Equipment	312
bucket, sugar (*use:* Bucket, Sap)	Food Processing Equipment	169
Bucket, Tar	Armament Accessories	266
Bucket, Water	Glass, Plastics & Clayworking T&E	192
Bucketline	Mining & Mineral Harvesting T&E	221
Buckle	Multiple Use T&E for Materials	227
Buckle, Belt	Clothing Accessories	84
Buckle, Clothing	Clothing Accessories	84
Buckle, Knee	Clothing Accessories	84
Buckle, Shoe	Clothing Accessories	84
Buckle, Tack	Land Transportation Accessories	420
Buckler	Body Armor	275
Bucksaw	Forestry T&E	191
Budget	Financial Records	469
Buffer, Glass	Glass, Plastics & Clayworking T&E	192
Buffer, Hoof	Farrier Equipment	140
Buffer, Nail	Beauty Supplies	117

Buffer, Recoil | Armament Accessories | 266
Buffer, Shoe | Clothing Care Objects | 105
Buffer, Skin | Beauty Supplies | 116
Buffet | Storage & Display Furniture | 54
Bugeye | Watercraft | 443
Buggy | Animal-Powered Vehicles | 423
Buggy, Dune | Motor Vehicles | 430
buggy, mountain (*use:* Stroller) | Human-Powered Vehicles | 427
Bugle | Musical Instruments | 370
Bugle, Key | Musical Instruments | 370
Bugle, Valve | Musical Instruments | 370
Building, Apartment | Dwellings | 32
Building, Entertainment | Cultural & Recreational Structures | 29
Building, Exhibition | Cultural & Recreational Structures | 29
Building, Fair | Cultural & Recreational Structures | 29
Building, Financial | Commercial Structures | 27
Building, Mine | Industrial Structures | 35
Building, Office | Other Structures | 41
Building, Performing Arts | Cultural & Recreational Structures | 29
Building, Public | Civic & Social Structures | 26
Building, Public Safety | Civic & Social Structures | 26
Building, Sawmill | Industrial Structures | 35
Building, Society | Civic & Social Structures | 26
building, storage (*use:* Warehouse) | Commercial Structures | 28
Building, Utility | Industrial Structures | 35
Building, Zoo | Cultural & Recreational Structures | 29
Bulb, Absorption | Labware | 292
Bulb, Black Light | Other Lighting Accessories | 72
Bulb, Connecting | Labware | 292
bulb, flash (*use:* Flashbulb) | Camera Equipment | 377
Bulb, Fluorescent | Other Lighting Accessories | 72
Bulb, Halogen | Other Lighting Accessories | 72
Bulb, Incandescent | Other Lighting Accessories | 72
Bulb, Laboratory | Labware | 292
Bulb, Light | Other Lighting Accessories | 72
Bulb, Neon | Other Lighting Accessories | 72
Bulb, Ultraviolet | Other Lighting Accessories | 72
bulker (*use:* Freighter, Bulk) | Watercraft | 446
Bulkhead | Other Structures | 41
Bull, Mechanical | Recreational Devices | 511
Bulldozer | Construction T&E | 295
Bullet | Ammunition | 263
Bullet, Armor-Piercing | Ammunition | 263
Bullet, Controlled Expansion | Ammunition | 263
Bullet, Expanding | Ammunition | 263
Bullet, Incendiary | Ammunition | 263
Bullet, Minie | Ammunition | 263
Bullet, Sling | Ammunition | 263
Bullet, Tracer | Ammunition | 263
Bulletin | Other Documents | 486
Bullhook | Animal Care Equipment | 136
Bullhorn | Sound Communication Devices | 392
Bull-Roarer | Religious Objects | 461
Bullseye | Water Transportation Accessories | 439
Bulwark | Water Transportation Accessories | 436
Bumper, Door | Finish Hardware | 10
bumper, vehicle (*use:* Fender, Vehicle) | Land Transportation Accessories | 417
bumper, watercraft (*use:* Fender, Watercraft) | Water Transportation Accessories | 437
Bundle, Medicine | Belief Symbols | 493
Bung | Food Storage Equipment | 170
Bung, Boat | Water Transportation Accessories | 437
Bungalow | Dwellings | 32
Bungstart | Woodworking T&E | 254
Bunk, Feed | Animal Care Equipment | 134
Bunker | Defense Structures | 31
Bunkhouse | Dwellings | 32
Bunting | Organizational Objects | 459
bunting (*use:* Barrowcoat) | Outerwear | 100
Buoy, Breeches | Water Transportation Accessories | 441
Buoy, Fishing | Fishing Equipment | 145
Buoy, Lobster | Fishing Equipment | 145
Buoy, Mooring | Water Transportation Accessories | 436
Buoy, Navigational | Navigational Equipment | 350
Buoy, Net | Fishing Equipment | 145
Bur, Dental | Dental Instruments | 322
bureau (*use:* Chest of Drawers) | Storage & Display Furniture | 53
Burette | Labware | 292
Burette, Geissler | Labware | 292
Burette, Mohr | Labware | 292
Burette, Stopcock | Labware | 293
Burette, Titration | Labware | 293
Burgonet | Body Armor | 275
Burin | Graphic Equipment | 384
Burin, Stone | Masonry & Stoneworking T&E | 204
Burka | Main Garments | 95
Burner, Alcohol | Labware | 292
Burner, Argand | Labware | 292
Burner, Bunsen | Labware | 292
burner, candle (*use:* Follower, Candle) | Other Lighting Accessories | 72
Burner, Incense | Other Household Accessories | 66
Burner, Laboratory | Labware | 292
Burner, Lamp | Other Lighting Accessories | 72

burner, pastille (*use:* Cassolette)		
Burner, Spirit	Other Household Accessories	66
Burnisher	Food Preparation Equipment	154
	Leather, Horn & Shellworking T&E	196
Burnisher, Dental	Dental Instruments	322
Burnisher, Metal	Metalworking T&E	208
Burnisher, Printmaking	Graphic Equipment	384
Burnous	Outerwear	100
Burse	Religious Objects	461
Burster	Data Processing Accessories	359
Bus	Motor Vehicles	428
Bus, School	Motor Vehicles	428
Busby	Headwear	91
Bushhammer	Masonry & Stoneworking T&E	204
Busk	Underwear	103
Buskin	Status Symbols	499
Bust	Art	454
Bustier	Underwear	103
Bustle	Underwear	103
Bustle, Ceremonial	Status Symbols	498
Bustle, Dance	Status Symbols	498
Butler, Silent	Housekeeping Equipment	311
Butsudan	Religious Objects	461
buttbag (*use:* Haversack)	Personal Carrying & Storage Gear	110
butteris (*use:* Trimmer, Hoof)	Farrier Equipment	140
Button	Needleworking Equipment	236
Button, Call	Sound Communication Devices	391
Button, Campaign	Belief Symbols	493
Button, Collar	Clothing Accessories	87
Button, Fraternal	Status Symbols	496
Button, Insignia	Status Symbols	496
Button, Intestinal	Medical Instruments	330
button, Jaboulay (*use:* Button, Intestinal)	Medical Instruments	330
Button, Law Enforcement	Status Symbols	496
Button, Membership	Status Symbols	496
Button, Military	Status Symbols	496
button, Murphy's (*use:* Button, Intestinal)	Medical Instruments	330
button, police (*use:* Button, Law Enforcement)	Status Symbols	496
Button, Political	Belief Symbols	493
Button, Promotional	Advertising Media	449
Button, Stud	Needleworking Equipment	236
Buttonhook	Personal Assistive Objects	107
Buttplate	Armament Accessories	266
Buttress	Supporting Elements	16
Butyrometer	Food Processing Equipment	167
Buzzer	Sound Communication Devices	391
Bylaws	Administrative Records	467
Cab, Hansom	Animal-Powered Vehicles	423
Cabasset	Body Armor	275
Caber	Sports Equipment	518
Cabin	Dwellings	32
Cabin, Log	Dwellings	32
Cabin, Tourist	Commercial Structures	27
Cabinet	Storage & Display Furniture	52
Cabinet, Autoclave	Medical Accessories	325
Cabinet, Barber's	Storage & Display Furniture	52
Cabinet, Card	Storage & Display Furniture	52
Cabinet, China	Storage & Display Furniture	52
Cabinet, Coin	Storage & Display Furniture	52
Cabinet, Corner	Storage & Display Furniture	52
Cabinet, Curio	Storage & Display Furniture	52
Cabinet, Dental	Dental Accessories	320
Cabinet, Display	Merchandising T&E	336
cabinet, display (*use:* Cabinet, Curio)	Storage & Display Furniture	52
Cabinet, Entertainment	Storage & Display Furniture	52
Cabinet, Filing	Storage & Display Furniture	52
Cabinet, Food Storage	Food Storage Equipment	170
Cabinet, Gun	Storage & Display Furniture	52
Cabinet, Hanging	Storage & Display Furniture	52
Cabinet, Hoosier	Storage & Display Furniture	52
Cabinet, Jewelry	Storage & Display Furniture	52
Cabinet, Key	Storage & Display Furniture	52
Cabinet, Kitchen	Storage & Display Furniture	52
Cabinet, Liquor	Storage & Display Furniture	52
Cabinet, Mail Sorting	Storage & Display Furniture	52
Cabinet, Media	Storage & Display Furniture	52
Cabinet, Medicine	Storage & Display Furniture	52
Cabinet, Music	Storage & Display Furniture	52
Cabinet, Office	Storage & Display Furniture	52
cabinet, parlor (*use:* Étagère)	Storage & Display Furniture	54
Cabinet, Phonograph	Storage & Display Furniture	52
Cabinet, Radio	Storage & Display Furniture	52
Cabinet, Record	Storage & Display Furniture	52
cabinet, sewing (*use:* Table, Sewing)	Support Furniture	57
Cabinet, Smoking	Storage & Display Furniture	52
Cabinet, Spice	Food Storage Equipment	170
Cabinet, Television	Storage & Display Furniture	52
Cabinet, Thread	Storage & Display Furniture	52
cabinet, trinket (*use:* Cabinet, Curio)	Storage & Display Furniture	52
Cabinet, Type Case	Typesetting Equipment	388
Cabinet, Utility	Storage & Display Furniture	52
Cabinet, Weapon	Storage & Display Furniture	52
Cabinet, X-Ray	Medical Accessories	325
Cable	Multiple Use T&E for Materials	226
Cable, Antenna Lead	Telecommunication Media	398
Cable, Coaxial	Telecommunication Media	398
Cable, Data	Data Processing Accessories	359

Term	Category	Page
Cable, Electric	Electrical System Components	300
Cable, Jumper	Land Transportation Accessories	416
Cable, Marine	Water Transportation Accessories	436
Cable, Network	Data Processing Accessories	359
Cable, Parallel	Data Processing Accessories	359
Cable, Power	Data Processing Accessories	359
Cable, Railway	Rail Transportation Accessories	431
Cable, Serial	Data Processing Accessories	359
Cable, Submarine	Telecommunication Media	398
Cable, Telecommunication	Telecommunication Media	398
Cable, Telephone	Telecommunication Media	398
Cable, USB	Data Processing Accessories	360
Caboose	Rail Vehicles	433
Cabriolet	Animal-Powered Vehicles	423
Cachepot	Horticultural Containers	62
Caddinet	Food Service Accessories	180
Caddy	Containers	414
Caddy, Bath	Hygiene Objects	120
Caddy, Belt	Personal Carrying & Storage Gear	111
caddy, coupon (*use:* Case, Coupon)	Personal Carrying & Storage Gear	111
Caddy, Drawer	Storage & Display Accessories	63
Caddy, Food	Food Storage Equipment	170
caddy, shower (*use:* Caddy, Bath)	Hygiene Objects	120
Caddy, Tea	Food Storage Equipment	170
Cadger	Mining & Mineral Harvesting T&E	221
Cadran, Gemologist's	Other T&E for Materials	260
Café	Commercial Structures	27
Caftan	Main Garments	95
Cage, Animal	Animal Care Equipment	134
Cage, Batting	Cultural & Recreational Structures	30
Cage, Bird	Animal Care Equipment	134
Cage, Drying	Leather, Horn & Shellworking T&E	196
Cage, Insect	Animal Care Equipment	134
Cage, Man	Mining & Mineral Harvesting T&E	221
Cage, Mining	Mining & Mineral Harvesting T&E	221
Cage, Pet	Pet Supplies	141
Cage, Sound	Acoustical T&E	261
Cage, Wrestling	Sports Equipment	519
Cairn	Site Features	20
Caisson	Animal-Powered Vehicles	424
Cake, Urinal	Housekeeping Equipment	311
Calash	Headwear	94
Calcimeter	Chemical Testing Devices	289
Calculator	Data Processing Devices	361
Calculator, Desktop	Data Processing Devices	361
Calculator, Pocket	Data Processing Devices	361
caldron (*use:* Cauldron)	Cooking Vessels	151
caldron, potash (*use:* Cauldron, Potash)	Other T&E for Materials	260
Caleche	Animal-Powered Vehicles	423
Calendar	Other Documents	480
Calendar, Perpetual	Other Documents	480
Calender, Embossing	Textile Manufacturing Equipment	239
Calender, Paper	Papermaking T&E	232
Calf, Downy	Footwear	89
Caliper	Weights & Measures T&E	357
Caliper, Artillery	Armament Accessories	266
Caliper, Double	Weights & Measures T&E	357
Caliper, Glassmaker's	Glass, Plastics & Clayworking T&E	192
Caliper, Gunner's	Armament Accessories	266
Caliper, Hermaphrodite	Weights & Measures T&E	357
Caliper, Inside	Weights & Measures T&E	357
Caliper, Machining	Metalworking T&E	208
Caliper, Medical	Medical Instruments	327
Caliper, Outside	Weights & Measures T&E	357
Caliper, Potter's	Glass, Plastics & Clayworking T&E	192
Caliper, Shell	Armament Accessories	266
Caliper, Timber	Forestry T&E	190
Caliper, Vernier	Weights & Measures T&E	357
Caliver	Firearms	280
Calk, Horseshoe	Farrier Equipment	139
Call, Game	Armament Accessories	266
Calligraphy	Art	452
Calliope	Musical Instruments	371
Calorimeter	Thermal T&E	354
calot (*use:* Skullcap)	Headwear	92
Calotype	Graphic Documents	472
Caltrop	Armament Accessories	266
Calumet	Organizational Objects	459
Camcorder	Camera Equipment	376
Came	Door & Window Elements	7
Cameo	Art	454
Camera	Camera Equipment	376
Camera Lucida	Visual Communication Devices	400
Camera Obscura	Visual Communication Devices	400
Camera, 35 mm	Camera Equipment	376
Camera, Box	Camera Equipment	376
Camera, Detective	Camera Equipment	376
Camera, Digital	Camera Equipment	376
Camera, Disposable	Camera Equipment	376
Camera, Folding	Camera Equipment	376
Camera, Instant	Camera Equipment	376
Camera, Kinescope	Camera Equipment	376
Camera, Motion Picture	Camera Equipment	376
Camera, Panoramic	Camera Equipment	376

Camera, Pinhole — Camera Equipment 376
Camera, Press — Camera Equipment 376
Camera, Process — Camera Equipment 376
Camera, Rangefinder — Camera Equipment 376
Camera, Reflex — Camera Equipment 376
Camera, Schmidt — Astronomical T&E 285
Camera, Single Lens Reflex — Camera Equipment 376
Camera, Stereoscopic — Camera Equipment 376
Camera, Television — Telecommunication Devices 396
Camera, Twin Lens Reflex — Camera Equipment 376
Camera, Video — Camera Equipment 376
Camera, View — Camera Equipment 376
Camiknickers — Underwear 103
Camisole — Underwear 104
Camper — Motor Vehicles 428
Campimeter — Medical Instruments 329
Campylometer — Drafting T&E 366
Can — Containers 414
Can, Blasting — Mining & Mineral Harvesting T&E 221
Can, Carbide — Mining & Mineral Harvesting T&E 221
Can, Cream — Food Processing Equipment 166
Can, Dairy — Food Processing Equipment 165
Can, Film — Photographic Accessories 378
Can, Food Storage — Food Storage Equipment 170
can, garbage (*use:* Can, Trash) — Housekeeping Equipment 311
Can, Gasoline — Land Transportation Accessories 416
Can, Grease — Food Storage Equipment 170
Can, Kerosene — Housekeeping Equipment 311
Can, Lard — Food Storage Equipment 170
Can, Milk — Food Processing Equipment 166
Can, Oil — Mechanical Devices 317
Can, Paint — Painting T&E 229
can, safety carbide (*use:* Can, Carbide) — Mining & Mineral Harvesting T&E 221
Can, Settling — Food Processing Equipment 166
Can, Trash — Housekeeping Equipment 311
Can, Watering — Groundskeeping Equipment 309
canary (*use:* Detector, Gas) — Protective Devices 345
Candelabrum — Lighting Holders 71
Candle — Other Lighting Accessories 72
Candle, Cake — Party Accessories 460
Candle, Pillar — Other Lighting Accessories 72
Candle, Votive — Religious Objects 461
Candleholder — Lighting Holders 71
Candlelighter — Other Lighting Accessories 72
Candlepin — Sports Equipment 513
Candler, Egg — Food Processing Equipment 167
Candlesnuffer — Other Lighting Accessories 72
Candlestand — Lighting Holders 71
Candlestick — Lighting Holders 71
Candlestick, Hogscraper — Lighting Holders 71
Candlestick, Miner's — Lighting Holders 71
Candlestick, Religious — Religious Objects 461
Cane — Personal Assistive Objects 109
Cane, Sword — Edged Weapons 278
Cangue — Regulative Devices 348
Canion — Clothing Accessories 84
Canister — Containers 414
Canister, Coffee — Food Storage Equipment 170
Canister, Film — Photographic Accessories 378
Canister, Flour — Food Storage Equipment 170
Canister, Food Storage — Food Storage Equipment 170
Canister, Sugar — Food Storage Equipment 170
Canister, Tea — Food Storage Equipment 171
Cann — Drinking Vessels 173
Canner — Food Processing Equipment 165
Cannery — Industrial Structures 35
Cannon — Artillery 274
Cannon, Hand — Firearms 282
cannon, petronel (*use:* Petronel) — Firearms 281
Cannon, Serpentine — Artillery 274
Cannonball — Ammunition 263
Cannula — Medical Instruments 334
Canoe — Watercraft 442
Canoe, Bark — Watercraft 442
canoe, birchbark (*use:* Canoe, Bark) — Watercraft 442
Canoe, Decked — Watercraft 442
Canoe, Dugout — Watercraft 442
Canoe, Outrigger — Watercraft 442
Canoe, Sailing — Watercraft 442
Canoe, War — Watercraft 442
canopy (*use:* Awning) — Door & Window Elements 6
canopy (*use:* Tent, Canopy) — Other Structures 41
Canopy, Bed — Bedding 43
Canteen — Drinking Vessels 173
Canterbury — Storage & Display Furniture 52
Cantir — Drinking Vessels 173
Canvas, Needlework — Needleworking Equipment 234
Cap — Headwear 91
Cap, Aviator's — Headwear 91
Cap, Baby — Headwear 91
Cap, Baseball — Headwear 91
Cap, Bathing — Headwear 91
Cap, BB — Ammunition 263
Cap, Bearskin — Headwear 91
Cap, Blasting — Mining & Mineral Harvesting T&E 221
Cap, Bottle — Food Processing Equipment 168
Cap, Boudoir — Headwear 91
Cap, Breakfast — Headwear 91
Cap, Chimney — Environmental Control Elements 8
Cap, China — Food Preparation Equipment 162

cap, day (*use:* Bonnet, Indoor) Headwear 91
Cap, Deerstalker Headwear 91
Cap, Dunce Regulative Devices 347
cap, flat (*use:* Flatcap) Headwear 92
Cap, Forage Headwear 91
Cap, Garrison Headwear 91
Cap, Gas Land Transportation Accessories 417
cap, gob (*use:* Cap, Sailor) Headwear 91
Cap, Golf Headwear 91
Cap, Grain Harvesting Equipment 127
cap, grease (*use:* Hubcap) Land Transportation Accessories 417
Cap, Horse Animal Care Equipment 134
Cap, Jockey Headwear 91
Cap, Lens Camera Equipment 376
cap, lounging (*use:* Cap, Smoking) Headwear 91
Cap, Military Headwear 91
Cap, Miner's Headwear 91
Cap, Musket Armament Accessories 266
Cap, Muzzle Armament Accessories 266
Cap, Newel Stair Elements 15
Cap, Nurse's Headwear 91
cap, officer's (*use:* Cap, Service) Headwear 91
cap, overseas (*use:* Cap, Garrison) Headwear 91
Cap, Percussion Armament Accessories 266
Cap, Ridge Roof Elements 14
Cap, Riding Headwear 91
Cap, Round-Eared Headwear 91
cap, sailing (*use:* Cap, Yachting) Headwear 91
Cap, Sailor Headwear 91
Cap, Scottish Headwear 91
Cap, Service Headwear 91
Cap, Smoking Headwear 91
Cap, Snap Armament Accessories 266
Cap, Sport Headwear 91
Cap, Stocking Headwear 92
Cap, Timber Mining & Mineral Harvesting T&E 225
Cap, Vent Environmental Control Elements 8
Cap, Watch Headwear 91
cap, wedge (*use:* Cap, Garrison) Headwear 91
Cap, Window Door & Window Elements 7
Cap, Yachting Headwear 91
Capacitor Electrical System Components 300
Capacitor, Electrolytic Electrical System Components 300
Capacitor, Variable Electrical System Components 300
Caparison Land Transportation Accessories 419
Cape Outerwear 100
Cape, Dressing Dressingwear & Nightwear 88
Cape, Hairdressing Protective Wear 102
Cape, Tippet Outerwear 100
Capelet Outerwear 100
Capital Supporting Elements 16
Capitol Civic & Social Structures 26
Capo Musical Accessories 369
Capote Outerwear 100
Capper, Bottle Food Processing Equipment 168
Capstan Water Transportation Accessories 437
Capsule, Pharmaceutical Medical Accessories 325
Capsule, Time Memorabilia 478
Capuchin Outerwear 100
car (*use:* Automobile) Motor Vehicles 428
Car, Armored Motor Vehicles 429
Car, Baggage Rail Vehicles 433
Car, Bilevel Rail Vehicles 433
Car, Bumper Recreational Devices 511
Car, Business Rail Vehicles 433
Car, Cable Rail Vehicles 435
car, chair (*use:* Coach, Rail) Rail Vehicles 433
car, chair lounge (*use:* Coach, Rail) Rail Vehicles 433
Car, Clearance Rail Vehicles 433
Car, Coal Rail Vehicles 433
Car, Coaster Recreational Devices 509
car, commuter (*use:* Coach, Rail) Rail Vehicles 433
Car, Container Rail Vehicles 433
Car, Crew Rail Vehicles 433
Car, Dining Rail Vehicles 433
Car, Dome Rail Vehicles 433
Car, Dump Rail Vehicles 433
Car, Dynamometer Rail Vehicles 433
car, express (*use:* Car, Baggage) Rail Vehicles 433
Car, Express Rail Vehicles 433
Car, Freight Rail Vehicles 433
Car, Funicular Rail Vehicles 434
Car, Gondola Rail Vehicles 433
Car, Hopper Rail Vehicles 433
Car, Instructional Rail Vehicles 433
Car, Kiddie Toys 524
Car, Lobster Fishing Equipment 145
Car, Lounge Rail Vehicles 433
Car, Man Mining & Mineral Harvesting T&E 221
Car, Midget Motor Vehicles 428
Car, Mine Ambulance Mining & Mineral Harvesting T&E 221
Car, Mining Mining & Mineral Harvesting T&E 221

Term	Category	Page
Car, Monorail	Rail Vehicles	434
Car, Ore	Mining & Mineral Harvesting T&E	221
Car, Passenger	Rail Vehicles	433
Car, Pedal	Toys	524
Car, Piggyback	Rail Vehicles	433
Car, Police	Motor Vehicles	428
car, pullman (*use:* Car, Sleeping)	Rail Vehicles	433
Car, Racing	Motor Vehicles	428
Car, Rack	Rail Vehicles	433
Car, Railroad	Rail Vehicles	433
Car, Refrigerator	Rail Vehicles	433
Car, Scale Test	Rail Vehicles	433
Car, Self-Propelled Train	Rail Vehicles	433
Car, Service	Rail Vehicles	433
Car, Slag	Metalworking T&E	208
Car, Sleeping	Rail Vehicles	433
Car, Snowplow	Rail Vehicles	433
car, soapbox (*use:* Car, Coaster)	Recreational Devices	509
Car, Steam	Motor Vehicles	430
Car, Stock	Rail Vehicles	433
Car, Stock Race	Motor Vehicles	428
Car, Subway	Rail Vehicles	434
Car, Tank	Rail Vehicles	433
Car, Tower	Rail Vehicles	434
Car, Track Geometry	Rail Vehicles	434
car, velocipede (*use:* Handcar)	Rail Vehicles	434
Carabiner	Sports Equipment	514
Caraco	Main Garments	96
Carafe	Serving Vessels	188
caravan (*use:* Van, Gypsy)	Animal-Powered Vehicles	424
Carbine	Firearms	280
Carbolimeter	Chemical Testing Devices	289
Carbonometer	Chemical Testing Devices	289
Carboy	Containers	415
Carburetor	Power Producing Equipment	303
Carburometer	Chemical Testing Devices	289
Carcass	Ammunition	264
Card, Activity	Toys	521
Card, Admittance	Exchange Media	490
Card, Advertising	Advertising Media	449
Card, Altar	Religious Objects	465
card, ATM (*use:* Card, Debit)	Exchange Media	487
Card, Attendance	Other Documents	480
Card, Autograph	Other Documents	480
Card, Baseball	Other Documents	481
Card, Bingo	Game Equipment	503
Card, Business	Personal Identification	495
card, cabinet (*use:* Photograph, Cabinet)	Graphic Documents	473
Card, Calling	Personal Identification	495
Card, Camera	Camera Equipment	376
Card, Catalog	Other Documents	480
card, charge (*use:* Card, Credit)	Exchange Media	487
card, cigarette (*use:* Card, Tobacco)	Advertising Media	449
Card, Collecting	Other Documents	481
Card, Commemorative	Memorabilia	478
Card, Compass	Navigational Equipment	349
Card, Congratulatory	Other Documents	481
Card, Courting	Other Documents	481
Card, Credit	Exchange Media	487
card, dance (*use:* Program, Dance)	Other Documents	485
Card, Data	Data Processing Media	363
Card, Debit	Exchange Media	487
Card, Devotional	Religious Objects	465
card, display (*use:* Card, Show)	Advertising Media	449
Card, Divider	Writing Accessories	402
Card, Documentary	Other Documents	480
Card, Draft	Personal Identification	495
Card, Edge-Notched	Data Processing Media	363
Card, Escort	Other Documents	481
Card, Flash	Instructional Documents	475
card, flirtation (*use:* Card, Courting)	Other Documents	481
card, funeral (*use:* Card, Mourning)	Funerary Objects	456
Card, Game	Game Equipment	501
Card, Get Well	Other Documents	481
card, gift (*use:* Card, Store)	Exchange Media	490
Card, Greeting	Other Documents	481
Card, Hand	Textile Manufacturing Equipment	239
Card, Holiday	Other Documents	481
Card, Identification	Personal Identification	495
Card, Index	Writing Media	408
Card, Inspirational	Other Documents	481
Card, Instruction	Instructional Documents	475
Card, Insurance	Other Documents	481
Card, Jacquard	Textile Manufacturing Equipment	239
Card, Key	Protective Devices	345
Card, Library	Personal Identification	495
Card, Lobby	Advertising Media	450
Card, Membership	Personal Identification	495
card, memorial (*use:* Card, Mourning)	Funerary Objects	456
card, memory (*use:* Drive, Flash)	Data Processing Media	363
Card, Money	Exchange Media	487
Card, Mourning	Funerary Objects	456
Card, Picker's	Harvesting Equipment	127
card, place (*use:* Placecard)	Other Documents	481
Card, Playing	Game Equipment	504

Term	Category	Page
Card, Pledge	Other Documents	485
Card, Political	Advertising Media	449
Card, Prayer	Religious Objects	465
Card, Punched	Data Processing Media	363
Card, QSL	Other Documents	481
Card, Recipe	Instructional Documents	475
Card, Report	Other Documents	481
Card, Sample	Merchandising T&E	338
card, score (*use:* Scorecard)	Other Documents	482
card, security (*use:* Card, Key)	Protective Devices	345
Card, Sewing	Toys	521
Card, Show	Advertising Media	449
Card, Signal	Visual Communication Devices	400
Card, Social Security	Personal Identification	495
Card, Souvenir	Memorabilia	478
card, stereoscope (*use:* Stereograph)	Graphic Documents	473
Card, Store	Exchange Media	490
Card, Sympathy	Other Documents	481
card, tally (*use:* Checklist)	Other Documents	483
card, tally (*use:* Scorecard)	Other Documents	482
Card, Tarot	Game Equipment	504
card, time (*use:* Timecard)	Financial Records	469
Card, Tobacco	Advertising Media	449
Card, Trade	Advertising Media	449
Card, Union	Personal Identification	495
card, visiting (*use:* Card, Calling)	Personal Identification	495
carder (*use:* Card, Hand)	Textile Manufacturing Equipment	239
Cardigan	Main Garments	99
Cardinal	Outerwear	100
Cardiograph	Medical Instruments	327
Carillon	Musical Instruments	371
Carlet	Leather, Horn & Shellworking T&E	201
Carousel	Recreational Devices	511
Carpet	Floor Coverings	45
Carpet, Broadloom	Floor Coverings	45
Carpet, Table	Furniture Coverings	61
carpet, wall-to-wall (*use:* Carpet, Broadloom)	Floor Coverings	45
Carpetbag	Personal Carrying & Storage Gear	110
Carport	Architectural Spaces	1
Carrack	Watercraft	444
Carriage	Animal-Powered Vehicles	423
Carriage, Artillery	Animal-Powered Vehicles	424
Carriage, Baby	Human-Powered Vehicles	427
Carriage, Cannon	Animal-Powered Vehicles	424
Carriage, Doll	Toys	520
Carriage, Runabout	Animal-Powered Vehicles	423
Carriage, Tunnel	Mining & Mineral Harvesting T&E	221
carrick (*use:* Greatcoat)	Outerwear	100
Carrier, Aircraft	Watercraft	447
Carrier, Amalgam	Dental Accessories	320
Carrier, Ammunition	Motor Vehicles	430
carrier, bulk (*use:* Freighter, Bulk)	Watercraft	446
Carrier, Cargo	Land Transportation Accessories	416
Carrier, Cheese	Food Processing Equipment	166
Carrier, Child	Human-Powered Vehicles	426
Carrier, Egg	Food Processing Equipment	167
Carrier, Ember	Heating Equipment Accessories	76
Carrier, Feed	Animal Care Equipment	134
carrier, flag (*use:* Belt, Flag)	Organizational Objects	459
Carrier, Food	Food Service Accessories	180
Carrier, Gas Mask	Protective Devices	345
Carrier, Gold Foil	Dental Accessories	320
carrier, lathe (*use:* Dog, Lathe)	Metalworking T&E	210
Carrier, Ligature	Medical Instruments	329
Carrier, Litter	Animal Care Equipment	134
Carrier, Log	Heating Equipment Accessories	76
carrier, luggage (*use:* Carrier, Cargo)	Land Transportation Accessories	416
Carrier, Luggage	Personal Carrying & Storage Gear	111
Carrier, Milk Bottle	Food Processing Equipment	166
Carrier, Personnel	Motor Vehicles	430
Carrier, Pet	Pet Supplies	141
Carrier, Timber	Forestry T&E	190
Carriole	Animal-Powered Vehicles	424
carrom (*use:* Game, Carrom)	Game Equipment	505
Carronade	Artillery	274
Cart	Animal-Powered Vehicles	424
Cart, Appliance	Support Furniture	56
cart, baggage (*use:* Cart, Luggage)	Human-Powered Vehicles	426
Cart, Batch	Glass, Plastics & Clayworking T&E	192
Cart, Beverage	Food Service Accessories	180
cart, breaking (*use:* Break, Skeleton)	Animal-Powered Vehicles	423
Cart, Computer	Support Furniture	56
Cart, Dish	Food Service Accessories	180
Cart, Dog	Animal-Powered Vehicles	424
cart, doll (*use:* Carriage, Doll)	Toys	520
Cart, Firehose	Human-Powered Vehicles	426
Cart, Food Service	Food Service Accessories	180
Cart, Golf	Motor Vehicles	430

Cart, Governess Animal-Powered Vehicles 424
Cart, Hotel Luggage Human-Powered Vehicles 426
Cart, Irish Jaunting Animal-Powered Vehicles 424
Cart, Janitorial Housekeeping Equipment 311
Cart, Luggage Human-Powered Vehicles 426
Cart, Lumber Animal-Powered Vehicles 424
Cart, Mail Animal-Powered Vehicles 424
Cart, Media Support Furniture 56
cart, ox (*use:* Oxcart) Animal-Powered Vehicles 424
Cart, Panel Human-Powered Vehicles 426
Cart, Portable Luggage Human-Powered Vehicles 426
Cart, Projector Visual Communication Accessories 399
Cart, Service Human-Powered Vehicles 426
Cart, Shopping Merchandising T&E 336
Cart, Street Sweeping Groundskeeping Equipment 309
Cart, Tea Support Furniture 56
cart, tractor grain (*use:* Trailer, Farm) Motor Vehicles 429
Cart, Tray Food Service Accessories 180
Cart, Utility Human-Powered Vehicles 426
Carte-de-visite Graphic Documents 473
Cartograph Graphic Documents 472
Carton Containers 414
Cartoon Graphic Documents 472
Cartridge Ammunition 263
cartridge, audiotape (*use:* Audiocassette) Sound Communication Media 393
Cartridge, Blank Ammunition 263
Cartridge, Caseless Ammunition 263
Cartridge, Center-Fire Ammunition 263
cartridge, data (*use:* Tape, Magnetic) Data Processing Media 363
Cartridge, Dummy Ammunition 263
Cartridge, Ink Writing Accessories 402
Cartridge, Linen Ammunition 263
Cartridge, Paper Ammunition 263
Cartridge, Phonograph Sound Communication Accessories 389
Cartridge, Pinfire Ammunition 263
Cartridge, Rimfire Ammunition 263
Cartridge, Toner Printing Accessories 386
cartridge, video game (*use:* Game, Console) Game Equipment 506
Carver, Dental Dental Instruments 322
Carving Art 454
Carving, Cathead Water Transportation Accessories 437
Carving, Marine Water Transportation Accessories 437
Carving, Paddlebox Water Transportation Accessories 437
Carving, Stern Water Transportation Accessories 437
Carving, Taffrail Water Transportation Accessories 437
Case Containers 414
Case, Armament Armament Accessories 267
Case, Artillery Shell Armament Accessories 267
Case, Astronomical Instrument Astronomical T&E 284
Case, Attaché Personal Carrying & Storage Gear 111
Case, Audio Equipment Sound Communication Accessories 389
Case, Audio Recording Sound Communication Accessories 389
Case, Audiotape Sound Communication Accessories 389
Case, Binoculars Optical T&E 343
Case, Biological Instrument Biological T&E 286
Case, Bodkin Needleworking Equipment 234
Case, Bow Armament Accessories 267
Case, Camera Photographic Accessories 378
Case, Camera Battery Photographic Accessories 378
Case, Card Personal Carrying & Storage Gear 111
Case, Cartridge Armament Accessories 267
Case, Chalice Religious Objects 461
Case, Chart Water Transportation Accessories 440
Case, Chemical Instrument Chemical Testing Devices 289
Case, Chopstick Food Service Accessories 180
Case, Ciborium Religious Objects 462
Case, Cigar Smoking & Recreational Drug Equipment 114
Case, Cigarette Smoking & Recreational Drug Equipment 114
Case, Clarinet Musical Accessories 368
Case, Comb Hair Care Objects 118
Case, Commemorative Memorabilia 478
Case, Compact Disc Data Processing Accessories 359
Case, Computer Equipment Data Processing Accessories 359
Case, Contact Lens Personal Carrying & Storage Gear 111
Case, Cosmetic Beauty Supplies 116
Case, Coupon Personal Carrying & Storage Gear 111
Case, Crochet Hook Textile Manufacturing Equipment 239
Case, Curio Storage & Display Accessories 63
Case, Daguerreotype Photographic Accessories 378
Case, Dental Dental Accessories 320
Case, Denture Personal Carrying & Storage Gear 111
Case, Digital Videodisc Data Processing Accessories 359
Case, Diskette Data Processing Accessories 359
Case, Display Merchandising T&E 336
case, display (*use:* Case, Curio) Storage & Display Accessories 63
Case, Document Writing Accessories 402

Case, Drafting Instrument — Drafting T&E 366
Case, Dressing — Personal Carrying & Storage Gear 111
Case, Eating Utensil — Food Service Accessories 180
Case, Epaulet — Personal Carrying & Storage Gear 111
Case, Eyeglass — Personal Carrying & Storage Gear 112
Case, Fife — Musical Accessories 368
Case, Firework — Public Entertainment Devices 507
Case, Fishing Gear — Fishing Equipment 145
Case, Fishing Rod — Fishing Equipment 145
Case, Flatware — Food Service Accessories 180
Case, Food Service — Food Service Accessories 180
Case, Game — Game Equipment 501
Case, Guitar — Musical Accessories 368
Case, Gun — Armament Accessories 267
Case, Hairpin — Personal Carrying & Storage Gear 112
case, jewel (*use:* Case, Compact Disc) — Data Processing Accessories 359
Case, Jewelry — Personal Carrying & Storage Gear 112
Case, Key — Personal Carrying & Storage Gear 112
Case, Knitting Needle — Textile Manufacturing Equipment 239
Case, Lancet — Medical Accessories 325
Case, Laptop Computer — Data Processing Accessories 359
Case, Manicure — Beauty Supplies 116
Case, Match — Personal Carrying & Storage Gear 112
Case, Measuring Instrument — Weights & Measures T&E 357
Case, Medical Instrument — Medical Accessories 325
Case, Medical Thermometer — Medical Accessories 325
Case, Medicine — Personal Carrying & Storage Gear 112
Case, Mezuzah — Religious Objects 462
Case, Microscope — Optical T&E 343
Case, Monstrance — Religious Objects 462
Case, Mummy — Funerary Objects 456
Case, Musical Instrument — Musical Accessories 368
Case, Napkin — Food Service Accessories 180
Case, Navigational Instrument — Navigational Equipment 349
Case, Necktie — Personal Carrying & Storage Gear 112
Case, Needle — Needleworking Equipment 234
Case, Needlework — Needleworking Equipment 234
Case, Octant — Navigational Equipment 349
Case, Optical Instrument — Optical T&E 343
Case, Parchment — Writing Accessories 402
Case, Pen — Writing Accessories 403
Case, Pencil — Writing Accessories 403
Case, Pencil Lead — Writing Accessories 403
Case, Personal — Personal Carrying & Storage Gear 111
Case, Phonograph — Sound Communication Accessories 389
Case, Photograph — Photographic Accessories 378
Case, Photographic Equipment — Photographic Accessories 378
case, pill (*use:* Pillbox) — Personal Carrying & Storage Gear 112
Case, Pin — Needleworking Equipment 235
Case, Pipe — Smoking & Recreational Drug Equipment 114
Case, Powder Box — Armament Accessories 267
Case, Projector — Visual Communication Accessories 399
Case, Prop — Public Entertainment Devices 507
Case, Public Entertainment — Public Entertainment Devices 507
Case, Punch — Leather, Horn & Shellworking T&E 196
Case, Puppet — Public Entertainment Devices 507
Case, Radiator — Barrier Elements 2
Case, Razor — Hair Care Objects 119
Case, Record — Sound Communication Accessories 389
Case, Sales Sample — Merchandising T&E 336
Case, Scale — Weights & Measures T&E 357
Case, Scissors — Needleworking Equipment 235
Case, Serving Utensil — Food Service Accessories 180
Case, Sextant — Navigational Equipment 349
Case, Shaving Brush — Hair Care Objects 119
case, shell (*use:* Case, Cartridge) — Armament Accessories 267
Case, Slipper — Personal Carrying & Storage Gear 112
Case, Snap — Glass, Plastics & Clayworking T&E 192
Case, Soap — Hygiene Objects 120
Case, Spool — Needleworking Equipment 235
Case, Stamp — Personal Carrying & Storage Gear 112
Case, Stud — Personal Carrying & Storage Gear 112
Case, Surveying Instrument — Surveying Equipment 352
Case, Surveyor's Compass — Surveying Equipment 352
Case, Sword — Armament Accessories 267
Case, Telecommunication Equipment — Telecommunication Accessories 394
Case, Telephone — Telecommunication Accessories 394
Case, Telescope — Optical T&E 343

Term	Category	Page
Case, Textilemaking Tool	Textile Manufacturing Equipment	239
Case, Thermal Instrument	Thermal T&E	354
Case, Thermometer	Thermal T&E	354
Case, Thimble	Needleworking Equipment	235
Case, Thread	Needleworking Equipment	235
Case, Timepiece	Timekeeping T&E	355
Case, Toilet Bottle	Hygiene Objects	120
Case, Toothbrush	Hygiene Objects	120
Case, Traveling	Personal Carrying & Storage Gear	112
Case, Type	Typesetting Equipment	388
Case, Typewriter	Writing Accessories	403
Case, Violin	Musical Accessories	369
Case, Visual Communication Equipment	Visual Communication Accessories	399
Case, Wardian	Horticultural Containers	62
Case, Watch	Timekeeping T&E	355
Case, Wig	Personal Carrying & Storage Gear	112
Case, Writing	Writing Accessories	403
Case, Writing Equipment	Writing Accessories	403
Cashbook	Financial Records	469
Cashbox	Merchandising T&E	336
Casing	Mining & Mineral Harvesting T&E	221
Casing, Bed	Bedding	43
Casino	Cultural & Recreational Structures	29
Cask	Containers	414
Cask, Bread	Food Storage Equipment	171
Cask, Food	Food Storage Equipment	171
Cask, Harness	Water Transportation Accessories	436
Cask, Rum	Food Storage Equipment	171
Cask, Water	Food Storage Equipment	171
Cask, Whiskey	Food Storage Equipment	171
Cask, Wine	Food Storage Equipment	171
Casket	Funerary Objects	456
Casserole	Cooking Vessels	150
Cassock	Status Symbols	499
Cassolette	Other Household Accessories	66
Cassone	Storage & Display Furniture	53
Cast, Dental	Dental Accessories	320
Cast, Medical	Medical Instruments	332
Castanet	Musical Instruments	372
caster (*use:* Castor)	Other Household Accessories	66
Caster	Serving Vessels	188
Caster, Mustard	Serving Vessels	188
Caster, Pepper	Serving Vessels	188
Caster, Pickle	Serving Vessels	188
Caster, Sugar	Serving Vessels	188
Casting	Art	454
Castle	Dwellings	32
Castor	Other Household Accessories	66
Catafalque	Funerary Objects	457
Catalog	Other Documents	481
Catalog, Auction	Advertising Media	449
Catalog, Mail Order	Advertising Media	449
Catalog, Sales	Advertising Media	449
Catalog, Trade	Advertising Media	449
Catamaran	Watercraft	443
Catapult	Percussive Weapons	283
Catboat	Watercraft	443
catcher, cow (*use:* Pilot, Locomotive)	Rail Transportation Accessories	431
Catcher, Fly	Other Household Accessories	66
Catcher, Grass	Groundskeeping Equipment	309
Catcher, Hog	Animal Care Equipment	135
Catcher, Poultry	Animal Care Equipment	135
catcher, tear (*use:* Bottle, Tear)	Funerary Objects	456
Catcher, Water	Other Household Accessories	66
Catcher, Whale	Watercraft	445
Catechism	Instructional Documents	475
Cathedra	Religious Objects	461
Cathedral	Ceremonial Structures	25
Catheter	Medical Instruments	334
Cathetometer	Surveying Equipment	352
Cathetometer, Laboratory	Chemical Testing Devices	290
Cathode	Electrical System Components	300
catling (*use:* Knife, Amputation)	Medical Instruments	331
Cat-o'-Nine-Tails	Regulative Devices	347
Catopter	Optical T&E	343
Catsuit	Main Garments	96
Catwalk	Architectural Spaces	1
Caul	Headwear	92
Cauldron	Cooking Vessels	151
Cauldron, Potash	Other T&E for Materials	260
cauldron, scalding (*use:* Scalder, Hog)	Food Processing Equipment	165
Caulk	Construction Materials	3
Cauterium	Painting T&E	230
Cauterizer	Medical Instruments	330
Cavalier	Defense Structures	31
Cavil	Masonry & Stoneworking T&E	203
CD (*use:* Disc, Compact)	Data Processing Media	363
Ceilometer	Meteorological T&E	339
Celesta	Musical Instruments	371
Cell, Bleaching	Papermaking T&E	232
Cell, Detention	Regulative Devices	347
Cell, Flotation	Mining & Mineral Harvesting T&E	221
Cell, Jail	Regulative Devices	347

Cellar	Architectural Spaces	1
Cellar, Root	Architectural Spaces	1
Cellar, Storm	Architectural Spaces	1
Cellar, Wine	Architectural Spaces	1
Cellarette	Storage & Display Furniture	53
Cello	Musical Instruments	373
Celt	Multiple Use T&E for Materials	226
Cenotaph	Site Features	21
Censer	Religious Objects	462
cent (*use:* Penny)	Exchange Media	488
Cent, Half	Exchange Media	487
Centavo	Exchange Media	487
Center, Community	Civic & Social Structures	26
center, entertainment (*use:* Cabinet, Entertainment)	Storage & Display Furniture	52
Center, Lathe	Woodworking T&E	246
Center, Shopping	Commercial Structures	27
Center, Welfare	Institutional Structures	37
Centerboard	Water Transportation Accessories	437
Centerdrill	Metalworking T&E	210
Centerpiece	Decorative Furnishings	60
Centime	Exchange Media	487
Centrifuge, Chemical	Labware	292
Centrifuge, Clinical	Labware	292
Centrifuge, Human	Biological T&E	286
Centrifuge, Laboratory	Labware	292
Centrolinead	Drafting T&E	366
Cephalometer	Medical Instruments	327
Cephalotribe	Medical Instruments	330
Certificate	Other Documents	481
Certificate of Deposit	Financial Records	469
Certificate, Achievement	Achievement Symbols	491
Certificate, Attendance	Other Documents	481
certificate, award (*use:* Certificate, Achievement)	Achievement Symbols	491
Certificate, Baptismal	Other Documents	481
Certificate, Birth	Government Records	470
certificate, burial (*use:* Record, Burial	Government Records)	
Certificate, Church	Other Documents	481
Certificate, Citizenship	Government Records	470
Certificate, Commemorative	Memorabilia	478
certificate, commendation (*use:* Certificate, Achievement)	Achievement Symbols	491
Certificate, Confirmation	Other Documents	481
Certificate, Death	Government Records	470
certificate, discharge (*use:* Discharge)	Legal Documents	476
Certificate, First Communion	Other Documents	481
Certificate, Gift	Exchange Media	487
Certificate, Gold	Exchange Media	489
Certificate, Marriage	Government Records	471
Certificate, Membership	Other Documents	481
certificate, merit (*use:* Reward of Merit)	Achievement Symbols	491
certificate, military service (*use:* Record, Service)	Government Records	470
certificate, naturalization (*use:* Certificate, Citizenship)	Government Records	470
certificate, registration (*use:* Registration)	Other Documents	484
Certificate, Silver	Exchange Media	489
Certificate, Stock	Financial Records	469
Cestrum	Painting T&E	230
Chad	Data Processing Accessories	359
Chain	Multiple Use T&E for Materials	226
Chain of Office	Status Symbols	498
Chain, Anchor	Water Transportation Accessories	436
Chain, Bicycle	Land Transportation Accessories	417
Chain, Brake	Forestry T&E	190
Chain, Curb	Land Transportation Accessories	419
Chain, Cycle	Land Transportation Accessories	417
Chain, Draught	Land Transportation Accessories	419
Chain, Engineer's	Surveying Equipment	352
Chain, Eyeglass	Personal Carrying & Storage Gear	112
Chain, Key	Personal Carrying & Storage Gear	112
Chain, Log	Forestry T&E	190
Chain, Lorgnette	Personal Carrying & Storage Gear	112
Chain, Marine	Water Transportation Accessories	436
Chain, Motorcycle	Land Transportation Accessories	417
Chain, Obstetrical	Veterinary Equipment	142
Chain, Restraining	Regulative Devices	348
Chain, Shoe	Personal Assistive Objects	107
Chain, Surveyor's	Surveying Equipment	352
Chain, Tire	Land Transportation Accessories	416
Chain, Watch	Personal Carrying & Storage Gear	112
chainsaw (*use:* Saw, Chain)	Forestry T&E	191
Chair	Seating Furniture	47
Chair, Adirondack	Seating Furniture	47
Chair, Altar	Religious Objects	461

chair, arm (*use:* Armchair)	Seating Furniture	47
Chair, Ballroom	Seating Furniture	48
Chair, Barber's	Seating Furniture	48
Chair, Bath	Seating Furniture	48
Chair, Beach	Seating Furniture	48
Chair, Beanbag	Seating Furniture	48
Chair, Bed	Seating Furniture	48
chair, bent-wire (*use:* Chair, Soda Fountain)	Seating Furniture	48
Chair, Boatswain's	Water Transportation Accessories	436
Chair, Camp	Seating Furniture	48
Chair, Captain's	Seating Furniture	49
Chair, Child's	Seating Furniture	48
Chair, Chiropody	Medical Accessories	325
Chair, Commode	Seating Furniture	48
Chair, Corner	Seating Furniture	48
Chair, Deck	Sleeping & Reclining Furniture	50
Chair, Dentist's	Dental Accessories	320
Chair, Desk	Seating Furniture	48
Chair, Dining	Seating Furniture	48
Chair, Director's	Seating Furniture	48
Chair, Easy	Seating Furniture	47
Chair, Electric	Regulative Devices	347
Chair, Examining	Medical Accessories	325
Chair, Fireplace	Seating Furniture	48
Chair, Folding	Seating Furniture	48
chair, gaffer's (*use:* Bench, Glassmaker's)	Glass, Plastics & Clayworking T&E	192
Chair, Garden	Seating Furniture	48
Chair, Gondola	Seating Furniture	47
Chair, Great	Seating Furniture	47
Chair, Hall	Seating Furniture	48
chair, high (*use:* Highchair)	Seating Furniture	48
Chair, Hitchcock	Seating Furniture	48
chair, ice-cream parlor (*use:* Chair, Soda Fountain)	Seating Furniture	48
Chair, Invalid	Seating Furniture	48
Chair, Kitchen	Seating Furniture	48
chair, ladder-back (*use:* Chair, Slat-Back)	Seating Furniture	48
chair, lawn (*use:* Chair, Garden)	Seating Furniture	48
Chair, Massage	Seating Furniture	48
Chair, Medical	Medical Accessories	325
Chair, Morris	Seating Furniture	47
Chair, Music	Musical Accessories	369
Chair, Office	Seating Furniture	48
Chair, Patio	Seating Furniture	48
chair, platform rocking (*use:* Rocker, Platform)	Seating Furniture	48
Chair, Porter's	Seating Furniture	47
Chair, Potty	Seating Furniture	48
Chair, Rail	Rail Vehicles	434
Chair, Reclining	Seating Furniture	48
Chair, Rocking	Seating Furniture	48
Chair, Sedan	Human-Powered Vehicles	426
Chair, Shoeshine	Seating Furniture	48
Chair, Side	Seating Furniture	48
Chair, Slat-Back	Seating Furniture	48
Chair, Slipper	Seating Furniture	48
Chair, Smoking	Seating Furniture	48
Chair, Soda Fountain	Seating Furniture	48
chair, spa (*use:* Chair, Touring)	Human-Powered Vehicles	426
Chair, Stacking	Seating Furniture	48
chair, stenographer's (*use:* Chair, Typing)	Seating Furniture	48
Chair, Step	Seating Furniture	48
Chair, Swivel	Seating Furniture	48
Chair, Tablet-Arm	Seating Furniture	47
Chair, Touring	Human-Powered Vehicles	426
Chair, Treatment	Medical Accessories	325
Chair, Typing	Seating Furniture	48
Chair, Window	Seating Furniture	49
Chair, Windsor	Seating Furniture	49
Chair, Wing	Seating Furniture	47
Chair-Table	Seating Furniture	47
Chaise	Animal-Powered Vehicles	423
chaise longue (*use:* Lounge)	Sleeping & Reclining Furniture	51
Chaise, Post	Animal-Powered Vehicles	423
Chalice	Religious Objects	462
Chalk	Writing Devices	406
Chalk, Billiard	Game Equipment	501
Chalk, Lumber	Woodworking T&E	248
Chalk, Tailor's	Needleworking Equipment	236
Chalk, Woodworking	Woodworking T&E	248
Chalkboard	Writing Media	408
Chalumeau	Musical Instruments	374
Chalwar	Main Garments	97
Chamber, Bubble	Nuclear Physics T&E	341
Chamber, Cloud	Nuclear Physics T&E	341
Chamber, Counting	Medical Instruments	327
chamber, film (*use:* Magazine, Film)	Visual Communication Accessories	399
Chamber, Heliotropic	Biological T&E	286
Chamber, Particle Detection	Nuclear Physics T&E	341
Chamber, Vacuum	Nuclear Physics T&E	341
Chamberstick	Lighting Holders	71
Chandelier	Lighting Devices	68
Changer, Belt Coin	Merchandising T&E	336
Changer, Bulb	Other Lighting Accessories	72
Changer, Light Bulb	Housekeeping Equipment	311
Changer, Money	Merchandising T&E	336
Changkol	Mining & Mineral Harvesting T&E	221
Channeler, Leather	Leather, Horn & Shellworking T&E	196

Channeler, Rock	Mining & Mineral Harvesting T&E	221
Chanter, Practice	Musical Instruments	374
Chanukiah	Religious Objects	461
Chapel	Ceremonial Structures	25
Chaperon	Headwear	92
chaplet (*use:* Rosary)	Belief Symbols	494
Chaplet	Headwear	92
Chaps	Protective Wear	102
Charcoal	Firemaking Equipment	74
Charge, Depth	Ammunition	263
Charger	Serving Vessels	187
Charger, Battery	Power Producing Equipment	303
Charger, Nipple	Armament Accessories	267
Chariot	Animal-Powered Vehicles	423
Charka	Drinking Vessels	173
Charm	Belief Symbols	493
charm (*use:* Pendant, Charm)	Body Adornments	81
Charm, Beverage	Food Service Accessories	180
charm, watch (*use:* Fob, Watch)	Personal Carrying & Storage Gear	112
Chart	Graphic Documents	472
Chart, Color	Graphic Documents	472
Chart, Flow	Graphic Documents	472
chart, genealogical (*use:* Tree, Family)	Graphic Documents	472
Chart, Instructional	Instructional Documents	475
chart, medical (*use:* Record, Medical)	Other Documents	485
Chart, Navigational	Graphic Documents	472
Chart, Organizational	Graphic Documents	472
Chart, Plotting	Graphic Documents	472
Chart, Seating	Graphic Documents	472
Chart, Visual Acuity	Medical Instruments	329
Charter	Legal Documents	476
Chartometer	Drafting T&E	366
Chase	Typesetting Equipment	388
Chaser	Metalworking T&E	209
Chaser, Submarine	Watercraft	447
Chasuble	Status Symbols	499
Chatelaine	Clothing Accessories	84
Chaveta	Other T&E for Materials	260
check, baggage (*use:* Tag, Luggage)	Other Documents	483
Check, Bank	Exchange Media	489
Check, Certified	Exchange Media	489
Check, Door	Finish Hardware	10
Check, Rain	Exchange Media	487
Check, Traveler's	Exchange Media	489
Checkbook	Financial Records	469
Checker	Game Equipment	502
Checkerboard	Game Equipment	501
checkers (*use:* Set, Checkers)	Game Equipment	503
checkers, Chinese (*use:*Set, Chinese Checkers)	Game Equipment	504
Checklist	Other Documents	483
checkwriter (*use:* Embosser, Check)	Writing Devices	406
Cheeseboard	Serving Vessels	187
Cheesecloth	Food Processing Equipment	166
Cheilvangroscope	Medical Instruments	327
chemise (*use:* Dress, Chemise)	Main Garments	95
Chemise	Underwear	103
Chemisette	Main Garments	95
cheque (*use:* Check, Bank)	Exchange Media	489
chess (*use:* Set, Chess)	Game Equipment	503
Chessboard	Game Equipment	501
chessman (*use:* Piece, Chess)	Game Equipment	502
Chest	Storage & Display Furniture	53
Chest of Drawers	Storage & Display Furniture	53
Chest on Chest	Storage & Display Furniture	53
Chest on Frame	Storage & Display Furniture	53
Chest, Ammunition	Armament Accessories	267
Chest, Apothecary	Storage & Display Furniture	53
Chest, Armament	Armament Accessories	267
Chest, Blanket	Storage & Display Furniture	53
chest, burial (*use:* Casket)	Funerary Objects	456
Chest, Campaign	Storage & Display Furniture	53
Chest, Chart	Water Transportation Accessories	440
Chest, Clothes	Storage & Display Furniture	53
Chest, Doll	Toys	520
chest, dower (*use:* Chest, Hope)	Storage & Display Furniture	53
Chest, Food Storage	Food Storage Equipment	171
Chest, High	Storage & Display Furniture	53
Chest, Hope	Storage & Display Furniture	53
chest, ice (*use:* Cooler)	Food Service Accessories	181
Chest, Liquor	Personal Carrying & Storage Gear	113
chest, low (*use:* Lowboy)	Storage & Display Furniture	53
Chest, Medicine	Storage & Display Accessories	63
Chest, Mess	Food Service Accessories	180
Chest, Sea	Personal Carrying & Storage Gear	113
Chest, Sewing	Storage & Display Furniture	53
Chest, Silver	Storage & Display Accessories	63
Chest, Spice	Food Storage Equipment	171
chest, spool (*use:* Cabinet, Thread)	Storage & Display Furniture	52
Chest, Tea	Food Storage Equipment	171
Chest, Tool	Multiple Use T&E for Materials	226
Chest, Veterinary	Veterinary Equipment	142

Term	Category	Page
Chesterfield	Outerwear	100
chesterfield (*use:* Sofa, Chesterfield)	Seating Furniture	49
Cheval de Frise	Defense Structures	31
Chevron	Status Symbols	497
Chiffonier	Storage & Display Furniture	53
Chifforobe	Storage & Display Furniture	53
Chiller	Environmental Control Elements	8
Chime	Sound Communication Devices	391
Chime, Door	Door & Window Elements	6
Chime, Musical	Musical Instruments	372
Chime, Wind	Musical Instruments	372
Chimere	Status Symbols	499
Chimney	Environmental Control Elements	8
Chimney, Lamp	Other Lighting Accessories	72
chimneypiece (*use:* Overmantel)	Surface Elements	18
Chink, Iron	Food Processing Equipment	164
Chinking	Construction Materials	3
Chinois	Food Preparation Equipment	162
Chip, Butter	Eating Vessels	176
Chip, Gambling	Game Equipment	502
Chip, Poker	Game Equipment	502
Chipper	Papermaking T&E	232
Chisel	Multiple Use T&E for Materials	226
Chisel, Barking	Forestry T&E	191
Chisel, Bench	Woodworking T&E	248
Chisel, Bent	Woodworking T&E	249
Chisel, Blocking	Masonry & Stoneworking T&E	203
Chisel, Boatbuilder's	Woodworking T&E	249
Chisel, Brick	Masonry & Stoneworking T&E	203
chisel, broad (*use:* Slick)	Woodworking T&E	249
chisel, bruzz (*use:* Chisel, Corner)	Woodworking T&E	248
Chisel, Butt	Woodworking T&E	248
chisel, cant (*use:* Chisel, Firmer)	Woodworking T&E	248
Chisel, Cape	Metalworking T&E	208
Chisel, Carving	Woodworking T&E	249
Chisel, Cold	Metalworking T&E	208
Chisel, Corner	Woodworking T&E	248
Chisel, Cutting	Masonry & Stoneworking T&E	203
Chisel, Dental	Dental Instruments	322
Chisel, Diamond-Point	Metalworking T&E	208
chisel, filecutter's (*use:* Chisel, Hot)	Metalworking T&E	208
Chisel, Firmer	Woodworking T&E	248
Chisel, Fishtail	Woodworking T&E	249
Chisel, Flat	Metalworking T&E	208
Chisel, Floor	Woodworking T&E	249
chisel, forming (*use:* Chisel, Firmer)	Woodworking T&E	249
chisel, framing (*use:* Chisel, Firmer)	Woodworking T&E	249
Chisel, Gooseneck	Woodworking T&E	249
Chisel, Grafting	Tending Equipment	133
Chisel, Half Round Nose	Metalworking T&E	208
Chisel, Hinge	Woodworking T&E	249
Chisel, Hoof	Farrier Equipment	140
Chisel, Hot	Metalworking T&E	208
Chisel, Ice	Mining & Mineral Harvesting T&E	225
Chisel, Metalworking	Metalworking T&E	208
Chisel, Mortise	Woodworking T&E	248
Chisel, Octagonal	Masonry & Stoneworking T&E	203
Chisel, Paring	Woodworking T&E	248
Chisel, Parting	Woodworking T&E	249
Chisel, Pitching	Masonry & Stoneworking T&E	203
Chisel, Plugging	Masonry & Stoneworking T&E	203
Chisel, Point	Masonry & Stoneworking T&E	203
Chisel, Pruning	Groundskeeping Equipment	310
Chisel, Ripping	Woodworking T&E	249
Chisel, Sash	Woodworking T&E	249
Chisel, Skew	Woodworking T&E	249
chisel, slice (*use:* Slick)	Woodworking T&E	249
Chisel, Socket	Woodworking T&E	249
Chisel, Splitting	Masonry & Stoneworking T&E	203
Chisel, Stone	Masonry & Stoneworking T&E	203
Chisel, Straight	Masonry & Stoneworking T&E	203
Chisel, Surgical	Medical Instruments	330
Chisel, Thonging	Leather, Horn & Shellworking T&E	196
Chisel, Tooth	Masonry & Stoneworking T&E	203
Chisel, Trephining	Medical Instruments	330
Chisel, Turning	Woodworking T&E	249
Chisel, Weeding	Cultivation Equipment	125
Chisel, Woodworking	Woodworking T&E	248
chlorometer (*use:* Blanchimeter)	Chemical Testing Devices	289
Chock	Mechanical Devices	317
Chock, Mast	Water Transportation Accessories	439
Chock, Wheel	Land Transportation Accessories	416
Choke, Electrical	Electrical System Components	300
Choker	Body Adornments	81
Choli	Main Garments	98
Chopine	Footwear	90

Term	Category	Page
Chopper	Multiple Use T&E for Materials	226
Chopper, Drum	Cultivation Equipment	123
chopper, ensilage (*use:* Cutter, Ensilage)	Feed Processing Equipment	126
Chopper, Feed	Feed Processing Equipment	126
chopper, fodder (*use:* Chopper, Feed)	Feed Processing Equipment	126
Chopper, Food	Food Preparation Equipment	158
chopper, hay (*use:* Chopper, Feed)	Feed Processing Equipment	126
Chopper, Meat	Food Preparation Equipment	158
chopper, silage (*use:* Cutter, Ensilage)	Feed Processing Equipment	126
chopper, stalk (*use:* Cutter, Stalk)	Cultivation Equipment	123
chopper, stalk (*use:* Chopper, Feed)	Feed Processing Equipment	126
chopper, stover (*use:* Chopper, Feed)	Feed Processing Equipment	126
Chopstick	Eating & Drinking Utensils	178
Chorograph	Surveying Equipment	352
Chrismatory	Religious Objects	462
Chromascope	Optical T&E	343
Chromatometer	Medical Instruments	329
Chromatoscope	Astronomical T&E	285
Chromatrope	Optical T&E	343
chromolithograph (*use:* Lithograph)	Graphic Documents	474
Chronograph	Timekeeping T&E	355
Chronometer	Navigational Equipment	349
chronometer, solar (*use:* Sundial)	Timekeeping T&E	356
Chronoscope	Timekeeping T&E	355
Chronothermometer	Thermal T&E	354
Chuck	Multiple Use T&E for Materials	226
Chuck, Drill	Multiple Use T&E for Materials	226
Chuck, Lathe	Multiple Use T&E for Materials	226
Chuck, Tap	Metalworking T&E	208
Chuckwagon	Animal-Powered Vehicles	425
Church	Ceremonial Structures	25
Churn	Food Processing Equipment	166
churn, ice cream (*use:* Freezer, Ice Cream)	Food Preparation Equipment	153
churn, syllabub (*use:* Whip, Cream)	Food Preparation Equipment	162
Chute	Conveyance Devices	5
Chute, Coal	Conveyance Devices	5
Chute, Deposit	Conveyance Devices	5
Chute, Drop	Masonry & Stoneworking T&E	203
Chute, Grain	Harvesting Equipment	128
Chute, Laundry	Conveyance Devices	5
Chute, Mail	Conveyance Devices	5
Chute, Refuse	Conveyance Devices	5
Chyometer	Chemical Testing Devices	290
Ciborium	Religious Objects	462
Cigar	Smoking & Recreational Drug Equipment	114
Cigarette	Smoking & Recreational Drug Equipment	114
Cimbalom	Musical Instruments	373
cinch (*use:* Girth)	Land Transportation Accessories	421
Cincher, Waist	Underwear	103
Cincture	Status Symbols	499
Cinema	Cultural & Recreational Structures	29
Circle, Azimuth	Surveying Equipment	352
Circle, Meridian	Astronomical T&E	284
Circle, Reflecting	Navigational Equipment	349
Circle, Repeating	Surveying Equipment	352
Circuit	Electrical System Components	300
Circular	Advertising Media	450
Circumferentor	Surveying Equipment	352
Cistern	Plumbing & Drainage Elements	12
Cittern	Musical Instruments	373
Cityscape	Art	453
Claim	Legal Documents	476
Clamp	Mechanical Devices	315
clamp, alligator (*use:* Clip, Alligator)	Electrical System Components	301
Clamp, Bar	Woodworking T&E	249
Clamp, Beam	Water Transportation Accessories	437
Clamp, Bench	Woodworking T&E	249
Clamp, Bone	Medical Instruments	330
Clamp, Bookbinding	Bookbinding Equipment	382
Clamp, Boot	Leather, Horn & Shellworking T&E	196
Clamp, Bowel	Medical Instruments	330
Clamp, C	Woodworking T&E	249
Clamp, Cervical	Medical Instruments	330
Clamp, Cigar	Other T&E for Materials	260
Clamp, Collar and Screw	Woodworking T&E	249
Clamp, Corner	Woodworking T&E	249
Clamp, Dental	Dental Instruments	322
Clamp, Flooring	Woodworking T&E	249
Clamp, Furniture	Woodworking T&E	249
clamp, G (*use:* Clamp, C)	Woodworking T&E	249
Clamp, Glassworking	Glass, Plastics & Clayworking T&E	192
Clamp, Hornworker's	Leather, Horn & Shellworking T&E	201
Clamp, Hosecock	Labware	292
Clamp, Joiner's	Woodworking T&E	249
Clamp, Laboratory	Labware	292

Term	Category	Page
Clamp, Last	Leather, Horn & Shellworking T&E	196
Clamp, Leatherworking	Leather, Horn & Shellworking T&E	196
Clamp, Needlework	Needleworking Equipment	234
Clamp, Panel	Woodworking T&E	249
Clamp, Quilting Frame	Needleworking Equipment	234
Clamp, Rectal	Medical Instruments	330
Clamp, Rigger's	Needleworking Equipment	234
Clamp, Saddler's	Leather, Horn & Shellworking T&E	196
Clamp, Saw	Woodworking T&E	249
Clamp, Screw	Woodworking T&E	249
Clamp, Sewing	Needleworking Equipment	234
Clamp, Slat-Bending	Woodworking T&E	249
Clamp, Spring	Woodworking T&E	249
Clamp, Stopcock	Labware	292
Clamp, Stretching	Leather, Horn & Shellworking T&E	197
Clamp, Surgical	Medical Instruments	330
Clamp, Suspension	Labware	292
Clamp, Universal	Woodworking T&E	249
Clamp, Web	Woodworking T&E	249
Clamp, Winding	Needleworking Equipment	234
Clamp, Woodworking	Woodworking T&E	249
Clapper	Sound Communication Devices	391
Clapper, Musical	Musical Accessories	368
clapper, stick (*use:* Stick, Clapper)	Musical Instruments	372
Clarinet	Musical Instruments	374
Clasp	Multiple Use T&E for Materials	227
Clasp, Clothing	Clothing Accessories	84
clasp, tie (*use:* Clip, Tie)	Clothing Accessories	84
Classboat	Watercraft	444
Classifier	Mining & Mineral Harvesting T&E	221
Clave	Musical Instruments	372
Clavichord	Musical Instruments	371
Clavicor	Musical Instruments	370
claw, tack (*use:* Puller, Tack)	Woodworking T&E	256
Clay, Modeling	Toys	524
Claymore	Edged Weapons	278
Cleaner, Ballast	Rail Vehicles	434
Cleaner, Carpet	Housekeeping Equipment	311
Cleaner, Cottonseed	Harvesting Equipment	127
Cleaner, Eyeglass	Personal Carrying & Storage Gear	112
Cleaner, Furnace	Heating Equipment Accessories	76
Cleaner, Grain	Food Processing Equipment	168
cleaner, grain (*use:* Mill, Fanning)	Harvesting Equipment	131
Cleaner, Knife	Dishwashing Equipment	308
Cleaner, Lamp Chimney	Housekeeping Equipment	311
Cleaner, Nail	Beauty Supplies	117
Cleaner, Pipe	Smoking & Recreational Drug Equipment	114
cleaner, pot (*use:* Scrubber, Pot)	Dishwashing Equipment	308
Cleaner, Record	Sound Communication Accessories	389
Cleaner, Shrimp	Food Preparation Equipment	153
Cleaner, Vacuum	Housekeeping Equipment	311
Cleat	Water Transportation Accessories	437
Cleat, Awning	Finish Hardware	10
Cleat, Shoe	Sports Equipment	512
Cleave	Fiberworking T&E	144
Cleaver	Food Preparation Equipment	159
clepsydra (*use:* Clock, Water)	Timekeeping T&E	356
Clevis	Mechanical Devices	315
clew (*use:* Iron, Clew)	Water Transportation Accessories	439
clicker (*use:* Press, Clicker)	Leather, Horn & Shellworking T&E	199
clickwheel (*use:* Wheel, Surveyor's)	Surveying Equipment	353
Climatometer	Medical Instruments	327
Climber	Recreational Devices	510
clinch (*use:* Block, Clinching)	Farrier Equipment	139
clincher (*use:* Tongs, Clinching)	Farrier Equipment	139
Clinic	Institutional Structures	37
Clinograph	Surveying Equipment	352
Clinometer	Surveying Equipment	352
Clinostat	Biological T&E	286
Clip	Multiple Use T&E for Materials	227
Clip, Alligator	Electrical System Components	301
Clip, Bedding	Bedding	43
Clip, Binder	Writing Accessories	404
Clip, Cartridge	Armament Accessories	267
Clip, Clothing	Clothing Accessories	84
Clip, Collar	Clothing Accessories	84
clip, cow (*use:* Holder, Cow Tail)	Animal Care Equipment	135
clip, crocodile (*use:* Clip, Alligator)	Electrical System Components	301
Clip, Dress	Clothing Accessories	84
Clip, Glove	Clothing Accessories	84
Clip, Grafting	Tending Equipment	133
Clip, Hair	Hair Adornments	83
Clip, Key	Personal Carrying & Storage Gear	112
Clip, Money	Personal Carrying & Storage Gear	112

Term	Category	Page
Clip, Music	Musical Accessories	369
Clip, Pacifier	Personal Carrying & Storage Gear	112
Clip, Paper	Writing Accessories	404
Clip, Pencil	Writing Accessories	402
Clip, Print	Photographic Accessories	378
Clip, Roach	Smoking & Recreational Drug Equipment	114
Clip, Scarf	Clothing Accessories	84
Clip, Shirt	Clothing Accessories	84
Clip, Shoe	Clothing Accessories	84
Clip, Stripper	Armament Accessories	267
Clip, Sweater	Clothing Accessories	84
Clip, Tie	Clothing Accessories	84
Clip, Truss	Supporting Elements	16
Clipboard	Writing Accessories	402
Clipper, Animal	Animal Care Equipment	136
Clipper, Baltimore	Watercraft	444
clipper, bolt (*use:* Cutter, Bolt)	Metalworking T&E	209
Clipper, Flower	Groundskeeping Equipment	309
Clipper, Hair	Hair Care Objects	118
Clipper, Nail	Beauty Supplies	117
Clipping	Other Documents	481
Clipping, Magazine	Other Documents	481
Clipping, Newspaper	Other Documents	481
Cloak	Outerwear	100
Cloche	Headwear	92
Clock	Timekeeping T&E	355
Clock, Alarm	Timekeeping T&E	355
Clock, Astronomical	Astronomical T&E	284
Clock, Bracket	Timekeeping T&E	355
Clock, Calendar	Timekeeping T&E	355
Clock, Carriage	Timekeeping T&E	355
Clock, Cuckoo	Timekeeping T&E	356
Clock, Digital	Timekeeping T&E	355
Clock, Dwarf Tall	Timekeeping T&E	355
Clock, Electronic	Timekeeping T&E	355
Clock, Floor	Timekeeping T&E	355
clock, grandfather (*use:* Clock, Tall Case)	Timekeeping T&E	355
clock, grandmother (*use:* Clock, Dwarf Tall)	Timekeeping T&E	355
Clock, Mantel	Timekeeping T&E	355
Clock, Mechanical	Timekeeping T&E	355
Clock, Musical	Timekeeping T&E	355
Clock, Pedestal	Timekeeping T&E	355
Clock, Quartz	Timekeeping T&E	355
Clock, Regulator	Timekeeping T&E	355
Clock, Self-Winding	Timekeeping T&E	355
Clock, Shelf	Timekeeping T&E	355
Clock, Ship's	Timekeeping T&E	355
Clock, Sidereal	Astronomical T&E	284
Clock, Table	Timekeeping T&E	355
Clock, Tall Case	Timekeeping T&E	355
Clock, Time Recording	Timekeeping T&E	355
clock, tower (*use:* Clock, Turret)	Timekeeping T&E	356
Clock, Travel	Timekeeping T&E	355
Clock, Turret	Timekeeping T&E	356
Clock, Wall	Timekeeping T&E	356
Clock, Water	Timekeeping T&E	356
Clog	Footwear	89
cloth, altar (*use:* Covering, Altar)	Religious Objects	463
cloth, bread basket (*use:* Napkin, Bread Basket)	Food Service Accessories	181
Cloth, Cleaning	Housekeeping Equipment	311
Cloth, Credence	Religious Objects	463
cloth, dish (*use:* Dishcloth)	Dishwashing Equipment	308
Cloth, Drop	Painting T&E	229
Cloth, Emery	Multiple Use T&E for Materials	226
Cloth, Fair Linen	Religious Objects	463
cloth, floor (*use:* Floorcloth)	Floor Coverings	45
Cloth, Flower	Art	452
Cloth, Forehead	Headwear	93
Cloth, Ground	Bedding	44
cloth, mantel (*use:* Lambrequin)	Furniture Coverings	61
Cloth, Mourning	Funerary Objects	456
Cloth, Polishing	Housekeeping Equipment	311
Cloth, Pressing	Laundry Equipment	313
Cloth, Story	Art	452
cloth, tammy (*use:* Riddle)	Food Preparation Equipment	162
Cloth, Tea	Food Service Accessories	181
Cloth, Tester	Bedding	44
clothes, doll (*use:* Clothing, Doll)	Toys	520
Clothesline	Laundry Equipment	313
Clothespin	Laundry Equipment	313
Clothing, Doll	Toys	520
Club	Percussive Weapons	283
club, billy (*use:* Nightstick)	Percussive Weapons	283
Club, Fish	Fishing Equipment	145
Club, Froe	Woodworking T&E	254
Club, Golf	Sports Equipment	515
Club, Health	Institutional Structures	37
Club, Indian	Recreational Devices	509
Club, Juggling	Public Entertainment Devices	508
Clubhouse	Civic & Social Structures	26
Coach	Animal-Powered Vehicles	423
Coach, Berlin	Animal-Powered Vehicles	423
Coach, Concord	Animal-Powered Vehicles	423
Coach, Rail	Rail Vehicles	433
Coach, Road	Animal-Powered Vehicles	423
coach, stage (*use:* Stagecoach)	Animal-Powered Vehicles	423

Coach, State Animal-Powered Vehicles 423
Coachee Animal-Powered Vehicles 423
Coagulometer Biological T&E 287
Coaming Water Transportation Accessories 437
Coaster Food Service Accessories 180
Coaster, Roller Recreational Devices 511
Coaster, Snow Recreational Devices 509
Coaster, Wine Food Service Accessories 180
Coat Main Garments 95
Coat of Arms Status Symbols 496
Coat, Blanket Outerwear 100
Coat, Buff Body Armor 275
coat, bunker (*use:* Coat, Turnout) Protective Wear 102
Coat, Car Outerwear 100
Coat, Cutaway Main Garments 95
coat, dinner (*use:* Jacket, Dinner) Main Garments 95
Coat, Duffle Outerwear 100
Coat, Dust Protective Wear 102
Coat, Evening Outerwear 100
Coat, Frock Main Garments 95
Coat, Laboratory Protective Wear 102
Coat, Morning Main Garments 95
coat, pea (*use:* Jacket, Pea) Outerwear 101
Coat, Riding Outerwear 100
Coat, Sack Main Garments 95
coat, sports (*use:* Sportcoat) Main Garments 95
Coat, Suit Main Garments 95
Coat, Tail Main Garments 95
Coat, Trench Outerwear 101
Coat, Turnout Protective Wear 102
Coat, Vest Outerwear 100
Coatdress Main Garments 95
Coatee Main Garments 95
Coathanger Clothing Care Objects 105
Coatrack Storage & Display Accessories 64
coat-tree (*use:* Tree, Coat) Support Furniture 55
Cob Exchange Media 487
Cockade Status Symbols 496
cockspur (*use:* Spur, Cockfighting) Sports Equipment 514
Coddler Food Preparation Equipment 154
Codpiece Main Garments 95
Coffeepot Serving Vessels 189
Coffer Storage & Display Furniture 53
Coffin Funerary Objects 456
Coggle Glass, Plastics & Clayworking T&E 192
cogwheel (*use:* Gear) Power Transmission Components 305
Coherer Telecommunication Devices 396
Coil, HVAC Environmental Control Elements 8
Coil, Induction Electrical System Components 301
Coil, Tesla Electrical System Components 301
Coin Exchange Media 487
Coin, Commemorative Memorabilia 478
Coin, Crown Exchange Media 487
Coin, Disappearing Public Entertainment Devices 508
Coin, Pagoda Exchange Media 487
Coin, Two-Dollar Exchange Media 487
Colander Food Preparation Equipment 162
Collage Art 452
collar (*use:* Gorget) Body Armor 275
Collar Clothing Accessories 84
Collar, Bark Training Pet Supplies 141
Collar, Bell Pet Supplies 141
Collar, Breast Land Transportation Accessories 419
Collar, Choke Pet Supplies 141
Collar, Clerical Status Symbols 499
Collar, Flea Pet Supplies 141
Collar, Horse Land Transportation Accessories 419
collar, livery (*use:* Chain of Office) Status Symbols 498
Collar, Pet Pet Supplies 141
Collar, Slave Regulative Devices 348
Collar, Wine Food Service Accessories 180
collarbone (*use:* Stay, Collar) Clothing Accessories 87
collator (*use:* Sorter, Card) Data Processing Accessories 360
collection, archival (*use:* Archive) Other Documents 480
Collier Watercraft 446
Collimator Nuclear Physics T&E 341
Collimator, Optical Optical T&E 343
Collotype Graphic Documents 473
Colonoscope Medical Instruments 330
Colorimeter Chemical Testing Devices 290
Columbarium Ceremonial Structures 25
Column Supporting Elements 16
Column, Memorial Site Features 21
Comal Food Preparation Equipment 154
Comb, Animal Animal Care Equipment 136
Comb, Broomcorn Fiberworking T&E 144
Comb, Carding Textile Manufacturing Equipment 239
Comb, Cock's Masonry & Stoneworking T&E 206
comb, curry (*use:* Currycomb) Animal Care Equipment 136

Comb, Eyebrow | Hair Care Objects | 118
Comb, Graining | Painting T&E | 229
Comb, Hair | Hair Care Objects | 118
Comb, Hand | Textile Manufacturing Equipment | 239
Comb, Hot | Hair Care Objects | 118
Comb, Lice | Hair Care Objects | 118
Comb, Mustache | Hair Care Objects | 118
Comb, Ornamental | Hair Adornments | 83
Comb, Side | Hair Adornments | 83
Comb, Textile | Textile Manufacturing Equipment | 239
Comb, Tuck | Hair Adornments | 83
Comb, Weaving | Textile Manufacturing Equipment | 239
Combination | Underwear | 103
Combine | Harvesting Equipment | 128
Combine, Corn | Harvesting Equipment | 128
Combine, Green Pea | Harvesting Equipment | 128
Combine, Hillside | Harvesting Equipment | 128
Combine, Peanut | Harvesting Equipment | 128
Combine, Pull-Type | Harvesting Equipment | 128
Combine, Self-Propelled | Harvesting Equipment | 128
combine, sidehill (*use:* Combine, Hillside) | Harvesting Equipment | 128
combinette (*use:* Pot, Chamber) | Hygiene Objects | 121
Comboliner | Rail Vehicles | 434
Come-Along | Mechanical Devices | 315
Comforter | Bedding | 43
Comic | Graphic Documents | 472
commander (*use:* Beetle) | Woodworking T&E | 254
Commemorative | Memorabilia | 478
Commission | Other Documents | 484
Commode | Storage & Display Furniture | 53
Compact | Beauty Supplies | 116
Compactor | Construction T&E | 295
Compactor, Trash | Housekeeping Equipment | 311
Comparator | Data Processing Devices | 361
Comparator, High Phosphate Slide | Chemical Testing Devices | 290
Comparator, Hydrogenation | Chemical Testing Devices | 290
Comparator, Laboratory | Chemical Testing Devices | 290
Comparator, Length | Weights & Measures T&E | 357
Comparator, Nessler Tube | Chemical Testing Devices | 290
Compass | Navigational Equipment | 349
Compass, Aircraft | Aerospace Transportation Accessories | 409
Compass, Beam | Drafting T&E | 366
Compass, Binnacle | Water Transportation Accessories | 437
Compass, Borehole | Surveying Equipment | 352
Compass, Bow | Drafting T&E | 366
Compass, Box | Water Transportation Accessories | 437
Compass, Dip | Surveying Equipment | 352
Compass, Drafting | Drafting T&E | 366
Compass, Drycard | Surveying Equipment | 352
Compass, Napier | Drafting T&E | 366
Compass, Pencil | Drafting T&E | 366
Compass, Pillar | Drafting T&E | 366
Compass, Potter's | Glass, Plastics & Clayworking T&E | 192
Compass, Proportional | Drafting T&E | 366
Compass, Radio | Navigational Equipment | 349
Compass, Scratch | Leather, Horn & Shellworking T&E | 197
Compass, Ship's | Water Transportation Accessories | 437
Compass, Solar | Surveying Equipment | 352
Compass, Surveyor's | Surveying Equipment | 352
Compass, Telltale | Navigational Equipment | 349
Compass, Wing | Drafting T&E | 366
Compass, Woodworking | Woodworking T&E | 249
Compass, Wrist | Navigational Equipment | 349
Compensator | Surveying Equipment | 352
Component, Aircraft | Aerospace Transportation Accessories | 409
Component, Bed | Sleeping & Reclining Furniture | 50
Component, Billiard | Game Equipment | 501
Component, Chimney | Environmental Control Elements | 8
Component, Fireplace | Environmental Control Elements | 8
Component, Game | Game Equipment | 501
Component, Musical Instrument | Musical Accessories | 369
Component, Rail Vehicle | Rail Transportation Accessories | 431
Component, Scale | Weights & Measures T&E | 357
Component, Stove | Heating Equipment Accessories | 76
Component, Timepiece | Timekeeping T&E | 356
Component, Track | Rail Transportation Accessories | 431
Component, Vehicle | Land Transportation Accessories | 416
Component, Video Game | Game Equipment | 501
Component, Watercraft | Water Transportation Accessories | 436
Composition, Musical | Literary Works | 477
Composter | Groundskeeping Equipment | 309
Compote | Serving Vessels | 186
Compound, Impression | Dental Accessories | 320
Compress | Medical Instruments | 333
Compressor | Power Producing Equipment | 303
Compressor, Blowing Engine | Power Producing Equipment | 303
Compressor, Dental | Dental Accessories | 320
Compressor, Duplex Air | Power Producing Equipment | 303

Term	Category	Page
Compressor, HVAC	Environmental Control Elements	8
Compressor, Rotary	Power Producing Equipment	303
Compressor, Sullivan Angle	Power Producing Equipment	303
Compressor, Turbo	Power Producing Equipment	303
Computer, Analog	Data Processing Devices	361
Computer, Desktop	Data Processing Devices	362
Computer, Digital	Data Processing Devices	362
Computer, Handheld	Data Processing Devices	362
Computer, Hybrid	Data Processing Devices	361
Computer, Laptop	Data Processing Devices	362
Computer, Mainframe	Data Processing Devices	362
computer, palmtop (*use:* Computer, Handheld)	Data Processing Devices	362
Computer, Tablet	Data Processing Devices	362
Concentrator	Metalworking T&E	208
Concentrator, Cyclone	Metalworking T&E	209
Concentrator, Electromagnetic	Metalworking T&E	209
Concentrator, Flotation	Metalworking T&E	209
Concentrator, Jig	Metalworking T&E	209
Concentrator, Mineral	Mining & Mineral Harvesting T&E	221
Concentrator, Shaking Table	Metalworking T&E	209
Concertina	Musical Instruments	371
Concho	Clothing Accessories	84
Conchometer	Biological T&E	287
Concrete	Construction Materials	3
condenser (*use:* Capacitor)	Electrical System Components	300
Condenser	Textile Manufacturing Equipment	239
Condenser, Amalgam	Dental Accessories	320
Condenser, Cotton	Textile Manufacturing Equipment	239
Condenser, Goulding	Textile Manufacturing Equipment	240
Condenser, HVAC	Environmental Control Elements	8
Condenser, Laboratory	Chemical Testing Devices	290
Condenser, Milk	Food Processing Equipment	166
Condenser, Optical	Optical T&E	343
Condenser, Rotating	Nuclear Physics T&E	341
Condenser, Rub-Apron	Textile Manufacturing Equipment	240
Condenser, Rub-Roll	Textile Manufacturing Equipment	240
Condenser, Tape	Textile Manufacturing Equipment	240
Conditioner, Air	Heating & Cooling Equipment	75
Conditioner, Central Air	Environmental Control Elements	8
Conditioner, Grain	Food Processing Equipment	168
Conditioner, Hay	Harvesting Equipment	127
Conditioner, Water	Plumbing & Drainage Elements	12
Conditioner, Wheat	Food Processing Equipment	168
Condom	Hygiene Objects	121
Condominium	Dwellings	32
Conduit	Hydraulic Structures	34
Conduit, Electric	Electrical System Components	300
Cone, Adjusting	Medical Instruments	329
Cone, Braiding	Textile Manufacturing Equipment	240
Cone, Imhoff	Chemical Testing Devices	290
Cone, Nose	Aerospace Transportation Accessories	409
Cone, Pyrometric	Glass, Plastics & Clayworking T&E	192
cone, tinkling (*use:* Tinkler)	Clothing Accessories	87
Cone, Tuning	Musical Accessories	369
Confectionery	Commercial Structures	27
Confessional	Religious Objects	461
Confetti	Party Accessories	460
Conformateur	Biological T&E	287
Connector, Cable	Telecommunication Accessories	394
Connector, Data	Data Processing Accessories	359
Conograph	Drafting T&E	366
Console, Bowling Scoring	Sports Equipment	513
Console, Computer	Peripherals	364
console, entertainment (*use:* Cabinet, Entertainment)	Storage & Display Furniture	52
Console, Lighting	Other Lighting Accessories	72
console, mixing (*use:* Mixer, Audio)	Sound Communication Devices	392
Console, Video Game	Game Equipment	501
Constitution	Administrative Records	467
Construction	Art	454
Container, Apothecary	Merchandising T&E	336
Container, Armament	Armament Accessories	267
Container, Bait	Fishing Equipment	145
Container, Ballot	Organizational Objects	459
Container, Biological Specimen	Biological T&E	287
Container, Chart	Water Transportation Accessories	440
Container, Cigar	Containers for Smoking & Tobacco	59
Container, Comb	Hair Care Objects	118
Container, Cosmetic	Beauty Supplies	116
Container, Crop	Harvesting Equipment	127
Container, Document	Writing Accessories	402
Container, Film	Photographic Accessories	378
Container, Fishing	Fishing Equipment	145
Container, Food Preparation	Food Preparation Equipment	153

Container, Food Processing	Food Processing Equipment	164
Container, Food Waste	Food Service Accessories	181
Container, Fuel	Heating Equipment Accessories	76
Container, Funerary	Funerary Objects	456
Container, Game	Game Equipment	502
Container, Hairpin	Personal Carrying & Storage Gear	112
Container, Laboratory	Labware	292
Container, Laundry	Laundry Equipment	313
Container, Mail	Containers	414
Container, Medicine	Medical Accessories	325
Container, Money	Merchandising T&E	336
Container, Needlework	Needleworking Equipment	234
Container, Offering	Religious Objects	461
Container, Ore	Mining & Mineral Harvesting T&E	221
Container, Postage Stamp	Writing Accessories	403
Container, Recycling	Housekeeping Equipment	312
Container, Ritual	Religious Objects	461
Container, Seed	Planting Equipment	132
Container, Shipping	Containers	414
Container, Shopping	Merchandising T&E	336
Container, Snuff	Smoking & Recreational Drug Equipment	114
Container, Soap	Hygiene Objects	120
Container, Specimen	Medical Accessories	325
Container, Spit	Containers for Smoking & Tobacco	59
Container, Tack	Land Transportation Accessories	418
Container, Tool	Multiple Use T&E for Materials	226
Container, Trick or Treat	Holiday Objects	458
Container, Writing Equipment	Writing Accessories	403
Contract	Legal Documents	476
control, antenna (*use:* Rotor, Antenna)	Telecommunication Accessories	395
Control, Remote	Telecommunication Devices	396
Controller, Sound	Acoustical T&E	261
Controller, Video Game	Game Equipment	501
Convector	Environmental Control Elements	8
converter (*use:* Furnace, Converter)	Metalworking T&E	211
Converter, AC-DC	Electrical System Components	300
converter, analog-to-digital (*use:* Digitizer)	Data Processing Devices	361
Converter, Cable	Telecommunication Accessories	394
Converter, Card-to-Tape	Data Processing Devices	361
Converter, Color	Telecommunication Accessories	394
Converter, Data	Data Processing Devices	361
Converter, Digital-to-Analog	Data Processing Devices	361
Converter, Pacific	Textile Manufacturing Equipment	240
Converter, Television	Telecommunication Accessories	394
Converter, UHF	Telecommunication Accessories	394
Convertible	Motor Vehicles	428
Conveyor	Mechanical Devices	315
Conveyor, Belt	Mechanical Devices	315
Conveyor, Bucket	Mechanical Devices	315
Conveyor, Crop	Harvesting Equipment	128
Cookbook	Instructional Documents	475
Cooker, Feed	Feed Processing Equipment	126
Cooker, Pressure	Food Preparation Equipment	154
Cooker, Rice	Food Preparation Equipment	154
cooker, slow (*use:* Crockpot)	Food Preparation Equipment	154
Cooker, Steam	Food Preparation Equipment	154
Cookstove	Food Preparation Equipment	154
Cookstove, Alcohol	Food Preparation Equipment	154
Cookstove, Coal	Food Preparation Equipment	154
Cookstove, Electric	Food Preparation Equipment	154
Cookstove, Gas	Food Preparation Equipment	154
Cookstove, Kerosene	Food Preparation Equipment	154
Cookstove, Portable	Food Preparation Equipment	154
Cookstove, Wood	Food Preparation Equipment	154
Cookware	Cooking Vessels	151
Cooler	Food Service Accessories	181
Cooler, Beer	Food Service Accessories	181
Cooler, Butter	Serving Vessels	186
Cooler, Dairy	Food Processing Equipment	166
Cooler, Hand	Personal Assistive Objects	107
Cooler, Lard	Food Processing Equipment	169
Cooler, Milk	Food Processing Equipment	166
Cooler, Water	Serving Vessels	189
Cooler, Wine	Food Service Accessories	181
Cooler, Wine Glass	Food Service Accessories	181
Coop, Chicken	Agricultural Structures	23
Coop, Poultry Shipping	Animal Care Equipment	134
Cope	Status Symbols	499
copier, xerographic (*use:* Photocopier)	Replication Equipment	387
copper, soldering (*use:* Iron, Soldering)	Metalworking T&E	213

Copy, Reprographic	Other Documents	481
Copybook	Instructional Documents	475
cor anglais (*use:* Horn, English)	Musical Instruments	375
cor, tenor (*use:* Mellophone)	Musical Instruments	370
Coracle	Watercraft	442
Corbel	Supporting Elements	16
Cord	Multiple Use T&E for Materials	226
cord, bungee (*use:* Cord, Elastic)	Multiple Use T&E for Materials	226
Cord, Elastic	Multiple Use T&E for Materials	226
Cord, Extension	Electrical System Components	300
Cord, Power	Electrical System Components	300
Cord, Sash	Finish Hardware	11
cord, shock (*use:* Cord, Elastic)	Multiple Use T&E for Materials	226
Cord, Sync	Camera Equipment	376
Cordage, Marine	Water Transportation Accessories	440
Core	Unclassifiable Objects	527
Corer, Fruit	Food Preparation Equipment	158
cork (*use:* Stopper, Bottle)	Food Service Accessories	182
Corker, Bottle	Food Processing Equipment	168
Corkscrew	Food Preparation Equipment	156
Corncrib	Agricultural Structures	23
Cornerstone	Construction Materials	3
Cornet	Musical Instruments	370
Cornet, Valve	Musical Instruments	370
Cornette	Headwear	92
Cornhusker	Harvesting Equipment	128
Cornhusker, Hand	Harvesting Equipment	128
Cornice	Supporting Elements	16
cornopean (*use:* Cornet)	Musical Instruments	370
Corona	Lighting Devices	68
Coronet	Status Symbols	498
Coronograph	Astronomical T&E	284
Corporal	Religious Objects	463
corral (*use:* Paddock)	Other Structures	41
Corrector, Course	Navigational Equipment	349
Correspondence	Other Documents	481
Corsage	Clothing Accessories	84
Corsage, Wrist	Clothing Accessories	85
Corselet	Underwear	103
Corset	Underwear	103
Corset, Surgical	Medical Instruments	332
Corvette	Watercraft	447
Cosmetic	Beauty Supplies	116
Cosmolabe	Astronomical T&E	284
Cosmosphere	Astronomical T&E	284
Costume, Academic	Status Symbols	498
Costume, Dance	Public Entertainment Devices	507
Costume, Dress-Up	Toys	521
Costume, Holiday	Holiday Objects	458
costume, judicial (*use:* Costume, Legal)	Status Symbols	498
Costume, Legal	Status Symbols	498
Costume, Performance	Public Entertainment Devices	507
costume, seasonal (*use:* Costume, Holiday)	Holiday Objects	458
Costume, Theater	Public Entertainment Devices	507
Cot	Sleeping & Reclining Furniture	50
cot, bath (*use:* Chair, Bath)	Seating Furniture	48
cot, finger (*use:* Fingerstall)	Leather, Horn & Shellworking T&E	197
Cote, Bell	Roof Elements	14
Cotta	Status Symbols	499
Cottage	Dwellings	32
Cotton, Dressing	Medical Instruments	333
Couch	Sleeping & Reclining Furniture	50
couch, fainting (*use:* Couch)	Sleeping & Reclining Furniture	50
couch, Grecian (*use:* Recamier)	Sleeping & Reclining Furniture	50
Counter	Storage & Display Furniture	53
counter (*use:* Fantail)	Water Transportation Accessories	437
Counter, Blood	Medical Instruments	327
Counter, Game	Game Equipment	502
Counter, Geiger	Nuclear Physics T&E	341
Counter, Sales	Merchandising T&E	336
Counter, Tally	Data Processing Devices	361
Counter, Thread	Textile Manufacturing Equipment	240
Counterbore	Metalworking T&E	210
Counterfeit	Exchange Media	487
counterpane (*use:* Bedspread)	Bedding	43
Counterpunch	Metalworking T&E	215
countershaft (*use:* Jackshaft)	Power Transmission Components	305
Countersink	Metalworking T&E	210
Counterweight, Lamp	Other Lighting Accessories	72
Counterweight, Sash	Finish Hardware	11
Coupe	Eating Vessels	176
Coupler, Acoustic	Data Processing Accessories	360
Coupler, Car	Rail Transportation Accessories	431
Coupler, Knuckle	Rail Transportation Accessories	431
Coupler, Link and Pin	Rail Transportation Accessories	431

Term	Category	Page
Coupling	Mechanical Devices	315
Coupling, Shaft	Power Transmission Components	305
Coupon	Exchange Media	487
Coupon, Ration	Exchange Media	487
Courthouse	Civic & Social Structures	26
Cover, Air Conditioner	Other Household Accessories	66
Cover, Ash	Other Household Accessories	66
Cover, Automotive	Land Transportation Accessories	418
Cover, Bakeware	Cooking Vessels	150
Cover, Boat	Water Transportation Accessories	440
Cover, Bolster	Bedding	43
Cover, Bonnet	Clothing Accessories	85
Cover, Canteen	Food Service Accessories	180
Cover, Cartridge Box	Armament Accessories	267
Cover, Chair Arm	Furniture Coverings	61
Cover, Chair Seat	Furniture Coverings	61
Cover, Checkbook	Personal Carrying & Storage Gear	112
Cover, Cookware	Cooking Vessels	151
Cover, Corset	Underwear	104
Cover, Crop	Tending Equipment	133
Cover, Cushion	Furniture Coverings	61
cover, deadlight (*use:* Shutter, Deadlight)	Water Transportation Accessories	439
Cover, Desk	Furniture Coverings	61
Cover, Diaper	Underwear	103
Cover, Document	Other Documents	482
Cover, Drain	Plumbing & Drainage Elements	12
Cover, Drinking Vessel	Drinking Vessels	173
Cover, Dust	Furniture Coverings	61
Cover, Duvet	Bedding	43
cover, field (*use:* Cloth, Ground)	Bedding	44
cover, fire (*use:* Curfew)	Heating Equipment Accessories	76
Cover, First Day	Memorabilia	478
Cover, Flue	Other Household Accessories	66
Cover, Food	Food Preparation Accessories	152
Cover, Food Storage	Food Storage Equipment	171
Cover, Furnishing	Furniture Coverings	61
Cover, Golf Club Head	Sports Equipment	515
Cover, Grill	Furniture Coverings	61
Cover, Hat	Clothing Accessories	85
Cover, Hatch	Water Transportation Accessories	437
Cover, Hawse	Water Transportation Accessories	437
Cover, Headwear	Clothing Accessories	85
Cover, Helmet	Body Armor	275
Cover, Horseshoe	Farrier Equipment	139
Cover, Ironing Board	Laundry Equipment	313
Cover, Lamp	Furniture Coverings	61
Cover, Manhole	Site Features	20
Cover, Map	Other Documents	482
Cover, Mattress	Bedding	43
Cover, Matzah	Holiday Objects	458
Cover, Motor	Water Transportation Accessories	440
Cover, Outlet	Finish Hardware	10
Cover, Parasol	Personal Assistive Objects	107
cover, piano (*use:* Throw)	Furniture Coverings	61
Cover, Pillow	Bedding	43
cover, quilt (*use:* Cover, Duvet)	Bedding	43
Cover, Record	Sound Communication Accessories	389
Cover, Rolling Pin	Food Preparation Accessories	152
Cover, Saddle	Land Transportation Accessories	418
Cover, Seat	Land Transportation Accessories	418
Cover, Serving Vessel	Serving Vessels	186
Cover, Shoe	Clothing Accessories	85
Cover, Socket	Electrical System Components	300
Cover, Stair	Floor Coverings	45
Cover, Steering Wheel	Land Transportation Accessories	418
cover, stirrup (*use:* Tapadera)	Land Transportation Accessories	421
Cover, Stool	Furniture Coverings	61
cover, table (*use:* Throw, Table)	Furniture Coverings	61
cover, telescope (*use:* Case, Telescope)	Optical T&E	343
Cover, Throw Pillow	Furniture Coverings	61
Cover, Tire	Land Transportation Accessories	418
Cover, Toilet Seat	Furniture Coverings	61
Cover, Truck Bed	Land Transportation Accessories	418
Cover, Typewriter	Writing Accessories	404
Cover, Vehicle	Land Transportation Accessories	418
Cover, Vent	Armament Accessories	268
cover, vent (*use:* Grate, Register)	Barrier Elements	2
Cover, Well	Site Features	20
cover, wheel (*use:* Hubcap)	Land Transportation Accessories	417
Coveralls	Protective Wear	102
Covering, Altar	Religious Objects	463
Covering, Animal	Animal Care Equipment	134
Covering, Wall	Surface Elements	18
Coverlet	Bedding	43

coverplate (*use:* Escutcheon) Finish Hardware 10
Cowbell Animal Care Equipment 134
Cowbell, Musical Musical Instruments 372
cowcatcher (*use:* Pilot, Locomotive) Rail Transportation Accessories 431
Cowl Status Symbols 498
Cozy Food Service Accessories 181
cozy, drink (*use:* Holder, Insulated Beverage) Food Service Accessories 181
Cozy, Tea Food Service Accessories 181
Cozy, Toilet Paper Storage & Display Accessories 63
CPU (*use:* Computer, Digital) Data Processing Devices 362
Crabber Watercraft 445
Cradle Sleeping & Reclining Furniture 50
Cradle with Spikes Regulative Devices 347
cradle, barley (*use:* Scythe, Cradle) Harvesting Equipment 130
Cradle, Basket Human-Powered Vehicles 426
Cradle, Boat Water Transportation Accessories 440
Cradle, Cannon Armament Accessories 268
Cradle, Doll Toys 520
cradle, grain (*use:* Scythe, Cradle) Harvesting Equipment 130
Cradle, Hub Woodworking T&E 249
cradle, rounding (*use:* Block, Bevel) Woodworking T&E 248
Cradle, Slat Human-Powered Vehicles 426
Cradleboard Human-Powered Vehicles 426
cradle-rocker (*use:* Bench, Cradle) Seating Furniture 47
Craft, Competition Watercraft 444
Craft, Landing Watercraft 447
Craft, Pleasure Watercraft 444
Crakow Footwear 90
cramp (*use:* Clamp, Woodworking) Woodworking T&E 249
Crampon Sports Equipment 514
Crane Mechanical Devices 315
Crane, Fireplace Food Preparation Equipment 162
crane, gooseneck (*use:* Truck, Boom) Motor Vehicles 429
Crane, Mail Transportation Structures 39
Cranioclast Medical Instruments 330
Craniometer Biological T&E 287
Crank Power Transmission Components 305
Crank, Phonograph Sound Communication Accessories 390
Crate Containers 414
Crate, Breeding Breeding Equipment 138
Crate, Hog Breeding Breeding Equipment 138
Crate, Shipping Containers 415
Crate, Storage Containers 415
Cravat Clothing Accessories 85
Crayon Painting T&E 229
Crayon, Lithographic Graphic Equipment 384
Crayon, Lumber Woodworking T&E 249
Crayon, Marking Writing Devices 406
creamer (*use:* Pitcher, Cream) Serving Vessels 189
Creaser Leather, Horn & Shellworking T&E 197
Creaser, Double Leather, Horn & Shellworking T&E 197
Creaser, Edge Leather, Horn & Shellworking T&E 197
Creaser, Screw Leather, Horn & Shellworking T&E 197
Creaser, Single Leather, Horn & Shellworking T&E 197
Creche Religious Objects 464
Credence Religious Objects 463
Credenza Storage & Display Furniture 54
Creel, Bobbin Textile Manufacturing Equipment 240
Creel, Fishing Fishing Equipment 145
Creeper Main Garments 96
Creeper, Ice Personal Assistive Objects 107
Cresset Lighting Holders 71
Cresset, Cooper's Woodworking T&E 249
Cresting Surface Elements 18
Crewelwork Art 452
Crib Sleeping & Reclining Furniture 50
crib, corn (*use:* Corncrib) Agricultural Structures 23
Crib, Cribbing Mining & Mineral Harvesting T&E 221
crib, tool (*use:* Toolshed) Outbuildings 38
cribbage (*use:* Set, Cribbage) Game Equipment 504
crimper (*use:* Machine, Metal Crimping) Metalworking T&E 214
Crimper, Blasting Cap Mining & Mineral Harvesting T&E 221
Crimper, Cap Armament Accessories 268
Crimper, Glass Glass, Plastics & Clayworking T&E 192
Crimper, Leather Leather, Horn & Shellworking T&E 197
crimper, pie (*use:* Wheel, Jagging) Food Preparation Equipment 159
Crinoline Underwear 103
Crinoline, Cage Underwear 103
Croat Exchange Media 487
Crochet Art 452
Crock Containers 415
Crock, Butter Food Storage Equipment 171
Crock, Food Storage Food Storage Equipment 171

Term	Category	Page
Crockpot	Food Preparation Equipment	154
crokinole (*use:* Game, Crokinole)	Game Equipment	505
Crook, Hay	Harvesting Equipment	128
Crook, Shepherd's	Animal Care Equipment	137
crook, throw (*use:* Tier, Corn Shock)	Harvesting Equipment	131
Crop, Riding	Land Transportation Accessories	419
Cropper, Shoe	Farrier Equipment	139
Crosier	Status Symbols	498
Cross	Religious Objects	464
Cross, Dish	Food Service Accessories	181
Cross, Teasel	Textile Manufacturing Equipment	240
crossbar (*use:* Cap, Timber)	Mining & Mineral Harvesting T&E	225
Crossbar, Pole Vault	Sports Equipment	518
Crossbeam	Supporting Elements	16
Crossbow	Edged Weapons	277
Cross-Staff	Surveying Equipment	352
Cross-Stitch	Art	452
Crosstie	Rail Transportation Accessories	432
Crowbar	Mechanical Devices	316
crown (*use:* Coin, Crown)	Exchange Media	487
Crown	Status Symbols	498
Crown, Death	Memorabilia	478
Crown, Dental	Dental Instruments	322
Crown, Half	Exchange Media	487
Crow's-Nest	Water Transportation Accessories	437
Croze	Woodworking T&E	254
crozier (*use:* Crosier)	Status Symbols	498
crucible (*use:* Pot, Melting)	Glass, Plastics & Clayworking T&E	194
Crucible, Laboratory	Labware	293
Crucible, Metal	Metalworking T&E	209
Crucifix	Religious Objects	465
Cruet	Serving Vessels	188
Cruet, Altar	Religious Objects	462
Cruiser, Cabin	Watercraft	444
Cruiser, Guided Missile	Watercraft	447
Cruiser, Heavy	Watercraft	447
Cruiser, Light	Watercraft	447
Crumbcloth	Floor Coverings	45
Crumber	Housekeeping Equipment	312
Crumhorn	Musical Instruments	374
Crupper	Land Transportation Accessories	421
Crusher, Ball	Mining & Mineral Harvesting T&E	221
Crusher, Cone	Mining & Mineral Harvesting T&E	221
Crusher, Corn	Feed Processing Equipment	126
Crusher, Gyratory	Mining & Mineral Harvesting T&E	221
Crusher, Hammer	Mining & Mineral Harvesting T&E	221
Crusher, Ice	Food Preparation Equipment	158
Crusher, Jaw	Mining & Mineral Harvesting T&E	221
Crusher, Mineral	Mining & Mineral Harvesting T&E	221
crusher, ore (*use:* Crusher, Mineral)	Mining & Mineral Harvesting T&E	221
crusher, rock (*use:* Crusher, Mineral)	Mining & Mineral Harvesting T&E	221
Crusher, Roller	Mining & Mineral Harvesting T&E	221
Crusher, Seed	Food Processing Equipment	164
Crusher, Stamp	Mining & Mineral Harvesting T&E	221
Crutch	Personal Assistive Objects	107
Crutch, Boom	Water Transportation Accessories	437
Crwth	Musical Instruments	374
Cryometer	Thermal T&E	354
Cryophorus	Thermal T&E	354
cryptocurrency (*use:* Medium, Digital Exchange)	Exchange Media	487
Cuber, Hay	Harvesting Equipment	128
cudgel (*use:* Club, Froe)	Woodworking T&E	254
Cue, Billiard	Game Equipment	501
Cue, Shuffleboard	Game Equipment	502
Cuff	Clothing Accessories	85
cuff, blood pressure (*use:* Sphygmomanometer)	Medical Instruments	327
cufflink (*use:* Link, Cuff)	Clothing Accessories	85
Cuirass	Body Armor	275
Cuirass, Medical	Medical Instruments	333
Cuisse	Body Armor	275
Culet	Body Armor	275
Culottes	Main Garments	97
Cultipacker	Cultivation Equipment	125
Cultivator	Cultivation Equipment	123
cultivator, chisel (*use:* Cultivator, Field)	Cultivation Equipment	123
Cultivator, Field	Cultivation Equipment	123
Cultivator, Garden	Cultivation Equipment	123
Cultivator, Hand	Cultivation Equipment	123
Cultivator, Rotary	Cultivation Equipment	123
Cultivator, Row Crop	Cultivation Equipment	123
Cultivator, Straddle-Row	Cultivation Equipment	123
Cultivator, Walking	Cultivation Equipment	123
cultivator, wheel hoe (*use:* Cultivator, Garden)	Cultivation Equipment	123
Culverin	Artillery	274
Culvert	Hydraulic Structures	34
Cummerbund	Clothing Accessories	86
Cup	Drinking Vessels	173

cup and ball (*use:* Toy, Cup and Ball) Toys 523
Cup, Amalgam Dental Accessories 320
Cup, Baptismal Religious Objects 462
Cup, Bleeding Medical Instruments 333
cup, bouillon (*use:* Cup, Soup) Eating Vessels 176
Cup, Bride's Wedding Objects 466
cup, candy (*use:* Cup, Favor) Eating Vessels 176
Cup, Canteen Drinking Vessels 173
Cup, Caster Other Household Accessories 66
Cup, Caudle Drinking Vessels 173
Cup, Chocolate Drinking Vessels 173
Cup, Coffee Drinking Vessels 173
Cup, Collapsible Drinking Vessels 173
Cup, Communion Religious Objects 462
Cup, Covered Drinking Vessels 173
cup, cupping (*use:* Cup, Bleeding) Medical Instruments 333
Cup, Custard Eating Vessels 176
Cup, Demitasse Drinking Vessels 173
Cup, Dental Dental Accessories 320
Cup, Dental Waste Dental Accessories 320
cup, dessert (*use:* Dish, Dessert) Eating Vessels 176
Cup, Dice Game Equipment 501
Cup, Disposable Drinking Vessels 173
Cup, Dram Drinking Vessels 173
Cup, Favor Eating Vessels 176
Cup, Fuddling Drinking Vessels 173
Cup, Grease Mechanical Devices 317
Cup, Grinder Metalworking T&E 209
Cup, Impression Dental Accessories 320
Cup, Invalid Drinking Vessels 173
cup, julep (*use:* Beaker, Drinking) Drinking Vessels 173
Cup, Kiddush Religious Objects 462
Cup, Libation Religious Objects 463
Cup, Loving Achievement Symbols 491
Cup, Measuring Food Preparation Equipment 156
Cup, Medicine Medical Instruments 333
Cup, Mustache Drinking Vessels 173
cup, mustard (*use:* Pot, Mustard) Serving Vessels 188
Cup, Nursing Drinking Vessels 173
cup, nut (*use:* Cup, Favor) Eating Vessels 176
Cup, Oil Metalworking T&E 209
Cup, Orange Eating Vessels 176
Cup, Palette Painting T&E 229
Cup, Pharmaceutical Measuring Medical Accessories 326
Cup, Prophylaxis Dental Accessories 320
Cup, Punch Drinking Vessels 173
Cup, Putting Sports Equipment 515
Cup, Saki Drinking Vessels 174
Cup, Slip-Trailing Glass, Plastics & Clayworking T&E 195
Cup, Soup Eating Vessels 176
Cup, Spout Drinking Vessels 174
Cup, Stacking Game Equipment 504
Cup, Standing Drinking Vessels 174
Cup, Stirrup Drinking Vessels 174
Cup, Straw Drinking Vessels 174
cup, tea (*use:* Teacup) Drinking Vessels 174
Cup, Traveling Drinking Vessels 174
Cup, Turpentine Forestry T&E 190
cup, vodka (*use:* Charka) Drinking Vessels 173
Cup, Wager Game Equipment 502
Cup, Washing Religious Objects 462
Cup, Wine Drinking Vessels 174
Cupboard Storage & Display Furniture 53
Cupboard, Corner Storage & Display Furniture 53
Cupboard, Food Storage Food Storage Equipment 171
Cupboard, Hanging Storage & Display Furniture 53
Cupboard, Jelly Food Storage Equipment 171
Cupboard, Press Storage & Display Furniture 53
Cupboard, Spice Food Storage Equipment 171
Cupel Metalworking T&E 209
Cupola Roof Elements 14
Curette Medical Instruments 330
Curette, Adenoid Medical Instruments 330
Curette, Alveolar Medical Instruments 331
Curette, Bone Medical Instruments 331
Curette, Periodontal Dental Instruments 322
Curfew Heating Equipment Accessories 76
Curler, Butter Food Preparation Equipment 157
Curler, Eyelash Beauty Supplies 117
curler, hair (*use:* Roller, Hair) Hair Care Objects 119
curler, wig (*use:* Roller, Hair) Hair Care Objects 119
Currency, Continental Exchange Media 489
Currency, Fractional Exchange Media 489
Curricle Animal-Powered Vehicles 423
Currycomb Animal Care Equipment 136
Curtain Window & Door Coverings 78
Curtain, Beaded Window & Door Coverings 78
Curtain, Bed Bedding 44
Curtain, Café Window & Door Coverings 78
Curtain, Case Bedding 44
Curtain, Cottage Window & Door Coverings 78
Curtain, Doorway Window & Door Coverings 78
Curtain, Dress Window & Door Coverings 78
Curtain, Festoon Window & Door Coverings 78
Curtain, Foot Bedding 44
Curtain, Head Bedding 44
Curtain, Priscilla Window & Door Coverings 78
Curtain, Sheer Window & Door Coverings 78
Curtain, Shower Other Household Accessories 66

Term	Category	Page
Curtain, Stage	Public Entertainment Devices	507
Curtain, Window	Window & Door Coverings	78
curtal (*use:* Dulcian)	Musical Instruments	374
Curve	Drafting T&E	366
Curve, Brook's	Drafting T&E	366
Curve, Flexible	Drafting T&E	366
Curve, French	Drafting T&E	366
curve, variable (*use:* Curve, Flexible)	Drafting T&E	366
Cushion	Other Household Accessories	66
Cushion, Air	Personal Assistive Objects	107
Cushion, Body	Personal Assistive Objects	107
Cushion, Emery	Needleworking Equipment	235
Cushion, Gilder's	Painting T&E	229
Cushion, Helmet	Clothing Accessories	85
Cushion, Lacemaker's	Textile Manufacturing Equipment	240
Cushion, Lead	Metalworking T&E	209
Cushion, Neck	Personal Assistive Objects	107
Cushion, Vehicle Seat	Land Transportation Accessories	418
cuspidor (*use:* Spittoon)	Containers for Smoking & Tobacco	59
Customhouse	Civic & Social Structures	26
Cutlass	Edged Weapons	278
Cutter	Animal-Powered Vehicles	424
cutter (*use:* Boat, Ship's)	Watercraft	448
Cutter, Albany	Animal-Powered Vehicles	424
Cutter, Bar	Metalworking T&E	209
Cutter, Base	Painting T&E	231
Cutter, Biscuit	Food Preparation Equipment	158
Cutter, Board	Bookbinding Equipment	382
Cutter, Bolt	Metalworking T&E	209
cutter, bone (*use:* Grinder, Bone)	Feed Processing Equipment	126
Cutter, Bone	Food Processing Equipment	165
cutter, bone (*use:* Cutter, Medical Bone)	Medical Instruments	331
cutter, box (*use:* Knife, Utility)	Multiple Use T&E for Materials	227
Cutter, Brush	Groundskeeping Equipment	309
Cutter, Butter	Food Preparation Equipment	158
Cutter, Cabbage	Food Preparation Equipment	158
Cutter, Cake	Armament Accessories	268
Cutter, Cast	Medical Accessories	325
Cutter, Cider Cheese	Food Processing Equipment	165
Cutter, Cigar	Smoking & Recreational Drug Equipment	114
Cutter, Clinch	Metalworking T&E	209
Cutter, Coal	Mining & Mineral Harvesting T&E	221
Cutter, Coast Guard	Watercraft	448
Cutter, Cookie	Food Preparation Equipment	158
cutter, corn (*use:* Scraper, Corn)	Food Preparation Equipment	159
Cutter, Country	Animal-Powered Vehicles	424
Cutter, Curd	Food Processing Equipment	166
Cutter, Dough	Food Preparation Equipment	158
Cutter, Doughnut	Food Preparation Equipment	158
Cutter, Dovetail	Woodworking T&E	249
cutter, dowel (*use:* Cutter, Peg)	Woodworking T&E	249
Cutter, Edge	Painting T&E	231
Cutter, Ensilage	Feed Processing Equipment	126
Cutter, Fabric	Needleworking Equipment	235
cutter, feed (*use:* Chopper, Feed)	Feed Processing Equipment	126
cutter, flail (*use:* Shredder, Flail)	Harvesting Equipment	131
cutter, fodder (*use:* Chopper, Feed)	Feed Processing Equipment	126
Cutter, French Fry	Food Preparation Equipment	158
Cutter, Fuze	Armament Accessories	268
cutter, gear (*use:* Machine, Gear Cutting)	Metalworking T&E	213
Cutter, Gem	Other T&E for Materials	260
Cutter, Glass	Glass, Plastics & Clayworking T&E	192
Cutter, Hair	Hair Care Objects	118
Cutter, Ice	Mining & Mineral Harvesting T&E	225
Cutter, Julienne	Food Preparation Equipment	158
cutter, kraut (*use:* Cutter, Cabbage)	Food Preparation Equipment	158
cutter, lead (*use:* Cutter, Slug)	Printing Accessories	386
Cutter, Leather	Leather, Horn & Shellworking T&E	197
Cutter, Mat	Painting T&E	229
Cutter, Medical Bone	Medical Instruments	331
Cutter, Metal	Metalworking T&E	209
Cutter, Microscopic Section	Biological T&E	287
Cutter, Milling	Metalworking T&E	209
Cutter, Miter	Woodworking T&E	249
Cutter, Molar	Veterinary Equipment	142
cutter, nail (*use:* Nipper, Nail)	Metalworking T&E	214
cutter, nail (*use:* Nipper, Toenail)	Pet Supplies	141
Cutter, Noodle	Food Preparation Equipment	158
cutter, paper (*use:* Machine, Paper Cutting)	Papermaking T&E	232

cutter, paper (*use:* Guillotine, Paper) | Printing Accessories | 386
Cutter, Paper | Writing Accessories | 404
Cutter, Pasta | Food Preparation Equipment | 158
cutter, pastry (*use:* Blender, Pastry) | Food Preparation Equipment | 158
Cutter, Peg | Woodworking T&E | 249
Cutter, Phonograph Needle | Sound Communication Accessories | 389
Cutter, Pinion | Metalworking T&E | 209
Cutter, Pipe | Metalworking T&E | 209
Cutter, Pizza | Food Preparation Equipment | 158
Cutter, Plug | Woodworking T&E | 248
Cutter, Portland | Animal-Powered Vehicles | 424
Cutter, Potato Seed | Harvesting Equipment | 129
Cutter, Quill | Writing Accessories | 404
Cutter, Revenue | Watercraft | 448
Cutter, Rivet | Metalworking T&E | 209
Cutter, Root | Cultivation Equipment | 123
Cutter, Rotary Leather | Leather, Horn & Shellworking T&E | 197
Cutter, Sailing | Watercraft | 443
Cutter, Set | Woodworking T&E | 250
Cutter, Shingle | Woodworking T&E | 250
cutter, silage (*use:* Cutter, Ensilage) | Feed Processing Equipment | 126
cutter, slaw (*use:* Cutter, Cabbage) | Food Preparation Equipment | 158
Cutter, Slug | Printing Accessories | 386
Cutter, Snout | Animal Care Equipment | 134
Cutter, Sod | Groundskeeping Equipment | 309
Cutter, Sprue | Metalworking T&E | 209
Cutter, Stalk | Cultivation Equipment | 123
cutter, stover (*use:* Chopper, Feed) | Feed Processing Equipment | 126
Cutter, Sugar | Food Preparation Equipment | 158
Cutter, Thread | Metalworking T&E | 209
Cutter, Tobacco | Merchandising T&E | 336
Cutter, Toggle | Glass, Plastics & Clayworking T&E | 192
Cutter, Tuck | Other T&E for Materials | 260
cutter, turf (*use:* Cutter, Sod) | Groundskeeping Equipment | 309
Cutter, Vegetable | Food Preparation Equipment | 158
Cutter, Wad | Armament Accessories | 268
Cutter, Wallpaper | Painting T&E | 231
Cutter, Washer | Metalworking T&E | 209
Cutter, Weed | Cultivation Equipment | 125
Cutter, Wire | Metalworking T&E | 209
cutter, wire-band (*use:* Shears, Band Cutter) | Harvesting Equipment | 131
Cutter, Wood | Woodworking T&E | 249
cutting, scissor (*use:* Work, Cut Paper) | Art | 455
Cuttoe | Edged Weapons | 279
Cyanometer | Astronomical T&E | 284
Cyanotype | Graphic Documents | 473
cyberglove (*use:* Glove, Data) | Peripherals | 364
Cycle | Human-Powered Vehicles | 426
cyclograph (*use:* Arcograph) | Drafting T&E | 366
Cycloidograph | Drafting T&E | 366
Cyclotron | Nuclear Physics T&E | 341
Cyclotron, AVF | Nuclear Physics T&E | 341
Cyclotron, Isochronous | Nuclear Physics T&E | 341
Cylinder, Audio | Sound Communication Media | 393
Cylinder, Dictation | Sound Communication Media | 393
cylinder, graduated (*use:* Graduate) | Labware | 293
Cylinder, Music Box | Musical Accessories | 369
Cylinder, Phonograph | Sound Communication Media | 393
Cymbal | Musical Instruments | 372
Cymograph | Drafting T&E | 366
cystoscope (*use:* Urethroscope) | Medical Instruments | 334
Dabber | Graphic Equipment | 385
Dagger | Edged Weapons | 277
Dagger, Stiletto | Edged Weapons | 277
Daggerboard | Water Transportation Accessories | 437
Daguerreotype | Graphic Documents | 473
Dalmatic | Status Symbols | 499
Dam | Hydraulic Structures | 34
Dam, Dental | Dental Instruments | 322
Damper, Fireplace | Environmental Control Elements | 8
Damper, Stovepipe | Heating Equipment Accessories | 76
Damper, Ventilator | Environmental Control Elements | 8
Damper, Vibration | Nuclear Physics T&E | 341
dandyhorse (*use:* Draisine) | Human-Powered Vehicles | 426
darby (*use:* Float, Long) | Masonry & Stoneworking T&E | 204
darner (*use:* Egg, Darning) | Needleworking Equipment | 235
Dart | Edged Weapons | 277
Dart, Game | Game Equipment | 501
dart, hair (*use:* Hairstick) | Hair Adornments | 83
Dart, Lawn | Game Equipment | 501
Dart, Spring | Mining & Mineral Harvesting T&E | 222
Dartboard | Game Equipment | 501
darts (*use:* Game, Dart) | Game Equipment | 504
Dasher, Churn | Food Processing Equipment | 166

Term	Category	Page
Dashiki	Outerwear	100
Dasymeter	Chemical Testing Devices	290
Database	Other Documents	482
dataglove (*use:* Glove, Data)	Peripherals	364
Daub	Construction Materials	3
Daughter, Scavenger's	Regulative Devices	347
Davenport	Seating Furniture	49
David	Watercraft	447
Davit	Water Transportation Accessories	437
Davit, Anchor	Water Transportation Accessories	437
Davit, Boat	Water Transportation Accessories	437
Daybed	Sleeping & Reclining Furniture	51
Daybook	Financial Records	469
Daysailer	Watercraft	443
Deadeye	Water Transportation Accessories	439
deadlight (*use:* Window, Fixed)	Door & Window Elements	7
deadlight (*use:* Shutter, Deadlight)	Water Transportation Accessories	439
deadlight (*use:* Window, Watercraft)	Water Transportation Accessories	440
Deanery	Dwellings	32
Debeaker	Veterinary Equipment	142
Debitage	Unclassifiable Objects	527
Decal	Other Documents	482
Decanter	Serving Vessels	189
Decanter, Bar	Serving Vessels	189
Decanter, Ship's	Serving Vessels	189
Decapper/Recapper	Armament Accessories	268
decision (*use:* Judgment)	Government Records	470
Deck	Architectural Spaces	1
deck, card (*use:* Card, Playing)	Game Equipment	504
deck, tape (*use:* Player, Tape)	Sound Communication Devices	392
Decking, Watercraft	Water Transportation Accessories	437
Deckle	Papermaking T&E	232
Declaration	Declaratory Documents	468
Declaration, Customs	Government Records	470
Declinometer	Electrical & Magnetic Measurement Devices	298
Decoder	Data Processing Devices	361
Decoration	Decorative Furnishings	60
Decoration of Honor	Achievement Symbols	491
Decoration, Cake	Party Accessories	460
Decoration, Holiday	Holiday Objects	458
Decoupage	Art	452
Decoy	Armament Accessories	268
Decoy, Fish	Fishing Equipment	147
Decree	Declaratory Documents	468
Deed	Legal Documents	476
Defibrillator	Medical Instruments	333
Deflector, Flow	Nuclear Physics T&E	341
Deflesher	Food Processing Equipment	165
Defroster, Windshield	Land Transportation Accessories	418
Dehorner	Veterinary Equipment	142
Dehumidifier	Environmental Control Elements	8
Dehydrator, Dental	Dental Accessories	320
Dehydrator, Food	Food Preparation Equipment	155
Demi-Cannon	Artillery	274
Demi-Culverin	Artillery	274
Demijohn	Containers	415
Dendrometer	Forestry T&E	190
dengelstock (*use:* Anvil, Scythe Sharpening)	Metalworking T&E	207
Denier	Exchange Media	487
Densimeter	Chemical Testing Devices	290
Densitometer	Chemical Testing Devices	290
Densitometer, Photographic	Photographic Accessories	379
Dentimeter	Dental Instruments	322
Denture	Personal Assistive Objects	109
Deposition	Legal Documents	476
Depot	Transportation Structures	39
Depot, Bus	Transportation Structures	39
Depot, Railroad	Transportation Structures	39
Depressor, Tongue	Medical Instruments	330
Derby	Headwear	92
Dermatome	Medical Instruments	331
Derrick	Mechanical Devices	315
Derrick, Grain	Harvesting Equipment	128
Derringer	Firearms	281
Descrambler	Telecommunication Accessories	394
Desiccator	Labware	293
Desiccator, Balance	Nuclear Physics T&E	341
Desk	Storage & Display Furniture	53
Desk, Butler's	Storage & Display Furniture	53
Desk, Campaign	Storage & Display Furniture	53
Desk, Computer	Storage & Display Furniture	53
desk, cylinder fall (*use:* Desk, Quarter-Cylinder)	Storage & Display Furniture	54
Desk, Drop-Front	Storage & Display Furniture	53
desk, fall-front (*use:* Desk, Drop-Front)	Storage & Display Furniture	53
Desk, Kneehole	Storage & Display Furniture	53
Desk, Partner's	Storage & Display Furniture	54
Desk, Portable	Writing Accessories	404
Desk, Quarter-Cylinder	Storage & Display Furniture	54
Desk, Rolltop	Storage & Display Furniture	54
Desk, School	Storage & Display Furniture	54
desk, sewing (*use:* Table, Sewing)	Support Furniture	57
Desk, Slant-Top	Storage & Display Furniture	53
Desk, Standing	Storage & Display Furniture	54

Desk, Tambour	Storage & Display Furniture	54
Desk, Writing	Storage & Display Furniture	54
Destroyer	Watercraft	447
Destroyer, Tank	Artillery	274
detector, fire (*use:* Alarm, Fire)	Protective Devices	345
Detector, Firedamp	Mining & Mineral Harvesting T&E	222
Detector, Gas	Protective Devices	345
Detector, Heatmount	Breeding Equipment	138
Detector, Metal	Surveying Equipment	353
Detector, Mine	Armament Accessories	268
Detector, Neutron	Nuclear Physics T&E	341
Detector, Radiation	Nuclear Physics T&E	341
detector, smoke (*use:* Alarm, Smoke)	Protective Devices	345
detector, stud (*use:* Finder, Stud)	Construction T&E	296
Detonator	Mining & Mineral Harvesting T&E	222
Deveiner, Shrimp	Food Preparation Equipment	160
Developer	Photoprocessing Equipment	381
Developer, Wrist	Recreational Devices	509
Device, Bingo	Game Equipment	502
Device, Blood Pressure	Medical Instruments	327
Device, Blood Testing	Medical Instruments	327
Device, Bloodletting	Medical Instruments	333
device, contraceptive (*use:* Prophylactic)	Hygiene Objects	121
Device, Cooking	Food Preparation Equipment	153
Device, Electronic Effects	Musical Instruments	371
Device, Execution	Regulative Devices	347
Device, Fire Protection	Protective Devices	345
Device, Fitness	Recreational Devices	509
Device, Flash	Camera Equipment	376
Device, Flashing Rear-End	Rail Transportation Accessories	431
Device, Gambling	Game Equipment	502
device, global positioning (*use:* Receiver, Global Positioning)	Navigational Equipment	350
Device, Hearing	Personal Assistive Objects	107
Device, Input	Peripherals	364
Device, Lottery	Game Equipment	503
Device, Massage	Personal Assistive Objects	107
Device, Morse Code Instruction	Telecommunication Accessories	394
Device, Output	Peripherals	364
device, personal floatation (*use:* Preserver, Life)	Water Transportation Accessories	437
Device, Pest Control	Other Household Accessories	66
Device, Playground	Recreational Devices	510
Device, Punishment	Regulative Devices	347
Device, Respiratory Testing	Medical Instruments	327
Device, Respiratory Treatment	Medical Instruments	333
Device, Securing	Finish Hardware	10
Device, Security	Protective Devices	345
Device, Sound Signaling	Sound Communication Devices	391
Device, Sounding	Navigational Equipment	349
Device, Tanning	Beauty Supplies	117
Device, Test Scoring	Data Processing Devices	361
Device, Torture	Regulative Devices	347
Device, Vision	Personal Assistive Objects	107
Device, Visual Signaling	Visual Communication Devices	400
Device, Voting	Organizational Objects	459
Device, Water Recreation	Recreational Devices	510
Dhow	Watercraft	443
Diabolo	Toys	525
Diadem	Status Symbols	498
Dial, Miner's	Mining & Mineral Harvesting T&E	222
Diaper	Underwear	103
Diaphanometer	Meteorological T&E	339
Diaphragm	Hygiene Objects	121
Diary	Other Documents	480
Diascope	Medical Instruments	327
diascope (*use:* Projector, Slide)	Visual Communication Devices	401
dibber (*use:* Dibble)	Planting Equipment	132
Dibble	Planting Equipment	132
dice (*use:* Die)	Game Equipment	502
Dichroscope	Optical T&E	343
Dickey	Clothing Accessories	85
Dictionary	Other Documents	480
Didgeridoo	Musical Instruments	374
Die	Game Equipment	502
Die, Binder	Bookbinding Equipment	382
Die, Coin	Metalworking T&E	210
Die, Forming	Multiple Use T&E for Materials	226
Die, Hornworker's	Leather, Horn & Shellworking T&E	201
Die, Loading	Armament Accessories	268
Die, Screw	Metalworking T&E	209
Die, Thread Cutting	Metalworking T&E	209
Die, Wire Drawing	Metalworking T&E	210
Diestock	Metalworking T&E	210
Differential	Power Transmission Components	305
Diffusiometer	Chemical Testing Devices	290
Digest	Other Documents	486
Digester	Papermaking T&E	232
Digger, Post Hole	Construction T&E	295
Digger, Potato	Harvesting Equipment	129
digger, thistle (*use:* Spud, Weeding)	Cultivation Equipment	125
digger, trench (*use:* Machine, Trenching)	Construction T&E	295

Term	Category	Page
Digitizer	Data Processing Devices	361
Dilatometer	Chemical Testing Devices	290
Dilator	Medical Instruments	331
Dilator, Cervical	Medical Instruments	331
Dilator, Uterine	Medical Instruments	331
Dildo	Personal Assistive Objects	108
diligence (*use:* Stagecoach)	Animal-Powered Vehicles	423
Dime	Exchange Media	487
Dime, Half	Exchange Media	487
Dimmer	Other Lighting Accessories	72
Dinar	Exchange Media	488
Diner	Commercial Structures	27
Dinghy	Watercraft	448
Dinghy, Abaco	Watercraft	443
dinghy, Bahama (*use:* Dinghy, Abaco)	Watercraft	443
Dinghy, Bermuda	Watercraft	443
dinghy, fitted (*use:* Dinghy, Bermuda)	Watercraft	443
Dinghy, Sailing	Watercraft	444
Diode	Electrical System Components	302
Diode, Light-Emitting	Other Lighting Accessories	72
Diorama	Other Documents	484
Diorama, Automata	Other Documents	484
dip (*use:* Rod, Gauge)	Woodworking T&E	256
Dipleidoscope	Astronomical T&E	284
Diploma	Achievement Symbols	491
Dipper	Serving Utensils	184
Dipper, Honey	Serving Utensils	184
Dipper, Syrup	Food Processing Equipment	169
Dipper, Turpentine	Forestry T&E	190
Dipper, Whale Oil	Fishing Equipment	148
Dipstick	Weights & Measures T&E	357
Diptych	Religious Objects	464
Directory	Other Documents	480
Directory, Business	Other Documents	480
Directory, City	Other Documents	480
Directory, County	Other Documents	480
Directory, Membership	Other Documents	480
Directory, Telephone	Other Documents	480
dirigible (*use:* Airship)	Aircraft	411
Dirk	Edged Weapons	277
Dirndl	Main Garments	98
Disc, Compact	Data Processing Media	363
Discharge	Legal Documents	476
Discharge, Military	Government Records	470
Discus	Sports Equipment	518
Disdrometer	Meteorological T&E	339
Disgorger	Fishing Equipment	147
Dish, Baking	Cooking Vessels	150
Dish, Banana Split	Eating Vessels	176
Dish, Baptismal	Religious Objects	462
Dish, Berry	Eating Vessels	176
Dish, Bonbon	Serving Vessels	186
Dish, Bone	Food Service Accessories	181
Dish, Butter	Serving Vessels	186
Dish, Candy	Serving Vessels	186
Dish, Celery	Serving Vessels	186
Dish, Chafing	Food Preparation Equipment	163
Dish, Cheese	Serving Vessels	186
Dish, Comb	Hair Care Objects	118
dish, condiment (*use:* Dish, Relish)	Serving Vessels	186
Dish, Corn	Eating Vessels	176
Dish, Culture	Labware	293
Dish, Dessert	Eating Vessels	176
Dish, Dissolving	Labware	293
Dish, Eating	Eating Vessels	176
Dish, Evaporating	Labware	293
Dish, Honey	Serving Vessels	186
Dish, Jelly	Serving Vessels	186
Dish, Laboratory	Labware	293
Dish, Nail	Leather, Horn & Shellworking T&E	197
Dish, Nut	Serving Vessels	186
Dish, Offering	Religious Objects	461
dish, olive (*use:* Dish, Relish)	Serving Vessels	186
Dish, Pet	Pet Supplies	141
Dish, Petri	Labware	293
dish, pickle (*use:* Dish, Relish)	Serving Vessels	186
Dish, Pudding	Eating Vessels	176
Dish, Quiche	Cooking Vessels	150
Dish, Relish	Serving Vessels	186
Dish, Ring	Personal Carrying & Storage Gear	112
Dish, Salt	Serving Vessels	188
Dish, Satellite	Telecommunication Devices	396
Dish, Sauce	Eating Vessels	176
Dish, Serving	Serving Vessels	186
Dish, Sherbet	Eating Vessels	176
Dish, Soap	Hygiene Objects	120
Dish, Soufflé	Cooking Vessels	150
Dish, Sundae	Eating Vessels	176
Dish, Sweetmeat	Serving Vessels	186
Dish, Tea Bag	Food Service Accessories	181
Dish, Vegetable	Serving Vessels	186
Dish, Waste	Food Service Accessories	181
Dishcloth	Dishwashing Equipment	308
disher (*use:* Scoop, Ice Cream)	Serving Utensils	184
Dishpan	Dishwashing Equipment	308
Dishwasher	Dishwashing Equipment	308
Disk, Abrasive Dental	Dental Accessories	320
disk, floppy (*use:* Diskette)	Data Processing Media	363
Disk, Flying	Toys	521
Disk, Magnetic	Data Processing Media	363
Disk, Music Box	Musical Accessories	369

Term	Category	Page
Disk, Optical	Data Processing Media	363
Disk, Pi	Funerary Objects	456
Disk, Shuffleboard	Game Equipment	502
Disk, Sight	Armament Accessories	268
Diskette	Data Processing Media	363
Dispatch	Other Documents	482
Dispenser, Beverage	Serving Vessels	189
Dispenser, Cap	Armament Accessories	268
Dispenser, Cigarette Paper	Smoking & Recreational Drug Equipment	114
Dispenser, Coin	Merchandising T&E	336
Dispenser, Cup	Food Service Accessories	181
Dispenser, Dental	Dental Accessories	320
Dispenser, Fabric Softener	Laundry Equipment	313
Dispenser, Food Service	Food Service Accessories	181
Dispenser, Fragrance	Other Household Accessories	66
Dispenser, Hand Towel	Hygiene Objects	120
Dispenser, Laboratory	Labware	293
Dispenser, Lotion	Beauty Supplies	117
Dispenser, Lottery Ball	Game Equipment	503
Dispenser, Napkin	Food Service Accessories	181
Dispenser, Plate	Food Service Accessories	181
Dispenser, Powder	Animal Care Equipment	134
Dispenser, Shaving Cream	Hair Care Objects	119
Dispenser, Soap	Hygiene Objects	120
Dispenser, Stamp	Writing Accessories	403
Dispenser, Straw	Food Service Accessories	181
Dispenser, Tape	Multiple Use T&E for Materials	226
Dispenser, Ticket	Merchandising T&E	336
Dispenser, Token	Merchandising T&E	336
Dispenser, Toothpick	Food Service Accessories	181
Display	Other Documents	482
Display, Head-Mounted	Peripherals	364
disposal, garbage (*use:* Disposer)	Plumbing & Drainage Elements	12
Disposer	Plumbing & Drainage Elements	12
Dissertation	Literary Works	477
Distaff	Textile Manufacturing Equipment	240
Distillery	Industrial Structures	35
Distributor, Fertilizer	Tending Equipment	133
Divan	Seating Furniture	49
Divider	Drafting T&E	366
Divider, Chart	Writing Accessories	404
Divider, File	Writing Accessories	404
divider, room (*use:* Partition)	Barrier Elements	2
Divider, Stitch	Leather, Horn & Shellworking T&E	197
Dividers, Carpenter's	Woodworking T&E	250
Dock	Transportation Structures	39
Dock, Prisoner's	Regulative Devices	347
Docker, Tail	Veterinary Equipment	142
Docket	Government Records	470
Document, Digital	Other Documents	482
Document, Scoring	Other Documents	482
Document, Surrender	Government Records	470
Document, Travel	Other Documents	482
Dod	Glass, Plastics & Clayworking T&E	192
Dodger	Photoprocessing Equipment	381
Dodger, Boat	Water Transportation Accessories	437
Dog	Woodworking T&E	250
Dog, Bench	Woodworking T&E	250
dog, hewing (*use:* Dog, Log)	Forestry T&E	190
Dog, Hooping	Woodworking T&E	250
Dog, Joiner's	Woodworking T&E	250
Dog, Lathe	Metalworking T&E	210
Dog, Log	Forestry T&E	190
dog, post (*use:* Dog, Log)	Forestry T&E	190
Dog, Raft	Forestry T&E	190
Dog, Ring	Forestry T&E	190
Dog, Shutter	Finish Hardware	11
Dog, Span	Forestry T&E	190
Dog, Spoke	Woodworking T&E	250
dog, timber (*use:* Dog, Log)	Forestry T&E	190
Doghouse	Site Features	20
Dogsled	Animal-Powered Vehicles	424
Doily	Furniture Coverings	61
Doll	Toys	521
Doll, Boudoir	Decorative Furnishings	60
Doll, Decorative	Decorative Furnishings	60
Doll, Mechanical	Toys	521
Doll, Nesting	Toys	521
Doll, Paper	Toys	521
Doll, Voodoo	Religious Objects	463
Dollar	Exchange Media	488
Dollar, Half	Exchange Media	488
dollar, Maria Theresa (*use:* Taler)	Exchange Media	489
dollar, quarter (*use:* Quarter)	Exchange Media	488
Dollhouse	Toys	521
Dolly	Human-Powered Vehicles	426
Dolly, Camera	Camera Equipment	377
Dolly, Metalworking	Metalworking T&E	210
Dolly, Motorized	Motor Vehicles	429
Dolly, Timber	Forestry T&E	190
Dolly, Wash	Laundry Equipment	313
dolman (*use:* Jacket, Dolman)	Outerwear	100
Dolmen	Ceremonial Structures	25
Dome, Cheese	Serving Vessels	187
dome, display (*use:* Jar, Bell)	Storage & Display Accessories	64
Dome, Food	Serving Vessels	187

Term	Category	Page
dome, snow (*use:* Globe, Snow)	Decorative Furnishings	60
Dominical	Belief Symbols	493
Domino	Game Equipment	505
donut (*use:* Chamber, Vacuum)	Nuclear Physics T&E	341
doodlebug (*use:* Car, Self-Propelled Train)	Rail Vehicles	433
Door	Door & Window Elements	6
Door, Accordion	Door & Window Elements	6
Door, Dutch	Door & Window Elements	6
Door, Fireplace	Environmental Control Elements	8
Door, French	Door & Window Elements	6
Door, Garage	Door & Window Elements	6
Door, Louver	Door & Window Elements	6
Door, Pet	Door & Window Elements	6
Door, Revolving	Door & Window Elements	6
Door, Screen	Door & Window Elements	6
Door, Sliding	Door & Window Elements	6
Door, Soot	Environmental Control Elements	8
Door, Storm	Door & Window Elements	6
Door, Vehicle	Land Transportation Accessories	417
Doorbell	Door & Window Elements	6
Doorcap	Door & Window Elements	6
Doorcase	Door & Window Elements	6
Doorframe	Door & Window Elements	6
Doorknob	Finish Hardware	10
Doormat	Floor Coverings	45
Doorplate	Finish Hardware	10
Doorsill	Door & Window Elements	6
Doorstone	Door & Window Elements	6
Doorstop	Other Household Accessories	67
Do-Rag	Headwear	93
Dormer	Roof Elements	14
Dormeuse	Headwear	92
Dormitory	Dwellings	32
Dory	Watercraft	445
Dory, Banks	Watercraft	445
dory, Chamberlain (*use:* Dory, Swampscott)	Watercraft	445
Dory, Swampscott	Watercraft	445
Dosimeter	Nuclear Physics T&E	341
Dossal	Religious Objects	463
Doubler, Telephone Line	Telecommunication Accessories	394
Doublet	Main Garments	95
Doubletree	Land Transportation Accessories	419
Doubloon	Exchange Media	488
Douche	Hygiene Objects	120
Douche, Nasal	Medical Instruments	330
Douter	Other Lighting Accessories	72
Dovecote	Site Features	20
Dowel	Woodworking T&E	250
Dowel, Cake	Food Preparation Equipment	155
downrigger (*use:* Rig, Trolling)	Fishing Equipment	147
Downshave, Cooper's	Woodworking T&E	252
Downspout	Plumbing & Drainage Elements	12
dozer (*use:* Bulldozer)	Construction T&E	295
Draft	Other Documents	482
Draft, Bank	Exchange Media	489
drag (*use:* Travois)	Animal-Powered Vehicles	424
drag (*use:* Litter)	Human-Powered Vehicles	427
Drag	Masonry & Stoneworking T&E	206
Drag, Park	Animal-Powered Vehicles	423
drag, plank (*use:* Drag, Smoothing)	Cultivation Equipment	123
Drag, Smoothing	Cultivation Equipment	123
Dragger	Watercraft	445
Drain	Plumbing & Drainage Elements	12
Drainboard	Dishwashing Equipment	308
Drainer, Dish	Dishwashing Equipment	308
Draisine	Human-Powered Vehicles	426
drape (*use:* Drapery)	Window & Door Coverings	78
Drapery	Window & Door Coverings	78
Drawbridge	Transportation Structures	39
Drawer, Cash	Merchandising T&E	336
Drawers	Underwear	104
Drawing	Art	452
Drawing, Architectural	Graphic Documents	474
drawing, engineer's (*use:* Drawing, Technical)	Graphic Documents	474
Drawing, Technical	Graphic Documents	474
Drawknife	Woodworking T&E	252
Drawknife, Backing	Woodworking T&E	252
Drawknife, Barking	Woodworking T&E	252
Drawknife, Carpenter's	Woodworking T&E	252
Drawknife, Chamfering	Woodworking T&E	252
Drawknife, Cooper's	Woodworking T&E	252
Drawknife, Handlemaker's	Woodworking T&E	252
Drawknife, Heading	Woodworking T&E	256
Drawknife, Hollowing	Woodworking T&E	253
Drawknife, Hornworker's	Leather, Horn & Shellworking T&E	201
Drawknife, Mast	Woodworking T&E	253
Drawknife, Wheelwright's	Woodworking T&E	253
drawshave (*use:* Drawknife)	Woodworking T&E	252
Dray	Animal-Powered Vehicles	424
dreadnought (*use:* Battleship)	Watercraft	447
dredge (*use:* Net, Dredge)	Fishing Equipment	146

Dredge	Watercraft	448
Dredge, Bucketline	Mining & Mineral Harvesting T&E	222
Dredge, Mining	Mining & Mineral Harvesting T&E	222
Dredge, Suction	Mining & Mineral Harvesting T&E	222
Dredger	Food Storage Equipment	171
dredger, pounce (*use:* Box, Pounce)	Writing Accessories	403
Dreidel	Toys	525
Drencher	Veterinary Equipment	142
Dress	Main Garments	95
Dress, Ballet	Main Garments	95
dress, baptismal (*use:* Gown, Baptismal)	Religious Objects	463
Dress, Bridesmaid	Wedding Objects	466
Dress, Chemise	Main Garments	95
dress, christening (*use:* Gown, Baptismal)	Religious Objects	463
dress, coat (*use:* Coatdress)	Main Garments	95
Dress, Cocktail	Main Garments	95
Dress, Confirmation	Religious Objects	463
Dress, Day	Main Garments	95
dress, evening (*use:* Gown, Evening)	Main Garments	96
Dress, House	Main Garments	95
Dress, Jingle	Religious Objects	463
Dress, Lingerie	Main Garments	95
Dress, Maternity	Main Garments	95
Dress, Maxi	Main Garments	95
Dress, Midi	Main Garments	95
Dress, Mini	Main Garments	95
Dress, Mourning	Funerary Objects	456
Dress, Redingote	Main Garments	95
dress, round (*use:* Gown, Round)	Main Garments	96
Dress, Sheath	Main Garments	95
Dress, Skating	Main Garments	95
dress, sun (*use:* Sundress)	Main Garments	96
Dress, Sweater	Main Garments	95
Dress, Wedding	Wedding Objects	466
Dress, Wrap	Main Garments	95
Dresser	Storage & Display Furniture	53
Dresser, Grinding Wheel	Metalworking T&E	210
Dresser, Kitchen	Storage & Display Furniture	53
Dresser, Warp	Textile Manufacturing Equipment	240
Dressing	Medical Instruments	333
Dressing, Torah	Religious Objects	463
Drift, Cutting	Metalworking T&E	210
Drift, Drill	Woodworking T&E	250
Driftbolt	Woodworking T&E	250
driftpin (*use:* Driftbolt)	Woodworking T&E	250
Driftsight	Navigational Equipment	349
Drill	Multiple Use T&E for Materials	226
drill, barrow (*use:* Drill, Seed)	Planting Equipment	132
Drill, Bone	Medical Instruments	331
Drill, Bow	Multiple Use T&E for Materials	226
Drill, Breast	Woodworking T&E	250
drill, calyx (*use:* Drill, Shot)	Mining & Mineral Harvesting T&E	222
Drill, Churn	Mining & Mineral Harvesting T&E	222
Drill, Core	Mining & Mineral Harvesting T&E	222
Drill, Dental	Dental Instruments	322
Drill, Diamond	Mining & Mineral Harvesting T&E	222
Drill, Disk	Planting Equipment	132
Drill, Double Disk	Planting Equipment	132
Drill, Drifter	Mining & Mineral Harvesting T&E	222
Drill, Electric	Multiple Use T&E for Materials	226
drill, fertilizer (*use:* Drill, Seed)	Planting Equipment	132
Drill, Firemaking	Firemaking Equipment	74
Drill, Flexible-Shaft	Glass, Plastics & Clayworking T&E	192
Drill, Gang	Mining & Mineral Harvesting T&E	222
drill, garden (*use:* Drill, Seed)	Planting Equipment	132
drill, grain (*use:* Drill, Seed)	Planting Equipment	132
Drill, Hand	Multiple Use T&E for Materials	226
drill, hand (*use:* Drill, Seed)	Planting Equipment	132
Drill, Hoe	Planting Equipment	132
Drill, Hurdy Gurdy	Mining & Mineral Harvesting T&E	222
Drill, Jetting	Mining & Mineral Harvesting T&E	222
Drill, Jumper	Mining & Mineral Harvesting T&E	222
Drill, Metalworking	Metalworking T&E	210
Drill, Mining	Mining & Mineral Harvesting T&E	222
Drill, Octagonal	Masonry & Stoneworking T&E	203
Drill, Percussive	Construction T&E	295
Drill, Percussive Mining	Mining & Mineral Harvesting T&E	222
Drill, Placer	Mining & Mineral Harvesting T&E	222
Drill, Pole	Mining & Mineral Harvesting T&E	222
Drill, Post	Metalworking T&E	210
Drill, Press	Planting Equipment	132

Drill, Pump Woodworking T&E 250
Drill, Push Woodworking T&E 250
Drill, Rotary Mining & Mineral Harvesting T&E 222
Drill, Round Masonry & Stoneworking T&E 203
Drill, Seed Planting Equipment 132
Drill, Shoe Planting Equipment 132
Drill, Shot Mining & Mineral Harvesting T&E 222
Drill, Single Disk Planting Equipment 132
Drill, Sinker Mining & Mineral Harvesting T&E 222
Drill, Star Masonry & Stoneworking T&E 203
Drill, Stone Masonry & Stoneworking T&E 203
Drill, Stopper Mining & Mineral Harvesting T&E 222
Drill, Turbo Mining & Mineral Harvesting T&E 222
drill, walking (*use:* Drill, Seed) Planting Equipment 132
drill, wheelbarrow (*use:* Drill, Seed) Planting Equipment 132
Drill, Woodworking Woodworking T&E 250
Drive, Data Peripherals 365
Drive, Disk Peripherals 365
Drive, Flash Data Processing Media 363
Drive, Hard Peripherals 365
Drive, Motorized Film Photographic Accessories 378
Drive, Tape Peripherals 365
Driveboat Watercraft 445
Driveline Power Transmission Components 305
Driver Sports Equipment 515
Driver, Calk Farrier Equipment 139
Driver, Hoop Woodworking T&E 250
Driver, Pile Construction T&E 295
Driver, Point Painting T&E 229
Driver, Stud Construction T&E 295
drivetrain (*use:* Driveline) Power Transmission Components 305
Drone Aircraft 411
Drop, Flat Public Entertainment Devices 507
Drop, Roll Public Entertainment Devices 507
Drop, Scrim Public Entertainment Devices 507
dropcloth (*use:* Cloth, Drop) Painting T&E 229
Droplight Lighting Devices 68
Dropper, Funnel Food Preparation Equipment 157
Dropper, Medicine Medical Instruments 333
Droshky Animal-Powered Vehicles 423
Drosometer Meteorological T&E 339
drug (*use:* Dolly, Timber) Forestry T&E 190
Drugget Floor Coverings 45
Drum Musical Instruments 372
Drum, Bass Musical Instruments 372
Drum, Bongo Musical Instruments 372
Drum, Friction Musical Instruments 371
drum, kettle (*use:* Timpanum) Musical Instruments 372
Drum, Magnetic Data Processing Media 363
Drum, Sawdust Leather, Horn & Shellworking T&E 197
Drum, Side Musical Instruments 372
Drum, Slit Musical Instruments 372
Drum, Snare Musical Instruments 372
Drum, Steel Musical Instruments 372
Drum, Storage Containers 415
Drum, Tenor Musical Instruments 372
Drumstick Musical Accessories 368
Dry-Dock, Floating Watercraft 448
Dryer, Clothes Laundry Equipment 313
Dryer, Corn Food Preparation Equipment 155
Dryer, Crop Harvesting Equipment 128
Dryer, Film Photoprocessing Equipment 381
Dryer, Food Food Preparation Equipment 155
Dryer, Fruit Food Preparation Equipment 155
Dryer, Glove Laundry Equipment 313
Dryer, Grain Harvesting Equipment 128
Dryer, Hair Hair Care Objects 118
Dryer, Hand Hygiene Objects 120
Dryer, Herb Food Preparation Equipment 155
Dryer, Loop Textile Manufacturing Equipment 240
dryer, milk (*use:* Evaporator, Milk) Food Processing Equipment 166
Dryer, Paper Papermaking T&E 232
Dryer, Portable Hair Hair Care Objects 118
Dryer, Print Photoprocessing Equipment 381
Dryer, Reel Textile Manufacturing Equipment 240
Dryer, Standing Hair Hair Care Objects 118
Dryer, Textile Textile Manufacturing Equipment 240
Dryer, Yarn Textile Manufacturing Equipment 240
Drysuit Protective Wear 102
Ducat Exchange Media 488
Duckboat Watercraft 442
ducker, Delaware (*use:* Boat, Gunning) Watercraft 442
Duckpin Sports Equipment 513
Duct, Air Environmental Control Elements 8

Ductilometer	Mechanical Measurement Equipment	318
Dulang	Mining & Mineral Harvesting T&E	223
Dulcian	Musical Instruments	374
Dulcimer	Musical Instruments	373
Dulcimer, Appalachian	Musical Instruments	373
Dulcimer, Hammered	Musical Instruments	373
Dumbbell	Recreational Devices	510
Dumbwaiter	Conveyance Devices	5
Dummy	Masonry & Stoneworking T&E	204
Dummy, Blocking	Sports Equipment	515
Dummy, Football	Sports Equipment	515
Dummy, Tackling	Sports Equipment	515
Dummy, Ventriloquist	Public Entertainment Devices	508
Duplex	Dwellings	32
Duplicator	Replication Equipment	387
Duplicator, Denture	Dental Accessories	320
Duplicator, X-Ray	Medical Accessories	325
Durometer	Chemical Testing Devices	290
dustcloth (*use:* Cloth, Cleaning)	Housekeeping Equipment	311
Duster	Housekeeping Equipment	312
duster (*use:* Coat, Dust)	Protective Wear	102
Duster, Bran	Food Processing Equipment	168
duster, cloth (*use:* Cloth, Cleaning)	Housekeeping Equipment	311
duster, potato (*use:* Duster, Powder)	Tending Equipment	133
Duster, Powder	Tending Equipment	133
duster, tobacco (*use:* Duster, Powder)	Tending Equipment	133
Dustpan	Housekeeping Equipment	312
Duvet	Bedding	43
DVD (*use:* Videodisc, Digital)	Data Processing Media	363
Dye, Hair	Hair Care Objects	118
Dye, Laboratory	Labware	293
Dynactinometer	Optical T&E	343
Dynameter	Optical T&E	343
dynamo (*use:* Generator)	Power Producing Equipment	304
Dynamometer	Mechanical Measurement Equipment	318
Dynamotor	Power Producing Equipment	303
Eagle	Exchange Media	488
Eagle, Double	Exchange Media	488
Eagle, Half	Exchange Media	488
eagle, pilothouse (*use:* Ornament, Pilothouse)	Water Transportation Accessories	438
Eagle, Quarter	Exchange Media	488
earbud (*use:* Earphone)	Sound Communication Devices	391
Earmuff	Headwear	92
Earphone	Sound Communication Devices	391
earplug (*use:* Earspool)	Body Adornments	81
Earplug	Personal Assistive Objects	108
Earring	Body Adornments	81
Earspool	Body Adornments	81
Earthmover	Construction T&E	295
Earthwork	Site Features	20
Easel	Support Furniture	55
Easel, Darkroom	Photoprocessing Equipment	381
Easel, Picture	Storage & Display Accessories	65
Easel, Studio	Painting T&E	229
Ebullioscope	Thermal T&E	354
Eccentrolinead	Drafting T&E	366
Echometer	Navigational Equipment	350
Echoppe	Graphic Equipment	384
Echoscope	Medical Instruments	327
Eclipsareon	Astronomical T&E	284
Ecofact	Unclassifiable Objects	527
Ecraseur	Medical Instruments	332
Écu	Exchange Media	488
Edger, Lawn	Groundskeeping Equipment	309
Edger, Leather	Leather, Horn & Shellworking T&E	197
Edger, Masonry	Masonry & Stoneworking T&E	203
edger, turf (*use:* Edger, Lawn)	Groundskeeping Equipment	309
Edging, Landscape	Groundskeeping Equipment	309
Editor, Film	Photographic Accessories	378
Editorial	Declaratory Documents	468
eductor (*use:* Ejector)	Mechanical Devices	315
Eelpot	Fishing Equipment	148
Effigy	Funerary Objects	457
Egg, Darning	Needleworking Equipment	235
Egg, Easter	Holiday Objects	458
Egg, Nest	Breeding Equipment	138
Eggbeater	Food Preparation Equipment	161
Eggcup	Eating Vessels	176
eidograph (*use:* Pantograph)	Drafting T&E	367
Eikonometer	Optical T&E	343
Ejector	Mechanical Devices	315
Elacometer	Chemical Testing Devices	290
Electrifier, Flour-Bleaching	Food Processing Equipment	168
Electrocardiograph	Medical Instruments	327
Electrode	Electrical System Components	300
Electrometer	Electrical & Magnetic Measurement Devices	297
Electroscope	Electrical & Magnetic Measurement Devices	297
Electrotome	Medical Instruments	331

Element, Door — Door & Window Elements 6
Element, Window — Door & Window Elements 6
Elevation — Graphic Documents 474
Elevator — Conveyance Devices 5
Elevator, Auger — Harvesting Equipment 128
Elevator, Bale — Harvesting Equipment 128
Elevator, Casing — Mining & Mineral Harvesting T&E 222
Elevator, Crop — Harvesting Equipment 128
Elevator, Dental — Dental Instruments 322
Elevator, Drilling — Mining & Mineral Harvesting T&E 222
Elevator, Grain — Agricultural Structures 23
Elevator, Malar — Medical Instruments 331
Elevator, Periosteal — Medical Instruments 331
Elevator, Rod — Mining & Mineral Harvesting T&E 222
Elevator, Root — Dental Instruments 322
Elevator, Surgical — Medical Instruments 331
Elevator, Trephining — Medical Instruments 331
Elevator, Tubing — Mining & Mineral Harvesting T&E 222
Eliminator, Nuclear Static — Nuclear Physics T&E 341
Ellipsograph — Drafting T&E 366
elliptograph (*use:* Ellipsograph) — Drafting T&E 366
e-mail (*use:* Mail, Electronic) — Other Documents 482
Emasculator — Veterinary Equipment 143
Embosser — Writing Devices 406
Embosser, Braille — Writing Devices 406
Embosser, Check — Writing Devices 406
Embosser, Label — Writing Devices 406
Embosser, Metal — Metalworking T&E 210
Embroidery — Art 452
Embroidery, Punched Paper — Art 452
Enclosure, Animal — Other Structures 41
Enclosure, Prisoner — Regulative Devices 347
Encoder — Data Processing Devices 361
Encyclopedia — Other Documents 480
end, wax (*use:* Bristle, Sewing) — Leather, Horn & Shellworking T&E 196
Endoscope — Medical Instruments 328
Enframement, Door — Door & Window Elements 6
Enframement, Fireplace — Surface Elements 18
Engine — Power Producing Equipment 303
Engine, Aircraft — Aerospace Transportation Accessories 409
Engine, Automotive — Land Transportation Accessories 417
Engine, Blowing — Metalworking T&E 208
engine, compression-ignition (*use:* Engine, Diesel) — Power Producing Equipment 303
Engine, Dental — Dental Accessories 320
Engine, Diesel — Power Producing Equipment 303
Engine, Difference — Data Processing Devices 361
Engine, Dividing — Drafting T&E 366
Engine, Gas — Power Producing Equipment 303
Engine, Gasoline — Power Producing Equipment 303
Engine, Hot Air — Power Producing Equipment 303
Engine, Liquid Fuel — Power Producing Equipment 303
Engine, Man — Mining & Mineral Harvesting T&E 222
Engine, Oil Traction — Power Producing Equipment 303
Engine, Radial — Power Producing Equipment 303
Engine, Ramjet — Aerospace Transportation Accessories 409
Engine, Reciprocating — Power Producing Equipment 303
Engine, Ruling — Drafting T&E 366
Engine, Spit — Food Preparation Equipment 163
Engine, Steam — Power Producing Equipment 303
Engine, Steam Gas — Power Producing Equipment 303
Engine, Steam Traction — Power Producing Equipment 304
Engine, Toy Steam — Toys 521
engine, train (*use:* Locomotive) — Rail Vehicles 434
Engine, Turbojet — Aerospace Transportation Accessories 409
Engine, Turboprop — Aerospace Transportation Accessories 409
Engine, Walking Beam — Power Producing Equipment 303
Engine, Watercraft — Water Transportation Accessories 437
engine, winding (*use:* Windlass) — Mechanical Devices 315
Engiscope — Optical T&E 344
Engraver, Metal — Metalworking T&E 210
Engraving — Graphic Documents 473
Engraving, Wood — Graphic Documents 474
Enlarger — Photoprocessing Equipment 381
Ensemble — Main Garments 96
Entablature — Supporting Elements 16
Envelope — Writing Accessories 402
Envelope, Money — Merchandising T&E 336
envelope, seed (*use:* Packet, Seed) — Planting Equipment 132
Envelope, Shipping — Containers 415
Epaulet — Status Symbols 496

Term	Category	Page
Épée	Sports Equipment	515
Epergne	Serving Vessels	187
Epilator	Hair Care Objects	119
equipment, exercise (*use:* Device, Fitness)	Recreational Devices	509
equipment, magician's (*use:* Prop, Magician's)	Public Entertainment Devices	508
equipment, playground (*use:* Device, Playground)	Recreational Devices	510
Eraser	Writing Accessories	404
Eraser, Audio Tape	Sound Communication Accessories	389
e-reader (*use:* Reader, Electronic)	Visual Communication Devices	401
Eriometer	Weights & Measures T&E	357
Escalator	Conveyance Devices	5
Escape, Fire	Stair Elements	15
Esclavage	Body Adornments	81
Escudo	Exchange Media	488
Escutcheon	Finish Hardware	10
Espadrille	Footwear	90
Essay	Literary Works	477
Esthesiometer	Biological T&E	287
Estimate	Financial Records	469
Estoque	Sports Equipment	514
Étagère	Storage & Display Furniture	54
Etching	Graphic Documents	473
Etching, Relief	Graphic Documents	474
Etui	Personal Carrying & Storage Gear	112
Eulogy	Literary Works	477
Euphonium	Musical Instruments	370
Euphroe	Water Transportation Accessories	437
Euro	Exchange Media	488
Evacuator, Dental	Dental Instruments	322
Evaporator, HVAC	Environmental Control Elements	9
Evaporator, Milk	Food Processing Equipment	166
Evaporator, Sugar	Food Processing Equipment	169
Evaporimeter	Meteorological T&E	339
Evener, Horse	Land Transportation Accessories	419
Ewer	Serving Vessels	189
Examination	Instructional Documents	475
Excavator	Construction T&E	295
Excavator, Dental	Dental Instruments	322
Exchange	Commercial Structures	27
Exciter	Power Producing Equipment	304
Excluder, Queen	Animal Care Equipment	136
Exedra	Site Features	21
Exercise, School	Instructional Documents	475
Expander, Metal	Metalworking T&E	210
Expander, Palatal	Dental Instruments	322
exploder (*use:* Detonator)	Mining & Mineral Harvesting T&E	222
Exploder, Cap	Toys	521
Explorer, Dental	Dental Instruments	323
Extender, Handle	Metalworking T&E	210
Extension, Hair	Hair Adornments	83
Extension, Sight	Armament Accessories	269
Extensometer	Weights & Measures T&E	357
Extinguisher, Candle	Other Lighting Accessories	72
Extinguisher, Fire	Protective Devices	345
Extractor, Bung	Woodworking T&E	250
Extractor, Calk	Farrier Equipment	139
Extractor, Cork	Food Preparation Equipment	156
Extractor, Dental	Dental Instruments	322
Extractor, Fetal	Veterinary Equipment	142
Extractor, Fuze	Armament Accessories	269
Extractor, Headless Shell	Armament Accessories	269
Extractor, Honey	Food Processing Equipment	164
extractor, juice (*use:* Juicer)	Food Preparation Equipment	160
Extractor, Laboratory	Labware	293
Extractor, Root	Dental Instruments	322
Extractor, Tooth	Dental Instruments	322
Extruder	Glass, Plastics & Clayworking T&E	192
Extruder, Metal	Metalworking T&E	210
Eyecup	Hygiene Objects	120
Eyedropper	Hygiene Objects	120
eyedropper (*use:* Dropper, Medicine)	Medical Instruments	333
Eyeglasses	Personal Assistive Objects	107
Eyeglasses, 3D	Visual Communication Accessories	399
Eyelash, False	Beauty Supplies	116
eyelet (*use:* Grommet)	Needleworking Equipment	236
Eyeliner	Beauty Supplies	116
Eyeshade	Headwear	94
Eyeshadow	Beauty Supplies	116
Face-Bow	Dental Instruments	323
Facility, Correctional	Institutional Structures	37
Facility, Health	Institutional Structures	37
Facility, Lodging	Commercial Structures	27
Faciometer	Medical Instruments	328
Facsimile	Other Documents	485
Factory	Industrial Structures	35
Factory, Metal	Industrial Structures	35
Fadeometer	Textile Manufacturing Equipment	244
Fairing	Memorabilia	479
Fairlead	Mechanical Devices	315
Falcon	Artillery	274
Falconet	Artillery	274
fall (*use:* Extension, Hair)	Hair Adornments	83
Falsework	Construction T&E	296
Falsie	Underwear	103
Fan, Brisé	Personal Assistive Objects	108
Fan, Ceiling	Heating & Cooling Equipment	75

Term	Category	Page
Fan, Cockade	Personal Assistive Objects	108
fan, dutch (*use:* Mill, Fanning)	Harvesting Equipment	131
Fan, Electric	Heating & Cooling Equipment	75
Fan, Exhaust	Environmental Control Elements	9
Fan, Fire	Heating Equipment Accessories	77
Fan, Fixed	Personal Assistive Objects	108
Fan, Hand	Personal Assistive Objects	108
Fan, Recirculating	Environmental Control Elements	9
Fan, Ventilation	Environmental Control Elements	9
fan, winnowing (*use:* Mill, Fanning)	Harvesting Equipment	131
Fanchon	Headwear	92
fancywork (*use:* Needlework)	Art	452
Fanlight	Door & Window Elements	7
Fantail	Water Transportation Accessories	437
Farmhouse	Dwellings	32
Farthing	Exchange Media	488
farthing, penny (*use:* Bicycle, Ordinary)	Human-Powered Vehicles	426
Farthingale	Underwear	103
Fascinator	Headwear	93
Fastener	Multiple Use T&E for Materials	227
Fastener, Anchor	Multiple Use T&E for Materials	227
Fastener, Button	Leather, Horn & Shellworking T&E	197
Fastener, Chain Bolt	Finish Hardware	10
Fastener, Curtain	Window & Door Coverings	78
Fastener, Hook and Eye	Needleworking Equipment	236
Fastener, Hook and Loop	Needleworking Equipment	236
Fastener, Metal	Metalworking T&E	210
Fastener, Paper	Writing Accessories	404
Fastener, Textile	Needleworking Equipment	236
Fastener, Wood	Woodworking T&E	250
fathometer (*use:* Finder, Depth)	Navigational Equipment	350
Fatigues	Status Symbols	500
Faucet	Plumbing & Drainage Elements	12
Fauchard	Edged Weapons	277
Fauld	Body Armor	275
Favor	Party Accessories	460
Feather	Masonry & Stoneworking T&E	203
Featherwork	Art	452
Feature, Garden	Site Features	20
Fecalyzer	Veterinary Equipment	142
Fedora	Headwear	92
Feedbag	Animal Care Equipment	134
Feeder, Animal	Animal Care Equipment	134
Feeder, Bird	Site Features	21
Feeder, Blending	Food Processing Equipment	168
Feeder, Deer	Site Features	21
feeder, diet (*use:* Wagon, Feeder)	Feed Processing Equipment	126
Feeder, Esophageal	Veterinary Equipment	142
Feeder, Flour-Bleaching	Food Processing Equipment	168
Feeder, Invalid	Eating Vessels	177
Feeder, Livestock	Animal Care Equipment	135
Feeder, Pet	Pet Supplies	141
Feeder, Poultry	Animal Care Equipment	135
Feeder, Roll	Food Processing Equipment	168
Feeder, Root	Tending Equipment	133
feeder, sick (*use:* Feeder, Invalid)	Eating Vessels	177
Feeder, Squirrel	Site Features	21
Feeder, Wildlife	Site Features	21
Felt, Game	Game Equipment	502
Felucca	Watercraft	443
Fence	Site Features	20
Fence, Barbed Wire	Site Features	20
Fence, Board	Site Features	20
Fence, Chain Link	Site Features	20
Fence, Electric	Site Features	20
fence, paling (*use:* Fence, Picket)	Site Features	20
Fence, Picket	Site Features	20
Fence, Rail	Site Features	20
Fence, Snow	Site Features	20
Fender	Heating Equipment Accessories	76
Fender, Vehicle	Land Transportation Accessories	417
Fender, Watercraft	Water Transportation Accessories	437
Ferronière	Headwear	93
ferrotype (*use:* Tintype)	Graphic Documents	473
Ferrule	Multiple Use T&E for Materials	227
Ferry	Watercraft	446
Ferry, Car	Watercraft	446
Fertilizer	Tending Equipment	133
festoon (*use:* Swag)	Window & Door Coverings	79
fetish (*use:* Talisman)	Belief Symbols	493
fetter (*use:* Shackle, Leg)	Regulative Devices	348
Fez	Headwear	92
Fichu	Clothing Accessories	86
Fid	Needleworking Equipment	235
Fid, Leatherworking	Leather, Horn & Shellworking T&E	197
Fiddle	Musical Instruments	373
Fiddle, Hardanger	Musical Instruments	373
Fife	Musical Instruments	374
fife-rail (*use:* Rail, Fife)	Water Transportation Accessories	438

Fighter	Aircraft	411
Figure, Action	Toys	521
Figure, Lay	Painting T&E	229
Figure, Mechanical	Toys	521
Figure, Religious	Religious Objects	465
Figure, Tobacconist's	Advertising Media	451
Figure, Toy	Toys	521
Figurehead	Water Transportation Accessories	437
Figurine	Art	454
File	Multiple Use T&E for Materials	227
File, Cabinet	Woodworking T&E	250
File, Dental	Dental Instruments	323
File, Document	Other Documents	482
file, double-cut (*use:* File, Machine)	Metalworking T&E	210
File, Flat	Metalworking T&E	210
File, Float	Woodworking T&E	250
File, Glass	Glass, Plastics & Clayworking T&E	192
File, Half Round	Metalworking T&E	210
File, Hornworker's	Leather, Horn & Shellworking T&E	201
File, Joint	Metalworking T&E	210
File, Knife	Woodworking T&E	250
File, Machine	Metalworking T&E	210
File, Metalworking	Metalworking T&E	210
File, Mill	Metalworking T&E	210
File, Nail	Beauty Supplies	117
File, Needle	Metalworking T&E	210
File, Portable	Writing Accessories	402
file, rat tail (*use:* File, Round)	Metalworking T&E	210
File, Riffler	Woodworking T&E	250
File, Round	Metalworking T&E	210
File, Saddler's	Leather, Horn & Shellworking T&E	197
File, Saw	Metalworking T&E	210
file, single-cut (*use:* File, Mill)	Metalworking T&E	210
File, Square	Metalworking T&E	210
File, Triangular	Metalworking T&E	210
File, Woodworking	Woodworking T&E	250
Filler, Bottle	Food Processing Equipment	168
Filler, Capsule	Medical Accessories	325
Filler, Lamp	Other Lighting Accessories	72
filler, silo (*use:* Blower, Ensilage)	Feed Processing Equipment	126
Fillet	Typesetting Equipment	388
film (*use:* Picture, Motion)	Other Documents	485
Film, Magazine	Photographic Media	380
Film, Motion Picture	Photographic Media	380
Film, Photographic	Photographic Media	380
Film, Roll	Photographic Media	380
Film, Self-Developing	Photographic Media	380
Film, Sheet	Photographic Media	380
Filmstrip	Other Documents	485
filter, air (*use:* Filter, HVAC)	Environmental Control Elements	9
filter, air (*use:* Purifier, Air)	Other Household Accessories	67
filter, air (*use:* Filter, Engine)	Power Transmission Components	305
Filter, Camera	Camera Equipment	377
Filter, Cloud	Camera Equipment	377
Filter, Coffee	Food Preparation Equipment	155
Filter, Color Correcting	Camera Equipment	377
Filter, Daylight	Camera Equipment	377
Filter, Engine	Power Transmission Components	305
Filter, HVAC	Environmental Control Elements	9
Filter, Laboratory	Labware	293
Filter, Polarizing	Camera Equipment	377
Filter, Seitz	Biological T&E	287
Filter, Serum	Biological T&E	287
Filter, Specimen	Biological T&E	287
Filter, Water	Food Preparation Equipment	155
Fin, Swim	Recreational Devices	510
Finder, Depth	Navigational Equipment	350
Finder, Direction	Navigational Equipment	350
Finder, Distance	Navigational Equipment	350
finder, laser range (*use:* Rangefinder, Laser)	Surveying Equipment	353
Finder, Radio Direction	Navigational Equipment	350
finder, radio range (*use:* Rangefinder, Radio)	Surveying Equipment	353
finder, range (*use:* Rangefinder)	Surveying Equipment	353
Finder, Star	Navigational Equipment	350
Finder, Stud	Construction T&E	296
Finger, Wool	Textile Manufacturing Equipment	240
Fingernail, Artificial	Beauty Supplies	116
Fingerstall	Leather, Horn & Shellworking T&E	197
Fingerstall, Shipwright's	Woodworking T&E	250
Finial	Roof Elements	14
Finial, Curtain Rod	Window & Door Coverings	78
Finial, Lamp	Other Lighting Accessories	72
Finisher, Flint-Glazing	Papermaking T&E	232
Finisher, Paper	Papermaking T&E	232
Finisher, Pebbling	Papermaking T&E	232
Fireback	Environmental Control Elements	8
Fireboard	Environmental Control Elements	8
Fireboat	Watercraft	446

Term	Category	Page
Firebrick	Construction Materials	3
Firecracker	Public Entertainment Devices	507
firedog (*use:* Andiron)	Heating Equipment Accessories	76
fireguard (*use:* Screen, Fire)	Heating Equipment Accessories	76
firehouse (*use:* Station, Fire)	Civic & Social Structures	26
Firepit	Site Features	21
Fireplace	Environmental Control Elements	9
fireplug (*use:* Hydrant)	Hydraulic Structures	34
Firepole	Conveyance Devices	5
Fireset	Heating Equipment Accessories	76
Firesteel	Firemaking Equipment	74
Firework	Public Entertainment Devices	507
Firkin	Food Storage Equipment	171
Fishbowl	Pet Supplies	141
fisherman (*use:* Trawler)	Watercraft	445
Fishhook	Fishing Equipment	147
Fishplate	Supporting Elements	16
Fishplate, Rail	Rail Transportation Accessories	432
Fitting, Blind	Window & Door Coverings	78
Fitting, Book	Writing Accessories	404
Fitting, Boom	Water Transportation Accessories	439
Fitting, Grease	Power Transmission Components	305
Fitting, Keyhole	Finish Hardware	10
Fitting, Oil	Mechanical Devices	317
Fitting, Pipe	Plumbing & Drainage Elements	12
Fixer	Photoprocessing Equipment	381
Fixture, Ceiling	Lighting Devices	68
Fixture, Combination	Lighting Devices	68
Fixture, Electric	Lighting Devices	68
Fixture, Gas	Lighting Devices	68
Fixture, Lighting	Lighting Devices	68
Fixture, Plumbing	Plumbing & Drainage Elements	12
Fixture, Store Display	Merchandising T&E	336
Fixture, Wall	Lighting Devices	68
Fixture, Wall Display	Merchandising T&E	337
Flabellum	Religious Objects	463
Flag	Organizational Objects	459
flag, code (*use:* Flag, Signal)	Visual Communication Devices	400
Flag, Football	Sports Equipment	515
Flag, Golf	Sports Equipment	516
Flag, Promotional	Advertising Media	449
Flag, Semaphore	Visual Communication Devices	400
Flag, Service	Declaratory Documents	468

Term	Category	Page
Flag, Signal	Visual Communication Devices	400
Flag, Water Ski	Recreational Devices	510
Flag, Wind	Armament Accessories	269
Flageolet	Musical Instruments	374
Flageolet, Double	Musical Instruments	374
Flageolet, Triple	Musical Instruments	374
Flagon	Serving Vessels	189
Flagpole	Site Features	21
Flagstaff, Watercraft	Water Transportation Accessories	437
flagstone (*use:* Stone, Paving)	Site Features	22
flail (*use:* Flail, Threshing)	Harvesting Equipment	128
Flail	Percussive Weapons	283
Flail, Ritual	Religious Objects	463
Flail, Threshing	Harvesting Equipment	128
Flake	Unclassifiable Objects	527
Flake, Modified	Unclassifiable Objects	527
Flake, Primary	Unclassifiable Objects	527
Flake, Secondary	Unclassifiable Objects	527
Flake, Tertiary	Unclassifiable Objects	527
Flaker	Multiple Use T&E for Materials	227
Flambeau	Lighting Holders	71
flamethrower (*use:* Weeder, Flame)	Cultivation Equipment	125
Flamethrower	Firearms	280
Flange	Multiple Use T&E for Materials	227
Flannel, Tobacco	Advertising Media	450
flare, distress (*use:* Flare, Signal)	Visual Communication Devices	400
Flare, Signal	Visual Communication Devices	400
Flash, Handheld	Camera Equipment	376
Flash, Stroboscopic	Camera Equipment	376
Flashbulb	Camera Equipment	377
Flashgun	Camera Equipment	377
Flashing	Construction Materials	3
Flashlight	Lighting Devices	68
Flask	Containers	415
Flask, Ammunition	Armament Accessories	267
Flask, Boiling	Labware	293
Flask, Culture	Labware	293
Flask, Denture Curing	Dental Accessories	320
flask, Dewar (*use:* Flask, Vacuum)	Labware	293
Flask, Distilling	Labware	293
Flask, Erlenmeyer	Labware	293
Flask, Filtering	Labware	293
flask, gemel (*use:* Bottle, Gemel)	Containers	415
Flask, Laboratory	Labware	293
Flask, Molding	Metalworking T&E	210
Flask, Pocket	Personal Carrying & Storage Gear	112

Flask, Powder — Armament Accessories 267
Flask, Priming — Armament Accessories 267
Flask, Shot — Armament Accessories 267
Flask, Snap — Metalworking T&E 210
Flask, Urinal — Hygiene Objects 121
Flask, Vacuum — Labware 293
flat (*use:* Drop, Flat) — Public Entertainment Devices 507
Flatcap — Headwear 92
Flatcar — Rail Vehicles 433
Flatiron — Laundry Equipment 313
Flatter — Metalworking T&E 211
Flatweave — Floor Coverings 45
Fleam — Medical Instruments 333
flesher (*use:* Deflesher) — Food Processing Equipment 165
Flier — Advertising Media 450
Flier, Political — Advertising Media 450
Flier, Trade — Advertising Media 450
Flint — Firemaking Equipment 74
Flint, Gun — Armament Accessories 269
Flip-Flop — Footwear 90
flipper-flopper (*use:* Ladder, Rope) — Recreational Devices 510
Float, Angle — Masonry & Stoneworking T&E 203
Float, Bull — Masonry & Stoneworking T&E 204
Float, Dental — Veterinary Equipment 142
Float, Devil — Masonry & Stoneworking T&E 206
Float, Fishing — Fishing Equipment 147
Float, Hand — Masonry & Stoneworking T&E 203
Float, Life — Water Transportation Accessories 441
Float, Long — Masonry & Stoneworking T&E 204
float, net (*use:* Buoy, Net) — Fishing Equipment 145
Float, Texture — Masonry & Stoneworking T&E 204
Float, Woodworking — Woodworking T&E 250
Floatstone — Masonry & Stoneworking T&E 204
flogger, bung (*use:* Bungstart) — Woodworking T&E 254
Floodgate — Hydraulic Structures 34
Floodlight — Lighting Devices 68
Floorcloth — Floor Coverings 45
Flooring — Surface Elements 18
Flooring, Hardwood — Surface Elements 18
Flooring, Puncheon — Surface Elements 18
Flooring, Vinyl — Surface Elements 18
Flora, Artificial — Decorative Furnishings 60
Flora, Pressed — Art 453
Floss, Dental — Hygiene Objects 121
flounce, bed (*use:* Bedskirt) — Bedding 44
Flower, Artificial — Decorative Furnishings 60
Flowerpot — Horticultural Containers 62
Flowerpot, Hanging — Horticultural Containers 62
Flue — Environmental Control Elements 8
Flugelhorn — Musical Instruments 370
Flume, Log — Hydraulic Structures 34
Fluoroscope — Medical Instruments 328
Flute — Musical Instruments 374
Flute, Courting — Musical Instruments 374
Fluxmeter — Electrical & Magnetic Measurement Devices 298
Fly, Artificial — Fishing Equipment 147
Flypaper — Other Household Accessories 66
Flytrap — Other Household Accessories 66
Flywheel — Mechanical Devices 315
Flywhisk — Other Household Accessories 66
Fob — Personal Carrying & Storage Gear 112
Fob, Key — Personal Carrying & Storage Gear 112
Fob, Watch — Personal Carrying & Storage Gear 112
Focometer — Optical T&E 343
Foghorn — Navigational Equipment 350
Foil — Sports Equipment 515
foil, aluminum (*use:* Foil, Cooking) — Food Preparation Equipment 155
Foil, Cooking — Food Preparation Equipment 155
Foil, Phonograph — Sound Communication Accessories 389
Folder, Bone — Printing Accessories 386
Folder, Coin — Personal Carrying & Storage Gear 113
Folder, File — Writing Accessories 402
folder, paper (*use:* Machine, Paper Folding) — Printing Accessories 386
Folio — Other Documents 483
Follower, Candle — Other Lighting Accessories 72
Folly — Site Features 21
Fonds — Other Documents 480
Font, Baptismal — Religious Objects 462
Font, Holy Water — Religious Objects 462
Football — Sports Equipment 515
Footbath — Plumbing & Drainage Elements 12
Footboard — Sleeping & Reclining Furniture 50
Footbridge — Transportation Structures 39
Footlight — Lighting Devices 70
Footlocker — Personal Carrying & Storage Gear 113

Term	Category	Page
Footrest, Vehicle	Land Transportation Accessories	418
footstick (*use:* Stick, Foot)	Typesetting Equipment	388
Footstone	Funerary Objects	457
Footstool	Seating Furniture	49
Forceps	Medical Instruments	331
Forceps, Bone Cutting	Medical Instruments	331
Forceps, Catch	Medical Instruments	331
Forceps, Dental	Dental Instruments	322
Forceps, Dissecting	Biological T&E	288
Forceps, Obstetrical	Medical Instruments	330
Forceps, Pill	Veterinary Equipment	142
Forceps, Trephining	Medical Instruments	331
Forecastle	Water Transportation Accessories	437
Foresail	Water Transportation Accessories	439
forestaff (*use:* Staff, Jacob's)	Surveying Equipment	353
Forge	Metalworking T&E	210
Forge, Blacksmith's	Metalworking T&E	210
forge, drop (*use:* Hammer, Drop)	Metalworking T&E	211
Forgery	Exchange Media	487
Fork, Alfalfa	Harvesting Equipment	128
Fork, Asparagus	Serving Utensils	184
Fork, Ballast	Rail Transportation Accessories	432
Fork, Barbecue	Food Preparation Equipment	160
Fork, Barley	Harvesting Equipment	128
Fork, Beet	Harvesting Equipment	128
Fork, Bending	Metalworking T&E	207
Fork, Berry	Eating & Drinking Utensils	178
Fork, Blubber	Fishing Equipment	148
Fork, Butter	Food Processing Equipment	166
Fork, Cabbage	Harvesting Equipment	128
Fork, Cake	Eating & Drinking Utensils	178
Fork, Carrying-In	Glass, Plastics & Clayworking T&E	192
Fork, Carving	Serving Utensils	184
fork, chaff (*use:* Fork, Header)	Harvesting Equipment	129
Fork, Cold-Meat	Serving Utensils	184
Fork, Cooking	Food Preparation Equipment	160
fork, cottonseed (*use:* Fork, Ensilage)	Feed Processing Equipment	126
Fork, Cultivating	Cultivation Equipment	123
Fork, Curd	Food Processing Equipment	166
Fork, Dessert	Eating & Drinking Utensils	178
fork, digging (*use:* Fork, Spading)	Cultivation Equipment	123
Fork, Dinner	Eating & Drinking Utensils	178
Fork, Eating	Eating & Drinking Utensils	178
Fork, Ensilage	Feed Processing Equipment	126
Fork, Fireplace	Heating Equipment Accessories	76
Fork, Fish	Eating & Drinking Utensils	178
Fork, Fish Serving	Serving Utensils	184
fork, flesh (*use:* Fork, Meat)	Food Preparation Equipment	160
Fork, Folding	Eating & Drinking Utensils	178
Fork, Fondue	Serving Utensils	184
fork, garden (*use:* Fork, Spading)	Cultivation Equipment	123
fork, grain (*use:* Fork, Header)	Harvesting Equipment	129
Fork, Grapple	Harvesting Equipment	128
Fork, Harpoon	Harvesting Equipment	128
Fork, Harvesting	Harvesting Equipment	128
fork, hay (*use:* Hayfork)	Harvesting Equipment	129
Fork, Hay Lifting	Harvesting Equipment	128
Fork, Header	Harvesting Equipment	129
Fork, Hors d'Oeuvre	Eating & Drinking Utensils	178
fork, horse hay (*use:* Fork, Hay Lifting)	Harvesting Equipment	128
Fork, Hot Shot	Armament Accessories	269
Fork, Ice Cream	Eating & Drinking Utensils	178
Fork, Laundry	Laundry Equipment	313
Fork, Lemon	Serving Utensils	184
fork, lobster (*use:* Pick, Seafood)	Eating & Drinking Utensils	178
Fork, Lobster	Eating & Drinking Utensils	178
Fork, Luncheon	Eating & Drinking Utensils	178
Fork, Manure	Tending Equipment	133
Fork, Meat	Food Preparation Equipment	160
Fork, Olive	Serving Utensils	184
Fork, Oyster	Eating & Drinking Utensils	178
Fork, Pastry	Eating & Drinking Utensils	178
Fork, Pickle	Serving Utensils	184
fork, pitch (*use:* Hayfork)	Harvesting Equipment	129
Fork, Potato	Harvesting Equipment	128
Fork, Salad	Eating & Drinking Utensils	178
Fork, Sardine	Serving Utensils	184
Fork, Serving	Serving Utensils	184
fork, silage (*use:* Fork, Ensilage)	Feed Processing Equipment	126
Fork, Sluice	Mining & Mineral Harvesting T&E	222
Fork, Spading	Cultivation Equipment	123
Fork, Straining	Leather, Horn & Shellworking T&E	198
fork, straw (*use:* Fork, Barley)	Harvesting Equipment	128
Fork, Sucket	Eating & Drinking Utensils	179
fork, table (*use:* Fork, Dinner)	Eating & Drinking Utensils	178
Fork, Thatching	Fiberworking T&E	144
Fork, Toasting	Food Preparation Equipment	163
Fork, Tuning	Acoustical T&E	261
Fork, Vegetable Scoop	Harvesting Equipment	128
Fork, Weeding	Cultivation Equipment	125

fork, winnowing (*use:* Fork, Harvesting)	Harvesting Equipment	128
Forklift	Motor Vehicles	429
Form	Other Documents	482
form, arch (*use:* Formwork)	Construction T&E	296
form, bust (*use:* Improver, Bust)	Underwear	103
Form, Collar	Laundry Equipment	313
Form, Dress	Needleworking Equipment	235
Form, Order	Other Documents	483
form, sleeve (*use:* Form, Dress)	Needleworking Equipment	235
form, tailoring (*use:* Form, Dress)	Needleworking Equipment	235
Former, Bite Rim	Dental Accessories	320
Formwork	Construction T&E	296
Fort	Defense Structures	31
Fortification	Defense Structures	31
Fortress	Defense Structures	31
Foundation	Supporting Elements	16
Foundation, Cosmetic	Beauty Supplies	116
Foundry	Industrial Structures	35
Fountain, Drinking	Plumbing & Drainage Elements	12
Fountain, Indoor	Plumbing & Drainage Elements	12
fountain, poultry (*use:* Waterer, Poultry)	Animal Care Equipment	137
Fountain, Soda	Serving Vessels	189
fountain, stock (*use:* Waterer, Livestock)	Animal Care Equipment	137
Fountain, Water	Site Features	21
four-in-hand (*use:* Coach)	Animal-Powered Vehicles	423
Fourragère	Status Symbols	496
Fowler	Firearms	282
Fragment	Unclassifiable Objects	527
Frame	Storage & Display Accessories	63
Frame, Contact Printing	Photoprocessing Equipment	381
Frame, Drawing	Textile Manufacturing Equipment	240
Frame, Embroidery	Needleworking Equipment	237
Frame, Futon	Sleeping & Reclining Furniture	51
Frame, Heating	Labware	293
Frame, Lace	Textile Manufacturing Equipment	240
Frame, Mirror	Storage & Display Accessories	63
Frame, Needlework	Needleworking Equipment	237
Frame, Ox-Shoeing	Farrier Equipment	139
Frame, Pack	Personal Carrying & Storage Gear	112
Frame, Picture	Storage & Display Accessories	63
Frame, Quilting	Needleworking Equipment	237
Frame, Ring	Textile Manufacturing Equipment	240
Frame, Roving	Textile Manufacturing Equipment	240
Frame, Sewing	Bookbinding Equipment	382
Frame, Slubbing	Textile Manufacturing Equipment	240
Frame, Spinning	Textile Manufacturing Equipment	240
frame, teasel (*use:* Napper)	Textile Manufacturing Equipment	243
Frame, Tenter	Textile Manufacturing Equipment	240
Frame, Throstle	Textile Manufacturing Equipment	240
Frame, Toggling	Leather, Horn & Shellworking T&E	198
Frame, Transom	Water Transportation Accessories	438
Frame, Twisting	Textile Manufacturing Equipment	240
Frame, Vehicle	Land Transportation Accessories	417
Frame, Warping	Textile Manufacturing Equipment	240
Frame, Watercraft	Water Transportation Accessories	438
Frame, Wheel	Woodworking T&E	250
Frame, Window	Door & Window Elements	7
Franc	Exchange Media	488
Freezer	Food Storage Equipment	171
Freezer, Chest	Food Storage Equipment	171
Freezer, Ice Cream	Food Preparation Equipment	153
Freezer, Upright	Food Storage Equipment	171
Freezer, Walk-In	Food Storage Equipment	171
Freighter, Bulk	Watercraft	446
Freshener, Air	Other Household Accessories	66
fret, meat (*use:* Maul, Meat)	Food Preparation Equipment	156
Fretsaw	Woodworking T&E	257
Fretwork	Art	452
Friend, Bosom	Underwear	103
Frieze	Supporting Elements	16
Frigate	Watercraft	447
Fringe	Needleworking Equipment	237
Frisbee	Toys	521
Frisket	Graphic Equipment	384
frock (*use:* Dress, Chemise)	Main Garments	95
Froe	Woodworking T&E	250
Froe, Cooper's	Woodworking T&E	250
Froe, Knife	Woodworking T&E	250
Froe, Lathmaker's	Woodworking T&E	251
Frog	Needleworking Equipment	236

Term	Category	Page
Frog, Flower	Horticultural Containers	62
Frog, Weapon	Armament Accessories	269
Frontal	Religious Objects	463
Frontispiece	Surface Elements	18
Frontlet	Headwear	93
frontlet (*use:* Superfrontal)	Religious Objects	463
frow (*use:* Froe)	Woodworking T&E	250
Fruit, Artificial	Decorative Furnishings	60
Fryer, Deep	Food Preparation Equipment	154
Fuel, Canned	Food Preparation Equipment	155
Fuller	Metalworking T&E	210
Fuller, Bottom	Metalworking T&E	211
Fuller, Top	Metalworking T&E	211
Funhouse	Cultural & Recreational Structures	29
Funnel	Multiple Use T&E for Materials	227
Funnel, Canning	Food Processing Equipment	165
Funnel, Filter	Labware	293
Funnel, Kitchen	Food Preparation Equipment	155
Funnel, Laboratory	Labware	293
Funnel, Pie	Food Preparation Equipment	155
Funnel, Wax	Glass, Plastics & Clayworking T&E	193
Funnel, Wine	Food Preparation Equipment	155
funnel-horn (*use:* Horn, Funnel)	Acoustical T&E	261
Furnace	Environmental Control Elements	9
furnace, agricultural (*use:* Cooker, Feed)	Feed Processing Equipment	126
Furnace, Annealing	Metalworking T&E	211
Furnace, Blast	Metalworking T&E	211
Furnace, Coal	Environmental Control Elements	9
Furnace, Converter	Metalworking T&E	211
Furnace, Cupola	Metalworking T&E	211
Furnace, Electric	Environmental Control Elements	9
Furnace, Glass	Glass, Plastics & Clayworking T&E	193
Furnace, Hearth	Metalworking T&E	211
Furnace, Metal	Metalworking T&E	211
Furnace, Muffle	Metalworking T&E	211
Furnace, Oil	Environmental Control Elements	9
Furnace, Reverberatory	Metalworking T&E	211
Furnace, Solar	Power Producing Equipment	304
Furnace, Test	Chemical Testing Devices	290
Furnishing, Dollhouse	Toys	521
Furniture, Doll	Toys	520
furniture, dollhouse (*use:* Furnishing, Dollhouse)	Toys	521
Furniture, Kiln	Glass, Plastics & Clayworking T&E	193
fuse (*use:* Breaker, Circuit)	Electrical System Components	300
Fuse, Detonating	Mining & Mineral Harvesting T&E	222
Fuselage	Aerospace Transportation Accessories	409
Fusil	Firearms	281
Futon	Bedding	44
Fuze	Ammunition	264
Gad	Mining & Mineral Harvesting T&E	222
Gadder	Mining & Mineral Harvesting T&E	222
Gaff	Water Transportation Accessories	440
Gaff, Cockfighting	Sports Equipment	514
Gaff, Fish	Fishing Equipment	146
gaff, hay (*use:* Crook, Hay)	Harvesting Equipment	128
Gaff, Sealing	Fishing Equipment	146
Gag	Regulative Devices	348
Gag, Canine	Pet Supplies	141
Gaiter	Footwear	89
Galactometer	Food Processing Equipment	167
Galleon	Watercraft	444
Gallery, Shooting	Game Equipment	503
Galley	Typesetting Equipment	388
Galley, Row	Watercraft	446
Gallipot	Medical Accessories	325
Gallows	Regulative Devices	347
Galosh	Footwear	90
Galvanometer	Electrical & Magnetic Measurement Devices	297
Galvanometer, Blasting	Mining & Mineral Harvesting T&E	222
Galvanoscope	Electrical & Magnetic Measurement Devices	297
Galvanothermometer	Thermal T&E	354
Gambrel	Food Processing Equipment	165
Game	Game Equipment	503
Game, Air Hockey	Game Equipment	505
Game, Arcade	Game Equipment	503
Game, Audio	Game Equipment	504
Game, Bagatelle	Game Equipment	505
Game, Bingo	Game Equipment	503
Game, Board	Game Equipment	503
Game, Bowling	Game Equipment	504
Game, Card	Game Equipment	504
game, carnival (*use:* Game, Arcade)	Game Equipment	503
Game, Carrom	Game Equipment	505

Game, Computer | Game Equipment | 506
Game, Console | Game Equipment | 506
Game, Crokinole | Game Equipment | 505
Game, Dart | Game Equipment | 504
Game, Dexterity | Game Equipment | 504
Game, Dice | Game Equipment | 504
Game, Educational | Game Equipment | 504
Game, Electronic | Game Equipment | 504
Game, Foosball | Game Equipment | 505
Game, Handheld Electronic | Game Equipment | 504
Game, Lotto | Game Equipment | 505
Game, Mechanical | Game Equipment | 505
Game, Memory | Game Equipment | 504
Game, Outdoor | Game Equipment | 505
Game, Paddle Ball | Game Equipment | 505
Game, Party | Game Equipment | 505
Game, Ring Toss | Game Equipment | 505
Game, Role-Playing | Game Equipment | 505
Game, Skee-Ball | Game Equipment | 503
Game, Table | Game Equipment | 505
Game, Tabletop Electronic | Game Equipment | 505
Game, Teletype | Game Equipment | 505
Game, Tile | Game Equipment | 505
Game, Tivoli | Game Equipment | 505
Game, Trivia | Game Equipment | 504
Game, Video | Game Equipment | 506
Game, Word | Game Equipment | 506
Gameboard | Game Equipment | 501
Gangplank | Water Transportation Accessories | 441
Gangway | Architectural Spaces | 1
gangway, nautical (*use:* Gangplank) | Water Transportation Accessories | 437
Gantry | Construction T&E | 296
Gantry, Signal | Transportation Structures | 39
Garage | Outbuildings | 38
Garden, Play | Toys | 522
Gargoyle | Plumbing & Drainage Elements | 13
Garland | Holiday Objects | 458
Garland, Shot | Armament Accessories | 268
Garment, Baptismal | Religious Objects | 463
Garment, Combination | Main Garments | 96
Garment, Foundation | Underwear | 103
Garment, Pet | Pet Supplies | 141
Garniture, Clock | Decorative Furnishings | 60
Garter | Clothing Accessories | 85
Garter, Sock | Clothing Accessories | 85
Garvey | Watercraft | 445
Gasket | Multiple Use T&E for Materials | 227
gasolier (*use:* Fixture, Gas) | Lighting Devices | 68
Gastroscope | Medical Instruments | 328
Gate | Site Features | 20
Gate, Casting | Metalworking T&E | 211
gate, child (*use:* Gate, Safety) | Other Household Accessories | 67
Gate, Pet | Pet Supplies | 141
Gate, Safety | Other Household Accessories | 67
Gate, Ski | Sports Equipment | 517
Gate, Swinging | Recreational Devices | 510
Gatehouse | Dwellings | 32
Gateway | Site Features | 20
gatherer, fruit (*use:* Picker, Fruit) | Harvesting Equipment | 129
Gauchos | Main Garments | 97
Gauge | Weights & Measures T&E | 357
Gauge, Air Pressure | Mechanical Measurement Equipment | 318
gauge, ammonia (*use:* Ammoniameter) | Chemical Testing Devices | 290
Gauge, Armament | Armament Accessories | 269
Gauge, Artillery | Armament Accessories | 269
Gauge, Barrel | Armament Accessories | 269
Gauge, Bevel | Woodworking T&E | 251
Gauge, Boring | Woodworking T&E | 251
Gauge, Bullet | Armament Accessories | 269
Gauge, Butt | Woodworking T&E | 251
Gauge, Cannonball | Armament Accessories | 269
Gauge, Center | Metalworking T&E | 211
Gauge, Clapboard | Woodworking T&E | 251
Gauge, Combination | Woodworking T&E | 251
Gauge, Composing Stick | Typesetting Equipment | 388
Gauge, Crown | Dental Accessories | 321
Gauge, Cutting | Woodworking T&E | 251
Gauge, Depth | Navigational Equipment | 350
Gauge, Dovetail | Woodworking T&E | 251
Gauge, Draw | Leather, Horn & Shellworking T&E | 198
Gauge, Drill | Metalworking T&E | 211
Gauge, Feeler | Weights & Measures T&E | 357
Gauge, Fruit | Harvesting Equipment | 128
gauge, grasshopper (*use:* Gauge, Monkey) | Woodworking T&E | 251
gauge, handrail (*use:* Gauge, Monkey) | Woodworking T&E | 251
Gauge, Hoof | Farrier Equipment | 140
Gauge, Ice | Mining & Mineral Harvesting T&E | 225
Gauge, Knitting Needle | Textile Manufacturing Equipment | 240
Gauge, Leather | Leather, Horn & Shellworking T&E | 198
Gauge, Line | Typesetting Equipment | 388
Gauge, Lobster | Fishing Equipment | 146
Gauge, Marking | Woodworking T&E | 251
Gauge, Metalworking | Metalworking T&E | 211
Gauge, Monkey | Woodworking T&E | 251
Gauge, Mortise | Woodworking T&E | 251
Gauge, Net | Textile Manufacturing Equipment | 240

Gauge, Panel	Woodworking T&E	251
gauge, patternmaker's (*use:* Gauge, Monkey)	Woodworking T&E	251
Gauge, Plate	Graphic Equipment	384
Gauge, Plough	Leather, Horn & Shellworking T&E	198
Gauge, Powder	Armament Accessories	269
Gauge, Precipitation	Meteorological T&E	339
Gauge, Pressure	Mechanical Measurement Equipment	318
Gauge, Rabbet	Woodworking T&E	251
Gauge, Railway	Rail Transportation Accessories	432
gauge, rain (*use:* Ombrometer)	Meteorological T&E	339
Gauge, Ring	Weights & Measures T&E	357
Gauge, Saw	Woodworking T&E	251
Gauge, Screw Pitch	Metalworking T&E	211
gauge, slitting (*use:* Gauge, Cutting)	Woodworking T&E	251
Gauge, Snow	Meteorological T&E	339
Gauge, Splint	Fiberworking T&E	144
Gauge, Stave	Woodworking T&E	251
Gauge, Steam Pressure	Mechanical Measurement Equipment	318
Gauge, Temperature	Thermal T&E	354
Gauge, Thread	Metalworking T&E	211
Gauge, Thumb	Woodworking T&E	251
Gauge, Tire Pressure	Land Transportation Accessories	418
Gauge, Tire Tread	Land Transportation Accessories	418
gauge, track (*use:* Gauge, Railway)	Rail Transportation Accessories	432
Gauge, Turner's	Woodworking T&E	251
Gauge, Type	Typesetting Equipment	388
Gauge, Vacuum	Mechanical Measurement Equipment	318
Gauge, Vent	Armament Accessories	269
Gauge, Water	Weights & Measures T&E	357
Gauge, Wheelwright's	Woodworking T&E	251
Gauge, Wind	Meteorological T&E	339
Gauge, Wire	Metalworking T&E	211
Gauge, Woodworking	Woodworking T&E	251
Gauntlet	Clothing Accessories	85
Gauntlet, Plate	Body Armor	275
Gavel	Organizational Objects	459
Gazebo	Site Features	21
Gazette	Other Documents	486
Gazetteer	Other Documents	480
Gear	Power Transmission Components	305
Gear, Animal Racing	Sports Equipment	512
Gear, Badminton	Sports Equipment	512
Gear, Baseball	Sports Equipment	512
Gear, Basketball	Sports Equipment	513
Gear, Bowling	Sports Equipment	513
Gear, Boxing	Sports Equipment	514
Gear, Bullfighting	Sports Equipment	514
gear, bunker (*use:* Gear, Turnout)	Protective Wear	102
Gear, Climbing	Sports Equipment	514
Gear, Cockfighting	Sports Equipment	514
Gear, Cricket	Sports Equipment	514
Gear, Croquet	Game Equipment	501
Gear, Curling	Sports Equipment	514
Gear, Cycling	Sports Equipment	514
Gear, Fencing	Sports Equipment	514
Gear, Field Hockey	Sports Equipment	515
Gear, Football	Sports Equipment	515
Gear, Golf	Sports Equipment	515
Gear, Gymnastics	Sports Equipment	516
Gear, Handball	Sports Equipment	516
Gear, Hockey	Sports Equipment	516
Gear, Jai Alai	Sports Equipment	516
Gear, Lacrosse	Sports Equipment	516
Gear, Landing	Aerospace Transportation Accessories	409
Gear, Pole Vault	Sports Equipment	518
Gear, Polo	Sports Equipment	517
Gear, Racquetball	Sports Equipment	517
Gear, Rugby	Sports Equipment	517
Gear, Shuffleboard	Game Equipment	502
Gear, Skating	Sports Equipment	517
Gear, Skiing	Sports Equipment	517
Gear, Sled Racing	Sports Equipment	517
Gear, Snowboarding	Sports Equipment	518
Gear, Soccer	Sports Equipment	518
Gear, Squash	Sports Equipment	518
Gear, Stickball	Sports Equipment	518
Gear, Table Tennis	Sports Equipment	518
Gear, Tennis	Sports Equipment	518
Gear, Track and Field	Sports Equipment	518
Gear, Turnout	Protective Wear	102
Gear, Volleyball	Sports Equipment	519
Gear, Water Polo	Sports Equipment	519
Gear, Wrestling	Sports Equipment	519
Generator	Power Producing Equipment	304
Generator, Cockcroft-Walton	Nuclear Physics T&E	341
Generator, Electrostatic	Electrical & Magnetic Measurement Devices	297
Generator, Gasoline	Power Producing Equipment	304
Generator, Sound	Acoustical T&E	261
Generator, Steam	Power Producing Equipment	304
Generator, Thermoelectric	Power Producing Equipment	304
Generator, Van de Graaf	Electrical & Magnetic Measurement Devices	297
Generator, Water	Power Producing Equipment	304

Term	Category	Page
Generator, Wind	Power Producing Equipment	304
Genoa	Water Transportation Accessories	439
Geodescope	Astronomical T&E	284
Geodolite	Surveying Equipment	352
Geoglyph	Site Features	20
Geophone	Geological T&E	307
Geospecimen	Geological T&E	307
Geothermometer	Thermal T&E	354
Germinator	Planting Equipment	132
Geta	Footwear	90
Ghillie	Footwear	90
giant, hydraulic (*use:* Monitor, Hydraulic)	Mining & Mineral Harvesting T&E	223
gibbet (*use:* Gallows)	Regulative Devices	347
Gibus	Headwear	93
Gig	Animal-Powered Vehicles	423
gig (*use:* Spear, Fish)	Edged Weapons	278
Gig, Napping	Textile Manufacturing Equipment	240
gig, teasel (*use:* Gig, Napping)	Textile Manufacturing Equipment	240
Gillnetter	Watercraft	445
Gimbal, Compass	Navigational Equipment	350
Gimlet	Woodworking T&E	251
Gimlet, Artillery	Armament Accessories	269
Gimlet, Fuze	Armament Accessories	269
Gimlet, Gunner's	Armament Accessories	269
Gin	Mechanical Devices	315
gin (*use:* Hoist, Mine)	Mining & Mineral Harvesting T&E	223
Gin, Cotton	Textile Manufacturing Equipment	240
Girandole	Lighting Holders	71
girdle (*use:* Belt, Girdle)	Clothing Accessories	84
Girdle	Underwear	103
Girdle, Panty	Underwear	103
Girt	Supporting Elements	16
Girth	Land Transportation Accessories	421
Gisarme	Edged Weapons	278
Gladius	Edged Weapons	278
Glaive	Edged Weapons	277
Glarimeter	Papermaking T&E	233
glass, ale (*use:* Glass, Malt Beverage)	Drinking Vessels	174
glass, beer (*use:* Glass, Malt Beverage)	Drinking Vessels	174
glass, brandy (*use:* Snifter)	Drinking Vessels	174
Glass, Champagne	Drinking Vessels	174
Glass, Cider	Drinking Vessels	174
glass, coaching (*use:* Cup, Stirrup)	Drinking Vessels	174
Glass, Cocktail	Drinking Vessels	174
Glass, Cordial	Drinking Vessels	174
glass, cupping (*use:* Cup, Bleeding)	Medical Instruments	333
Glass, Custard	Eating Vessels	176
Glass, Dessert	Eating Vessels	176
Glass, Dram	Drinking Vessels	174
Glass, Dressing	Other Furniture	58
Glass, Drinking	Drinking Vessels	174
glass, egg (*use:* Timer, Egg)	Food Preparation Equipment	158
Glass, Flip	Drinking Vessels	174
Glass, Flute	Drinking Vessels	174
Glass, Gin	Drinking Vessels	174
glass, goblet (*use:* Goblet)	Drinking Vessels	174
glass, hock (*use:* Glass, Wine)	Drinking Vessels	174
Glass, Hurricane	Other Lighting Accessories	72
Glass, Jelly	Eating Vessels	176
Glass, Juice	Drinking Vessels	174
Glass, Lemonade	Drinking Vessels	174
glass, liqueur (*use:* Glass, Cordial)	Drinking Vessels	174
glass, looking (*use:* Mirror, Cheval)	Other Furniture	58
Glass, Magnifying	Optical T&E	344
Glass, Malt Beverage	Drinking Vessels	174
Glass, Mead	Drinking Vessels	174
Glass, Measuring	Food Preparation Equipment	156
Glass, Opera	Personal Assistive Objects	108
Glass, Picture Frame	Other Household Accessories	67
Glass, Pier	Other Furniture	58
Glass, Reducing	Optical T&E	344
glass, sherry (*use:* Glass, Wine)	Drinking Vessels	174
Glass, Shot	Drinking Vessels	174
Glass, Soda Fountain	Drinking Vessels	174
Glass, Sweetmeat	Eating Vessels	176
Glass, Syllabub	Drinking Vessels	174
Glass, Toasting	Wedding Objects	466
Glass, Trick	Drinking Vessels	174
Glass, Watch	Labware	293
Glass, Water	Drinking Vessels	174
Glass, Whiskey	Drinking Vessels	174
Glass, Wine	Drinking Vessels	174
Glasses, Data	Peripherals	364
glasses, eye (*use:* Eyeglasses)	Personal Assistive Objects	107
Glasses, Field	Optical T&E	343
Glasses, Safety	Personal Assistive Objects	107
Glaze	Glass, Plastics & Clayworking T&E	193
Glazer	Leather, Horn & Shellworking T&E	198
Glengarry	Headwear	91
Glider	Aircraft	411

Glider, Hang | Aircraft | 411
Glider, Playground | Recreational Devices | 510
Glider, Porch | Seating Furniture | 49
Globe | Graphic Documents | 472
Globe, Celestial | Astronomical T&E | 284
Globe, Lace | Textile Manufacturing Equipment | 240
Globe, Lamp | Other Lighting Accessories | 72
Globe, Rolling | Public Entertainment Devices | 507
Globe, Snow | Decorative Furnishings | 60
Globulimeter | Medical Instruments | 327
Glockenspiel | Musical Instruments | 372
Glove | Clothing Accessories | 85
Glove, Baseball | Sports Equipment | 512
Glove, Batting | Sports Equipment | 512
Glove, Bowling | Sports Equipment | 513
Glove, Boxing | Sports Equipment | 514
Glove, Data | Peripherals | 364
Glove, Disposable | Clothing Accessories | 85
Glove, Driving | Clothing Accessories | 85
Glove, Evening | Clothing Accessories | 85
Glove, Fencing | Sports Equipment | 515
Glove, Field Hockey | Sports Equipment | 515
Glove, Fielder's | Sports Equipment | 512
Glove, Golf | Sports Equipment | 516
Glove, Hockey | Sports Equipment | 516
glove, hockey goalie (*use:* Blocker) | Sports Equipment | 516
Glove, Lacrosse | Sports Equipment | 517
Glove, Ski | Sports Equipment | 517
Glove, Soccer Goalie | Sports Equipment | 518
Glove, Softball | Sports Equipment | 512
Glove, Target Shooter's | Armament Accessories | 269
Glove, Wicket Keeping | Sports Equipment | 514
glove, wired (*use:* Glove, Data) | Peripherals | 364
Glove, Work | Clothing Accessories | 85
Glucometer | Medical Instruments | 328
Gluepot | Woodworking T&E | 251
Gnomon | Timekeeping T&E | 356
goad (*use:* Prod, Stock) | Animal Care Equipment | 137
Goal, Field Hockey | Sports Equipment | 515
Goal, Ice Hockey | Sports Equipment | 516
Goal, Soccer | Sports Equipment | 518
Goal, Water Polo | Sports Equipment | 519
Goalpost | Cultural & Recreational Structures | 30
Goblet | Drinking Vessels | 174
Goffer | Bookbinding Equipment | 382
Goggles | Personal Assistive Objects | 108
Goggles, Aviator's | Personal Assistive Objects | 108
goggles, data (*use:* Glasses, Data) | Peripherals | 364
Goggles, Driving | Personal Assistive Objects | 108
Goggles, Field Hockey | Sports Equipment | 515
Goggles, Night Vision | Personal Assistive Objects | 108
Goggles, Skating | Sports Equipment | 517
Goggles, Snow | Personal Assistive Objects | 108
Goggles, Swim | Recreational Devices | 510
Goggles, Welder's | Personal Assistive Objects | 108
Gondola | Watercraft | 442
Gong | Sound Communication Devices | 391
Gong, Musical | Musical Instruments | 372
Goniometer | Chemical Testing Devices | 290
goniometer (*use:* Finder, Direction) | Navigational Equipment | 350
Goniometer, Medical | Medical Instruments | 328
Goniophotometer | Optical T&E | 344
Gonioscope | Medical Instruments | 329
Good, Grave | Funerary Objects | 456
Good, Trade | Exchange Media | 487
Gorge, Fish | Fishing Equipment | 147
Gorget | Body Armor | 275
gorget (*use:* Pendant, Gorget) | Status Symbols | 497
Gorget, Ornamental | Body Adornments | 81
Goschen | Exchange Media | 488
Gouge, Adjustable | Leather, Horn & Shellworking T&E | 198
Gouge, Bent | Woodworking T&E | 251
Gouge, Bowl | Woodworking T&E | 251
Gouge, Carving | Woodworking T&E | 251
Gouge, Channel | Leather, Horn & Shellworking T&E | 198
Gouge, Firmer | Woodworking T&E | 251
Gouge, Fishtail | Woodworking T&E | 251
Gouge, Fluting | Woodworking T&E | 251
Gouge, Fuze | Armament Accessories | 269
Gouge, Leather | Leather, Horn & Shellworking T&E | 198
Gouge, Paring | Woodworking T&E | 251
Gouge, Parting | Woodworking T&E | 251
Gouge, Turning | Woodworking T&E | 251
Gouge, V | Leather, Horn & Shellworking T&E | 198
Gouge, Wheelwright's | Woodworking T&E | 251
Gouge, Woodworking | Woodworking T&E | 251
Governor | Power Transmission Components | 305
Governor, Mine Hoist | Mining & Mineral Harvesting T&E | 223
Gown | Main Garments | 95
Gown, Academic | Status Symbols | 498
Gown, Baptismal | Religious Objects | 463
Gown, Barrister's | Status Symbols | 498
gown, christening (*use:* Gown, Baptismal) | Religious Objects | 463
Gown, Dressing | Dressingwear & Nightwear | 88
Gown, Evening | Main Garments | 96
Gown, Geneva | Status Symbols | 499
Gown, Hospital | Dressingwear & Nightwear | 88
gown, night (*use:* Nightgown) | Dressingwear & Nightwear | 88

Term	Category	Page
Gown, Open	Main Garments	95
gown, pulpit (*use:* Gown, Geneva)	Status Symbols	499
Gown, Round	Main Garments	96
Gown, Scrub	Protective Wear	102
Gown, Tea	Main Garments	96
gown, wedding (*use:* Dress, Wedding)	Wedding Objects	466
Grabber, Fish	Fishing Equipment	146
Grader	Construction T&E	295
grader, bean (*use:* Sorter, Bean)	Food Processing Equipment	164
Grader, Egg	Food Processing Equipment	167
Grader, Fruit	Food Processing Equipment	168
Gradiometer	Surveying Equipment	352
Graduate	Labware	293
Graduator	Drafting T&E	366
Grager	Religious Objects	463
Graille	Leather, Horn & Shellworking T&E	201
grainer (*use:* Comb, Graining)	Painting T&E	229
Grammar	Instructional Documents	475
Gramophone	Sound Communication Devices	392
Granary	Agricultural Structures	23
Grandstand	Cultural & Recreational Structures	30
Granometer	Biological T&E	287
Grapeshot	Ammunition	264
Graph	Graphic Documents	472
Graphometer	Surveying Equipment	352
Graphoscope	Visual Communication Devices	400
Graphotype	Metalworking T&E	210
Grapnel	Mining & Mineral Harvesting T&E	223
Grapple	Mechanical Devices	315
Grate, Fireplace	Heating Equipment Accessories	76
Grate, Hot Shot	Armament Accessories	269
Grate, Register	Barrier Elements	2
Grate, Stove	Heating Equipment Accessories	76
Grate, Tree	Site Features	21
Grater	Food Preparation Equipment	158
Grater, Bread	Food Preparation Equipment	158
Grater, Cheese	Food Preparation Equipment	158
grater, nutmeg (*use:* Grater, Spice)	Food Preparation Equipment	158
Grater, Soap	Laundry Equipment	313
Grater, Spice	Food Preparation Equipment	158
Grater, Tobacco	Smoking & Recreational Drug Equipment	114
grating (*use:* Grille)	Barrier Elements	2
Gravehouse	Ceremonial Structures	25
graver (*use:* Burin)	Graphic Equipment	384
Graver, Metal	Metalworking T&E	211
Graver, Stone	Masonry & Stoneworking T&E	204
gravestone (*use:* Tombstone)	Funerary Objects	457
Gravimeter	Mechanical Measurement Equipment	318
Greaser, Pan	Food Preparation Equipment	155
Greatcoat	Outerwear	100
Greave	Body Armor	275
greenback (*use:* Note, United States)	Exchange Media	489
Greenhouse	Agricultural Structures	23
Grenade	Ammunition	264
Grenade, Antipersonnel	Ammunition	264
Grenade, Antitank	Ammunition	264
Grenade, Hand	Ammunition	264
Grenade, Incendiary	Ammunition	264
Grenade, Rifle	Ammunition	264
Grenade, Smoke	Ammunition	264
Grenade, Tear Gas	Ammunition	264
Griddle	Food Preparation Equipment	154
Gridiron	Food Preparation Equipment	163
Grill	Food Preparation Equipment	154
Grill, Charcoal	Food Preparation Equipment	154
Grill, Electric	Food Preparation Equipment	154
Grill, Gas	Food Preparation Equipment	154
Grille	Barrier Elements	2
Grille, Ventilator	Barrier Elements	2
Grille, Window	Barrier Elements	2
grinder (*use:* Chipper)	Papermaking T&E	232
Grinder, Alfalfa	Feed Processing Equipment	126
Grinder, Bone	Feed Processing Equipment	126
Grinder, Bran	Food Processing Equipment	168
Grinder, Card	Textile Manufacturing Equipment	240
grinder, coffee (*use:* Mill, Coffee)	Food Preparation Equipment	160
Grinder, Cylindrical	Metalworking T&E	211
Grinder, Feed	Feed Processing Equipment	126
Grinder, Food	Food Preparation Equipment	160
Grinder, Herb	Food Preparation Equipment	160
Grinder, Meat	Food Preparation Equipment	160
Grinder, Metal	Metalworking T&E	211

grinder, middlings (*use:* Mill, Middlings)	Food Processing Equipment	169
Grinder, Mower Knife	Metalworking T&E	211
Grinder, Paint	Painting T&E	229
Grinder, Planer Knife	Metalworking T&E	211
Grinder, Soil	Cultivation Equipment	123
grinder, spice (*use:* Mill, Spice)	Food Preparation Equipment	160
Grinder, Stump	Groundskeeping Equipment	309
Grinder, Surface	Metalworking T&E	211
Grinder, Tool	Metalworking T&E	211
Grinder, Valve	Metalworking T&E	211
Grindstone	Metalworking T&E	211
grip, besom (*use:* Horse, Broom)	Fiberworking T&E	144
Gripper	Mechanical Devices	315
Gripper, Hand	Recreational Devices	509
Grisett	Other Lighting Accessories	72
Grizzly	Mining & Mineral Harvesting T&E	224
Groma	Surveying Equipment	352
Grommet	Needleworking Equipment	236
Groover	Masonry & Stoneworking T&E	204
Groover, Hand	Metalworking T&E	211
Groover, Hoof	Farrier Equipment	139
Groover, Stitching	Leather, Horn & Shellworking T&E	198
Grout	Construction Materials	3
Growler	Electrical Maintenance & Repair Equipment	299
Growler, Beer	Serving Vessels	189
grozer (*use:* Pliers, Glass)	Glass, Plastics & Clayworking T&E	194
G-String	Underwear	103
Guaranty	Legal Documents	476
Guard, Arm	Armament Accessories	269
Guard, Batting Helmet	Sports Equipment	513
Guard, Chest	Sports Equipment	519
Guard, Ear	Sports Equipment	519
Guard, Eye	Sports Equipment	519
Guard, Fingernail	Personal Assistive Objects	108
Guard, Foot	Sports Equipment	519
Guard, Hand	Personal Assistive Objects	108
Guard, Hanger	Clothing Care Objects	105
Guard, Hoof	Farrier Equipment	139
Guard, Key	Personal Carrying & Storage Gear	113
Guard, Knuckle	Armament Accessories	269
Guard, Leg	Sports Equipment	513
Guard, Lingerie	Clothing Accessories	84
Guard, Neck	Sports Equipment	513
Guard, Pant	Clothing Accessories	85
Guard, Pants	Clothing Care Objects	105
Guard, Shin	Sports Equipment	519
Guard, Skate	Sports Equipment	517
guard, spark (*use:* Screen, Fire)	Heating Equipment Accessories	76
Guard, Sword	Armament Accessories	269
Guard, Trigger	Armament Accessories	269
guard, trouser (*use:* Guard, Pant)	Clothing Accessories	85
Guard, Weapon	Armament Accessories	269
Guard, Wrist	Armament Accessories	269
Guardhouse	Defense Structures	31
Guardrail	Site Features	20
Guernsey	Main Garments	99
Guestbook	Other Documents	483
Guesthouse	Dwellings	32
Guide, Buttonhole	Needleworking Equipment	235
Guide, Lettering	Writing Accessories	404
Guide, Seam	Needleworking Equipment	235
Guide, Sharpening	Metalworking T&E	211
Guideboat	Watercraft	442
Guideboat, Adirondack	Watercraft	442
Guidebook	Instructional Documents	475
Guidepost	Visual Communication Devices	401
Guidon	Organizational Objects	459
Guillotine	Regulative Devices	347
guillotine, paper (*use:* Machine, Paper Cutting)	Papermaking T&E	232
Guillotine, Paper	Printing Accessories	386
guimpe (*use:* Chemisette)	Main Garments	95
Guinea	Exchange Media	488
Guitar	Musical Instruments	373
Guitar, 12-String	Musical Instruments	373
Guitar, Bass	Musical Instruments	373
guitar, dobro (*use:* Guitar, Resonator)	Musical Instruments	373
Guitar, Electric	Musical Instruments	373
Guitar, Resonator	Musical Instruments	373
Guitar, Steel	Musical Instruments	373
Guitar, Tenor	Musical Instruments	373
Gum, Bee	Animal Care Equipment	136
Gun, Air	Firearms	280
Gun, Animal Marking	Animal Care Equipment	136
Gun, Antiaircraft	Artillery	274
Gun, Antitank	Artillery	274
Gun, Balling	Veterinary Equipment	142
Gun, BB	Firearms	280
Gun, Bellows	Firearms	280
gun, bird (*use:* Fowler)	Firearms	282
Gun, Bomb	Firearms	280
gun, burp (*use:* Gun, Submachine)	Firearms	280
Gun, Calking	Multiple Use T&E for Materials	227
Gun, Cane	Firearms	280
Gun, Cap	Toys	521
gun, capture (*use:* Gun, Tranquilizer)	Firearms	280
Gun, Combination	Firearms	280
Gun, Dart	Firearms	280

gun, dose (*use:* Drencher)	Veterinary Equipment	142
gun, dusting (*use:* Duster, Powder)	Tending Equipment	133
Gun, Field	Artillery	274
Gun, Flare	Visual Communication Devices	400
Gun, Folding	Firearms	280
Gun, Garrison	Artillery	274
Gun, Gatling	Firearms	280
gun, grease (*use:* Gun, Submachine)	Firearms	280
Gun, Grease	Land Transportation Accessories	421
Gun, Harpoon	Firearms	280
Gun, Hunting	Firearms	280
gun, insect powder (*use:* Duster, Powder)	Tending Equipment	133
Gun, Laser Tag	Toys	521
Gun, Line-Throwing	Water Transportation Accessories	441
Gun, Livestock Tattoo	Animal Care Equipment	136
Gun, Lyle	Water Transportation Accessories	441
Gun, Machine	Firearms	280
Gun, Naval	Artillery	274
Gun, Paintball	Toys	521
Gun, Pellet	Firearms	280
Gun, Piercing	Beauty Supplies	117
gun, pneumatic (*use:* Gun, Air)	Firearms	280
Gun, Price Label	Merchandising T&E	337
Gun, Pump-Up	Firearms	280
Gun, Punt	Firearms	282
Gun, Radar	Mechanical Measurement Equipment	319
Gun, Railway	Artillery	274
gun, rapid-fire (*use:* Gun, Machine)	Firearms	280
Gun, Recoilless	Artillery	274
Gun, Riot	Firearms	280
Gun, Sea-Coast	Artillery	274
Gun, Self-Propelled	Artillery	274
Gun, Siege	Artillery	274
Gun, Soldering	Metalworking T&E	211
Gun, Spear	Firearms	280
Gun, Spray	Painting T&E	229
Gun, Spring Air	Firearms	280
gun, squirt (*use:* Gun, Water)	Toys	521
Gun, Staple	Multiple Use T&E for Materials	227
Gun, Stud	Construction T&E	295
Gun, Stun	Firearms	280
Gun, Submachine	Firearms	280
Gun, Swivel	Artillery	274
Gun, Tagging	Merchandising T&E	337
gun, tattoo (*use:* Gun, Livestock Tattoo)	Animal Care Equipment	136
gun, tattoo (*use:* Machine, Tattoo)	Beauty Supplies	117
Gun, Tear Gas	Firearms	280
Gun, Toy	Toys	521
Gun, Toy Air	Toys	521
Gun, Toy Dart	Toys	521
Gun, Tranquilizer	Firearms	280
Gun, Volley	Artillery	274
Gun, Wall	Firearms	280
Gun, Water	Toys	521
gun, whaling (*use:* Gun, Harpoon)	Firearms	280
Gunboat, Patrol	Watercraft	447
Gundalow	Watercraft	446
Gunflint	Armament Accessories	269
Gunpowder	Ammunition	264
Gurdy	Fishing Equipment	146
Gurney	Human-Powered Vehicles	426
Gutter	Plumbing & Drainage Elements	12
Guy	Multiple Use T&E for Materials	226
Gym, Home	Recreational Devices	509
gym, jungle (*use:* Junglegym)	Recreational Devices	510
Gymnasium	Cultural & Recreational Structures	30
Gyrocompass	Navigational Equipment	349
Gyrocompass, Aircraft	Aerospace Transportation Accessories	409
Gyrojet	Firearms	280
Gyroscope	Mechanical Measurement Equipment	318
Gyrostat	Mechanical Measurement Equipment	318
Habit	Status Symbols	498
Habit, Monk's	Status Symbols	499
Habit, Nun's	Status Symbols	499
Habit, Riding	Main Garments	99
Habitat, Pet	Pet Supplies	141
Hack	Animal-Powered Vehicles	423
Hack, Turpentine	Forestry T&E	190
Hackamore	Land Transportation Accessories	419
hackle (*use:* Hatchel)	Textile Manufacturing Equipment	239
Hacksaw	Metalworking T&E	216
haemacytometer (*use:* Hemocytometer)	Biological T&E	287
haematometer (*use:* Hemocytometer)	Biological T&E	287
haemoscope (*use:* Hemoscope)	Medical Instruments	327
Haft, Sewing	Leather, Horn & Shellworking T&E	198
Hairbag	Hair Adornments	83
Hairband	Hair Adornments	83

Hairbrush	Hair Care Objects	118
Hairnet	Headwear	92
Hairpiece	Hair Adornments	83
Hairpin	Hair Adornments	83
Hairstick	Hair Adornments	83
Hairwork	Art	452
Halberd	Edged Weapons	278
half-cent (*use:* Cent, Half)	Exchange Media	487
half-dime (*use:* Dime, Half)	Exchange Media	487
half-dollar (*use:* Dollar, Half)	Exchange Media	488
Half-Figure	Decorative Furnishings	60
half-model (*use:* Model, Half)	Other Documents	484
Halfpenny	Exchange Media	488
Hall, Assembly	Civic & Social Structures	26
Hall, Bingo	Cultural & Recreational Structures	29
Hall, Concert	Cultural & Recreational Structures	29
Hall, Dance	Cultural & Recreational Structures	29
Hall, Drill	Defense Structures	31
Hall, Grange	Civic & Social Structures	26
Hall, Pool	Cultural & Recreational Structures	29
Hall, Town	Civic & Social Structures	26
Hall, Union	Civic & Social Structures	26
Hallstand	Support Furniture	55
hall-tree (*use:* Tree, Coat)	Support Furniture	55
Halometer	Chemical Testing Devices	290
Halter	Land Transportation Accessories	419
halter (*use:* Top, Halter)	Main Garments	99
Halter, Show	Animal Care Equipment	135
Halyard	Water Transportation Accessories	439
Ham, Tailor's	Needleworking Equipment	235
Hame	Land Transportation Accessories	420
Hame, Covered	Land Transportation Accessories	420
Hame, Plated	Land Transportation Accessories	420
Hammer	Woodworking T&E	251
hammer, adz eye (*use:* Hammer, Claw)	Woodworking T&E	251
Hammer, Ax	Masonry & Stoneworking T&E	204
Hammer, Backing	Bookbinding Equipment	382
Hammer, Ball-Peen	Metalworking T&E	211
Hammer, Blast	Metalworking T&E	211
Hammer, Board	Metalworking T&E	211
Hammer, Brick	Masonry & Stoneworking T&E	204
Hammer, Broom Maker's	Fiberworking T&E	144
hammer, bush (*use:* Bushhammer)	Masonry & Stoneworking T&E	204
Hammer, Chipping	Metalworking T&E	211
Hammer, Claw	Woodworking T&E	251
Hammer, Clench	Woodworking T&E	251
Hammer, Cobbler's	Leather, Horn & Shellworking T&E	198
Hammer, Cooper's	Woodworking T&E	251
Hammer, Crandall	Masonry & Stoneworking T&E	204
Hammer, Cross-Peen	Metalworking T&E	211
Hammer, Dental	Dental Instruments	323
Hammer, Driving	Farrier Equipment	139
Hammer, Drop	Metalworking T&E	211
hammer, engineer's (*use:* Hammer, Ball-Peen)	Metalworking T&E	211
Hammer, Face	Masonry & Stoneworking T&E	204
Hammer, Farrier's	Farrier Equipment	139
Hammer, File-Cutting	Metalworking T&E	212
Hammer, Fitting	Farrier Equipment	139
hammer, flooring (*use:* Hammer, Clench)	Woodworking T&E	251
Hammer, Foot-Powered	Metalworking T&E	212
Hammer, Forging	Metalworking T&E	212
Hammer, Framing	Woodworking T&E	251
Hammer, Hand	Mining & Mineral Harvesting T&E	222
Hammer, Heel	Leather, Horn & Shellworking T&E	198
Hammer, Helve	Metalworking T&E	212
Hammer, Ironing	Metalworking T&E	212
Hammer, Jeweler's	Metalworking T&E	212
Hammer, Joiner's	Woodworking T&E	251
hammer, killing (*use:* Hammer, Slaughtering)	Food Processing Equipment	165
Hammer, Knapping	Masonry & Stoneworking T&E	204
Hammer, Leatherworking	Leather, Horn & Shellworking T&E	198
Hammer, Marking	Forestry T&E	190
Hammer, Mason's	Masonry & Stoneworking T&E	204
hammer, meat (*use:* Maul, Meat)	Food Preparation Equipment	156
Hammer, Medical	Medical Instruments	328
Hammer, Metalworking	Metalworking T&E	211
Hammer, Patent	Masonry & Stoneworking T&E	204
Hammer, Patternmaker's	Woodworking T&E	251
Hammer, Percussion	Musical Accessories	368
Hammer, Pewterer's	Metalworking T&E	212
Hammer, Pick	Mining & Mineral Harvesting T&E	223
Hammer, Planishing	Metalworking T&E	212

Hammer, Plow	Metalworking T&E	212
hammer, power (*use:* Drill, Percussive)	Construction T&E	295
Hammer, Railroad Spike	Rail Transportation Accessories	432
Hammer, Raising	Metalworking T&E	212
Hammer, Reflex	Medical Instruments	328
Hammer, Riveting	Metalworking T&E	212
hammer, roofing (*use:* Hammer, Clench)	Woodworking T&E	251
hammer, rounding (*use:* Hammer, Turning)	Metalworking T&E	212
Hammer, Saddler's	Leather, Horn & Shellworking T&E	198
Hammer, Set	Metalworking T&E	212
Hammer, Setting	Metalworking T&E	212
Hammer, Sharpening	Metalworking T&E	212
hammer, ship's maul (*use:* Hammer, Top Maul)	Woodworking T&E	252
hammer, shoeing (*use:* Hammer, Driving)	Farrier Equipment	139
Hammer, Shoemaker's	Leather, Horn & Shellworking T&E	198
hammer, shoe-turning (*use:* Hammer, Turning)	Metalworking T&E	212
Hammer, Slater's	Masonry & Stoneworking T&E	204
Hammer, Slaughtering	Food Processing Equipment	165
hammer, sledge (*use:* Sledgehammer)	Metalworking T&E	212
hammer, sound (*use:* Sounder, Telegraph)	Telecommunication Devices	396
Hammer, Spalling	Masonry & Stoneworking T&E	204
hammer, steak (*use:* Maul, Meat)	Food Preparation Equipment	156
Hammer, Steam	Metalworking T&E	212
Hammer, Stone	Masonry & Stoneworking T&E	204
Hammer, Straight-Peen	Metalworking T&E	212
hammer, striking (*use:* Sledgehammer)	Metalworking T&E	212
Hammer, Sugar	Serving Utensils	184
Hammer, Swage	Metalworking T&E	212
Hammer, Tack	Woodworking T&E	252
Hammer, Throwing	Sports Equipment	519
Hammer, Tilt	Metalworking T&E	212
Hammer, Top Maul	Woodworking T&E	252
Hammer, Trimmer's	Woodworking T&E	252
hammer, trip (*use:* Hammer, Helve)	Metalworking T&E	212
Hammer, Turning	Metalworking T&E	212
Hammer, Turn-Shoe	Leather, Horn & Shellworking T&E	198
Hammer, Veneer	Woodworking T&E	252
Hammer, War	Percussive Weapons	283
Hammer, Welding	Metalworking T&E	212
Hammer, Xylophone	Musical Accessories	368
hammermill (*use:* Mill, Hammer)	Food Processing Equipment	169
hammerstone (*use:* Mortar, Food)	Food Preparation Equipment	160
Hammerstone	Masonry & Stoneworking T&E	204
Hammock	Sleeping & Reclining Furniture	51
Hamper	Laundry Equipment	313
Hamper, Picnic	Food Service Accessories	180
Hand, Artificial	Personal Assistive Objects	109
hand, butter (*use:* Hand, Scotch)	Food Preparation Equipment	157
Hand, Helping	Metalworking T&E	213
Hand, Scotch	Food Preparation Equipment	157
handbag (*use:* Purse)	Personal Carrying & Storage Gear	111
Handball	Sports Equipment	516
Handbell	Musical Instruments	372
Handbill	Advertising Media	450
handbook (*use:* Manual)	Instructional Documents	475
Handcar	Rail Vehicles	434
Handcart	Human-Powered Vehicles	426
Handcuff	Regulative Devices	348
handgun (*use:* Pistol)	Firearms	281
handgun (*use:* Revolver)	Firearms	281
Handkerchief	Personal Assistive Objects	108
Handle, Controller	Rail Transportation Accessories	431
Handle, Dental	Dental Instruments	323
Handle, Door	Finish Hardware	11
Handle, Traction	Medical Instruments	330
Handpiece, Dental	Dental Instruments	323
Handpress	Replication Equipment	387
Handrail	Barrier Elements	2
handsaw (*use:* Saw, Hand)	Woodworking T&E	258
Handspike	Mechanical Devices	316
Handspike, Gunner's	Armament Accessories	269
Handsteel	Mining & Mineral Harvesting T&E	222
Handstone	Food Processing Equipment	168
Hangar	Transportation Structures	39
Hanger	Storage & Display Accessories	63
Hanger, Clothes	Clothing Care Objects	105
Hanger, Door	Advertising Media	450
Hanger, Film	Photoprocessing Equipment	381
Hanger, Hosiery	Laundry Equipment	313
hanger, lamp (*use:* Holder, Lamp)	Lighting Holders	71

Hanger, Pants Clothing Care Objects 105
Hanger, Picture Storage & Display Accessories 63
Hanger, Plant Storage & Display Accessories 63
Hanger, Plate Storage & Display Accessories 63
Hanger, Shaft Power Transmission Components 305
Hanger, Skirt Clothing Care Objects 105
Hanging, Bed Bedding 44
Hanging, Wall Decorative Furnishings 60
Hank, Jib Water Transportation Accessories 439
Harbick Textile Manufacturing Equipment 240
Hardware, Door Finish Hardware 11
Hardware, Harness Land Transportation Accessories 420
Hardware, Vehicle Land Transportation Accessories 417
Hardware, Window Finish Hardware 11
Hardy Metalworking T&E 212
Hardy, Half Round Metalworking T&E 212
Hardy, Side Cut Metalworking T&E 212
Hardy, Straight Metalworking T&E 212
Harmonica Musical Instruments 375
Harmonica, Glass Musical Instruments 371
harmonium (*use:* Organ, Reed) Musical Instruments 371
Harmonometer Acoustical T&E 261
Harness, Animal Land Transportation Accessories 420
Harness, Buggy Land Transportation Accessories 420
Harness, Casting Animal Care Equipment 135
Harness, Climbing Sports Equipment 514
Harness, Dog Land Transportation Accessories 420
Harness, Donkey Land Transportation Accessories 420
Harness, Express Land Transportation Accessories 420
Harness, Farm Land Transportation Accessories 420
Harness, Foot Public Entertainment Devices 507
harness, heavy truck (*use:* Harness, Express) Land Transportation Accessories 420
Harness, Horse Land Transportation Accessories 420
Harness, Marking Breeding Equipment 138
Harness, Ox Land Transportation Accessories 420
Harness, Pony Land Transportation Accessories 420
Harness, Runabout Land Transportation Accessories 420
Harness, Safety Regulative Devices 348
harness, team (*use:* Harness, Farm) Land Transportation Accessories 420
Harness, Track Land Transportation Accessories 420
Harp Musical Instruments 373
Harp, Aeolian Musical Instruments 374
harp, aluminum (*use:* Harp, Friction) Musical Instruments 371
Harp, Celtic Musical Instruments 374
Harp, Friction Musical Instruments 371
Harp, Jaw Musical Instruments 372
harp, Jews' (*use:* Harp, Jaw) Musical Instruments 372
Harp, Lamp Other Lighting Accessories 72
Harp, Pedal Musical Instruments 374
Harpoon Edged Weapons 277
Harpoon, Single Flue Edged Weapons 277
Harpoon, Toggling Edged Weapons 277
Harpoon, Two Flue Edged Weapons 277
Harpsichord Musical Instruments 371
Harquebus Firearms 280
Harrow Cultivation Equipment 123
Harrow, Acme Cultivation Equipment 123
Harrow, Disk Cultivation Equipment 124
harrow, drag (*use:* Harrow, Spike-tooth) Cultivation Equipment 124
Harrow, Spading Cultivation Equipment 124
Harrow, Spike-Tooth Cultivation Equipment 124
Harrow, Spring-Tooth Cultivation Equipment 124
Harrow, Tine-Tooth Cultivation Equipment 124
Harvester Harvesting Equipment 128
Harvester, Bean Harvesting Equipment 128
Harvester, Carrot Harvesting Equipment 128
harvester, combine (*use:* Combine) Harvesting Equipment 128
Harvester, Corn Harvesting Equipment 129
Harvester, Forage Harvesting Equipment 129
Harvester, Onion Harvesting Equipment 129
Harvester, Potato Harvesting Equipment 129
Harvester, Sugar Beet Harvesting Equipment 129
Harvester, Sugarcane Harvesting Equipment 129
Harvester, Tomato Harvesting Equipment 129
harvester-thresher (*use:* Combine) Harvesting Equipment 128
hasher (*use:* Grinder, Meat) Food Preparation Equipment 160
Hasp Finish Hardware 10
Hassock Seating Furniture 49
Hat Headwear 92
Hat, Alpine Headwear 92
Hat, Beekeper's Headwear 93
Hat, Bergère Headwear 93
Hat, Campaign Headwear 92
Hat, Castor Headwear 92
hat, chef's (*use:* Toque) Headwear 92

Term	Category	Page
Hat, Cocked	Headwear	92
Hat, Conductor	Headwear	92
Hat, Cowboy	Headwear	92
hat, derby (*use:* Derby)	Headwear	92
Hat, Ecclesiastical	Status Symbols	499
Hat, Fraternal	Status Symbols	496
Hat, Hard	Headwear	94
hat, homberg (*use:* Homberg)	Headwear	93
Hat, Jungle	Headwear	92
Hat, Kettle	Body Armor	275
Hat, Magic	Public Entertainment Devices	508
Hat, Mushroom	Headwear	92
hat, opera (*use:* Gibus)	Headwear	93
Hat, Panama	Headwear	93
Hat, Party	Party Accessories	460
Hat, Picture	Headwear	93
Hat, Pillbox	Headwear	93
Hat, Pork Pie	Headwear	93
Hat, Rain	Headwear	93
hat, safety (*use:* Hat, Hard)	Headwear	94
Hat, Shovel	Headwear	93
Hat, Slouch	Headwear	93
Hat, Snap-Brim	Headwear	93
Hat, Straw	Headwear	93
Hat, Sun	Headwear	93
Hat, Top	Headwear	93
Hatband	Clothing Accessories	86
Hatbox	Personal Carrying & Storage Gear	111
Hatchback	Motor Vehicles	428
Hatchel	Textile Manufacturing Equipment	239
Hatchel, Wigmaker's	Fiberworking T&E	144
Hatcher, Poultry	Breeding Equipment	138
Hatchet	Woodworking T&E	247
Hatchet, Candy	Food Preparation Equipment	158
Hatchet, Claw	Woodworking T&E	247
Hatchet, Dental	Dental Instruments	323
Hatchet, Hewing	Woodworking T&E	247
Hatchet, Lathing	Woodworking T&E	247
Hatchet, Shingling	Woodworking T&E	247
Hatpin	Clothing Accessories	86
hatstand (*use:* Stand, Hat)	Support Furniture	55
Hauberk	Body Armor	275
hautboy (*use:* Oboe)	Musical Instruments	375
Havelock	Headwear	93
Haversack	Personal Carrying & Storage Gear	110
Haversack, Gunner's	Armament Accessories	269
Hawk	Masonry & Stoneworking T&E	205
Hawser	Water Transportation Accessories	441
Hayfork	Harvesting Equipment	129
hay-loader (*use:* Loader, Hay)	Harvesting Equipment	130
hay-loader, bale (*use:* Loader, Bale Hay)	Harvesting Equipment	130
Head, Casing	Mining & Mineral Harvesting T&E	223
Head, Doll	Toys	521
Head, Shower	Plumbing & Drainage Elements	12
head, trophy (*use:* Trophy, Game)	Achievement Symbols	492
Headband	Headwear	93
Headband, Tightening	Regulative Devices	347
Headboard	Sleeping & Reclining Furniture	50
Headcloth	Headwear	93
Headcloth, Bed	Bedding	44
Headdress	Status Symbols	499
Headdress, Roach	Status Symbols	499
Header, Barrel	Woodworking T&E	252
Header, Bolt	Metalworking T&E	218
Header, Grain	Harvesting Equipment	129
Header, Nail	Metalworking T&E	218
Headgear, Orthodontic	Dental Instruments	322
headkerchief (*use:* Kerchief)	Headwear	93
Headlamp	Land Transportation Accessories	417
Headlamp, Locomotive	Rail Transportation Accessories	431
Headphone	Sound Communication Devices	391
Headpiece	Headwear	94
Headrest	Bedding	44
Headrest, Photographer's	Photographic Accessories	378
Headring	Personal Assistive Objects	107
Headsail	Water Transportation Accessories	439
Headscarf	Headwear	93
Headset	Telecommunication Devices	396
Headset, Radio	Telecommunication Accessories	394
Headstall	Land Transportation Accessories	420
Headstone	Funerary Objects	457
Headtie	Headwear	93
Hearse, Candle	Funerary Objects	456
Hearse, Horse-Drawn	Animal-Powered Vehicles	423
Hearse, Motor	Motor Vehicles	428
Hearth	Environmental Control Elements	8
Hearth, Front	Environmental Control Elements	8
Hearthstone	Environmental Control Elements	8
heat, canned (*use:* Fuel, Canned)	Food Preparation Equipment	155

Heater — Heating & Cooling Equipment 75
Heater, Alcohol — Heating & Cooling Equipment 75
heater, baseboard (*use:* Unit, Baseboard) — Environmental Control Elements 9
Heater, Block — Land Transportation Accessories 417
Heater, Branding Iron — Metalworking T&E 212
Heater, Calrod — Glass, Plastics & Clayworking T&E 193
Heater, Coal — Heating & Cooling Equipment 75
Heater, Convention — Environmental Control Elements 9
Heater, Curling Iron — Hair Care Objects 118
Heater, Electric — Heating & Cooling Equipment 75
Heater, Fan — Heating & Cooling Equipment 75
Heater, Gas — Heating & Cooling Equipment 75
Heater, Iron — Laundry Equipment 313
Heater, Kerosene — Heating & Cooling Equipment 75
Heater, Lamp — Heating & Cooling Equipment 75
Heater, Milk — Food Processing Equipment 166
Heater, Oil — Heating & Cooling Equipment 75
Heater, Orchard — Tending Equipment 133
Heater, Radiant — Heating & Cooling Equipment 75
Heater, Strip — Glass, Plastics & Clayworking T&E 193
Heater, Thermoforming — Glass, Plastics & Clayworking T&E 193
Heater, Vehicle — Land Transportation Accessories 417
Heater, Water — Plumbing & Drainage Elements 12
heater, wheat (*use:* Conditioner, Wheat) — Food Processing Equipment 168
Heater, Wood — Heating & Cooling Equipment 75
Heaume — Body Armor 275
Heaver — Mechanical Devices 315
Heaver, Stitch — Needleworking Equipment 235
heckle (*use:* Hatchel) — Textile Manufacturing Equipment 239
Hectograph — Replication Equipment 387
Heddle — Textile Manufacturing Equipment 240
Helicograph — Drafting T&E 366
Helicon — Musical Instruments 370
Helicopter — Aircraft 412
Heliograph — Visual Communication Devices 400
Heliometer — Astronomical T&E 284
Helioscope — Astronomical T&E 284
Heliostat — Astronomical T&E 285
heliostat (*use:* Heliotrope) — Surveying Equipment 352
Heliotrope — Surveying Equipment 352
Heller — Exchange Media 488
Helm — Body Armor 275
Helmet — Headwear 94
Helmet, Aviator's — Headwear 94
Helmet, Baseball — Sports Equipment 513
Helmet, Batter's — Sports Equipment 513
Helmet, Catcher's — Sports Equipment 513
Helmet, Crash — Headwear 94
Helmet, Cricket — Sports Equipment 514
Helmet, Cycling — Sports Equipment 514
Helmet, Diver's — Recreational Devices 510
Helmet, Fencing — Sports Equipment 515
Helmet, Field Hockey — Sports Equipment 515
Helmet, Firefighter's — Headwear 94
Helmet, Flight — Headwear 94
Helmet, Football — Sports Equipment 515
Helmet, Ice Hockey — Sports Equipment 516
Helmet, Lacrosse — Sports Equipment 517
Helmet, Military — Headwear 94
Helmet, Miner's — Headwear 94
Helmet, Pith — Headwear 94
Helmet, Plate — Body Armor 275
Helmet, Polo — Sports Equipment 517
Helmet, Ski — Sports Equipment 517
Hemocytometer — Biological T&E 287
Hemoglobinometer — Biological T&E 287
Hemoscope — Medical Instruments 327
Hemostat — Medical Instruments 331
Hen, Tappit — Drinking Vessels 174
Hennin — Headwear 94
hetchel (*use:* Hatchel) — Textile Manufacturing Equipment 239
Hibachi — Food Preparation Equipment 153
Hide — Leather, Horn & Shellworking T&E 199
Highboy — Storage & Display Furniture 53
Highchair — Seating Furniture 48
highlighter (*use:* Pen, Marker) — Writing Devices 406
highwheeler (*use:* Bicycle, Ordinary) — Human-Powered Vehicles 426
Hijab — Headwear 93
hilac (*use:* Accelerator, Linear) — Nuclear Physics T&E 341
Hinge — Finish Hardware 11
Hinge, Butt — Finish Hardware 11
Hinge, Strap — Finish Hardware 11
Hiphuggers — Main Garments 97
History — Literary Works 477

Hitch, Trailer — Land Transportation Accessories 418
Hoard — Unclassifiable Objects 527
Hobble — Animal Care Equipment 135
hobbyhorse (*use:* Draisine) — Human-Powered Vehicles 426
Hobbyhorse — Toys 524
Hobnail — Leather, Horn & Shellworking T&E 199
Hod — Masonry & Stoneworking T&E 205
Hod, Coal — Heating Equipment Accessories 77
hodometer (*use:* Wheel, Surveyor's) — Surveying Equipment 353
Hoe — Cultivation Equipment 124
hoe, bog (*use:* Hoe, Grub) — Cultivation Equipment 124
hoe, broad (*use:* Hoe, Garden) — Cultivation Equipment 124
Hoe, Celery — Cultivation Equipment 124
Hoe, Clamming — Fishing Equipment 146
Hoe, Corn — Cultivation Equipment 124
Hoe, Cotton — Cultivation Equipment 124
hoe, cultivator (*use:* Hoe, Weeding) — Cultivation Equipment 125
hoe, Dutch (*use:* Hoe, Scuffle) — Cultivation Equipment 124
Hoe, Garden — Cultivation Equipment 124
Hoe, Grape — Cultivation Equipment 124
hoe, grass (*use:* Hoe, Meadow) — Cultivation Equipment 124
Hoe, Grub — Cultivation Equipment 124
Hoe, Hop — Cultivation Equipment 124
hoe, horse (*use:* Cultivator, Row Crop) — Cultivation Equipment 123
Hoe, Mattock — Cultivation Equipment 124
Hoe, Meadow — Cultivation Equipment 124
hoe, narrow (*use:* Hoe, Grub) — Cultivation Equipment 124
Hoe, Nursery — Cultivation Equipment 124
Hoe, Periodontal — Dental Instruments 323
hoe, plantation (*use:* Hoe, Cotton) — Cultivation Equipment 124
hoe, planter (*use:* Hoe, Cotton) — Cultivation Equipment 124
Hoe, Potato — Harvesting Equipment 129
hoe, rotary (*use:* Tiller, Rotary) — Cultivation Equipment 125
Hoe, Scuffle — Cultivation Equipment 124
hoe, shuffle (*use:* Hoe, Scuffle) — Cultivation Equipment 124
Hoe, Sugar Beet — Cultivation Equipment 124
Hoe, Tobacco — Cultivation Equipment 124
Hoe, Turnip — Cultivation Equipment 124
Hoe, Warren — Cultivation Equipment 124
Hoe, Weeding — Cultivation Equipment 125
hoe, wheel (*use:* Cultivator, Garden) — Cultivation Equipment 123
Hogan — Dwellings 32
Hoist — Mechanical Devices 315
Hoist, Dressing — Food Processing Equipment 165
Hoist, Mine — Mining & Mineral Harvesting T&E 223
Hoist, Mining — Mining & Mineral Harvesting T&E 223
Hoist, Quarry — Mining & Mineral Harvesting T&E 223
holdback (*use:* Tieback) — Window & Door Coverings 78
Holder — Storage & Display Accessories 63
Holder, Ammunition — Armament Accessories 268
Holder, Ampul — Medical Accessories 325
Holder, Bag — Merchandising T&E 337
Holder, Beverage — Food Service Accessories 181
Holder, Bottle — Storage & Display Accessories 63
Holder, Bouquet — Personal Carrying & Storage Gear 113
Holder, Broach — Dental Accessories 321
Holder, Broom — Housekeeping Equipment 312
Holder, Brush — Painting T&E 229
holder, candle (*use:* Candleholder) — Lighting Holders 71
Holder, Card — Game Equipment 502
Holder, Card File — Writing Accessories 402
Holder, Cartridge — Armament Accessories 268
Holder, Casserole — Food Service Accessories 181
Holder, Chalk — Writing Accessories 403
Holder, Cigar — Smoking & Recreational Drug Equipment 114
holder, cigar (*use:* Box, Cigar) — Containers for Smoking & Tobacco 59
Holder, Cigarette — Smoking & Recreational Drug Equipment 114
Holder, Cleaning Brush — Housekeeping Equipment 312
Holder, Clip — Armament Accessories 268
Holder, Clothespin — Laundry Equipment 313
Holder, Coaster — Food Service Accessories 181
Holder, Coin — Personal Carrying & Storage Gear 113
Holder, Corn — Eating & Drinking Utensils 178
Holder, Cow Tail — Animal Care Equipment 135
Holder, Cuff — Clothing Accessories 84
Holder, Cup — Food Service Accessories 181
Holder, Cut Film — Camera Equipment 377
Holder, Dental Bur — Dental Accessories 321
Holder, Dental Equipment — Dental Accessories 321
Holder, Dental Film — Dental Accessories 321
Holder, Dental Instrument — Dental Accessories 321
holder, desk blotter (*use:* Pad, Desk) — Writing Accessories 404

Holder, Die	Metalworking T&E	212
Holder, Drill Bit	Woodworking T&E	252
Holder, Duster	Housekeeping Equipment	312
Holder, Film	Camera Equipment	377
Holder, Fire Extinguisher	Protective Devices	345
holder, fireplace tool (*use:* Stand, Fireset)	Heating Equipment Accessories	76
Holder, Fishhook	Fishing Equipment	145
Holder, Fishing Gear	Fishing Equipment	145
Holder, Fishing Line	Fishing Equipment	145
Holder, Fishing Rod	Fishing Equipment	145
Holder, Flagpole	Organizational Objects	459
Holder, Flash Powder	Camera Equipment	377
Holder, Flax	Textile Manufacturing Equipment	240
Holder, Garden Sphere	Site Features	21
Holder, Grain Bag	Food Processing Equipment	168
Holder, Handkerchief	Personal Carrying & Storage Gear	113
Holder, Hatpin	Personal Carrying & Storage Gear	113
Holder, Hog	Animal Care Equipment	135
Holder, Housekeeping Equipment	Housekeeping Equipment	312
holder, incense (*use:* Censer)	Religious Objects	462
Holder, Insulated Beverage	Food Service Accessories	181
Holder, Label	Writing Accessories	402
Holder, Lamp	Lighting Holders	71
Holder, Letter	Writing Accessories	403
Holder, Marking Stamp	Writing Accessories	403
Holder, Match	Storage & Display Accessories	63
Holder, Medical Supply	Medical Accessories	325
Holder, Menu	Food Service Accessories	181
Holder, Metalworking Tool	Metalworking T&E	212
Holder, Nail	Woodworking T&E	252
Holder, Napkin	Food Service Accessories	181
Holder, Needle	Needleworking Equipment	235
Holder, Needlework	Needleworking Equipment	235
Holder, Nosegay	Personal Carrying & Storage Gear	113
Holder, Page	Writing Accessories	404
holder, paper (*use:* Tray, Paper)	Writing Accessories	403
Holder, Paper Clip	Writing Accessories	403
Holder, Paper Towel	Housekeeping Equipment	312
Holder, Pen	Writing Accessories	403
Holder, Pencil	Writing Accessories	403
Holder, Photograph	Photographic Accessories	378
Holder, Photographic Plate	Camera Equipment	377
Holder, Pipe	Containers for Smoking & Tobacco	59
Holder, Pipe Cleaner	Containers for Smoking & Tobacco	59
Holder, Placecard	Food Service Accessories	181
Holder, Plume	Clothing Accessories	86
Holder, Retort	Labware	293
Holder, Roll Film	Camera Equipment	377
Holder, Rotary Card File	Writing Accessories	402
Holder, Rubber Dam	Dental Accessories	321
Holder, Rushlight	Lighting Holders	71
Holder, Sash	Clothing Accessories	85
Holder, Scarf	Storage & Display Accessories	63
Holder, Scythe Sharpener	Metalworking T&E	212
Holder, Shaving Paper	Hair Care Objects	119
Holder, Sheet Film	Camera Equipment	377
Holder, Shell	Armament Accessories	268
holder, ship's bell (*use:* Bracket, Ship's Bell)	Water Transportation Accessories	436
Holder, Shoe	Storage & Display Accessories	64
Holder, Sign	Visual Communication Accessories	399
Holder, Skewer	Food Preparation Accessories	152
Holder, Slide	Visual Communication Accessories	399
Holder, Soldering Iron	Metalworking T&E	213
Holder, Spill	Storage & Display Accessories	64
Holder, Splint	Lighting Holders	71
Holder, Spool	Needleworking Equipment	235
holder, spoon (*use:* Spooner)	Food Service Accessories	182
holder, stair carpet (*use:* Rod, Stair)	Finish Hardware	11
Holder, Stitch	Textile Manufacturing Equipment	240
Holder, Stocking	Holiday Objects	458
Holder, String	Merchandising T&E	337
Holder, Surgical Needle	Medical Instruments	331
Holder, Tape	Needleworking Equipment	235
Holder, Taper	Lighting Holders	71
Holder, Thimble	Needleworking Equipment	235
Holder, Thread	Needleworking Equipment	235
Holder, Tire Bolt	Metalworking T&E	213
Holder, Tissue	Hygiene Objects	120
holder, tobacco (*use:* Pouch, Tobacco)	Smoking & Recreational Drug Equipment	115
Holder, Toilet Paper	Storage & Display Accessories	64
Holder, Toothbrush	Hygiene Objects	120
Holder, Toothpick	Food Service Accessories	181
Holder, Torch	Lighting Holders	71
Holder, Tree	Holiday Objects	458
holder, umbrella (*use:* Stand, Umbrella)	Support Furniture	55
Holder, Watch	Storage & Display Accessories	64

Holder, Whip	Land Transportation Accessories	418
Holder, Whisk Broom	Housekeeping Equipment	312
Holder, Writing Equipment	Writing Accessories	403
Holder, X-Ray	Medical Accessories	326
Holdfast	Woodworking T&E	252
Hologram	Graphic Documents	472
Holometer	Weights & Measures T&E	357
Holophote	Optical T&E	343
Holster	Armament Accessories	268
Holystone	Housekeeping Equipment	312
Homberg	Headwear	93
Home, Funeral	Ceremonial Structures	25
Home, Mobile	Dwellings	32
Home, Nursing	Institutional Structures	37
Homogenizer, Milk	Food Processing Equipment	166
hone (*use:* Whetstone)	Metalworking T&E	216
Hone, Razor	Hair Care Objects	119
Hood	Headwear	94
Hood, Academic	Status Symbols	498
Hood, Chimney	Environmental Control Elements	8
Hood, Falconry	Animal Care Equipment	135
Hood, Focusing	Camera Equipment	377
Hood, Gallows	Regulative Devices	347
hood, hawking (*use:* Hood, Falconry)	Animal Care Equipment	135
Hood, Lens	Camera Equipment	377
Hood, Stove	Heating Equipment Accessories	76
Hood, Sweat	Animal Care Equipment	134
Hook	Mechanical Devices	315
hook, bagging (*use:* Hook, Reaping)	Harvesting Equipment	129
Hook, Bench	Woodworking T&E	252
hook, bill (*use:* Bill)	Edged Weapons	278
hook, bill (*use:* Billhook)	Groundskeeping Equipment	310
Hook, Blubber	Fishing Equipment	148
Hook, Blunt	Medical Instruments	330
Hook, Boat	Water Transportation Accessories	441
Hook, Boot	Personal Assistive Objects	108
hook, bramble (*use:* Hook, Brush)	Groundskeeping Equipment	309
Hook, Brush	Groundskeeping Equipment	309
hook, bull (*use:* Bullhook)	Animal Care Equipment	136
hook, bush (*use:* Hook, Brush)	Groundskeeping Equipment	309
hook, button (*use:* Buttonhook)	Personal Assistive Objects	107
Hook, Cant	Forestry T&E	190
hook, carcass (*use:* Hook, Meat)	Food Processing Equipment	165
Hook, Cargo	Mechanical Devices	315
Hook, Caulking	Woodworking T&E	252
Hook, Ceiling	Storage & Display Accessories	64
Hook, Chain	Mechanical Devices	315
Hook, Circle	Fishing Equipment	147
Hook, Coat	Storage & Display Accessories	64
Hook, Corn	Harvesting Equipment	129
Hook, Crochet	Textile Manufacturing Equipment	240
Hook, Curtain	Window & Door Coverings	78
Hook, Dough	Food Preparation Equipment	161
Hook, Drill	Harvesting Equipment	129
hook, fagging (*use:* Hook, Reaping)	Harvesting Equipment	129
Hook, Fire	Protective Devices	345
hook, fireplace (*use:* Crane, Fireplace)	Food Preparation Equipment	162
Hook, Forge	Metalworking T&E	213
Hook, Glassworker's	Glass, Plastics & Clayworking T&E	193
Hook, Grab	Mining & Mineral Harvesting T&E	223
Hook, Grappling	Forestry T&E	190
Hook, Grass	Groundskeeping Equipment	309
Hook, Grub	Cultivation Equipment	124
hook, hay (*use:* Crook, Hay)	Harvesting Equipment	128
Hook, Hay Bale	Harvesting Equipment	129
Hook, Hedge	Groundskeeping Equipment	310
Hook, Household	Storage & Display Accessories	64
hook, husking (*use:* Cornhusker, Hand)	Harvesting Equipment	128
Hook, Ice	Mining & Mineral Harvesting T&E	225
Hook, Last	Leather, Horn & Shellworking T&E	198
Hook, Lobster	Fishing Equipment	146
Hook, Logging	Forestry T&E	190
hook, lug (*use:* Carrier, Timber)	Forestry T&E	190
Hook, Manure	Cultivation Equipment	124
Hook, Meat	Food Processing Equipment	165
Hook, Ornament	Holiday Objects	458
Hook, Picture	Storage & Display Accessories	64
hook, pot (*use:* Pothook)	Food Preparation Equipment	163
Hook, Potato	Harvesting Equipment	129
Hook, Pruning	Groundskeeping Equipment	310
Hook, Pullman Porter's	Rail Transportation Accessories	432
Hook, Pulp	Forestry T&E	190
Hook, Raft	Forestry T&E	190
Hook, Reaping	Harvesting Equipment	129
Hook, Reed	Textile Manufacturing Equipment	240

Hook, Rug	Textile Manufacturing Equipment	241
hook, sheer board (*use:* Harbick)	Textile Manufacturing Equipment	240
Hook, Shell	Armament Accessories	269
Hook, Shoelace	Personal Assistive Objects	108
Hook, Sister	Mechanical Devices	315
Hook, Surgical	Medical Instruments	331
Hook, Swamp	Forestry T&E	190
Hook, Swivel	Mechanical Devices	315
Hook, Tambour	Needleworking Equipment	237
Hook, Tendon	Medical Instruments	331
Hook, Tieback	Window & Door Coverings	78
Hook, Towel	Storage & Display Accessories	64
Hook, Wall	Storage & Display Accessories	64
Hook, Wardrobe	Storage & Display Accessories	64
Hook, Weeding	Cultivation Equipment	124
Hookah	Personal Assistive Objects	107
Hookah, Smoking	Smoking & Recreational Drug Equipment	114
Hookaroon	Forestry T&E	190
Hoop, Barrel	Woodworking T&E	252
Hoop, Basketball	Sports Equipment	513
Hoop, Embroidery	Needleworking Equipment	237
Hoop, Hula	Toys	521
Hoop, Mast	Water Transportation Accessories	439
Hoop, Needlework	Needleworking Equipment	237
Hoop, Quilting	Needleworking Equipment	237
Hoop, Rolling	Toys	521
Hoop, Skirt	Underwear	103
Hoop, Toy	Toys	521
Hoop, Train Order	Rail Transportation Accessories	432
hoop, truss (*use:* Hoop, Barrel)	Woodworking T&E	252
Hopper, Grain	Harvesting Equipment	128
hoppit (*use:* Kibble)	Mining & Mineral Harvesting T&E	221
Horizon, Artificial	Aerospace Transportation Accessories	409
horn (*use:* Instrument, Brass)	Musical Instruments	370
Horn	Sound Communication Devices	391
Horn, Alto	Musical Instruments	370
Horn, Baritone	Musical Instruments	370
Horn, Bass	Musical Instruments	370
Horn, Basset	Musical Instruments	374
Horn, Bicycle	Land Transportation Accessories	418
Horn, Buffalo	Leather, Horn & Shellworking T&E	199
Horn, Coach	Sound Communication Devices	391
Horn, Dinner	Sound Communication Devices	391
Horn, Drinking	Drinking Vessels	174
Horn, English	Musical Instruments	375
Horn, French	Musical Instruments	370
Horn, Funnel	Acoustical T&E	261
Horn, Grease	Multiple Use T&E for Materials	227
Horn, Hunting	Sound Communication Devices	391
Horn, Locomotive	Rail Transportation Accessories	431
Horn, Miner's	Mining & Mineral Harvesting T&E	224
Horn, Phonograph	Sound Communication Devices	391
Horn, Post	Sound Communication Devices	391
Horn, Powder	Armament Accessories	267
Horn, Tenor	Musical Instruments	370
horn, train (*use:* Horn, Locomotive)	Rail Transportation Accessories	431
Horn, Vehicle	Land Transportation Accessories	418
Hornbook	Instructional Documents	475
Horometer	Timekeeping T&E	356
Horse, Anvil	Metalworking T&E	207
Horse, Broom	Fiberworking T&E	144
Horse, Clothes	Laundry Equipment	313
Horse, Froe	Woodworking T&E	247
Horse, Hornworker's	Leather, Horn & Shellworking T&E	201
Horse, Pommel	Sports Equipment	516
Horse, Punishment	Regulative Devices	347
Horse, Rocking	Toys	524
horse, saw (*use:* Sawhorse)	Woodworking T&E	259
Horse, Saw-Sharpening	Woodworking T&E	247
Horse, Shaving	Woodworking T&E	247
Horse, Sheet	Water Transportation Accessories	438
horse, shingling (*use:* Horse, Froe)	Woodworking T&E	247
Horse, Side	Sports Equipment	516
horse, stick (*use:* Hobbyhorse)	Toys	524
horse, stitching (*use:* Bench, Harness Maker's)	Leather, Horn & Shellworking T&E	196
Horse, Vaulting	Sports Equipment	516
Horsecar	Rail Vehicles	435
Horseshoe	Farrier Equipment	139
Horseshoe, Pitching	Game Equipment	505
hose (*use:* Hosiery)	Footwear	89

Hose Multiple Use T&E for Materials 227
Hose, Air Multiple Use T&E for Materials 227
Hose, Bath Hygiene Objects 120
Hose, Enema Medical Instruments 330
Hose, Fire Protective Devices 345
Hose, Garden Groundskeeping Equipment 309
Hose, Irrigation Tending Equipment 133
hose, nose (*use:* Airway, Nasopharyngeal) Medical Instruments 335
Hosiery Footwear 89
Hospital Institutional Structures 37
Host Religious Objects 463
Hotel Commercial Structures 27
Hourglass Timekeeping T&E 356
House Dwellings 32
House, Broiler Agricultural Structures 23
House, Brooder Agricultural Structures 23
House, Cape Cod Dwellings 32
House, Carriage Outbuildings 38
House, Charnel Ceremonial Structures 25
House, Clergy Dwellings 32
House, Cow Agricultural Structures 23
house, doll (*use:* Dollhouse) Toys 521
House, Double-Pen Dwellings 32
House, Foursquare Dwellings 32
House, Fraternity Dwellings 32
House, Fruit Drying Agricultural Structures 23
House, Garrison Dwellings 32
house, hog (*use:* House, Swine) Agricultural Structures 23
House, Kitchen Outbuildings 38
House, Manor Dwellings 32
house, pig (*use:* House, Swine) Agricultural Structures 23
House, Pilot Water Transportation Accessories 438
House, Plantation Dwellings 32
House, Potato Agricultural Structures 23
House, Poultry Agricultural Structures 23
house, powder (*use:* Magazine, Powder) Defense Structures 31
House, Ranch Dwellings 32
House, Row Dwellings 32
House, Saltbox Dwellings 32
House, Settlement Institutional Structures 37
House, Shotgun Dwellings 32
House, Single-Pen Dwellings 32
House, Sorority Dwellings 32
House, Split-Level Dwellings 32
House, Sugar Agricultural Structures 23
House, Swine Agricultural Structures 23
house, toll (*use:* Tollhouse) Transportation Structures 40
House, Tree Cultural & Recreational Structures 29
house, well (*use:* Wellhouse) Outbuildings 38
Houseboat Watercraft 444
Housecoat Dressingwear & Nightwear 88
Housewife Needleworking Equipment 235
housing, bearing (*use:* Block, Bearing) Power Transmission Components 305
Housing, Clutch Power Transmission Components 305
Hovercraft Aircraft 412
Howdah Land Transportation Accessories 420
Howitzer Artillery 274
Huarache Footwear 90
Hub, Wheel Land Transportation Accessories 417
Hubcap Land Transportation Accessories 417
Hull Water Transportation Accessories 438
Huller Food Processing Equipment 164
Huller, Nut Food Processing Equipment 164
Huller, Pea Food Processing Equipment 164
Huller, Seed Food Processing Equipment 164
Huller, Strawberry Food Preparation Equipment 160
Humidifier Environmental Control Elements 9
Humidor Containers for Smoking & Tobacco 59
hummeler (*use:* Bearder, Barley) Harvesting Equipment 127
Huntboard Storage & Display Furniture 54
Huppah Wedding Objects 466
Hurdle Sports Equipment 519
hurdy-gurdy (*use:* Gurdy) Fishing Equipment 146
hurdy-gurdy (*use:* Drill, Hurdy Gurdy) Mining & Mineral Harvesting T&E 222
Hurdy-Gurdy Musical Instruments 372
husker, corn (*use:* Cornhusker) Harvesting Equipment 128
Husker-Shredder, Corn Harvesting Equipment 128
Husle Musical Instruments 373
Hut Dwellings 32
Hut, Quonset Other Structures 41
Hutch Storage & Display Furniture 54
Hyalograph Drafting T&E 366
Hydrant Hydraulic Structures 34
Hydria Storage & Display Accessories 64
hydrocrystolophone (*use:* Harmonica, Glass) Musical Instruments 371
Hydrodynamometer Mechanical Measurement Equipment 318

Hydrofoil	Watercraft	447
Hydrometer	Chemical Testing Devices	290
Hydrophore	Chemical Testing Devices	290
Hydroplane	Watercraft	447
hydropyrometer (*use:* Pyrometer)	Thermal T&E	354
hydroscope (*use:* Hygrometer)	Meteorological T&E	339
Hyfrecator	Medical Instruments	331
Hygrograph	Meteorological T&E	339
Hygrometer	Meteorological T&E	339
hygrophant (*use:* Hygrometer)	Meteorological T&E	339
Hygrothermograph	Meteorological T&E	339
Hymnal	Religious Objects	463
Hypsometer	Thermal T&E	354
hysteroscope (*use:* Metroscope)	Medical Instruments	330
Iceboat	Watercraft	443
Icebox	Food Storage Equipment	172
Icebreaker	Watercraft	448
Icehouse	Outbuildings	38
Icon	Religious Objects	465
Idler	Power Transmission Components	305
Idol	Religious Objects	465
igniter (*use:* Detonator)	Mining & Mineral Harvesting T&E	222
Igniter, Portable	Firemaking Equipment	74
Imbrex	Surface Elements	19
Impactor	Metalworking T&E	213
Implant, Breast	Personal Assistive Objects	108
Imprinter	Writing Devices	406
Imprinter, Credit Card	Merchandising T&E	337
Improver, Bust	Underwear	103
Incense	Other Household Accessories	67
Incinerator	Housekeeping Equipment	312
Inclinometer	Surveying Equipment	352
Incubator	Breeding Equipment	138
Incubator, Biological	Biological T&E	287
Incubator, Fish	Breeding Equipment	138
Incubator, Poultry	Breeding Equipment	138
Incubator, Yogurt	Food Preparation Equipment	154
Indenture	Legal Documents	476
Index	Other Documents	483
Indicator, Airspeed	Aerospace Transportation Accessories	409
indicator, attitude (*use:* Horizon, Artificial)	Aerospace Transportation Accessories	409
indicator, bank (*use:* Indicator, Turn and Bank)	Aerospace Transportation Accessories	409
Indicator, Bite	Fishing Equipment	147
Indicator, Borehole Drift	Mining & Mineral Harvesting T&E	223
indicator, climb (*use:* Indicator, Rate-of-Climb)	Aerospace Transportation Accessories	409
Indicator, Drift	Aerospace Transportation Accessories	409
indicator, drift (*use:* Indicator, Borehole Drift)	Mining & Mineral Harvesting T&E	223
Indicator, Floor	Conveyance Devices	5
Indicator, Height-Range	Navigational Equipment	350
Indicator, Horsepower	Power Transmission Components	305
Indicator, Position	Navigational Equipment	350
Indicator, Rate-of-Climb	Aerospace Transportation Accessories	409
Indicator, Strain	Electrical & Magnetic Measurement Devices	297
indicator, turn (*use:* Indicator, Turn and Bank)	Aerospace Transportation Accessories	409
Indicator, Turn and Bank	Aerospace Transportation Accessories	409
indicator, vertical speed (*use:* Indicator, Rate-of-Climb)	Aerospace Transportation Accessories	409
Indicator, Volume Change	Chemical Testing Devices	290
Indicator, Water Stability	Chemical Testing Devices	290
Indictment	Legal Documents	476
Indigometer	Chemical Testing Devices	290
indiscope (*use:* Ophthalmoscope)	Medical Instruments	329
Inductometer	Electrical & Magnetic Measurement Devices	297
Infirmary	Institutional Structures	37
Infuser, Tea	Food Preparation Equipment	155
Ingot	Metalworking T&E	217
Inhalator	Medical Instruments	333
Inhaler	Medical Instruments	333
Injector, Cement	Mining & Mineral Harvesting T&E	223
Injector, Fertilizer	Tending Equipment	133
Injector, Marinade	Food Preparation Equipment	155
Ink	Writing Accessories	404
Ink, Printer's	Printing Accessories	386
Inkball	Graphic Equipment	385
Inkpad	Writing Accessories	404
Inkstand	Writing Accessories	403
Inkstone	Printing Accessories	386
Inkwell	Writing Accessories	403
Inn	Commercial Structures	27
Inro	Personal Carrying & Storage Gear	113
Insert, Fireplace	Heating Equipment Accessories	76

Term	Category	Page
Insignia	Status Symbols	496
Insignia, Shoulder	Status Symbols	496
Insole	Clothing Accessories	85
Instructograph	Telecommunication Accessories	394
Instrument, Anesthetic	Medical Instruments	327
Instrument, Astronomical	Astronomical T&E	284
Instrument, Azimuth	Astronomical T&E	284
Instrument, Biological	Biological T&E	287
Instrument, Brass	Musical Instruments	370
Instrument, Chemical	Chemical Testing Devices	291
Instrument, Diagnostic	Medical Instruments	327
Instrument, Drafting	Drafting T&E	366
Instrument, Ear	Medical Instruments	328
Instrument, Electrical	Electrical & Magnetic Measurement Devices	297
Instrument, Electronic	Musical Instruments	370
Instrument, Embalming	Medical Instruments	328
Instrument, Eye	Medical Instruments	329
Instrument, Flight	Aerospace Transportation Accessories	409
Instrument, Friction	Musical Instruments	371
Instrument, Gynecological	Medical Instruments	329
Instrument, Keyboard	Musical Instruments	371
Instrument, Magnetic	Electrical & Magnetic Measurement Devices	298
Instrument, Mechanical	Musical Instruments	371
Instrument, Meteorological	Meteorological T&E	339
Instrument, Nasal	Medical Instruments	330
Instrument, Navigational	Navigational Equipment	350
Instrument, Obstetrical	Medical Instruments	330
Instrument, Optical	Optical T&E	343
Instrument, Oral	Medical Instruments	330
Instrument, Percussion	Musical Instruments	372
Instrument, Rectal	Medical Instruments	330
Instrument, Stringed	Musical Instruments	373
Instrument, Surgical	Medical Instruments	330
Instrument, Surveying	Surveying Equipment	352
Instrument, Therapeutic	Medical Instruments	332
Instrument, Thermal	Thermal T&E	354
Instrument, Urological	Medical Instruments	334
Instrument, Woodwind	Musical Instruments	374
Insulation	Construction Materials	3
Insulator	Electrical System Components	300
Insulator, Antenna	Telecommunication Accessories	394
Insulator, Communication	Telecommunication Accessories	394
Insulator, Telegraph Wire	Telecommunication Accessories	394
Insulator, Telephone Wire	Telecommunication Accessories	394
Intaglio	Art	454
Integrator	Data Processing Devices	361
Intercom	Sound Communication Devices	391
Interferometer, Optical	Optical T&E	343
Interferometer, Radio	Astronomical T&E	284
Inventionshorn	Musical Instruments	370
Inventory	Other Documents	483
Inverness	Outerwear	100
Invitation	Other Documents	485
Invoice	Financial Records	469
Iron	Laundry Equipment	313
Iron, Balling	Veterinary Equipment	142
Iron, Barking	Forestry T&E	191
iron, bick (*use:* Beakiron)	Metalworking T&E	207
Iron, Branding	Writing Devices	406
Iron, Bucking	Mining & Mineral Harvesting T&E	223
Iron, Caulking	Woodworking T&E	252
iron, cauterizing (*use:* Cauterizer)	Medical Instruments	330
Iron, Cauterizing	Veterinary Equipment	142
Iron, Clew	Water Transportation Accessories	439
Iron, Cooking	Food Preparation Equipment	154
Iron, Cooper's Burning	Woodworking T&E	252
iron, creasing (*use:* Iron, Making)	Woodworking T&E	252
Iron, Crimping	Hair Care Objects	118
Iron, Curling	Hair Care Objects	118
Iron, Electric	Laundry Equipment	313
iron, fire (*use:* Fireset)	Heating Equipment Accessories	76
Iron, Flagging	Woodworking T&E	252
iron, flat (*use:* Flatiron)	Laundry Equipment	313
Iron, Fluting	Laundry Equipment	313
Iron, Gathering	Glass, Plastics & Clayworking T&E	193
iron, glazing (*use:* Slicker, Edge)	Leather, Horn & Shellworking T&E	200
iron, goffering (*use:* Iron, Fluting)	Laundry Equipment	313
Iron, Grab	Rail Transportation Accessories	431
Iron, Grafting	Tending Equipment	133
Iron, Hair	Hair Care Objects	118
Iron, Hoof-Searing	Farrier Equipment	140
Iron, Horsing	Woodworking T&E	252
Iron, Knocking-Down	Bookbinding Equipment	382
iron, knocking-up (*use:* Iron, Raising)	Woodworking T&E	252
iron, leg (*use:* Shackle, Leg)	Regulative Devices	348
Iron, Lily	Edged Weapons	277
Iron, Making	Woodworking T&E	252
Iron, Marking	Woodworking T&E	252
Iron, Metalworking	Metalworking T&E	213
Iron, Mulling	Food Preparation Equipment	154

Term	Category	Page
iron, pinching (*use:* Iron, Straightening)	Hair Care Objects	118
Iron, Pinking	Leather, Horn & Shellworking T&E	198
Iron, Polishing	Bookbinding Equipment	382
Iron, Raising	Woodworking T&E	252
Iron, Rapping	Fiberworking T&E	144
Iron, Rosette	Food Preparation Equipment	154
Iron, Seat	Leather, Horn & Shellworking T&E	198
iron, sharp (*use:* Iron, Caulking)	Woodworking T&E	252
Iron, Shipwright's Caulking	Woodworking T&E	252
Iron, Shipwright's Meaking	Woodworking T&E	252
Iron, Snarling	Metalworking T&E	213
Iron, Soldering	Metalworking T&E	213
Iron, Straightening	Hair Care Objects	118
Iron, Switch	Rail Transportation Accessories	432
Iron, Tacking	Photoprocessing Equipment	381
Iron, Tailor's	Laundry Equipment	313
Iron, Tire	Land Transportation Accessories	421
Iron, Veneering	Woodworking T&E	252
Iron, Wafer	Food Preparation Equipment	154
Iron, Waffle	Food Preparation Equipment	154
Iron, Wheelwright's Burning	Woodworking T&E	252
Iron, Woodworking	Woodworking T&E	252
Ironworks	Industrial Structures	35
Irrigator	Medical Instruments	333
Irrigator, Dental	Dental Instruments	323
Irrigator, Uterine	Medical Instruments	330
Island, Kitchen	Storage & Display Furniture	53
Isograph	Drafting T&E	366
Itinerary	Other Documents	482
Jabot	Clothing Accessories	85
jack (*use:* Pucella)	Glass, Plastics & Clayworking T&E	194
Jack	Mechanical Devices	316
Jack, Automotive	Land Transportation Accessories	419
Jack, Bottle	Food Preparation Equipment	163
Jack, Clock	Timekeeping T&E	356
Jack, Fence	Mechanical Devices	316
Jack, Furniture	Mechanical Devices	316
Jack, Glazing	Leather, Horn & Shellworking T&E	198
Jack, Hoisting	Mechanical Devices	316
Jack, Jumping	Toys	521
Jack, Last	Leather, Horn & Shellworking T&E	198
Jack, Leather	Drinking Vessels	174
Jack, Lifting	Mechanical Devices	316
Jack, Miter	Woodworking T&E	248
Jack, Pallet	Human-Powered Vehicles	427
Jack, Pulling	Mechanical Devices	316
jack, pump (*use:* Pumpjack)	Mechanical Devices	316
Jack, Roasting	Food Preparation Equipment	163
jack, single (*use:* Hammer, Hand)	Mining & Mineral Harvesting T&E	222
Jack, Spinning	Textile Manufacturing Equipment	241
Jack, Stagecoach	Land Transportation Accessories	419
Jack, Telephone	Telecommunication Accessories	395
Jack, Toy	Game Equipment	502
Jack, Track	Rail Transportation Accessories	432
Jack, Vehicle	Land Transportation Accessories	418
Jack, Wagon	Land Transportation Accessories	419
Jack, Wax	Lighting Holders	71
Jackboot	Footwear	89
Jacket	Main Garments	96
Jacket, Baptismal	Religious Objects	463
Jacket, Battle	Main Garments	96
Jacket, Bed	Dressingwear & Nightwear	88
jacket, bomber (*use:* Jacket, Flight)	Outerwear	100
Jacket, Book	Other Documents	482
Jacket, Bush	Outerwear	100
jacket, combing (*use:* Jacket, Dressing)	Dressingwear & Nightwear	88
Jacket, Dinner	Main Garments	95
Jacket, Dolman	Outerwear	100
Jacket, Dressing	Dressingwear & Nightwear	88
jacket, dust (*use:* Jacket, Book)	Other Documents	482
Jacket, Fire Hose	Protective Devices	345
jacket, flak (*use:* Vest, Flak)	Body Armor	276
Jacket, Flight	Outerwear	100
Jacket, Hunting	Main Garments	96
Jacket, Jean	Main Garments	96
Jacket, Life	Water Transportation Accessories	441
Jacket, Mess	Main Garments	96
Jacket, Nehru	Main Garments	96
Jacket, Norfolk	Main Garments	96
Jacket, Pea	Outerwear	101
Jacket, Record	Sound Communication Accessories	389
Jacket, Riding	Main Garments	97
jacket, safari (*use:* Jacket, Bush)	Outerwear	100

Term	Category	Page
Jacket, Shirt	Main Garments	97
Jacket, Shooting	Outerwear	101
Jacket, Ski	Outerwear	101
Jacket, Smoking	Main Garments	97
Jacket, Spencer	Main Garments	97
jacket, sport (*use:* Sportcoat)	Main Garments	95
jacket, suit (*use:* Coat, Suit)	Main Garments	95
Jacket, Target Shooter's	Armament Accessories	269
jacket, tuxedo (*use:* Jacket, Dinner)	Main Garments	95
Jacket, Waiter's	Main Garments	97
Jackhammer	Construction T&E	295
Jack-in-the-Box	Toys	521
Jackknife	Personal Assistive Objects	108
jackleg (*use:* Leg, Air)	Mining & Mineral Harvesting T&E	223
Jacklight	Lighting Devices	68
Jackshaft	Power Transmission Components	305
Jackstaff	Water Transportation Accessories	437
jackstraw (*use:* Stick, Pick-Up)	Game Equipment	504
Jag, Cleaning	Armament Accessories	269
Jail	Institutional Structures	37
Jalousie	Door & Window Elements	7
Jamb, Door	Door & Window Elements	6
Jamb, Window	Door & Window Elements	7
Jar	Containers	415
Jar, Apothecary	Merchandising T&E	336
Jar, Battery	Electrical System Components	301
Jar, Bell	Storage & Display Accessories	64
jar, canning (*use:* Jar, Preserving)	Food Processing Equipment	165
Jar, Canopic	Funerary Objects	456
Jar, Condiment	Serving Vessels	188
Jar, Confectionery	Merchandising T&E	337
Jar, Cookie	Food Storage Equipment	171
Jar, Cosmetic	Beauty Supplies	116
Jar, Display	Merchandising T&E	337
Jar, Food Storage	Food Storage Equipment	171
jar, fruit (*use:* Jar, Preserving)	Food Processing Equipment	165
Jar, Ginger	Food Storage Equipment	171
Jar, Honey	Serving Vessels	188
jar, jam (*use:* Pot, Jam)	Serving Vessels	188
jar, mortuary (*use:* Urn, Cremation)	Funerary Objects	456
jar, mustard (*use:* Pot, Mustard)	Serving Vessels	188
Jar, Ointment	Medical Accessories	325
Jar, Pickle	Serving Vessels	188
Jar, Potpourri	Other Household Accessories	66
Jar, Preserving	Food Processing Equipment	165
Jar, Seed	Planting Equipment	132
Jar, Slop	Housekeeping Equipment	312
Jar, Snuff	Containers for Smoking & Tobacco	59
Jar, Specimen	Medical Accessories	325
Jar, Strawberry	Horticultural Containers	62
Jar, Syringe	Medical Accessories	326
jar, tobacco (*use:* Humidor)	Containers for Smoking & Tobacco	59
Jar, Vacuum	Mechanical Measurement Equipment	318
Jar, Watch	Storage & Display Accessories	64
Jar, Water	Storage & Display Accessories	64
Jardinière	Horticultural Containers	62
Javelin	Edged Weapons	278
Javelin, Track and Field	Sports Equipment	519
Jeans	Main Garments	97
Jeep	Motor Vehicles	428
Jenny, Spinning	Textile Manufacturing Equipment	241
Jerkin	Main Garments	97
Jersey	Main Garments	97
Jess	Animal Care Equipment	135
jet (*use:* Airplane, Jet)	Aircraft	411
Jewelry	Body Adornments	81
Jib	Water Transportation Accessories	439
Jibboom	Water Transportation Accessories	440
Jig	Multiple Use T&E for Materials	227
Jig, Fishing	Fishing Equipment	147
Jig, Metalworking	Metalworking T&E	213
Jig, Woodworking	Woodworking T&E	252
Jigger	Woodworking T&E	253
Jigger, Measuring	Food Preparation Equipment	156
jigger, pastry (*use:* Wheel, Jagging)	Food Preparation Equipment	159
Jigsaw	Woodworking T&E	257
Jingle	Musical Instruments	372
Jockstrap	Underwear	104
Jodhpur	Main Garments	97
Johnboat	Watercraft	443
johns, long (*use:* Underwear, Long)	Underwear	104
Joint, Universal	Power Transmission Components	305
Jointer	Woodworking T&E	253
Jointer, Masonry	Masonry & Stoneworking T&E	204
Jointer-Planer	Woodworking T&E	253
Joist	Supporting Elements	16
Joist, Ceiling	Supporting Elements	16

Joist, Floor | Supporting Elements | 16
jolly, beach (*use:* Boat, Jolly) | Watercraft | 448
Journal | Other Documents | 480
Joystick | Peripherals | 364
Judgment | Government Records | 470
Jug | Containers | 415
Jug, Bartmann | Containers | 415
jug, Bellarmine (*use:* Jug, Bartmann) | Containers | 415
Jug, Bunghole | Serving Vessels | 189
Jug, Claret | Serving Vessels | 189
Jug, Face | Art | 454
Jug, Food Storage | Food Storage Equipment | 171
Jug, Libation | Religious Objects | 463
Jug, Milk | Serving Vessels | 189
Jug, Monkey | Serving Vessels | 189
Jug, Puzzle | Drinking Vessels | 175
Jug, Serving | Serving Vessels | 189
Jug, Syrup | Food Storage Equipment | 171
Jug, Toby | Serving Vessels | 189
Jug, Whiskey | Food Storage Equipment | 171
Juicer | Food Preparation Equipment | 160
Jukebox | Sound Communication Devices | 391
Jumbo | Mining & Mineral Harvesting T&E | 223
Jump | Underwear | 104
Jumper | Main Garments | 96
jumper (*use:* Iron, Raising) | Woodworking T&E | 252
Jumpsuit | Main Garments | 96
Junglegym | Recreational Devices | 510
Junk | Watercraft | 444
Kachina | Religious Objects | 465
Kaffiyeh | Headwear | 93
Kaleidoscope | Toys | 523
kamak (*use:* Mukluk) | Footwear | 89
Kamelaukion | Status Symbols | 499
kanzashi (*use:* Ornament, Hair) | Hair Adornments | 83
Kas | Storage & Display Furniture | 54
Kayak | Watercraft | 442
Kazoo | Musical Instruments | 375
Keel | Water Transportation Accessories | 438
Keeler | Food Preparation Equipment | 153
Keelson | Water Transportation Accessories | 438
keeper, grease (*use:* Keeper, Oil) | Food Storage Equipment | 171
Keeper, Oil | Food Storage Equipment | 171
Keeper, Sling | Armament Accessories | 269
keepsake (*use:* Souvenir) | Memorabilia | 478
keeve (*use:* Concentrator) | Metalworking T&E | 208
Keg | Containers | 415
Keg, Beer | Food Storage Equipment | 171
Keg, Food Storage | Food Storage Equipment | 171
Keg, Paint | Painting T&E | 229
Keg, Powder | Armament Accessories | 268
Kennel | Other Structures | 41
Kepi | Headwear | 91
Keratome | Medical Instruments | 331
keratometer (*use:* Ophthalmometer) | Medical Instruments | 329
Kerchief | Headwear | 93
Ketch | Watercraft | 443
Kettle | Cooking Vessels | 151
Kettle, Dyeing | Textile Manufacturing Equipment | 241
Kettle, Fish | Cooking Vessels | 151
Kettle, Frying | Cooking Vessels | 151
Kettle, Hornworker's | Leather, Horn & Shellworking T&E | 201
Kettle, Lard Rendering | Food Processing Equipment | 169
kettle, lard settling (*use:* Tank, Lard Settling) | Food Processing Equipment | 169
Kettle, Preserving | Cooking Vessels | 151
kettle, tea (*use:* Teakettle) | Cooking Vessels | 151
Key | Protective Devices | 345
key, bed (*use:* Bedkey) | Other Household Accessories | 66
Key, Chuck | Woodworking T&E | 252
Key, Church | Food Preparation Equipment | 156
Key, Clock | Timekeeping T&E | 356
Key, Commemorative | Memorabilia | 478
key, cotter (*use:* Pin, Cotter) | Metalworking T&E | 210
Key, Handcuff | Regulative Devices | 347
Key, Ignition | Land Transportation Accessories | 419
Key, Jail | Regulative Devices | 347
key, nipple (*use:* Wrench, Nipple) | Armament Accessories | 273
Key, Paint Can | Painting T&E | 229
Key, Phonograph | Sound Communication Accessories | 390
Key, Quoin | Typesetting Equipment | 388
Key, Skate | Sports Equipment | 517
Key, Switch | Rail Transportation Accessories | 432
key, tap (*use:* Spigot) | Food Service Accessories | 182
Key, Telegraph | Telecommunication Devices | 396
Key, Timepiece | Timekeeping T&E | 356
key, tooth (*use:* Toothkey) | Dental Instruments | 323
Key, Watch | Timekeeping T&E | 356
Keyboard, Computer | Peripherals | 364
Keyboard, Electronic | Musical Instruments | 371
Keypad, Security | Protective Devices | 346
Keystone | Construction Materials | 4
Khimar | Headwear | 94

Kibble — Mining & Mineral Harvesting T&E 221
Kickboard — Recreational Devices 510
Kicker — Leather, Horn & Shellworking T&E 198
Kickplate — Finish Hardware 10
Kick-Stop — Animal Care Equipment 135
kiddie-car (*use:* Car, Kiddie) — Toys 524
Kidney — Glass, Plastics & Clayworking T&E 193
killer, poultry (*use:* Knife, Poultry Killing) — Food Processing Equipment 165
killik (*use:* Anchor) — Water Transportation Accessories 436
Kiln — Glass, Plastics & Clayworking T&E 193
Kiln, Brick — Masonry & Stoneworking T&E 204
Kiln, Cement — Masonry & Stoneworking T&E 204
Kiln, Lime — Masonry & Stoneworking T&E 204
Kiln, Mold — Glass, Plastics & Clayworking T&E 193
Kiln, Pot — Glass, Plastics & Clayworking T&E 193
Kilt — Main Garments 98
Kimono — Main Garments 97
Kinara — Religious Objects 461
Kindling — Firemaking Equipment 74
Kinetophone — Visual Communication Devices 400
Kinetoscope — Visual Communication Devices 400
Kit — Musical Instruments 373
Kit, Automotive Tool — Land Transportation Accessories 421
Kit, Bicycle Tool — Land Transportation Accessories 421
Kit, Chemical Test — Chemical Testing Devices 291
Kit, Cocaine — Smoking & Recreational Drug Equipment 114
Kit, Cosmetic — Beauty Supplies 117
Kit, Cupping — Medical Instruments 333
Kit, Dental Filling — Dental Instruments 323
Kit, Dissecting — Biological T&E 287
kit, dop (*use:* Kit, Toilet) — Personal Carrying & Storage Gear 112
kit, drafting (*use:* Set, Drafting) — Drafting T&E 367
Kit, First Aid — Medical Instruments 333
kit, fishing (*use:* Tackle, Fishing) — Fishing Equipment 147
Kit, Gun Cleaning — Armament Accessories 269
Kit, Gun Loading — Armament Accessories 269
Kit, Hosiery Mending — Clothing Care Objects 105
Kit, Insemination — Breeding Equipment 138
Kit, Learning — Instructional Documents 475
Kit, Medical — Medical Instruments 333
Kit, Medicine — Medical Instruments 333
Kit, Mess — Food Service Sets 183
Kit, Midwife — Medical Instruments 333
Kit, Model — Toys 521
Kit, Needlework — Needleworking Equipment 235
Kit, Pregnancy Test — Medical Instruments 328
Kit, Press — Declaratory Documents 468
Kit, Repair — Multiple Use T&E for Materials 227
Kit, Sailmaker's — Needleworking Equipment 235
Kit, Sales Sample — Merchandising T&E 338
Kit, Science — Toys 522
Kit, Sewing — Needleworking Equipment 235
Kit, Shaving — Hair Care Objects 119
Kit, Shoeshine — Clothing Care Objects 105
kit, shotgun reloading (*use:* Kit, Gun Loading) — Armament Accessories 269
Kit, Soil Testing — Tending Equipment 133
Kit, Suction — Medical Instruments 333
Kit, Surgical — Medical Instruments 331
Kit, Thermo-Cautery — Medical Instruments 331
Kit, Toilet — Personal Carrying & Storage Gear 112
Kit, Tool — Multiple Use T&E for Materials 226
Kit, Toy — Toys 522
Kit, Water Analysis — Chemical Testing Devices 291
Kitchen, Play — Toys 522
Kitchen, Tin — Food Preparation Equipment 163
Kite — Aircraft 412
Kite, Fishing — Fishing Equipment 146
Kite, Toy — Toys 522
Kittel — Funerary Objects 457
Kiva — Ceremonial Structures 25
Klismos — Seating Furniture 49
klomp (*use:* Sabot) — Footwear 90
Klystron — Nuclear Physics T&E 342
knapsack (*use:* Backpack) — Personal Carrying & Storage Gear 110
Knee, Watercraft — Water Transportation Accessories 438
kneecap, horse (*use:* Pad, Horse Knee) — Land Transportation Accessories 420
Kneeler — Religious Objects 463
Knickers — Main Garments 97
Knickknack — Decorative Furnishings 60
Knife — Multiple Use T&E for Materials 227
Knife, Amputation — Medical Instruments 331
Knife, Band-Cutter — Harvesting Equipment 129
knife, beaming (*use:* Knife, Fleshing) — Leather, Horn & Shellworking T&E 198
Knife, Beet-Topping — Harvesting Equipment 129

Knife, Bench — Woodworking T&E 253
Knife, Bleeding — Edged Weapons 277
Knife, Block — Woodworking T&E 253
Knife, Blubber — Fishing Equipment 148
Knife, Boarding — Fishing Equipment 148
Knife, Boning — Food Preparation Equipment 159
Knife, Bowie — Edged Weapons 277
Knife, Bread — Serving Utensils 184
Knife, Brush — Forestry T&E 191
knife, budding (*use:* Knife, Grafting) — Tending Equipment 133
Knife, Butcher — Food Preparation Equipment 159
Knife, Butter — Serving Utensils 184
Knife, Cake — Serving Utensils 184
Knife, Callus — Beauty Supplies 117
Knife, Carpet — Needleworking Equipment 235
Knife, Cartilage — Medical Instruments 331
Knife, Carving — Serving Utensils 184
knife, carving (*use:* Knife, Woodcarving) — Woodworking T&E 253
Knife, Castrating — Veterinary Equipment 143
Knife, Cheese — Food Processing Equipment 166
Knife, Cheese Serving — Serving Utensils 184
Knife, Chef's — Food Preparation Equipment 159
Knife, Chest — Glass, Plastics & Clayworking T&E 193
Knife, Chopping — Food Preparation Equipment 159
Knife, Cigar — Other T&E for Materials 260
Knife, Circumcision — Medical Instruments 331
Knife, Clasp — Personal Assistive Objects 108
knife, cook's (*use:* Knife, Chef's) — Food Preparation Equipment 159
knife, corn (*use:* Knife, Callus) — Beauty Supplies 117
Knife, Corn — Harvesting Equipment 129
Knife, Crooked — Woodworking T&E 253
knife, crumb (*use:* Crumber) — Housekeeping Equipment 312
Knife, Curd — Food Processing Equipment 166
Knife, Currier's — Leather, Horn & Shellworking T&E 197
Knife, Cuticle — Beauty Supplies 117
Knife, Decapping — Animal Care Equipment 136
Knife, Dehorning — Veterinary Equipment 142
Knife, Dessert — Eating & Drinking Utensils 178
Knife, Dinner — Eating & Drinking Utensils 178
Knife, Draw — Leather, Horn & Shellworking T&E 197
Knife, Eating — Eating & Drinking Utensils 178
knife, edging (*use:* Edger, Lawn) — Groundskeeping Equipment 309
Knife, Elastic — Masonry & Stoneworking T&E 205
Knife, Etching — Graphic Equipment 384
Knife, Farrier's — Farrier Equipment 139
Knife, Feathering — Leather, Horn & Shellworking T&E 197
Knife, Fettling — Glass, Plastics & Clayworking T&E 193
Knife, Fillet — Food Preparation Equipment 159
Knife, Film — Photographic Accessories 378
Knife, Finger — Woodworking T&E 253
Knife, Fish — Eating & Drinking Utensils 178
Knife, Fleshing — Leather, Horn & Shellworking T&E 198
Knife, Folding — Printing Accessories 386
knife, froe (*use:* Froe, Knife) — Woodworking T&E 250
Knife, Fruit — Eating & Drinking Utensils 178
Knife, Gilder's — Painting T&E 229
Knife, Grafting — Tending Equipment 133
Knife, Grain-Heading — Harvesting Equipment 129
Knife, Graining — Painting T&E 229
Knife, Grapefruit — Food Preparation Equipment 159
knife, half-moon (*use:* Knife, Currier's) — Leather, Horn & Shellworking T&E 197
Knife, Ham — Food Preparation Equipment 159
Knife, Harvesting — Harvesting Equipment 129
Knife, Hay — Harvesting Equipment 129
Knife, Head — Leather, Horn & Shellworking T&E 197
Knife, Hoof — Farrier Equipment 140
Knife, Hoop-Notching — Woodworking T&E 253
Knife, Hunting — Edged Weapons 277
Knife, Ice Cream — Serving Utensils 184
Knife, Jelly — Serving Utensils 184
Knife, Kitchen — Food Preparation Equipment 158
knife, lathmaker's (*use:* Froe, Knife) — Woodworking T&E 250
Knife, Leaning — Fishing Equipment 148
Knife, Leather — Leather, Horn & Shellworking T&E 197
Knife, Luncheon — Eating & Drinking Utensils 178
Knife, Magician's — Public Entertainment Devices 508
Knife, Marking — Woodworking T&E 253
Knife, Mat — Painting T&E 229
Knife, Mescal — Harvesting Equipment 129
Knife, Mincing — Fishing Equipment 148
knife, mincing (*use:* Knife, Chopping) — Food Preparation Equipment 159
Knife, Orange — Food Preparation Equipment 159
Knife, Oyster — Food Preparation Equipment 159
Knife, Painting — Painting T&E 229

Knife, Palette	Painting T&E	229
knife, paper (*use:* Guillotine, Paper)	Printing Accessories	386
knife, paper (*use:* Opener, Letter)	Writing Accessories	404
Knife, Paring	Food Preparation Equipment	159
Knife, Pastry	Food Preparation Equipment	159
Knife, Patch	Armament Accessories	269
Knife, Picking	Fiberworking T&E	144
Knife, Pipe	Smoking & Recreational Drug Equipment	114
Knife, Plaster	Masonry & Stoneworking T&E	205
Knife, Pocket	Personal Assistive Objects	108
knife, potato (*use:* Cutter, Potato Seed)	Harvesting Equipment	129
Knife, Poultry Killing	Food Processing Equipment	165
Knife, Produce	Food Processing Equipment	164
Knife, Pruning	Groundskeeping Equipment	310
Knife, Putty	Painting T&E	229
knife, race (*use:* Scribe, Timber)	Forestry T&E	191
Knife, Sacrificial	Religious Objects	463
Knife, Sailmaker's	Needleworking Equipment	235
Knife, Santoku	Food Preparation Equipment	159
knife, scaling (*use:* Scaler, Fish)	Food Preparation Equipment	157
Knife, Scuba	Recreational Devices	510
Knife, Scutching	Textile Manufacturing Equipment	241
Knife, Serving	Serving Utensils	184
Knife, Shaving	Woodworking T&E	253
Knife, Shearing	Forestry T&E	191
Knife, Sheath	Edged Weapons	277
Knife, Sheeter	Printing Accessories	386
knife, shoeing (*use:* Knife, Hoof)	Farrier Equipment	140
Knife, Sinew	Other T&E for Materials	260
Knife, Skinning	Food Processing Equipment	165
Knife, Skiving	Leather, Horn & Shellworking T&E	197
Knife, Slate Trimming	Masonry & Stoneworking T&E	204
knife, slaughtering (*use:* Knife, Sticking)	Food Processing Equipment	165
Knife, Snow	Other T&E for Materials	260
Knife, Sole	Farrier Equipment	139
Knife, Square Point	Leather, Horn & Shellworking T&E	197
Knife, Steak	Eating & Drinking Utensils	178
Knife, Sticking	Food Processing Equipment	165
Knife, Stopping	Glass, Plastics & Clayworking T&E	193
Knife, Stretching	Leather, Horn & Shellworking T&E	197
Knife, Sugarcane	Harvesting Equipment	130
Knife, Surgical	Medical Instruments	331
knife, swingling (*use:* Knife, Scutching)	Textile Manufacturing Equipment	241
Knife, Switchblade	Edged Weapons	277
knife, table (*use:* Knife, Dinner)	Eating & Drinking Utensils	178
Knife, Teat	Veterinary Equipment	142
Knife, Throwing	Edged Weapons	277
Knife, Tobacco	Harvesting Equipment	130
Knife, Toe	Farrier Equipment	139
Knife, Trench	Edged Weapons	277
Knife, Trimmer	Printing Accessories	386
Knife, Uncapping	Food Processing Equipment	164
Knife, Unhairing	Leather, Horn & Shellworking T&E	198
Knife, Utility	Multiple Use T&E for Materials	227
Knife, Wallpaper	Painting T&E	231
Knife, Weapon	Edged Weapons	277
Knife, Welt	Leather, Horn & Shellworking T&E	197
Knife, Willow	Fiberworking T&E	144
Knife, Woodcarving	Woodworking T&E	253
Knife, Woodworking	Woodworking T&E	252
Knifeboard	Food Preparation Accessories	152
Knighthead	Water Transportation Accessories	438
Knitwork	Art	453
Knob, Tieback	Window & Door Coverings	78
Knockabout	Watercraft	443
Knocker	Finish Hardware	11
Knocker, Snow	Farrier Equipment	139
Knork	Eating & Drinking Utensils	178
Knot, Ornamental	Art	452
Knot, Shoulder	Status Symbols	496
Knot, Sword	Status Symbols	497
Knotter	Textile Manufacturing Equipment	241
Knout	Regulative Devices	347
Knuckles, Brass	Percussive Weapons	283
Koban	Exchange Media	488
kogai (*use:* Ornament, Hair)	Hair Adornments	83
Koniscope	Meteorological T&E	339
Kopek	Exchange Media	488
Koran	Religious Objects	465
Kris	Edged Weapons	277
Kubbestol	Seating Furniture	49
Kymograph	Mechanical Measurement Equipment	318
Kymoscope	Medical Instruments	327
Label	Writing Media	408
Label, Address	Other Documents	483
Label, Decanter	Food Service Accessories	181
Label, Identification	Other Documents	483

Label, Product — Merchandising T&E 337
Label, Shipping — Other Documents 483
Labret — Body Adornments 81
Lace — Needleworking Equipment 237
lace, boot (*use:* Shoelace) — Clothing Accessories 86
Lace, Corset — Clothing Accessories 85
Lactobutyrometer — Food Processing Equipment 167
Lactometer — Food Processing Equipment 167
lactorium (*use:* Parlor, Milking) — Agricultural Structures 23
Ladder — Other Household Accessories 67
Ladder, Fire — Protective Devices 345
ladder, fruit picking (*use:* Ladder, Orchard) — Harvesting Equipment 130
Ladder, Horizontal — Recreational Devices 510
ladder, Jacob's (*use:* Ladder, Rope) — Recreational Devices 510
Ladder, Jacob's — Water Transportation Accessories 441
Ladder, Orchard — Harvesting Equipment 130
Ladder, Rope — Recreational Devices 510
Ladder, Ship's — Water Transportation Accessories 441
ladder, step (*use:* Stepladder) — Other Household Accessories 67
Ladder, Watercraft — Water Transportation Accessories 441
Ladle, Apothecary — Medical Accessories 326
Ladle, Cinder — Metalworking T&E 213
Ladle, Cream — Serving Utensils 184
Ladle, Foundry — Metalworking T&E 213
Ladle, Gravy — Serving Utensils 184
Ladle, Hot Metal — Metalworking T&E 213
Ladle, Hot Shot — Armament Accessories 270
Ladle, Kitchen — Food Preparation Equipment 160
Ladle, Mayonnaise — Serving Utensils 184
Ladle, Melting — Glass, Plastics & Clayworking T&E 193
Ladle, Punch — Serving Utensils 184
Ladle, Sauce — Serving Utensils 184
Ladle, Serving — Serving Utensils 184
Ladle, Shipwright's Caulking — Woodworking T&E 253
Ladle, Slag — Metalworking T&E 213
Ladle, Soup — Serving Utensils 184
Ladle, Toddy — Serving Utensils 184
Ladle, Wax — Glass, Plastics & Clayworking T&E 193
Ladle, Wok — Food Preparation Equipment 160
Lagging — Mechanical Devices 316
Lambrequin — Furniture Coverings 61
Laminator — Writing Accessories 404
Lamp — Lighting Devices 68
lamp, acetylene (*use:* Lamp, Carbide) — Lighting Devices 68
Lamp, Aircraft — Aerospace Transportation Accessories 409
Lamp, Alarm — Visual Communication Devices 400
lamp, alcohol (*use:* Lamp, Spirit) — Lighting Devices 69
Lamp, Aldis — Visual Communication Devices 400
Lamp, Anchor — Water Transportation Accessories 438
Lamp, Argand — Lighting Devices 69
Lamp, Astral — Lighting Devices 69
Lamp, Banquet — Lighting Devices 69
Lamp, Battery Operated — Lighting Devices 68
Lamp, Betty — Lighting Devices 69
Lamp, Bicycle — Land Transportation Accessories 417
Lamp, Binnacle — Water Transportation Accessories 438
lamp, brazing (*use:* Lamp, Soldering) — Metalworking T&E 213
Lamp, Burning Fluid — Lighting Devices 68
Lamp, Camphene — Lighting Devices 68
Lamp, Candle — Lighting Devices 68
Lamp, Carbide — Lighting Devices 68
Lamp, Carcel — Lighting Devices 69
Lamp, Carriage — Land Transportation Accessories 417
Lamp, Crusie — Lighting Devices 69
Lamp, Davy — Lighting Devices 69
Lamp, Desk — Lighting Devices 68
Lamp, Electric — Lighting Devices 68
Lamp, Fairy — Lighting Devices 68
lamp, flame safety (*use:* Lamp, Safety) — Lighting Devices 69
Lamp, Floor — Lighting Devices 68
Lamp, Food Heat — Food Preparation Equipment 163
Lamp, Gas — Lighting Devices 68
Lamp, Gasoline — Lighting Devices 68
Lamp, Grease — Lighting Devices 69
Lamp, Hanukkah — Religious Objects 464
Lamp, Heat — Heating & Cooling Equipment 75
Lamp, Hitchcock — Lighting Devices 69
lamp, jeweler's (*use:* Torch, Alcohol) — Metalworking T&E 208
Lamp, Kerosene — Lighting Devices 69
Lamp, Landing — Aerospace Transportation Accessories 410
Lamp, Lard — Lighting Devices 69
Lamp, Lava — Decorative Furnishings 60
Lamp, Mantel — Lighting Devices 69
lamp, masthead (*use:* Light, Masthead) — Water Transportation Accessories 438
Lamp, Moderator — Lighting Devices 69
Lamp, Mosque — Religious Objects 464

Term	Category	Page
lamp, navigation (*use:* Light, Navigation)	Water Transportation Accessories	438
Lamp, Oil	Lighting Devices	69
Lamp, Opium	Smoking & Recreational Drug Equipment	114
Lamp, Photoflood	Camera Equipment	377
Lamp, Pole	Lighting Devices	69
Lamp, Position	Aerospace Transportation Accessories	410
lamp, railroad (*use:* Lantern, Railroad)	Visual Communication Devices	400
Lamp, Reflector	Lighting Devices	69
Lamp, Religious	Religious Objects	464
Lamp, Rumford	Lighting Devices	69
Lamp, Sabbath	Religious Objects	464
Lamp, Safety	Lighting Devices	69
Lamp, Sanctuary	Religious Objects	464
Lamp, Semaphore	Visual Communication Devices	400
Lamp, Semiliquid	Lighting Devices	69
Lamp, Signal	Visual Communication Devices	400
Lamp, Soldering	Metalworking T&E	213
Lamp, Spark	Lighting Devices	69
Lamp, Spirit	Lighting Devices	69
Lamp, Spout	Lighting Devices	69
Lamp, Stephenson	Lighting Devices	69
Lamp, Stern	Water Transportation Accessories	438
Lamp, Student	Lighting Devices	69
lamp, sun (*use:* Lamp, Tanning)	Beauty Supplies	117
Lamp, Table	Lighting Devices	69
Lamp, Tanning	Beauty Supplies	117
Lamp, Teeth Whitening	Dental Instruments	323
Lamp, Vehicle	Land Transportation Accessories	417
Lamp, Votive	Religious Objects	464
Lamp, Wanzer	Lighting Devices	69
Lamp, Watercraft	Water Transportation Accessories	438
Lampion	Lighting Devices	69
Lamppost	Site Features	21
Lampshade	Other Lighting Accessories	73
Lance	Edged Weapons	278
Lance, Bomb	Edged Weapons	277
Lance, Whale	Edged Weapons	278
Lancet	Medical Instruments	331
Lancet, Animal	Veterinary Equipment	142
Lancet, Vaccine	Medical Instruments	333
Landau	Animal-Powered Vehicles	423
Landaulet	Animal-Powered Vehicles	423
Landing, Marine	Transportation Structures	39
Landscape	Art	453
Lantern	Lighting Devices	69
Lantern, Battle	Water Transportation Accessories	438
Lantern, Candle	Lighting Devices	69
Lantern, Carbide	Lighting Devices	69
Lantern, Dark	Lighting Devices	69
Lantern, Electric	Lighting Devices	69
Lantern, Gasoline	Lighting Devices	69
Lantern, Kerosene	Lighting Devices	69
lantern, magic (*use:* Projector, Lantern Slide)	Visual Communication Devices	400
Lantern, Oil	Lighting Devices	69
Lantern, Paper	Other Lighting Accessories	73
Lantern, Railroad	Visual Communication Devices	400
Lantern, Ship's	Water Transportation Accessories	441
Lantern, Signal	Visual Communication Devices	400
Lanyard	Personal Carrying & Storage Gear	113
Lanyard, Weapon	Armament Accessories	270
Lapboard	Writing Accessories	402
Lapboard, Basketmaker's	Fiberworking T&E	144
Lappet	Clothing Accessories	86
Lapstone	Leather, Horn & Shellworking T&E	198
Lariat	Animal Care Equipment	135
Laryngoscope	Medical Instruments	330
lasso (*use:* Lariat)	Animal Care Equipment	135
Last	Leather, Horn & Shellworking T&E	198
Last, Boot	Leather, Horn & Shellworking T&E	198
Last, Saddle	Leather, Horn & Shellworking T&E	198
Last, Shoe	Leather, Horn & Shellworking T&E	198
Latch	Finish Hardware	10
Lath	Construction Materials	3
Lathe	Glass, Plastics & Clayworking T&E	193
Lathe, Boring	Woodworking T&E	253
Lathe, Dental	Dental Instruments	323
Lathe, Duplicating	Woodworking T&E	253
Lathe, Engine	Metalworking T&E	213
Lathe, Foot	Metalworking T&E	213
Lathe, Hand	Metalworking T&E	213
Lathe, Metalworking	Metalworking T&E	213
Lathe, Pole	Woodworking T&E	253
Lathe, Spoke	Woodworking T&E	253
Lathe, Turret	Metalworking T&E	213
Lathe, Wheel	Woodworking T&E	253
Lathe, Woodworking	Woodworking T&E	253
Lattice	Barrier Elements	2
Launch	Watercraft	448
Launch, Diesel	Watercraft	443
Launch, Gasoline	Watercraft	443
Launch, Naphtha	Watercraft	443
Launch, Steam	Watercraft	443

Term	Category	Page
Launcher, Fireworks	Public Entertainment Devices	507
Launcher, Grenade	Firearms	280
Launcher, Kite	Aerospace Transportation Accessories	410
launcher, pyrotechnic (*use:* Launcher, Fireworks)	Public Entertainment Devices	507
Launcher, Rocket	Artillery	274
launcher, skeet (*use:* Trap, Skeet)	Armament Accessories	272
Launcher, Target	Armament Accessories	270
Laundry	Commercial Structures	27
Lavabo	Religious Objects	464
Lavaliere	Body Adornments	81
lavallière (*use:* Ascot)	Clothing Accessories	85
Lavatory	Plumbing & Drainage Elements	12
laver (*use:* Lavabo)	Religious Objects	464
Layout	Other Documents	482
Lazy Susan	Food Service Accessories	182
Lead, Pencil	Writing Accessories	404
Lead, Sounding	Navigational Equipment	349
Leader, Cattle	Animal Care Equipment	135
Leader, Livestock	Animal Care Equipment	135
leader, ribbon (*use:* Bodkin)	Needleworking Equipment	237
Leaf	Other Documents	483
Leaf, Metal	Painting T&E	229
Leaflet	Other Documents	483
Lean-To	Other Structures	41
Lease	Legal Documents	476
Leash	Animal Care Equipment	135
Leash, Child	Regulative Devices	348
Leash, Pet	Pet Supplies	141
Lectern	Support Furniture	55
Lecture	Literary Works	477
Lederhosen	Main Garments	97
Ledger	Financial Records	469
Leeboard	Water Transportation Accessories	438
Leg, Air	Mining & Mineral Harvesting T&E	223
Leg, Artificial	Personal Assistive Objects	109
Legging	Main Garments	97
Legharness	Body Armor	275
Lehr	Glass, Plastics & Clayworking T&E	193
leister (*use:* Spear, Fish)	Edged Weapons	278
Lencoscope	Medical Instruments	329
Lens	Optical T&E	344
Lens, Anastigmatic	Optical T&E	344
Lens, Camera	Camera Equipment	377
Lens, Contact	Personal Assistive Objects	108
Lens, Fisheye	Camera Equipment	377
Lens, Macro	Camera Equipment	377
Lens, Stenopaic	Medical Instruments	329
Lens, Telephoto	Camera Equipment	377
Lens, Water	Optical T&E	344
Lens, Wide Angle	Camera Equipment	377
Lens, Zoom	Camera Equipment	377
Leotard	Main Garments	96
Letter	Other Documents	482
Letter of Credit	Exchange Media	489
Letter, Form	Other Documents	482
Letter, Recommendation	Other Documents	482
Letter, Referral	Other Documents	482
letterhead (*use:* Stationery)	Writing Media	408
Letterpress	Replication Equipment	387
Lettre de Cachet	Government Records	470
Level, Automatic	Surveying Equipment	353
Level, Carpenter's	Woodworking T&E	253
Level, Dumpy	Surveying Equipment	353
Level, Gunner's	Armament Accessories	270
Level, Mason's	Masonry & Stoneworking T&E	204
Level, Plumb	Woodworking T&E	253
Level, Spirit	Woodworking T&E	253
Level, Surveyor's	Surveying Equipment	352
Level, Track	Rail Transportation Accessories	432
Level, Wye	Surveying Equipment	353
Leveler, Hoof	Farrier Equipment	140
Leveler, Land	Cultivation Equipment	124
Lever	Mechanical Devices	316
Lever, Throttle	Rail Transportation Accessories	431
Levigator	Graphic Equipment	384
Lewis	Masonry & Stoneworking T&E	204
Library	Civic & Social Structures	26
License	Other Documents	484
License, Animal	Other Documents	484
license, driver's (*use:* License, Transportation)	Other Documents	484
license, fishing (*use:* License, Sporting)	Other Documents	484
license, hunting (*use:* License, Sporting)	Other Documents	484
License, Marriage	Government Records	471
License, Occupational	Other Documents	484
License, Sporting	Other Documents	484
License, Transportation	Other Documents	484
Lid, Dish	Serving Vessels	187
Lid, Drinking Vessel	Drinking Vessels	175
Lid, Stove	Heating Equipment Accessories	77
Lifeboat	Watercraft	446
Lifeboat, Rescue	Watercraft	446
Lifeboat, Ship's	Watercraft	446
Lifecar	Watercraft	446
lifesaver (*use:* Ring, Life)	Water Transportation Accessories	441

Lift, Chair	Rail Vehicles	434
Lift, Cow	Veterinary Equipment	142
Lift, Drawing	Mining & Mineral Harvesting T&E	223
Lift, Gondola	Rail Vehicles	434
Lift, Hydraulic	Mechanical Devices	316
Lift, Levitation	Public Entertainment Devices	508
Lift, Sash	Finish Hardware	11
Lift, Stair	Conveyance Devices	5
Lifter, Jar	Food Processing Equipment	165
Lifter, Pie	Food Preparation Equipment	160
Lifter, Plate	Food Preparation Accessories	152
Lifter, Pot	Food Preparation Accessories	152
Lifter, Roast	Food Preparation Equipment	160
Lifter, Sand	Metalworking T&E	213
Lifter, Skirt	Clothing Accessories	85
Lifter, Sod	Groundskeeping Equipment	309
Lifter, Stove	Heating Equipment Accessories	77
lifter, stump (*use:* Puller, Stump)	Cultivation Equipment	125
Lifter, Toddy	Serving Vessels	189
Ligature	Medical Instruments	331
Light, Aiming Post	Armament Accessories	270
Light, Aircraft Running	Aerospace Transportation Accessories	410
light, black (*use:* Bulb, Ultraviolet)	Other Lighting Accessories	72
Light, Bollard	Lighting Devices	70
Light, Channel	Navigational Equipment	350
Light, Christmas Tree	Holiday Objects	458
Light, Dental Curing	Dental Accessories	321
Light, Emergency	Lighting Devices	69
Light, Holiday	Holiday Objects	458
Light, Masthead	Water Transportation Accessories	438
Light, Navigation	Water Transportation Accessories	438
light, neon (*use:* Bulb, Neon)	Other Lighting Accessories	72
Light, Night	Lighting Devices	69
Light, Outdoor	Lighting Devices	69
Light, Overtaking	Water Transportation Accessories	438
Light, Pendant	Lighting Devices	68
Light, Plaque	Dental Instruments	323
Light, Recessed	Lighting Devices	68
Light, Rope	Lighting Devices	70
light, signal (*use:* Lamp, Signal)	Visual Communication Devices	400
Light, Solar	Lighting Devices	70
light, stop (*use:* Signal, Traffic)	Visual Communication Devices	400
Light, String	Lighting Devices	70
Light, Strobe	Lighting Devices	70
Light, Track	Lighting Devices	68
Light, Vehicle Running	Land Transportation Accessories	417
Light, Watercraft Running	Water Transportation Accessories	438
Lighter	Smoking & Recreational Drug Equipment	114
Lighter, Friction	Metalworking T&E	213
Lighter, Marine	Watercraft	446
Lighthouse	Transportation Structures	39
lightpen (*use:* Pen, Light)	Peripherals	364
Lightship	Watercraft	448
Lightstick	Other Lighting Accessories	72
Limb, Artificial	Personal Assistive Objects	108
limber (*use:* Caisson)	Animal-Powered Vehicles	424
Limber, Artillery	Armament Accessories	270
Limousine	Motor Vehicles	428
linac (*use:* Accelerator, Linear)	Nuclear Physics T&E	341
Linchpin	Land Transportation Accessories	417
Line, Aircraft Mooring	Aerospace Transportation Accessories	410
Line, Chalk	Woodworking T&E	248
Line, Fishing	Fishing Equipment	147
Line, Power	Electrical System Components	301
Line, Tack	Water Transportation Accessories	439
line, tow (*use:* Hawser)	Water Transportation Accessories	441
linen, stair (*use:* Cover, Stair)	Floor Coverings	45
Linen, Table	Food Service Accessories	181
Liner, Boot	Footwear	90
Liner, Commode	Hygiene Objects	120
Liner, Cylinder	Metalworking T&E	213
Liner, Helmet	Body Armor	275
Liner, Inkwell	Writing Accessories	403
Liner, Ocean	Watercraft	446
Liner, Platter	Food Service Accessories	182
Liner, Toilet Seat	Hygiene Objects	120
Lineshaft	Power Transmission Components	305
Lining, Flue	Environmental Control Elements	8
Lining, Garment	Clothing Accessories	85
Link, Cuff	Clothing Accessories	85
Link, Snap	Multiple Use T&E for Materials	227
Linocut	Graphic Documents	474
Linoleum	Surface Elements	18

Term	Category	Page
linotype (*use:* Machine, Type Casting)	Typesetting Equipment	388
Linstock	Armament Accessories	270
Lintel	Supporting Elements	16
linter, cottonseed (*use:* Cleaner, Cottonseed)	Harvesting Equipment	127
Lipstick	Beauty Supplies	117
Lira	Exchange Media	488
lira (*use:* Lyra)	Musical Instruments	374
List	Other Documents	483
List, Attendance	Other Documents	483
List, Mailing	Other Documents	483
List, Membership	Other Documents	483
List, Passenger	Other Documents	483
list, price (*use:* Pricelist)	Other Documents	483
List, Subscription	Other Documents	483
List, Voters'	Other Documents	483
Lithograph	Graphic Documents	474
Lithophane	Decorative Furnishings	60
litho-press (*use:* Press, Lithographic)	Replication Equipment	387
Lithotrite	Medical Instruments	334
Litrameter	Chemical Testing Devices	290
Litter	Human-Powered Vehicles	427
loader (*use:* Machine, Loading)	Mining & Mineral Harvesting T&E	223
Loader, Ammunition	Armament Accessories	270
Loader, Ammunition Belt	Armament Accessories	270
Loader, Bale Hay	Harvesting Equipment	130
loader, bucket (*use:* Loader, Front End)	Construction T&E	295
Loader, Corn Shock	Harvesting Equipment	130
Loader, Crop	Harvesting Equipment	130
Loader, Front End	Construction T&E	295
Loader, Hay	Harvesting Equipment	130
Loader, Shell	Armament Accessories	270
Loader, Skid	Construction T&E	295
Loafer	Footwear	90
Lobsterboat	Watercraft	445
Locator, Cable Fault	Electrical Maintenance & Repair Equipment	299
Lock	Hydraulic Structures	34
Lock, Cannon	Armament Accessories	270
Lock, Door	Finish Hardware	10
lock, load (*use:* Bar, Load)	Land Transportation Accessories	416
Lock, Security	Protective Devices	346
Lock, Window	Finish Hardware	10
Locker	Storage & Display Furniture	54
Locker, Arms	Armament Accessories	268
Locker, Flag	Visual Communication Accessories	399
Locket	Body Adornments	81
Locknut	Multiple Use T&E for Materials	227

Term	Category	Page
Locksaw	Woodworking T&E	257
Locomotive	Rail Vehicles	434
Locomotive, Articulated	Rail Vehicles	434
Locomotive, Diesel-Electric	Rail Vehicles	434
Locomotive, Diesel-Hydraulic	Rail Vehicles	434
Locomotive, Electric	Rail Vehicles	434
Locomotive, Gasoline	Rail Vehicles	434
Locomotive, Gasoline-Electric	Rail Vehicles	434
Locomotive, Gear	Rail Vehicles	434
Locomotive, Geared	Rail Vehicles	434
Locomotive, Mine	Mining & Mineral Harvesting T&E	223
Locomotive, Steam	Rail Vehicles	434
Locomotive, Tank	Rail Vehicles	434
Locomotive, Turbine	Rail Vehicles	434
Lodge	Commercial Structures	27
Lodge, Fishing	Cultural & Recreational Structures	30
Lodge, Fraternal	Civic & Social Structures	26
Lodge, Hunting	Cultural & Recreational Structures	30
Lodge, Sporting	Cultural & Recreational Structures	30
Log	Other Documents	484
Log, Artificial	Decorative Furnishings	60
Log, Flight	Other Documents	484
Log, Impeller	Water Transportation Accessories	441
Log, Lithology	Mining & Mineral Harvesting T&E	223
Log, Nautical	Water Transportation Accessories	441
Log, Neutron	Mining & Mineral Harvesting T&E	223
Log, Pit	Water Transportation Accessories	441
Log, Ship's	Other Documents	484
Log, Taffrail	Water Transportation Accessories	441
Log, Timber	Construction Materials	3
Loggia	Architectural Spaces	1
Logograph	Acoustical T&E	261
Logometer	Chemical Testing Devices	291
Loincloth	Main Garments	97
Longboat	Watercraft	448
Longbow	Edged Weapons	277
Longhouse	Dwellings	33
Longline	Fishing Equipment	147
Longliner	Watercraft	445
Loom	Textile Manufacturing Equipment	241
loom, apron (*use:* Loom, Bow)	Textile Manufacturing Equipment	241
Loom, Backstrap	Textile Manufacturing Equipment	241

Term	Category	Page
Loom, Bead	Textile Manufacturing Equipment	241
Loom, Belt	Textile Manufacturing Equipment	241
Loom, Bow	Textile Manufacturing Equipment	241
Loom, Broad	Textile Manufacturing Equipment	241
Loom, Cam	Textile Manufacturing Equipment	241
Loom, Carpet	Textile Manufacturing Equipment	241
Loom, Counterbalance	Textile Manufacturing Equipment	241
Loom, Countermarch	Textile Manufacturing Equipment	241
Loom, Dobby	Textile Manufacturing Equipment	241
loom, doup (*use:* Loom, Leno)	Textile Manufacturing Equipment	241
Loom, Draw	Textile Manufacturing Equipment	241
Loom, Frame	Textile Manufacturing Equipment	241
Loom, Ground	Textile Manufacturing Equipment	241
Loom, Hand	Textile Manufacturing Equipment	241
Loom, Inkle	Textile Manufacturing Equipment	241
Loom, Jack	Textile Manufacturing Equipment	241
Loom, Jacquard	Textile Manufacturing Equipment	241
Loom, Lace	Textile Manufacturing Equipment	241
Loom, Leno	Textile Manufacturing Equipment	241
Loom, Needlepoint	Textile Manufacturing Equipment	241
Loom, Pile Fabric	Textile Manufacturing Equipment	241
loom, power (*use:* Powerloom)	Textile Manufacturing Equipment	241
Loom, Rapier	Textile Manufacturing Equipment	241
Loom, Rigid Heddle	Textile Manufacturing Equipment	241
Loom, Shuttleless	Textile Manufacturing Equipment	241
Loom, Swivel	Textile Manufacturing Equipment	241
Loom, Table	Textile Manufacturing Equipment	241
Loom, Tablet	Textile Manufacturing Equipment	241
Loom, Tape	Textile Manufacturing Equipment	241
Loom, Treadle	Textile Manufacturing Equipment	241
Loom, Warp-Weighted	Textile Manufacturing Equipment	241
Loom, Water-Jet	Textile Manufacturing Equipment	241
Loomweight	Textile Manufacturing Equipment	242
loonie (*use:* Dollar)	Exchange Media	488
Loop, Bacteriology	Biological T&E	287
loop, curtain (*use:* Loop, Tieback)	Window & Door Coverings	78
Loop, Shoulder	Status Symbols	496
Loop, Tieback	Window & Door Coverings	78
lopper (*use:* Pruner, Tree)	Groundskeeping Equipment	310
Lorgnette	Personal Assistive Objects	108
lotto (*use:* Game, Lotto)	Game Equipment	505
loudspeaker (*use:* Speaker)	Sound Communication Devices	392
Louis d'Or	Exchange Media	488
Lounge	Sleeping & Reclining Furniture	51
Loupe	Optical T&E	344
Loupe, Focusing	Photographic Accessories	378
Lowboy	Storage & Display Furniture	53
LP (*use:* Record, 33 1/3 RPM)	Sound Communication Media	393
Lubricator, Pressure	Mechanical Devices	317
Lubricator-Sizer	Armament Accessories	270
Lucet	Textile Manufacturing Equipment	242
lucimeter (*use:* Photometer)	Optical T&E	344
Luge	Sports Equipment	517
Lumber	Construction Materials	3
Luminometer	Optical T&E	344
Lunchbox	Food Service Accessories	180
Lung, Iron	Medical Instruments	333
Lure	Fishing Equipment	147
Lure, Dog Track	Sports Equipment	512
Lure, Plug	Fishing Equipment	147
Lure, Soft	Fishing Equipment	147
Lure, Spoon	Fishing Equipment	147
Lure, Surface	Fishing Equipment	147
Luster	Other Lighting Accessories	73
Lute	Musical Instruments	374
Lyra	Musical Instruments	374
Lyre	Musical Instruments	374
Lyre-Guitar	Musical Instruments	373
Lysimeter	Biological T&E	287
Mace	Percussive Weapons	283
Mace, Ceremonial	Status Symbols	498
mace-head (*use:* Mattoir)	Graphic Equipment	384
Machete	Harvesting Equipment	130
Machine, Adding	Data Processing Devices	361

Term	Category	Page
Machine, Addressing	Replication Equipment	387
Machine, Answering	Telecommunication Devices	396
machine, arc welding (*use:* Welder, Electric)	Metalworking T&E	219
machine, arcade (*use:* Game, Arcade)	Game Equipment	503
Machine, Automatic Teller	Merchandising T&E	337
Machine, Backfilling	Textile Manufacturing Equipment	242
Machine, Backstripping	Bookbinding Equipment	382
Machine, Bag Closing	Food Processing Equipment	168
Machine, Bag Forming	Papermaking T&E	232
Machine, Bag Sewing	Food Processing Equipment	168
Machine, Bag Tying	Food Processing Equipment	168
Machine, Banding	Printing Accessories	386
Machine, Batcher-Jogger	Bookbinding Equipment	382
Machine, Batt Making	Textile Manufacturing Equipment	242
Machine, Beading	Metalworking T&E	213
Machine, Beaming	Leather, Horn & Shellworking T&E	198
Machine, Beating	Leather, Horn & Shellworking T&E	198
Machine, Bedding	Woodworking T&E	253
Machine, Beetle	Textile Manufacturing Equipment	242
Machine, Billing	Data Processing Devices	361
Machine, Binding	Bookbinding Equipment	382
Machine, Bleaching	Textile Manufacturing Equipment	242
Machine, Blending	Textile Manufacturing Equipment	242
machine, Bloomberg (*use:* Ticker, Stock)	Telecommunication Devices	396
Machine, Blowing	Glass, Plastics & Clayworking T&E	193
Machine, Blueprint	Drafting T&E	367
Machine, Bolt Heading	Metalworking T&E	213
Machine, Bonding	Textile Manufacturing Equipment	242
Machine, Book Smashing	Bookbinding Equipment	382
Machine, Book Stitching	Bookbinding Equipment	382
Machine, Book Trimming	Bookbinding Equipment	382
Machine, Bookkeeping	Data Processing Devices	361
machine, boring (*use:* Machine, Metal Boring)	Metalworking T&E	214
machine, boring (*use:* Machine, Wood Boring)	Woodworking T&E	254
Machine, Bottling	Food Processing Equipment	168
Machine, Brading	Metalworking T&E	213
Machine, Braiding	Textile Manufacturing Equipment	242
machine, bread (*use:* Maker, Bread)	Food Preparation Equipment	154
Machine, Brick	Masonry & Stoneworking T&E	204
Machine, Broaching	Metalworking T&E	213
Machine, Broom	Fiberworking T&E	144
Machine, Brush	Food Processing Equipment	164
machine, brushing (*use:* Machine, Leather Brushing)	Leather, Horn & Shellworking T&E	199
machine, brushing (*use:* Machine, Textile Brushing)	Textile Manufacturing Equipment	243
machine, buffing (*use:* Machine, Leather Buffing)	Leather, Horn & Shellworking T&E	199
machine, buffing (*use:* Machine, Metal Buffing)	Metalworking T&E	214
Machine, Bulking	Textile Manufacturing Equipment	242
Machine, Burling	Textile Manufacturing Equipment	242
Machine, Burring	Metalworking T&E	213
Machine, Calculating	Data Processing Devices	361
Machine, Can Capping	Food Processing Equipment	168
Machine, Cappuccino	Food Preparation Equipment	154
Machine, Card Clothing	Textile Manufacturing Equipment	242
Machine, Card Punching	Textile Manufacturing Equipment	242
machine, carding (*use:* Machine, Leather Carding)	Leather, Horn & Shellworking T&E	199
machine, carding (*use:* Machine, Textile Carding)	Textile Manufacturing Equipment	243
Machine, Cartoning	Food Processing Equipment	168
Machine, Casemaking	Bookbinding Equipment	382
Machine, Casing-In	Bookbinding Equipment	382
Machine, Change	Merchandising T&E	336
Machine, Charging	Metalworking T&E	213
Machine, Chinchilla	Textile Manufacturing Equipment	242
Machine, Cipher	Writing Devices	406
Machine, Clay Coating	Glass, Plastics & Clayworking T&E	193
machine, coating (*use:* Machine, Clay Coating)	Glass, Plastics & Clayworking T&E	193
machine, coating (*use:* Machine, Paper Coating)	Papermaking T&E	232
machine, coating (*use:* Machine, Textile Coating)	Textile Manufacturing Equipment	243
Machine, Coffee Roasting	Food Preparation Equipment	155

Machine, Collating	Bookbinding Equipment	382
machine, composing (*use:* Typesetter)	Typesetting Equipment	388
Machine, Concrete Finishing	Masonry & Stoneworking T&E	204
Machine, Cone	Metalworking T&E	213
machine, copying (*use:* Photocopier)	Replication Equipment	387
Machine, Cork	Food Processing Equipment	168
Machine, Cotton Candy	Food Preparation Equipment	155
Machine, Crabbing	Textile Manufacturing Equipment	242
machine, creasing (*use:* Machine, Leather Creasing)	Leather, Horn & Shellworking T&E	199
machine, creasing (*use:* Machine, Metal Creasing)	Metalworking T&E	214
Machine, Credit Card	Merchandising T&E	337
machine, crimping (*use:* Machine, Metal Crimping)	Metalworking T&E	214
machine, crimping (*use:* Machine, Textile Crimping)	Textile Manufacturing Equipment	243
Machine, Crocheting	Textile Manufacturing Equipment	242
Machine, Cutting	Mining & Mineral Harvesting T&E	223
Machine, Cylinder	Papermaking T&E	232
Machine, Deburring	Leather, Horn & Shellworking T&E	198
Machine, Decating	Textile Manufacturing Equipment	242
Machine, Dehairing	Leather, Horn & Shellworking T&E	198
Machine, Diathermy	Medical Instruments	334
Machine, Dibbling	Planting Equipment	132
Machine, Dictating	Sound Communication Devices	392
machine, die cutting (*use:* Press, Clicker)	Leather, Horn & Shellworking T&E	199
Machine, Die Cutting	Metalworking T&E	213
machine, ditching (*use:* Machine, Trenching)	Construction T&E	295
Machine, Ditching	Cultivation Equipment	124
Machine, Ditto	Replication Equipment	387
Machine, Double Seaming	Metalworking T&E	213
Machine, Dovetailing	Woodworking T&E	253
Machine, Drafting	Drafting T&E	366
Machine, Drawing-In	Textile Manufacturing Equipment	242
Machine, Dry Cleaning	Laundry Equipment	313
Machine, Drying	Leather, Horn & Shellworking T&E	198
machine, duplicating (*use:* Duplicator)	Replication Equipment	387
Machine, Dyeing	Textile Manufacturing Equipment	242
Machine, Electrotherapy	Medical Instruments	334
Machine, Elliptical	Recreational Devices	509
Machine, Embroidery	Needleworking Equipment	235
Machine, Engraving	Glass, Plastics & Clayworking T&E	193
Machine, Espresso	Food Preparation Equipment	154
Machine, Exercise	Recreational Devices	509
Machine, Eyelet	Leather, Horn & Shellworking T&E	198
Machine, Fall	Mechanical Devices	316
Machine, Felting	Textile Manufacturing Equipment	242
Machine, Filament Winding	Glass, Plastics & Clayworking T&E	193
Machine, Fleshing	Leather, Horn & Shellworking T&E	199
Machine, Float Cutting	Textile Manufacturing Equipment	242
Machine, Flocking	Textile Manufacturing Equipment	242
Machine, Foam	Glass, Plastics & Clayworking T&E	193
Machine, Foam Cutting	Glass, Plastics & Clayworking T&E	193
machine, folding (*use:* Machine, Metal Folding)	Metalworking T&E	214
machine, folding (*use:* Machine, Paper Folding)	Printing Accessories	386
machine, folding (*use:* Machine, Textile Folding)	Textile Manufacturing Equipment	243
Machine, Food Packing	Food Processing Equipment	168
machine, forming (*use:* Machine, Plastic Forming)	Glass, Plastics & Clayworking T&E	193
machine, forming (*use:* Machine, Metal Forming)	Metalworking T&E	214
Machine, Fourdrinier	Papermaking T&E	232
Machine, Fulling	Textile Manufacturing Equipment	242
Machine, Garnett	Textile Manufacturing Equipment	242
Machine, Gear Cutting	Metalworking T&E	213
Machine, Gigging	Textile Manufacturing Equipment	242
Machine, Gluing	Bookbinding Equipment	382
Machine, Grooving	Metalworking T&E	213

machine, grout (*use:* Injector, Cement)	Mining & Mineral Harvesting T&E	223
Machine, Gunite	Masonry & Stoneworking T&E	204
Machine, Heat Setting	Textile Manufacturing Equipment	242
Machine, Hemstitching	Needleworking Equipment	236
Machine, Hornworker's	Leather, Horn & Shellworking T&E	201
machine, husking (*use:* Husker-Shredder, Corn)	Harvesting Equipment	128
Machine, Interlocking	Rail Transportation Accessories	432
machine, ironing (*use:* Machine, Leather Ironing)	Leather, Horn & Shellworking T&E	199
Machine, Key Cutting	Metalworking T&E	213
Machine, Knitting	Textile Manufacturing Equipment	242
Machine, Knitting Sewing	Needleworking Equipment	236
Machine, Leather Brushing	Leather, Horn & Shellworking T&E	199
Machine, Leather Buffing	Leather, Horn & Shellworking T&E	199
Machine, Leather Carding	Leather, Horn & Shellworking T&E	199
Machine, Leather Creasing	Leather, Horn & Shellworking T&E	199
Machine, Leather Ironing	Leather, Horn & Shellworking T&E	199
Machine, Leather Sewing	Leather, Horn & Shellworking T&E	199
Machine, Leather Shearing	Leather, Horn & Shellworking T&E	199
Machine, Leather Stretching	Leather, Horn & Shellworking T&E	199
Machine, Leatherworking	Leather, Horn & Shellworking T&E	198
Machine, Loading	Mining & Mineral Harvesting T&E	223
Machine, Looping	Textile Manufacturing Equipment	242
Machine, Mailing	Writing Accessories	404
Machine, Medical X-Ray	Medical Instruments	328
Machine, Mercerizing	Textile Manufacturing Equipment	242
machine, message (*use:* Machine, Answering)	Telecommunication Devices	396
Machine, Metal Boring	Metalworking T&E	214
Machine, Metal Buffing	Metalworking T&E	214
Machine, Metal Casting	Dental Accessories	321
Machine, Metal Creasing	Metalworking T&E	214
Machine, Metal Crimping	Metalworking T&E	214
Machine, Metal Folding	Metalworking T&E	214
Machine, Metal Forming	Metalworking T&E	214
Machine, Metal Shearing	Metalworking T&E	214
Machine, Metalworking	Metalworking T&E	213
Machine, Metering	Glass, Plastics & Clayworking T&E	193
Machine, Milking	Food Processing Equipment	166
Machine, Milling	Metalworking T&E	214
Machine, Mitering	Woodworking T&E	253
Machine, Molding	Glass, Plastics & Clayworking T&E	193
Machine, Mortising	Woodworking T&E	253
machine, mower (*use:* Mower)	Harvesting Equipment	130
Machine, Mucking	Mining & Mineral Harvesting T&E	223
Machine, Nail Cutting	Metalworking T&E	214
Machine, Needlework	Needleworking Equipment	235
Machine, Numbering	Printing Accessories	386
Machine, Oxygen	Medical Instruments	333
Machine, Pachinko	Game Equipment	503
Machine, Package Changing	Textile Manufacturing Equipment	242
Machine, Packaging	Food Processing Equipment	168
Machine, Pad	Textile Manufacturing Equipment	242
Machine, Paper	Papermaking T&E	232
Machine, Paper Coating	Papermaking T&E	232
Machine, Paper Cutting	Papermaking T&E	232
Machine, Paper Folding	Printing Accessories	386
machine, paper making (*use:* Machine, Paper)	Papermaking T&E	232
Machine, Paper Packing	Papermaking T&E	232
Machine, Paper Trimming	Papermaking T&E	232
machine, peepshow (*use:* Peepshow)	Toys	524
machine, perfusion (*use:* Pump, Perfusion)	Medical Instruments	334
Machine, Perlock	Textile Manufacturing Equipment	242
Machine, Permanent Wave	Hair Care Objects	118
Machine, Pill	Medical Accessories	326
Machine, Pillow	Textile Manufacturing Equipment	243
Machine, Pinball	Game Equipment	503
Machine, Pinking	Textile Manufacturing Equipment	242
Machine, Pipe Threading	Metalworking T&E	214
Machine, Plastering	Masonry & Stoneworking T&E	206
Machine, Plastic Forming	Glass, Plastics & Clayworking T&E	193
Machine, Pleating	Textile Manufacturing Equipment	242
Machine, Polishing	Metalworking T&E	214
Machine, Popcorn	Food Preparation Equipment	155

Machine, Preform — Glass, Plastics & Clayworking T&E 193
Machine, Pressing — Mining & Mineral Harvesting T&E 223
Machine, Profiling — Woodworking T&E 253
Machine, Pulling — Leather, Horn & Shellworking T&E 199
Machine, Pulp Washing — Papermaking T&E 232
Machine, Pumping — Glass, Plastics & Clayworking T&E 193
Machine, Quarrying — Mining & Mineral Harvesting T&E 223
Machine, Quilting — Needleworking Equipment 236
Machine, Receipt — Writing Accessories 404
Machine, Rifling — Metalworking T&E 214
Machine, Rivet Making — Metalworking T&E 214
Machine, Riveting — Leather, Horn & Shellworking T&E 199
Machine, Ropemaking — Textile Manufacturing Equipment 242
Machine, Round Cornering — Bookbinding Equipment 382
Machine, Rowing — Recreational Devices 509
Machine, Ruling — Bookbinding Equipment 382
Machine, Saw Sharpening — Metalworking T&E 214
Machine, Scoring — Papermaking T&E 232
Machine, Screw Cutting — Metalworking T&E 213
Machine, Setting Down — Metalworking T&E 214
machine, sewing (*use:* Machine, Leather Sewing) — Leather, Horn & Shellworking T&E 199
Machine, Sewing — Needleworking Equipment 236
Machine, Shaving — Woodworking T&E 253
Machine, Shaving Lather — Hair Care Objects 119
machine, shearing (*use:* Machine, Leather Shearing) — Leather, Horn & Shellworking T&E 199
machine, shearing (*use:* Machine, Metal Shearing) — Metalworking T&E 214
machine, shearing (*use:* Machine, Textile Shearing) — Textile Manufacturing Equipment 243
Machine, Shoemaking — Leather, Horn & Shellworking T&E 199
Machine, Shrinking — Textile Manufacturing Equipment 242
Machine, Signature — Writing Devices 406
Machine, Simplex — Textile Manufacturing Equipment 243
Machine, Sintering — Metalworking T&E 214
Machine, Ski — Recreational Devices 509
Machine, Skiving — Leather, Horn & Shellworking T&E 199
Machine, Slot — Game Equipment 503
Machine, Sno-Cone — Food Preparation Equipment 156
Machine, Soldering — Metalworking T&E 214
Machine, Sounding — Navigational Equipment 349
Machine, Splitting — Leather, Horn & Shellworking T&E 199
Machine, Spotting — Woodworking T&E 253
Machine, Stamping — Glass, Plastics & Clayworking T&E 193
Machine, Stencil — Writing Accessories 404
Machine, Step — Recreational Devices 509
Machine, Stitching — Bookbinding Equipment 382
Machine, Stock Compressing — Printing Accessories 386
Machine, Straightening — Metalworking T&E 214
machine, stretching (*use:* Machine, Leather Stretching) — Leather, Horn & Shellworking T&E 199
machine, stretching (*use:* Machine, Textile Stretching) — Textile Manufacturing Equipment 243
Machine, Stuffing — Textile Manufacturing Equipment 243
Machine, Sueding — Textile Manufacturing Equipment 243
Machine, Tab Cutting — Printing Accessories 386
Machine, Tabulating — Data Processing Devices 361
Machine, Taffy Pulling — Food Preparation Equipment 156
Machine, Tandem — Nuclear Physics T&E 341
Machine, Tapping — Metalworking T&E 214
Machine, Tattoo — Beauty Supplies 117
Machine, Teaching — Data Processing Devices 361
Machine, Tenoning — Woodworking T&E 253
Machine, Textile — Textile Manufacturing Equipment 242
Machine, Textile Brushing — Textile Manufacturing Equipment 243
Machine, Textile Carding — Textile Manufacturing Equipment 243
Machine, Textile Coating — Textile Manufacturing Equipment 243
Machine, Textile Crimping — Textile Manufacturing Equipment 243
Machine, Textile Folding — Textile Manufacturing Equipment 243
Machine, Textile Shearing — Textile Manufacturing Equipment 243
Machine, Textile Stretching — Textile Manufacturing Equipment 243
Machine, Texturing — Textile Manufacturing Equipment 243
machine, threshing (*use:* Thresher) — Harvesting Equipment 131
Machine, Throwing — Textile Manufacturing Equipment 243
Machine, Ticker Tape — Telecommunication Devices 396
Machine, Ticket Punch — Merchandising T&E 337
Machine, Tiering — Construction T&E 296

Machine, Tipping	Bookbinding Equipment	382
Machine, Tire Bending	Metalworking T&E	214
Machine, Tobacco	Other T&E for Materials	260
Machine, Toll Collection	Transportation Structures	40
Machine, Tongue and Groove	Woodworking T&E	253
Machine, Transplanting	Planting Equipment	132
Machine, Treenailing	Woodworking T&E	254
Machine, Trenching	Construction T&E	295
Machine, Trimming	Woodworking T&E	254
Machine, Tufting	Textile Manufacturing Equipment	243
Machine, Turning	Metalworking T&E	214
Machine, Twinning	Leather, Horn & Shellworking T&E	201
Machine, Tying-In	Textile Manufacturing Equipment	243
Machine, Type Casting	Typesetting Equipment	388
Machine, Vending	Merchandising T&E	337
machine, voice mail (*use:* Machine, Answering)	Telecommunication Devices	396
Machine, Voting	Organizational Objects	459
Machine, Vulcanizing	Glass, Plastics & Clayworking T&E	193
machine, washing (*use:* Washer, Clothes)	Laundry Equipment	314
Machine, Waste	Textile Manufacturing Equipment	243
Machine, Weight	Recreational Devices	509
Machine, Wheel Making	Woodworking T&E	254
machine, winnowing (*use:* Mill, Fanning)	Harvesting Equipment	131
Machine, Wiring	Metalworking T&E	214
Machine, Wood Bending	Woodworking T&E	254
Machine, Wood Boring	Woodworking T&E	254
Machine, Woodworking	Woodworking T&E	253
Machine, Wrapping	Food Processing Equipment	168
machine, x-ray (*use:* Machine, Medical X-Ray)	Medical Instruments	328
machine, x-ray (*use:* Scanner, X-Ray Security)	Protective Devices	346
Machine, Yankee	Papermaking T&E	232
Mackinaw	Outerwear	101
Mackintosh	Outerwear	101
Magazine	Other Documents	486
magazine, comic (*use:* Book, Comic)	Graphic Documents	472
Magazine, Film	Visual Communication Accessories	399
Magazine, Firearm	Armament Accessories	270
Magazine, Powder	Defense Structures	31
Magazine, Slide	Visual Communication Accessories	399
Magnet	Electrical & Magnetic Measurement Devices	298
Magnet, Accelerator	Nuclear Physics T&E	342
Magnet, Bending	Nuclear Physics T&E	342
Magnet, Drum	Food Processing Equipment	164
Magnet, Quadruple	Nuclear Physics T&E	342
Magnet, Refrigerator	Storage & Display Accessories	64
Magnet, Sextuple	Nuclear Physics T&E	342
Magneto	Power Producing Equipment	304
Magnetograph	Astronomical T&E	285
Magnetometer	Surveying Equipment	353
Magnetron	Electrical System Components	302
mah-jongg (*use:* Set, Mah-Jongg)	Game Equipment	505
mahlstick (*use:* Maulstick)	Painting T&E	230
Mail	Body Armor	275
Mail, Electronic	Other Documents	482
mail, electronic (*use:* Correspondence)	Other Documents	481
Mail, Irish	Toys	524
mail, victory (*use:* V-Mail)	Other Documents	482
Mailbag	Containers	414
Mailbox	Containers	414
Main, Water	Hydraulic Structures	34
Mainsail	Water Transportation Accessories	439
Maker, Bread	Food Preparation Equipment	154
Maker, Coffee	Food Preparation Equipment	154
Maker, Dimple	Medical Instruments	334
maker, ice cream (*use:* Freezer, Ice Cream)	Food Preparation Equipment	153
maker, label (*use:* Embosser, Label)	Writing Devices	406
Maker, Pasta	Food Preparation Equipment	156
maker, yogurt (*use:* Incubator, Yogurt)	Food Preparation Equipment	154
Mall, Shopping	Commercial Structures	27
Mallet	Woodworking T&E	254
Mallet, Carpenter's	Woodworking T&E	254
Mallet, Carver's	Woodworking T&E	254
Mallet, Caulking	Woodworking T&E	254
Mallet, Croquet	Game Equipment	501
Mallet, Dead-Blow	Woodworking T&E	254
Mallet, Dental	Dental Instruments	323
Mallet, Fuze	Armament Accessories	270
Mallet, Gong	Sound Communication Devices	391
Mallet, Grafting	Tending Equipment	133
Mallet, Leatherworking	Leather, Horn & Shellworking T&E	199

Term	Category	Page
Mallet, Mason's	Masonry & Stoneworking T&E	204
Mallet, Oral Surgery	Dental Instruments	323
Mallet, Printer's	Graphic Equipment	384
Mallet, Serving	Textile Manufacturing Equipment	243
Mallet, Shipwright's	Woodworking T&E	254
Mallet, Stone	Masonry & Stoneworking T&E	204
Mallet, Stonecarver's	Masonry & Stoneworking T&E	204
Mallet, Surgical	Medical Instruments	331
Mallet, Wood Carver's	Woodworking T&E	254
Malthouse	Agricultural Structures	23
manacle (*use:* Handcuff)	Regulative Devices	348
Manchette	Clothing Accessories	86
Mandocello	Musical Instruments	374
mandolin (*use:* Slicer, Vegetable)	Food Preparation Equipment	159
Mandolin	Musical Instruments	374
Mandore	Musical Instruments	374
Mandrel	Metalworking T&E	214
Mandrel, Dental	Dental Instruments	323
Mandrel, Hornworker's	Leather, Horn & Shellworking T&E	201
Mandrel, Phonograph	Sound Communication Accessories	389
Mangle	Laundry Equipment	314
Mangonel	Percussive Weapons	283
Manifest	Administrative Records	467
Manifesto	Declaratory Documents	468
Manifold	Power Transmission Components	305
Manikin, Display	Merchandising T&E	337
manikin, dress (*use:* Form, Dress)	Needleworking Equipment	235
Manikin, Teaching	Instructional Documents	475
Maniple	Status Symbols	499
mannequin (*use:* Manikin, Display)	Merchandising T&E	337
mannequin, dress (*use:* Form, Dress)	Needleworking Equipment	235
mannequin, teaching (*use:* Manikin, Teaching)	Instructional Documents	475
Mano	Food Preparation Equipment	160
man-of-war (*use:* Warship)	Watercraft	447
Manometer	Chemical Testing Devices	291
Manoptoscope	Medical Instruments	329
Mansion	Dwellings	33
Mantel	Environmental Control Elements	8
Mantelet	Outerwear	100
mantelshelf (*use:* Mantel)	Environmental Control Elements	8
Mantilla	Headwear	94
Mantle	Outerwear	100
Mantle, Ecclesiastical	Status Symbols	500
Mantle, Lamp	Other Lighting Accessories	73
Mantua	Main Garments	97
Manual	Instructional Documents	475
Manual, Employee	Instructional Documents	475
Manual, Training	Instructional Documents	475
Manuscript	Other Documents	484
Manuterge	Religious Objects	464
Map	Graphic Documents	472
Map, Road	Graphic Documents	472
Maquette	Art	454
Maraca	Musical Instruments	372
Marble	Game Equipment	504
Marble, Voting	Organizational Objects	459
Marimba	Musical Instruments	372
Marionette	Public Entertainment Devices	508
Mark	Exchange Media	488
Mark, Fire	Other Documents	485
marker (*use:* Pen, Marker)	Writing Devices	406
Marker, Boundary	Site Features	21
Marker, Clapboard	Woodworking T&E	254
Marker, Concrete	Surveying Equipment	353
Marker, Distance	Site Features	21
Marker, Fabric	Needleworking Equipment	236
Marker, Game	Game Equipment	502
Marker, Golf Ball	Sports Equipment	516
Marker, Grave	Funerary Objects	457
Marker, Hem	Needleworking Equipment	236
Marker, Ice	Mining & Mineral Harvesting T&E	225
Marker, Mason's	Masonry & Stoneworking T&E	204
marker, mile (*use:* Marker, Distance)	Site Features	21
Marker, Navigational	Navigational Equipment	350
Marker, Pattern	Needleworking Equipment	236
Marker, Ream	Papermaking T&E	232
Marker, Site	Site Features	21
Marker, Survey	Surveying Equipment	353
Marlinespike	Needleworking Equipment	236
Marotte	Toys	521
Marquee	Advertising Media	451
Martingale	Land Transportation Accessories	421
Marver	Glass, Plastics & Clayworking T&E	194
Mascara	Beauty Supplies	117
Masher	Food Preparation Equipment	156
Masher, Kraut	Food Preparation Equipment	156
Masher, Potato	Food Preparation Equipment	156

Term	Category	Page
Mask, Anesthesia	Medical Instruments	327
Mask, Burial	Funerary Objects	456
Mask, Catcher's	Sports Equipment	513
Mask, Cold Weather	Headwear	94
Mask, Cup	Personal Assistive Objects	107
Mask, Death	Memorabilia	478
Mask, Diving	Recreational Devices	510
mask, dust (*use:* Mask, Cup)	Personal Assistive Objects	107
Mask, Fencing	Sports Equipment	515
Mask, Gas	Protective Devices	346
Mask, Goalie	Sports Equipment	516
Mask, Holiday	Holiday Objects	458
Mask, Life	Art	454
Mask, Lip	Glass, Plastics & Clayworking T&E	194
Mask, Oxygen	Medical Instruments	333
Mask, Photographic	Photoprocessing Equipment	381
Mask, Plug	Glass, Plastics & Clayworking T&E	194
Mask, Respirator	Personal Assistive Objects	107
Mask, Ritual	Religious Objects	464
mask, scuba (*use:* Mask, Diving)	Recreational Devices	510
Mask, Sleep	Personal Assistive Objects	107
Mask, Surgical	Medical Accessories	326
Mask, Swim	Recreational Devices	510
Mask, Theatrical	Public Entertainment Devices	507
Mask, Welder's	Metalworking T&E	214
Masker, Audio	Acoustical T&E	261
Massager, Belt	Recreational Devices	509
Massager, Scalp	Personal Assistive Objects	107
Mast	Water Transportation Accessories	440
Mat	Floor Coverings	45
Mat, Bath	Floor Coverings	45
Mat, Bed	Bedding	44
mat, bureau (*use:* Mat, Furniture)	Furniture Coverings	61
Mat, Chair	Floor Coverings	45
Mat, Counter	Merchandising T&E	337
Mat, Exercise	Recreational Devices	509
Mat, Furniture	Furniture Coverings	61
Mat, Game	Game Equipment	502
Mat, Gymnastics	Sports Equipment	516
Mat, Picture	Photographic Accessories	378
mat, place (*use:* Placemat)	Food Service Accessories	181
Mat, Sleeping	Bedding	44
mat, stove (*use:* Pad, Stove)	Floor Coverings	45
Mat, Table	Furniture Coverings	61
Mat, Vehicle Floor	Land Transportation Accessories	419
Mat, Wrestling	Sports Equipment	519
Match	Firemaking Equipment	74
Matchbook	Firemaking Equipment	74
Matchbox	Firemaking Equipment	74
Material, Animal	Leather, Horn & Shellworking T&E	199
Material, Fragrance	Other Household Accessories	67
Material, Worked	Unclassifiable Objects	527
matrix, seal (*use:* Press, Seal)	Writing Devices	406
Matte	Camera Equipment	377
Mattock	Cultivation Equipment	124
Mattoir	Graphic Equipment	384
Mattress	Bedding	44
Mattress, Air	Bedding	44
Mattress, Feather	Bedding	44
Mattress, Foam	Bedding	44
Mattress, Horsehair	Bedding	44
Mattress, Spring	Bedding	44
Maul	Woodworking T&E	254
Maul, Chime	Woodworking T&E	254
Maul, Grab	Forestry T&E	191
Maul, Meat	Food Preparation Equipment	156
Maul, Post	Woodworking T&E	254
Maul, Rawhide	Leather, Horn & Shellworking T&E	199
Maul, Spike	Metalworking T&E	212
Maulstick	Painting T&E	230
Mausoleum	Ceremonial Structures	25
Maxiskirt	Main Garments	98
Maypole	Ceremonial Structures	25
Mazarine	Food Preparation Equipment	162
Mazer	Drinking Vessels	173
Measure, Culinary	Food Preparation Equipment	156
Measure, Dry	Weights & Measures T&E	357
Measure, Liquid	Weights & Measures T&E	357
Measure, Pharmaceutical	Medical Accessories	326
Measure, Powder	Armament Accessories	270
Measure, Spring	Weights & Measures T&E	358
Measure, Tape	Weights & Measures T&E	358
Measurer, Sound	Acoustical T&E	261
meat-ax (*use:* Cleaver)	Food Preparation Equipment	159
meatoscope (*use:* Speculum)	Medical Instruments	328
Medal	Achievement Symbols	491
Medal, Commemorative	Memorabilia	478
medal, fraternal (*use:* Pendant, Fraternal)	Status Symbols	497
Medal, Peace	Organizational Objects	459
Medal, Political	Belief Symbols	493
Medal, Prize	Achievement Symbols	491
medallion (*use:* Medal, Commemorative)	Memorabilia	478
Medium, Digital Exchange	Exchange Media	487
Meetinghouse	Ceremonial Structures	25

Term	Category	Page
Megalethoscope	Visual Communication Devices	400
Megaphone	Sound Communication Devices	391
megascope (*use:* Projector, Lantern Slide)	Visual Communication Devices	400
Megger	Electrical & Magnetic Measurement Devices	297
Melanoscope	Chemical Testing Devices	291
Mellophone	Musical Instruments	370
Mellotron	Musical Instruments	371
Melodeon	Musical Instruments	371
melonseed (*use:* Boat, Gunning)	Watercraft	442
memento (*use:* Souvenir)	Memorabilia	478
Memoir	Literary Works	477
Memorandum	Other Documents	482
menat (*use:* Amulet)	Belief Symbols	493
Mender, Pot	Food Preparation Accessories	152
Menhir	Site Features	21
Menorah	Religious Objects	461
Menu	Other Documents	483
Méridienne	Seating Furniture	49
Merry-Go-Round	Recreational Devices	510
Mesoscaphe	Watercraft	448
messtin (*use:* Tin, Mess)	Cooking Vessels	151
Metalcut	Graphic Documents	474
Metate	Food Processing Equipment	169
Meteorograph	Meteorological T&E	340
Meteorometer	Meteorological T&E	339
Meteoroscope	Astronomical T&E	285
Meter, Air	Meteorological T&E	339
Meter, Angle	Surveying Equipment	353
Meter, Electric	Electrical & Magnetic Measurement Devices	297
Meter, Exposure	Photographic Accessories	379
Meter, Gas	Mechanical Measurement Equipment	318
Meter, Light	Photographic Accessories	378
Meter, Parking	Transportation Structures	39
Meter, Peak Flow	Medical Instruments	327
Meter, Phase	Electrical & Magnetic Measurement Devices	297
Meter, Postage	Writing Accessories	404
Meter, Water	Mechanical Measurement Equipment	318
meter, watthour (*use:* Meter, Electric)	Electrical & Magnetic Measurement Devices	297
Meter, Yaw	Navigational Equipment	350
Meterstick	Weights & Measures T&E	358
Mether	Drinking Vessels	173
Metope	Supporting Elements	16
Metrochrome	Optical T&E	344
Metronome	Musical Accessories	369
Metroscope	Medical Instruments	330
Mezuzah	Religious Objects	465
Mezzaluna	Food Preparation Equipment	159
Microcassette	Sound Communication Media	393
microcomputer (*use:* Computer, Desktop)	Data Processing Devices	362
microcomputer (*use:* Computer, Handheld)	Data Processing Devices	362
microcomputer (*use:* Computer, Laptop)	Data Processing Devices	362
Microfiche	Other Documents	484
Microfilm	Other Documents	484
Microform	Other Documents	484
Micrograph	Drafting T&E	366
Micromanometer	Chemical Testing Devices	291
Micrometer	Weights & Measures T&E	358
Microphone	Sound Communication Devices	392
Microphone, Clip	Sound Communication Devices	392
Microscope	Optical T&E	344
Microscope, Binocular	Optical T&E	344
Microscope, Confocal	Optical T&E	344
Microscope, Electron	Optical T&E	344
Microscope, Fluorescence	Optical T&E	344
Microscope, Petrographic	Geological T&E	307
Microscope, Phase Contrast	Optical T&E	344
Microscope, Scanning Electron	Optical T&E	344
Microscope, Transmission Electron	Optical T&E	344
Microspectroscope	Optical T&E	344
Microtome	Biological T&E	287
Middlebuster	Cultivation Equipment	124
milepost (*use:* Milestone)	Site Features	21
Milestone	Site Features	21
Milker, Surge	Food Processing Equipment	166
Milkometer	Food Processing Equipment	167
mill (*use:* Factory)	Industrial Structures	35
Mill, Apple	Food Processing Equipment	165
Mill, Ball	Painting T&E	230
Mill, Bark	Forestry T&E	191
Mill, Buhr	Food Processing Equipment	169
Mill, Cane	Food Processing Equipment	164
Mill, Coffee	Food Preparation Equipment	160
Mill, Corn	Food Processing Equipment	169
Mill, Cotton	Industrial Structures	35
Mill, Culinary	Food Preparation Equipment	160
Mill, Curd	Food Processing Equipment	166
Mill, Drug	Medical Accessories	326

Term	Category	Page
mill, fan (*use:* Mill, Fanning)	Harvesting Equipment	131
Mill, Fanning	Harvesting Equipment	131
mill, feed (*use:* Grinder, Feed)	Feed Processing Equipment	126
Mill, Flint	Mining & Mineral Harvesting T&E	223
Mill, Flour	Food Processing Equipment	169
Mill, Food	Food Preparation Equipment	160
Mill, Fulling	Textile Manufacturing Equipment	243
Mill, Glaze	Glass, Plastics & Clayworking T&E	194
Mill, Gold Rolling	Dental Accessories	321
Mill, Grain	Food Processing Equipment	168
mill, hammer (*use:* Grinder, Feed)	Feed Processing Equipment	126
Mill, Hammer	Food Processing Equipment	169
Mill, Middlings	Food Processing Equipment	169
Mill, Nut	Food Preparation Equipment	160
Mill, Paper	Industrial Structures	35
Mill, Pepper	Serving Vessels	188
mill, pharmaceutical (*use:* Mill, Drug)	Medical Accessories	326
Mill, Powder	Industrial Structures	35
Mill, Pug	Glass, Plastics & Clayworking T&E	192
Mill, Pulp	Industrial Structures	35
Mill, Quartz	Mining & Mineral Harvesting T&E	221
Mill, Rail	Metalworking T&E	214
Mill, Roller	Food Processing Equipment	169
mill, roller (*use:* Grinder, Paint)	Painting T&E	229
Mill, Rolling	Metalworking T&E	214
Mill, Sampling	Metalworking T&E	214
Mill, Slitting	Metalworking T&E	214
Mill, Sorghum	Food Processing Equipment	169
Mill, Spice	Food Preparation Equipment	160
mill, stamp (*use:* Crusher, Stamp)	Mining & Mineral Harvesting T&E	221
Mill, Stamping	Metalworking T&E	214
Mill, Steel	Industrial Structures	35
mill, steel (*use:* Mill, Flint)	Mining & Mineral Harvesting T&E	223
mill, stone (*use:* Mill, Buhr)	Food Processing Equipment	169
Mill, Textile	Industrial Structures	35
Mill, Tube	Metalworking T&E	214
Mill, Warping	Textile Manufacturing Equipment	243
mill, winnowing (*use:* Mill, Fanning)	Harvesting Equipment	131
Mill, Wire	Metalworking T&E	214
Mill, Woolen	Industrial Structures	35
Milliammeter	Electrical & Magnetic Measurement Devices	297
Millivoltmeter	Electrical & Magnetic Measurement Devices	298
Millrace	Hydraulic Structures	34
Millstone	Food Processing Equipment	169
Mimeograph	Replication Equipment	387
mimeoscope (*use:* Table, Light)	Visual Communication Accessories	399
Mine	Ammunition	264
Mine, Aerial	Ammunition	264
Mine, Industrial	Industrial Structures	35
Mine, Land	Ammunition	264
Mine, Underwater	Ammunition	264
Minelayer	Watercraft	447
Miner, Continuous	Mining & Mineral Harvesting T&E	223
miner, mechanical (*use:* Miner, Continuous)	Mining & Mineral Harvesting T&E	223
Minesweeper	Watercraft	447
Miniature	Art	454
Miniblind	Window & Door Coverings	78
Minicassette	Sound Communication Media	393
Minicomputer	Data Processing Devices	362
minieball (*use:* Bullet, Minie)	Ammunition	263
Minion	Artillery	274
Miniskirt	Main Garments	98
Minivan	Motor Vehicles	428
Minutes	Administrative Records	467
Mirror	Other Furniture	58
Mirror, Architectural	Other Furniture	58
Mirror, Astronomical	Astronomical T&E	285
Mirror, Cheval	Other Furniture	58
Mirror, Cloud	Meteorological T&E	340
Mirror, Curved	Other Furniture	58
Mirror, Dresser	Other Furniture	58
Mirror, Eye Observation	Medical Instruments	329
Mirror, Girandole	Other Furniture	58
Mirror, Hall	Other Furniture	58
Mirror, Hand	Beauty Supplies	117
Mirror, Mantel	Other Furniture	58
Mirror, Mouth	Dental Instruments	323
mirror, oral examining (*use:* Mirror, Mouth)	Dental Instruments	323
mirror, pier (*use:* Glass, Pier)	Other Furniture	58
Mirror, Shaving	Hair Care Objects	119
Mirror, Signaling	Visual Communication Devices	400
mirror, tabernacle (*use:* Mirror, Architectural)	Other Furniture	58
Mirror, Wall	Other Furniture	58

Misericorde	Edged Weapons	278
Missal	Religious Objects	465
Missile	Ammunition	264
Missile, Air-to-Air	Ammunition	264
Missile, Air-to-Surface	Ammunition	264
Missile, Air-to-Underwater	Ammunition	264
Missile, Air-to-Water	Ammunition	264
missile, antiaircraft (*use:* Missile, Surface-to-Air)	Ammunition	264
Missile, Antimissile	Ammunition	264
Missile, Ballistic	Ammunition	264
Missile, Guided	Ammunition	264
Missile, Surface-to-Air	Ammunition	264
Missile, Surface-to-Surface	Ammunition	264
Missile, Underwater-to-Surface	Ammunition	264
Miter	Status Symbols	500
Mitt	Clothing Accessories	85
Mitt, Bath	Hygiene Objects	120
Mitt, Catcher's	Sports Equipment	512
Mitt, First Baseman's	Sports Equipment	512
Mitt, Oven	Food Preparation Accessories	152
Mitten	Clothing Accessories	85
Mitten, Target Shooter's	Armament Accessories	270
Mixer, Audio	Sound Communication Devices	392
Mixer, Cake	Food Preparation Equipment	161
mixer, cement (*use:* Mixer, Concrete)	Masonry & Stoneworking T&E	204
Mixer, Concrete	Masonry & Stoneworking T&E	204
Mixer, Dental Casting	Dental Accessories	321
Mixer, Dough	Food Preparation Equipment	161
Mixer, Drink	Food Preparation Equipment	161
Mixer, Electric Hand	Food Preparation Equipment	161
Mixer, Electric Stand	Food Preparation Equipment	161
Mixer, Feed	Feed Processing Equipment	126
Mixer, Food	Food Preparation Equipment	161
Mixer, Ice Cream	Food Preparation Equipment	161
Mixer, Jiffler	Masonry & Stoneworking T&E	204
Mixer, Masonry	Masonry & Stoneworking T&E	204
Mixer, Mayonnaise	Food Preparation Equipment	161
Mixer, Meat	Food Preparation Equipment	161
Mixer, Pharmaceutical	Medical Accessories	326
mixer, stand (*use:* Mixer, Electric Stand)	Food Preparation Equipment	161
Mizzen	Water Transportation Accessories	439
Mobcap	Headwear	92
Mobile	Art	454
Mobile, Toy	Toys	522
Moccasin	Footwear	90
Mochila	Land Transportation Accessories	416
Mocock	Personal Carrying & Storage Gear	113
Model	Other Documents	484
Model, Anatomical	Medical Accessories	326
Model, Architect's	Other Documents	484
model, artist's (*use:* Figure, Lay)	Painting T&E	229
Model, Geometric	Drafting T&E	367
Model, Half	Other Documents	484
Model, Instructional	Other Documents	484
Model, Patent	Other Documents	484
Model, Product	Advertising Media	450
model, site (*use:* Model, Architect's)	Other Documents	484
model, site (*use:* Model, Topographic)	Other Documents	484
Model, Topographic	Other Documents	484
Modem	Peripherals	365
Modesty	Clothing Accessories	85
Modulator, Electrical	Electrical System Components	301
Modulator, Single Side Band	Electrical System Components	301
Module, Airlock	Aerospace Transportation Accessories	410
Module, Command	Spacecraft	413
Module, Lunar	Spacecraft	413
Moil	Mining & Mineral Harvesting T&E	222
Moistener	Writing Accessories	404
Mola	Art	452
Mold	Glass, Plastics & Clayworking T&E	194
Mold, Ammunition	Armament Accessories	270
Mold, Ball	Armament Accessories	270
Mold, Basket Weaving	Fiberworking T&E	144
mold, blancmange (*use:* Mold, Gelatin)	Food Preparation Equipment	157
mold, border (*use:* Mold, Ring)	Food Preparation Equipment	157
Mold, Brick	Masonry & Stoneworking T&E	205
Mold, Bullet	Armament Accessories	270
Mold, Butter	Food Preparation Equipment	157
Mold, Cake	Food Preparation Equipment	157

Mold, Candle — Glass, Plastics & Clayworking T&E 194
Mold, Candy — Food Preparation Equipment 157
Mold, Casting — Metalworking T&E 214
Mold, Cheese — Food Processing Equipment 166
Mold, Chocolate — Food Preparation Equipment 157
Mold, Cigar — Other T&E for Materials 260
Mold, Cookie — Food Preparation Equipment 157
Mold, Cutlet — Food Preparation Equipment 157
Mold, Dental Casting — Dental Accessories 321
Mold, Doughnut — Food Preparation Equipment 157
Mold, Food — Food Preparation Equipment 157
Mold, Gelatin — Food Preparation Equipment 157
Mold, Glass — Glass, Plastics & Clayworking T&E 194
Mold, Hat — Textile Manufacturing Equipment 243
Mold, Ice Cream — Food Preparation Equipment 157
Mold, Jelly — Food Preparation Equipment 157
Mold, Jewelry — Other T&E for Materials 260
Mold, Maple Sugar — Food Processing Equipment 169
Mold, Papermaking — Papermaking T&E 232
Mold, Pastry — Food Preparation Equipment 157
Mold, Piece — Glass, Plastics & Clayworking T&E 194
Mold, Plate — Glass, Plastics & Clayworking T&E 194
Mold, Pottery — Glass, Plastics & Clayworking T&E 194
Mold, Pudding — Food Preparation Equipment 157
Mold, Revolving — Other T&E for Materials 260
Mold, Rice — Food Preparation Equipment 157
Mold, Ring — Food Preparation Equipment 157
Mold, Soap — Other T&E for Materials 260
mold, springerle (*use:* Mold, Cookie) — Food Preparation Equipment 157
Mold, Sugar — Food Preparation Equipment 157
Mold, Suppository — Medical Accessories 326
Mold, Wad — Armament Accessories 270
Molding — Surface Elements 18
Molding, Cap — Surface Elements 18
Molinet — Food Preparation Equipment 161
molly (*use:* Bolt, Molly) — Multiple Use T&E for Materials 227
Money — Exchange Media 487
Money, Paper — Exchange Media 489
Money, Play — Game Equipment 502
Money, Shell — Exchange Media 489
moneychanger (*use:* Changer, Money) — Merchandising T&E 336
Monitor, Computer — Peripherals 364
Monitor, Hydraulic — Mining & Mineral Harvesting T&E 223
Monitor, Video — Telecommunication Devices 396
Monocle — Personal Assistive Objects 108
Monograph — Literary Works 477
Monoplane — Aircraft 411
Monopod, Camera — Camera Equipment 377
Monopod, Shooting — Armament Accessories 270
Monotype — Graphic Documents 474
Monstrance — Religious Objects 462
Montage — Art 452
Monteith — Food Service Accessories 182
Montera — Headwear 93
Monument — Site Features 21
Mood — Unclassifiable Objects 527
Moondial — Timekeeping T&E 356
Mop — Housekeeping Equipment 312
Mop, Pitch — Woodworking T&E 254
mop, rag (*use:* Mop, String) — Housekeeping Equipment 312
Mop, Sponge — Housekeeping Equipment 312
Mop, String — Housekeeping Equipment 312
Moped — Motor Vehicles 428
Morion — Body Armor 275
Morse — Status Symbols 500
Mortar — Construction Materials 3
Mortar, Artillery — Artillery 274
mortar, bomb (*use:* Mortar, Artillery) — Artillery 274
Mortar, Food — Food Preparation Equipment 160
Mortar, Grain — Food Processing Equipment 169
Mortar, Laboratory — Labware 293
Mortar, Pharmaceutical — Medical Accessories 326
Mortar, Proving — Artillery 274
mortar, samp (*use:* Mortar, Stamp) — Food Processing Equipment 169
Mortar, Stamp — Food Processing Equipment 169
Mortarboard — Status Symbols 498
Mortgage — Financial Records 469
Mortiser — Woodworking T&E 254
Mosaic — Surface Elements 18
Mosque — Ceremonial Structures 25
Motel — Commercial Structures 27
Motor — Power Producing Equipment 304
Motor, Electric — Power Producing Equipment 304

Motor, Hydraulic | Power Producing Equipment | 304
Motor, Outboard | Water Transportation Accessories | 441
Motor, Pneumatic | Power Producing Equipment | 304
Motorbike | Motor Vehicles | 428
Motorboat | Watercraft | 443
Motorcycle | Motor Vehicles | 428
Motorhome | Motor Vehicles | 430
Motorsailer | Watercraft | 443
Motorship | Watercraft | 446
Moulder | Woodworking T&E | 254
Mound | Site Features | 20
Mound, Conical | Site Features | 20
Mound, Effigy | Site Features | 20
Mound, Linear | Site Features | 20
Mound, Platform | Site Features | 20
mound, ridge-top (*use:* Mound, Linear) | Site Features | 20
Mount, Bridle | Land Transportation Accessories | 418
Mount, Engine | Power Transmission Components | 305
Mount, Gun | Armament Accessories | 270
Mount, Panama | Defense Structures | 31
Mount, Sight | Armament Accessories | 270
Mount, Specimen | Biological T&E | 287
Mount, Taxidermy | Decorative Furnishings | 60
Mouse | Peripherals | 364
Mousetrap | Other Household Accessories | 66
Mouthguard | Sports Equipment | 519
Mouthpiece | Musical Accessories | 369
Mouthpiece, Iron Jaw | Public Entertainment Devices | 507
Mouthpiece, Saliva Ejector | Dental Instruments | 323
Mover, Rail Car | Rail Vehicles | 434
Mower | Harvesting Equipment | 130
Mower, Gang Reel | Groundskeeping Equipment | 309
Mower, Horse-Drawn | Harvesting Equipment | 130
Mower, Lawn | Groundskeeping Equipment | 309
Mower, Power | Groundskeeping Equipment | 309
Mower, Reel | Groundskeeping Equipment | 309
Mower, Riding | Groundskeeping Equipment | 309
Mower, Tractor-Drawn | Harvesting Equipment | 130
mower-conditioner (*use:* Windrower) | Harvesting Equipment | 130
Mozzetta | Status Symbols | 500
Muddler | Food Preparation Equipment | 162
Mudflap | Land Transportation Accessories | 419
Muff | Clothing Accessories | 85
Muffineer | Serving Vessels | 188
Muffler | Clothing Accessories | 86
Muffler, Automotive | Land Transportation Accessories | 417
Mug | Drinking Vessels | 175
Mug, Coffee | Drinking Vessels | 175
Mug, Decorative | Decorative Furnishings | 60
Mug, Fraternal | Status Symbols | 497
Mug, Shaving | Hair Care Objects | 119
Mug, Travel | Drinking Vessels | 175
Mukluk | Footwear | 89
mukuk (*use:* Mocock) | Personal Carrying & Storage Gear | 113
Mulcher | Cultivation Equipment | 124
Mule | Footwear | 90
Muleshoe | Farrier Equipment | 139
Muleta | Sports Equipment | 514
muller (*use:* Mano) | Food Preparation Equipment | 160
Muller | Painting T&E | 230
Mullion | Door & Window Elements | 7
Multihull | Watercraft | 443
Multimeter | Electrical & Magnetic Measurement Devices | 297
Multiplexer | Data Processing Accessories | 360
Multiplier, Voltage | Electrical System Components | 301
Muniment | Legal Documents | 476
Mural | Art | 452
Museum | Cultural & Recreational Structures | 29
Music, Sheet | Literary Works | 477
Musket | Firearms | 280
Musket, Cartridge | Firearms | 280
Musket, Flintlock | Firearms | 280
Musket, Matchlock | Firearms | 281
Musket, Percussion | Firearms | 281
Musket, Wheelock | Firearms | 281
Musketoon | Firearms | 281
Mutascope | Toys | 524
Mutch | Headwear | 92
Mute | Musical Accessories | 369
Muumuu | Main Garments | 96
Muzzle | Animal Care Equipment | 135
Muzzle, False | Armament Accessories | 270
Muzzle, Pet | Pet Supplies | 141
Mydynamometer | Medical Instruments | 328
Myograph | Medical Instruments | 328
Myriopticon | Toys | 524
Nail | Woodworking T&E | 250
Nail, Cobbler's | Leather, Horn & Shellworking T&E | 199
Nail, Horseshoe | Farrier Equipment | 139
Nail, Picture | Storage & Display Accessories | 64
Nail, Shoeing | Farrier Equipment | 139
nameboard (*use:* Signboard) | Visual Communication Devices | 401
Nameplate | Other Documents | 485

Nametag	Personal Identification	495
Napkin	Food Service Accessories	181
Napkin, Bread Basket	Food Service Accessories	181
Napkin, Sanitary	Hygiene Objects	120
Napper	Textile Manufacturing Equipment	243
Nappy	Serving Vessels	186
Narrative	Literary Works	477
Natrometer	Telecommunication Accessories	394
Navette	Religious Objects	462
Nebulizer	Medical Instruments	333
Neckcloth	Clothing Accessories	85
Neckerchief	Clothing Accessories	85
Necklace	Body Adornments	81
Neckpiece	Clothing Accessories	85
Necktie	Clothing Accessories	85
Needle, Binding	Bookbinding Equipment	383
Needle, Blood Collecting	Medical Instruments	327
Needle, Carpet	Needleworking Equipment	237
Needle, Darning	Needleworking Equipment	237
Needle, Dental	Dental Instruments	323
Needle, Dipping	Mining & Mineral Harvesting T&E	223
Needle, Dissecting	Biological T&E	288
Needle, Embroidery	Needleworking Equipment	237
Needle, Etching	Graphic Equipment	384
Needle, Finishing	Textile Manufacturing Equipment	243
Needle, Gillmore	Chemical Testing Devices	291
Needle, Glover's	Leather, Horn & Shellworking T&E	199
Needle, Harness	Leather, Horn & Shellworking T&E	199
Needle, Hypodermic	Medical Instruments	334
Needle, Injection	Medical Instruments	334
Needle, Inoculating	Biological T&E	287
Needle, Knitting	Textile Manufacturing Equipment	243
Needle, Lacing	Leather, Horn & Shellworking T&E	199
Needle, Larding	Food Preparation Equipment	156
Needle, Leatherworking	Leather, Horn & Shellworking T&E	199
Needle, Ligating	Medical Instruments	331
Needle, Netmaking	Textile Manufacturing Equipment	243
Needle, Phonograph	Sound Communication Accessories	389
Needle, Sailmaker's	Needleworking Equipment	237
Needle, Sewing	Needleworking Equipment	237
Needle, Spinal	Medical Instruments	334
Needle, Surgical	Medical Instruments	331
Needle, Suturing	Medical Instruments	331
Needle, Textile Making	Textile Manufacturing Equipment	243
Needle, Thatching	Fiberworking T&E	144
Needle, Trussing	Food Preparation Equipment	156
Needle, Upholsterer's	Needleworking Equipment	238
Needlepin, Inoculating	Veterinary Equipment	142
Needlepoint	Art	453
Needlework	Art	452
Negative	Graphic Documents	472
Negative, Glass Plate	Graphic Documents	473
Negative, Roll Film	Graphic Documents	473
Negative, Sheet Film	Graphic Documents	473
Negligee	Dressingwear & Nightwear	88
Nephoscope	Meteorological T&E	340
nest, crow's (*use:* Crow's-Nest)	Water Transportation Accessories	437
Net, Animal	Animal Care Equipment	135
Net, Badminton	Sports Equipment	512
Net, Basketball	Sports Equipment	513
Net, Blanket	Fishing Equipment	146
Net, Bottom-Set	Fishing Equipment	146
Net, Brail	Fishing Equipment	146
Net, Casting	Fishing Equipment	146
Net, Climbing	Recreational Devices	510
Net, Crab	Fishing Equipment	146
Net, Dip	Fishing Equipment	146
Net, Dredge	Fishing Equipment	146
Net, Drift	Fishing Equipment	146
Net, Fishing	Fishing Equipment	146
Net, Fly	Animal Care Equipment	134
Net, Fyke	Fishing Equipment	146
Net, Gill	Fishing Equipment	146
Net, Harvesting	Harvesting Equipment	130
Net, Head	Headwear	94
Net, Helmet	Body Armor	275
Net, Hoop	Fishing Equipment	146
Net, Landing	Fishing Equipment	146
Net, Lift	Fishing Equipment	146
Net, Luggage	Land Transportation Accessories	416
Net, Mosquito	Bedding	44
net, ping pong (*use:* Net, Table Tennis)	Sports Equipment	518
Net, Pound	Fishing Equipment	146
Net, Purse	Fishing Equipment	146
Net, Reef	Fishing Equipment	146
Net, Safety	Public Entertainment Devices	507
Net, Scoop	Fishing Equipment	146
Net, Seine	Fishing Equipment	146
Net, Surrounding	Fishing Equipment	146
Net, Table Tennis	Sports Equipment	518
Net, Tennis	Sports Equipment	518
net, throw (*use:* Net, Casting)	Fishing Equipment	146
Net, Torpedo	Water Transportation Accessories	441
Net, Trap	Fishing Equipment	146

Net, Trawl	Fishing Equipment	146
Net, Volleyball	Sports Equipment	519
netsinker (*use:* Weight, Net)	Fishing Equipment	147
Netsuke	Personal Carrying & Storage Gear	113
Newel	Stair Elements	15
Newsletter	Other Documents	486
Newspaper	Other Documents	486
Newsstand	Commercial Structures	27
Nib, Pen	Writing Devices	406
Nibbler	Metalworking T&E	209
Nickel	Exchange Media	488
nickelodeon (*use:* Jukebox)	Sound Communication Devices	391
Niddy-Noddy	Textile Manufacturing Equipment	244
Nightcap	Headwear	92
Nightclub	Cultural & Recreational Structures	29
Nightgown	Dressingwear & Nightwear	88
nightlight (*use:* Light, Night)	Lighting Devices	69
Nightshirt	Dressingwear & Nightwear	88
nightstand (*use:* Table, Night)	Support Furniture	57
Nightstick	Percussive Weapons	283
ninepins (*use:* Set, Ninepins)	Game Equipment	504
Nipper	Leather, Horn & Shellworking T&E	199
Nipper, Band	Bookbinding Equipment	383
nipper, hoof (*use:* Parer, Hoof)	Farrier Equipment	140
Nipper, Metal	Metalworking T&E	214
Nipper, Nail	Metalworking T&E	214
Nipper, Pulling	Metalworking T&E	214
Nipper, Sheet	Metalworking T&E	214
nipper, sugar (*use:* Cutter, Sugar)	Food Preparation Equipment	158
nipper, sugar (*use:* Tongs, Sugar)	Serving Utensils	185
Nipper, Tile	Masonry & Stoneworking T&E	205
Nipper, Toenail	Pet Supplies	141
Nipple, Nursing	Animal Care Equipment	135
Niqab	Headwear	94
Nitrometer	Chemical Testing Devices	291
Nocturnal	Navigational Equipment	350
Nogging	Construction Materials	3
Noisemaker	Toys	524
noisemaker, ratchet (*use:* Rattle, Ratchet)	Sound Communication Devices	391
Nomogram	Data Processing Devices	361
Noose, Hangman's	Regulative Devices	347
nosebag (*use:* Feedbag)	Animal Care Equipment	134
Noseplug	Personal Assistive Objects	108
Notcher, Ear	Animal Care Equipment	136
Note	Other Documents	484
note, bank (*use:* Money, Paper)	Exchange Media	489
Note, Confederate	Exchange Media	489
Note, Federal Reserve	Exchange Media	489
Note, Field	Other Documents	484
Note, Private Bank	Exchange Media	489
Note, Promissory	Exchange Media	489
Note, United States	Exchange Media	489
Notebook	Writing Media	408
Notecard	Writing Media	408
Notepad	Writing Media	408
Notepad, Adhesive	Writing Media	408
notice (*use:* Announcement)	Declaratory Documents	468
Notice, Legal	Declaratory Documents	468
Notion	Needleworking Equipment	236
Novel	Literary Works	477
Novel, Graphic	Graphic Documents	472
Novelty, Promotional	Advertising Media	450
Nozzle, Fire Hose	Protective Devices	345
Nozzle, Garden Hose	Groundskeeping Equipment	309
Nozzle, Hydraulic	Mining & Mineral Harvesting T&E	223
Nut	Multiple Use T&E for Materials	227
Nut, Adjusting	Multiple Use T&E for Materials	227
Nut, Back	Multiple Use T&E for Materials	227
Nut, Wing	Multiple Use T&E for Materials	227
Nut, Wire	Electrical System Components	301
Nutcracker	Food Preparation Equipment	160
Nutpick	Food Preparation Equipment	160
nylon (*use:* Stocking)	Footwear	89
Oakum	Construction Materials	3
Oar	Water Transportation Accessories	441
Oar, Sculling	Water Transportation Accessories	441
Oar, Steering	Water Transportation Accessories	441
Oar, Sweep	Water Transportation Accessories	441
Oarlock	Water Transportation Accessories	438
Oath	Legal Documents	476
Oban	Exchange Media	488
Obelisk	Site Features	21
Obi	Clothing Accessories	86
Obituary	Declaratory Documents	468
Object, Devotional	Belief Symbols	493

Object, Divination	Religious Objects	464
Object, Unidentified	Unclassifiable Objects	527
Oboe	Musical Instruments	375
Oboe d'Amore	Musical Instruments	375
Observatory, Orbiting Solar	Spacecraft	413
Ocarina	Musical Instruments	375
Occluder, Eye	Medical Instruments	329
Octant	Navigational Equipment	350
Octavin	Musical Instruments	375
Odometer	Weights & Measures T&E	358
Odontograph	Drafting T&E	366
Oenometer	Food Processing Equipment	164
Office, Post	Civic & Social Structures	26
Office, Railway Post	Rail Vehicles	433
Office, Telegraph	Other Structures	41
Ohmeter	Electrical & Magnetic Measurement Devices	297
Oilcan	Metalworking T&E	214
Oiler	Watercraft	446
Oiler, Hog	Animal Care Equipment	135
Oilskin	Protective Wear	102
Oilstone	Metalworking T&E	216
Ojime	Personal Carrying & Storage Gear	113
okimono (*use:* Figurine)	Art	454
Oleometer	Chemical Testing Devices	290
olla (*use:* Jar, Food Storage)	Food Storage Equipment	171
ombrometer (*use:* Pluviometer)	Meteorological T&E	339
Ombrometer	Meteorological T&E	339
Omnibus	Animal-Powered Vehicles	424
Omnigraph	Telecommunication Accessories	394
Omnimeter	Surveying Equipment	353
omophorion (*use:* Stole, Ecclesiastical)	Status Symbols	500
Oncometer	Medical Instruments	328
oomiak (*use:* Umiak)	Watercraft	442
Opacimeter	Papermaking T&E	233
Opeidoscope	Acoustical T&E	261
Opener, Bottle	Food Preparation Equipment	156
Opener, Can	Food Preparation Equipment	156
Opener, Electric Can	Food Preparation Equipment	156
Opener, Food Container	Food Preparation Equipment	156
Opener, Garage Door	Door & Window Elements	6
Opener, Jar	Food Preparation Equipment	156
Opener, Lead	Glass, Plastics & Clayworking T&E	194
Opener, Letter	Writing Accessories	404
opener-picker (*use:* Picker, Fiber)	Textile Manufacturing Equipment	243
Operameter	Mechanical Measurement Equipment	318
Ophthalmometer	Medical Instruments	329
Ophthalmoscope	Medical Instruments	329
Opisometer	Navigational Equipment	350
opsiometer (*use:* Optometer)	Medical Instruments	329
Optometer	Medical Instruments	329
Optophone	Sound Communication Devices	392
Orb	Status Symbols	499
Orbiter	Spacecraft	413
Orchestrion	Musical Instruments	371
Order, Money	Exchange Media	489
Order, Pay	Exchange Media	489
Order, Purchase	Financial Records	469
order, shipping (*use:* Bill of Lading)	Administrative Records	467
Order, Work	Administrative Records	467
Orders, Military	Government Records	470
ordinance (*use:* Statute)	Government Records	470
ordinary (*use:* Bicycle, Ordinary)	Human-Powered Vehicles	426
Organ	Musical Instruments	371
Organ, Band	Musical Instruments	372
Organ, Barrel	Musical Instruments	371
organ, bowl (*use:* Harmonica, Glass)	Musical Instruments	371
Organ, Chamber	Musical Instruments	371
Organ, Laboratory	Acoustical T&E	261
Organ, Parlor	Musical Instruments	371
Organ, Pipe	Musical Instruments	371
Organ, Reed	Musical Instruments	371
Organette	Musical Instruments	372
Organizer, Desk	Writing Accessories	403
Organizer, File	Writing Accessories	403
ornament, antenna (*use:* Topper, Antenna)	Land Transportation Accessories	422
Ornament, Bridle	Land Transportation Accessories	420
Ornament, Ceiling	Surface Elements	19
Ornament, Christmas Tree	Holiday Objects	458
Ornament, Ear	Body Adornments	81
Ornament, Fireplace	Surface Elements	19
Ornament, Footwear	Clothing Accessories	86
Ornament, Furniture	Decorative Furnishings	60
Ornament, Garden	Site Features	21
Ornament, Hair	Hair Adornments	83
Ornament, Harness	Land Transportation Accessories	420
Ornament, Headwear	Clothing Accessories	86
Ornament, Holiday	Holiday Objects	458

Term	Category	Page
Ornament, Hood	Land Transportation Accessories	417
ornament, lawn (*use:* Ornament, Garden)	Site Features	21
Ornament, Masthead	Water Transportation Accessories	438
Ornament, Mourning	Funerary Objects	457
Ornament, Nose	Body Adornments	81
ornament, package (*use:* Wrap, Gift)	Party Accessories	460
Ornament, Party	Party Accessories	460
Ornament, Pilothouse	Water Transportation Accessories	438
Ornament, Shoe	Clothing Accessories	86
Ornament, Surface	Surface Elements	18
Ornament, Tack	Land Transportation Accessories	420
Ornament, Transfer	Visual Communication Accessories	399
Ornament, Vehicle	Land Transportation Accessories	417
Ornament, Wall	Surface Elements	19
Ornament, Watercraft	Water Transportation Accessories	438
Ornament, Window	Decorative Furnishings	60
Ornament, Yacht	Water Transportation Accessories	438
Ornithopter	Aircraft	412
Orograph	Surveying Equipment	353
Orphanage	Institutional Structures	37
orphicleide (*use:* Bugle, Key)	Musical Instruments	370
Orrery	Astronomical T&E	285
Orthoscanner	Peripherals	364
Orthoscope	Medical Instruments	329
Oscillator	Electrical System Components	301
Oscillator, Audio	Acoustical T&E	261
Oscillograph	Electrical & Magnetic Measurement Devices	297
Oscillometer	Navigational Equipment	350
Oscilloscope	Electrical & Magnetic Measurement Devices	297
Osmometer	Chemical Testing Devices	291
Osmoscope	Biological T&E	287
Ossuary	Funerary Objects	456
Osteophone	Medical Instruments	334
Otacoustic	Medical Instruments	328
Otheoscope	Optical T&E	344
Otoscope	Medical Instruments	328
Ottoman	Seating Furniture	49
Outboard	Watercraft	443
Outhouse	Outbuildings	38
Outlet, Electrical	Electrical System Components	301
Outrigger	Water Transportation Accessories	438
Outwork	Defense Structures	31
Oven	Food Preparation Equipment	154
Oven, Bake	Food Preparation Equipment	154
Oven, Beehive	Site Features	21
Oven, Coke	Metalworking T&E	211
Oven, Convection	Food Preparation Equipment	155
Oven, Curing	Glass, Plastics & Clayworking T&E	193
Oven, Dutch	Cooking Vessels	151
Oven, Electric	Food Preparation Equipment	155
Oven, Microwave	Food Preparation Equipment	155
Oven, Reflector	Food Preparation Equipment	163
Oven, Solar	Food Preparation Equipment	155
Oven, Toaster	Food Preparation Equipment	155
Oven, Warming	Food Preparation Equipment	155
Overalls	Main Garments	96
Overblouse	Main Garments	98
Overcoat	Outerwear	100
Overdress	Main Garments	96
Overmantel	Surface Elements	18
Overshoe	Footwear	90
Overskirt	Main Garments	98
Oversleeve	Clothing Accessories	86
oxbow (*use:* Yoke, Animal)	Land Transportation Accessories	421
Oxcart	Animal-Powered Vehicles	424
Oxford	Footwear	90
Oxshoe	Farrier Equipment	139
Ozonometer	Meteorological T&E	340
Pac	Footwear	89
Pacemaker	Medical Instruments	334
pachisi (*use:* Set, Parcheesi)	Game Equipment	504
Pachymeter	Medical Instruments	329
Pacifier	Personal Assistive Objects	108
Pack	Containers	415
pack, belt (*use:* Pack, Fanny)	Personal Carrying & Storage Gear	110
Pack, Fanny	Personal Carrying & Storage Gear	110
pack, jet (*use:* Belt, Rocket)	Aircraft	411
Package, Product	Merchandising T&E	337
Packer, Barrel	Food Processing Equipment	168
packer, bran (*use:* Packer, Barrel)	Food Processing Equipment	168
Packer, Butter	Food Processing Equipment	166
Packer, Cigar	Other T&E for Materials	260

Term	Category	Page
packer, feed (*use:* Packer, Barrel)	Food Processing Equipment	168
packer, flour (*use:* Packer, Barrel)	Food Processing Equipment	168
packer, surface (*use:* Roller, Land)	Cultivation Equipment	125
Packet	Containers	415
packet (*use:* Ship, Packet)	Watercraft	446
Packet, Seed	Planting Equipment	132
Pad, Animal	Land Transportation Accessories	420
Pad, Buckle	Land Transportation Accessories	420
Pad, Bunion	Personal Assistive Objects	108
Pad, Bustle	Underwear	103
Pad, Carpet	Floor Coverings	45
Pad, Chair	Other Household Accessories	66
Pad, Collar	Land Transportation Accessories	420
Pad, Desk	Writing Accessories	404
Pad, Flip Chart	Writing Media	408
Pad, Furniture	Other Household Accessories	67
Pad, Garment Shoulder	Underwear	103
Pad, Heating	Personal Assistive Objects	109
Pad, Hip	Sports Equipment	519
Pad, Horse Knee	Land Transportation Accessories	420
Pad, Horseshoe	Farrier Equipment	139
Pad, Hot	Food Preparation Accessories	152
Pad, Knee	Protective Wear	102
Pad, Leg	Sports Equipment	519
Pad, Legal	Writing Media	408
Pad, Mouse	Data Processing Accessories	360
Pad, Nursing	Clothing Accessories	86
Pad, Paint	Painting T&E	230
pad, receipt (*use:* Book, Receipt)	Financial Records	469
Pad, Rib	Sports Equipment	519
Pad, Saddle	Land Transportation Accessories	420
Pad, Scouring	Dishwashing Equipment	308
Pad, Shoulder	Sports Equipment	519
pad, shoulder (*use:* Pad, Garment Shoulder)	Underwear	103
pad, sketch (*use:* Sketchbook)	Painting T&E	230
pad, soap (*use:* Pad, Scouring)	Dishwashing Equipment	308
Pad, Stove	Floor Coverings	45
Pad, Table	Food Service Accessories	181
pad, table (*use:* Mat, Table)	Furniture Coverings	61
Pad, Withers	Land Transportation Accessories	420
pad, writing (*use:* Notepad)	Writing Media	408
Paddle	Regulative Devices	347
Paddle, Angle	Masonry & Stoneworking T&E	206
Paddle, Apple Butter	Food Preparation Equipment	161
Paddle, Boat	Water Transportation Accessories	441
Paddle, Butter	Food Processing Equipment	166
Paddle, Canoe	Water Transportation Accessories	441
Paddle, Croupier's	Game Equipment	503
Paddle, Double-Bladed	Water Transportation Accessories	441
Paddle, Food	Food Preparation Equipment	161
Paddle, Fraternal	Status Symbols	497
paddle, glassworker's (*use:* Battledore)	Glass, Plastics & Clayworking T&E	192
Paddle, Lard	Food Processing Equipment	169
paddle, ping pong (*use:* Paddle, Table Tennis)	Sports Equipment	518
Paddle, Table Tennis	Sports Equipment	518
Paddle, Tennis	Sports Equipment	518
paddleboard (*use:* Surfboard)	Recreational Devices	511
Paddock	Other Structures	41
Padlock	Protective Devices	346
Page	Other Documents	483
Pager	Telecommunication Devices	396
Pagoda	Ceremonial Structures	25
pagoda (*use:* Coin, Pagoda)	Exchange Media	487
Pagoscope	Meteorological T&E	340
Paho	Religious Objects	464
Pail	Housekeeping Equipment	312
Pail, Diaper	Laundry Equipment	313
Pail, Dinner	Food Service Accessories	180
pail, flour (*use:* Bucket, Flour)	Food Storage Equipment	170
pail, lard (*use:* Can, Lard)	Food Storage Equipment	170
Pail, Milking	Food Processing Equipment	166
Pail, Toy	Toys	522
Paint	Painting T&E	230
paintbrush (*use:* Brush, Paint)	Painting T&E	229
Painting	Art	453
Painting, Bark	Art	453
Painting, Ceiling	Art	453
Painting, Miniature	Art	453
Painting, Panel	Art	453
painting, rock (*use:* Pictograph)	Graphic Documents	473
Painting, Wall	Art	453
Pajamas	Dressingwear & Nightwear	88

Pajamas, Baby Doll	Dressingwear & Nightwear	88
Palanquin	Human-Powered Vehicles	427
Paletot	Outerwear	101
Palette	Painting T&E	230
Palette, Arm	Painting T&E	230
paling (*use:* Fence, Picket)	Site Features	20
Palinurus	Navigational Equipment	350
Palisade	Defense Structures	31
Pall, Funeral	Funerary Objects	457
Pallet, Bookbinding	Bookbinding Equipment	383
Palm	Leather, Horn & Shellworking T&E	199
Palm, Sailmaker's	Needleworking Equipment	237
Palstave	Multiple Use T&E for Materials	228
paltock (*use:* Tunic)	Main Garments	99
Pamphlet	Other Documents	484
Pamphlet, Instruction	Instructional Documents	475
Pan, Amalgamating	Metalworking T&E	214
Pan, Baking	Cooking Vessels	150
pan, braising (*use:* Brazier, Cooking)	Food Preparation Equipment	153
Pan, Bread	Cooking Vessels	150
Pan, Breadstick	Cooking Vessels	150
Pan, Broiler	Cooking Vessels	151
Pan, Bundt	Cooking Vessels	150
Pan, Cake	Cooking Vessels	150
Pan, Comfit	Food Preparation Equipment	153
Pan, Cornstick	Cooking Vessels	150
pan, cream (*use:* Pan, Milk)	Food Processing Equipment	166
Pan, Crepe	Cooking Vessels	151
Pan, Douche	Hygiene Objects	120
Pan, Drip	Glass, Plastics & Clayworking T&E	194
Pan, Dripping	Cooking Vessels	150
Pan, Ebelskiver	Cooking Vessels	151
Pan, Electric Frying	Food Preparation Equipment	155
Pan, Freezer	Food Storage Equipment	171
Pan, Frying	Cooking Vessels	151
pan, gem (*use:* Pan, Muffin)	Cooking Vessels	150
Pan, Jam	Cooking Vessels	150
Pan, Jelly Roll	Cooking Vessels	150
Pan, Madeleine	Cooking Vessels	150
Pan, Milk	Food Processing Equipment	166
Pan, Miner's	Mining & Mineral Harvesting T&E	223
Pan, Muffin	Cooking Vessels	150
Pan, Omelet	Cooking Vessels	151
Pan, Paella	Cooking Vessels	151
Pan, Patty	Cooking Vessels	150
Pan, Pie	Cooking Vessels	150
Pan, Popover	Cooking Vessels	150
Pan, Pudding	Cooking Vessels	150
Pan, Roasting	Cooking Vessels	151
pan, roll (*use:* Pan, Muffin)	Cooking Vessels	150
Pan, Salt	Food Processing Equipment	164
Pan, Sap	Food Processing Equipment	169
pan, sauce (*use:* Saucepan)	Cooking Vessels	151
Pan, Sheet	Cooking Vessels	150
Pan, Soldering	Metalworking T&E	215
Pan, Springform	Cooking Vessels	150
Pan, Stew	Cooking Vessels	151
Pan, Stool	Hygiene Objects	121
Pan, Taco Shell	Cooking Vessels	150
Pan, Tart	Cooking Vessels	150
Pan, Track	Rail Transportation Accessories	432
Pan, Tube	Cooking Vessels	150
pandau (*use:* Cloth, Flower)	Art	452
Pane	Door & Window Elements	7
Panel	Surface Elements	19
Panel, Aerial Marker	Visual Communication Devices	400
Panel, Data Patch	Data Processing Accessories	360
Panel, Dispatcher's	Rail Transportation Accessories	432
panel, electrical (*use:* Box, Electrical)	Electrical System Components	300
Panel, Fretwork	Surface Elements	19
panel, photovoltaic (*use:* Panel, Solar)	Power Producing Equipment	304
Panel, Solar	Power Producing Equipment	304
Panel, Solar Thermal	Environmental Control Elements	9
Paneling	Surface Elements	18
Pannier	Underwear	103
pannier, bicycle (*use:* Bag, Bicycle)	Land Transportation Accessories	416
Pannier, Motorcycle	Land Transportation Accessories	416
Pannikin	Drinking Vessels	175
Panorama, Toy	Toys	524
Panpipe	Musical Instruments	375
Pantalettes	Underwear	104
Pantaloons	Main Garments	97
pantaloons (*use:* Drawers)	Underwear	104
Panties	Underwear	104
Panties, Control	Underwear	103
Pantile	Surface Elements	19
Pantograph	Drafting T&E	367
Pantograph, Rail	Rail Transportation Accessories	431
Pantometer	Surveying Equipment	353
Pants	Main Garments	97
Pants, Bazooka	Armament Accessories	270
pants, bunker (*use:* Pants, Turnout)	Protective Wear	102

Term	Category	Page
Pants, Capri	Main Garments	97
pants, harem (*use:* Chalwar)	Main Garments	97
Pants, Hot	Main Garments	98
Pants, Palazzo	Main Garments	97
Pants, Scrub	Protective Wear	102
Pants, Ski	Outerwear	101
Pants, Snow	Outerwear	101
pants, sweat (*use:* Sweatpants)	Main Garments	97
Pants, Tap	Underwear	104
Pants, Toreador	Main Garments	97
Pants, Training	Underwear	104
Pants, Turnout	Protective Wear	102
Pantsuit	Main Garments	99
Pantyhose	Footwear	89
Papboat	Eating Vessels	177
Paper	Writing Media	408
Paper, Adhesive Note	Writing Media	408
Paper, Art	Painting T&E	230
Paper, Articulating	Dental Instruments	323
paper, blotter (*use:* Blotter, Desk)	Writing Accessories	402
Paper, Carbon	Writing Media	408
paper, cigarette (*use:* Paper, Rolling)	Smoking & Recreational Drug Equipment	114
Paper, Construction	Toys	523
Paper, Copy	Writing Media	408
Paper, Craft	Toys	523
Paper, Filter	Biological T&E	287
paper, fly (*use:* Flypaper)	Other Household Accessories	66
paper, letterhead (*use:* Stationery)	Writing Media	408
Paper, Litmus	Labware	293
paper, music (*use:* Paper, Staff)	Writing Media	408
Paper, Onionskin	Writing Media	408
Paper, Origami	Toys	523
Paper, Pattern Tracing	Needleworking Equipment	237
Paper, Photographic	Photographic Media	380
Paper, Rolling	Smoking & Recreational Drug Equipment	114
paper, roofing (*use:* Paper, Tar)	Construction Materials	3
Paper, Shaving	Hair Care Objects	119
Paper, Shelf	Housekeeping Equipment	312
Paper, Staff	Writing Media	408
Paper, Stencil	Painting T&E	230
Paper, Tar	Construction Materials	3
Paper, Toilet	Hygiene Objects	120
Paper, Typing	Writing Media	408
Paper, Wrapping	Merchandising T&E	337
Paper, Writing	Writing Media	408
Paperweight	Writing Accessories	404
Parachute	Aerospace Transportation Accessories	410
Parachute, Cargo	Aerospace Transportation Accessories	410
Parachute, Drogue	Aerospace Transportation Accessories	410
Parachute, Personnel	Aerospace Transportation Accessories	410
Paraglider	Aircraft	411
Parapet	Supporting Elements	17
Parasol	Personal Assistive Objects	109
Parasol, Carriage	Land Transportation Accessories	419
Parbuckle	Mechanical Devices	316
Pardon	Government Records	470
parer (*use:* Peeler)	Food Preparation Equipment	159
Parer, Hoof	Farrier Equipment	140
Parfleche	Personal Carrying & Storage Gear	110
Parka	Outerwear	101
Parlor, Beauty	Commercial Structures	27
Parlor, Milking	Agricultural Structures	23
Parrel	Water Transportation Accessories	439
Parsonage	Dwellings	32
Partisan	Edged Weapons	278
Partition	Barrier Elements	2
Partition, Demountable	Barrier Elements	2
Partition, Folding	Barrier Elements	2
Pass	Exchange Media	490
Pass, Boarding	Exchange Media	490
Passer, Catheter	Medical Instruments	332
Passglas	Drinking Vessels	173
passometer (*use:* Pedometer)	Recreational Devices	509
Passport	Other Documents	482
Pastel	Art	453
pastel (*use:* Crayon)	Painting T&E	229
Pasteurizer, Milk	Food Processing Equipment	166
Pasty	Body Adornments	82
Patch, Eye	Medical Instruments	329
Patch, Fire	Status Symbols	497
Patch, Fraternal	Status Symbols	497
Patch, Gun Cleaning	Armament Accessories	270
Patch, Insignia	Status Symbols	497
Patch, Law Enforcement	Status Symbols	497
Patch, Membership	Status Symbols	497
patch, merit (*use:* Badge, Merit)	Achievement Symbols	491
Patch, Military	Status Symbols	497
Patch, Textile	Needleworking Equipment	236
Patch, Tire	Land Transportation Accessories	419
Paten	Religious Objects	462
Patent	Government Records	470
Patent, Letters	Government Records	470
Patten	Footwear	90
Pattern	Needleworking Equipment	237

Term	Category	Page
Pattern, Casting	Metalworking T&E	217
Pattern, Clothes	Needleworking Equipment	237
Pattern, Ear	Animal Care Equipment	136
Pattern, Leather	Leather, Horn & Shellworking T&E	201
Pattern, Masonry	Masonry & Stoneworking T&E	205
Pattern, Metalworking	Metalworking T&E	217
Pattern, Needlework	Needleworking Equipment	237
Pattern, Quilt	Needleworking Equipment	237
Pattern, Sole	Leather, Horn & Shellworking T&E	201
Pattern, Tracing	Metalworking T&E	217
Pattern, Woodworking	Woodworking T&E	259
Pauldron	Body Armor	275
Pavement	Site Features	21
Paver	Site Features	22
Pavilion, Garden	Site Features	21
Pavilion, Recreation	Cultural & Recreational Structures	29
Pavis	Body Armor	275
Pax	Religious Objects	465
Paybook	Financial Records	469
Payroll	Financial Records	469
PDA (*use:* Computer, Handheld)	Data Processing Devices	362
Peapod	Watercraft	443
Peavy	Forestry T&E	190
Pedal, Effects	Musical Instruments	371
pedal, tremolo (*use:* Pedal, Effects)	Musical Instruments	371
pedal, wa-wa (*use:* Pedal, Effects)	Musical Instruments	371
pedestal (*use:* Stand, Pedestal)	Support Furniture	55
Pedestal	Supporting Elements	16
Pedestal, Garden	Site Features	21
Pedestal, Wheel	Water Transportation Accessories	438
pedigree (*use:* Tree, Family)	Graphic Documents	472
Pediment	Surface Elements	19
Pedometer	Recreational Devices	509
pedrero (*use:* Perrier)	Artillery	274
Peel	Food Preparation Equipment	161
Peel, Bread	Food Preparation Equipment	161
Peel, Pizza	Food Preparation Equipment	161
Peel, Printer's	Printing Accessories	386
Peeler	Food Preparation Equipment	159
Peeler, Fruit	Food Preparation Equipment	159
Peeler, Vegetable	Food Preparation Equipment	159
peeler, willow (*use:* Brake, Peeling)	Fiberworking T&E	144
Peepshow	Toys	524
Peg	Woodworking T&E	248
peg, husking (*use:* Cornhusker, Hand)	Harvesting Equipment	128
Peg, Lobster	Fishing Equipment	146
Peg, Shoe	Leather, Horn & Shellworking T&E	200
Pegboard	Surface Elements	18
Peignoir	Dressingwear & Nightwear	88
Pelerine	Outerwear	100
Pelican	Dental Instruments	322
Pelisse	Outerwear	100
Pelorus	Navigational Equipment	349
Pelt	Leather, Horn & Shellworking T&E	199
Pelvimeter	Medical Instruments	328
Pen	Writing Devices	406
Pen, Ballpoint	Writing Devices	406
pen, cartridge (*use:* Pen, Fountain)	Writing Devices	406
Pen, Dip	Writing Devices	406
Pen, Drafting	Drafting T&E	367
pen, felt tip (*use:* Pen, Marker)	Writing Devices	406
Pen, Fountain	Writing Devices	406
Pen, Gel	Writing Devices	406
Pen, Lettering	Writing Devices	406
Pen, Light	Peripherals	364
Pen, Marker	Writing Devices	406
Pen, Metal Nib	Writing Devices	406
Pen, Pyrography	Multiple Use T&E for Materials	228
Pen, Quill	Writing Devices	406
Pen, Reed	Writing Devices	406
Pen, Reservoir	Writing Devices	406
Pen, Ruling	Drafting T&E	367
pence, new (*use:* Penny, New)	Exchange Media	488
Pencil	Writing Devices	406
Pencil, Art	Painting T&E	230
Pencil, Carpenter's	Woodworking T&E	254
Pencil, Colored	Writing Devices	406
Pencil, Coloring	Painting T&E	230
Pencil, Eyebrow	Beauty Supplies	117
Pencil, Grease	Writing Devices	406
Pencil, Mechanical	Writing Devices	406
Pencil, Paint	Painting T&E	230
Pencil, Skin Marking	Biological T&E	287
Pencil, Slate	Writing Devices	406
Pencil, Styptic	Hair Care Objects	119
Pendant	Body Adornments	81
Pendant, Architectural	Roof Elements	14
Pendant, Charm	Body Adornments	81
Pendant, Fraternal	Status Symbols	497

Term	Category	Page
Pendant, Gorget	Status Symbols	497
Pendant, Insignia	Status Symbols	497
Pendant, Religious	Belief Symbols	494
Pendulum	Mechanical Devices	316
Pendulum, Ballistic	Armament Accessories	270
Pendulum, Sound	Acoustical T&E	261
Penetrometer	Chemical Testing Devices	291
Penknife	Personal Assistive Objects	108
Pennant	Organizational Objects	459
Pennant, Promotional	Advertising Media	450
Pennon	Organizational Objects	459
Penny	Exchange Media	488
Penny, English	Exchange Media	488
Penny, New	Exchange Media	488
Penstock	Hydraulic Structures	34
Pepperbox	Firearms	281
pepperbox (*use:* Shaker, Pepper)	Serving Vessels	188
perambulator (*use:* Carriage, Baby)	Human-Powered Vehicles	427
perambulator (*use:* Wheel, Surveyor's)	Surveying Equipment	353
perambulator, doll (*use:* Carriage, Doll)	Toys	520
Perch	Animal Care Equipment	135
Percolator	Food Preparation Equipment	154
Percolator, Laboratory	Labware	293
Percussor	Medical Instruments	328
Perforator	Writing Accessories	404
Perforator, Obstetrical	Medical Instruments	330
Perforator, Printing	Printing Accessories	386
Perforator, Surgical	Medical Instruments	332
Pergola	Site Features	21
Perimeter	Medical Instruments	329
Perimeter, Sound	Acoustical T&E	261
Periodical	Other Documents	486
Periscope	Optical T&E	344
periwig (*use:* Peruke)	Hair Adornments	83
Permission	Other Documents	484
Permit	Other Documents	484
Permit, Building	Other Documents	485
Permit, Business	Other Documents	485
Permit, Interment	Other Documents	485
Perrier	Artillery	274
Perspectograph	Drafting T&E	367
Perspectoscope	Medical Instruments	329
Peruke	Hair Adornments	83
Peso	Exchange Media	488
Pessary	Medical Instruments	334
Pestle, Food	Food Preparation Equipment	160
Pestle, Laboratory	Labware	293
Pestle, Paint	Painting T&E	230
Pestle, Pharmaceutical	Medical Accessories	326
Petard	Ammunition	264
Petition	Other Documents	485
Petroform	Site Features	22
Petroglyph	Art	453
Petrograph	Art	453
Petronel	Firearms	281
Petticoat	Underwear	104
Pew	Seating Furniture	47
Pfennig	Exchange Media	488
Phaeton	Animal-Powered Vehicles	423
Phanarogrisonmeter	Mining & Mineral Harvesting T&E	223
phantoscope (*use:* Projector, Motion Picture)	Visual Communication Devices	401
Pharmacy	Commercial Structures	27
Phenakistoscope	Toys	524
Phiale	Religious Objects	462
phone (*use:* Telephone)	Telecommunication Devices	396
phone, pay (*use:* Telephone, Coin-Operated)	Telecommunication Devices	396
Phoneidoscope	Optical T&E	344
Phonelescope	Acoustical T&E	261
Phonodeik	Acoustical T&E	261
Phonograph	Sound Communication Devices	392
Phonograph, Console	Sound Communication Devices	392
Phonograph, Cylinder	Sound Communication Devices	392
Phonograph, Portable	Sound Communication Devices	392
Phonometer	Acoustical T&E	261
Phono-Projectoscope	Acoustical T&E	261
Phonorganon	Acoustical T&E	261
Phonoscope	Acoustical T&E	261
Phosphoroscope	Chemical Testing Devices	291
Photoclinometer	Mining & Mineral Harvesting T&E	223
Photocoagulator	Medical Instruments	332
Photocopier	Replication Equipment	387
Photocopy	Other Documents	481
Photodrome	Optical T&E	344
Photoengraving	Graphic Documents	473
Photograph	Graphic Documents	472
Photograph, Black-and-White	Graphic Documents	473
Photograph, Cabinet	Graphic Documents	473
Photograph, Color	Graphic Documents	473
Photogravure	Graphic Documents	473
Photoheliograph	Astronomical T&E	285
Photolithograph	Graphic Documents	474
Photometer	Optical T&E	344
Photometer, Photoelectric	Astronomical T&E	285
Photometer, Polarizing	Optical T&E	344
Photophone	Acoustical T&E	262
Photosynthometer	Biological T&E	287

Term	Category	Page
Phototypesetter	Typesetting Equipment	388
Phrenograph	Medical Instruments	328
phylactery (*use:* Tefillin)	Belief Symbols	494
Piano	Musical Instruments	371
Piano, Baby Grand	Musical Instruments	371
piano, barrel (*use:* Piano, Upright)	Musical Instruments	371
Piano, Grand	Musical Instruments	371
Piano, Player	Musical Instruments	372
piano, reproducing (*use:* Piano, Player)	Musical Instruments	372
Piano, Square	Musical Instruments	371
Piano, Upright	Musical Instruments	371
Piccolo	Musical Instruments	375
Pick	Construction T&E	296
Pick, Coal	Heating Equipment Accessories	77
Pick, Dental	Dental Instruments	323
Pick, Double-Pointed	Mining & Mineral Harvesting T&E	223
Pick, Drifting	Mining & Mineral Harvesting T&E	223
Pick, Driving	Mining & Mineral Harvesting T&E	223
Pick, Eating	Eating & Drinking Utensils	178
Pick, Flinting	Masonry & Stoneworking T&E	205
Pick, Floral	Party Accessories	460
Pick, Hair	Hair Care Objects	118
pick, holing (*use:* Pick, Undercutting)	Mining & Mineral Harvesting T&E	224
Pick, Hoof	Animal Care Equipment	136
Pick, Hors d'Oeuvre	Eating & Drinking Utensils	178
Pick, Ice	Food Preparation Equipment	159
Pick, Instrument	Musical Accessories	369
pick, lobster (*use:* Pick, Seafood)	Eating & Drinking Utensils	178
Pick, Mason's	Masonry & Stoneworking T&E	205
Pick, Mill	Masonry & Stoneworking T&E	205
Pick, Mining	Mining & Mineral Harvesting T&E	223
Pick, Paleontologist's	Geological T&E	307
Pick, Poll	Mining & Mineral Harvesting T&E	223
Pick, Seafood	Eating & Drinking Utensils	178
Pick, Slate	Masonry & Stoneworking T&E	205
Pick, Stone	Masonry & Stoneworking T&E	205
Pick, Undercutting	Mining & Mineral Harvesting T&E	224
Pick, Water	Hygiene Objects	121
Pick, Wick	Other Lighting Accessories	73
Pickaroon	Forestry T&E	190
Picker, Cherry	Construction T&E	296
Picker, Corn	Harvesting Equipment	129
Picker, Cotton	Harvesting Equipment	129
Picker, Crop	Harvesting Equipment	129
Picker, Fiber	Textile Manufacturing Equipment	243
Picker, Fruit	Harvesting Equipment	129
picker, rock (*use:* Picker, Stone)	Cultivation Equipment	124
Picker, Stone	Cultivation Equipment	124
pickup (*use:* Truck, Pickup)	Motor Vehicles	429
Pickup, Acoustic	Musical Accessories	369
pickup, phonograph (*use:* Cartridge, Phonograph)	Sound Communication Accessories	389
Pictograph	Graphic Documents	473
Picture	Art	453
Picture, Animal	Art	453
Picture, Flora	Art	453
Picture, Genre	Art	453
Picture, History	Art	453
Picture, Leaf	Art	453
Picture, Motion	Other Documents	485
Picture, Seed	Art	453
Picture, Woven	Art	453
Piece of Eight	Exchange Media	488
Piece, Chess	Game Equipment	502
Piece, Display	Advertising Media	450
piece, fifty-cent (*use:* Dollar, Half)	Exchange Media	488
piece, five-cent (*use:* Nickel)	Exchange Media	488
Piece, Floral	Art	453
Piece, Game	Game Equipment	502
piece, one-cent (*use:* Penny)	Exchange Media	488
Piece, Presentation	Achievement Symbols	491
piece, ten-cent (*use:* Dime, Half)	Exchange Media	487
Piece, Three-Cent	Exchange Media	488
Pier	Transportation Structures	39
Pier, Supporting	Supporting Elements	16
Piezometer	Mechanical Measurement Equipment	318
Pig	Glass, Plastics & Clayworking T&E	194
pigeon, clay (*use:* Target, Skeet)	Armament Accessories	272
Piggin, Milking	Food Processing Equipment	166
Pigment, Paint	Painting T&E	230
Pigsty	Agricultural Structures	23
Pike	Edged Weapons	278
Pike, Awl	Edged Weapons	278
Pike, Boarding	Edged Weapons	278
Pike, Jam	Forestry T&E	191
Pike, Pole	Forestry T&E	191

Term	Category	Page
Pilaster	Supporting Elements	16
Pillar	Supporting Elements	16
pillbox (*use:* Hat, Pillbox)	Headwear	93
Pillbox	Personal Carrying & Storage Gear	112
Pillory	Regulative Devices	347
Pillow	Bedding	44
Pillow, Air	Bedding	44
pillow, bobbin lace (*use:* Cushion, Lacemaker's)	Textile Manufacturing Equipment	240
Pillow, Body	Bedding	44
Pillow, Coffin	Funerary Objects	457
Pillow, Feather	Bedding	44
Pillow, Foam	Bedding	44
Pillow, Medicinal	Medical Instruments	334
Pillow, Neck	Personal Assistive Objects	108
Pillow, Ring	Wedding Objects	466
Pillow, Throw	Other Household Accessories	67
Pillowcase	Bedding	44
Pilot, Locomotive	Rail Transportation Accessories	431
pilothouse (*use:* House, Pilot)	Water Transportation Accessories	438
Pin, Award	Achievement Symbols	491
pin, baby (*use:* Pin, Scatter)	Clothing Accessories	86
Pin, Bandage	Veterinary Equipment	142
Pin, Bar	Clothing Accessories	86
Pin, Belaying	Water Transportation Accessories	438
Pin, Bobby	Hair Adornments	83
Pin, Boom	Forestry T&E	191
Pin, Bowling	Sports Equipment	513
Pin, Campaign	Belief Symbols	493
Pin, Chaining	Surveying Equipment	353
Pin, Clothing	Clothing Accessories	86
Pin, Collar	Clothing Accessories	86
Pin, Cotter	Metalworking T&E	210
Pin, Coupling	Rail Transportation Accessories	431
Pin, Diaper	Clothing Accessories	86
Pin, Draw Bore	Woodworking T&E	254
pin, drift (*use:* Punch, Drift)	Metalworking T&E	215
Pin, Fire	Status Symbols	497
Pin, Fraternal	Status Symbols	497
pin, husking (*use:* Cornhusker, Hand)	Harvesting Equipment	128
Pin, Insignia	Status Symbols	497
Pin, Inspirational	Belief Symbols	494
Pin, Juggling	Public Entertainment Devices	508
Pin, Lapel	Clothing Accessories	86
Pin, Law Enforcement	Status Symbols	497

Term	Category	Page
pin, linch (*use:* Linchpin)	Land Transportation Accessories	417
Pin, Line	Masonry & Stoneworking T&E	205
Pin, Membership	Status Symbols	497
Pin, Military	Status Symbols	497
Pin, Occupational	Status Symbols	497
Pin, Picket	Animal Care Equipment	135
Pin, Political	Belief Symbols	493
Pin, Priming	Armament Accessories	270
Pin, Prolapse	Veterinary Equipment	142
Pin, Promotional	Advertising Media	450
Pin, Rolling	Food Preparation Equipment	156
Pin, Safety	Needleworking Equipment	236
Pin, Scatter	Clothing Accessories	86
Pin, Skirt	Clothing Accessories	86
Pin, Sororital	Status Symbols	497
Pin, Stake	Pet Supplies	141
Pin, Straight	Needleworking Equipment	236
Pin, Surgical	Medical Instruments	332
Pin, Thole	Water Transportation Accessories	438
pin, tie (*use:* Stickpin)	Clothing Accessories	86
Pin, Truss	Supporting Elements	16
Pin, Watch	Clothing Accessories	86
Pinafore	Protective Wear	102
Piñata	Game Equipment	505
Pinboard	Data Processing Accessories	360
Pince-Nez	Personal Assistive Objects	108
Pincers	Glass, Plastics & Clayworking T&E	194
Pincers, Farrier's	Farrier Equipment	139
Pincers, Gunner's	Armament Accessories	270
Pincers, Lasting	Leather, Horn & Shellworking T&E	200
Pincers, Wire	Metalworking T&E	215
Pincers, Woodworking	Woodworking T&E	254
Pinchbar	Mechanical Devices	316
Pincushion	Needleworking Equipment	235
Pink	Watercraft	443
Pinky	Watercraft	444
Pinnace	Watercraft	448
Pinner	Headwear	92
Pinrail	Water Transportation Accessories	438
Pinsetter	Sports Equipment	513
Pinwheel	Toys	525
Pioscope	Food Processing Equipment	167
Pipe	Construction Materials	3
Pipe, Boatswain's	Sound Communication Devices	391
pipe, bosun's (*use:* Pipe, Boatswain's)	Sound Communication Devices	391
Pipe, Bubble	Toys	523
Pipe, Coupling	Metalworking T&E	215
Pipe, Drainage	Plumbing & Drainage Elements	13

Pipe, Draught | Labware | 293
Pipe, Exhaust | Power Transmission Components | 305
Pipe, Irrigation | Tending Equipment | 133
Pipe, Opium | Smoking & Recreational Drug Equipment | 114
Pipe, Organ | Musical Accessories | 369
pipe, peace (*use:* Calumet) | Organizational Objects | 459
Pipe, Pitch | Musical Accessories | 369
Pipe, Plumbing | Plumbing & Drainage Elements | 12
pipe, reed (*use:* Reedpipe) | Musical Instruments | 375
Pipe, Riser | Plumbing & Drainage Elements | 13
Pipe, Scupper | Water Transportation Accessories | 438
Pipe, Smoking | Smoking & Recreational Drug Equipment | 114
Pipe, Tabor | Musical Instruments | 375
pipe, tobacco (*use:* Pipe, Smoking) | Smoking & Recreational Drug Equipment | 114
Pipe, Water | Smoking & Recreational Drug Equipment | 114
Pipe, Water Supply | Plumbing & Drainage Elements | 13
pipe, whistle (*use:* Whistle, Toy) | Toys | 524
Pipette | Labware | 294
Pipette, Absorption | Labware | 294
Pipette, Intrauterine | Breeding Equipment | 138
Pipette, Volumetric | Labware | 294
Piping | Needleworking Equipment | 237
Pipkin | Cooking Vessels | 151
pirogue (*use:* Canoe, Dugout) | Watercraft | 442
piscina (*use:* Lavabo) | Religious Objects | 464
Pistol | Firearms | 281
Pistol, Automatic | Firearms | 281
Pistol, Belt | Firearms | 281
Pistol, Blank | Firearms | 281
Pistol, Blunderbuss | Firearms | 281
pistol, cap (*use:* Gun, Cap) | Toys | 521
Pistol, Cartridge | Firearms | 281
Pistol, Dueling | Firearms | 281
pistol, firecracker (*use:* Gun, Cap) | Toys | 521
Pistol, Flintlock | Firearms | 281
Pistol, Holster | Firearms | 281
Pistol, Line Throwing | Water Transportation Accessories | 441
pistol, machine (*use:* Gun, Submachine) | Firearms | 280
Pistol, Matchlock | Firearms | 281
pistol, paintball (*use:* Gun, Paintball) | Toys | 521
Pistol, Palm | Firearms | 281
Pistol, Percussion | Firearms | 281
Pistol, Pocket | Firearms | 281
Pistol, Saddle | Firearms | 281
Pistol, Semi-Automatic | Firearms | 281
pistol, signal (*use:* Gun, Flare) | Visual Communication Devices | 400
Pistol, Starter | Sound Communication Devices | 391
Pistol, Target | Firearms | 281
pistol, tinder (*use:* Tinderpistol) | Firemaking Equipment | 74
pistol, very (*use:* Gun, Flare) | Visual Communication Devices | 400
pistol, water (*use:* Gun, Water) | Toys | 521
Pistol, Wheelock | Firearms | 281
Piston | Power Transmission Components | 305
Pit, Ball | Recreational Devices | 510
Pitcher | Serving Vessels | 189
Pitcher, Batter | Food Preparation Equipment | 153
Pitcher, Beer | Serving Vessels | 189
Pitcher, Communion | Religious Objects | 462
Pitcher, Cream | Serving Vessels | 189
Pitcher, Hot Water | Serving Vessels | 189
Pitcher, Ice Water | Serving Vessels | 189
Pitcher, Measuring | Food Preparation Equipment | 156
Pitcher, Milk | Serving Vessels | 189
Pitcher, Syrup | Serving Vessels | 189
Pitcher, Wash | Hygiene Objects | 120
Pitcher, Water | Serving Vessels | 189
pitchfork (*use:* Hayfork) | Harvesting Equipment | 129
pitometer (*use:* Log, Pit) | Water Transportation Accessories | 441
Piton | Sports Equipment | 514
Pitter, Fruit | Food Preparation Equipment | 160
Placard | Advertising Media | 450
Placecard | Other Documents | 481
Placemat | Food Service Accessories | 181
plagiograph (*use:* Pantograph) | Drafting T&E | 367
Plaid | Main Garments | 97
Plan | Graphic Documents | 474
Plan, Floor | Graphic Documents | 474
Plan, Site | Graphic Documents | 474
Plane | Woodworking T&E | 254
Plane, Angle | Masonry & Stoneworking T&E | 206
Plane, Astragal | Woodworking T&E | 255
Plane, Badger | Woodworking T&E | 254
Plane, Banding | Woodworking T&E | 254
plane, bead molding (*use:* Plane, Astragal) | Woodworking T&E | 254

Term	Category	Page
plane, beading (*use:* Plane, Astragal)	Woodworking T&E	254
Plane, Block	Woodworking T&E	255
Plane, Bullnose	Woodworking T&E	254
Plane, Cargo	Aircraft	411
plane, centerbead (*use:* Plane, Centerboard)	Woodworking T&E	255
Plane, Centerboard	Woodworking T&E	255
plane, chisel (*use:* Plane, Edge)	Woodworking T&E	254
plane, chiv (*use:* Plane, Howell)	Woodworking T&E	255
plane, cluster-bead (*use:* Plane, Molding)	Woodworking T&E	255
Plane, Coach	Woodworking T&E	254
Plane, Combination	Woodworking T&E	254
Plane, Compass	Woodworking T&E	255
Plane, Cooper's Stoup	Woodworking T&E	255
Plane, Cornice	Woodworking T&E	255
Plane, Cove	Woodworking T&E	255
plane, crown (*use:* Plane, Cornice)	Woodworking T&E	255
plane, croze (*use:* Croze)	Woodworking T&E	254
Plane, Dado	Woodworking T&E	254
Plane, Drawer	Woodworking T&E	254
Plane, Edge	Woodworking T&E	254
Plane, Fillister	Woodworking T&E	254
Plane, Finger	Woodworking T&E	255
Plane, Float	Aircraft	411
Plane, Floor	Woodworking T&E	255
Plane, Fore	Woodworking T&E	255
plane, forkstaff (*use:* Plane, Hollow)	Woodworking T&E	255
Plane, Grooving	Woodworking T&E	254
Plane, Guttering	Woodworking T&E	255
Plane, Handrail	Woodworking T&E	255
Plane, Hollow	Woodworking T&E	255
Plane, Howell	Woodworking T&E	255
Plane, Inclined	Mechanical Devices	316
Plane, Jack	Woodworking T&E	255
Plane, Jointer	Woodworking T&E	255
Plane, Leveling	Woodworking T&E	255
Plane, Miter	Woodworking T&E	255
Plane, Modeling	Woodworking T&E	255
Plane, Molding	Woodworking T&E	255
Plane, Nosing	Woodworking T&E	255
Plane, Ogee	Woodworking T&E	255
plane, old woman's tooth (*use:* Plane, Router)	Woodworking T&E	255
Plane, Ovolo	Woodworking T&E	255
Plane, Panel	Woodworking T&E	255
plane, panel fielding (*use:* Plane, Raising)	Woodworking T&E	256
Plane, Passenger	Aircraft	411
Plane, Plow	Woodworking T&E	255
plane, pull (*use:* Plane, Jointer)	Woodworking T&E	255
Plane, Pulping	Harvesting Equipment	130
Plane, Rabbet	Woodworking T&E	255
Plane, Raising	Woodworking T&E	256
plane, rebate (*use:* Plane, Rabbet)	Woodworking T&E	255
Plane, Roughing	Woodworking T&E	256
Plane, Round	Woodworking T&E	255
Plane, Rounder	Woodworking T&E	256
Plane, Router	Woodworking T&E	255
Plane, Sash	Woodworking T&E	255
plane, scaleboard (*use:* Plane, Splint)	Woodworking T&E	256
Plane, Scoopmaker	Woodworking T&E	256
Plane, Shoulder	Woodworking T&E	255
Plane, Side Rabbet	Woodworking T&E	255
plane, skew (*use:* Plane, Rabbet)	Woodworking T&E	255
Plane, Smoothing	Woodworking T&E	255
Plane, Splint	Woodworking T&E	256
Plane, Spoke	Woodworking T&E	256
plane, spy (*use:* Airplane, Reconnaissance)	Aircraft	411
Plane, Stairbuilder's	Woodworking T&E	255
Plane, Sun	Woodworking T&E	255
Plane, Thumb	Woodworking T&E	256
Plane, Tongue and Groove	Woodworking T&E	255
Plane, Tonguing	Woodworking T&E	255
Plane, Toothing	Woodworking T&E	255
plane, topping (*use:* Plane, Sun)	Woodworking T&E	255
plane, trolling (*use:* Rig, Trolling)	Fishing Equipment	147
Plane, Trying	Woodworking T&E	255
Plane, Violinmaker's	Woodworking T&E	256
plane, witchet (*use:* Plane, Rounder)	Woodworking T&E	256
Planer, Metal	Metalworking T&E	215
Planer, Printer's	Graphic Equipment	384
Planer, Wood	Woodworking T&E	254
planetarium (*use:* Projector, Planetarium)	Astronomical T&E	285
Planetarium	Cultural & Recreational Structures	29
planigraph (*use:* Pantograph)	Drafting T&E	367
Planimeter	Data Processing Devices	361
planimeter (*use:* Platometer)	Surveying Equipment	353
Planisphere	Astronomical T&E	285
plank (*use:* Board)	Construction Materials	3
planking, watercraft (*use:* Decking, Watercraft)	Water Transportation Accessories	437
Plansifter	Food Processing Equipment	169
Plant, Artificial	Decorative Furnishings	60

Plant, Assembly	Industrial Structures	35
plant, batch (*use:* Batcher)	Masonry & Stoneworking T&E	204
Plant, Beverage	Industrial Structures	35
Plant, Bottling	Industrial Structures	35
Plant, Chemical	Industrial Structures	35
Plant, Dairy	Industrial Structures	35
Plant, Food	Industrial Structures	35
plant, industrial (*use:* Factory)	Industrial Structures	35
Plant, Nuclear Power	Industrial Structures	35
Plant, Packing	Industrial Structures	35
Plant, Power	Industrial Structures	35
Planter	Horticultural Containers	62
Planter, Corn	Planting Equipment	132
Planter, Garden	Site Features	21
Planter, Garden Seed	Planting Equipment	132
Planter, Hand	Planting Equipment	132
Planter, Lister	Planting Equipment	132
Planter, Potato	Planting Equipment	132
Planter, Precision	Planting Equipment	132
Planter, Seed	Planting Equipment	132
Planter, Walking	Planting Equipment	132
planter, walking-stick (*use:* Planter, Hand)	Planting Equipment	132
planter, wheel (*use:* Planter, Garden Seed)	Planting Equipment	132
Plaque	Organizational Objects	459
Plaque, Award	Achievement Symbols	491
Plaque, Date	Other Documents	485
Plaque, Decorative	Art	454
Plaque, Insignia	Status Symbols	497
Plaque, Religious	Religious Objects	464
Plaster	Construction Materials	3
Plaster, Cough	Medical Instruments	334
Plastron	Sports Equipment	515
Plat	Graphic Documents	472
plate, amalgam (*use:* Table, Amalgamating)	Metalworking T&E	217
Plate, Anchor	Supporting Elements	16
Plate, Armor	Body Armor	275
Plate, Belt	Status Symbols	497
Plate, Bench	Metalworking T&E	215
Plate, Bite	Dental Instruments	323
plate, bread (*use:* Plate, Butter)	Eating Vessels	176
Plate, Builder's	Other Documents	485
Plate, Butter	Eating Vessels	176
Plate, Cake	Serving Vessels	187
Plate, Circumcision	Medical Instruments	332
Plate, Coffin	Funerary Objects	457
plate, collection (*use:* Plate, Offering)	Religious Objects	461
Plate, Commemorative	Memorabilia	478
Plate, Communion	Religious Objects	462
Plate, Cup	Eating Vessels	176
Plate, Decorative	Decorative Furnishings	60
Plate, Dessert	Eating Vessels	176
Plate, Dinner	Eating Vessels	176
plate, doorknob (*use:* Escutcheon)	Finish Hardware	10
plate, dowel (*use:* Cutter, Peg)	Woodworking T&E	249
Plate, Dry	Photographic Media	380
Plate, Electrotype	Graphic Equipment	384
Plate, Embossing	Graphic Equipment	384
plate, engraving (*use:* Block, Engraving)	Graphic Equipment	384
Plate, Ferrotype	Photoprocessing Equipment	381
Plate, Food	Eating Vessels	176
Plate, Fruit	Serving Vessels	187
Plate, Glue	Woodworking T&E	256
plate, griddle (*use:* Griddle)	Food Preparation Equipment	154
Plate, Heel	Clothing Accessories	86
Plate, Helmet	Status Symbols	497
Plate, Hot	Food Preparation Equipment	155
Plate, Identification	Other Documents	485
Plate, Insignia	Status Symbols	497
Plate, Jamb	Finish Hardware	10
Plate, Juggling	Public Entertainment Devices	508
Plate, Key	Finish Hardware	10
plate, keyhole (*use:* Escutcheon)	Finish Hardware	10
plate, letter-box (*use:* Slot, Mail)	Finish Hardware	11
Plate, License	Land Transportation Accessories	419
Plate, Lithograph	Graphic Equipment	384
Plate, Luncheon	Eating Vessels	176
Plate, Mayonnaise Bowl	Serving Vessels	187
plate, name (*use:* Nameplate)	Other Documents	485
Plate, Number	Other Documents	485
Plate, Offering	Religious Objects	461
Plate, Offset	Graphic Equipment	384
Plate, Oyster	Serving Vessels	187
Plate, Photographic	Photographic Media	380
plate, pie (*use:* Pan, Pie)	Cooking Vessels	150
Plate, Place	Eating Vessels	176
Plate, Printing	Graphic Equipment	384
Plate, Salad	Eating Vessels	177
Plate, Sauceboat	Serving Vessels	187
Plate, Screw	Metalworking T&E	209
Plate, Seder	Religious Objects	462
Plate, Serving	Serving Vessels	187
plate, shoulder (*use:* Pauldron)	Body Armor	275
Plate, Sill	Supporting Elements	17
Plate, Snatch	Mining & Mineral Harvesting T&E	224

Plate, Soup Eating Vessels 177
Plate, Spice Serving Vessels 187
Plate, Spinning Public Entertainment Devices 508
Plate, Stereotype Graphic Equipment 384
Plate, Stove Heating Equipment Accessories 76
Plate, Strike Finish Hardware 10
Plate, Switch Finish Hardware 10
Plate, Tarnish Remover Housekeeping Equipment 312
Plate, Tea Eating Vessels 177
plate, tie (*use:* Fishplate, Rail) Rail Transportation Accessories 432
Plate, Toddy Serving Vessels 187
Plate, Tracing Dental Instruments 323
Plate, Vegetable Serving Vessels 187
Plate, Warming Food Preparation Equipment 163
Plate, Wet Photographic Media 380
plate, wiredrawing (*use:* Die, Wire Drawing) Metalworking T&E 210
Plateau Food Service Accessories 182
plateholder, photographic (*use:* Holder, Photographic Plate) Camera Equipment 377
Platform Architectural Spaces 1
Platform, Roofing Construction T&E 296
Platform, Working Construction T&E 296
Platometer Surveying Equipment 353
Platter Serving Vessels 187
Platter, Well Serving Vessels 187
Platymeter Electrical & Magnetic Measurement Devices 297
Play Literary Works 477
Player, Audio Sound Communication Devices 392
Player, Audiocassette Sound Communication Devices 392
player, CD (*use:* Player, Compact Disc) Sound Communication Devices 392
Player, Compact Disc Sound Communication Devices 392
player, data cassette (*use:* Drive, Tape) Peripherals 365
Player, Digital Audio Sound Communication Devices 392
Player, Digital Videodisc Visual Communication Devices 400
player, DVD (*use:* Player, Digital Videodisc) Visual Communication Devices 400
Player, Eight-Track Sound Communication Devices 392
player, MP3 (*use:* Player, Digital Audio) Sound Communication Devices 392
Player, Record Sound Communication Devices 392
Player, Reel-to-Reel Tape Sound Communication Devices 392
player, solid state (*use:* Player, Digital Audio) Sound Communication Devices 392
Player, Tape Sound Communication Devices 392
Playhouse Toys 522
Playpen Other Furniture 58
Playsuit Main Garments 96
Plaza, Shopping Commercial Structures 27
plectrum (*use:* Pick, Instrument) Musical Accessories 369
Pledge Other Documents 485
Pledget Medical Instruments 333
Plethysmograph Medical Instruments 328
Pliers Multiple Use T&E for Materials 228
pliers, band soldering (*use:* Tweezers, Soldering) Dental Accessories 321
Pliers, Combination Multiple Use T&E for Materials 228
Pliers, Contouring Dental Accessories 321
Pliers, Dental Dental Instruments 323
Pliers, Dressing Dental Instruments 323
Pliers, Elastrator Veterinary Equipment 143
Pliers, Electrician's Electrical Maintenance & Repair Equipment 299
Pliers, Fence Construction T&E 296
Pliers, Gas Metalworking T&E 215
Pliers, Glass Glass, Plastics & Clayworking T&E 194
Pliers, Lacing Leather, Horn & Shellworking T&E 200
Pliers, Leatherworking Leather, Horn & Shellworking T&E 200
Pliers, Metalworking Metalworking T&E 215
Pliers, Needlenose Multiple Use T&E for Materials 228
Pliers, Pad Screw Leather, Horn & Shellworking T&E 200
Pliers, Setting Metalworking T&E 215
Pliers, Stretching Painting T&E 230
Plinth Supporting Elements 17
Plotter Peripherals 364
Plow Cultivation Equipment 124
Plow, Angle Masonry & Stoneworking T&E 206
Plow, Bog Cultivation Equipment 124
Plow, Bookbinding Bookbinding Equipment 383
Plow, Breaking Cultivation Equipment 124
plow, chisel (*use:* Plow, Subsoil) Cultivation Equipment 125
Plow, Disk Cultivation Equipment 124
Plow, Gang Cultivation Equipment 124
Plow, Garden Cultivation Equipment 124
Plow, Hillside Cultivation Equipment 124

Term	Category	Page
Plow, Ice	Mining & Mineral Harvesting T&E	225
plow, lister (*use:* Middlebuster)	Cultivation Equipment	124
plow, middlebuster (*use:* Middlebuster)	Cultivation Equipment	124
Plow, Moldboard	Cultivation Equipment	124
plow, peat (*use:* Plow, Bog)	Cultivation Equipment	124
plow, potato (*use:* Middlebuster)	Cultivation Equipment	124
Plow, Ridging	Cultivation Equipment	124
Plow, Scratch	Cultivation Equipment	125
Plow, Shovel	Cultivation Equipment	125
plow, sidehill (*use:* Plow, Hillside)	Cultivation Equipment	124
plow, snow (*use:* Snowplow, Horse-Drawn)	Animal-Powered Vehicles	424
plow, snow (*use:* Blade, Snow)	Land Transportation Accessories	416
plow, snow (*use:* Snowplow)	Motor Vehicles	429
Plow, Stubble	Cultivation Equipment	125
Plow, Subsoil	Cultivation Equipment	125
Plow, Sulky	Cultivation Equipment	125
plow, swing (*use:* Plow, Hillside)	Cultivation Equipment	124
Plow, Two-Way	Cultivation Equipment	125
Plow, Wheel	Cultivation Equipment	125
Plug, Drain	Other Household Accessories	67
Plug, Electrical	Electrical System Components	301
Plug, Masonry	Masonry & Stoneworking T&E	205
Plug, Nose	Body Adornments	81
plug, nose (*use:* Noseplug)	Personal Assistive Objects	108
Plug, Receptacle	Electrical System Components	301
Plug, Socket	Electrical System Components	301
plug, spark (*use:* Sparkplug)	Power Transmission Components	305
Plugger, Dental	Dental Accessories	321
plume (*use:* Aigrette)	Hair Adornments	83
Plume	Status Symbols	497
Plume, Hat	Clothing Accessories	86
plummet (*use:* Bob, Plumb)	Construction T&E	295
Plunger	Housekeeping Equipment	312
Pluviograph	Meteorological T&E	339
Pluviometer	Meteorological T&E	339
pneometer (*use:* Spirometer)	Medical Instruments	327
Poacher	Cooking Vessels	151
Poacher, Egg	Cooking Vessels	151
Poacher, Fish	Cooking Vessels	151
Pocket	Personal Carrying & Storage Gear	110
Pocket, Crib	Storage & Display Accessories	64
Pocket, Wall	Storage & Display Accessories	64
pocketbook (*use:* Purse)	Personal Carrying & Storage Gear	111
Podium	Support Furniture	55
Poem	Literary Works	477
Pogamoggan	Percussive Weapons	283
poignard (*use:* Poniard)	Edged Weapons	277
Point	Masonry & Stoneworking T&E	203
Point, Cautery	Medical Instruments	332
Point, Dental	Dental Instruments	323
point, engraving (*use:* Burin)	Graphic Equipment	384
Point, Glazier's	Glass, Plastics & Clayworking T&E	194
Point, Lithographic	Graphic Equipment	384
Point, Projectile	Edged Weapons	278
Point, Pyrography	Multiple Use T&E for Materials	228
Point, Spear	Edged Weapons	278
Point, Steam Thawing	Mining & Mineral Harvesting T&E	224
Pointer	Visual Communication Devices	400
Pointer, Laser	Visual Communication Devices	400
Pointer, Picket	Woodworking T&E	256
Pointer, Spoke	Woodworking T&E	256
Pointer, Station	Navigational Equipment	350
Poise, Air	Meteorological T&E	340
Pokal	Drinking Vessels	174
Poke	Animal Care Equipment	135
Poker	Heating Equipment Accessories	77
Poker, Blacksmith's	Metalworking T&E	215
Poker, Bond	Fiberworking T&E	144
Poker, Kiln	Masonry & Stoneworking T&E	205
Polarimeter	Optical T&E	344
Polariscope	Optical T&E	344
Pole, Balancing	Public Entertainment Devices	507
Pole, Barber	Advertising Media	451
pole, barge (*use:* Quant)	Water Transportation Accessories	441
Pole, Basketball	Sports Equipment	513
pole, fishing (*use:* Rod, Fishing)	Fishing Equipment	147
Pole, Gin	Mechanical Devices	315
Pole, Lamplighter	Other Lighting Accessories	73

Term	Category	Page
Pole, Pick	Construction T&E	296
Pole, Picket	Surveying Equipment	353
pole, pike (*use:* Pole, Pick)	Construction T&E	296
pole, pike (*use:* Hook, Raft)	Forestry T&E	190
pole, pike (*use:* Hook, Fire)	Protective Devices	345
Pole, Push	Rail Transportation Accessories	432
pole, quant (*use:* Quant)	Water Transportation Accessories	441
Pole, Sash	Other Household Accessories	67
Pole, Ski	Sports Equipment	517
Pole, Sliding	Recreational Devices	510
pole, spike (*use:* Pole, Pick)	Construction T&E	296
Pole, Spinnaker	Water Transportation Accessories	440
Pole, Spring	Mining & Mineral Harvesting T&E	224
Pole, Telephone	Other Structures	41
Pole, Tent	Supporting Elements	17
Pole, Totem	Art	454
Pole, Utility	Other Structures	41
Pole, Vaulting	Sports Equipment	518
Pole-Arm	Edged Weapons	278
Poleax	Edged Weapons	278
poleax (*use:* Ax, Slaughtering)	Food Processing Equipment	165
Polemoscope	Optical T&E	343
Poleyn	Body Armor	275
Policy, Insurance	Financial Records	469
Polish, Nail	Beauty Supplies	117
polish, shoe (*use:* Wax, Shoe)	Clothing Care Objects	106
Polisher, Dental	Dental Instruments	323
Polisher, Floor	Housekeeping Equipment	312
Polisher, Porte	Dental Instruments	323
pollbook (*use:* List, Voters')	Other Documents	483
Polonaise	Main Garments	96
polygonoscope (*use:* Kaleidoscope)	Toys	523
Polygraph	Medical Instruments	328
Pomander	Personal Assistive Objects	108
Pompon	Needleworking Equipment	236
Poncho	Outerwear	101
Poniard	Edged Weapons	277
Pontil	Glass, Plastics & Clayworking T&E	194
Pontoon	Watercraft	448
Pony, Lacing	Leather, Horn & Shellworking T&E	200
Pool	Hydraulic Structures	34
Pool, Swimming	Cultural & Recreational Structures	30
Pool, Wading	Recreational Devices	511
Pooper-Scooper	Pet Supplies	141
Popgun	Toys	521
Popper, Corn	Food Preparation Equipment	155
Popper, Electric	Food Preparation Equipment	155
Popper, Stovetop	Food Preparation Equipment	155
Porch	Architectural Spaces	1
porch, carriage (*use:* Porte-Cochere)	Architectural Spaces	1
Porch, Sleeping	Architectural Spaces	1
Porringer	Eating Vessels	177
Porro	Drinking Vessels	175
Portcullis	Door & Window Elements	6
porte, screw (*use:* Extractor, Root)	Dental Instruments	322
Porte-Cochère	Architectural Spaces	1
Portfolio	Writing Accessories	403
Porthole	Water Transportation Accessories	440
Portico	Architectural Spaces	1
Portiere	Window & Door Coverings	78
portmanteau (*use:* Suitcase)	Personal Carrying & Storage Gear	112
Portrait	Art	453
Positive, Direct	Graphic Documents	473
Posnet	Cooking Vessels	151
Post	Supporting Elements	17
Post, Aiming	Armament Accessories	270
Post, Binding	Electrical System Components	301
Post, Croquet	Game Equipment	501
Post, Dental	Dental Instruments	323
Post, Fence	Site Features	20
Post, Gate	Site Features	20
Post, Hitching	Transportation Structures	39
Post, Observation	Defense Structures	31
Post, Scratching	Pet Supplies	141
Post, Tennis	Sports Equipment	518
Post, Whipping	Regulative Devices	347
Postcard	Writing Media	408
Postcard, Picture	Writing Media	408
Poster	Advertising Media	450
Poster, Instructional	Instructional Documents	475
Poster, Music	Advertising Media	450
Poster, Political	Advertising Media	450
Poster, Theater	Advertising Media	450
Posturometer	Biological T&E	287
pot, babbitt (*use:* Crucible, Metal)	Metalworking T&E	209
Pot, Baking	Cooking Vessels	151
pot, bean (*use:* Beanpot)	Cooking Vessels	151
Pot, Blow	Aerospace Transportation Accessories	410
Pot, Chamber	Hygiene Objects	121
Pot, Chimney	Environmental Control Elements	8

Pot, Chocolate	Serving Vessels	189
pot, coffee (*use:* Coffeepot)	Serving Vessels	186
Pot, Crab	Fishing Equipment	148
pot, crock (*use:* Crockpot)	Food Preparation Equipment	154
pot, eel (*use:* Eelpot)	Fishing Equipment	148
Pot, Fish	Fishing Equipment	148
pot, flower (*use:* Flowerpot)	Horticultural Containers	62
Pot, Fondue	Food Preparation Equipment	155
pot, fuming (*use:* Burner, Incense)	Other Household Accessories	66
Pot, Glue	Printing Accessories	386
pot, grease (*use:* Keeper, Oil)	Food Storage Equipment	171
pot, hot water (*use:* Urn, Hot Water)	Serving Vessels	189
Pot, Jam	Serving Vessels	188
Pot, Lobster	Fishing Equipment	148
Pot, Melting	Glass, Plastics & Clayworking T&E	194
Pot, Mustard	Serving Vessels	188
Pot, Ollio	Serving Vessels	188
Pot, Paste	Other Household Accessories	67
pot, pepper (*use:* Shaker, Pepper)	Serving Vessels	188
Pot, Posset	Drinking Vessels	175
pot, pounce (*use:* Box, Pounce)	Writing Accessories	403
pot, smudge (*use:* Heater, Orchard)	Tending Equipment	133
Pot, Smudge	Visual Communication Devices	400
Pot, Soldering	Metalworking T&E	215
pot, stock (*use:* Stockpot)	Cooking Vessels	151
pot, tea (*use:* Teapot)	Serving Vessels	189
Pot, Try	Fishing Equipment	148
pot, unguent (*use:* Jar, Ointment)	Medical Accessories	325
Potentiometer	Electrical & Magnetic Measurement Devices	297
Potholder	Food Preparation Accessories	152
Pothook	Food Preparation Equipment	163
Potometer	Biological T&E	287
Potpourri	Other Household Accessories	67
Potsherd	Unclassifiable Objects	527
Pottery	Industrial Structures	35
potty (*use:* Pot, Chamber)	Hygiene Objects	121
Pouch	Containers	415
Pouch, Arms	Armament Accessories	268
Pouch, Cap	Armament Accessories	268
Pouch, Carrying	Personal Carrying & Storage Gear	110
Pouch, Cartridge	Armament Accessories	268
Pouch, Gunner's	Armament Accessories	268
Pouch, Nail	Woodworking T&E	256
Pouch, Primer	Armament Accessories	268
Pouch, Shot	Armament Accessories	268
Pouch, Tobacco	Smoking & Recreational Drug Equipment	115
pouf (*use:* Hassock)	Seating Furniture	49
Pouffe	Seating Furniture	49
poulaine (*use:* Crakow)	Footwear	89
Pound	Exchange Media	488
pounder (*use:* Pestle, Food)	Food Preparation Equipment	160
pounder, meat (*use:* Maul, Meat)	Food Preparation Equipment	156
Pounder, Poi	Food Preparation Equipment	160
Powder, Bronze	Painting T&E	230
Powder, Developing	Photoprocessing Equipment	381
Powder, Ink	Writing Accessories	404
Power of Attorney	Legal Documents	476
power, tread (*use:* Treadmill)	Power Producing Equipment	304
Powerhouse	Industrial Structures	35
Powerloom	Textile Manufacturing Equipment	241
Pram	Watercraft	443
pram, doll (*use:* Carriage, Doll)	Toys	520
Pram, Sailing	Watercraft	443
Praxinoscope	Toys	524
Prayer	Literary Works	477
Preener, Record	Sound Communication Accessories	389
Preform	Unclassifiable Objects	527
Premium	Advertising Media	450
premium, cigarette (*use:* Premium, Tobacco)	Advertising Media	450
Premium, Tobacco	Advertising Media	450
Prescription	Other Documents	485
Preserver, Life	Water Transportation Accessories	441
press, baling (*use:* Baler)	Harvesting Equipment	127
Press, Blocking	Bookbinding Equipment	383
Press, Book	Replication Equipment	387
Press, Bookbinding	Bookbinding Equipment	383
Press, Butter	Food Preparation Equipment	159
Press, Candy	Food Preparation Equipment	156
Press, Cheese	Food Processing Equipment	166
Press, Cider	Food Processing Equipment	165
Press, Cigar	Other T&E for Materials	260
Press, Cigar Mold	Other T&E for Materials	260

Term	Category	Page
Press, Cigar Packer's	Other T&E for Materials	260
Press, Clicker	Leather, Horn & Shellworking T&E	199
Press, Cloth	Textile Manufacturing Equipment	243
Press, Clothes	Storage & Display Furniture	53
Press, Coffee	Food Preparation Equipment	154
Press, Cookie	Food Preparation Equipment	156
Press, Cork	Woodworking T&E	256
Press, Crown	Dental Accessories	321
Press, Culinary	Food Preparation Equipment	156
Press, Cutting	Bookbinding Equipment	383
Press, Cylinder	Replication Equipment	387
Press, Drill	Metalworking T&E	215
Press, Dry Mount	Visual Communication Accessories	399
Press, Embossing	Replication Equipment	387
press, etching (*use:* Press, Rolling)	Replication Equipment	387
Press, Finishing	Bookbinding Equipment	383
press, fly (*use:* Press, Embossing)	Replication Equipment	387
Press, Fruit	Food Preparation Equipment	160
Press, Fur	Leather, Horn & Shellworking T&E	200
Press, Garlic	Food Preparation Equipment	156
press, hand (*use:* Handpress)	Replication Equipment	387
press, hay (*use:* Baler, Hay)	Harvesting Equipment	127
Press, Hornworker's	Leather, Horn & Shellworking T&E	201
Press, Hot-Head	Laundry Equipment	314
press, jelly (*use:* Press, Fruit)	Food Preparation Equipment	160
Press, Lard	Food Processing Equipment	169
Press, Laundry	Laundry Equipment	313
press, letter (*use:* Letterpress)	Replication Equipment	387
Press, Linen	Storage & Display Furniture	53
Press, Lithographic	Replication Equipment	387
Press, Lying	Bookbinding Equipment	383
Press, Meat	Food Preparation Equipment	156
Press, Metal	Metalworking T&E	215
Press, Mold	Glass, Plastics & Clayworking T&E	194
press, multilith (*use:* Press, Offset)	Replication Equipment	387
Press, Newspaper	Replication Equipment	387
Press, Nipping	Bookbinding Equipment	383
Press, Offset	Replication Equipment	387
Press, Oil	Food Preparation Equipment	156
Press, Pants	Laundry Equipment	314
Press, Plant	Biological T&E	287
Press, Priming	Armament Accessories	271
Press, Printing	Replication Equipment	387
Press, Punch	Metalworking T&E	215
Press, Ravioli	Food Preparation Equipment	156
Press, Rolling	Replication Equipment	387
Press, Rotary	Replication Equipment	387
Press, Seal	Writing Devices	406
Press, Smoothing	Papermaking T&E	232
Press, Stamping	Metalworking T&E	215
Press, Standing	Bookbinding Equipment	383
Press, Straw	Fiberworking T&E	144
Press, Tankage	Food Processing Equipment	169
Press, Tennis Racket	Sports Equipment	518
Press, Tobacco	Harvesting Equipment	130
Press, Toggle	Replication Equipment	387
Press, Tortilla	Food Preparation Equipment	156
Press, Vacuum	Glass, Plastics & Clayworking T&E	194
Press, Veneer	Woodworking T&E	256
Press, Wafer	Food Preparation Equipment	156
Press, Wine	Food Preparation Equipment	160
Pricelist	Other Documents	483
Pricker	Mining & Mineral Harvesting T&E	224
pricker (*use:* Pick, Wick)	Other Lighting Accessories	73
Pricker, Military	Armament Accessories	271
Pricker, Sailmaker's	Needleworking Equipment	237
pricker, wheel (*use:* Wheel, Pricking)	Leather, Horn & Shellworking T&E	202
Prie-Dieu	Religious Objects	463
Primer	Instructional Documents	475
Primer, Detonation	Ammunition	264
Primer, Friction	Ammunition	264
Primer, Nipple	Armament Accessories	271
Print	Graphic Documents	473
Print, Albumen	Graphic Documents	473
print, blueline (*use:* Blueprint)	Other Documents	481
Print, Digital	Graphic Documents	473
Print, Dye Transfer	Graphic Documents	474
Print, Embossed	Graphic Documents	473
Print, Intaglio	Graphic Documents	473
Print, Photographic	Graphic Documents	473
Print, Photomechanical	Graphic Documents	473
Print, Planographic	Graphic Documents	474
Print, Platinum	Graphic Documents	473
Print, Relief	Graphic Documents	474
Print, Salted Paper	Graphic Documents	473
Print, Screen	Graphic Documents	474

Printer	Peripherals	364
Printer, 3D	Multiple Use T&E for Materials	228
Printer, Barcode	Writing Devices	406
printer, butter (*use:* Press, Butter)	Food Preparation Equipment	159
Printer, Character Impact	Peripherals	364
Printer, Contact	Photoprocessing Equipment	381
Printer, Daisywheel	Peripherals	364
Printer, Dot Matrix	Peripherals	364
printer, electrostatic (*use:* Photocopier)	Replication Equipment	387
Printer, Inkjet	Peripherals	364
Printer, Keyboard	Peripherals	365
Printer, Label	Writing Devices	406
Printer, Laser	Peripherals	364
Printer, Line	Peripherals	364
printer, matrix (*use:* Printer, Dot Matrix)	Peripherals	364
Printer, On-the-Fly	Peripherals	365
Printer, Serial	Peripherals	365
Printer, Telegraph	Telecommunication Devices	396
Printer, Thermal	Peripherals	365
Prism	Other Lighting Accessories	73
Prism, Deck	Water Transportation Accessories	438
Prism, Objective	Astronomical T&E	285
Prison	Institutional Structures	37
Pritchel	Metalworking T&E	215
Privateer	Watercraft	447
privy (*use:* Outhouse)	Outbuildings	38
Prize	Achievement Symbols	491
Probang	Medical Instruments	332
Probate	Government Records	470
Probe	Medical Instruments	328
Probe, Bullet	Medical Instruments	332
Probe, Dental	Dental Instruments	323
Probe, Periodontal	Dental Instruments	323
Probe, Uterine	Medical Instruments	330
Proceedings	Administrative Records	467
Processor, Analog Data	Data Processing Devices	361
Processor, Card	Peripherals	365
Processor, Digital Data	Data Processing Devices	361
Processor, Food	Food Preparation Equipment	156
processor, hybrid (*use:* Computer, Hybrid)	Data Processing Devices	361
Proclamation	Declaratory Documents	468
Proctoscope	Medical Instruments	330
Prod, Cattle	Animal Care Equipment	137
Prod, Stock	Animal Care Equipment	137
Product, Feminine Hygiene	Hygiene Objects	120
Product, Oral Care	Hygiene Objects	120
Product, Shaving	Hair Care Objects	118
Profile, Bricklaying	Masonry & Stoneworking T&E	205
Program	Other Documents	485
program, computer (*use:* Software)	Data Processing Accessories	360
Program, Concert	Other Documents	485
Program, Dance	Other Documents	485
Program, Theater	Other Documents	485
Projection	Graphic Documents	474
Projector	Visual Communication Devices	400
Projector, Filmstrip	Visual Communication Devices	400
Projector, Lantern Slide	Visual Communication Devices	400
Projector, Light	Lighting Devices	70
Projector, Motion Picture	Visual Communication Devices	401
Projector, Opaque	Visual Communication Devices	401
Projector, Overhead	Visual Communication Devices	401
Projector, Planetarium	Astronomical T&E	285
Projector, Postcard	Visual Communication Devices	401
Projector, Slide	Visual Communication Devices	401
Proof, Printing	Other Documents	482
Prop	Public Entertainment Devices	507
Prop, Aerialist's	Public Entertainment Devices	507
Prop, Juggler's	Public Entertainment Devices	508
Prop, Magician's	Public Entertainment Devices	508
prop, mouth (*use:* Block, Bite)	Dental Instruments	322
Prop, Sawyer's	Woodworking T&E	258
Prop, Theatrical	Public Entertainment Devices	508
Propeller, Adjustable-Pitch	Aerospace Transportation Accessories	410
Propeller, Aircraft	Aerospace Transportation Accessories	410
Propeller, Fixed-Pitch	Aerospace Transportation Accessories	410
Propeller, Watercraft	Water Transportation Accessories	438
property (*use:* Prop)	Public Entertainment Devices	507
Prophylactic	Hygiene Objects	121
Prospectus	Administrative Records	467
Prosthesis	Personal Assistive Objects	108
Prosthesis, Dental	Personal Assistive Objects	109
Protector, Body	Sports Equipment	519
protector, check (*use:* Embosser, Check)	Writing Devices	406
Protector, Chest	Sports Equipment	519

Term	Category	Page
protector, paper (*use:* Protector, Sheet)	Writing Accessories	404
Protector, Pocket	Clothing Accessories	86
Protector, Sheet	Writing Accessories	404
Protector, Sleeve	Protective Wear	102
Protector, Throat	Armament Accessories	271
Protector, Tree Trunk	Groundskeeping Equipment	309
Protractor	Drafting T&E	367
Protractor, Hoof	Farrier Equipment	140
Prover, Linen	Textile Manufacturing Equipment	244
pruner, hand (*use:* Shears, Pruning)	Groundskeeping Equipment	310
Pruner, Tree	Groundskeeping Equipment	310
prybar (*use:* Crowbar)	Mechanical Devices	316
Psaltery	Musical Instruments	374
Pschent	Status Symbols	499
Pseudophone	Acoustical T&E	262
Pseudoscope	Optical T&E	344
Pseudoscope, Lenticular	Medical Instruments	329
Psychrometer	Meteorological T&E	339
Pucella	Glass, Plastics & Clayworking T&E	194
Puck, Hockey	Sports Equipment	516
Pueblo	Dwellings	33
Puff, Powder	Beauty Supplies	116
Pulaski	Protective Devices	345
pull, door (*use:* Handle, Door)	Finish Hardware	11
Pull, Shade	Window & Door Coverings	78
Puller, Bullet	Armament Accessories	271
Puller, Calf	Veterinary Equipment	142
Puller, Crosstie	Rail Transportation Accessories	432
Puller, Fastener	Woodworking T&E	256
Puller, Fuse	Electrical Maintenance & Repair Equipment	299
Puller, Gear	Mechanical Devices	316
Puller, Nail	Woodworking T&E	256
Puller, Pole	Construction T&E	296
Puller, Rail Spike	Rail Transportation Accessories	432
puller, shoe (*use:* Pincers, Farrier's)	Farrier Equipment	139
Puller, Slate	Masonry & Stoneworking T&E	205
Puller, Stake	Construction T&E	296
Puller, Staple	Woodworking T&E	256
Puller, Stump	Cultivation Equipment	125
Puller, Tack	Woodworking T&E	256
Puller, Wire	Metalworking T&E	215
Pulley	Mechanical Devices	316
Pulley, Crown	Mechanical Devices	316
Pulley, Exercise	Recreational Devices	509
Pulley, Heddle	Textile Manufacturing Equipment	243
Pullover	Main Garments	97
Pulper	Papermaking T&E	232
Pulper, Root	Cultivation Equipment	125
Pulpit	Religious Objects	464
pulverizer, surface (*use:* Roller, Land)	Cultivation Equipment	125
pump (*use:* Shoe, Pump)	Footwear	90
Pump	Mechanical Devices	316
Pump, Backpack	Protective Devices	345
Pump, Barrel	Mechanical Devices	316
Pump, Bilge	Water Transportation Accessories	441
Pump, Breast	Personal Assistive Objects	109
Pump, Centrifugal	Mechanical Devices	316
Pump, Concrete	Masonry & Stoneworking T&E	205
Pump, Diver's	Mechanical Devices	316
Pump, Double-Action	Mechanical Devices	316
Pump, Embalming	Medical Instruments	329
Pump, Fuel	Power Transmission Components	305
Pump, Gasoline	Transportation Structures	39
Pump, Heat	Environmental Control Elements	9
Pump, Hydrostatic Test	Mechanical Devices	316
pump, Indian (*use:* Pump, Backpack)	Protective Devices	345
Pump, Infusion	Medical Instruments	334
Pump, Milk	Food Processing Equipment	166
Pump, Perfusion	Medical Instruments	334
Pump, Piston	Mechanical Devices	316
Pump, Plumbing	Plumbing & Drainage Elements	13
Pump, Plunger	Mechanical Devices	316
Pump, Single-Action	Mechanical Devices	316
Pump, Submersible	Mechanical Devices	316
Pump, Sump	Plumbing & Drainage Elements	13
Pump, Tire	Land Transportation Accessories	419
Pump, Water	Plumbing & Drainage Elements	13
Pumper, Hand-Drawn Fire	Human-Powered Vehicles	427
Pumper, Hand-Drawn Hand	Human-Powered Vehicles	427
Pumper, Hand-Drawn Steam	Human-Powered Vehicles	427
Pumper, Horse-Drawn Hand	Animal-Powered Vehicles	425
Pumper, Horse-Drawn Steam	Animal-Powered Vehicles	425
Pumphouse	Industrial Structures	35
Pumpjack	Mechanical Devices	316
Punch	Multiple Use T&E for Materials	228
Punch, Arch	Leather, Horn & Shellworking T&E	200
Punch, Backing-Out	Metalworking T&E	215

Punch, Belt	Leather, Horn & Shellworking T&E	200
Punch, Biopsy	Medical Instruments	328
punch, bob (*use:* Countersink)	Metalworking T&E	210
Punch, Button Hole	Leather, Horn & Shellworking T&E	200
punch, card (*use:* Punch, Keyboard)	Data Processing Devices	362
Punch, Carver's	Woodworking T&E	256
Punch, Center	Metalworking T&E	215
Punch, Cooper's	Woodworking T&E	256
Punch, Dapping	Metalworking T&E	215
Punch, Data	Data Processing Devices	362
Punch, Drift	Metalworking T&E	215
Punch, Drive	Leather, Horn & Shellworking T&E	200
punch, ear (*use:* Notcher, Ear)	Animal Care Equipment	136
Punch, Ear Tag	Animal Care Equipment	136
Punch, Egg	Food Preparation Equipment	156
Punch, Embroidery	Needleworking Equipment	238
Punch, Eyelet	Leather, Horn & Shellworking T&E	200
Punch, Fabric	Needleworking Equipment	238
Punch, Fore	Metalworking T&E	215
Punch, Gang	Data Processing Devices	362
Punch, Grommet	Needleworking Equipment	238
Punch, Hand	Leather, Horn & Shellworking T&E	200
Punch, Handrail	Woodworking T&E	256
Punch, Hole	Leather, Horn & Shellworking T&E	200
Punch, Hollow	Metalworking T&E	215
Punch, Keyboard	Data Processing Devices	362
Punch, Leather	Leather, Horn & Shellworking T&E	200
Punch, Line	Leather, Horn & Shellworking T&E	200
Punch, Marking	Woodworking T&E	256
Punch, Metal	Metalworking T&E	215
Punch, Nail	Woodworking T&E	256
Punch, Oblong	Leather, Horn & Shellworking T&E	200
Punch, Oval	Metalworking T&E	215
Punch, Paper	Writing Accessories	404
Punch, Piercing	Leather, Horn & Shellworking T&E	200
punch, pin (*use:* Punch, Backing-out)	Metalworking T&E	215
Punch, Poultry	Animal Care Equipment	136
Punch, Prick	Metalworking T&E	215
Punch, Revolving	Leather, Horn & Shellworking T&E	200
punch, rivet (*use:* Punch, Starting)	Woodworking T&E	256
Punch, Round	Metalworking T&E	215
Punch, Rubber Dam	Dental Instruments	323
Punch, Saddler's	Leather, Horn & Shellworking T&E	200
Punch, Sailmaker's	Needleworking Equipment	238
Punch, Scalloping	Leather, Horn & Shellworking T&E	200
Punch, Shingle	Woodworking T&E	256
Punch, Slater's	Masonry & Stoneworking T&E	205
Punch, Spot	Data Processing Devices	362
Punch, Square	Metalworking T&E	215
Punch, Starting	Woodworking T&E	256
Punch, Strap End	Leather, Horn & Shellworking T&E	200
Punch, Summary	Data Processing Devices	362
Punch, Ticket	Merchandising T&E	337
Punch, Veneer	Woodworking T&E	256
Punch, Vent	Armament Accessories	271
Punch, Wood	Woodworking T&E	256
Punchboard	Game Equipment	503
punchclock (*use:* Clock, Time Recording)	Timekeeping T&E	355
puncheon (*use:* Cask)	Containers	414
Puncheon	Supporting Elements	17
puncheon (*use:* Flooring, Puncheon)	Surface Elements	18
Pung	Animal-Powered Vehicles	424
Punk	Firemaking Equipment	74
Punkah	Heating & Cooling Equipment	75
Punt	Watercraft	443
punty (*use:* Pontil)	Glass, Plastics & Clayworking T&E	194
Pupilometer	Medical Instruments	329
Puppet	Public Entertainment Devices	508
Puppet, Finger	Public Entertainment Devices	508
Puppet, Hand	Public Entertainment Devices	508
Puppet, Rod	Public Entertainment Devices	508
Puppet, Shadow	Public Entertainment Devices	508
Purificator	Religious Objects	463
Purifier, Air	Other Household Accessories	67
Purifier, Middlings	Food Processing Equipment	169
Purse	Personal Carrying & Storage Gear	111
Purse, Change	Personal Carrying & Storage Gear	111
Purse, Cosmetic	Beauty Supplies	116
purse, hairpin (*use:* Case, Hairpin)	Personal Carrying & Storage Gear	112
Pushcart	Human-Powered Vehicles	426

Term	Category	Page
Pusher, Food	Eating & Drinking Utensils	179
Pushers, Pedal	Main Garments	97
Pushpin	Writing Accessories	404
Pushplate	Finish Hardware	10
Puttee	Footwear	90
Putter	Sports Equipment	515
Putty, Play	Toys	524
Puzzle	Toys	522
puzzle, Chinese (*use:* Block, Parquetry)	Toys	520
Puzzle, Crossword	Game Equipment	506
Puzzle, Dexterity	Toys	522
Puzzle, Jigsaw	Toys	522
Puzzle, Mental	Toys	522
Puzzle, Number	Toys	522
Puzzle, Slide	Toys	522
Puzzle, Word	Toys	522
Pycnometer	Chemical Testing Devices	290
pyjamas (*use:* Pajamas)	Dressingwear & Nightwear	88
Pyramid, Dessert	Serving Vessels	187
Pyrheliometer	Astronomical T&E	285
Pyrometer	Thermal T&E	354
Pyx	Religious Objects	462
Quad	Typesetting Equipment	388
Quadrant	Navigational Equipment	350
Quadrant, Astronomical	Astronomical T&E	285
Quadrant, Gunner's	Armament Accessories	271
Quadricycle	Human-Powered Vehicles	426
quadruple (*use:* Truck, Fire)	Motor Vehicles	429
Quant	Water Transportation Accessories	441
Quarnet, Hornworker's	Leather, Horn & Shellworking T&E	201
quarrel (*use:* Bolt, Crossbow)	Edged Weapons	277
Quarry	Industrial Structures	36
Quarter	Exchange Media	488
Quarterboard	Water Transportation Accessories	440
Quarters, Slave	Dwellings	33
Quarterstaff	Percussive Weapons	283
Quern	Food Preparation Equipment	160
Questionnaire	Other Documents	485
Quickdraw	Sports Equipment	514
Quid	Unclassifiable Objects	527
Quiller	Textile Manufacturing Equipment	245
Quillwork	Art	454
Quilt	Art	453
Quilt, Bed	Bedding	43
Quilt, Crib	Bedding	43
Quilt, Memory	Memorabilia	478
Quilt, Mourning	Funerary Objects	457
Quirt	Land Transportation Accessories	421
Quiver	Armament Accessories	268
quoin (*use:* Stone, Quoin)	Construction Materials	4
Quoin	Typesetting Equipment	388
Quoin, Artillery	Armament Accessories	271
Quoit	Game Equipment	505
Rab	Masonry & Stoneworking T&E	206
Rabble	Metalworking T&E	215
race (*use:* Millrace)	Hydraulic Structures	34
Raceboat	Watercraft	444
raceway, electric (*use:* Conduit, Electric)	Electrical System Components	300
Rack	Storage & Display Accessories	64
Rack, Arms	Armament Accessories	268
Rack, Bicycle	Transportation Structures	39
Rack, Billiard Ball	Game Equipment	501
Rack, Blowpipe	Glass, Plastics & Clayworking T&E	194
Rack, Bomb	Armament Accessories	268
Rack, Book	Storage & Display Accessories	64
Rack, Boot	Storage & Display Accessories	64
Rack, Bottle Serving	Food Service Accessories	182
Rack, Bottle Storage	Food Storage Equipment	171
Rack, Canning	Food Processing Equipment	165
Rack, Cigar Bundling	Other T&E for Materials	260
rack, clothing (*use:* Rack, Garment)	Merchandising T&E	337
Rack, Cooling	Food Preparation Equipment	156
Rack, Cue	Game Equipment	502
rack, dish (*use:* Drainer, Dish)	Dishwashing Equipment	308
Rack, Dish	Dishwashing Equipment	308
Rack, Display	Merchandising T&E	337
Rack, Drying	Laundry Equipment	314
Rack, Fire Bucket	Protective Devices	345
Rack, Fire Hose	Protective Devices	345
Rack, Firewood	Storage & Display Accessories	64
Rack, Food Storage	Food Storage Equipment	171
Rack, Garment	Merchandising T&E	337
Rack, Gun	Storage & Display Accessories	64
rack, hall (*use:* Rack, Hat)	Storage & Display Accessories	64
Rack, Harness	Land Transportation Accessories	418
Rack, Hat	Storage & Display Accessories	64
Rack, Herb Drying	Food Preparation Equipment	155
Rack, Horseshoeing	Farrier Equipment	139
Rack, Key	Storage & Display Accessories	64

Rack, Kitchenware | Food Preparation Accessories | 152
Rack, Knife | Food Preparation Accessories | 152
Rack, Laboratory | Labware | 294
rack, letter (*use:* Holder, Letter) | Writing Accessories | 403
Rack, Life Ring | Water Transportation Accessories | 438
Rack, Luggage | Land Transportation Accessories | 416
Rack, Magazine | Storage & Display Accessories | 64
Rack, Meat | Food Preparation Equipment | 156
Rack, Media | Storage & Display Accessories | 64
Rack, Music | Storage & Display Accessories | 64
Rack, Needlework | Needleworking Equipment | 235
Rack, Newspaper | Storage & Display Accessories | 64
rack, pen (*use:* Holder, Pen) | Writing Accessories | 403
Rack, Pie | Food Service Accessories | 182
Rack, Pipe | Containers for Smoking & Tobacco | 59
Rack, Plant | Storage & Display Accessories | 65
Rack, Plate | Storage & Display Accessories | 65
Rack, Poker Chip | Game Equipment | 503
Rack, Pot | Food Preparation Accessories | 152
Rack, Record | Storage & Display Accessories | 64
Rack, Recycling | Housekeeping Equipment | 312
Rack, Saddle | Land Transportation Accessories | 418
Rack, Safety Pin | Needleworking Equipment | 235
Rack, Saucepan | Food Preparation Accessories | 152
Rack, Signal Flag | Water Transportation Accessories | 438
Rack, Spice | Food Storage Equipment | 172
Rack, Spit | Food Preparation Accessories | 152
Rack, Spool | Needleworking Equipment | 235
Rack, Spoon | Storage & Display Accessories | 65
rack, stamp (*use:* Holder, Marking Stamp) | Writing Accessories | 403
Rack, Tack | Land Transportation Accessories | 418
Rack, Test Tube | Labware | 294
Rack, Tie | Storage & Display Accessories | 65
Rack, Toast | Serving Vessels | 187
Rack, Tobacco | Harvesting Equipment | 130
Rack, Tool | Storage & Display Accessories | 65
Rack, Torture | Regulative Devices | 347
Rack, Towel | Storage & Display Accessories | 65
Rack, Tray | Food Service Accessories | 182
rack, umbrella (*use:* Stand, Umbrella) | Support Furniture | 55
Rack, Utensil | Food Preparation Accessories | 152
Rack, Weight | Recreational Devices | 509
Rack, Wine | Food Storage Equipment | 171
Racket | Musical Instruments | 375
Racket, Badminton | Sports Equipment | 512
Racket, Racquetball | Sports Equipment | 517
Racket, Squash | Sports Equipment | 518
Racket, Tennis | Sports Equipment | 518
Radiator | Environmental Control Elements | 9
Radiator, Automotive | Land Transportation Accessories | 417
Radio | Telecommunication Devices | 396
Radio, Car | Telecommunication Devices | 396
Radio, CB | Telecommunication Devices | 397
Radio, Console | Telecommunication Devices | 396
Radio, Crystal | Telecommunication Devices | 396
Radio, Portable | Telecommunication Devices | 396
Radio, Table | Telecommunication Devices | 396
Radio, Transistor | Telecommunication Devices | 396
Radiogram | Graphic Documents | 473
Radiometer | Electrical & Magnetic Measurement Devices | 297
Radiophone | Telecommunication Devices | 397
Radiosonde | Meteorological T&E | 340
Raft | Watercraft | 444
Raft, Life | Watercraft | 446
Raft, Lumber | Watercraft | 446
Raft, Pool | Recreational Devices | 511
Rafter | Roof Elements | 14
Rafter, Show | Roof Elements | 14
Rag, Pine Tar | Sports Equipment | 513
Rail | Rail Transportation Accessories | 432
Rail, Bar | Finish Hardware | 11
Rail, Chair | Surface Elements | 18
Rail, Fife | Water Transportation Accessories | 438
Rail, Peg | Surface Elements | 18
Rail, Picture | Surface Elements | 18
rail, pin (*use:* Pinrail) | Water Transportation Accessories | 438
Rail, Plate | Surface Elements | 18
Rail, Safety | Other Household Accessories | 67
Rail, Toilet Safety | Other Household Accessories | 67

Rail, Wall	Surface Elements	18
Rail, Watercraft	Water Transportation Accessories	438
Railgrinder	Rail Vehicles	434
railway, centrifugal (*use:* Coaster, Roller)	Recreational Devices	511
Raincoat	Outerwear	101
Rake	Harvesting Equipment	130
rake, ash (*use:* Scraper, Ash)	Heating Equipment Accessories	77
Rake, Blacksmith's	Metalworking T&E	215
Rake, Blueberry	Harvesting Equipment	130
rake, buck (*use:* Rake, Sweep)	Harvesting Equipment	130
rake, bull (*use:* Rake, Clam)	Fishing Equipment	146
rake, bull (*use:* Rake, Sweep)	Harvesting Equipment	130
Rake, Carpet	Housekeeping Equipment	312
Rake, Clam	Fishing Equipment	146
Rake, Clover	Harvesting Equipment	130
Rake, Common Hay	Harvesting Equipment	130
Rake, Cranberry	Harvesting Equipment	130
Rake, Curd	Food Processing Equipment	166
Rake, Dump	Harvesting Equipment	130
Rake, Fireplace	Heating Equipment Accessories	76
Rake, Fishing	Fishing Equipment	146
rake, flip-flop (*use:* Rake, Revolving Hay)	Harvesting Equipment	130
rake, floral (*use:* Rake, Garden)	Cultivation Equipment	125
rake, furnace (*use:* Scraper, Ash)	Heating Equipment Accessories	77
Rake, Garden	Cultivation Equipment	125
Rake, Grading	Construction T&E	296
rake, grain (*use:* Rake, Hay)	Harvesting Equipment	130
Rake, Grain Binder's	Harvesting Equipment	130
Rake, Hand Hay	Harvesting Equipment	130
Rake, Hay	Harvesting Equipment	130
rake, hay-bunching (*use:* Rake, Sweep)	Harvesting Equipment	130
Rake, Herring	Fishing Equipment	146
Rake, Hot Shot	Armament Accessories	271
Rake, Kiln	Glass, Plastics & Clayworking T&E	194
Rake, Lawn	Groundskeeping Equipment	309
rake, man (*use:* Rake, Hand Hay)	Harvesting Equipment	130
Rake, Onion	Harvesting Equipment	130
Rake, Pomace	Food Processing Equipment	165
Rake, Potato	Food Preparation Equipment	163
Rake, Reaper Platform	Harvesting Equipment	130
rake, reel-type (*use:* Rake, Side Delivery)	Harvesting Equipment	130
Rake, Revolving Hay	Harvesting Equipment	130
Rake, Shellfish	Fishing Equipment	146
Rake, Side Delivery	Harvesting Equipment	130
rake, spring-tooth (*use:* Rake, Dump)	Harvesting Equipment	130
rake, stove (*use:* Scraper, Ash)	Heating Equipment Accessories	77
rake, sulky (*use:* Rake, Dump)	Harvesting Equipment	130
Rake, Sweep	Harvesting Equipment	130
Raker	Masonry & Stoneworking T&E	205
Ram	Watercraft	447
Ram, Battering	Percussive Weapons	283
Ram, Hydraulic	Mechanical Devices	316
Ramekin	Cooking Vessels	150
rammer (*use:* Ramrod)	Armament Accessories	271
Rammer, Paver's	Construction T&E	295
Rammer, Sand	Metalworking T&E	215
Ramp	Stair Elements	15
Ramp, Boat Launching	Transportation Structures	39
Ramp, Skateboard	Sports Equipment	517
Ramp, Wheelchair	Stair Elements	15
Rampart	Defense Structures	31
Ramrod	Armament Accessories	271
range (*use:* Cookstove)	Food Preparation Equipment	154
Rangefinder	Surveying Equipment	353
Rangefinder, Laser	Surveying Equipment	353
Rangefinder, Radio	Surveying Equipment	353
Rapier	Edged Weapons	278
Rasp	Woodworking T&E	250
Rasp, Bread	Food Preparation Equipment	158
Rasp, Cabinet	Woodworking T&E	250
Rasp, Hoof	Farrier Equipment	140
Rasp, Riffler	Woodworking T&E	250
Rasp, Shoemaker's	Leather, Horn & Shellworking T&E	200
Rasp, Stone	Masonry & Stoneworking T&E	205
rasp, tooth (*use:* Float, Dental)	Veterinary Equipment	142
Rat, Hair	Hair Adornments	83
Ratchet	Mechanical Devices	316
ratchet (*use:* Wheel, Scraped)	Musical Instruments	373
Ratchet, Thread	Metalworking T&E	215
Ratemeter	Nuclear Physics T&E	341
Rattle	Sound Communication Devices	391
Rattle, Baby	Toys	522
Rattle, Ceremonial	Religious Objects	464
Rattle, Combination	Toys	522
rattle, gas (*use:* Rattle)	Sound Communication Devices	391
Rattle, Musical	Musical Instruments	372

Rattle, Ratchet	Sound Communication Devices	391
Rattrap	Other Household Accessories	66
Rawinsonde	Meteorological T&E	340
Razor	Hair Care Objects	119
Razor, Disposable	Hair Care Objects	119
Razor, Electric	Hair Care Objects	119
Razor, Safety	Hair Care Objects	119
Razor, Straight	Hair Care Objects	119
Reactor, Nuclear	Power Producing Equipment	304
Reader	Peripherals	364
Reader, Card	Peripherals	364
Reader, Character	Peripherals	364
Reader, Credit Card	Merchandising T&E	337
Reader, Electronic	Visual Communication Devices	401
Reader, Magnetic Tape	Peripherals	364
Reader, Microfiche	Visual Communication Devices	401
Reader, Microfilm	Visual Communication Devices	401
Reader, Microform	Visual Communication Devices	401
Reader, Punched Tape	Peripherals	364
Reader, Security Card	Protective Devices	346
Reader, Tape	Data Processing Devices	362
reader, wireless (*use:* Computer, Handheld)	Data Processing Devices	362
Real	Exchange Media	488
Reamer	Glass, Plastics & Clayworking T&E	194
Reamer, Broach	Woodworking T&E	256
Reamer, Chamber	Armament Accessories	271
Reamer, Endodontic	Dental Instruments	323
Reamer, Fuze Plug	Armament Accessories	271
Reamer, Hooked	Woodworking T&E	256
Reamer, Hornworker's	Leather, Horn & Shellworking T&E	201
Reamer, Juice	Food Preparation Equipment	160
Reamer, Metalworking	Metalworking T&E	215
Reamer, Woodworking	Woodworking T&E	256
Reaper	Harvesting Equipment	129
Reaper, Hand-Rake	Harvesting Equipment	129
Reaper, Self-Rake	Harvesting Equipment	129
rebar (*use:* Bar, Reinforcing)	Supporting Elements	16
Rebec	Musical Instruments	374
Rebus	Other Documents	485
Recamier	Sleeping & Reclining Furniture	50
Receipt	Financial Records	469
Receiver, Beacon	Navigational Equipment	350
Receiver, Card	Storage & Display Accessories	65
Receiver, Distilling	Chemical Testing Devices	289
Receiver, Global Positioning	Navigational Equipment	350
receiver, GPS (*use:* Receiver, Global Positioning)	Navigational Equipment	350
Receiver, Hair	Hair Care Objects	119
Receiver, Hairpin	Personal Carrying & Storage Gear	112
Receiver, Loran	Navigational Equipment	350
Receiver, Radar	Navigational Equipment	350
receiver, radio (*use:* Radio)	Telecommunication Devices	396
Receiver, Sound	Acoustical T&E	262
receiver, television (*use:* Television)	Telecommunication Devices	397
Receiver, Tracking	Navigational Equipment	350
receptacle, electric (*use:* Outlet, Electrical)	Electrical System Components	301
Receptacle, Human Waste	Hygiene Objects	121
Recipe	Instructional Documents	475
Record, 33 1/3 RPM	Sound Communication Media	393
Record, 45 RPM	Sound Communication Media	393
Record, 78 RPM	Sound Communication Media	393
Record, Birth	Government Records	470
Record, Bookkeeping	Financial Records	469
Record, Burial	Government Records	470
Record, Census	Government Records	470
Record, Customs	Government Records	470
Record, Death	Government Records	470
Record, Divorce	Government Records	471
Record, Executive	Government Records	470
Record, Immigration	Government Records	470
Record, Insurance	Financial Records	469
Record, Judicial	Government Records	470
Record, Legislative	Government Records	470
record, long-playing (*use:* Record, 33 1/3 RPM)	Sound Communication Media	393
Record, Marriage	Government Records	471
Record, Medical	Other Documents	485
Record, Military	Government Records	470
record, naturalization (*use:* Certificate, Citizenship)	Government Records	470
Record, Payroll	Financial Records	469
Record, Personnel	Administrative Records	467
Record, Phonograph	Sound Communication Media	393
Record, Sales	Financial Records	469
Record, Service	Government Records	470
Record, Shipping	Administrative Records	467
Record, Student	Other Documents	485
Record, Vital	Government Records	470

Recorder — Musical Instruments 375
Recorder, Audio — Sound Communication Devices 392
Recorder, Audio Disk — Sound Communication Devices 392
Recorder, Audio Tape — Sound Communication Devices 392
Recorder, Audio Wire — Sound Communication Devices 392
Recorder, Audiocassette — Sound Communication Devices 392
recorder, dictation (*use:* Machine, Dictating) — Sound Communication Devices 392
Recorder, Film — Peripherals 365
Recorder, Flight — Aerospace Transportation Accessories 410
Recorder, Reel-to-Reel Tape — Sound Communication Devices 392
Recorder, Sceptre — Navigational Equipment 350
Recorder, Sound — Acoustical T&E 262
Recorder, Sunshine — Meteorological T&E 340
Recorder, Train Event — Rail Transportation Accessories 432
recorder, videocassette (*use:* Recorder, Videotape) — Visual Communication Devices 401
Recorder, Videotape — Visual Communication Devices 401
Recording — Other Documents 485
Recording, Audio — Other Documents 485
Recording, Video — Other Documents 485
rectifier (*use:* Converter, AC-DC) — Electrical System Components 300
Rectory — Dwellings 32
Redingote — Outerwear 101
Redoubt — Defense Structures 31
Reducer, Bust — Underwear 103
reducer, tubing (*use:* Adapter, Tubing) — Labware 292
Reed, Textile — Textile Manufacturing Equipment 243
Reedpipe — Musical Instruments 375
Reel — Mechanical Devices 316
Reel, Bait Casting — Fishing Equipment 147
Reel, Candle Dipping — Glass, Plastics & Clayworking T&E 194
Reel, Chalk — Woodworking T&E 248
Reel, Clock — Textile Manufacturing Equipment 245
Reel, Clothesline — Laundry Equipment 314
Reel, Film — Visual Communication Accessories 399
Reel, Fire Hose — Protective Devices 345
Reel, Fishing — Fishing Equipment 147
Reel, Fly — Fishing Equipment 147
Reel, Garden Hose — Groundskeeping Equipment 309
Reel, Horse-Drawn Hose — Animal-Powered Vehicles 425
Reel, Kite — Aerospace Transportation Accessories 410
Reel, Log — Navigational Equipment 350
Reel, Spin Cast — Fishing Equipment 147
Reel, Spinning — Fishing Equipment 147
Reel, Tape — Sound Communication Accessories 390
Reel, Warping — Textile Manufacturing Equipment 245
Reel, Yarn — Textile Manufacturing Equipment 245
reference (*use:* Letter, Recommendation) — Other Documents 482
Refinery, Sugar — Industrial Structures 35
Reflector — Other Lighting Accessories 73
Reflector, Solar — Other Energy Production T&E 306
Reflector, Studio — Photographic Accessories 379
Reflector, Vehicle — Land Transportation Accessories 417
Reformatory — Institutional Structures 37
Refractometer — Chemical Testing Devices 291
Refrigerator — Food Storage Equipment 172
refrigerator, dairy (*use:* Cooler, Dairy) — Food Processing Equipment 166
Refrigerator, Portable — Food Storage Equipment 172
Refrigerator, Window — Food Storage Equipment 172
Regalia — Status Symbols 498
Register — Other Documents 483
Register, Birth — Government Records 470
Register, Cash — Merchandising T&E 338
Register, Death — Government Records 471
Register, Family — Other Documents 483
register, guest (*use:* Guestbook) — Other Documents 483
Register, Marriage — Government Records 471
register, taffrail log (*use:* Log, Taffrail) — Water Transportation Accessories 441
Registration — Other Documents 484
Regulation — Government Records 470
Regulator, Breathing — Personal Assistive Objects 107
Regulator, Gas — Mechanical Devices 316
Regulator, Scuba — Recreational Devices 511
Regulator, Voltage — Electrical System Components 301
Rein — Land Transportation Accessories 420
Rein, Check — Land Transportation Accessories 420
Rein, Driving — Land Transportation Accessories 420
Rejon — Sports Equipment 514
Relay — Electrical System Components 301
Release, Bomb — Armament Accessories 271
Release, Cable — Camera Equipment 377

Release, News	Declaratory Documents	468
release, press (*use:* Release, News)	Declaratory Documents	468
Relic, Historic	Memorabilia	478
Relic, Religious	Religious Objects	464
Relief	Art	454
Relief, High	Art	454
Reliquary	Religious Objects	462
Reminiscence	Literary Works	477
Remover, Blade	Medical Instruments	332
Remover, Burr	Textile Manufacturing Equipment	243
Remover, Case	Armament Accessories	271
Remover, Hair	Hair Care Objects	119
Remover, Staple	Writing Accessories	404
Replica	Other Documents	485
Report	Administrative Records	467
Report, Administrative	Administrative Records	467
Report, Annual	Administrative Records	467
report, financial (*use:* Statement, Financial)	Financial Records	469
Report, Quarterly	Administrative Records	467
Report, Technical	Administrative Records	467
Repositor, Uterine	Medical Instruments	330
Reprint	Other Documents	481
Reproducer, Card	Data Processing Devices	362
Reproducer, Data	Data Processing Devices	362
Reproducer, Sound	Acoustical T&E	262
Reproducer, Tape	Data Processing Devices	362
Reproduction	Other Documents	485
Request	Other Documents	485
Requisition	Financial Records	469
Resectoscope	Medical Instruments	334
Reservoir	Hydraulic Structures	34
Resistor	Electrical System Components	301
Resolution	Administrative Records	467
Resonator	Acoustical T&E	262
Respirator	Medical Instruments	333
Respirometer	Biological T&E	287
Rest, Chin	Musical Accessories	369
Rest, Firearm	Armament Accessories	270
Rest, Iron	Laundry Equipment	314
Rest, Knife	Food Service Accessories	182
Rest, Machine	Armament Accessories	270
Rest, Musical Instrument	Musical Accessories	369
Rest, Musket	Armament Accessories	270
rest, pen (*use:* Holder, Pen)	Writing Accessories	403
rest, pot (*use:* Trivet)	Food Preparation Accessories	152
Rest, Shoulder	Musical Accessories	369
Rest, Spoon	Food Preparation Accessories	152
Rest, Tool	Multiple Use T&E for Materials	226
Restaurant	Commercial Structures	27
Restaurant, Drive-In	Commercial Structures	27
Restraint	Regulative Devices	347
Restraint, Animal	Animal Care Equipment	135
Restraint, Bird	Animal Care Equipment	135
Resume	Administrative Records	467
Resuscitator	Medical Instruments	333
Retable	Religious Objects	464
Retainer, Matrix	Dental Instruments	323
Retainer, Orthodontic	Dental Instruments	322
Reticule	Personal Carrying & Storage Gear	111
Retinoscope	Medical Instruments	329
Retort	Chemical Testing Devices	289
Retort, Amalgam	Metalworking T&E	215
Retort, Canning	Food Processing Equipment	165
Retractor	Medical Instruments	332
Return, Bowling Ball	Sports Equipment	513
Return, Tax	Financial Records	469
Reverberator	Acoustical T&E	262
Review	Literary Works	477
Revolver	Firearms	281
Revolver, Cartridge	Firearms	281
Revolver, Percussion	Firearms	281
Reward of Merit	Achievement Symbols	491
Rewinder	Papermaking T&E	233
Rheometer	Mechanical Measurement Equipment	318
Rheoscope	Electrical & Magnetic Measurement Devices	297
Rheostat	Electrical System Components	301
Rheotome	Electrical System Components	301
Rhinoscope	Medical Instruments	330
Rhumboscope	Drafting T&E	367
rhythmometer (*use:* Metronome)	Musical Accessories	369
rhyton (*use:* Horn, Drinking)	Drinking Vessels	174
Rib, Potter's	Glass, Plastics & Clayworking T&E	195
Rib, Vault	Supporting Elements	17
Rib, Watercraft	Water Transportation Accessories	439
Ribbon, Adding Machine	Writing Accessories	405
Ribbon, Campaign	Belief Symbols	493
Ribbon, Cigar	Advertising Media	450
Ribbon, Commemorative	Memorabilia	478
Ribbon, Fraternal	Status Symbols	497
Ribbon, Gift Wrap	Party Accessories	460
Ribbon, Hair	Hair Adornments	83
Ribbon, Hat	Clothing Accessories	86
Ribbon, Insignia	Status Symbols	497
Ribbon, Membership	Status Symbols	497
Ribbon, Political	Belief Symbols	493
Ribbon, Prize	Achievement Symbols	491

Term	Category	Page
Ribbon, Promotional	Advertising Media	450
ribbon, service (*use:* Bar, Ribbon)	Achievement Symbols	491
Ribbon, Textile	Needleworking Equipment	237
Ribbon, Typewriter	Writing Accessories	405
Ribbonwork	Art	454
Ricer	Food Preparation Equipment	156
Rickshaw	Human-Powered Vehicles	427
Riddle	Food Preparation Equipment	154
Riddle, Foundry	Metalworking T&E	215
Riddle, Grain	Harvesting Equipment	131
riddle, winnowing (*use:* Riddle, Grain)	Harvesting Equipment	131
Ride, Amusement	Recreational Devices	511
Rider, Spring	Recreational Devices	510
Riffle	Mining & Mineral Harvesting T&E	224
riffler (*use:* File, Riffler)	Woodworking T&E	250
riffler (*use:* Rasp, Riffler)	Woodworking T&E	250
Rifle	Firearms	281
Rifle, Assault	Firearms	281
Rifle, Cartridge	Firearms	281
Rifle, Field	Artillery	274
Rifle, Flintlock	Firearms	281
Rifle, Half Stock	Firearms	281
Rifle, Hunting	Firearms	281
Rifle, Jaeger	Firearms	281
rifle, Kentucky (*use:* Rifle, Long)	Firearms	281
Rifle, Long	Firearms	281
Rifle, Matchlock	Firearms	281
Rifle, Military	Firearms	281
Rifle, Over and Under	Firearms	281
rifle, Pennsylvania (*use:* Rifle, Long)	Firearms	281
Rifle, Percussion	Firearms	282
Rifle, Plains	Firearms	282
Rifle, Recoilless	Artillery	274
Rifle, Repeating	Firearms	282
Rifle, Schuetzen	Firearms	282
rifle, sea-coast (*use:* Gun, Sea-Coast)	Artillery	274
Rifle, Spotting	Artillery	274
Rifle, Target	Firearms	282
Rifle, Training	Firearms	282
Rifle, Wheelock	Firearms	282
Rig, Fishing	Fishing Equipment	147
Rig, Trolling	Fishing Equipment	147
Rigging	Water Transportation Accessories	439
Rigging, Aerial	Public Entertainment Devices	508
Rigging, Tent	Supporting Elements	17
rimsherd (*use:* Sherd, Rim)	Unclassifiable Objects	527
Ring, Adapter	Photographic Accessories	379
Ring, Animal Nose	Animal Care Equipment	135
Ring, Boxing	Sports Equipment	514
Ring, Burner	Labware	294
Ring, Cinch	Land Transportation Accessories	420
Ring, Class	Status Symbols	497
Ring, Clinch	Metalworking T&E	215
Ring, Curtain	Window & Door Coverings	78
Ring, Deck Tennis	Sports Equipment	518
Ring, Dish	Food Service Accessories	182
Ring, Door	Finish Hardware	11
Ring, Eternity	Body Adornments	81
Ring, Exercise	Recreational Devices	509
Ring, Finger	Body Adornments	81
Ring, Forge	Metalworking T&E	215
Ring, Fraternal	Status Symbols	497
Ring, Gimmel	Body Adornments	82
Ring, Gymnastics	Sports Equipment	516
ring, harness (*use:* Terret)	Land Transportation Accessories	420
Ring, Harness	Land Transportation Accessories	420
Ring, Insignia	Status Symbols	497
Ring, Juggling	Public Entertainment Devices	508
Ring, Key	Personal Carrying & Storage Gear	113
Ring, Life	Water Transportation Accessories	441
ring, marriage (*use:* Ring, Wedding)	Wedding Objects	466
Ring, Mourning	Funerary Objects	457
Ring, Napkin	Food Service Accessories	182
Ring, Nipple	Body Adornments	82
Ring, Nose	Body Adornments	81
Ring, Pastoral	Status Symbols	499
Ring, Rectal	Veterinary Equipment	142
Ring, Shower Curtain	Other Household Accessories	67
Ring, Signet	Personal Identification	495
Ring, Snub	Forestry T&E	191
Ring, Teething	Personal Assistive Objects	109
Ring, Toe	Body Adornments	82
Ring, Tong	Metalworking T&E	215
Ring, Wedding	Wedding Objects	466
Ringer, Animal Nose	Animal Care Equipment	135
Rink, Skating	Cultural & Recreational Structures	30
Ripper	Construction T&E	295
Ripper, Slater's	Masonry & Stoneworking T&E	205
Ripper, Stitch	Needleworking Equipment	237
Ripple	Textile Manufacturing Equipment	239
Ripsaw	Woodworking T&E	257
Riser, Stair	Stair Elements	15

Riverboat	Watercraft	446
Rivet, Leather	Leather, Horn & Shellworking T&E	200
Rivet, Metal	Metalworking T&E	210
Rivet, Tong	Metalworking T&E	210
Rivière	Body Adornments	81
roach (*use:* Headdress, Roach)	Status Symbols	499
Roadster	Motor Vehicles	428
roaster (*use:* Pan, Roasting)	Cooking Vessels	151
Roaster, Apple	Food Preparation Equipment	163
Roaster, Bird	Food Preparation Equipment	163
Roaster, Chestnut	Food Preparation Equipment	163
Roaster, Coffee	Food Preparation Equipment	155
Roaster, Fish	Food Preparation Equipment	163
Roaster, Ore	Metalworking T&E	215
Robe	Main Garments	97
robe, barrister's (*use:* Gown, Barrister's)	Status Symbols	498
robe, buffalo (*use:* Robe, Lap)	Land Transportation Accessories	419
robe, button (*use:* Blanket, Button)	Status Symbols	498
Robe, Judicial	Status Symbols	498
Robe, Lap	Land Transportation Accessories	419
robe, nobility (*use:* Blanket, Nobility)	Status Symbols	498
robe, open (*use:* Gown, Open)	Main Garments	95
robe, preaching (*use:* Gown, Geneva)	Status Symbols	499
robe, pulpit (*use:* Gown, Geneva)	Status Symbols	499
Robe, Séance	Religious Objects	464
Robinet	Artillery	274
Robot	Data Processing Devices	362
Robot, Industrial	Data Processing Devices	362
Rochet	Status Symbols	500
Rockaway	Animal-Powered Vehicles	424
Rocker	Graphic Equipment	384
rocker (*use:* Chair, Rocking)	Seating Furniture	48
rocker, cradle (*use:* Bench, Cradle)	Seating Furniture	47
Rocker, Ore	Mining & Mineral Harvesting T&E	224
Rocker, Platform	Seating Furniture	48
rocket (*use:* Missile)	Ammunition	264
Rocket, Signal	Visual Communication Devices	400
Rod, Boning	Surveying Equipment	353
Rod, Calculating	Data Processing Devices	361
Rod, Casting	Fishing Equipment	147
Rod, Closet	Storage & Display Accessories	65
Rod, Connecting	Power Transmission Components	305
Rod, Curtain	Window & Door Coverings	78
Rod, Divining	Mining & Mineral Harvesting T&E	224
Rod, Fishing	Fishing Equipment	147
Rod, Fly	Fishing Equipment	147
Rod, Gauge	Woodworking T&E	256
Rod, Grounding	Telecommunication Accessories	395
Rod, Gun Cleaning	Armament Accessories	271
Rod, Heddle	Textile Manufacturing Equipment	243
Rod, Knockout	Armament Accessories	271
Rod, Leveling	Surveying Equipment	353
Rod, Lightning	Roof Elements	14
Rod, Nuclear Control	Power Transmission Components	305
Rod, Sea	Fishing Equipment	147
Rod, Spinning	Fishing Equipment	147
Rod, Stadia	Surveying Equipment	353
Rod, Stair	Finish Hardware	11
Rod, Stirring	Photoprocessing Equipment	381
Rod, Stuffing	Leather, Horn & Shellworking T&E	200
Rod, Sucker	Mining & Mineral Harvesting T&E	224
Rod, Tie	Supporting Elements	16
Rod, Trolling	Fishing Equipment	147
Rod, Tungsten	Glass, Plastics & Clayworking T&E	194
Rod, Wantage	Weights & Measures T&E	358
Rode, Anchor	Water Transportation Accessories	439
Roemer	Drinking Vessels	174
Rola Bola	Public Entertainment Devices	507
roll (*use:* Roster)	Other Documents	484
Roll, Bucking	Land Transportation Accessories	420
roll, Cornish (*use:* Crusher, Roller)	Mining & Mineral Harvesting T&E	221
Roll, Dandy	Papermaking T&E	233
Roll, Lard	Food Processing Equipment	169
Roll, Music	Musical Accessories	369
Roll, Muster	Government Records	470
roll, pillow (*use:* Bolster)	Bedding	43
roll, pillow (*use:* Pillow, Neck)	Personal Assistive Objects	108
roll, player piano (*use:* Roll, Music)	Musical Accessories	369
Roll, Tax	Government Records	470

Rollator Personal Assistive Objects 109
Roller Construction T&E 295
Roller, Bandage Medical Accessories 326
Roller, Cigar Other T&E for Materials 260
Roller, Cigarette Other T&E for Materials 260
roller, corrugated (*use:* Roller, Land) Cultivation Equipment 125
Roller, Felting Textile Manufacturing Equipment 243
roller, field (*use:* Roller, Land) Cultivation Equipment 125
roller, fulling (*use:* Roller, Felting) Textile Manufacturing Equipment 243
Roller, Garden Groundskeeping Equipment 309
Roller, Graining Painting T&E 230
Roller, Hair Hair Care Objects 119
Roller, Impregnating Glass, Plastics & Clayworking T&E 194
Roller, Ink Graphic Equipment 385
Roller, Land Cultivation Equipment 125
roller, lawn (*use:* Roller, Garden) Groundskeeping Equipment 309
Roller, Lint Clothing Care Objects 105
Roller, Metal Metalworking T&E 216
Roller, Paint Painting T&E 230
Roller, Pill Medical Accessories 326
Roller, Potter's Glass, Plastics & Clayworking T&E 194
Roller, Print Photoprocessing Equipment 381
Roller, Seam Painting T&E 231
Roller, Snow Animal-Powered Vehicles 424
Roller, Springerle Food Preparation Equipment 159
Roller, Tobacco Other T&E for Materials 260
Roller, Towel Storage & Display Accessories 65
Roller, Wallpaper Painting T&E 231
roller, warp (*use:* Beam, Warp) Textile Manufacturing Equipment 239
Rolly-Doll Toys 521
rommelpot (*use:* Drum, Friction) Musical Instruments 371
Romper Main Garments 96
Rongeur Medical Instruments 332
Roof Roof Elements 14
Room, Miniature Other Documents 484
Rope Multiple Use T&E for Materials 226
Rope, Climbing Sports Equipment 514
Rope, Gym Recreational Devices 509
Rope, Jump Toys 522
rope, marine (*use:* Cordage, Marine) Water Transportation Accessories 440
rope, sheet (*use:* Sheet) Water Transportation Accessories 439
rope, skipping (*use:* Rope, Jump) Toys 522
Rosary Belief Symbols 494
Rosette Finish Hardware 10
rosette, bridle (*use:* Ornament, Bridle) Land Transportation Accessories 420
Rosin, Bowstring Musical Accessories 369
Roster Other Documents 484
Rotisserie Food Preparation Equipment 155
Rotor Power Transmission Components 305
Rotor, Aircraft Aerospace Transportation Accessories 410
Rotor, Antenna Telecommunication Accessories 395
Rotorplane Aircraft 412
Roulette Graphic Equipment 384
Roulette, Potter's Glass, Plastics & Clayworking T&E 194
Rounder Leather, Horn & Shellworking T&E 200
rounder (*use:* Plane, Rounder) Woodworking T&E 256
Rounder, Pill Medical Accessories 326
Roundhouse Transportation Structures 39
Router Woodworking T&E 256
Router, Data Data Processing Accessories 360
Rowboat Watercraft 443
rowlock (*use:* Oarlock) Water Transportation Accessories 438
Rubber Footwear 90
rubber, grain (*use:* Mano) Food Preparation Equipment 160
Rubber, Sailmaker's Needleworking Equipment 237
Rubbing Graphic Documents 474
Ruche Needleworking Equipment 236
rucksack (*use:* Backpack) Personal Carrying & Storage Gear 110
Rudder Water Transportation Accessories 439
Ruff Clothing Accessories 84
ruffle, dust (*use:* Bedskirt) Bedding 44
Rug Floor Coverings 45
Rug, Area Floor Coverings 45
Rug, Bed Bedding 43
Rug, Hearth Floor Coverings 45
Rug, Knotted Floor Coverings 45
Rug, Linoleum Floor Coverings 45
Rug, Loop Floor Coverings 45
Rug, Oriental Floor Coverings 45
Rug, Pelt Floor Coverings 45
Rug, Pictorial Floor Coverings 45
Rug, Prayer Religious Objects 464
Rug, Rag Floor Coverings 45
rug, scatter (*use:* Rug, Throw) Floor Coverings 45
Rug, Shag Floor Coverings 45

Rug, Stair	Floor Coverings	45
Rug, Throw	Floor Coverings	45
Rule, Bench	Woodworking T&E	256
Rule, Board	Woodworking T&E	256
Rule, Caliper	Woodworking T&E	256
Rule, Carpenter's	Woodworking T&E	256
Rule, Composing	Typesetting Equipment	388
Rule, Extension	Weights & Measures T&E	358
Rule, Featheredge	Masonry & Stoneworking T&E	206
Rule, Folding	Weights & Measures T&E	358
Rule, Foot	Weights & Measures T&E	358
Rule, Jointing	Masonry & Stoneworking T&E	205
rule, line (*use:* Gauge, Line)	Typesetting Equipment	388
Rule, Log	Forestry T&E	191
Rule, Makeup	Typesetting Equipment	388
Rule, Parallel	Drafting T&E	367
Rule, Patternmaker's	Woodworking T&E	257
Rule, Protractor	Woodworking T&E	257
Rule, Retractable	Weights & Measures T&E	358
Rule, Slide	Data Processing Devices	361
Rule, Trunnion	Armament Accessories	271
Rule, Woodworking	Woodworking T&E	256
Ruler	Weights & Measures T&E	358
ruler, fish (*use:* Board, Fish Measuring)	Fishing Equipment	145
Ruler, Parallel	Navigational Equipment	350
Ruler, Pica	Typesetting Equipment	388
Rules	Administrative Records	467
Rummer	Drinking Vessels	174
runabout (*use:* Carriage, Runabout)	Animal-Powered Vehicles	423
Runabout	Watercraft	444
runestone (*use:* Stone, Rune)	Site Features	21
Runner, Edge	Papermaking T&E	233
Runner, Floor	Floor Coverings	45
Runner, Furniture	Furniture Coverings	61
Runner, Gig	Land Transportation Accessories	417
Runner, Sleigh	Land Transportation Accessories	417
Runner, Table	Furniture Coverings	61
Runner, Vehicle	Land Transportation Accessories	417
Rushlight	Other Lighting Accessories	73
Sabaton	Body Armor	275
Saber	Edged Weapons	278
Saber, Fencing	Sports Equipment	515
Saber, Short	Edged Weapons	279
Sabot	Footwear	90
Sabot, Ammunition	Ammunition	264
Sabratache	Personal Carrying & Storage Gear	111
sabre, fencing (*use:* Saber, Fencing)	Sports Equipment	515
Saccharimeter	Chemical Testing Devices	291
Sachet	Clothing Care Objects	105
sack (*use:* Bag)	Containers	414
Sack	Main Garments	96
sack, feed (*use:* Feedbag)	Animal Care Equipment	134
Sack, Gunny	Containers	414
Sack, Hacky	Game Equipment	505
Sackbut	Musical Instruments	370
sacque (*use:* Sack)	Main Garments	96
sacrarium (*use:* Lavabo)	Religious Objects	464
Saddle	Land Transportation Accessories	420
Saddle, Pack	Land Transportation Accessories	420
Saddle, Pad	Land Transportation Accessories	420
Saddle, Racing	Land Transportation Accessories	420
Saddle, Riding	Land Transportation Accessories	420
Saddle, Stock	Land Transportation Accessories	420
Saddlebag	Land Transportation Accessories	416
Sadiron	Laundry Equipment	313
Safe	Storage & Display Furniture	54
Safe, Candle	Storage & Display Accessories	65
safe, food (*use:* Safe, Kitchen)	Food Storage Equipment	171
Safe, Gun	Storage & Display Furniture	54
Safe, Kitchen	Food Storage Equipment	171
Safe, Match	Storage & Display Accessories	65
safe, pie (*use:* Safe, Kitchen)	Food Storage Equipment	171
Safelight	Photoprocessing Equipment	381
Safety, Grip	Armament Accessories	271
Sagemono	Personal Carrying & Storage Gear	113
Sagger	Glass, Plastics & Clayworking T&E	193
Sail	Water Transportation Accessories	439
Sail, Fore-and-Aft	Water Transportation Accessories	439
Sail, Square	Water Transportation Accessories	439
Sailboard	Recreational Devices	511
Sailboat	Watercraft	443
sailboat, Comet (*use:* Classboat)	Watercraft	444
sailboat, Penguin (*use:* Classboat)	Watercraft	444
Sailplane	Aircraft	411
Saker	Artillery	274
Salamander	Food Preparation Equipment	157

Term	Category	Page
Salimeter	Chemical Testing Devices	290
salinometer (*use:* Salimeter)	Chemical Testing Devices	290
Sallet	Body Armor	275
Saloon	Commercial Structures	27
Salt, Standing	Serving Vessels	188
Saltcellar	Serving Vessels	188
Saltshaker	Serving Vessels	188
Salver	Serving Vessels	187
salver, cake (*use:* Stand, Cake)	Serving Vessels	187
Samovar	Serving Vessels	189
Sampan	Watercraft	443
Sample, Food	Food Processing Equipment	164
Sample, Material	Unclassifiable Objects	527
Sample, Sales	Merchandising T&E	338
Sample, Tissue	Biological T&E	287
Sampler	Art	453
Sampler, Effluent	Chemical Testing Devices	291
Sampler, Milk	Food Processing Equipment	166
Sampler, Music	Musical Instruments	371
Sampler, Sidewall	Mining & Mineral Harvesting T&E	224
Sanatorium	Institutional Structures	37
Sandal	Footwear	90
Sandbag	Protective Devices	346
Sandbagger	Watercraft	443
Sandbox	Recreational Devices	510
sandbox (*use:* Box, Pounce)	Writing Accessories	403
Sandbox, Locomotive	Rail Transportation Accessories	431
Sander	Woodworking T&E	257
sander (*use:* Shaker, Sand)	Writing Accessories	405
Sander, Belt	Woodworking T&E	257
Sander, Contour	Woodworking T&E	257
Sander, Disk	Woodworking T&E	257
Sander, Spindle	Woodworking T&E	257
Sandglass	Timekeeping T&E	356
Sandpaper	Woodworking T&E	257
sandshaker (*use:* Box, Pounce)	Writing Accessories	403
Sarape	Outerwear	100
Sarcophagus	Funerary Objects	456
Sari	Main Garments	97
Sarong	Main Garments	97
Sarrusophone	Musical Instruments	375
Sash	Clothing Accessories	86
Sash, Window	Door & Window Elements	7
Satchel	Personal Carrying & Storage Gear	111
Satellite	Spacecraft	413
Satellite, Communications	Spacecraft	413
Satellite, Datasphere	Spacecraft	413
Satellite, Meteorological	Spacecraft	413
Sauceboat	Serving Vessels	187
Saucepan	Cooking Vessels	151
Saucer	Eating Vessels	177
Saucer, Berry	Eating Vessels	177
Saucer, Bouillon Cup	Eating Vessels	177
Saucer, Demitasse	Eating Vessels	177
Saucer, Flowerpot	Horticultural Containers	62
Saucer, Nest	Painting T&E	230
Saucer, Snow	Recreational Devices	509
Sauna	Other Structures	41
Sautoir	Body Adornments	81
Save-All	Papermaking T&E	233
saver, life (*use:* Ring, Life)	Water Transportation Accessories	441
Saver, Soap	Dishwashing Equipment	308
Saw	Multiple Use T&E for Materials	228
Saw, Amputation	Medical Instruments	332
saw, angle (*use:* Saw, Dovetail)	Woodworking T&E	257
saw, back (*use:* Backsaw)	Woodworking T&E	257
Saw, Band	Woodworking T&E	257
Saw, Bead	Woodworking T&E	257
Saw, Bench	Woodworking T&E	257
Saw, Blitz	Woodworking T&E	257
saw, board (*use:* Saw, Pit)	Woodworking T&E	258
Saw, Bow	Woodworking T&E	257
saw, bracket (*use:* Fretsaw)	Woodworking T&E	257
Saw, Brick	Masonry & Stoneworking T&E	205
saw, buck (*use:* Bucksaw)	Forestry T&E	191
saw, buhl (*use:* Fretsaw)	Woodworking T&E	257
Saw, Cabinet	Woodworking T&E	257
Saw, Carcass	Woodworking T&E	257
Saw, Chain	Forestry T&E	191
saw, chairmaker's (*use:* Saw, Felloe)	Woodworking T&E	257
Saw, Cheese	Food Processing Equipment	166
Saw, Circular	Woodworking T&E	257
Saw, Compass	Woodworking T&E	257
Saw, Concrete	Construction T&E	296
Saw, Coping	Woodworking T&E	257
Saw, Crosscut	Forestry T&E	191
Saw, Crown	Woodworking T&E	257
Saw, Dehorning	Veterinary Equipment	142
Saw, Dental	Dental Instruments	323
Saw, Dovetail	Woodworking T&E	257
Saw, Drunken	Woodworking T&E	257
Saw, Electric Portable	Woodworking T&E	257
Saw, Felloe	Woodworking T&E	257
Saw, Flooring	Woodworking T&E	258
Saw, Frame	Woodworking T&E	257
Saw, Framed Veneer	Woodworking T&E	258
saw, fret (*use:* Fretsaw)	Woodworking T&E	257
Saw, Fuze	Armament Accessories	271
Saw, Grub	Masonry & Stoneworking T&E	205

saw, hack (*use:* Hacksaw)	Metalworking T&E	216
Saw, Hand	Woodworking T&E	258
Saw, Heading	Woodworking T&E	258
Saw, Ice	Mining & Mineral Harvesting T&E	225
saw, jig (*use:* Jigsaw)	Woodworking T&E	257
Saw, Keyhole	Woodworking T&E	257
saw, lock (*use:* Locksaw)	Woodworking T&E	257
saw, long (*use:* Saw, Crosscut)	Forestry T&E	191
Saw, Mason's	Masonry & Stoneworking T&E	205
Saw, Meat	Food Processing Equipment	165
Saw, Metalworking	Metalworking T&E	216
Saw, Miter-Box	Woodworking T&E	257
Saw, Musical	Musical Instruments	372
Saw, One-Handed Crosscut	Forestry T&E	191
Saw, Open Pit	Woodworking T&E	258
Saw, Panel	Woodworking T&E	258
Saw, Patternmaker's	Woodworking T&E	258
Saw, Piercing	Metalworking T&E	216
Saw, Pit	Woodworking T&E	258
Saw, Pruning	Groundskeeping Equipment	310
Saw, Rabbet	Woodworking T&E	257
Saw, Radial Arm	Woodworking T&E	257
saw, rip (*use:* Ripsaw)	Woodworking T&E	257
Saw, Saber	Woodworking T&E	258
Saw, Scroll	Woodworking T&E	258
saw, skill (*use:* Saw, Electric Portable)	Woodworking T&E	257
saw, snow (*use:* Knife, Snow)	Other T&E for Materials	260
Saw, Square Hole	Woodworking T&E	257
Saw, Stairbuilder's	Woodworking T&E	257
Saw, Stone	Masonry & Stoneworking T&E	205
Saw, Surgical	Medical Instruments	332
Saw, Table	Woodworking T&E	257
Saw, Tenon	Woodworking T&E	257
saw, thwart (*use:* Saw, Two-Handed Crosscut)	Forestry T&E	191
Saw, Timber	Forestry T&E	191
Saw, Treadle	Woodworking T&E	258
Saw, Two-Handed Crosscut	Forestry T&E	191
saw, two-man crosscut (*use:* Saw, Two-Handed Crosscut)	Forestry T&E	191
Saw, Vellum	Woodworking T&E	258
Saw, Veneer	Woodworking T&E	257
saw, web (*use:* Saw, Bow)	Woodworking T&E	257
saw, woodcutter's (*use:* Bucksaw)	Forestry T&E	191
Saw, Woodworking	Woodworking T&E	257
Sawbuck	Woodworking T&E	259
Sawhorse	Woodworking T&E	259

sawmill (*use:* Building, Sawmill)	Industrial Structures	35
Sawmill	Woodworking T&E	258
Sawmill, Band	Woodworking T&E	258
Sawmill, Circular	Woodworking T&E	258
Sawmill, Gang	Woodworking T&E	258
Sawmill, Gate-Type	Woodworking T&E	258
Sawmill, Muley	Woodworking T&E	258
sawmill, sash (*use:* Sawmill, Gate-Type)	Woodworking T&E	258
Sawmill, Up-and-Down	Woodworking T&E	258
Saw-Set	Metalworking T&E	216
saxhorn (*use:* Bugle, Valve)	Musical Instruments	370
Saxophone	Musical Instruments	375
Saxophone, Alto	Musical Instruments	375
Saxophone, Baritone	Musical Instruments	375
Saxophone, Soprano	Musical Instruments	375
Saxophone, Tenor	Musical Instruments	375
Scabbard	Armament Accessories	268
Scabbard, Bayonet	Armament Accessories	268
Scabbard, Carbine	Armament Accessories	268
Scabbard, Dagger	Armament Accessories	268
Scabbard, Machete	Harvesting Equipment	130
Scabbard, Sword	Armament Accessories	268
Scaffold	Construction T&E	296
Scalder, Hog	Food Processing Equipment	165
Scale	Weights & Measures T&E	358
Scale, Animal	Animal Care Equipment	135
Scale, Apothecary	Weights & Measures T&E	358
Scale, Architect's	Drafting T&E	367
scale, balance (*use:* Balance)	Weights and Measures T&E	358
scale, barrel (*use:* Scale, Cylinder)	Weights and Measures T&E	358
Scale, Bathroom	Weights & Measures T&E	358
Scale, Butter	Food Processing Equipment	166
Scale, Computing	Weights & Measures T&E	358
Scale, Cylinder	Weights & Measures T&E	358
Scale, Dairy	Food Processing Equipment	166
scale, drum (*use:* Scale, Cylinder)	Weights and Measures T&E	358
scale, egg (*use:* Grader, Egg)	Food Processing Equipment	167
Scale, Grain	Food Processing Equipment	169
Scale, Hemoglobin	Medical Instruments	327
Scale, Hopper	Weights & Measures T&E	358
Scale, Kitchen	Food Preparation Equipment	157
Scale, Lever	Weights & Measures T&E	358
Scale, Livestock	Animal Care Equipment	135
Scale, Market	Merchandising T&E	338
Scale, Meat	Food Preparation Equipment	157
Scale, Milk	Food Processing Equipment	166
Scale, Navigational	Navigational Equipment	351

Scale, Nutritional | Food Preparation Equipment | 157
Scale, Pet | Pet Supplies | 141
Scale, Platform | Weights & Measures T&E | 358
Scale, Postal | Weights & Measures T&E | 358
Scale, Spice | Food Preparation Equipment | 157
Scale, Spring | Weights & Measures T&E | 358
Scale, Surveyor's | Surveying Equipment | 353
Scale, Timber | Forestry T&E | 191
Scale, Triangular | Weights & Measures T&E | 358
Scale, Truck | Weights & Measures T&E | 358
Scaler, Dental | Dental Instruments | 323
Scaler, Fish | Food Preparation Equipment | 157
Scaler, Nuclear | Nuclear Physics T&E | 341
Scalp | Achievement Symbols | 491
Scalpel | Medical Instruments | 331
Scalpel, Dental | Dental Instruments | 323
Scanner, Barcode | Peripherals | 364
Scanner, Flatbed | Peripherals | 364
Scanner, Handheld | Peripherals | 364
Scanner, Optical | Peripherals | 364
Scanner, Price | Merchandising T&E | 338
Scanner, Radio | Telecommunication Devices | 396
Scanner, Security | Protective Devices | 346
Scanner, X-Ray Security | Protective Devices | 346
Scapular | Status Symbols | 500
Scarf | Clothing Accessories | 86
Scarf, Bureau | Furniture Coverings | 61
scarf, dresser (*use:* Scarf, Bureau) | Furniture Coverings | 61
Scarf, Furniture | Furniture Coverings | 61
scarf, head (*use:* Headscarf) | Headwear | 93
Scarf, Neck | Clothing Accessories | 86
Scarf, Piano | Furniture Coverings | 61
Scarf, Table | Furniture Coverings | 61
scarf, washstand (*use:* Scarf, Furniture) | Furniture Coverings | 61
Scarificator | Medical Instruments | 333
Scarifier | Construction T&E | 295
Scarifier, Plaster | Masonry & Stoneworking T&E | 206
scene, nativity (*use:* Creche) | Religious Objects | 464
scenery, theatrical (*use:* Set, Stage) | Public Entertainment Devices | 508
Scepter | Status Symbols | 499
Schedule | Other Documents | 486
Schedule, Fee | Other Documents | 486
Schilling | Exchange Media | 488
schnelle (*use:* Tankard) | Drinking Vessels | 175
School | Institutional Structures | 37
Schooner | Watercraft | 444
Schooner, Fishing | Watercraft | 445
schooner, Grand Banks (*use:* Banker) | Watercraft | 445
Schooner, Prairie | Animal-Powered Vehicles | 425
Scimitar | Edged Weapons | 279
Sciopticon | Visual Communication Devices | 400
Scissors | Multiple Use T&E for Materials | 228
Scissors, Bandage | Medical Accessories | 326
Scissors, Circumcision | Medical Instruments | 332
Scissors, Dental | Dental Instruments | 324
Scissors, Dissecting | Biological T&E | 288
scissors, egg (*use:* Topper, Egg) | Food Preparation Equipment | 159
Scissors, Fabric | Needleworking Equipment | 235
scissors, grape (*use:* Shears, Grape) | Serving Utensils | 185
Scissors, Hair | Hair Care Objects | 118
Scissors, Manicure | Beauty Supplies | 117
scissors, pineapple (*use:* Snip, Pineapple) | Food Preparation Equipment | 159
scissors, poultry (*use:* Shears, Poultry) | Food Preparation Equipment | 159
Scissors, Surgical | Medical Instruments | 332
Scissors, Vine | Harvesting Equipment | 130
Scissors, Wallpaper | Painting T&E | 231
Sclerometer | Chemical Testing Devices | 290
Sconce | Lighting Devices | 68
Scoop | Multiple Use T&E for Materials | 228
Scoop, Butter | Food Processing Equipment | 167
Scoop, Cheese | Serving Utensils | 184
Scoop, Coffee | Food Preparation Equipment | 161
scoop, cranberry (*use:* Rake, Cranberry) | Harvesting Equipment | 130
Scoop, Curd | Food Processing Equipment | 167
Scoop, Digging | Multiple Use T&E for Materials | 228
scoop, ear (*use:* Spoon, Ear Wax) | Hygiene Objects | 121
Scoop, Feed | Animal Care Equipment | 135
Scoop, Flour | Food Preparation Equipment | 161
Scoop, Food | Food Preparation Equipment | 161
scoop, grain (*use:* Shovel, Grain) | Harvesting Equipment | 131
Scoop, Ice | Food Preparation Equipment | 161
Scoop, Ice Cream | Serving Utensils | 184
Scoop, Limpet | Fishing Equipment | 146
Scoop, Litter | Pet Supplies | 141
Scoop, Marrow | Eating & Drinking Utensils | 178
Scoop, Nut | Serving Utensils | 184
Scoop, Pet Waste | Pet Supplies | 141
scoop, potato (*use:* Fork, Vegetable Scoop) | Harvesting Equipment | 128
Scoop, Salt | Serving Utensils | 184
Scoop, Scale | Weights & Measures T&E | 357

Scoop, Serving	Serving Utensils	184
Scoop, Sugar	Serving Utensils	184
Scoop, Turtle	Fishing Equipment	146
scoop, winnowing (*use:* Basket, Winnowing)	Harvesting Equipment	131
Scooter	Toys	524
scooter, ice (*use:* Iceboat)	Watercraft	443
Scooter, Motor	Motor Vehicles	428
scope, rangefinder (*use:* Sight, Telescope)	Armament Accessories	271
scope, sniper's (*use:* Sight, Telescope)	Armament Accessories	271
scope, target (*use:* Sight, Telescope)	Armament Accessories	271
Score	Literary Works	477
Scoreboard	Cultural & Recreational Structures	30
Scorebook	Other Documents	482
Scorecard	Other Documents	482
scorepad (*use:* Scorebook)	Other Documents	482
Scorper	Woodworking T&E	258
Scorper, Closed	Woodworking T&E	258
Scorper, Open	Woodworking T&E	258
Scotch	Masonry & Stoneworking T&E	205
Scotoscope	Optical T&E	344
Scourer, Grain	Food Processing Equipment	168
scourer, wheat (*use:* Scourer, Grain)	Food Processing Equipment	168
scourge (*use:* Whip)	Regulative Devices	347
Scow	Watercraft	446
Scrambler	Telecommunication Accessories	395
Scrap	Unclassifiable Objects	527
Scrapbook	Memorabilia	478
Scraper	Glass, Plastics & Clayworking T&E	195
Scraper, Armament	Armament Accessories	271
Scraper, Ash	Heating Equipment Accessories	77
Scraper, Band	Armament Accessories	271
scraper, bench (*use:* Scraper, Dough)	Food Preparation Equipment	158
Scraper, Block	Masonry & Stoneworking T&E	205
Scraper, Boot	Other Household Accessories	67
Scraper, Box	Woodworking T&E	258
Scraper, Cabinet	Woodworking T&E	258
Scraper, Casing	Food Processing Equipment	165
Scraper, Corn	Food Preparation Equipment	159
Scraper, Cotton	Harvesting Equipment	130
scraper, crab (*use:* Skipjack)	Watercraft	445
Scraper, Dental	Dental Instruments	324
Scraper, Dough	Food Preparation Equipment	158
Scraper, Earth	Construction T&E	295
Scraper, End	Leather, Horn & Shellworking T&E	200
Scraper, Flat	Metalworking T&E	216
Scraper, Floor	Housekeeping Equipment	312
Scraper, Gun Barrel	Armament Accessories	271
Scraper, Half-Round	Metalworking T&E	216
Scraper, Hide	Leather, Horn & Shellworking T&E	200
Scraper, Hoe	Mining & Mineral Harvesting T&E	224
Scraper, Hog	Food Processing Equipment	165
Scraper, Hook	Metalworking T&E	216
Scraper, Ice	Land Transportation Accessories	419
Scraper, Metal	Metalworking T&E	216
Scraper, Mortar	Armament Accessories	271
Scraper, Musical	Musical Instruments	372
Scraper, Press	Graphic Equipment	384
scraper, road (*use:* Grader)	Construction T&E	295
Scraper, Shell	Armament Accessories	271
Scraper, Side	Leather, Horn & Shellworking T&E	200
scraper, snow (*use:* Blade, Snow)	Land Transportation Accessories	416
scraper, snow (*use:* Scraper, Ice)	Land Transportation Accessories	419
Scraper, Snow	Rail Transportation Accessories	432
Scraper, Stove	Heating Equipment Accessories	77
Scraper, Sweat	Animal Care Equipment	136
Scraper, Three-Cornered	Metalworking T&E	216
Scraper, Thumbnail	Leather, Horn & Shellworking T&E	200
Scraper, Tongue	Hygiene Objects	121
Scraper, Tree	Forestry T&E	191
Scraper, Turpentine	Forestry T&E	191
Scraper, Wall	Painting T&E	230
Scraper, Wood	Woodworking T&E	258
Scratcher, Back	Personal Assistive Objects	109
Screed	Masonry & Stoneworking T&E	205
Screen	Other Furniture	58
Screen, Candle	Other Household Accessories	67
Screen, Fire	Heating Equipment Accessories	76
Screen, Folding	Other Furniture	58
Screen, Food	Food Preparation Accessories	152
screen, foundry (*use:* Riddle, Foundry)	Metalworking T&E	215
Screen, Meat	Food Preparation Equipment	163

Term	Category	Page
Screen, Pole	Heating Equipment Accessories	76
Screen, Projection	Visual Communication Accessories	399
Screen, Rear Projection	Visual Communication Accessories	399
screen, revolving (*use:* Screen, Rolling)	Food Processing Equipment	168
Screen, Rolling	Food Processing Equipment	168
screen, silk (*use:* Silkscreen)	Graphic Equipment	384
Screen, Splatter	Food Preparation Accessories	152
Screen, Table	Decorative Furnishings	60
screen, touch (*use:* Touchscreen)	Peripherals	364
Screen, Trommel	Mining & Mineral Harvesting T&E	224
Screen, Window	Door & Window Elements	7
Screen, Winnowing	Harvesting Equipment	131
Screw	Multiple Use T&E for Materials	227
Screw, Archimedean	Mechanical Devices	316
Screw, Machine	Metalworking T&E	216
Screw, Metalworking	Metalworking T&E	216
Screw, Riggers	Metalworking T&E	216
Screw, Rigging	Water Transportation Accessories	439
Screw, Sheet Metal	Metalworking T&E	216
Screw, Wood	Woodworking T&E	250
Screwdriver	Multiple Use T&E for Materials	228
Screwdriver, Offset	Multiple Use T&E for Materials	228
Screwdriver, Ratchet	Multiple Use T&E for Materials	228
Scribe, Metal	Metalworking T&E	216
Scribe, Timber	Forestry T&E	191
Scribe, Wood	Woodworking T&E	258
Scrimshaw	Art	454
Scrip	Exchange Media	489
Script	Literary Works	477
Scroll	Other Documents	486
Scroll, Prayer	Religious Objects	465
Scrub	Protective Wear	102
Scrubber	Housekeeping Equipment	312
Scrubber, Pot	Dishwashing Equipment	308
Scrunchie	Hair Adornments	83
scuff (*use:* Slipper, Bathing)	Footwear	90
scull (*use:* Shell)	Watercraft	444
Sculpture	Art	454
Sculpture, Funerary	Funerary Objects	457
Sculpture, Origami	Art	454
Scupper	Plumbing & Drainage Elements	13
Scutch	Masonry & Stoneworking T&E	205
scutcheon (*use:* Escutcheon)	Finish Hardware	10
scutcher, flax (*use:* Knife, Scutching)	Textile Manufacturing Equipment	241
scuttle, coal (*use:* Hod, Coal)	Heating Equipment Accessories	77
Scuttle, Deadlight	Water Transportation Accessories	439
Scuttle, Deck	Water Transportation Accessories	439
Scythe	Harvesting Equipment	130
Scythe, Brush	Groundskeeping Equipment	309
Scythe, Cradle	Harvesting Equipment	130
Scythe, Flemish	Harvesting Equipment	130
Scythe, Grass	Groundskeeping Equipment	309
scythe, Hainault (*use:* Scythe, Flemish)	Harvesting Equipment	130
Scythe, Weed	Cultivation Equipment	125
Seacock	Water Transportation Accessories	439
Seal	Personal Identification	495
seal (*use:* Sticker, Seal)	Writing Accessories	405
Seal, Jar Lid	Food Processing Equipment	165
Seal, Railcar	Rail Transportation Accessories	431
Sealant	Construction Materials	3
Sealer, Heat	Merchandising T&E	338
Sealer, Tree	Groundskeeping Equipment	309
Sealer, Vacuum	Food Processing Equipment	168
Seamer, Metal	Metalworking T&E	216
Seaplane	Aircraft	411
Searcher, Vent	Armament Accessories	271
Searchlight	Lighting Devices	70
Seascape	Art	453
Seat, Aircraft	Aerospace Transportation Accessories	410
Seat, Automotive	Land Transportation Accessories	417
Seat, Bicycle	Land Transportation Accessories	417
Seat, Child Safety	Land Transportation Accessories	419
Seat, Ejection	Aerospace Transportation Accessories	410
Seat, Folding	Land Transportation Accessories	417
seat, garden (*use:* Bench, Garden)	Seating Furniture	47
Seat, Love	Seating Furniture	49
Seat, Music	Musical Accessories	369
Seat, Railway	Rail Transportation Accessories	431
Seat, Theater	Seating Furniture	49
Seat, Toilet	Other Household Accessories	67
Seat, Vehicle	Land Transportation Accessories	417

Seat, Wagon	Land Transportation Accessories	417
Seat, Watercraft	Water Transportation Accessories	439
Seat, Window	Door & Window Elements	7
Seater, Bullet	Armament Accessories	271
Secretary	Storage & Display Furniture	54
Section	Graphic Documents	474
section, magazine (*use:* Supplement, Newspaper)	Other Documents	486
Sectograph	Drafting T&E	367
sedan (*use:* Chair, Sedan)	Human-Powered Vehicles	426
Sedan	Motor Vehicles	428
seed, melon (*use:* Boat, Gunning)	Watercraft	442
seeder, broadcast (*use:* Broadcaster)	Planting Equipment	132
Seeder, Centrifugal	Planting Equipment	132
seeder, endgate (*use:* Seeder, Centrifugal)	Planting Equipment	132
Seeder, Grass	Groundskeeping Equipment	309
Seeder, Hand Centrifugal	Planting Equipment	132
Seeder, Hand Seedbox	Planting Equipment	132
Seeder, Raisin	Food Preparation Equipment	160
seeder, rotary (*use:* Seeder, Centrifugal)	Planting Equipment	132
Seeder, Seedbox	Planting Equipment	132
seeder, wheelbarrow (*use:* Seeder, Hand Seedbox)	Planting Equipment	132
Seesaw	Recreational Devices	510
Seesaw, Spring	Recreational Devices	510
seine (*use:* Net, Seine)	Fishing Equipment	146
Seiner	Watercraft	445
Seismograph	Geological T&E	307
Seismophone	Geological T&E	307
Selenotrope	Astronomical T&E	285
Semaphore, Railroad	Visual Communication Devices	400
semicircle (*use:* Graphometer)	Surveying Equipment	352
Semicircumferentor	Surveying Equipment	353
Semisubmersible	Watercraft	444
Semitrailer	Motor Vehicles	428
Sensor, Occupancy	Electrical System Components	301
separator (*use:* Thresher-Separator)	Harvesting Equipment	131
Separator, Beam	Nuclear Physics T&E	342
Separator, Cradle	Mining & Mineral Harvesting T&E	224
Separator, Cream	Food Processing Equipment	167
Separator, Disk	Food Processing Equipment	169
Separator, Egg	Food Preparation Equipment	162
Separator, Electromagnetic	Mining & Mineral Harvesting T&E	224
Separator, Electrostatic	Mining & Mineral Harvesting T&E	224
Separator, Frame	Mining & Mineral Harvesting T&E	224
Separator, Grading	Food Processing Equipment	169
Separator, Grain	Food Processing Equipment	169
Separator, Gravy	Food Preparation Equipment	162
Separator, Jig	Mining & Mineral Harvesting T&E	224
Separator, Laboratory	Labware	294
Separator, Metal	Metalworking T&E	216
Separator, Milling	Food Processing Equipment	169
Separator, Mineral	Mining & Mineral Harvesting T&E	224
Separator, Receiving	Food Processing Equipment	169
Separator, Teeth	Dental Instruments	324
Separator, Toe	Beauty Supplies	117
separator, warehouse (*use:* Separator, Receiving)	Food Processing Equipment	169
Separator, Washer	Mining & Mineral Harvesting T&E	224
Sequin	Needleworking Equipment	237
serape (*use:* Sarape)	Outerwear	100
Serial	Other Documents	486
serigraph (*use:* Print, Screen)	Graphic Documents	474
Sermon	Literary Works	477
Serpent	Musical Instruments	370
Serrefine	Medical Instruments	331
Server	Serving Utensils	185
server (*use:* Table, Serving)	Support Furniture	57
Server, Cake	Serving Utensils	185
Server, Cheese	Serving Utensils	185
Server, Ice Cream	Serving Utensils	185
Server, Lemon	Serving Utensils	185
Server, Network	Data Processing Devices	361
Server, Pie	Serving Utensils	185
Server, Salad	Serving Utensils	185
Server, Tomato	Serving Utensils	185
Service, Coffee	Food Service Sets	183
Service, Dessert	Food Service Sets	183
Service, Tea	Food Service Sets	183
serviette (*use:* Napkin)	Food Service Accessories	181
Servo, Remote	Telecommunication Devices	396
Set, Activity	Toys	522
Set, Arts and Crafts	Toys	523
Set, Backgammon	Game Equipment	503
Set, Barber's	Hair Care Objects	119
Set, Beverage	Food Service Sets	183
Set, Biopsy	Medical Instruments	328

Term	Category	Page
Set, Bleeding	Medical Instruments	333
Set, Blood Collecting	Medical Instruments	327
set, bridge (*use:* Set, Luncheon)	Food Service Sets	183
Set, Carpet Bowls	Game Equipment	504
Set, Carving	Food Service Sets	183
Set, Checkers	Game Equipment	503
Set, Chemistry	Toys	522
Set, Chess	Game Equipment	503
Set, Chinese Checkers	Game Equipment	504
Set, Communion	Religious Objects	462
Set, Condiment	Food Service Sets	183
Set, Construction	Toys	522
set, cosmetic (*use:* Kit, Cosmetic)	Beauty Supplies	117
Set, Cribbage	Game Equipment	504
Set, Croquet	Game Equipment	505
Set, Cup and Saucer	Food Service Sets	183
Set, Decanter	Food Service Sets	183
Set, Desk	Writing Accessories	405
set, dish (*use:* Set, Tableware)	Food Service Sets	183
Set, Dissecting	Biological T&E	287
Set, Drafting	Drafting T&E	367
Set, Drawing	Painting T&E	230
Set, Dresser	Hair Care Objects	119
set, erector (*use:* Set, Construction)	Toys	522
Set, Flatware	Food Service Sets	183
Set, Golf	Sports Equipment	516
Set, Hair Care	Hair Care Objects	119
Set, Halma	Game Equipment	504
Set, Hopscotch	Game Equipment	505
Set, Inoculating	Medical Instruments	334
Set, Intravenous	Medical Instruments	334
set, IV (*use:* Set, Intravenous)	Medical Instruments	334
Set, Jacks	Game Equipment	504
Set, Jewelry	Body Adornments	82
Set, Lawn Dart	Game Equipment	505
set, lemonade (*use:* Set, Beverage)	Food Service Sets	183
Set, Lens	Medical Instruments	329
Set, Livestock Tattoo	Animal Care Equipment	136
Set, Loading Tool	Armament Accessories	271
Set, Luncheon	Food Service Sets	183
Set, Magic	Toys	522
Set, Magnet	Toys	522
Set, Mah-Jongg	Game Equipment	505
Set, Mancala	Game Equipment	504
Set, Manicure	Beauty Supplies	117
Set, Mayonnaise	Food Service Sets	183
Set, Ninepins	Game Equipment	504
Set, Ouija	Toys	523
Set, Paint	Painting T&E	230
Set, Paint By Numbers	Painting T&E	230
Set, Parcheesi	Game Equipment	504
Set, Pin the Tail on the Donkey	Game Equipment	505
set, ping pong (*use:* Set, Table Tennis)	Sports Equipment	518
set, pitcher and cordial (*use:* Set, Beverage)	Food Service Sets	183
Set, Play	Toys	522
Set, Pyrography	Toys	523
Set, Racetrack	Toys	522
Set, Salt and Pepper	Food Service Sets	183
Set, Scribe	Writing Devices	406
Set, Shaving	Hair Care Objects	119
Set, Shuffleboard	Game Equipment	505
Set, Skittle	Game Equipment	505
Set, Spoon and Salt	Food Service Sets	183
Set, Stage	Public Entertainment Devices	508
Set, Sugar and Creamer	Food Service Sets	183
set, surgical instrument (*use:* Kit, Surgical)	Medical Instruments	334
Set, Table Croquet	Game Equipment	505
Set, Table Tennis	Sports Equipment	518
Set, Tablecloth	Food Service Sets	183
Set, Tableware	Food Service Sets	183
Set, Tap and Die	Metalworking T&E	209
set, tea (*use:* Service, Tea)	Food Service Sets	183
Set, Tenpins	Game Equipment	504
Set, Tiddlywinks	Game Equipment	504
Set, Toilet	Hygiene Objects	121
Set, Train	Toys	522
set, washstand (*use:* Set, Toilet)	Hygiene Objects	121
set, water (*use:* Set, Beverage)	Food Service Sets	183
set, water analysis (*use:* Kit, Water Analysis)	Chemical Testing Devices	291
Setscrew	Multiple Use T&E for Materials	227
Settee	Seating Furniture	49
Setter	Leather, Horn & Shellworking T&E	200
Setter, Fuze	Armament Accessories	271
Setter, Grommet	Leather, Horn & Shellworking T&E	200
Setter, Rivet	Leather, Horn & Shellworking T&E	200
Setter, Seedling	Planting Equipment	132
Setter, Trap	Trapping Equipment	149
Settle	Seating Furniture	47
Sextant	Navigational Equipment	351
Shack	Dwellings	33
Shack, Ice Fishing	Cultural & Recreational Structures	30
Shackle	Regulative Devices	348
Shackle, Bomb	Aerospace Transportation Accessories	410

shackle, drag (*use:* Dog, Span) — Forestry T&E 190
Shackle, Leg — Regulative Devices 348
Shackle, Raft — Forestry T&E 191
Shade — Window & Door Coverings 78
Shade, Accordion — Window & Door Coverings 78
Shade, Austrian — Window & Door Coverings 78
Shade, Balloon — Window & Door Coverings 79
Shade, Candle — Other Lighting Accessories 73
Shade, Horizon Glass — Navigational Equipment 351
Shade, Index — Navigational Equipment 351
Shade, Lighting — Other Lighting Accessories 73
Shade, Roller — Window & Door Coverings 79
Shade, Roman — Window & Door Coverings 79
Shade, Sextant — Navigational Equipment 351
Shade, Smoke — Other Lighting Accessories 73
Shaft — Power Transmission Components 305
Shaft, Column — Supporting Elements 17
Shaft, Drive — Land Transportation Accessories 417
Shafthouse — Industrial Structures 35
shaker (*use:* Dredger) — Food Storage Equipment 171
Shaker, Beverage — Food Preparation Equipment 153
Shaker, Cocktail — Food Preparation Equipment 153
shaker, dice (*use:* Cup, Dice) — Game Equipment 501
Shaker, Flour — Food Storage Equipment 171
Shaker, Grate — Heating Equipment Accessories 77
Shaker, Laboratory — Labware 294
Shaker, Paint — Painting T&E 230
Shaker, Pepper — Serving Vessels 188
Shaker, Pipette — Labware 294
Shaker, Powder — Beauty Supplies 116
shaker, salt (*use:* Saltshaker) — Serving Vessels 188
Shaker, Sand — Writing Accessories 405
Shaker, Soap — Hygiene Objects 121
Shaker, Sugar — Serving Vessels 188
Shaker, Tree — Harvesting Equipment 130
Shaker, Water Bath — Labware 294
Shako — Headwear 91
shalwar (*use:* Chalwar) — Main Garments 97
Sham — Bedding 44
Sham, Bolster — Bedding 44
Sham, Pillow — Bedding 44
Shampooer, Carpet — Housekeeping Equipment 311
shanty, ice fishing (*use:* Shack, Ice Fishing) — Cultural & Recreational Structures 30
Shaper, Body — Underwear 103
Shaper, Food — Food Preparation Equipment 157
Shaper, Metal — Metalworking T&E 216
Shaper, Wood — Woodworking T&E 254
Sharpener, Knife — Metalworking T&E 216
Sharpener, Metal — Metalworking T&E 216
Sharpener, Needle — Needleworking Equipment 237
Sharpener, Pencil — Writing Accessories 405
Sharpener, Razor — Hair Care Objects 119
Sharpener, Scissors — Metalworking T&E 216
sharpener, sickle-bar (*use:* Grinder, Mower Knife) — Metalworking T&E 211
Sharpener, Tool — Metalworking T&E 216
Sharpie — Watercraft 443
sharpie, New Haven (*use:* Boat, Tonging) — Watercraft 445
Shatter — Unclassifiable Objects 527
shave (*use:* Drawknife) — Woodworking T&E 201
Shave, Basket — Fiberworking T&E 144
Shave, Edge — Leather, Horn & Shellworking T&E 197
Shave, Heel — Leather, Horn & Shellworking T&E 197
Shave, Ice — Food Preparation Equipment 159
Shave, Leather — Leather, Horn & Shellworking T&E 197
shave, round (*use:* Scorper) — Woodworking T&E 258
Shave, Skirt — Leather, Horn & Shellworking T&E 197
Shave, Upright — Fiberworking T&E 144
Shaver, Dictating Machine — Sound Communication Accessories 390
Shawabti — Funerary Objects 457
Shawl — Outerwear 101
Shawl, Maiden — Outerwear 100
shawl, prayer (*use:* Tallith) — Belief Symbols 494
Shawm — Musical Instruments 375
shay (*use:* Chaise) — Animal-Powered Vehicles 423
shears, alligator (*use:* Shears, Lever) — Metalworking T&E 209
Shears, Animal — Animal Care Equipment 136
Shears, Band Cutter — Harvesting Equipment 131
Shears, Basketmaker's — Fiberworking T&E 144
Shears, Bench — Metalworking T&E 209
Shears, Circle — Metalworking T&E 209
Shears, Dental — Veterinary Equipment 142
Shears, Dressmaker's — Needleworking Equipment 235
Shears, Fabric — Needleworking Equipment 235
Shears, Fetlock — Animal Care Equipment 136
Shears, Fishing — Fishing Equipment 147
Shears, Fuller's — Needleworking Equipment 235
shears, garden (*use:* Shears, Pruning) — Groundskeeping Equipment 310
Shears, Glass — Glass, Plastics & Clayworking T&E 194
Shears, Grape — Serving Utensils 185

Term	Category	Page
Shears, Grass	Groundskeeping Equipment	309
Shears, Hedge	Groundskeeping Equipment	309
Shears, Horse	Animal Care Equipment	136
shears, lawn (*use:* Shears, Grass)	Groundskeeping Equipment	309
Shears, Leather	Leather, Horn & Shellworking T&E	197
Shears, Lever	Metalworking T&E	209
Shears, Medical	Medical Accessories	326
Shears, Metal	Metalworking T&E	209
Shears, Pinking	Needleworking Equipment	235
Shears, Portfire	Armament Accessories	271
Shears, Poultry	Food Preparation Equipment	159
Shears, Pruning	Groundskeeping Equipment	310
Shears, Rib	Medical Instruments	332
Shears, Sheep	Animal Care Equipment	136
Shears, Squaring	Metalworking T&E	209
Shears, Thinning	Hair Care Objects	118
Sheath	Armament Accessories	268
sheath (*use:* Dress, Sheath)	Main Garments	95
Sheath, Ax	Woodworking T&E	258
Sheath, Kitchen Knife	Food Preparation Accessories	152
Sheath, Knitting	Textile Manufacturing Equipment	243
Sheath, Marlinespike	Needleworking Equipment	237
Sheath, Penis	Main Garments	97
Sheath, Tool	Multiple Use T&E for Materials	226
Sheave, Winding	Mechanical Devices	316
Shed	Outbuildings	38
Shed, Cattle	Agricultural Structures	24
Shed, Livestock	Agricultural Structures	23
Shed, Sheep	Agricultural Structures	24
sheet (*use:* Bedsheet)	Bedding	43
Sheet	Water Transportation Accessories	439
Sheet, Blanket	Bedding	43
Sheet, Cookie	Cooking Vessels	150
Sheet, Dryer	Laundry Equipment	314
Sheet, Fitted	Bedding	43
Sheet, Flat	Bedding	43
sheet, ground (*use:* Cloth, Ground)	Bedding	44
Sheet, Instruction	Instructional Documents	475
Sheet, Plate Backing	Graphic Equipment	384
Sheet, Pledge	Other Documents	485
Sheet, Song	Literary Works	477
sheet, tally (*use:* Checklist)	Other Documents	483
sheet, tally (*use:* Scorecard)	Other Documents	482
sheet, tear (*use:* Tearsheet)	Other Documents	483
sheet, time (*use:* Timesheet)	Financial Records	469
sheet, winter (*use:* Sheet, Blanket)	Bedding	43
Shelf	Support Furniture	55
Shelf, Corner	Support Furniture	55
Shelf, Display	Merchandising T&E	337
Shell	Watercraft	444
Shell, Armament	Ammunition	264
Shell, Artillery	Ammunition	264
Shell, Band	Cultural & Recreational Structures	29
shell, baptismal (*use:* Dish, Baptismal)	Religious Objects	462
Shell, Bat	Sports Equipment	513
Shell, Mortar	Ammunition	264
Shell, Shotgun	Ammunition	264
shell, sugar (*use:* Spoon, Sugar)	Serving Utensils	185
Sheller	Harvesting Equipment	131
Sheller, Bean	Harvesting Equipment	131
Sheller, Corn	Harvesting Equipment	131
Sheller, Nut	Food Preparation Equipment	160
sheller, pea (*use:* Huller, Seed)	Food Processing Equipment	164
Shellwork	Art	454
Shelter, Animal	Institutional Structures	37
Shelter, Bomb	Defense Structures	31
Shelter, Bus	Transportation Structures	40
Shelter, Gun	Defense Structures	31
Sherd	Unclassifiable Objects	527
Sherd, Base	Unclassifiable Objects	527
Sherd, Body	Unclassifiable Objects	527
Sherd, Rim	Unclassifiable Objects	527
Shield	Body Armor	275
Shield, Dress	Clothing Accessories	86
Shield, Erasing	Drafting T&E	367
Shield, Heat	Aerospace Transportation Accessories	410
Shield, Insignia	Status Symbols	497
Shield, Magnetic	Electrical & Magnetic Measurement Devices	298
Shield, Mining	Mining & Mineral Harvesting T&E	224
Shield, Solar	Other Energy Production T&E	306
Shield, X-Ray	Medical Accessories	326
shift (*use:* Chemise)	Underwear	103
Shillelagh	Percussive Weapons	283
Shilling	Exchange Media	488
Shingle	Surface Elements	19
Shingle, Asphalt	Surface Elements	19
Shingle, Fish Scale	Surface Elements	19
Shingle, Shake	Surface Elements	19
Ship	Watercraft	444
ship in a bottle (*use:* Bottle, Impossible)	Art	454
Ship, Clipper	Watercraft	446

Ship, Container	Watercraft	446
Ship, Cruise	Watercraft	446
Ship, Factory	Watercraft	445
Ship, Hospital	Watercraft	447
ship, landing (*use:* Craft, Landing)	Watercraft	447
Ship, Packet	Watercraft	446
Ship, Sailing	Watercraft	444
Ship, Training	Watercraft	444
ship, whaling (*use:* Whaler)	Watercraft	445
Shirt	Main Garments	97
Shirt of Mail	Body Armor	276
Shirt, Aloha	Main Garments	98
Shirt, Dress	Main Garments	98
shirt, Hawaiian (*use:* Shirt, Aloha)	Main Garments	98
Shirt, Maternity	Main Garments	98
Shirt, Polo	Main Garments	98
Shirt, Scrub	Protective Wear	102
Shirt, Shell	Main Garments	98
Shirt, Shooter's	Main Garments	98
shirt, T (*use:* T-Shirt)	Main Garments	98
Shirtwaist	Main Garments	98
shiv (*use:* Knife, Weapon)	Edged Weapons	277
Shocker, Corn	Harvesting Equipment	131
Shocker, Grain	Harvesting Equipment	131
Shoe	Footwear	90
shoe (*use:* Shoe, Card)	Game Equipment	502
Shoe, Animal	Farrier Equipment	139
shoe, ballet (*use:* Slipper, Ballet)	Footwear	90
Shoe, Baseball	Sports Equipment	513
Shoe, Basketball	Sports Equipment	513
Shoe, Bathing	Footwear	90
Shoe, Bowling	Sports Equipment	513
Shoe, Brogan	Footwear	90
Shoe, Card	Game Equipment	502
Shoe, Clown	Footwear	90
Shoe, Deck	Footwear	90
Shoe, Diving	Recreational Devices	511
Shoe, Football	Sports Equipment	515
Shoe, Golf	Sports Equipment	516
shoe, gunny (*use:* Sack, Gunny)	Containers	414
shoe, ox (*use:* Oxshoe)	Farrier Equipment	139
Shoe, Platform	Footwear	90
Shoe, Pump	Footwear	90
Shoe, Saddle	Footwear	90
Shoe, Sport	Footwear	90
Shoe, Tap	Footwear	90
Shoe, Tennis	Sports Equipment	518
Shoe, Third Rail	Rail Transportation Accessories	431
Shoe, Toe	Footwear	90
Shoe, Track	Sports Equipment	519
Shoe, Trigger	Armament Accessories	271
Shoehorn	Personal Assistive Objects	109
Shoelace	Clothing Accessories	86
Shofar	Religious Objects	464
Shop	Commercial Structures	27
shop, blacksmith (*use:* Smithy)	Industrial Structures	36
Shop, Butcher	Commercial Structures	27
Shop, Cabinetmaking	Industrial Structures	36
Shop, Florist	Commercial Structures	27
Shop, Machine	Industrial Structures	36
Shop, Pet	Commercial Structures	28
Shop, Print	Commercial Structures	28
Shop, Repair	Commercial Structures	27
Shop, Wheelwright	Industrial Structures	36
Shorts	Main Garments	98
Shorts, Athletic	Main Garments	98
Shorts, Bermuda	Main Garments	98
Shorts, Boxer	Underwear	104
shorts, gym (*use:* Shorts, Athletic)	Main Garments	98
Shorts, Hockey	Sports Equipment	516
Shorts, Jockey	Underwear	104
Shorts, Short	Main Garments	98
Shorts, Sliding	Sports Equipment	513
Shot	Ammunition	264
Shot, Bar	Ammunition	265
Shot, BB	Ammunition	265
shot, canister (*use:* Shot, Case)	Ammunition	265
Shot, Case	Ammunition	265
Shot, Chain	Ammunition	265
Shot, Solid	Ammunition	265
Shotgun	Firearms	282
Shotgun, Cartridge	Firearms	282
Shotgun, Double-Barrel	Firearms	282
Shotgun, Flintlock	Firearms	282
Shotgun, Multi-Barrel	Firearms	282
Shotgun, Percussion	Firearms	282
Shotgun, Repeating	Firearms	282
Shotgun, Single-Barrel	Firearms	282
Shotgun, Skeet	Firearms	282
Shotgun, Trap	Firearms	282
Shotput	Sports Equipment	519
Shovel	Construction T&E	296
Shovel, Blacksmith's	Metalworking T&E	216
Shovel, Coal	Heating Equipment Accessories	77
Shovel, Fireplace	Heating Equipment Accessories	76
Shovel, Grain	Harvesting Equipment	131
Shovel, Incense	Religious Objects	465
Shovel, Mining	Mining & Mineral Harvesting T&E	224
shovel, potato (*use:* Fork, Vegetable Scoop)	Harvesting Equipment	128
Shovel, Power	Construction T&E	295
Shovel, Snow	Groundskeeping Equipment	309

Term	Category	Page
Shovel, Steam	Construction T&E	295
Shovel, Stove	Heating Equipment Accessories	77
shovel, sugar (*use:* Scoop, Sugar)	Serving Utensils	185
Shovel, Toy	Toys	522
showcase (*use:* Case, Display)	Merchandising T&E	336
Shower	Plumbing & Drainage Elements	12
Shrank	Storage & Display Furniture	54
Shrapnel	Ammunition	265
Shredder, Bark	Forestry T&E	191
Shredder, Flail	Harvesting Equipment	131
Shredder, Paper	Writing Accessories	405
shredder, stalk (*use:* Cutter, Stalk)	Cultivation Equipment	123
Shrine	Ceremonial Structures	25
shrinker, tire (*use:* Upsetter, Tire)	Metalworking T&E	218
Shroud	Water Transportation Accessories	439
Shroud, Burial	Funerary Objects	457
shroud, chimney (*use:* Hood, Chimney)	Environmental Control Elements	8
Shrug	Main Garments	98
Shuffler, Card	Game Equipment	502
Shunt, Electrical	Electrical System Components	301
Shunt, Medical	Medical Instruments	334
Shutter, Camera	Camera Equipment	377
Shutter, Deadlight	Water Transportation Accessories	439
Shutter, Exterior	Door & Window Elements	7
Shutter, Interior	Window & Door Coverings	79
Shutter, Louvered	Door & Window Elements	7
Shuttle	Textile Manufacturing Equipment	243
Shuttle, Netting	Textile Manufacturing Equipment	243
Shuttle, Space	Spacecraft	413
Shuttle, Tatting	Textile Manufacturing Equipment	243
Shuttle, Weaving	Textile Manufacturing Equipment	244
Shuttlecock	Sports Equipment	512
Sickle	Harvesting Equipment	129
sickle, grass (*use:* Hook, Grass)	Groundskeeping Equipment	309
siddur (*use:* Book, Prayer)	Religious Objects	465
Sideboard	Storage & Display Furniture	54
Sidecar, Motorcycle	Motor Vehicles	428
Sidelight	Door & Window Elements	7
Siderail	Sleeping & Reclining Furniture	50
Sideroscope	Electrical & Magnetic Measurement Devices	298
Siderostat	Astronomical T&E	285
Sidesaddle	Land Transportation Accessories	421
Sidewalk	Site Features	22
Sidewalk, Moving	Conveyance Devices	5
side-wheeler (*use:* Steamer, Paddle)	Watercraft	445
Siding	Surface Elements	18
Siding, Asphalt	Surface Elements	18
Siding, Board and Batten	Surface Elements	18
Siding, Clapboard	Surface Elements	18
Siding, Shiplap	Surface Elements	18
Siding, Vinyl	Surface Elements	18
Sieve	Food Preparation Equipment	162
sieve, compost (*use:* Sifter, Compost)	Tending Equipment	133
sieve, grain (*use:* Riddle, Grain)	Harvesting Equipment	131
Sieve, Hair	Food Preparation Equipment	162
sieve, soil (*use:* Sifter, Soil)	Cultivation Equipment	125
sieve, winnowing (*use:* Riddle, Grain)	Harvesting Equipment	131
Sifter	Food Preparation Equipment	162
Sifter, Ash	Housekeeping Equipment	312
Sifter, Compost	Tending Equipment	133
Sifter, Flour	Food Preparation Equipment	162
Sifter, Soil	Cultivation Equipment	125
Sight	Armament Accessories	271
Sight, Globe	Armament Accessories	271
Sight, Micrometer	Armament Accessories	271
Sight, Military	Armament Accessories	271
Sight, Tang	Armament Accessories	271
Sight, Telescope	Armament Accessories	271
Sight, Vernier	Armament Accessories	271
Sight, Windgauge	Armament Accessories	271
Sign	Visual Communication Devices	401
Sign, Advertising	Advertising Media	450
Sign, Directional	Visual Communication Devices	401
Sign, Identification	Visual Communication Devices	401
Sign, Informational	Visual Communication Devices	401
Sign, Instructional	Visual Communication Devices	401
Sign, Nautical	Water Transportation Accessories	440
Sign, Picket	Advertising Media	450
Sign, Regulatory	Visual Communication Devices	401
sign, shop (*use:* Sign, Trade)	Advertising Media	451

Sign, Trade — Advertising Media 451
Sign, Traffic — Visual Communication Devices 401
Sign, Yard — Advertising Media 451
Signal, Railroad — Visual Communication Devices 400
Signal, Traffic — Visual Communication Devices 400
Signboard — Visual Communication Devices 401
signet (*use:* Ring, Signet) — Personal Identification 495
Silencer — Armament Accessories 271
Silhouette — Art 455
Silk, Tobacco — Advertising Media 450
silkscreen (*use:* Print, Screen) — Graphic Documents 474
Silkscreen — Graphic Equipment 384
sill, door (*use:* Doorsill) — Door & Window Elements 6
Sill, Window — Door & Window Elements 7
Silo — Agricultural Structures 24
Silverer, Pill — Medical Accessories 326
Simulator — Data Processing Devices 362
Simulator, Air Flight — Aerospace Transportation Accessories 410
Simulator, Flight — Aerospace Transportation Accessories 410
Simulator, Sound Effect — Sound Communication Devices 392
Simulator, Space Flight — Aerospace Transportation Accessories 410
Singlet — Underwear 104
Singlet, Wrestling — Main Garments 96
Singletree — Land Transportation Accessories 419
Sink — Plumbing & Drainage Elements 12
Sink, Bathroom — Plumbing & Drainage Elements 12
Sink, Curd — Food Processing Equipment 167
Sink, Dry — Storage & Display Furniture 53
Sink, Kitchen — Plumbing & Drainage Elements 12
Sink, Pedestal — Plumbing & Drainage Elements 12
Sink, Slop — Plumbing & Drainage Elements 12
Sinker — Fishing Equipment 147
sinker, net (*use:* Weight, Net) — Fishing Equipment 147
sinker, net (*use:* Weight, Net) — Fishing Equipment 147
Siphon — Labware 294
siphon, soda (*use:* Bottle, Seltzer) — Serving Vessels 188
Siren — Sound Communication Devices 391
siren, fire (*use:* Alarm, Fire) — Protective Devices 345
Sitar — Musical Instruments 374
sith (*use:* Scythe, Flemish) — Harvesting Equipment 130
Sixpence — Exchange Media 488
sizer, potato (*use:* Sorter, Potato) — Food Processing Equipment 164
Skate, Ice — Sports Equipment 517
Skate, Inline — Sports Equipment 517
Skate, Roller — Sports Equipment 517
Skateboard — Sports Equipment 517
skeeter (*use:* Iceboat) — Watercraft 443
Skeiner — Textile Manufacturing Equipment 245
Skep, Bee — Animal Care Equipment 136
Sketch — Art 455
Sketchbook — Painting T&E 230
Skewer — Food Preparation Equipment 157
Skewer, Butchering — Food Processing Equipment 165
Ski, Aircraft — Aerospace Transportation Accessories 410
Ski, Cross-Country — Sports Equipment 517
Ski, Downhill — Sports Equipment 517
Ski, Jet — Watercraft 444
Ski, Snow — Sports Equipment 517
Ski, Water — Recreational Devices 511
Skid — Papermaking T&E 233
skife (*use:* Beveler, Safety) — Leather, Horn & Shellworking T&E 197
Skiff — Watercraft 443
skiff, Chesapeake Bay (*use:* Skiff, Crabbing) — Watercraft 445
Skiff, Crabbing — Watercraft 445
Skiff, Flatiron — Watercraft 443
skiff, gunning (*use:* Boat, Gunning) — Watercraft 442
skiff, oyster (*use:* Boat, Tonging) — Watercraft 445
skiff, oyster (*use:* Vessel, Dredging) — Watercraft 445
skiff, pole (*use:* Skiff, Rail) — Watercraft 442
skiff, push (*use:* Skiff, Rail) — Watercraft 442
Skiff, Rail — Watercraft 442
skiff, Seabright (*use:* Skiff) — Watercraft 443
Skiff, St. Lawrence River — Watercraft 444
skiff, Yankee (*use:* Skiff) — Watercraft 443
skillet (*use:* Pan, Frying) — Cooking Vessels 151
skillet (*use:* Spider) — Cooking Vessels 151
Skimmer — Metalworking T&E 216
Skimmer, Cream — Food Processing Equipment 167
skimmer, ice (*use:* Strainer, Ice) — Fishing Equipment 147
Skimmer, Kitchen — Food Preparation Equipment 162
Skimmer, Molasses — Food Processing Equipment 164
Skimmer, Syrup — Food Processing Equipment 169

Skimmer, Whale Oil | Fishing Equipment | 148
Skimmer, Wok | Food Preparation Equipment | 161
skin, speedskating (*use:* Suit, Speedskating) | Sports Equipment | 517
Skip | Mining & Mineral Harvesting T&E | 224
Skipjack | Watercraft | 445
Skirt | Main Garments | 98
Skirt, Bell | Main Garments | 98
Skirt, Bubble | Main Garments | 98
Skirt, Circular | Main Garments | 98
Skirt, Harem | Main Garments | 98
Skirt, Hobble | Main Garments | 98
Skirt, Hoop | Main Garments | 98
Skirt, Hula | Main Garments | 98
Skirt, Peg-Top | Main Garments | 98
Skirt, Pencil | Main Garments | 98
Skirt, Poodle | Main Garments | 98
Skirt, Riding | Main Garments | 98
Skirt, Trumpet | Main Garments | 98
Skirt, Umbrella | Main Garments | 99
Skirt, Walking | Main Garments | 99
Skirt, Wrap | Main Garments | 99
Skullcap | Headwear | 92
Skybridge | Transportation Structures | 39
Skylight | Door & Window Elements | 7
Slab, Candy Making | Food Preparation Equipment | 157
Slab, Cooking | Food Preparation Equipment | 155
Slab, Dental Mixing | Dental Accessories | 321
Slab, Graphite | Glass, Plastics & Clayworking T&E | 194
slab, grave (*use:* Slab, Tomb) | Funerary Objects | 457
Slab, Grinding | Multiple Use T&E for Materials | 228
Slab, Tomb | Funerary Objects | 457
Slacks | Main Garments | 97
Slapper, Livestock | Animal Care Equipment | 137
Slasher | Textile Manufacturing Equipment | 244
Slat, Bed | Sleeping & Reclining Furniture | 50
Slate, Braille | Writing Devices | 406
Slate, Roofing | Surface Elements | 19
Slate, Writing | Writing Media | 408
Slaver | Watercraft | 446
Sled | Recreational Devices | 509
Sled, Artillery | Armament Accessories | 272
Sled, Dog Racing | Sports Equipment | 512
Sled, Log | Animal-Powered Vehicles | 424
Sled, Rocket | Rail Vehicles | 434
Sled, Skeleton | Sports Equipment | 518
Sled, Water | Recreational Devices | 511
Sledge | Animal-Powered Vehicles | 424
sledge (*use:* Sledgehammer) | Metalworking T&E | 212
Sledge, Cross-Peen | Metalworking T&E | 212
Sledge, Double-Face | Metalworking T&E | 212
Sledge, Shoe-Turning | Metalworking T&E | 212
Sledge, Straight-Peen | Metalworking T&E | 212
Sledgehammer | Metalworking T&E | 212
Sleeper | Dressingwear & Nightwear | 88
Sleeve | Clothing Accessories | 86
Sleeve, Disk | Data Processing Accessories | 360
Sleeve, Gunner's | Armament Accessories | 272
Sleeve, Record | Sound Communication Accessories | 389
Sleigh | Animal-Powered Vehicles | 424
Sleigh, Runabout | Animal-Powered Vehicles | 424
Sleigh, Surrey | Animal-Powered Vehicles | 424
Slice, Fish | Serving Utensils | 185
Slicer, Cheese | Food Preparation Equipment | 159
Slicer, Ear Corn | Harvesting Equipment | 131
Slicer, Egg | Food Preparation Equipment | 159
Slicer, Food | Food Preparation Equipment | 159
Slicer, Fruit | Food Preparation Equipment | 159
Slicer, Mandoline | Food Preparation Equipment | 159
Slicer, Meat | Food Preparation Equipment | 159
Slicer, Vegetable | Food Preparation Equipment | 159
Slick | Woodworking T&E | 249
Slicker | Outerwear | 101
Slicker, Edge | Leather, Horn & Shellworking T&E | 200
slide (*use:* Transparency, Lantern Slide) | Graphic Documents | 473
slide (*use:* Transparency, Slide) | Graphic Documents | 473
Slide | Recreational Devices | 510
Slide, Bolo | Clothing Accessories | 87
Slide, Guitar | Musical Accessories | 369
slide, lantern (*use:* Transparency, Lantern Slide) | Graphic Documents | 473
Slide, Microscope | Biological T&E | 287
Slide, Scarf | Clothing Accessories | 87
Slide, Water | Recreational Devices | 511
Sling | Percussive Weapons | 283
Sling, Arm | Personal Assistive Objects | 109
sling, flag (*use:* Belt, Flag) | Organizational Objects | 459
sling, grain (*use:* Sling, Hay) | Harvesting Equipment | 131
Sling, Hay | Harvesting Equipment | 131
Sling, Hoist | Mechanical Devices | 316

Sling, Infant | Human-Powered Vehicles | 426
Slingback | Footwear | 90
Slingshot | Percussive Weapons | 283
Slinky | Toys | 524
Slip | Underwear | 104
Slip, Bank | Exchange Media | 489
slip, building (*use:* Slipway) | Transportation Structures | 40
Slip, Call | Other Documents | 483
Slip, Deposit | Exchange Media | 489
Slip, Full | Underwear | 104
Slip, Half | Underwear | 104
Slip, Packing | Administrative Records | 467
slip, pillow (*use:* Pillowcase) | Bedding | 44
Slip, Withdrawal | Exchange Media | 489
Slipcase | Writing Accessories | 403
Slipcase, Book | Other Documents | 482
Slipcover | Furniture Coverings | 61
Slipper | Footwear | 90
Slipper, Ballet | Footwear | 90
Slipper, Bathing | Footwear | 90
Slipper, Bedroom | Footwear | 90
Slipway | Transportation Structures | 40
Slitter, Crown | Dental Instruments | 324
Slitter, Paper | Papermaking T&E | 232
Slitter, Teat | Veterinary Equipment | 142
Sloop | Watercraft | 443
Sloop, Fishing | Watercraft | 445
Sloop, Friendship | Watercraft | 445
Sloop, Noank | Watercraft | 445
Sloop-of-War | Watercraft | 447
Slot, Mail | Finish Hardware | 11
slubber (*use:* Billy, Slubbing) | Textile Manufacturing Equipment | 239
Slug | Exchange Media | 487
Slug, Type | Typesetting Equipment | 388
Sluice | Hydraulic Structures | 34
Slusher | Mining & Mineral Harvesting T&E | 224
Smallsword | Edged Weapons | 279
Smartphone | Data Processing Devices | 362
smasher, atom (*use:* Accelerator, Particle) | Nuclear Physics T&E | 341
Smelter | Industrial Structures | 35
Smithy | Industrial Structures | 36
Smock | Protective Wear | 102
Smokehouse | Outbuildings | 38
Smokejack | Food Preparation Equipment | 163
Smoker | Containers for Smoking & Tobacco | 59
Smoker, Bee | Animal Care Equipment | 136
Smoker, Fish | Food Preparation Equipment | 157
Smoker, Food | Food Preparation Equipment | 157
Smoker, Meat | Food Preparation Equipment | 157
Smokestack | Environmental Control Elements | 8
Smoother | Leather, Horn & Shellworking T&E | 200
Smoother, Bed | Housekeeping Equipment | 312
Smoother, Linen | Textile Manufacturing Equipment | 244
Smoother, Wallpaper | Painting T&E | 231
Smutter | Food Processing Equipment | 168
Snap | Needleworking Equipment | 236
Snapper, Corn | Harvesting Equipment | 129
Snapsetter | Needleworking Equipment | 237
Snapshot | Graphic Documents | 473
Snare | Trapping Equipment | 149
Snare, Surgical | Medical Instruments | 332
Sneakbox | Watercraft | 442
Sneaker | Footwear | 90
Snifter | Drinking Vessels | 174
Snip, Pineapple | Food Preparation Equipment | 159
Snip, Sheet Metal | Metalworking T&E | 209
Snip, Tin | Metalworking T&E | 209
Snood | Headwear | 92
Snore | Mining & Mineral Harvesting T&E | 224
snorkel (*use:* Truck, Boom) | Motor Vehicles | 429
Snorkel | Recreational Devices | 511
Snowblower | Groundskeeping Equipment | 310
Snowboard | Sports Equipment | 518
snowglobe (*use:* Globe, Snow) | Decorative Furnishings | 60
Snowmobile | Motor Vehicles | 430
snowplow (*use:* Blade, Snow) | Land Transportation Accessories | 416
Snowplow | Motor Vehicles | 429
Snowplow, Horse-Drawn | Animal-Powered Vehicles | 424
Snowshed | Transportation Structures | 40
Snowshoe | Human-Powered Vehicles | 427
Snowsuit | Outerwear | 101
Snuff | Smoking & Recreational Drug Equipment | 115
Snuffbox | Smoking & Recreational Drug Equipment | 114
snuffer, candle (*use:* Candlesnuffer) | Other Lighting Accessories | 72
Soap | Hygiene Objects | 121
Soap, Laundry | Laundry Equipment | 314
Sociable | Animal-Powered Vehicles | 424
sociable (*use:* Bicycle, Side-By-Side) | Human-Powered Vehicles | 426
sociable (*use:* Tricycle, Side-By-Side) | Human-Powered Vehicles | 426
Sock | Footwear | 89
Sock, Ankle | Footwear | 89

Term	Category	Page
Sock, Knee	Footwear	89
Sock, Sport	Footwear	89
Sock, Water	Footwear	89
Sock, Wind	Meteorological T&E	339
Socket	Metalworking T&E	216
Socket, Rope	Mining & Mineral Harvesting T&E	224
Socket, Tube	Electrical System Components	301
socket, wall (*use:* Outlet, Electrical)	Electrical System Components	301
socket, whip (*use:* Holder, Whip)	Land Transportation Accessories	418
Sofa	Seating Furniture	49
Sofa, Chesterfield	Seating Furniture	49
Sofa, Conversational	Seating Furniture	49
Sofa, Sectional	Seating Furniture	49
sofa, sleeper (*use:* Bed, Sofa)	Seating Furniture	49
Softball	Sports Equipment	512
Software	Data Processing Accessories	360
software, antiviral (*use:* Software, Security)	Data Processing Accessories	360
Software, Browser	Data Processing Accessories	360
Software, Database	Data Processing Accessories	360
Software, Diagnostic	Data Processing Accessories	360
Software, Email	Data Processing Accessories	360
software, firewall (*use:* Software, Security)	Data Processing Accessories	360
Software, Gaming	Data Processing Accessories	360
Software, Graphics	Data Processing Accessories	360
Software, Multifunction System	Data Processing Accessories	360
Software, Operating System	Data Processing Accessories	360
Software, Security	Data Processing Accessories	360
Software, Specialty	Data Processing Accessories	360
Software, Spreadsheet	Data Processing Accessories	360
software, suite (*use:* Software, Multifunction)	Data Processing Accessories	360
Software, Utility	Data Processing Accessories	360
Software, Word Processing	Data Processing Accessories	360
Solander	Writing Accessories	403
Soldier, Toy	Toys	521
Solenoid	Electrical System Components	301
Solophone	Musical Instruments	374
Sombrero	Headwear	93
Sondograph	Navigational Equipment	349
Songbook	Literary Works	477
Sonometer	Acoustical T&E	262
Sorter, Apple	Food Processing Equipment	164
Sorter, Bean	Food Processing Equipment	164
Sorter, Card	Data Processing Accessories	360
Sorter, Cranberry	Food Processing Equipment	164
Sorter, Food	Food Processing Equipment	164
sorter, mail (*use:* Cabinet, Mail Sorting)	Storage & Display Furniture	52
Sorter, Mail	Writing Accessories	404
sorter, pea (*use:* Sorter, Bean)	Food Processing Equipment	164
Sorter, Potato	Food Processing Equipment	164
Sorter, Wire	Electrical Maintenance & Repair Equipment	299
Sound	Medical Instruments	328
soundboard (*use:* Board, Sounding)	Sound Communication Accessories	389
soundboard (*use:* Mixer, Audio)	Sound Communication Devices	392
Sounder, Telegraph	Telecommunication Devices	396
Sous Marqué	Exchange Media	488
Sousaphone	Musical Instruments	370
Souvenir	Memorabilia	478
Sovereign	Exchange Media	489
sower, broadcast (*use:* Broadcaster)	Planting Equipment	132
sower, seedbox (*use:* Seeder, Seedbox)	Planting Equipment	132
spa, home (*use:* Tub, Hot)	Plumbing & Drainage Elements	12
Spacecraft, Manned	Spacecraft	413
Spacecraft, Unmanned	Spacecraft	413
Spaceprobe	Spacecraft	413
Spacer, Kiln	Glass, Plastics & Clayworking T&E	193
Spade	Cultivation Equipment	125
Spade, Blubber	Fishing Equipment	148
Spade, Boat	Fishing Equipment	148
Spade, Bone	Fishing Equipment	148
spade, butter-working (*use:* Paddle, Butter)	Food Processing Equipment	166
Spade, Ditching	Cultivation Equipment	125
Spade, Drain	Cultivation Equipment	125
spade, folding (*use:* Tool, Entrenching)	Construction T&E	296
spade, folding (*use:* Tool, Entrenching)	Construction T&E	296
Spade, Garden	Cultivation Equipment	125
Spade, Gouge	Fishing Equipment	148
Spade, Grafting	Mining & Mineral Harvesting T&E	224
Spade, Hay	Harvesting Equipment	129
Spade, Head	Fishing Equipment	148
Spade, Peat	Cultivation Equipment	125
Spade, Tree	Forestry T&E	191
spade, turf (*use:* Lifter, Sod)	Groundskeeping Equipment	309
Spade, Whaling	Fishing Equipment	148
Spall	Unclassifiable Objects	527
spangle (*use:* Sequin)	Needleworking Equipment	237

Spanker | Water Transportation Accessories | 439
spanner (*use:* Wrench) | Metalworking T&E | 219
Spar | Water Transportation Accessories | 440
Sparkler | Public Entertainment Devices | 507
Sparkplug | Power Transmission Components | 305
Sparver | Bedding | 44
Spat | Footwear | 89
Spatula, Artist's | Painting T&E | 230
Spatula, Dental | Dental Instruments | 324
Spatula, Kiln | Glass, Plastics & Clayworking T&E | 194
Spatula, Kitchen | Food Preparation Equipment | 161
Spatula, Offset | Food Preparation Equipment | 161
Spatula, Plasterer's | Masonry & Stoneworking T&E | 205
Spatula, Surgical | Medical Instruments | 332
Spatula, Wok | Food Preparation Equipment | 161
Spaudler | Body Armor | 275
Speaker | Sound Communication Devices | 392
Speaker, Jukebox | Sound Communication Devices | 392
Spear | Edged Weapons | 278
Spear, Eel | Edged Weapons | 278
Spear, Fish | Edged Weapons | 278
Spear, Hunting | Edged Weapons | 278
Spear, Muskrat | Edged Weapons | 278
Spear, Squid | Edged Weapons | 278
Spear, Tobacco | Harvesting Equipment | 131
spearhead (*use:* Point, Spear) | Edged Weapons | 278
Specification | Other Documents | 486
Specimen, Animal | Biological T&E | 286
specimen, biological (*use:* Biospecimen) | Biological T&E | 286
specimen, geological (*use:* Geospecimen) | Geological T&E | 307
Specimen, Plant | Biological T&E | 286
Spectacles | Personal Assistive Objects | 108
Spectrogram, Sound | Acoustical T&E | 262
Spectrograph | Optical T&E | 344
Spectrograph, Mass | Nuclear Physics T&E | 342
Spectrograph, Sound | Acoustical T&E | 262
Spectroheliograph | Astronomical T&E | 285
Spectrometer | Optical T&E | 344
Spectrometer, Mass | Nuclear Physics T&E | 342
Spectrophotometer | Optical T&E | 344
Spectroscope | Optical T&E | 344
Spectroscope, Mass | Nuclear Physics T&E | 342
Speculum | Medical Instruments | 328
Speculum, Animal | Veterinary Equipment | 142
Speculum, Ear | Medical Instruments | 328
Speculum, Nasal | Medical Instruments | 330
Speculum, Vaginal | Medical Instruments | 330
Speech | Literary Works | 477
Speedboat | Watercraft | 443
Speeder | Rail Vehicles | 434
Speedometer | Mechanical Measurement Equipment | 318
Sphere, Armillary | Astronomical T&E | 284
Sphere, Garden | Site Features | 21
Spherograph | Navigational Equipment | 351
Spherometer | Weights & Measures T&E | 358
Spheroscope | Astronomical T&E | 285
Sphygmomanometer | Medical Instruments | 327
Spider | Cooking Vessels | 151
Spider, Burner | Labware | 294
Spife | Eating & Drinking Utensils | 178
Spigot | Food Service Accessories | 182
spigot (*use:* Faucet) | Plumbing & Drainage Elements | 12
Spike | Multiple Use T&E for Materials | 227
Spike, Barge | Woodworking T&E | 250
Spike, Cannon | Armament Accessories | 272
Spike, Gutter | Plumbing & Drainage Elements | 13
Spike, Rail | Rail Transportation Accessories | 432
Spike, Tree Climbing | Forestry T&E | 191
Spiker, Railway | Rail Vehicles | 434
spile (*use:* Spout, Sap) | Food Processing Equipment | 169
Spill | Firemaking Equipment | 74
spillikin (*use:* Stick, Pick-up) | Game Equipment | 504
Spillway | Hydraulic Structures | 34
Spindle | Textile Manufacturing Equipment | 244
Spindle, Paper | Writing Accessories | 405
Spindle, Ropemaking | Textile Manufacturing Equipment | 244
Spinet | Musical Instruments | 371
Spinnaker | Water Transportation Accessories | 439
Spinner, Game | Game Equipment | 502
Spinner, Salad | Food Preparation Equipment | 157
Spinnerbait | Fishing Equipment | 147
Spinneret | Textile Manufacturing Equipment | 244
Spinthariscope | Chemical Testing Devices | 291
Spire | Roof Elements | 14
Spirograph | Medical Instruments | 327
Spirometer | Medical Instruments | 327
Spit | Food Preparation Equipment | 163
Spit, Basket | Food Preparation Equipment | 163

Spit, Bird Food Preparation Equipment 163
Spit, Dangle Food Preparation Equipment 163
Spittoon Containers for Smoking & Tobacco 59
Splicer, Film Photographic Accessories 379
Splint Medical Instruments 334
Splint, Jaw Medical Instruments 334
Splint, Lighting Other Lighting Accessories 73
Splint, Thomas Medical Instruments 334
Splitter, Bond Fiberworking T&E 144
Splitter, Pill Personal Assistive Objects 109
Splitter, Sample Mining & Mineral Harvesting T&E 224
Splitter, Signal Telecommunication Accessories 395
Spokeshave Woodworking T&E 253
Spokeshave, Leather Leather, Horn & Shellworking T&E 197
Sponge Housekeeping Equipment 312
Sponge, Artillery Armament Accessories 272
Sponge, Bath Hygiene Objects 121
Sponge, Contraceptive Hygiene Objects 121
Sponge, Cosmetic Beauty Supplies 116
Sponge, Dish Dishwashing Equipment 308
Sponge, Paint Painting T&E 230
Sponge, Surgical Medical Instruments 332
Spontoon Edged Weapons 278
Spool Containers 415
spool, ear (*use:* Earspool) Body Adornments 81
Spool, Sewing Needleworking Equipment 237
Spooler Textile Manufacturing Equipment 245
Spoon, Baby Eating & Drinking Utensils 179
spoon, bar (*use:* Barspoon) Food Preparation Equipment 161
Spoon, Basting Food Preparation Equipment 157
Spoon, Berry Serving Utensils 185
Spoon, Blacksmith's Metalworking T&E 216
Spoon, Bonbon Serving Utensils 185
Spoon, Bouillon Eating & Drinking Utensils 179
Spoon, Caddy Serving Utensils 185
Spoon, Cereal Eating & Drinking Utensils 178
Spoon, Chocolate Eating & Drinking Utensils 178
Spoon, Claret Serving Utensils 185
Spoon, Cocaine Smoking & Recreational Drug Equipment 115
Spoon, Coffee Eating & Drinking Utensils 178
Spoon, Communion Religious Objects 462
Spoon, Cream Eating & Drinking Utensils 179
Spoon, Demitasse Eating & Drinking Utensils 178
Spoon, Dessert Eating & Drinking Utensils 179
Spoon, Ear Wax Hygiene Objects 121
Spoon, Eating Eating & Drinking Utensils 178
Spoon, Egg Eating & Drinking Utensils 179
Spoon, Feeding Eating & Drinking Utensils 179
Spoon, Folding Eating & Drinking Utensils 179
Spoon, Fruit Eating & Drinking Utensils 179
Spoon, Grapefruit Eating & Drinking Utensils 179
Spoon, Ice Cream Eating & Drinking Utensils 179
Spoon, Iced Tea Eating & Drinking Utensils 179
Spoon, Incense Religious Objects 465
Spoon, Jam Serving Utensils 185
Spoon, Lemonade Eating & Drinking Utensils 179
Spoon, Marrow Eating & Drinking Utensils 179
Spoon, Measuring Food Preparation Equipment 156
Spoon, Medical Medical Accessories 326
Spoon, Miner's Mining & Mineral Harvesting T&E 224
Spoon, Mixing Food Preparation Equipment 161
Spoon, Mud Masonry & Stoneworking T&E 205
Spoon, Mustard Serving Utensils 185
Spoon, Olive Serving Utensils 185
Spoon, Orange Eating & Drinking Utensils 179
Spoon, Pap Eating & Drinking Utensils 179
Spoon, Pharmaceutical Measuring Medical Accessories 326
Spoon, Salt Serving Utensils 185
Spoon, Serving Serving Utensils 185
Spoon, Sherbet Eating & Drinking Utensils 179
Spoon, Snuff Smoking & Recreational Drug Equipment 115
Spoon, Soda Eating & Drinking Utensils 179
Spoon, Soup Eating & Drinking Utensils 179
Spoon, Souvenir Memorabilia 479
Spoon, Strainer Food Preparation Equipment 162
Spoon, Sugar Serving Utensils 185
spoon, table (*use:* Tablespoon) Serving Utensils 185
spoon, tea (*use:* Teaspoon) Eating & Drinking Utensils 179
Spooner Food Service Accessories 182
Spork Eating & Drinking Utensils 179
Sporran Personal Carrying & Storage Gear 111
Sportcoat Main Garments 95
Sportfisherman Watercraft 444
Spotlight Lighting Devices 70
spout, drain (*use:* Waterspout) Plumbing & Drainage Elements 13
Spout, Ear Medical Instruments 328
Spout, Sap Food Processing Equipment 169
Sprag Mining & Mineral Harvesting T&E 225
Sprayer Tending Equipment 133
Sprayer, Bucket Tending Equipment 133
sprayer, flame (*use:* Weeder, Flame) Cultivation Equipment 125

Sprayer, Hand	Tending Equipment	133
Sprayer, Knapsack	Tending Equipment	133
Sprayer, Power	Tending Equipment	133
Sprayer, Sink	Plumbing & Drainage Elements	13
Sprayer, Wheelbarrow	Tending Equipment	133
Spread, Summer	Bedding	43
Spreader	Water Transportation Accessories	439
Spreader, Asphalt	Construction T&E	296
Spreader, Butter	Eating & Drinking Utensils	178
Spreader, Collar	Clothing Accessories	87
Spreader, Concrete	Masonry & Stoneworking T&E	205
spreader, garden manure (*use:* Spreader, Wheelbarrow)	Tending Equipment	133
Spreader, Hydraulic	Mechanical Devices	317
Spreader, Jaw	Dental Instruments	324
Spreader, Lawn	Groundskeeping Equipment	310
Spreader, Load	Mechanical Devices	317
Spreader, Manure	Tending Equipment	133
Spreader, Mineral	Tending Equipment	133
Spreader, Paving	Construction T&E	296
spreader, shoe (*use:* Tongs, Shoe-Spreading)	Farrier Equipment	139
Spreader, Tire	Land Transportation Accessories	421
Spreader, Wheelbarrow	Tending Equipment	133
Spreadsheet	Other Documents	482
Spring	Mechanical Devices	317
Spring, Box	Bedding	43
Spring, Indicator	Mechanical Devices	317
Spring, Leaf	Land Transportation Accessories	418
Spring, Pressure	Mechanical Devices	317
Spring, Spiral	Mechanical Devices	317
Spring, Vehicle	Land Transportation Accessories	418
Springboard	Sports Equipment	516
Springer	Construction Materials	4
Springhouse	Outbuildings	38
Sprinkler	Recreational Devices	511
Sprinkler, Blacksmith's	Metalworking T&E	216
Sprinkler, Fire	Protective Devices	345
sprinkler, holy water (*use:* Aspergillum)	Religious Objects	461
Sprinkler, Irrigation	Tending Equipment	133
sprinkler, knapsack (*use:* Sprayer, Knapsack)	Tending Equipment	133
Sprinkler, Laundry	Laundry Equipment	314
Sprinkler, Lawn	Groundskeeping Equipment	310
Sprinkler, Tobacco	Other T&E for Materials	260
Sprit	Water Transportation Accessories	440
Spud	Mining & Mineral Harvesting T&E	224
spud, barking (*use:* Iron, Barking)	Forestry T&E	191
Spud, Eye	Medical Instruments	329
Spud, Weeding	Cultivation Equipment	125
Spur	Land Transportation Accessories	421
Spur, Box	Land Transportation Accessories	421
Spur, Climbing	Sports Equipment	514
Spur, Cockfighting	Sports Equipment	514
Spur, Prick	Land Transportation Accessories	421
Spur, Rowel	Land Transportation Accessories	421
spur, tree climbing (*use:* Spike, Tree Climbing)	Forestry T&E	191
Spurtle	Food Preparation Equipment	162
squails (*use:* Set, Tiddlywinks)	Game Equipment	504
Square	Woodworking T&E	258
Square, Bevel	Woodworking T&E	258
Square, Carpenter's	Woodworking T&E	258
Square, Drill Point	Woodworking T&E	258
Square, Mason's	Masonry & Stoneworking T&E	205
Square, Miter	Woodworking T&E	258
Square, Optical	Surveying Equipment	353
Square, Set	Woodworking T&E	258
Square, Sliding	Woodworking T&E	258
Square, Tailor's	Needleworking Equipment	237
square, tee (*use:* T-Square)	Drafting T&E	367
Square, Try	Woodworking T&E	258
Squeaker	Toys	524
Squeegee	Housekeeping Equipment	312
Squeegee, Silkscreen	Graphic Equipment	384
Squeezer, Curd	Food Processing Equipment	167
Squeezer, Fruit	Food Preparation Equipment	160
Squeezer, Lard	Food Preparation Equipment	160
Squib	Mining & Mineral Harvesting T&E	224
Stabilizer, Armament	Armament Accessories	272
Stable	Agricultural Structures	24
Stable, Livery	Commercial Structures	27
stacker, cable (*use:* Stacker, Hay)	Harvesting Equipment	130
stacker, derrick (*use:* Stacker, Hay)	Harvesting Equipment	130
Stacker, Diaper	Storage & Display Accessories	64
Stacker, Hay	Harvesting Equipment	130

Term	Category	Page
stacker, overshot (*use:* Stacker, Hay)	Harvesting Equipment	130
stacker, swinging (*use:* Stacker, Hay)	Harvesting Equipment	130
stacker, tripod (*use:* Stacker, Hay)	Harvesting Equipment	130
Staddle	Supporting Elements	17
Stadimeter	Surveying Equipment	353
Stadium	Cultural & Recreational Structures	30
Staff, Dance	Religious Objects	464
Staff, Ensign	Water Transportation Accessories	437
Staff, Jacob's	Surveying Equipment	353
Staff, Leading	Edged Weapons	278
staff, leveling (*use:* Rod, Leveling)	Surveying Equipment	353
staff, pastoral (*use:* Crosier)	Status Symbols	498
Staff, Station	Surveying Equipment	353
Staff, Walking	Personal Assistive Objects	109
Stage	Architectural Spaces	1
Stage, Puppet	Public Entertainment Devices	508
Stagecoach	Animal-Powered Vehicles	423
Staircase	Stair Elements	15
Staircase, Spiral	Stair Elements	15
Stairstep	Stair Elements	15
stake (*use:* Anvil, Stake)	Metalworking T&E	207
Stake, Beakhorn	Metalworking T&E	207
Stake, Blowhorn	Metalworking T&E	207
Stake, Candlemold	Metalworking T&E	207
Stake, Creasing	Metalworking T&E	207
Stake, Double-Creasing	Metalworking T&E	207
Stake, Hatchet	Metalworking T&E	207
Stake, Hollow Mandrel	Metalworking T&E	207
Stake, Impalement	Regulative Devices	347
Stake, Needle Case	Metalworking T&E	207
Stake, Planishing	Metalworking T&E	207
Stake, Seaming	Metalworking T&E	207
Stake, Slater's	Masonry & Stoneworking T&E	205
Stake, Square	Metalworking T&E	207
Stake, Survey	Surveying Equipment	353
Stake, Tent	Supporting Elements	17
Stalagmometer	Mechanical Measurement Equipment	318
Stall, Animal	Other Structures	41
Stall, Shower	Architectural Spaces	1
Stall, Toilet	Architectural Spaces	1
Stalljack	Farrier Equipment	139
Stamp	Exchange Media	489
Stamp, Address	Writing Devices	407
stamp, butter (*use:* Press, Butter)	Food Preparation Equipment	159
Stamp, Cancellation	Writing Devices	407
Stamp, Date	Writing Devices	407
Stamp, Die	Metalworking T&E	216
Stamp, Embroidery	Replication Equipment	387
Stamp, Leather	Leather, Horn & Shellworking T&E	200
Stamp, Marking	Writing Devices	407
Stamp, Message	Writing Devices	407
Stamp, Metal	Metalworking T&E	216
Stamp, Name	Writing Devices	407
Stamp, Notary	Writing Devices	407
Stamp, Numbering	Writing Devices	407
Stamp, Postage	Exchange Media	489
Stamp, Postmark	Writing Devices	407
Stamp, Ration	Exchange Media	489
Stamp, Tax	Exchange Media	489
Stamp, Telegraph	Exchange Media	489
Stamp, Trading	Exchange Media	489
stamper (*use:* Rammer, Paver's)	Construction T&E	295
stamper, multipost (*use:* Affixer, Stamp)	Writing Accessories	402
stamper, pulp (*use:* Pulper)	Papermaking T&E	232
Stanchion	Barrier Elements	2
Stanchion, Watercraft	Water Transportation Accessories	440
Stand	Storage & Display Accessories	65
Stand, Animal	Public Entertainment Devices	508
Stand, Awl	Leather, Horn & Shellworking T&E	200
Stand, Basin	Support Furniture	55
Stand, Basket	Support Furniture	55
Stand, Bellows	Heating Equipment Accessories	77
Stand, Bicycle	Land Transportation Accessories	419
Stand, Bidet	Seating Furniture	49
Stand, Birdcage	Support Furniture	55
Stand, Blacksmith's	Metalworking T&E	216
stand, book (*use:* Bookstand)	Support Furniture	55
Stand, Cabinet	Support Furniture	55
Stand, Cake	Serving Vessels	187
stand, cake (*use:* Stand, Muffin)	Support Furniture	55
stand, candle (*use:* Candlestand)	Lighting Holders	71
Stand, Carafe	Food Service Accessories	182
Stand, Card	Support Furniture	55
Stand, Cask	Food Storage Equipment	171
stand, casket (*use:* Stand, Funerary)	Funerary Objects	457
stand, casserole (*use:* Holder, Casserole)	Food Service Accessories	181
stand, Christmas tree (*use:* Holder, Tree)	Holiday Objects	458

Term	Category	Page
Stand, Churn	Food Processing Equipment	167
Stand, Cobbler's	Leather, Horn & Shellworking T&E	200
stand, coffin (*use:* Bier)	Funerary Objects	457
stand, coffin (*use:* Stand, Funerary)	Funerary Objects	457
Stand, Croquet	Game Equipment	501
Stand, Crucible	Metalworking T&E	216
Stand, Cruet	Serving Vessels	187
stand, curio (*use:* Étagère)	Storage & Display Furniture	54
Stand, Curling Iron	Hair Care Objects	119
Stand, Deer	Cultural & Recreational Structures	30
Stand, Display	Merchandising T&E	337
Stand, Doll	Toys	520
Stand, Dressing	Support Furniture	55
Stand, Drinking	Support Furniture	55
Stand, Drum	Musical Accessories	369
Stand, Egg	Serving Vessels	187
Stand, Fireset	Heating Equipment Accessories	76
stand, flag (*use:* Holder, Flagpole)	Organizational Objects	459
Stand, Floor	Support Furniture	55
Stand, Flower	Storage & Display Accessories	65
Stand, Food	Commercial Structures	27
stand, frame (*use:* Easel, Picture)	Storage & Display Accessories	65
Stand, Funerary	Funerary Objects	457
stand, gentleman's dressing (*use:* Valet)	Support Furniture	55
Stand, Globe	Support Furniture	55
Stand, Hair Care	Hair Care Objects	119
stand, hall (*use:* Hallstand)	Support Furniture	55
Stand, Ham	Serving Vessels	187
Stand, Hat	Support Furniture	55
stand, heating (*use:* Tripod, Laboratory)	Labware	294
Stand, Laboratory	Labware	294
stand, lamp (*use:* Holder, Lamp)	Lighting Holders	71
stand, last (*use:* Jack, Last)	Leather, Horn & Shellworking T&E	198
Stand, Map	Support Furniture	55
Stand, Merchant's	Commercial Structures	27
Stand, Microphone	Sound Communication Accessories	390
Stand, Mirror	Beauty Supplies	117
Stand, Missal	Religious Objects	464
Stand, Mucilage	Storage & Display Accessories	65
Stand, Muffin	Support Furniture	55
Stand, Music	Musical Accessories	369
Stand, Pedestal	Support Furniture	55
Stand, Pipe	Containers for Smoking & Tobacco	59
Stand, Plant	Support Furniture	55
Stand, Plate	Storage & Display Accessories	65
Stand, Portfolio	Support Furniture	55
Stand, Printer	Support Furniture	55
Stand, Produce	Commercial Structures	27
Stand, Rolling Pin	Food Preparation Accessories	152
Stand, Saw	Woodworking T&E	258
Stand, Sculpting	Glass, Plastics & Clayworking T&E	194
Stand, Serving	Serving Vessels	187
Stand, Shaft	Woodworking T&E	259
Stand, Shaving	Support Furniture	55
stand, shoe repair (*use:* Stand, Cobbler's)	Leather, Horn & Shellworking T&E	200
Stand, Shoeing	Farrier Equipment	139
stand, shoeshine (*use:* Chair, Shoeshine)	Seating Furniture	48
Stand, Smoking	Containers for Smoking & Tobacco	59
Stand, Spoon	Serving Vessels	187
stand, stamp (*use:* Holder, Marking Stamp)	Writing Accessories	403
Stand, Surveyor's	Surveying Equipment	353
Stand, Sweetmeat	Serving Vessels	187
Stand, Teapot	Serving Vessels	187
Stand, Television	Support Furniture	55
Stand, Ticket	Cultural & Recreational Structures	29
Stand, Tiered	Support Furniture	55
Stand, Towel	Support Furniture	55
Stand, Tray	Support Furniture	55
stand, tree (*use:* Holder, Tree)	Holiday Objects	458
Stand, Truing	Land Transportation Accessories	419
Stand, Typewriter	Support Furniture	55
Stand, Umbrella	Support Furniture	55
Stand, Watch	Storage & Display Accessories	65
Stand, Water Heater	Plumbing & Drainage Elements	13
stand, wheel (*use:* Pedestal, Wheel)	Water Transportation Accessories	438
Stand, Wig	Personal Carrying & Storage Gear	113
Standard	Organizational Objects	459
Standard, Pole Vault	Sports Equipment	518
Standard, Religious	Religious Objects	465
Stanhope	Animal-Powered Vehicles	423
Staple	Writing Accessories	404
Staple, Fence	Construction T&E	296
Staple, Wood	Woodworking T&E	250
stapler (*use:* Gun, Staple)	Multiple Use T&E for Materials	227

Stapler, Paper	Writing Accessories	405
stapler, turbo (*use:* Machine, Perlock)	Textile Manufacturing Equipment	242
Stapler, Upholstery	Needleworking Equipment	237
Starter, Bullet	Armament Accessories	272
statehouse (*use:* Capitol)	Civic & Social Structures	26
Statement, Bank	Financial Records	469
Statement, Financial	Financial Records	469
Station of the Cross	Religious Objects	465
station, bus (*use:* Depot, Bus)	Transportation Structures	39
Station, Comfort	Institutional Structures	37
Station, Fire	Civic & Social Structures	26
Station, Police	Civic & Social Structures	26
Station, Railroad	Transportation Structures	40
Station, Service	Transportation Structures	40
Station, Space	Other Structures	41
Station, Subway	Transportation Structures	39
Station, Weigh	Transportation Structures	40
Stationery	Writing Media	408
Statue	Art	454
Statue, Garden	Art	454
statuette (*use:* Figurine)	Art	454
Statute	Government Records	470
Stauroscope	Optical T&E	344
Stave	Woodworking T&E	259
Stay	Water Transportation Accessories	439
Stay, Casement	Door & Window Elements	7
Stay, Collar	Clothing Accessories	87
Stay, Corset	Clothing Accessories	87
Stayband	Headwear	93
Staysail	Water Transportation Accessories	439
Steamboat	Watercraft	445
Steamer	Cooking Vessels	151
Steamer, Carpet	Housekeeping Equipment	311
Steamer, Menhaden	Watercraft	445
Steamer, Paddle	Watercraft	445
Steamer, Wallpaper	Painting T&E	231
steamer, wheat (*use:* Conditioner, Wheat)	Food Processing Equipment	168
Steamroller	Construction T&E	295
Steamship	Watercraft	445
steel (*use:* Firesteel)	Firemaking Equipment	74
Steel	Metalworking T&E	216
Steel, Carving	Food Preparation Accessories	152
Steel, Finger	Leather, Horn & Shellworking T&E	200
Steel, Turning	Leather, Horn & Shellworking T&E	201
steelyard (*use:* Scale, Lever)	Weights and Measures T&E	358
Steeple	Roof Elements	14
Stein	Drinking Vessels	175
Stela	Site Features	21
Stem, Drill	Mining & Mineral Harvesting T&E	224
Stem, Pipe	Smoking & Recreational Drug Equipment	115
Stemmer	Mining & Mineral Harvesting T&E	220
Stencil	Multiple Use T&E for Materials	228
Stencil, Cake Decorating	Food Preparation Equipment	159
Stencil, Film	Graphic Equipment	384
Stencil, Leather	Leather, Horn & Shellworking T&E	201
Stencil, Letter	Writing Accessories	405
Stencil, Metal	Metalworking T&E	217
Stencil, Paint	Painting T&E	230
Stencil, Printing	Printing Accessories	386
Step	Support Furniture	55
Step, Aerobics	Recreational Devices	509
Step, Bed	Support Furniture	55
Step, Library	Support Furniture	56
Step, Vehicle	Land Transportation Accessories	418
Stepladder	Other Household Accessories	67
Stereogram	Medical Instruments	329
Stereograph	Graphic Documents	473
Stereometer	Mechanical Measurement Equipment	319
stereopticon (*use:* Projector, Lantern Slide)	Visual Communication Devices	400
Stereoscope	Visual Communication Devices	401
Stereoscope, Medical	Medical Instruments	329
Stereoview	Graphic Documents	473
Stereoviewer	Visual Communication Devices	401
Sterilizer	Medical Accessories	326
Sterilizer, Bottle	Food Preparation Equipment	157
sternlight (*use:* Light, Overtaking)	Water Transportation Accessories	438
Sternpost	Water Transportation Accessories	440
stern-wheeler (*use:* Steamer, Paddle)	Watercraft	445
Stethogoniometer	Biological T&E	288
Stethometer	Medical Instruments	327
Stethoscope	Medical Instruments	328
Stevengraph	Art	453
Stick, Aircraft Control	Aerospace Transportation Accessories	410
stick, button polishing (*use:* Board, Button Polishing)	Clothing Care Objects	105

Term	Category	Page
Stick, Clapper	Musical Instruments	372
Stick, Composing	Typesetting Equipment	388
stick, concussion (*use:* Stick, Clapper)	Musical Instruments	372
Stick, Coup	Achievement Symbols	491
Stick, Cuticle	Beauty Supplies	117
Stick, Digging	Cultivation Equipment	125
Stick, Field Hockey	Sports Equipment	515
Stick, Foot	Typesetting Equipment	388
Stick, Gaming	Game Equipment	503
stick, glow (*use:* Lightstick)	Other Lighting Accessories	72
Stick, Goalie	Sports Equipment	516
stick, hair (*use:* Hairstick)	Hair Adornments	83
Stick, Harvesting	Harvesting Equipment	131
Stick, Hockey	Sports Equipment	516
Stick, Hoop	Toys	522
Stick, Incense	Other Household Accessories	67
Stick, Jigging	Fishing Equipment	147
stick, job (*use:* Stick, Composing)	Typesetting Equipment	388
Stick, Lacrosse	Sports Equipment	517
Stick, Laundry	Laundry Equipment	314
stick, light (*use:* Lightstick)	Other Lighting Accessories	72
Stick, Litter	Groundskeeping Equipment	310
Stick, Mixing	Food Preparation Equipment	161
stick, mush (*use:* Stick, Mixing)	Food Preparation Equipment	161
Stick, Pick-Up	Game Equipment	504
Stick, Piñata	Game Equipment	505
stick, planting (*use:* Dibble)	Planting Equipment	132
Stick, Pogo	Toys	524
Stick, Pointer	Visual Communication Devices	400
Stick, Polo	Sports Equipment	517
Stick, Prayer	Religious Objects	464
Stick, Printer's Shooting	Typesetting Equipment	388
stick, pudding (*use:* Stick, Mixing)	Food Preparation Equipment	161
stick, rabbit (*use:* Stick, Throwing)	Percussive Weapons	283
Stick, Ricing	Harvesting Equipment	131
Stick, Selfie	Camera Equipment	377
Stick, Shaving	Hair Care Objects	119
Stick, Shooting	Armament Accessories	270
stick, shooting (*use:* Stick, Printer's Shooting)	Typesetting Equipment	388
Stick, Show	Animal Care Equipment	137
Stick, Size	Leather, Horn & Shellworking T&E	201
Stick, Snuff	Smoking & Recreational Drug Equipment	115
Stick, Soap	Other T&E for Materials	260
Stick, Steam	Glass, Plastics & Clayworking T&E	194
Stick, Stickball	Sports Equipment	518
stick, stirring (*use:* Stirrer)	Food Preparation Equipment	161
Stick, Swagger	Status Symbols	499
Stick, Swizzle	Food Preparation Equipment	162
Stick, Talking	Organizational Objects	459
Stick, Tally	Data Processing Devices	361
stick, tally (*use:* Rule, Log)	Forestry T&E	191
Stick, Tempil	Thermal T&E	354
Stick, Throwing	Percussive Weapons	283
Stick, Tobacco	Other T&E for Materials	260
Stick, Toddy	Food Preparation Equipment	162
Stick, Walking	Personal Assistive Objects	109
stick, weaving (*use:* Batten, Weaving)	Textile Manufacturing Equipment	239
Sticker	Other Documents	486
Sticker, Bumper	Other Documents	486
Sticker, Seal	Writing Accessories	405
Stickpin	Clothing Accessories	86
Stile	Site Features	22
stiletto (*use:* Dagger, Stiletto)	Edged Weapons	277
Stiletto	Needleworking Equipment	238
Still	Food Processing Equipment	164
Still, Solar	Food Processing Equipment	164
Still-Life	Art	453
Stilt	Toys	522
Stilt, Kiln	Glass, Plastics & Clayworking T&E	194
Stilt, Pruning	Groundskeeping Equipment	310
Stimulator, Gum	Dental Instruments	324
Stimulator, Sound	Acoustical T&E	262
Stirrer	Food Preparation Equipment	161
Stirrer, Apple Butter	Food Preparation Equipment	162
Stirrer, Curd	Food Processing Equipment	167
Stirrer, Laboratory	Labware	294
Stirrer, Lard	Food Processing Equipment	169
Stirrer, Milk	Food Processing Equipment	167
Stirrer, Paint	Painting T&E	230
Stirrer, Scrapple	Food Preparation Equipment	162
Stirrup	Land Transportation Accessories	421
stitch-heaver, rigger's (*use:* Heaver, Stitch)	Needleworking Equipment	235
Stock	Clothing Accessories	85
stock, die (*use:* Diestock)	Metalworking T&E	210
stock, drill (*use:* Drill, Woodworking)	Woodworking T&E	250
Stock, Metal	Metalworking T&E	217

Stock, Portfire | Armament Accessories | 272
Stockade | Defense Structures | 31
Stocking | Footwear | 89
Stocking, Christmas | Holiday Objects | 458
Stockpot | Cooking Vessels | 151
Stocks | Regulative Devices | 347
Stoker, Locomotive | Rail Transportation Accessories | 431
Stole | Outerwear | 101
Stole, Ecclesiastical | Status Symbols | 500
Stomacher | Clothing Accessories | 87
Stomatoscope | Medical Instruments | 330
stomper, kraut (*use:* Masher, Kraut) | Food Preparation Equipment | 156
Stomper, Romper | Toys | 522
stone, altar (*use:* Altar) | Religious Objects | 461
Stone, Ballast | Water Transportation Accessories | 441
Stone, Building | Construction Materials | 3
stone, burnishing (*use:* Stone, Polishing) | Glass, Plastics & Clayworking T&E | 194
Stone, Commemorative | Site Features | 21
Stone, Cooking | Food Preparation Equipment | 154
Stone, Curling | Sports Equipment | 514
Stone, Date | Construction Materials | 4
Stone, Dimension | Construction Materials | 4
Stone, Dressed | Construction Materials | 4
stone, grinding (*use:* Metate) | Food Processing Equipment | 169
stone, imposing (*use:* Table, Imposing) | Graphic Equipment | 385
Stone, Lightning | Religious Objects | 464
Stone, Lithograph | Graphic Equipment | 384
Stone, Nutting | Food Preparation Equipment | 160
Stone, Paint | Painting T&E | 230
Stone, Paving | Site Features | 22
Stone, Polishing | Glass, Plastics & Clayworking T&E | 194
Stone, Pumice | Beauty Supplies | 116
Stone, Quoin | Construction Materials | 4
Stone, Ringing | Musical Instruments | 373
stone, rubbing (*use:* Floatstone) | Masonry & Stoneworking T&E | 204
Stone, Rune | Site Features | 21
Stone, Scythe Sharpening | Metalworking T&E | 216
stone, sharpening (*use:* Whetstone) | Metalworking T&E | 216
Stone, Sinew | Other T&E for Materials | 260
Stone, Spirit | Belief Symbols | 494
Stone, Tethering | Trapping Equipment | 149
Stoneboat | Cultivation Equipment | 125
Stoner, Cherry | Food Preparation Equipment | 160
Stoner, Peach | Food Preparation Equipment | 160
Stool | Seating Furniture | 49
stool, bar (*use:* Barstool) | Seating Furniture | 49
Stool, Box | Seating Furniture | 49
Stool, Camp | Seating Furniture | 49
Stool, Caulker's | Woodworking T&E | 259
Stool, Counter | Seating Furniture | 49
Stool, Dressing | Seating Furniture | 49
Stool, Ducking | Regulative Devices | 347
Stool, Folding | Seating Furniture | 49
Stool, Gout | Seating Furniture | 49
Stool, Kitchen | Seating Furniture | 49
Stool, Milking | Seating Furniture | 49
Stool, Music | Musical Accessories | 369
Stool, Piano | Musical Accessories | 369
Stool, Stacking | Seating Furniture | 49
Stool, Step | Seating Furniture | 49
stool, vanity (*use:* Stool, Dressing) | Seating Furniture | 49
Stoop | Architectural Spaces | 1
Stop, Bench | Woodworking T&E | 259
Stopcock | Labware | 294
Stopper | Food Storage Equipment | 172
Stopper, Bottle | Food Service Accessories | 182
Stopper, Laboratory | Labware | 294
Stopper, Muzzle | Armament Accessories | 272
Stopper, Pipe | Smoking & Recreational Drug Equipment | 115
Stopper, Sink | Plumbing & Drainage Elements | 13
Stopwatch | Timekeeping T&E | 356
Store | Commercial Structures | 27
Store, Clothing | Commercial Structures | 28
store, drug (*use:* Pharmacy) | Commercial Structures | 27
Store, General | Commercial Structures | 28
Store, Grocery | Commercial Structures | 28
Store, Hardware | Commercial Structures | 28
store, millinery (*use:* Store, Clothing) | Commercial Structures | 28
storehouse (*use:* Warehouse) | Commercial Structures | 28
Storyboard | Graphic Documents | 474
storycloth (*use:* Cloth, Story) | Art | 452
Stoup | Drinking Vessels | 175
stoup (*use:* Font, Holy Water) | Religious Objects | 462
stove, camp (*use:* Cookstove, Portable) | Food Preparation Equipment | 154
Stove, Charcoal Heating | Heating & Cooling Equipment | 75
Stove, Coal Heating | Heating & Cooling Equipment | 75
stove, cook (*use:* Cookstove) | Food Preparation Equipment | 154
Stove, Finishing | Bookbinding Equipment | 383

Term	Category	Page
Stove, Heating	Heating & Cooling Equipment	75
Stove, Laundry	Laundry Equipment	314
Stove, Oil Heating	Heating & Cooling Equipment	75
Stove, Pellet	Heating & Cooling Equipment	75
Stove, Wood Heating	Heating & Cooling Equipment	75
Stovepipe	Heating Equipment Accessories	76
Strabismometer	Medical Instruments	329
Straightedge	Drafting T&E	367
Straightener, Arrow	Armament Accessories	272
Straightener, Cloth	Textile Manufacturing Equipment	244
Strainer, Beverage	Food Preparation Equipment	162
strainer, cream (*use:* Strainer, Milk)	Food Processing Equipment	167
Strainer, Gravy	Food Preparation Equipment	162
Strainer, Grease	Food Preparation Equipment	162
Strainer, Ice	Fishing Equipment	147
Strainer, Jelly	Food Preparation Equipment	162
Strainer, Kitchen	Food Preparation Equipment	162
Strainer, Lye	Other T&E for Materials	260
Strainer, Milk	Food Processing Equipment	167
Strainer, Punch	Food Preparation Equipment	162
Strainer, Sink	Dishwashing Equipment	308
Strainer, Tea	Food Preparation Equipment	162
Strainer, Whey	Food Processing Equipment	167
Straitjacket	Regulative Devices	348
Strake, Blanket	Mining & Mineral Harvesting T&E	225
Strap	Multiple Use T&E for Materials	227
strap (*use:* Blackjack)	Percussive Weapons	283
Strap, Carrying	Personal Carrying & Storage Gear	113
Strap, Harness	Land Transportation Accessories	421
Strap, Instrument	Musical Accessories	369
strap, razor (*use:* Strop)	Hair Care Objects	119
Strap, Reinforcing	Multiple Use T&E for Materials	227
Strap, Restraining	Regulative Devices	348
Strap, Shoulder	Status Symbols	496
Strap, Spur	Land Transportation Accessories	421
Straw	Eating & Drinking Utensils	179
Streamer	Party Accessories	460
Streetcar	Rail Vehicles	434
streetcar, electric (*use:* Trolley)	Rail Vehicles	435
streetcar, horse-drawn (*use:* Horsecar)	Rail Vehicles	435
Streetlamp	Lighting Devices	70
Stretcher	Human-Powered Vehicles	427
Stretcher, Canvas	Painting T&E	230
Stretcher, Carpet	Housekeeping Equipment	312
Stretcher, Cloth	Textile Manufacturing Equipment	244
Stretcher, Clothes	Laundry Equipment	314
Stretcher, Curtain	Laundry Equipment	314
Stretcher, Fence Wire	Construction T&E	296
Stretcher, Glove	Clothing Care Objects	105
Stretcher, Hat	Clothing Care Objects	105
Stretcher, Needlework	Needleworking Equipment	237
Stretcher, Pelt	Leather, Horn & Shellworking T&E	201
Stretcher, Shoe	Clothing Care Objects	105
Stretcher, Sock	Laundry Equipment	314
Stretcher, Tie	Clothing Care Objects	105
Stretcher, Web	Leather, Horn & Shellworking T&E	201
strickle (*use:* Stone, Scythe Sharpening)	Metalworking T&E	216
Strigil	Hygiene Objects	121
Strike-a-Light	Firemaking Equipment	74
Striker, Match	Firemaking Equipment	74
String	Multiple Use T&E for Materials	226
String, Instrument	Musical Accessories	369
Stringer	Stair Elements	15
Stringer, Fence Wire	Construction T&E	296
Strip, Comic	Graphic Documents	472
Strip, Nasal	Personal Assistive Objects	109
strip, neck (*use:* Paper, Shaving)	Hair Care Objects	119
Strip, Weather	Door & Window Elements	7
Strip, Zoetrope	Graphic Documents	474
Stripe, Service	Achievement Symbols	491
Striplight	Lighting Devices	70
Stripper, Cotton	Harvesting Equipment	129
Stripper, Crop	Harvesting Equipment	129
Stripper, Grain	Harvesting Equipment	129
Stripper, Rib	Medical Instruments	332
Stripper, Sugar Cane	Harvesting Equipment	129
Stripper, Vein	Medical Instruments	332
Stripper, Wire	Electrical Maintenance & Repair Equipment	299
Strobilion	Acoustical T&E	262
Stroboscope	Mechanical Measurement Equipment	318
stroboscope (*use:* Phenakistoscope)	Toys	524
Stroller	Human-Powered Vehicles	427
Stroller, Doll	Toys	520

Strongbox	Storage & Display Accessories	63
Strop	Hair Care Objects	119
Structure, Funerary	Ceremonial Structures	25
Structure, Play	Toys	522
Structure, Religious	Ceremonial Structures	25
Structure, Sports	Cultural & Recreational Structures	29
Structure, Toll	Transportation Structures	40
Structure, Utility	Other Structures	41
Stucco	Construction Materials	3
stud (*use:* Button, Stud)	Needleworking Equipment	236
Stud	Supporting Elements	17
Stud, Clothing	Clothing Accessories	87
stud, collar (*use:* Button, Collar)	Clothing Accessories	87
Stud, Cuff	Clothing Accessories	87
Stud, Fraternal	Status Symbols	496
Stud, Nose	Body Adornments	81
Stud, Shirt	Clothing Accessories	87
Stud, Tongue	Body Adornments	82
Stuffer, Sausage	Food Preparation Equipment	157
Stull	Mining & Mineral Harvesting T&E	225
Stump	Painting T&E	230
Stylograph	Drafting T&E	367
Stylus, Clay	Glass, Plastics & Clayworking T&E	195
Stylus, Drawing	Drafting T&E	367
stylus, light (*use:* Pen, Light)	Peripherals	364
Submarine	Watercraft	448
Submarine, Attack	Watercraft	447
Submarine, Ballistic Missile	Watercraft	447
Submarine, Commercial	Watercraft	446
Submarine, Naval	Watercraft	447
Submarine, Research	Watercraft	447
Submersible	Watercraft	448
Subpoena	Government Records	470
subsoiler (*use:* Plow, Subsoil)	Cultivation Equipment	125
Suit	Main Garments	99
Suit, Bathing	Main Garments	99
Suit, Bicycle	Main Garments	99
Suit, Buster	Main Garments	99
suit, cat (*use:* Catsuit)	Main Garments	96
Suit, Diver's	Protective Wear	102
Suit, Evening	Main Garments	99
Suit, Exercise	Main Garments	99
suit, exposure (*use:* Suit, Diver's)	Protective Wear	102
Suit, Flier's	Protective Wear	102
Suit, Gym	Main Garments	99
Suit, Hiking	Main Garments	99
suit, jump (*use:* Jumpsuit)	Main Garments	96
Suit, Leisure	Main Garments	99
Suit, Norfolk	Main Garments	99
suit, pants (*use:* Pantsuit)	Main Garments	99
Suit, Pressure	Protective Wear	102
Suit, Proximity	Protective Wear	102
Suit, Sailor	Main Garments	99
Suit, Skeleton	Main Garments	99
Suit, Ski	Outerwear	101
Suit, Space	Protective Wear	102
Suit, Speedskating	Sports Equipment	517
suit, sweat (*use:* Sweatsuit)	Main Garments	99
Suit, Tank	Main Garments	99
suit, track (*use:* Sweatsuit)	Main Garments	99
suit, turnout (*use:* Suit, Proximity)	Protective Wear	102
Suit, Union	Underwear	103
Suit, Walking	Main Garments	99
Suitcase	Personal Carrying & Storage Gear	112
Suite, Bedroom	Furniture Sets	46
Suite, Dining	Furniture Sets	46
Suite, Garden	Furniture Sets	46
Suite, Hall	Furniture Sets	46
Suite, Library	Furniture Sets	46
suite, living room (*use:* Suite, Parlor)	Furniture Sets	46
Suite, Nursery	Furniture Sets	46
Suite, Parlor	Furniture Sets	46
Sukkah	Other Structures	41
Sulky	Animal-Powered Vehicles	424
Summons	Government Records	470
Sunbonnet	Headwear	92
suncatcher (*use:* Ornament, Window)	Decorative Furnishings	60
Sundial	Timekeeping T&E	356
Sundress	Main Garments	96
Sunglasses	Personal Assistive Objects	108
Sunsuit	Main Garments	96
Supercalender	Papermaking T&E	233
Superfrontal	Religious Objects	463
Supplement, Newspaper	Other Documents	486
Support, Imhoff Cone	Chemical Testing Devices	291
Support, Mine	Mining & Mineral Harvesting T&E	225
Support, Powered	Mining & Mineral Harvesting T&E	225
Support, Stove	Heating Equipment Accessories	76
Supporter	Underwear	104
supporter, athletic (*use:* Jockstrap)	Underwear	104
Suppressor, Flash	Armament Accessories	272
Surcingle	Land Transportation Accessories	421
Surface, Printing	Graphic Equipment	384

Surfboard	Recreational Devices	511
Surfboat	Watercraft	446
Surplice	Status Symbols	500
Surrey	Animal-Powered Vehicles	424
Surtout	Outerwear	100
Survey, Land	Graphic Documents	472
Suspender, File	Writing Accessories	405
Suspenders	Clothing Accessories	87
Suture	Medical Instruments	332
Swab	Medical Accessories	326
Swag	Window & Door Coverings	79
Swage	Metalworking T&E	217
Swage, Anvil	Metalworking T&E	217
Swage, Bolt Heading	Metalworking T&E	217
Swage, Bottom	Metalworking T&E	217
Swage, Creasing	Metalworking T&E	217
Swage, Forming	Metalworking T&E	217
Swage, Half-Round Top	Metalworking T&E	217
Swage, Hatchet	Metalworking T&E	217
Swage, Mandrel	Metalworking T&E	217
Swage, Necking	Metalworking T&E	217
Swage, Nut	Metalworking T&E	217
Swage, Spring	Metalworking T&E	217
Swage, Top	Metalworking T&E	217
Swage, V-Shaped	Metalworking T&E	217
Swatch	Merchandising T&E	338
swather (*use:* Windrower)	Harvesting Equipment	130
Swatter, Fly	Other Household Accessories	66
Sweatband	Headwear	93
Sweater	Main Garments	99
Sweatpants	Main Garments	97
Sweatshirt	Main Garments	98
Sweatsuit	Main Garments	99
swedge (*use:* Swage)	Metalworking T&E	212
Sweep	Power Producing Equipment	304
sweep (*use:* Oar, Sweep)	Water Transportation Accessories	441
Sweep, Animal-Powered	Power Producing Equipment	304
Sweep, Door	Door & Window Elements	6
Sweep, Human-Powered	Power Producing Equipment	304
Sweep, Well	Site Features	22
Sweeper, Carpet	Housekeeping Equipment	312
Sweeper, Lawn	Groundskeeping Equipment	310
Sweeper, Street	Motor Vehicles	429
Swift	Textile Manufacturing Equipment	245
Swift, Umbrella	Textile Manufacturing Equipment	245
Swimbait	Fishing Equipment	147
Swing	Recreational Devices	510
Swing, Circle	Recreational Devices	510
Swing, Porch	Seating Furniture	49
swingle, flax (*use:* Knife, Scutching)	Textile Manufacturing Equipment	241
Switch	Percussive Weapons	283
Switch, Dimmer	Electrical System Components	301
Switch, Electrical	Electrical System Components	301
Switch, Fly	Animal Care Equipment	136
Switch, Knife	Electrical System Components	301
Switch, Railroad	Rail Transportation Accessories	432
Switch, Solenoid	Electrical System Components	301
Switch, Time	Electrical System Components	301
Switch, Transfer	Electrical System Components	301
Switchboard, Telephone	Telecommunication Devices	396
Swivel	Mechanical Devices	317
Swivel, Lariat	Animal Care Equipment	136
Sword	Edged Weapons	278
Sword, Artillery	Edged Weapons	279
Sword, Fencing	Sports Equipment	515
Sword, Hanger	Edged Weapons	279
Sword, Hunting	Edged Weapons	279
sword, small (*use:* Smallsword)	Edged Weapons	279
sword, town (*use:* Smallsword)	Edged Weapons	279
sword, walking (*use:* Smallsword)	Edged Weapons	279
Syllabus	Instructional Documents	475
Symbol, Political	Belief Symbols	493
Symbol, Religious	Religious Objects	464
Symbol, Social	Belief Symbols	493
Symbol, Spiritual	Belief Symbols	493
Symbol, Trade	Advertising Media	451
Sympiesometer	Meteorological T&E	339
Synagogue	Ceremonial Structures	25
Synchrocyclotron	Nuclear Physics T&E	341
Synchronizer	Timekeeping T&E	356
Synchrotron	Nuclear Physics T&E	341
Synchrotron, Alternating Gradient	Nuclear Physics T&E	341
Synchrotron, Constant Gradient	Nuclear Physics T&E	341
Synchrotron, Proton	Nuclear Physics T&E	341
Synchrotron, Zero Gradient	Nuclear Physics T&E	341
Synthesizer	Musical Instruments	371
Syringe	Multiple Use T&E for Materials	228
Syringe, Bulb	Medical Instruments	334
Syringe, Dental	Dental Instruments	324
Syringe, Dose	Veterinary Equipment	142
Syringe, Icing	Food Preparation Equipment	159
Syringe, Medical	Medical Instruments	334
Syringe, Piston	Medical Instruments	334

Term	Category	Page
Syringe, Slip-Trailing	Glass, Plastics & Clayworking T&E	195
System, Fire Alarm	Protective Devices	345
Tab, Archery	Armament Accessories	272
Tab, Barrister's	Status Symbols	498
tab, finger (*use:* Tab, Archery)	Armament Accessories	272
Tab, Index	Writing Accessories	405
Tabard	Outerwear	101
Tabernacle	Religious Objects	462
Tabi	Footwear	89
Table	Support Furniture	56
table, air (*use:* Concentrator)	Metalworking T&E	208
Table, Amalgamating	Metalworking T&E	217
table, banquet (*use:* Table, Dining)	Support Furniture	56
Table, Billiard	Game Equipment	505
Table, Bindery	Bookbinding Equipment	383
Table, Breakfast	Support Furniture	56
Table, Café	Support Furniture	56
table, calling card (*use:* Stand, Card)	Support Furniture	55
Table, Card	Support Furniture	56
Table, Cart	Support Furniture	56
Table, Center	Support Furniture	56
table, chair (*use:* Chair-Table)	Seating Furniture	47
Table, Changing	Sleeping & Reclining Furniture	51
Table, Chart	Support Furniture	56
Table, Cocktail	Support Furniture	56
Table, Coffee	Support Furniture	56
Table, Commode	Support Furniture	56
Table, Communion	Religious Objects	465
Table, Console	Support Furniture	57
Table, Corner	Support Furniture	56
Table, Dental Instrument	Dental Accessories	321
Table, Dining	Support Furniture	56
Table, Display	Merchandising T&E	337
Table, Drafting	Drafting T&E	367
Table, Dressing	Support Furniture	56
Table, Dropleaf	Support Furniture	56
Table, Embalming	Medical Accessories	326
Table, End	Support Furniture	57
Table, Etching	Graphic Equipment	384
Table, Examination	Medical Accessories	326
Table, Extension Dining	Support Furniture	56
Table, Flow	Chemical Testing Devices	291
Table, Folding	Support Furniture	56
Table, Game	Support Furniture	56
Table, Gaming	Game Equipment	503
Table, Garden	Support Furniture	56
Table, Gateleg	Support Furniture	56
table, handkerchief (*use:* Table, Corner)	Support Furniture	56
Table, Imposing	Graphic Equipment	385
Table, Inversion	Medical Instruments	334
Table, Ironing	Laundry Equipment	313
Table, Kitchen	Support Furniture	56
Table, Kneading	Food Preparation Equipment	157
Table, Knitting	Support Furniture	57
Table, Library	Storage & Display Furniture	54
Table, Light	Visual Communication Accessories	399
Table, Manicure	Support Furniture	56
Table, Massage	Sleeping & Reclining Furniture	51
Table, Meat Cutting	Food Processing Equipment	165
Table, Medical	Medical Accessories	326
Table, Mess	Support Furniture	56
Table, Metalworking	Metalworking T&E	217
Table, Nesting	Support Furniture	56
Table, Night	Support Furniture	57
Table, Occasional	Support Furniture	56
Table, Operating	Medical Accessories	326
Table, Oscillating	Mechanical Devices	317
Table, Parlor	Support Furniture	56
Table, Parsons	Support Furniture	56
Table, Pasting	Painting T&E	231
Table, Patio	Support Furniture	56
Table, Pedestal	Support Furniture	56
Table, Pembroke	Support Furniture	56
Table, Picnic	Support Furniture	56
Table, Pier	Support Furniture	57
table, ping pong (*use:* Table, Table Tennis)	Sports Equipment	518
Table, Plane	Surveying Equipment	353
Table, Pool	Game Equipment	505
Table, Rent	Support Furniture	56
Table, Restaurant	Support Furniture	57
Table, Serving	Support Furniture	57
Table, Settle	Seating Furniture	47
Table, Sewing	Support Furniture	57
Table, Side	Support Furniture	57
table, sideboard (*use:* Table, Serving)	Support Furniture	57
Table, Snack	Support Furniture	57
Table, Sofa	Support Furniture	57
table, stacking (*use:* Table, Nesting)	Support Furniture	56
Table, Steam	Food Preparation Equipment	163
Table, Stripping	Printing Accessories	386
Table, Table Tennis	Sports Equipment	518
Table, Tea	Support Furniture	57
table, tiered (*use:* Stand, Tiered)	Support Furniture	55
Table, Tilt-Top	Support Furniture	57
table, tray (*use:* Table, Snack)	Support Furniture	57
Table, Trestle	Support Furniture	57

Table, Tripod	Support Furniture	57
table, TV (*use:* Table, Snack)	Support Furniture	57
Table, Vesting	Support Furniture	57
Table, Welding	Metalworking T&E	217
Table, Work	Support Furniture	57
Table, Writing	Storage & Display Furniture	54
Tablecloth	Food Service Accessories	181
Tablespoon	Serving Utensils	185
tablet (*use:* Computer, Tablet)	Data Processing Devices	362
Tablet	Other Documents	486
Tablet, Graphics	Peripherals	364
Tablet, Weaving	Textile Manufacturing Equipment	244
Tablet, Writing	Writing Media	408
Tablita	Status Symbols	499
Tabor	Musical Instruments	372
Taboret	Seating Furniture	49
Tachistoscope	Visual Communication Devices	401
Tachometer	Mechanical Measurement Equipment	318
tachymeter (*use:* Alidade)	Surveying Equipment	352
tachymeter (*use:* Theodolite)	Surveying Equipment	353
tachymeter (*use:* Transit)	Surveying Equipment	353
Tack	Multiple Use T&E for Materials	227
tack (*use:* Line, Tack)	Water Transportation Accessories	439
Tack, Animal	Land Transportation Accessories	419
Tack, Carpet	Housekeeping Equipment	312
Tack, Tie	Clothing Accessories	86
Tack, Upholstery	Needleworking Equipment	236
Tacker, Carpet	Housekeeping Equipment	312
tackle (*use:* Block and Tackle)	Mechanical Devices	315
Tackle, Breaking	Animal Care Equipment	135
Tackle, Fishing	Fishing Equipment	147
Tackle, Sawing	Woodworking T&E	259
Taffrail	Water Transportation Accessories	440
Tag	Writing Media	408
Tag, Animal	Animal Care Equipment	136
Tag, Carcass	Other Documents	483
Tag, Dog	Personal Identification	495
Tag, Gift	Party Accessories	460
Tag, Identification	Other Documents	483
Tag, Inventory	Other Documents	483
Tag, Luggage	Other Documents	483
Tag, Merchandise	Other Documents	483
tag, registration (*use:* Registration)	Other Documents	484
Tag, Shipping	Other Documents	483
Tagine	Cooking Vessels	151
Tailgate	Land Transportation Accessories	418
Taillamp	Land Transportation Accessories	417
Tailrace	Hydraulic Structures	34
Taj	Headwear	92
Taler	Exchange Media	489
Talisman	Belief Symbols	493
Tallith	Belief Symbols	494
Tally	Financial Records	469
tallyho (*use:* Coach, Road)	Animal-Powered Vehicles	423
tambour (*use:* Hoop, Embroidery)	Needleworking Equipment	237
Tambourine	Musical Instruments	373
Tambouritza	Musical Instruments	374
tamer, hog (*use:* Cutter, Snout)	Animal Care Equipment	134
tamis (*use:* Riddle)	Food Preparation Equipment	162
Tam-o'-Shanter	Headwear	91
Tamp, Butter	Food Preparation Equipment	161
Tamper	Construction T&E	295
tamper (*use:* Tamp, Butter)	Food Preparation Equipment	161
Tamper, Ballast	Rail Vehicles	434
tamper, kraut (*use:* Masher, Kraut)	Food Preparation Equipment	156
tamper, pipe (*use:* Stopper, Pipe)	Smoking & Recreational Drug Equipment	115
tampion (*use:* Tompion)	Armament Accessories	272
Tampon	Hygiene Objects	120
Tam-Tam	Musical Instruments	372
Tanakh	Religious Objects	465
Tank	Containers	415
Tank, Breathing	Personal Assistive Objects	107
Tank, Cooling	Food Processing Equipment	166
Tank, Developing	Photoprocessing Equipment	381
tank, diver's (*use:* Tank, Scuba)	Recreational Devices	511
Tank, Food Processing	Food Processing Equipment	164
Tank, Food Storage	Food Storage Equipment	172
Tank, Lard Settling	Food Processing Equipment	169
Tank, Libation	Religious Objects	463
Tank, Military	Motor Vehicles	430
Tank, Oil	Heating Equipment Accessories	77
Tank, Scuba	Recreational Devices	511
Tankard	Drinking Vessels	175
Tanker	Watercraft	446
Tannery	Industrial Structures	35
Tantalus	Food Storage Equipment	172
Tap	Metalworking T&E	209
Tap, Beer	Food Service Accessories	182
Tap, Bottom	Metalworking T&E	209
Tap, Plug	Metalworking T&E	209

Term	Category	Page
Tap, Screw	Woodworking T&E	259
Tap, Taper	Metalworking T&E	210
Tapadera	Land Transportation Accessories	421
Tape, Adhesive	Multiple Use T&E for Materials	228
tape, audio (*use:* Audiotape)	Sound Communication Media	393
Tape, Audio Reel	Sound Communication Media	393
tape, audiocassette (*use:* Audiocassette)	Sound Communication Media	393
Tape, Bat Grip	Sports Equipment	513
Tape, Bias	Needleworking Equipment	236
Tape, Drafting	Drafting T&E	367
Tape, Duct	Multiple Use T&E for Materials	228
Tape, Eight-Track	Sound Communication Media	393
Tape, Electrical	Electrical Maintenance & Repair Equipment	299
Tape, Magnetic	Data Processing Media	363
Tape, Masking	Multiple Use T&E for Materials	228
Tape, Medical	Medical Accessories	326
Tape, Mending	Needleworking Equipment	236
Tape, Packaging	Multiple Use T&E for Materials	228
Tape, Painter's	Painting T&E	230
Tape, Paper	Data Processing Media	363
Tape, Register	Merchandising T&E	338
Tape, Seed	Planting Equipment	132
Tape, Steel	Weights & Measures T&E	358
Tape, Surveyor's	Surveying Equipment	353
Tape, Ticker	Telecommunication Media	398
Tape, Transparent	Multiple Use T&E for Materials	228
Tape, Twill	Needleworking Equipment	236
Tape, Umbilical	Medical Accessories	326
Taper	Other Lighting Accessories	72
Tapestry	Art	455
Targe	Body Armor	276
Target	Armament Accessories	272
Target, Archery	Armament Accessories	272
Target, Gallery	Game Equipment	502
Target, Skeet	Armament Accessories	272
Tarogato	Musical Instruments	375
tarp, field (*use:* Cloth, Ground)	Bedding	44
Tarpaulin	Multiple Use T&E for Materials	228
Tarpot	Land Transportation Accessories	421
Tasimeter	Mechanical Measurement Equipment	318
Tassel	Needleworking Equipment	237
Tassel, Academic	Status Symbols	498
Tasset	Body Armor	276
Taster, Wine	Drinking Vessels	174
Tatami	Floor Coverings	45
Tattoo, Temporary	Body Adornments	82
Tavern	Commercial Structures	28
Taxi, Water	Watercraft	446
Taxicab	Motor Vehicles	428
Taximeter	Land Transportation Accessories	421
Tazza	Drinking Vessels	174
TDD	Telecommunication Devices	397
Teacup	Drinking Vessels	174
Teahouse	Ceremonial Structures	25
Teakettle	Cooking Vessels	151
Teapot	Serving Vessels	189
teapoy (*use:* Table, Tea)	Support Furniture	57
Tearsheet	Other Documents	483
Teaspoon	Eating & Drinking Utensils	179
Tedder	Harvesting Equipment	130
Teddy	Underwear	103
Tee, Batting	Sports Equipment	513
Tee, Football	Sports Equipment	515
Tee, Golf	Sports Equipment	516
teepee (*use:* Tipi)	Other Structures	41
Teeterboard	Public Entertainment Devices	507
teeter-totter (*use:* Seesaw)	Recreational Devices	510
teeth, false (*use:* Denture)	Personal Assistive Objects	109
Tefillin	Belief Symbols	494
tegula (*use:* Pantile)	Surface Elements	19
Teinoscope	Optical T&E	344
Telegram	Other Documents	482
Telegraph	Telecommunication Devices	396
telegraph, engine room (*use:* Telegraph, Ship's)	Water Transportation Accessories	440
Telegraph, Ship's	Water Transportation Accessories	440
Telemeter	Telecommunication Devices	396
Telengiscope	Astronomical T&E	285
Telephone	Telecommunication Devices	396
Telephone, Cellular	Telecommunication Devices	396
Telephone, Coin-Operated	Telecommunication Devices	396
Telephone, Cordless	Telecommunication Devices	397
Telephone, Desk	Telecommunication Devices	397
Telephone, Field	Telecommunication Devices	397
Telephone, Magneto	Telecommunication Devices	397
Telephone, Satellite	Telecommunication Devices	397
Telephone, Wall	Telecommunication Devices	397
telephone, wireless (*use:* Telephone, Cellular)	Telecommunication Devices	396
Telepolariscope	Astronomical T&E	285
Teleprinter	Telecommunication Devices	397
Telescope	Optical T&E	344
Telescope, Achromatic	Astronomical T&E	285
Telescope, Astronomical	Astronomical T&E	285

Telescope, Cassegrain	Astronomical T&E	285
Telescope, Equatorial	Astronomical T&E	285
Telescope, Galilean	Astronomical T&E	285
Telescope, Navigational	Navigational Equipment	351
Telescope, Orbiting	Astronomical T&E	285
Telescope, Quadrant	Navigational Equipment	351
Telescope, Radio	Astronomical T&E	285
Telescope, Reflecting	Astronomical T&E	285
Telescope, Refracting	Astronomical T&E	285
telescope, Schmidt (*use:* Camera, Schmidt)	Astronomical T&E	285
Telescope, Sextant	Navigational Equipment	351
Telescope, Solar	Astronomical T&E	285
Telescope, Spotting	Armament Accessories	272
Telespectroscope	Astronomical T&E	285
telethermometer (*use:* Pyrometer)	Thermal T&E	354
Teletype	Telecommunication Devices	397
Teletypewriter	Telecommunication Devices	397
Television	Telecommunication Devices	397
Television, Console	Telecommunication Devices	397
Television, Portable	Telecommunication Devices	397
Telltale	Water Transportation Accessories	441
Tellurometer	Surveying Equipment	353
Telpher	Rail Vehicles	435
Template, Dental	Dental Accessories	321
Template, Drafting	Drafting T&E	367
Template, Keyboard	Data Processing Accessories	360
Template, Leather	Leather, Horn & Shellworking T&E	201
Template, Lettering	Drafting T&E	367
Template, Metalworking	Metalworking T&E	217
Template, Woodworking	Woodworking T&E	259
Temple	Ceremonial Structures	25
Temple, Weaving Machine	Textile Manufacturing Equipment	244
Tenaculum	Medical Instruments	332
Tender	Rail Vehicles	433
Tender, Buoy	Watercraft	448
Tender, Submarine	Watercraft	447
Tender, Yacht	Watercraft	448
tenderizer, meat (*use:* Maul, Meat)	Food Preparation Equipment	156
Tenement	Dwellings	32
Tenoroon	Musical Instruments	375
tenpin (*use:* Pin, Bowling)	Sports Equipment	513
Tensiometer	Mechanical Measurement Equipment	318
Tensometer	Mechanical Measurement Equipment	319
Tent	Other Structures	41
Tent, Camping	Other Structures	41
Tent, Canopy	Other Structures	41
Tent, Circus	Cultural & Recreational Structures	29
Tent, Oxygen	Medical Instruments	333
Tent, Play	Toys	523
tenter (*use:* Frame, Tenter)	Textile Manufacturing Equipment	240
Tenterhook	Textile Manufacturing Equipment	244
tepoy (*use:* Table, Tea)	Support Furniture	57
Terminal	Transportation Structures	40
Terminal, Airport	Transportation Structures	40
Terminal, Bus	Transportation Structures	40
Terminal, Computer	Peripherals	365
Terminal, CRT	Peripherals	365
Terminal, Electrical	Electrical System Components	301
Terminal, Magnetic Tape	Peripherals	365
Terminal, Marine	Transportation Structures	40
Terminal, Railroad	Transportation Structures	40
Terminal, Truck	Transportation Structures	40
Terminal, Typewriter	Peripherals	365
Terrarium	Pet Supplies	141
Terret	Land Transportation Accessories	421
Terrine	Cooking Vessels	150
Tessera	Surface Elements	19
test (*use:* Examination)	Instructional Documents	475
Test, Color Perception	Medical Instruments	329
Test, Oven	Glass, Plastics & Clayworking T&E	195
Tester	Sleeping & Reclining Furniture	50
Tester, Acidity	Food Processing Equipment	167
Tester, Alcohol	Food Processing Equipment	164
Tester, Babcock	Food Processing Equipment	167
Tester, Battery	Electrical Maintenance & Repair Equipment	299
Tester, Burst	Textile Manufacturing Equipment	244
Tester, Cake	Food Preparation Equipment	158
Tester, Casing	Mining & Mineral Harvesting T&E	225
Tester, Cheese	Food Processing Equipment	167
Tester, Circuit	Electrical Maintenance & Repair Equipment	299
Tester, Color Sense	Medical Instruments	329
Tester, Crimp	Textile Manufacturing Equipment	244
Tester, Dental Pulp	Dental Instruments	324
Tester, Electrical	Electrical Maintenance & Repair Equipment	299
Tester, Fabric	Textile Manufacturing Equipment	244
Tester, Fiber Fineness	Textile Manufacturing Equipment	244
Tester, Fineness	Chemical Testing Devices	291
Tester, Fire Resistance	Textile Manufacturing Equipment	244
Tester, Hoof	Veterinary Equipment	142

Tester, Magneto and Coil — Electrical Maintenance & Repair Equipment 299
Tester, Milk — Food Processing Equipment 167
Tester, Milk Sediment — Food Processing Equipment 167
Tester, Mullen — Papermaking T&E 233
Tester, Nep — Textile Manufacturing Equipment 244
Tester, Overrun — Food Processing Equipment 167
Tester, Paper — Papermaking T&E 233
Tester, Paper Moisture — Papermaking T&E 233
Tester, Powder — Armament Accessories 272
Tester, Schopper — Papermaking T&E 233
Tester, Scorch — Textile Manufacturing Equipment 244
Tester, Sediment — Chemical Testing Devices 291
Tester, Shrinkage — Textile Manufacturing Equipment 244
Tester, Sliver — Textile Manufacturing Equipment 244
Tester, Soundness — Chemical Testing Devices 291
Tester, Tear — Textile Manufacturing Equipment 244
Tester, Torsion — Mechanical Measurement Equipment 319
Tester, Tube — Electrical Maintenance & Repair Equipment 299
Tester, Tubing — Mining & Mineral Harvesting T&E 225
Tester, Twist — Textile Manufacturing Equipment 244
Tester, Washfastness — Textile Manufacturing Equipment 244
Testimonial — Declaratory Documents 468
Testimony — Legal Documents 476
Testone — Exchange Media 489
Testudo — Armament Accessories 272
Tetanometer — Medical Instruments 328
tête-à-tête (*use:* Sofa, Conversational) — Seating Furniture 49
Tetherball — Game Equipment 505
Text, Religious — Religious Objects 465
Textbook — Instructional Documents 475
thaler (*use:* Taler) — Exchange Media 489
Thaumatrope — Toys 524
Thawb — Main Garments 99
Theater — Cultural & Recreational Structures 29
theater, movie (*use:* Cinema) — Cultural & Recreational Structures 29
Theodolite — Surveying Equipment 353
Theorobo — Musical Instruments 374
Theremin — Musical Instruments 371
Thermoammeter — Electrical & Magnetic Measurement Devices 297
Thermocouple — Thermal T&E 354
Thermograph — Thermal T&E 354
Thermohydrometer — Thermal T&E 354
Thermometer — Thermal T&E 354
Thermometer, Candy — Food Preparation Equipment 158
Thermometer, Culinary — Food Preparation Equipment 158
Thermometer, Darkroom — Photoprocessing Equipment 381
Thermometer, Deep Frying — Food Preparation Equipment 158
Thermometer, Incubator — Breeding Equipment 138
Thermometer, Meat — Food Preparation Equipment 158
Thermometer, Medical — Medical Instruments 328
Thermometer, Meteorological — Meteorological T&E 340
Thermometer, Milk — Food Processing Equipment 167
Thermometer, Oven — Food Preparation Equipment 158
thermometrograph (*use:* Thermograph) — Thermal T&E 354
Thermomultiplier — Thermal T&E 354
Thermoscope — Thermal T&E 354
Thermostat — Environmental Control Elements 9
Thesaurus — Other Documents 480
Thesis — Literary Works 477
Thief, Wine — Food Processing Equipment 164
Thimble — Needleworking Equipment 237
Thinner, Fruit — Tending Equipment 133
Tholia — Headwear 93
thong (*use:* Flip-Flop) — Footwear 90
thong (*use:* Underwear, Thong) — Underwear 104
Thread — Needleworking Equipment 236
Threader — Needleworking Equipment 237
threader, pipe (*use:* Machine, Pipe Threading) — Metalworking T&E 214
Thresher — Harvesting Equipment 131
Thresher, Groundhog — Harvesting Equipment 131
Thresher, Peanut — Harvesting Equipment 131
Thresher, Portable — Harvesting Equipment 131
Thresher, Simple — Harvesting Equipment 131
Thresher, Stationary — Harvesting Equipment 131
Thresher-Separator — Harvesting Equipment 131
Threshold — Door & Window Elements 6
Throw — Furniture Coverings 61
throw, bed (*use:* Bedspread) — Bedding 43
Throw, Chair — Furniture Coverings 61
Throw, Sofa — Furniture Coverings 61
Throw, Table — Furniture Coverings 61
thrower, skeet (*use:* Trap, Skeet) — Armament Accessories 272
thrower, snow (*use:* Snowblower) — Groundskeeping Equipment 310
thrower, spear (*use:* Atlatl) — Edged Weapons 277

Thumbscrew	Regulative Devices	347
Thumbstall	Armament Accessories	272
Thumbtack	Writing Accessories	404
thurible (*use:* Censer)	Religious Objects	462
Tiara	Status Symbols	499
tick (*use:* Cover, Mattress)	Bedding	43
Ticker, Stock	Telecommunication Devices	396
Ticket	Exchange Media	489
Ticket, Admission	Exchange Media	490
Ticket, Lottery	Game Equipment	503
Ticket, Meal	Exchange Media	490
ticket, ration (*use:* Coupon, Ration)	Exchange Media	487
Ticket, Traffic	Legal Documents	476
Ticket, Transfer	Exchange Media	490
Ticket, Transportation	Exchange Media	490
Tic-Tac-Toe	Game Equipment	506
tiddlywinks (*use:* Set, Tiddlywinks)	Game Equipment	504
tidy (*use:* Antimacassar)	Furniture Coverings	61
Tie, Anchor	Supporting Elements	16
Tie, Bolo	Clothing Accessories	85
Tie, Bow	Clothing Accessories	85
Tie, Cattle	Animal Care Equipment	135
Tie, Fastener	Multiple Use T&E for Materials	227
Tie, Hair	Hair Adornments	83
tie, neck (*use:* Necktie)	Clothing Accessories	85
tie, railroad (*use:* Crosstie)	Rail Transportation Accessories	432
Tie, String	Clothing Accessories	85
Tie, Twist	Multiple Use T&E for Materials	227
Tie, Wall	Masonry & Stoneworking T&E	205
Tieback	Window & Door Coverings	78
Tieback, Bed Curtain	Bedding	44
tiepin (*use:* Stickpin)	Clothing Accessories	86
Tier, Corn Shock	Harvesting Equipment	131
Tightener, Chain	Land Transportation Accessories	421
Tights	Footwear	89
Tiki	Religious Objects	465
Tilbury	Animal-Powered Vehicles	423
Tile	Surface Elements	19
Tile, Acoustical	Surface Elements	19
Tile, Carpet	Floor Coverings	45
Tile, Ceiling	Surface Elements	19
Tile, Decorative	Surface Elements	19
Tile, Drain	Plumbing & Drainage Elements	13
Tile, Floor	Surface Elements	19
Tile, Game	Game Equipment	502
Tile, Hearth	Surface Elements	19
Tile, Hip	Surface Elements	19
Tile, Pill	Medical Accessories	326
Tile, Pressed Metal Ceiling	Surface Elements	19
Tile, Ridge	Surface Elements	19
Tile, Roof	Surface Elements	19
tile, stove (*use:* Tile, Hearth)	Surface Elements	19
Tile, Wall	Surface Elements	19
till (*use:* Box, Money)	Merchandising T&E	336
Tiller	Water Transportation Accessories	440
Tiller, Garden Rotary	Cultivation Equipment	125
Tiller, Rotary	Cultivation Equipment	125
Tilter, Platter	Food Service Accessories	182
Tilter, Pot	Serving Vessels	187
Timbale	Food Preparation Equipment	157
Timber	Construction Materials	3
Timber, Mine	Mining & Mineral Harvesting T&E	225
Timecard	Financial Records	469
timeclock (*use:* Clock, Time Recording)	Timekeeping T&E	355
Timepiece	Timekeeping T&E	356
Timer	Timekeeping T&E	356
Timer, Darkroom	Photoprocessing Equipment	381
Timer, Egg	Food Preparation Equipment	158
Timer, Game	Game Equipment	502
Timer, Kitchen	Food Preparation Equipment	158
Timer, Light	Other Lighting Accessories	73
Timer, Pill	Personal Carrying & Storage Gear	112
Timer, Watering	Groundskeeping Equipment	310
Timesheet	Financial Records	469
Timetable	Other Documents	486
Timpanum	Musical Instruments	372
Tin	Containers	414
Tin, Mess	Cooking Vessels	151
Tin, Pressing	Bookbinding Equipment	383
Tinder	Firemaking Equipment	74
Tinderbox	Heating Equipment Accessories	77
Tinderbox, Pocket	Armament Accessories	272
Tinderpistol	Firemaking Equipment	74
Tinkler	Clothing Accessories	87
Tinsel	Holiday Objects	458
Tintometer	Textile Manufacturing Equipment	244
Tintype	Graphic Documents	473
Tip, Cake Decorating	Food Preparation Equipment	159
Tip, Gilder's	Painting T&E	230
tip, wing (*use:* Brogue)	Footwear	90
Tipi	Other Structures	41
Tiple	Musical Instruments	374
Tippet	Clothing Accessories	87
tip-up (*use:* Jig, Fishing)	Fishing Equipment	147
Tire	Land Transportation Accessories	418

Tissue	Hygiene Objects	121
Tissue, Dry Mount	Visual Communication Accessories	399
Tissue, Lens	Photographic Accessories	379
Tithonometer	Chemical Testing Devices	291
Titrator	Labware	294
Titrometer	Chemical Testing Devices	291
tivoli (*use:* Game, Tivoli)	Game Equipment	505
Toaster	Food Preparation Equipment	155
Toaster, Cheese	Food Preparation Equipment	163
Tobacco	Smoking & Recreational Drug Equipment	115
Tobacco, Chewing	Smoking & Recreational Drug Equipment	115
Toboggan	Recreational Devices	509
Toga	Main Garments	99
Toggle	Needleworking Equipment	236
Toilet	Plumbing & Drainage Elements	12
Token	Exchange Media	490
Token, Commemorative	Memorabilia	478
Token, Communion	Exchange Media	490
Token, Ration	Exchange Media	490
Token, Store	Exchange Media	490
Token, Tax	Exchange Media	490
Token, Transportation	Exchange Media	490
Tollbooth	Transportation Structures	40
Tollgate	Transportation Structures	40
Tollhouse	Transportation Structures	40
Tom, Long	Mining & Mineral Harvesting T&E	224
Tomahawk	Edged Weapons	279
Tomb	Ceremonial Structures	25
Tombstone	Funerary Objects	457
Tompion	Armament Accessories	272
Tomtom	Musical Instruments	372
Toner	Printing Accessories	386
tong, curling (*use:* Iron, Curling)	Hair Care Objects	118
tongs, anvil (*use:* Tongs, Pickup)	Metalworking T&E	218
Tongs, Asparagus	Serving Utensils	185
Tongs, Beaker	Labware	294
Tongs, Bending	Metalworking T&E	217
Tongs, Block Ice	Mining & Mineral Harvesting T&E	225
Tongs, Bolt	Metalworking T&E	218
Tongs, Box	Metalworking T&E	217
Tongs, Box Hammer	Metalworking T&E	218
Tongs, Brazing	Metalworking T&E	217
Tongs, Brick	Masonry & Stoneworking T&E	205
Tongs, Chain	Metalworking T&E	219
Tongs, Clam	Fishing Equipment	148
Tongs, Clinching	Farrier Equipment	139
Tongs, Clip	Metalworking T&E	217
Tongs, Crook-Bit	Metalworking T&E	218
Tongs, Darkroom	Photoprocessing Equipment	381
tongs, dental (*use:* Forceps, Dental)	Dental Instruments	322
Tongs, Dipping	Glass, Plastics & Clayworking T&E	195
Tongs, Double Box	Metalworking T&E	217
Tongs, Drawing	Metalworking T&E	217
tongs, eye (*use:* Tongs, Hammer)	Metalworking T&E	218
Tongs, Farrier's	Farrier Equipment	139
Tongs, Fireplace	Heating Equipment Accessories	76
Tongs, Fishing	Fishing Equipment	148
Tongs, Flask	Labware	294
Tongs, Flat	Metalworking T&E	217
Tongs, Gad	Metalworking T&E	218
Tongs, Half-Round	Metalworking T&E	218
Tongs, Hammer	Metalworking T&E	218
Tongs, Hog	Animal Care Equipment	135
Tongs, Hollow-Bit	Metalworking T&E	218
Tongs, Hoop	Metalworking T&E	218
Tongs, Hornworker's	Leather, Horn & Shellworking T&E	201
tongs, ice (*use:* Tongs, Block Ice)	Mining & Mineral Harvesting T&E	225
Tongs, Ice	Serving Utensils	185
Tongs, Incense	Religious Objects	465
Tongs, Kitchen	Food Preparation Equipment	161
Tongs, Laboratory	Labware	294
Tongs, Laundry	Laundry Equipment	314
Tongs, Link	Metalworking T&E	218
Tongs, Mercury	Labware	294
Tongs, Metalworking	Metalworking T&E	217
Tongs, Nail	Metalworking T&E	218
Tongs, Oyster	Fishing Equipment	148
Tongs, Pickup	Metalworking T&E	218
Tongs, Pincer	Metalworking T&E	218
Tongs, Pipe	Smoking & Recreational Drug Equipment	115
Tongs, Plow	Metalworking T&E	218
Tongs, Pottery	Glass, Plastics & Clayworking T&E	195
Tongs, Raku	Glass, Plastics & Clayworking T&E	195
tongs, right-angle bit (*use:* Tongs, Side)	Metalworking T&E	218
Tongs, Rocket	Armament Accessories	272
Tongs, Roofing	Metalworking T&E	218
Tongs, Round-Lip	Metalworking T&E	218
Tongs, Salad	Serving Utensils	185
Tongs, Sandwich	Serving Utensils	185
Tongs, Serving	Serving Utensils	185
Tongs, Shelf	Merchandising T&E	338
Tongs, Shoe	Metalworking T&E	218

Tongs, Shoe-Spreading	Farrier Equipment	139
Tongs, Side	Metalworking T&E	218
Tongs, Skidding	Forestry T&E	191
Tongs, Sliding	Metalworking T&E	218
tongs, smoking (*use:* Tongs, Pipe)	Smoking & Recreational Drug Equipment	115
Tongs, Spaghetti	Serving Utensils	185
tongs, straight-lip (*use:* Tongs, Flat)	Metalworking T&E	217
Tongs, Sugar	Serving Utensils	185
Tongs, Swivel Jaw	Metalworking T&E	218
Tongs, Tanner's	Leather, Horn & Shellworking T&E	201
Tongs, Tire	Metalworking T&E	218
Tongs, Toast	Food Preparation Equipment	161
tongs, v-lip (*use:* Tongs, Hollow-bit)	Metalworking T&E	218
Tongue, Vehicle	Land Transportation Accessories	418
Tonlet	Body Armor	276
Tonometer	Mechanical Measurement Equipment	319
Tonometer, Acoustical	Acoustical T&E	262
Tonometer, Ocular	Medical Instruments	329
Tonoscope	Acoustical T&E	262
Tonsillotome	Medical Instruments	332
Tool, Angle-Bending	Metalworking T&E	207
Tool, Animal Grooming	Animal Care Equipment	136
Tool, Animal Identification	Animal Care Equipment	136
Tool, Animal Obstetrical	Veterinary Equipment	142
Tool, Barking	Forestry T&E	191
Tool, Beekeeping	Animal Care Equipment	136
Tool, Boring	Metalworking T&E	218
Tool, Butchering	Food Processing Equipment	165
Tool, Calk	Farrier Equipment	139
Tool, Canning	Food Processing Equipment	165
Tool, Castration	Veterinary Equipment	143
Tool, Cider Making	Food Processing Equipment	165
Tool, Cigar Making	Other T&E for Materials	260
Tool, Combination	Multiple Use T&E for Materials	228
Tool, Dairy	Food Processing Equipment	165
Tool, Dissecting	Biological T&E	288
Tool, Ear Marking	Animal Care Equipment	136
Tool, Egg Processing	Food Processing Equipment	167
Tool, Entrenching	Construction T&E	296
Tool, Fabric Piercing	Needleworking Equipment	237
Tool, Fence	Construction T&E	296
Tool, Fertilizing	Tending Equipment	133
Tool, Fiber Plaiting	Fiberworking T&E	144
Tool, Finishing	Glass, Plastics & Clayworking T&E	195
tool, fishing (*use:* Tool, Well Fishing)	Mining & Mineral Harvesting T&E	225
Tool, Flaring	Glass, Plastics & Clayworking T&E	195
Tool, Flensing	Fishing Equipment	148
Tool, Fly Tying	Fishing Equipment	148
Tool, Foam Cutting	Glass, Plastics & Clayworking T&E	195
Tool, Food Cutting	Food Preparation Equipment	158
Tool, Food Decorating	Food Preparation Equipment	159
Tool, Food Extracting	Food Preparation Equipment	159
Tool, Food Grinding	Food Preparation Equipment	160
Tool, Food Handling	Food Preparation Equipment	160
Tool, Food Mixing	Food Preparation Equipment	161
Tool, Food Packaging	Food Processing Equipment	168
Tool, Food Separating	Food Preparation Equipment	162
Tool, Forming	Glass, Plastics & Clayworking T&E	195
Tool, Fruit Processing	Food Processing Equipment	168
Tool, Grafting	Tending Equipment	133
Tool, Grain Processing	Food Processing Equipment	168
Tool, Heading	Metalworking T&E	218
Tool, Hearth Cooking	Food Preparation Equipment	162
Tool, Herding	Animal Care Equipment	136
Tool, Hoof	Farrier Equipment	140
Tool, Hornworker's	Leather, Horn & Shellworking T&E	201
Tool, Ice Harvesting	Mining & Mineral Harvesting T&E	225
Tool, Incense	Religious Objects	465
Tool, Incising	Glass, Plastics & Clayworking T&E	195
Tool, Inking	Graphic Equipment	385
Tool, Irrigation	Tending Equipment	133
Tool, Knurling	Metalworking T&E	218
Tool, Lapidary	Other T&E for Materials	260
Tool, Lard Processing	Food Processing Equipment	169
Tool, Loop	Glass, Plastics & Clayworking T&E	195
Tool, Lubrication	Mechanical Devices	317
Tool, Manicure	Beauty Supplies	117
Tool, Maple Sugaring	Food Processing Equipment	169
Tool, Modeling	Glass, Plastics & Clayworking T&E	195
Tool, Needle	Glass, Plastics & Clayworking T&E	195
tool, parting (*use:* Gouge, Parting)	Woodworking T&E	251
Tool, Pharmaceutical	Medical Accessories	326
Tool, Plastering	Masonry & Stoneworking T&E	205
Tool, Pot-Setting	Glass, Plastics & Clayworking T&E	195

Tool, Pruning — Groundskeeping Equipment 310
Tool, Pyrography — Multiple Use T&E for Materials 228
Tool, Radius — Masonry & Stoneworking T&E 206
tool, rib (*use:* Rib, Potter's) — Glass, Plastics & Clayworking T&E 195
Tool, Scarification — Beauty Supplies 117
Tool, Scratch — Masonry & Stoneworking T&E 206
Tool, Sinew — Other T&E for Materials 260
Tool, Soapmaking — Other T&E for Materials 260
Tool, Stove — Heating Equipment Accessories 77
Tool, Tint — Graphic Equipment 384
Tool, Tong — Armament Accessories 272
Tool, Toy Sculpting — Toys 524
Tool, Track — Rail Transportation Accessories 432
Tool, Turning — Glass, Plastics & Clayworking T&E 195
Tool, Vehicle — Land Transportation Accessories 421
Tool, Wallpapering — Painting T&E 230
Tool, Well Fishing — Mining & Mineral Harvesting T&E 225
Tool, Whale Blubber — Fishing Equipment 148
Tool, Wigmaking — Fiberworking T&E 144
Toolbox — Multiple Use T&E for Materials 226
tools, fireplace (*use:* Fireset) — Heating Equipment Accessories 76
Toolshed — Outbuildings 38
toonie (*use:* Coin, Two-Dollar) — Exchange Media 487
Toothbrush — Hygiene Objects 121
Toothbrush, Electric — Hygiene Objects 121
Toothkey — Dental Instruments 323
Toothpick — Hygiene Objects 121
Top — Toys 525
top, bimini (*use:* Bimini) — Water Transportation Accessories 436
Top, Bowstring — Toys 525
Top, Gyroscope — Toys 525
Top, Halter — Main Garments 99
Top, Magnetic — Toys 525
Top, Peg — Toys 525
Top, Tank — Main Garments 98
Top, Tube — Main Garments 99
Top, Whip — Toys 525
topcoat (*use:* Overcoat) — Outerwear 100
topee (*use:* Helmet, Pith) — Headwear 94
Topophone — Acoustical T&E 262
Topper, Antenna — Land Transportation Accessories 422
Topper, Barrel — Woodworking T&E 259
Topper, Egg — Food Preparation Equipment 159
Topper, Hornworker's — Leather, Horn & Shellworking T&E 201
Topsail — Water Transportation Accessories 439
Toque — Headwear 92
Torah, Sepher — Religious Objects 465
torc (*use:* Torque) — Body Adornments 81
torch (*use:* Blowtorch) — Metalworking T&E 208
Torch — Lighting Holders 71
Torch, Acetylene — Metalworking T&E 208
Torch, Alcohol — Metalworking T&E 208
Torch, Campaign — Organizational Objects 459
Torch, Drip — Forestry T&E 191
Torch, Gas — Metalworking T&E 208
Torch, Gasoline — Metalworking T&E 208
Torch, Juggling — Public Entertainment Devices 508
Torch, Kerosene — Metalworking T&E 208
Torch, Oxyacetylene — Metalworking T&E 208
Torch, Oxyhydrogen — Metalworking T&E 208
Torch, Propane — Metalworking T&E 208
Torch, Tiki — Lighting Holders 71
Torchère — Lighting Holders 71
Torpedo — Ammunition 264
Torpedo, Aerial — Aircraft 411
Torpedo, Well — Mining & Mineral Harvesting T&E 225
Torque — Body Adornments 81
Tortillon — Painting T&E 230
Totem — Belief Symbols 494
Touchpad — Peripherals 364
Touchscreen — Peripherals 364
Toupee — Hair Adornments 83
Tourniquet — Medical Instruments 334
Towboat — Watercraft 448
Towel — Hygiene Objects 121
Towel, Bath — Hygiene Objects 121
Towel, Beach — Hygiene Objects 121
Towel, Bowling — Sports Equipment 514
Towel, Dish — Dishwashing Equipment 308
Towel, Face — Hygiene Objects 121
Towel, Fingertip — Hygiene Objects 121
Towel, Hand — Hygiene Objects 121
Towel, Paper — Housekeeping Equipment 312
Towel, Show — Decorative Furnishings 60
Towelette — Hygiene Objects 121
Tower — Other Structures 41
Tower, Bell — Other Structures 41
Tower, Church — Architectural Spaces 1
Tower, Clock — Other Structures 41
Tower, Control — Transportation Structures 40
Tower, Cooling — Environmental Control Elements 9
Tower, Fire — Other Structures 41
tower, observation (*use:* Watchtower) — Other Structures 41
Tower, Radio — Other Structures 41
Tower, Shot — Industrial Structures 35

Term	Category	Page
Tower, Signal	Transportation Structures	40
Tower, Television	Other Structures	41
Tower, Transmitting	Other Structures	41
Tower, Water	Hydraulic Structures	34
towline (*use:* Hawser)	Water Transportation Accessories	441
Towline, Vehicle	Land Transportation Accessories	422
Towline, Water Ski	Recreational Devices	511
Townscape	Art	453
Toy	Toys	523
Toy, Balance	Toys	523
Toy, Bath	Toys	523
Toy, Bell	Toys	523
Toy, Bubble	Toys	523
Toy, Car	Toys	523
Toy, Craft	Toys	523
Toy, Crib	Toys	523
Toy, Cup and Ball	Toys	523
Toy, Dexterity	Toys	523
Toy, Drawing	Toys	523
Toy, Educational	Toys	523
Toy, Fortune Telling	Toys	523
Toy, Inflatable	Toys	523
Toy, Magnetic	Toys	523
Toy, Mechanical	Toys	523
Toy, Musical	Toys	523
Toy, Optical	Toys	523
Toy, Pegboard	Toys	523
Toy, Penny	Toys	524
Toy, Pet	Pet Supplies	141
Toy, Pounding	Toys	524
Toy, Pull	Toys	524
Toy, Push	Toys	524
Toy, Riding	Toys	524
toy, rocking (*use:* Tumbler, Toy)	Toys	521
Toy, Sand	Toys	524
Toy, Scissor	Toys	524
Toy, Sculpting	Toys	524
Toy, Sound	Toys	524
toy, spinning (*use:* Whirligig)	Toys	525
Toy, Spring	Toys	524
Toy, Stacking	Toys	524
Toy, Stuffed	Toys	524
Toy, Teething	Toys	525
toy, trundle (*use:* Toy, Push)	Toys	524
Trace	Land Transportation Accessories	421
Tracer	Glass, Plastics & Clayworking T&E	195
tracer, curve (*use:* Curve, Flexible)	Drafting T&E	366
Track	Rail Transportation Accessories	432
Track, Door	Door & Window Elements	6
Trackball	Peripherals	364
Tracker, Head	Peripherals	364
tracksuit (*use:* Sweatsuit)	Main Garments	99
Tract	Literary Works	477
Tractor	Motor Vehicles	428
Tractor, Artillery	Motor Vehicles	430
Tractor, Crawler	Construction T&E	295
Tractor, Farm	Motor Vehicles	428
Tractor, Garden	Groundskeeping Equipment	310
tractor, lawn (*use:* Mower, Riding)	Groundskeeping Equipment	309
Tractor, Truck	Motor Vehicles	429
Trailboard	Water Transportation Accessories	437
Trailer	Motor Vehicles	428
Trailer, Animal	Motor Vehicles	428
Trailer, Bicycle	Human-Powered Vehicles	427
Trailer, Boat	Motor Vehicles	429
trailer, camping (*use:* Camper)	Motor Vehicles	428
Trailer, Farm	Motor Vehicles	429
Trailer, Horse	Motor Vehicles	428
Trailer, House	Motor Vehicles	429
Trailer, Slip	Glass, Plastics & Clayworking T&E	195
Trailer, Snowmobile	Motor Vehicles	429
trailer, tractor-drawn (*use:* Trailer, Farm)	Motor Vehicles	429
Trailer, Travel	Motor Vehicles	429
Train	Rail Vehicles	434
Train, Dress	Clothing Accessories	87
Train, Freight	Rail Vehicles	434
Train, Passenger	Rail Vehicles	434
Train, Scouring	Textile Manufacturing Equipment	244
train, toy (*use:* Set, Train)	Toys	522
tram (*use:* Streetcar)	Rail Vehicles	434
Tram, Mine	Mining & Mineral Harvesting T&E	221
Trammel	Food Preparation Equipment	163
Trampoline	Sports Equipment	516
Transceiver	Telecommunication Devices	397
Transcript	Literary Works	477
Transducer	Power Producing Equipment	304
Transformer	Electrical System Components	301
Transformer, Impedance	Electrical System Components	301
Transformer, Resonant	Electrical System Components	301
Transilluminator	Medical Instruments	328
Transistor	Electrical System Components	301
Transit	Surveying Equipment	353
Transmitter	Telecommunication Devices	397
Transmitter, Radio	Telecommunication Devices	397

Transmitter, Sound — Acoustical T&E 262
Transmitter, Television — Telecommunication Devices 397
Transom — Door & Window Elements 7
transom (*use:* Frame, Transom) — Water Transportation Accessories 438
Transparency — Graphic Documents 473
Transparency, Lantern Slide — Graphic Documents 473
transparency, magic lantern (*use:* Transparency, Lantern Slide) — Graphic Documents 473
Transparency, Roll Film — Graphic Documents 473
Transparency, Slide — Graphic Documents 473
Transplanter — Planting Equipment 132
Transplanter, Hand — Planting Equipment 132
Transponder — Telecommunication Devices 397
Transport, Naval — Watercraft 447
Transporter, Personal — Motor Vehicles 429
Trap — Animal-Powered Vehicles 424
Trap, Animal — Trapping Equipment 149
Trap, Bear — Trapping Equipment 149
Trap, Beaver — Trapping Equipment 149
Trap, Bullet — Armament Accessories 272
Trap, Cage — Trapping Equipment 149
trap, cartridge (*use:* Trap, Bullet) — Armament Accessories 272
Trap, Fish — Fishing Equipment 148
trap, fly (*use:* Flytrap) — Other Household Accessories 66
Trap, Foothold — Trapping Equipment 149
Trap, Hand — Armament Accessories 272
Trap, Insect — Other Household Accessories 66
trap, lobster (*use:* Pot, Lobster) — Fishing Equipment 148
trap, mouse (*use:* Mousetrap) — Other Household Accessories 66
trap, rat (*use:* Rattrap) — Other Household Accessories 66
Trap, Roach — Other Household Accessories 66
Trap, Rodent — Other Household Accessories 66
Trap, Skeet — Armament Accessories 272
Trapeze — Public Entertainment Devices 508
Trapeze, Playground — Recreational Devices 510
Traveler — Metalworking T&E 218
Travelogue — Literary Works 477
Travois — Animal-Powered Vehicles 424
trawl (*use:* Net, Trawl) — Fishing Equipment 146
trawl, tub (*use:* Longline) — Fishing Equipment 147
Trawler — Watercraft 445
Tray — Containers 415
Tray, Ammunition — Armament Accessories 268
tray, baking (*use:* Pan, Sheet) — Cooking Vessels 150
Tray, Bed — Food Service Accessories 182
Tray, Bread — Serving Vessels 187
Tray, Butler's — Food Service Accessories 182
Tray, Butter — Serving Vessels 187
Tray, Cafeteria — Food Service Accessories 182
tray, calling card (*use:* Receiver, Card) — Storage & Display Accessories 65
Tray, Candlesnuffer — Storage & Display Accessories 65
Tray, Chopping — Food Preparation Equipment 153
Tray, Cracker — Serving Vessels 187
tray, crumb (*use:* Butler, Silent) — Housekeeping Equipment 311
tray, cutlery (*use:* Tray, Flatware) — Food Service Accessories 182
Tray, Darkroom — Photoprocessing Equipment 381
Tray, Dental Accessory — Dental Accessories 321
Tray, Desk — Writing Accessories 404
Tray, Display — Merchandising T&E 337
Tray, Dresser — Storage & Display Accessories 65
Tray, Drying — Food Preparation Equipment 155
Tray, Flatware — Food Service Accessories 182
Tray, Food Service — Food Service Accessories 182
Tray, Frozen Dinner — Eating Vessels 177
Tray, Fruit — Serving Vessels 187
Tray, Gambling — Game Equipment 503
Tray, Household — Storage & Display Accessories 65
Tray, Ice Cream — Serving Vessels 187
Tray, Ice Cube — Food Preparation Equipment 153
Tray, Impression — Dental Accessories 321
Tray, Mess — Eating Vessels 177
Tray, Money — Merchandising T&E 336
Tray, Needlework — Needleworking Equipment 235
Tray, Offering — Religious Objects 461
Tray, Ore — Mining & Mineral Harvesting T&E 221
Tray, Organ — Medical Accessories 326
Tray, Paint — Painting T&E 231
Tray, Paper — Writing Accessories 403
Tray, Peg — Leather, Horn & Shellworking T&E 201
Tray, Pen — Writing Accessories 404
Tray, Pin — Needleworking Equipment 235
Tray, Relish — Serving Vessels 188
Tray, Sauceboat — Serving Vessels 188
Tray, Serving — Serving Vessels 187
Tray, Slide — Visual Communication Accessories 399
Tray, Tea — Serving Vessels 188
tray, threshing (*use:* Basket, Winnowing) — Harvesting Equipment 131
Tray, Tureen — Serving Vessels 188

Tray, Vending	Merchandising T&E	338
Tray, Winnowing	Harvesting Equipment	131
Tray, Writing Equipment	Writing Accessories	404
Tread, Stair	Stair Elements	15
Treadle	Power Producing Equipment	304
Treadle, Railway	Rail Transportation Accessories	432
Treadmill	Power Producing Equipment	304
Treadmill, Animal	Power Producing Equipment	304
Treadmill, Exercise	Recreational Devices	509
Treadmill, Human	Power Producing Equipment	304
Treatise	Literary Works	477
Treaty	Legal Documents	476
Trebucket	Percussive Weapons	283
trechometer (*use:* Wheel, Surveyor's)	Surveying Equipment	353
Tree, Boot	Clothing Care Objects	106
Tree, Christmas	Holiday Objects	458
Tree, Coat	Support Furniture	55
Tree, Family	Graphic Documents	472
Tree, Footwear	Clothing Care Objects	106
tree, hall (*use:* Tree, Coat)	Support Furniture	55
Tree, Holiday	Holiday Objects	458
Tree, Saddle	Land Transportation Accessories	421
Tree, Shoe	Clothing Care Objects	106
Treenail	Woodworking T&E	250
Trellis	Site Features	21
Trellis, Plant	Other Household Accessories	67
trembleuse (*use:* Set, Cup and Saucer)	Food Service Sets	183
Trench	Site Features	20
Trencher	Serving Vessels	187
Trephine	Medical Instruments	332
Trestle	Transportation Structures	39
Triangle, 30-60-90	Drafting T&E	367
Triangle, 45-45-90	Drafting T&E	367
Triangle, Adjustable	Drafting T&E	367
Triangle, Drafting	Drafting T&E	367
Triangle, Musical	Musical Instruments	373
Tribometer	Mechanical Measurement Equipment	319
Tricorn	Headwear	92
Tricycle	Human-Powered Vehicles	426
Tricycle, Gasoline	Motor Vehicles	428
Tricycle, Side-By-Side	Human-Powered Vehicles	426
Tricycle, Steam	Motor Vehicles	430
Tricycle, Tandem	Human-Powered Vehicles	426
Tricycle, Two-Track	Human-Powered Vehicles	426
Trident	Edged Weapons	278
Trier, Butter	Food Processing Equipment	167
Trier, Cheese	Food Processing Equipment	167
Trigger, Flash	Camera Equipment	377
Triglyph	Supporting Elements	16
Trim, Furnishing	Decorative Furnishings	60
Trim, Textile	Needleworking Equipment	236
Trimaran	Watercraft	443
trimmer, base (*use:* Cutter, Base)	Painting T&E	231
Trimmer, Beard	Hair Care Objects	118
Trimmer, Dental	Dental Instruments	324
Trimmer, Ear	Animal Care Equipment	136
Trimmer, Edge	Leather, Horn & Shellworking T&E	197
trimmer, edge (*use:* Cutter, Base)	Painting T&E	231
trimmer, hair (*use:* Clipper, Hair)	Hair Care Objects	118
Trimmer, Hedge	Groundskeeping Equipment	310
Trimmer, Hoof	Farrier Equipment	140
Trimmer, Leather	Leather, Horn & Shellworking T&E	197
Trimmer, Log	Forestry T&E	191
Trimmer, Nose Hair	Hair Care Objects	118
trimmer, paper (*use:* Machine, Paper Trimming)	Papermaking T&E	232
Trimmer, Paper	Writing Accessories	405
Trimmer, Photograph	Photoprocessing Equipment	381
trimmer, pie (*use:* Wheel, Jagging)	Food Preparation Equipment	159
Trimmer, String	Groundskeeping Equipment	310
Trimmer, Welt	Leather, Horn & Shellworking T&E	197
Trimmer, Wick	Other Lighting Accessories	73
Trindle	Bookbinding Equipment	383
trip-hammer (*use:* Hammer, Helve)	Metalworking T&E	212
Trip-Hammer	Papermaking T&E	233
triple (*use:* Truck, Fire)	Motor Vehicles	429
Tripletree	Land Transportation Accessories	419
Tripod	Support Furniture	55
Tripod, Camera	Camera Equipment	377
Tripod, Hearth	Food Preparation Equipment	163
Tripod, Laboratory	Labware	294
Tripod, Mining	Mining & Mineral Harvesting T&E	225
Tripod, Shooting	Armament Accessories	270
Tripod, Surveyor's	Surveying Equipment	353
Triptych	Religious Objects	464
Trivet	Food Preparation Accessories	152
Trivet, Ironing	Laundry Equipment	314
Trocar	Medical Instruments	332
troffer (*use:* Light, Recessed)	Lighting Devices	68
Trolley	Rail Vehicles	435

trolley, trackless (*use:* Trolleybus)	Motor Vehicles	428
Trolleybus	Motor Vehicles	428
Trombone	Musical Instruments	370
Trombone, Slide	Musical Instruments	370
Trombone, Valve	Musical Instruments	370
Tromometer	Geological T&E	307
Trophy	Achievement Symbols	492
Trophy, Game	Achievement Symbols	492
Tropostereoscope	Medical Instruments	329
Trough, Dough	Food Preparation Equipment	153
Trough, Feeding	Animal Care Equipment	135
Trough, Meat Salting	Food Processing Equipment	164
Trough, Mixing	Masonry & Stoneworking T&E	206
Trough, Pneumatic	Chemical Testing Devices	291
trough, powdering (*use:* Tub, Salting)	Food Preparation Equipment	153
Trough, Sap	Forestry T&E	191
trough, scalding (*use:* Scalder, Hog)	Food Processing Equipment	165
Trough, Watering	Animal Care Equipment	137
trousers (*use:* Pants)	Main Garments	97
Trousers, Bell-Bottom	Main Garments	97
Trowel	Masonry & Stoneworking T&E	206
Trowel, Brick	Masonry & Stoneworking T&E	206
Trowel, Buttering	Masonry & Stoneworking T&E	206
Trowel, Corner	Masonry & Stoneworking T&E	206
Trowel, Fraternal	Status Symbols	497
Trowel, Garden	Cultivation Equipment	125
Trowel, Grouting	Masonry & Stoneworking T&E	206
Trowel, Margin	Masonry & Stoneworking T&E	206
Trowel, Mechanical	Masonry & Stoneworking T&E	206
Trowel, Molder's	Metalworking T&E	218
trowel, nursery (*use:* Trowel, Garden)	Cultivation Equipment	125
Trowel, Pointing	Masonry & Stoneworking T&E	206
Trowel, Smoothing	Masonry & Stoneworking T&E	206
Truck	Motor Vehicles	429
Truck, Aerial Ladder	Motor Vehicles	429
Truck, Baggage	Motor Vehicles	429
Truck, Boom	Motor Vehicles	429
Truck, Crash	Motor Vehicles	429
Truck, Delivery	Motor Vehicles	429
Truck, Dump	Motor Vehicles	429
Truck, Fire	Motor Vehicles	429
Truck, Flatbed	Motor Vehicles	429
Truck, Garment	Human-Powered Vehicles	427
Truck, Hand	Human-Powered Vehicles	427
Truck, Hook and Ladder	Motor Vehicles	429
truck, ladder (*use:* Truck, Hook and Ladder)	Motor Vehicles	429
Truck, Lighting	Motor Vehicles	429
Truck, Lumber	Motor Vehicles	429
Truck, Mail	Motor Vehicles	429
Truck, Maintenance	Motor Vehicles	429
Truck, Milk	Motor Vehicles	429
Truck, Ordnance Workshop	Motor Vehicles	430
Truck, Panel	Motor Vehicles	429
Truck, Pickup	Motor Vehicles	429
Truck, Pumper	Motor Vehicles	429
Truck, Pumper Ladder	Motor Vehicles	429
Truck, Pumper/Aerial Ladder	Motor Vehicles	429
Truck, Stake	Motor Vehicles	429
Truck, Tank	Motor Vehicles	429
Truck, Tow	Motor Vehicles	429
Truck, Troop	Motor Vehicles	430
trug (*use:* Basket, Gathering)	Harvesting Equipment	127
Trumpet	Musical Instruments	370
Trumpet, Ear	Personal Assistive Objects	107
Trumpet, Fire	Sound Communication Devices	392
Trumpet, Hailing	Sound Communication Devices	391
Trumpet, Key	Musical Instruments	370
Trumpet, Marine	Musical Instruments	374
trumpet, nasal (*use:* Airway, Nasopharyngeal)	Medical Instruments	335
trumpet, natural (*use:* Trumpet, Slide)	Musical Instruments	370
Trumpet, Slide	Musical Instruments	370
Trumpet, Speaking	Sound Communication Devices	392
Trumpet, Valve	Musical Instruments	370
truncheon (*use:* Nightstick)	Percussive Weapons	283
Trunk	Personal Carrying & Storage Gear	113
Trunk, Document	Writing Accessories	403
Trunk, Doll	Toys	520
Trunk, Escape	Public Entertainment Devices	508
Trunks	Main Garments	98
trunnel (*use:* Treenail)	Woodworking T&E	250
Trunnion	Armament Accessories	272
Truss	Supporting Elements	17
Truss, Hernia	Medical Instruments	334
T-Shirt	Main Garments	98
T-Square	Drafting T&E	367
TTY (*use:* Teletypewriter)	Telecommunication Devices	397

Tub	Containers	415
Tub, Butter	Food Processing Equipment	167
Tub, Food Storage	Food Storage Equipment	172
Tub, Hot	Plumbing & Drainage Elements	12
Tub, Iron Cooling	Glass, Plastics & Clayworking T&E	195
Tub, Laundry	Plumbing & Drainage Elements	12
tub, powdering (*use:* Tub, Salting)	Food Preparation Equipment	153
Tub, Salting	Food Preparation Equipment	153
Tub, Slack	Metalworking T&E	218
tub, wash (*use:* Washtub)	Laundry Equipment	314
Tuba	Musical Instruments	370
Tuba, Wagner	Musical Instruments	370
Tube	Containers	415
Tube, Ballast	Electrical System Components	301
Tube, Barometer	Labware	293
Tube, Blood Collecting	Medical Instruments	327
Tube, Boiling	Labware	293
Tube, Capillary	Labware	293
Tube, Centrifuge	Labware	293
Tube, Combustion	Labware	293
tube, culture (*use:* Tube, Test)	Labware	293
Tube, Document	Writing Accessories	403
Tube, Electrical	Electrical System Components	301
Tube, Electron	Electrical System Components	302
Tube, Enema	Veterinary Equipment	143
Tube, Fluorescent	Other Lighting Accessories	72
Tube, Grouting	Masonry & Stoneworking T&E	206
Tube, Ink	Printing Accessories	386
Tube, Laboratory	Labware	293
Tube, Medical	Medical Instruments	334
Tube, Milk	Food Processing Equipment	167
Tube, Percussion	Armament Accessories	272
Tube, Pneumatic	Conveyance Devices	5
Tube, Pool	Recreational Devices	511
Tube, Quincke's	Acoustical T&E	262
tube, silage (*use:* Bag, Silage)	Feed Processing Equipment	126
Tube, Ski	Recreational Devices	511
Tube, Sounding	Navigational Equipment	349
Tube, Speaking	Sound Communication Devices	392
Tube, Stomach	Medical Instruments	335
Tube, Sucking	Medical Instruments	335
tube, teat (*use:* Tube, Milk)	Food Processing Equipment	167
Tube, Test	Labware	293
Tube, Tracheostomy	Medical Instruments	332
Tube, Tracheotomy	Veterinary Equipment	143
Tube, Vacuum	Electrical System Components	302
Tubing, Laboratory	Labware	294
tubing, reducer (*use:* Adapter, Tubing)	Labware	292
Tucker	Clothing Accessories	87
Tug, Shaft	Land Transportation Accessories	421
Tugboat	Watercraft	448
tug-towboat (*use:* Towboat)	Watercraft	448
Tumbler	Drinking Vessels	174
Tumbler, Bingo	Game Equipment	503
Tumbler, Toy	Toys	521
Tumbrel	Animal-Powered Vehicles	424
Tumpline	Personal Carrying & Storage Gear	113
Tuner, Radio	Telecommunication Devices	396
Tuner, Television	Telecommunication Accessories	395
Tunic	Main Garments	99
Tunnel	Transportation Structures	40
Tunnel, Amusement	Cultural & Recreational Structures	29
Tunnel, Play	Toys	523
Tunnel, Railroad	Transportation Structures	40
Tunnel, Water	Hydraulic Structures	34
Tunnel, Wind	Mechanical Measurement Equipment	319
Tuque	Headwear	92
Turban	Headwear	94
Turbidimeter	Mechanical Measurement Equipment	319
Turbine	Power Producing Equipment	304
Turbine, Gas	Power Producing Equipment	304
Turbine, Hydraulic	Power Producing Equipment	304
Turbine, Impulse	Power Producing Equipment	304
Turbine, Internal Combustion	Power Producing Equipment	304
Turbine, Steam	Power Producing Equipment	304
turbine, tub (*use:* Waterwheel, Tub)	Power Producing Equipment	304
Tureen	Serving Vessels	188
Tureen, Sauce	Serving Vessels	188
Tureen, Soup	Serving Vessels	188
Turf, Artificial	Floor Coverings	45
Turnbuckle	Mechanical Devices	317
turnbuckle (*use:* Screw, Rigging)	Water Transportation Accessories	439
Turner, Cake	Food Preparation Equipment	161

Turner, Seam	Leather, Horn & Shellworking T&E	201
turnkey, dental (*use:* Toothkey)	Dental Instruments	323
Turnstile	Site Features	20
Turntable, Phonograph	Sound Communication Accessories	390
Turntable, Railroad	Transportation Structures	40
Turret	Architectural Spaces	1
Turret, Machine Gun	Armament Accessories	270
Turtleneck	Main Garments	99
Tutu	Main Garments	99
Tuxedo	Main Garments	99
Tuyere	Metalworking T&E	218
Tweezers	Multiple Use T&E for Materials	228
Tweezers, Glassworking	Glass, Plastics & Clayworking T&E	195
Tweezers, Hair	Hair Care Objects	119
Tweezers, Soldering	Dental Accessories	321
Tweezers, Surgical	Medical Instruments	332
Twibil	Woodworking T&E	247
Twiffler	Eating Vessels	177
Twine	Multiple Use T&E for Materials	226
Twirler	Food Preparation Equipment	162
Twister	Textile Manufacturing Equipment	244
Twister, Nose	Animal Care Equipment	135
Twister, Wire	Metalworking T&E	218
twitch, nose (*use:* Twister, Nose)	Animal Care Equipment	135
Tyg	Drinking Vessels	174
Tympanum	Surface Elements	19
Type	Typesetting Equipment	388
Typescript	Other Documents	486
Typesetter	Typesetting Equipment	388
Typesetter, Computer	Typesetting Equipment	388
Typesetter, Keyboard	Typesetting Equipment	388
typesetter, linotype (*use:* Typesetter, Keyboard)	Typesetting Equipment	388
typesetter, monotype (*use:* Typesetter, Keyboard)	Typesetting Equipment	388
typesetter, photo (*use:* Phototypesetter)	Typesetting Equipment	388
Typewriter	Writing Devices	407
typewriter, braille (*use:* Embosser, Braille)	Writing Devices	406
typewriter, console (*use:* Typewriter, Encoding)	Data Processing Devices	362
Typewriter, Electric	Writing Devices	407
Typewriter, Encoding	Data Processing Devices	362
Typewriter, Magnetic Card	Data Processing Devices	362
Typewriter, Magnetic Disk	Data Processing Devices	362
Typewriter, Magnetic Tape	Data Processing Devices	362
Typewriter, Manual	Writing Devices	407
Typewriter, Paper Tape	Data Processing Devices	362
udometer (*use:* Pluviometer)	Meteorological T&E	339
Udometer	Meteorological T&E	339
Ukelin	Musical Instruments	374
Ukulele	Musical Instruments	373
ukulele, banjo (*use:* Banjolele)	Musical Instruments	373
Ulu	Multiple Use T&E for Materials	227
Umbrella	Personal Assistive Objects	109
Umiak	Watercraft	442
Underbodice	Underwear	104
Undercurrent	Mining & Mineral Harvesting T&E	225
Undercurtain	Window & Door Coverings	78
Underdress	Underwear	104
Underpants	Underwear	104
Underpants, Bikini	Underwear	104
Underpants, Long	Underwear	104
Underpants, Maternity	Underwear	104
Underpants, Protective	Underwear	104
Undershirt	Underwear	104
Underskirt	Underwear	104
Undersleeve	Clothing Accessories	87
undervest (*use:* Undershirt)	Underwear	104
Underwear, Long	Underwear	104
underwear, shaping (*use:* Garment, Foundation)	Underwear	103
Underwear, Thong	Underwear	104
Unicycle	Human-Powered Vehicles	426
Uniface	Unclassifiable Objects	527
Uniform	Status Symbols	500
Uniform, Fire	Status Symbols	500
Uniform, Law Enforcement	Status Symbols	500
Uniform, Military	Status Symbols	500
Uniform, Military Dress	Status Symbols	500
Uniform, Occupational	Status Symbols	500
Uniform, Organizational	Status Symbols	500
Uniform, Sports	Status Symbols	500
Unit, Air Handling	Environmental Control Elements	9
unit, assembly (*use:* Robot, Industrial)	Data Processing Devices	362
Unit, Audio Response	Peripherals	365
Unit, Baseboard	Environmental Control Elements	9
unit, card sensing-punching (*use:* Processor, Card)	Peripherals	365

unit, central processing (*use:* Computer, Digital) | Data Processing Devices | 362
Unit, Denture Curing | Dental Accessories | 321
unit, disk (*use:* Drive, Disk) | Peripherals | 365
Unit, Gondola Shelving | Merchandising T&E | 337
Unit, Hydrostatic Release | Water Transportation Accessories | 440
Unit, Peripheral Control | Peripherals | 365
Unit, Prophylaxis | Dental Accessories | 321
Unit, Shelving | Storage & Display Furniture | 54
unit, tape (*use:* Drive, Tape) | Peripherals | 365
unit, visual display (*use:* Monitor, Computer) | Peripherals | 364
Unitard | Main Garments | 96
Upsetter, Tire | Metalworking T&E | 218
Ureometer | Medical Instruments | 334
Urethroscope | Medical Instruments | 334
Urethrotome | Medical Instruments | 334
Uricometer | Medical Instruments | 334
Urinal | Plumbing & Drainage Elements | 12
Urinal, Portable | Hygiene Objects | 121
Urinometer | Medical Instruments | 334
Urn, Beverage | Serving Vessels | 189
urn, burial (*use:* Urn, Cremation) | Funerary Objects | 456
urn, cinerary (*use:* Urn, Cremation) | Funerary Objects | 456
Urn, Coffee | Serving Vessels | 189
Urn, Cremation | Funerary Objects | 456
Urn, Decorative | Decorative Furnishings | 60
Urn, Garden | Site Features | 21
Urn, Hot Water | Serving Vessels | 189
Urn, Tea | Serving Vessels | 189
Utensil, Infant | Eating & Drinking Utensils | 179
uteroscope (*use:* Metroscope) | Medical Instruments | 330
uvrou (*use:* Euphroe) | Water Transportation Accessories | 437
Vacuum, Canister | Housekeeping Equipment | 311
Vacuum, Handheld | Housekeeping Equipment | 311
Vacuum, Upright | Housekeeping Equipment | 311
Vacuum, Wet | Housekeeping Equipment | 311
Vacuum, Wet/Dry | Housekeeping Equipment | 311
Valance | Window & Door Coverings | 79
valance, base (*use:* Bedskirt) | Bedding | 44
Valance, Bed | Bedding | 44
Valance, Double | Bedding | 44
valance, shelf (*use:* Lambrequin) | Furniture Coverings | 61
Valentine | Other Documents | 482
Valentine, Sailor's | Art | 454
Valet | Support Furniture | 55
valise (*use:* Suitcase) | Personal Carrying & Storage Gear | 112
Valve | Finish Hardware | 11
Valve, Pipe | Finish Hardware | 11
Valve, Standing | Mining & Mineral Harvesting T&E | 225
Valve, Steam | Power Transmission Components | 305
Valve, Well Pump | Mining & Mineral Harvesting T&E | 225
Valve, Working | Mining & Mineral Harvesting T&E | 225
Vambrace | Body Armor | 276
Van | Motor Vehicles | 429
Van, Gypsy | Animal-Powered Vehicles | 424
vanity (*use:* Table, Dressing) | Support Furniture | 56
Vanner | Mining & Mineral Harvesting T&E | 224
Vaporimeter | Chemical Testing Devices | 291
Vaporizer | Medical Instruments | 333
Vargueño | Storage & Display Furniture | 53
Variator, Stern | Acoustical T&E | 262
Varioplex | Telecommunication Devices | 397
Vasculum | Biological T&E | 287
Vase | Horticultural Containers | 62
Vase, Altar | Religious Objects | 462
Vase, Automobile | Land Transportation Accessories | 422
Vase, Bud | Horticultural Containers | 62
Vase, Celery | Serving Vessels | 188
Vase, Flower | Horticultural Containers | 62
vase, incense (*use:* Censer) | Religious Objects | 462
Vase, Libation | Religious Objects | 463
vase, potpourri (*use:* Jar, Potpourri) | Other Household Accessories | 66
Vase, Temple | Religious Objects | 462
Vase, Wall | Horticultural Containers | 62
Vat, Cheese | Food Processing Equipment | 167
Vat, Cooling | Food Processing Equipment | 164
vat, cream (*use:* Vat, Cheese) | Food Processing Equipment | 167
Vat, Cyanidation | Mining & Mineral Harvesting T&E | 225
Vat, Food Processing | Food Processing Equipment | 164
Vat, Food Storage | Food Storage Equipment | 172
Vat, Fulling | Textile Manufacturing Equipment | 244
Vat, Leather Bleaching | Leather, Horn & Shellworking T&E | 201
Vat, Leather Dyeing | Leather, Horn & Shellworking T&E | 201
Vat, Leather Pickling | Leather, Horn & Shellworking T&E | 201
Vat, Leather Processing | Leather, Horn & Shellworking T&E | 201

Vat, Pulp Papermaking T&E 233
Vat, Storage Containers 415
Vat, Textile Dyeing Textile Manufacturing Equipment 244
Vault Architectural Spaces 1
Vault, Burial Funerary Objects 456
V-Block Glass, Plastics & Clayworking T&E 195
VCR (*use:* Recorder, Videotape) Visual Communication Devices 401
Vehicle, All Terrain Motor Vehicles 430
Vehicle, Amusement Ride Recreational Devices 511
Vehicle, Child Transport Human-Powered Vehicles 427
Vehicle, Lunar Motor Vehicles 430
Vehicle, Military Motor Vehicles 430
Vehicle, Recreational Motor Vehicles 430
Vehicle, Sport Utility Motor Vehicles 428
Vehicle, Steam Motor Vehicles 430
Vehicle, Transit Railway Rail Vehicles 434
Veil Headwear 93
Veil, Chalice Religious Objects 463
Veil, Ciborium Religious Objects 463
Veil, Hat Headwear 94
Veil, Humeral Status Symbols 500
Veil, Mourning Funerary Objects 457
Veil, Tabernacle Religious Objects 463
Veil, Wedding Wedding Objects 466
Veilleuse Seating Furniture 49
Veiner Woodworking T&E 249
Velocimeter Mechanical Measurement Equipment 319
Velocipede Human-Powered Vehicles 426
Ventilator Environmental Control Elements 9
Ventilator, Medical Medical Instruments 333
Ventilator, Window Door & Window Elements 7
Verifier Data Processing Devices 362
vertimeter (*use:* Indicator, Rate-of-Climb) Aerospace Transportation Accessories 409
Vertimeter Surveying Equipment 353
Vervel Animal Care Equipment 135
Vessel Containers 415
Vessel, Baptismal Religious Objects 462
Vessel, Bomb Watercraft 447
vessel, canopic (*use:* Jar, Canopic) Funerary Objects 456
Vessel, Cargo Watercraft 446
vessel, cinerary (*use:* Urn, Cremation) Funerary Objects 456
Vessel, Commercial Fishing Watercraft 445
Vessel, Communion Religious Objects 462
Vessel, Condiment Serving Vessels 188
Vessel, Dredging Watercraft 445
Vessel, Drink Serving Serving Vessels 188
Vessel, Emergency Watercraft 446
vessel, excursion (*use:* Boat, Excursion) Watercraft 446
Vessel, Handlining Watercraft 445
Vessel, Holy Water Religious Objects 462
Vessel, Libation Religious Objects 462
Vessel, Line Fishing Watercraft 445
Vessel, Merchant Watercraft 446
vessel, milking (*use:* Pail, Milking) Food Processing Equipment 166
Vessel, Naval Watercraft 446
Vessel, Net Fishing Watercraft 445
Vessel, Parting Metalworking T&E 218
Vessel, Passenger Watercraft 446
Vessel, Petroleum Service Watercraft 448
Vessel, Planing Watercraft 447
Vessel, Refrigerator Watercraft 446
Vessel, Remotely Operated Watercraft 447
Vessel, Research Watercraft 447
Vessel, Service Watercraft 447
vessel, shari (*use:* Reliquary) Religious Objects 462
Vessel, Survey Watercraft 447
Vessel, Trapping Watercraft 445
vessel, whaling (*use:* Whaler) Watercraft 445
Vest Main Garments 99
vest (*use:* Undershirt) Underwear 104
Vest, Bulletproof Body Armor 276
Vest, Flak Body Armor 276
vest, life (*use:* Jacket, Life) Water Transportation Accessories 441
Vest, Safety Protective Wear 102
vest, tactical (*use:* Vest, Bulletproof) Body Armor 276
Vestee Clothing Accessories 87
Vestment Status Symbols 499
Vial Containers 415
Vibraphone Musical Instruments 373
Vibrator Personal Assistive Objects 107
Vibrator, Dental Dental Accessories 321
Vibroscope Acoustical T&E 262
Victoria Animal-Powered Vehicles 424
Videodisc Photographic Media 380
Videodisc, Digital Data Processing Media 363
Videotape Photographic Media 380
Viewer, Filmstrip Visual Communication Accessories 399
Viewer, Slide Visual Communication Accessories 399
Viewer, X-Ray Medical Instruments 328
Viewfinder Camera Equipment 377
Viga Supporting Elements 16
Village, Toy Toys 522
Vinaigrette Personal Assistive Objects 107
Viner, Pea Harvesting Equipment 131
Vinylcut Graphic Documents 474
Viol Musical Instruments 373
Viola Musical Instruments 373
Viola d'Amore Musical Instruments 373

Term	Category	Page
Violin	Musical Instruments	373
Violoncello	Musical Instruments	373
Virginal	Musical Instruments	371
Visa	Other Documents	482
Vis-à-Vis	Animal-Powered Vehicles	424
viscometer (*use:* Viscosimeter)	Mechanical Measurement Equipment	319
Viscosimeter	Mechanical Measurement Equipment	319
Vise	Mechanical Devices	317
Vise, Armament	Armament Accessories	272
Vise, Bench	Metalworking T&E	218
Vise, Blacksmith's	Metalworking T&E	218
Vise, Box	Woodworking T&E	259
Vise, Breeching	Armament Accessories	272
vise, broom maker's (*use:* Horse, Broom)	Fiberworking T&E	144
Vise, Carving	Woodworking T&E	259
Vise, Chair	Woodworking T&E	259
Vise, Hammer Spring	Armament Accessories	272
Vise, Hand	Metalworking T&E	218
Vise, Harness Maker's	Leather, Horn & Shellworking T&E	201
Vise, Leatherworking	Leather, Horn & Shellworking T&E	201
Vise, Leg	Metalworking T&E	218
Vise, Lock Spring	Armament Accessories	272
Vise, Machine	Metalworking T&E	218
Vise, Metalworking	Metalworking T&E	218
Vise, Pipe	Metalworking T&E	218
Vise, Shell	Armament Accessories	272
Vise, Wire	Metalworking T&E	219
Vise, Woodworking	Woodworking T&E	259
Visiometer	Medical Instruments	328
Visor	Headwear	94
vitrine (*use:* Case, Display)	Merchandising T&E	336
vitrine (*use:* Case, Curio)	Storage & Display Accessories	63
vitrine (*use:* Cabinet, Curio)	Storage & Display Furniture	52
vizard (*use:* Mask, Theatrical)	Public Entertainment Devices	507
V-Mail	Other Documents	482
Volleyball	Sports Equipment	519
Voltmeter	Electrical & Magnetic Measurement Devices	297
Voluminometer	Mechanical Measurement Equipment	319
Voucher	Financial Records	469
Voussoir	Construction Materials	4
Vulcanizer, Dental	Dental Accessories	321
Vuvuzela	Sound Communication Devices	391
Wad, Gun	Ammunition	265
wader (*use:* Boot, Hip)	Footwear	89
Wafer	Personal Identification	495
wafer, communion (*use:* Host)	Religious Objects	463
Wagon	Animal-Powered Vehicles	424
Wagon, Baggage	Animal-Powered Vehicles	425
Wagon, Battery	Animal-Powered Vehicles	425
Wagon, Chemical	Animal-Powered Vehicles	425
Wagon, Child's	Toys	524
Wagon, Circus	Animal-Powered Vehicles	425
Wagon, Conestoga	Animal-Powered Vehicles	425
Wagon, Covered	Animal-Powered Vehicles	425
Wagon, Delivery	Animal-Powered Vehicles	425
Wagon, Farm	Animal-Powered Vehicles	425
Wagon, Feeder	Feed Processing Equipment	126
Wagon, Fire	Animal-Powered Vehicles	425
Wagon, Hay	Animal-Powered Vehicles	425
Wagon, Hook and Ladder	Animal-Powered Vehicles	425
Wagon, Hose	Animal-Powered Vehicles	425
Wagon, Ice	Animal-Powered Vehicles	425
Wagon, Log	Animal-Powered Vehicles	425
Wagon, Market	Animal-Powered Vehicles	425
Wagon, Mortar	Animal-Powered Vehicles	425
Wagon, Mountain	Animal-Powered Vehicles	425
wagon, paddy (*use:* Wagon, Patrol)	Animal-Powered Vehicles	425
Wagon, Patrol	Animal-Powered Vehicles	425
Wagon, Peddler's	Animal-Powered Vehicles	425
Wagon, Sheep	Animal-Powered Vehicles	425
Wagon, Station	Motor Vehicles	428
wagon, tea (*use:* Cart, Tea)	Support Furniture	56
Wagon, Thoroughbrace	Animal-Powered Vehicles	425
wagon, tractor-drawn (*use:* Trailer, Farm)	Motor Vehicles	429
Wagon, Tray	Animal-Powered Vehicles	425
Wainscoting	Surface Elements	18
waist (*use:* Bodice)	Main Garments	95
Waist, Corset	Underwear	104
Waistband	Clothing Accessories	87
Waistcoat	Main Garments	99
Walk, Widow's	Roof Elements	14
Walker	Personal Assistive Objects	109
Walker, Baby	Personal Assistive Objects	109
Walker, Invalid	Personal Assistive Objects	109
Walkie-Talkie	Telecommunication Devices	397
Wall	Supporting Elements	17
Wall, Boundary	Site Features	20
Wall, Climbing	Recreational Devices	510
Wall, Defensive	Defense Structures	31
Wall, Modular	Other Furniture	58
wall, partition (*use:* Partition)	Barrier Elements	2
Wallet	Personal Carrying & Storage Gear	112
Wallpaper	Surface Elements	18
Wampum	Exchange Media	487
Wanagan	Other Structures	41
Wand, Bubble	Toys	523

Wand, Hair Removal | Hair Care Objects | 119
Wand, Magic | Public Entertainment Devices | 508
Wardrobe | Storage & Display Furniture | 54
Warehouse | Commercial Structures | 28
Warmer, Bed | Other Household Accessories | 67
Warmer, Beverage | Food Preparation Equipment | 163
Warmer, Body | Personal Assistive Objects | 109
Warmer, Bottle | Food Preparation Equipment | 163
Warmer, Brandy | Food Preparation Equipment | 163
Warmer, Egg | Serving Vessels | 189
Warmer, Electric Plate | Food Preparation Accessories | 152
Warmer, Food | Food Preparation Equipment | 163
Warmer, Foot | Personal Assistive Objects | 109
Warmer, Frame | Medical Accessories | 326
warmer, gravy (*use:* Argyle) | Serving Vessels | 186
Warmer, Hand | Personal Assistive Objects | 109
Warmer, Knee | Footwear | 89
Warmer, Leg | Footwear | 90
Warmer, Plate | Food Preparation Accessories | 152
Warmer, Spoon | Food Preparation Accessories | 152
Warrant | Government Records | 470
Warrant, Dividend | Exchange Media | 489
Warranty | Legal Documents | 476
Warship | Watercraft | 447
Wash, Eye | Medical Instruments | 329
Washbasin | Hygiene Objects | 121
Washboard | Laundry Equipment | 314
washboiler (*use:* Boiler, Laundry) | Laundry Equipment | 313
washbowl (*use:* Washbasin) | Hygiene Objects | 121
Washcloth | Hygiene Objects | 121
Washer | Multiple Use T&E for Materials | 227
Washer, Brush | Painting T&E | 231
Washer, Clothes | Laundry Equipment | 314
Washer, Dry | Mining & Mineral Harvesting T&E | 224
Washer, Egg | Food Processing Equipment | 167
Washer, Film | Photoprocessing Equipment | 381
Washer, Glassware | Labware | 294
Washer, Grain | Food Processing Equipment | 169
Washer, Milk Bottle | Food Processing Equipment | 167
Washer, Milk Can | Food Processing Equipment | 167
Washer, Ore | Mining & Mineral Harvesting T&E | 224
Washer, Power | Housekeeping Equipment | 312
washer, pressure (*use:* Washer, Power) | Housekeeping Equipment | 312
Washer, Print | Photoprocessing Equipment | 381
Washer, Salad | Food Preparation Equipment | 163
Washer, Wheat | Food Processing Equipment | 169
Washfountain | Plumbing & Drainage Elements | 12
Washhouse | Outbuildings | 38
Wash-Pounder | Laundry Equipment | 314
Washstand | Support Furniture | 55
Washtub | Laundry Equipment | 314
Wastebasket | Housekeeping Equipment | 312
Watch | Timekeeping T&E | 356
Watch, Calendar | Timekeeping T&E | 356
Watch, Clock | Timekeeping T&E | 356
Watch, Digital | Timekeeping T&E | 356
Watch, Electronic | Timekeeping T&E | 356
Watch, Mechanical | Timekeeping T&E | 356
Watch, Pendant | Timekeeping T&E | 356
Watch, Pocket | Timekeeping T&E | 356
Watch, Quartz | Timekeeping T&E | 356
Watch, Self-Winding | Timekeeping T&E | 356
Watchclock | Timekeeping T&E | 355
Watchtower | Other Structures | 41
Watercraft, Subsurface | Watercraft | 448
Waterer, Animal | Animal Care Equipment | 137
Waterer, Livestock | Animal Care Equipment | 137
Waterer, Poultry | Animal Care Equipment | 137
Waterspout | Plumbing & Drainage Elements | 13
Waterwheel | Power Producing Equipment | 304
Waterwheel, Breast | Power Producing Equipment | 304
Waterwheel, Overshot | Power Producing Equipment | 304
Waterwheel, Tub | Power Producing Equipment | 304
Waterwheel, Undershot | Power Producing Equipment | 304
Wattle | Construction Materials | 4
Wattmeter | Electrical & Magnetic Measurement Devices | 298
Wavemeter | Electrical & Magnetic Measurement Devices | 298
Wax, Dental | Dental Accessories | 321
Wax, Lithographic | Printing Accessories | 386
Wax, Sealing | Writing Accessories | 405
Wax, Shoe | Clothing Care Objects | 106
Wax, Ski | Sports Equipment | 517
Waxer, Iron | Laundry Equipment | 314
way (*use:* Slipway) | Transportation Structures | 40
Waybill | Administrative Records | 467
waywiser (*use:* Wheel, Surveyor's) | Surveying Equipment | 353
Weaner, Calf | Animal Care Equipment | 135

weapon, automatic (*use:* Gun, Machine)	Firearms	280
weapon, automatic (*use:* Gun, Submachine)	Firearms	280
Weapon, Ax	Edged Weapons	279
weatherstrip (*use:* Strip, Weather)	Door & Window Elements	7
Weathervane	Meteorological T&E	339
Wedge	Mechanical Devices	317
Wedge, Deflection	Mining & Mineral Harvesting T&E	225
Wedge, Dental	Dental Instruments	324
Wedge, Felling	Forestry T&E	191
wedge, mast (*use:* Chock, Mast)	Water Transportation Accessories	439
Wedge, Splitting	Woodworking T&E	259
Weeder	Cultivation Equipment	125
Weeder, Flame	Cultivation Equipment	125
Weeder, Rod	Cultivation Equipment	125
Weeder, Spring-Tooth	Cultivation Equipment	125
Weight, Atlatl	Armament Accessories	272
Weight, Balance	Weights & Measures T&E	357
weight, barrel (*use:* Stabilizer, Armament)	Armament Accessories	272
Weight, Bat	Sports Equipment	513
Weight, Coin	Weights & Measures T&E	357
weight, counter (*use:* Counterweight, Sash)	Finish Hardware	11
Weight, Curtain	Window & Door Coverings	79
Weight, Door	Door & Window Elements	6
Weight, Exercise	Recreational Devices	510
Weight, Fishing	Fishing Equipment	147
Weight, Heaving Line	Water Transportation Accessories	441
Weight, Hitching	Land Transportation Accessories	422
Weight, Horn	Animal Care Equipment	135
weight, loom (*use:* Loomweight)	Textile Manufacturing Equipment	242
Weight, Loom	Textile Manufacturing Equipment	244
Weight, Net	Fishing Equipment	147
Weight, Rubber Dam	Dental Instruments	324
Weight, Safety Blow Off	Power Transmission Components	305
Weight, Skirt	Clothing Accessories	87
Weight, Toe	Farrier Equipment	140
Weight, Wheel	Land Transportation Accessories	422
Weight, Windmill	Power Transmission Components	305
Weightbelt	Recreational Devices	511
Weir	Fishing Equipment	148
welder, arc (*use:* Welder, Electric)	Metalworking T&E	219
Welder, Electric	Metalworking T&E	219
welder, gas (*use:* Torch, Gas)	Metalworking T&E	208
Well, Water	Hydraulic Structures	34
Wellhouse	Outbuildings	38
Wetsuit	Protective Wear	102
Whaleboat	Watercraft	445
Whaler	Watercraft	445
Whaler, Tancook	Watercraft	445
Whaleship	Watercraft	445
Wharf	Transportation Structures	39
whatnot (*use:* Étagère)	Storage & Display Furniture	54
Wheel	Mechanical Devices	317
Wheel of Fortune	Game Equipment	503
wheel of life (*use:* Zoetrope)	Toys	524
Wheel, Banding	Glass, Plastics & Clayworking T&E	195
Wheel, Bench	Glass, Plastics & Clayworking T&E	195
Wheel, Bicycle	Land Transportation Accessories	418
Wheel, Buffing	Other T&E for Materials	260
Wheel, Bull	Mechanical Devices	317
Wheel, Carriage	Land Transportation Accessories	418
Wheel, Caulking	Woodworking T&E	259
wheel, coggling (*use:* Wheel, Jagging)	Food Preparation Equipment	159
wheel, color (*use:* Chart, Color)	Graphic Documents	472
Wheel, Cutting	Glass, Plastics & Clayworking T&E	195
Wheel, Drafting	Drafting T&E	367
Wheel, Embossing	Leather, Horn & Shellworking T&E	202
Wheel, Ferris	Recreational Devices	511
Wheel, Finishing	Leather, Horn & Shellworking T&E	202
Wheel, Fish	Fishing Equipment	148
Wheel, Glassworking	Glass, Plastics & Clayworking T&E	195
wheel, godet (*use:* Wheel, Stretching)	Textile Manufacturing Equipment	244
Wheel, Grinding	Glass, Plastics & Clayworking T&E	195
Wheel, Hand	Textile Manufacturing Equipment	244
Wheel, Jagging	Food Preparation Equipment	159
Wheel, Jury	Organizational Objects	459
Wheel, Kick	Glass, Plastics & Clayworking T&E	195
Wheel, Lace	Textile Manufacturing Equipment	244
Wheel, Lapping	Glass, Plastics & Clayworking T&E	195

Wheel, Leatherworking — Leather, Horn & Shellworking T&E 201
Wheel, Log — Forestry T&E 191
Wheel, Medicine — Site Features 22
Wheel, Pelton — Power Producing Equipment 304
Wheel, Polishing — Glass, Plastics & Clayworking T&E 195
Wheel, Polishing/Sanding — Leather, Horn & Shellworking T&E 202
Wheel, Potter's — Glass, Plastics & Clayworking T&E 195
Wheel, Prayer — Religious Objects 465
Wheel, Pricking — Leather, Horn & Shellworking T&E 202
Wheel, Quilling — Textile Manufacturing Equipment 245
Wheel, Roulette — Game Equipment 503
Wheel, Savart — Acoustical T&E 262
Wheel, Scraped — Musical Instruments 373
Wheel, Ship's — Water Transportation Accessories 440
Wheel, Spinning — Textile Manufacturing Equipment 244
wheel, steering (*use:* Wheel, Vehicle Steering) — Land Transportation Accessories 418
wheel, steering (*use:* Wheel, Watercraft Steering) — Water Transportation Accessories 440
Wheel, Stretching — Textile Manufacturing Equipment 244
Wheel, Surveyor's — Surveying Equipment 353
wheel, tire-measuring (*use:* Traveler) — Metalworking T&E 218
Wheel, Tracing — Needleworking Equipment 236
Wheel, Vehicle — Land Transportation Accessories 418
Wheel, Vehicle Steering — Land Transportation Accessories 418
Wheel, Wagon — Land Transportation Accessories 418
Wheel, Watercraft Steering — Water Transportation Accessories 440
Wheel, Well — Site Features 22
Wheelbarrow — Human-Powered Vehicles 427
Wheelbox — Water Transportation Accessories 440
Wheelchair — Personal Assistive Objects 109
Wheelchair, Motorized — Personal Assistive Objects 109
Wherry — Watercraft 443
Wherry, Salmon — Watercraft 446
Whetstone — Metalworking T&E 216
Whimsey — Art 454
Whip — Regulative Devices 347
Whip, Animal — Animal Care Equipment 137
Whip, Buggy — Land Transportation Accessories 421
Whip, Coach — Land Transportation Accessories 421
Whip, Cream — Food Preparation Equipment 162
Whip, Curd — Food Processing Equipment 167
Whip, Driving — Land Transportation Accessories 421
whip, egg (*use:* Whisk) — Food Preparation Equipment 162
Whip, Musical — Musical Instruments 373
Whip, Riding — Land Transportation Accessories 421
Whip, Training — Animal Care Equipment 137
whippletree (*use:* Singletree) — Land Transportation Accessories 419
whipstock (*use:* Wedge, Deflection) — Mining & Mineral Harvesting T&E 225
Whirl — Recreational Devices 511
Whirligig — Toys 525
Whisk — Food Preparation Equipment 162
Whisky — Animal-Powered Vehicles 425
whist (*use:* Game, Card) — Game Equipment 504
Whistle — Sound Communication Devices 391
Whistle, Boat — Water Transportation Accessories 440
whistle, boatswain's (*use:* Pipe, Boatswain's) — Sound Communication Devices 391
Whistle, Calliope — Musical Accessories 369
Whistle, Factory — Sound Communication Devices 391
Whistle, Galton — Acoustical T&E 262
Whistle, Locomotive — Rail Transportation Accessories 431
Whistle, Musical — Musical Instruments 375
Whistle, Ship — Water Transportation Accessories 440
Whistle, Steam — Sound Communication Devices 391
Whistle, Toy — Toys 524
whistle, train (*use:* Whistle, Locomotive) — Rail Transportation Accessories 432
Whistle, Watercraft — Water Transportation Accessories 440
Whiteboard — Writing Media 408
Whitehall — Watercraft 443
Whorl, Spindle — Textile Manufacturing Equipment 244
Wick — Other Lighting Accessories 73
wick, pick (*use:* Pick, Wick) — Other Lighting Accessories 73
Wicket, Croquet — Game Equipment 502
Wickiup — Dwellings 33
widowmaker (*use:* Drill, Mining) — Mining & Mineral Harvesting T&E 222

Wig	Hair Adornments	83
Wig, Barrister's	Status Symbols	498
Wig, Bob	Hair Adornments	83
Wig, Tie	Hair Adornments	83
Wigwam	Dwellings	33
Will	Legal Documents	476
Wimple	Headwear	94
Winch	Mechanical Devices	315
Windbreak	Site Features	22
Windbreaker	Outerwear	101
Winder, Bobbin	Needleworking Equipment	238
Winder, Cone	Textile Manufacturing Equipment	245
Winder, Phonograph	Sound Communication Accessories	390
Winder, Spool	Needleworking Equipment	238
Winder, Spring	Metalworking T&E	219
Winder, Thread	Needleworking Equipment	238
Winder, Yarn	Textile Manufacturing Equipment	244
Windlass	Mechanical Devices	315
Windlass, Hand	Mechanical Devices	315
Windlass, Ship's	Water Transportation Accessories	440
Windmill	Power Producing Equipment	304
Window	Door & Window Elements	7
Window, Bay	Door & Window Elements	7
Window, Casement	Door & Window Elements	7
Window, Fixed	Door & Window Elements	7
Window, Leaded	Door & Window Elements	7
Window, Palladian	Door & Window Elements	7
Window, Screen	Door & Window Elements	7
Window, Sliding	Door & Window Elements	7
window, stained glass (*use:* Window, Leaded)	Door & Window Elements	7
Window, Storm	Door & Window Elements	7
Window, Watercraft	Water Transportation Accessories	440
Window, Wheel	Door & Window Elements	7
windowpane (*use:* Pane)	Door & Window Elements	7
Windrower	Harvesting Equipment	130
Windshield, Aircraft	Aerospace Transportation Accessories	410
Windshield, Vehicle	Land Transportation Accessories	418
Winery	Industrial Structures	35
Wineskin	Food Storage Equipment	172
Wing, Water	Recreational Devices	511
Winnower	Harvesting Equipment	131
wipe, wet (*use:* Towelette)	Hygiene Objects	121
Wiper, Pen	Writing Accessories	405
Wire, Aircraft	Aerospace Transportation Accessories	410
Wire, Antenna	Telecommunication Media	398
Wire, Antidrag	Aerospace Transportation Accessories	410
Wire, Antiflutter	Aerospace Transportation Accessories	410
Wire, Audio Recording	Sound Communication Media	393
Wire, Baling	Harvesting Equipment	131
Wire, Barbed	Barrier Elements	2
Wire, Barrier	Barrier Elements	2
Wire, Electric	Electrical System Components	302
Wire, Fairing	Aerospace Transportation Accessories	410
wire, guy (*use:* Guy)	Multiple Use T&E for Materials	226
Wire, High	Public Entertainment Devices	508
Wire, Orthodontic	Dental Instruments	322
Wire, Priming	Armament Accessories	272
Wire, Stagger	Aerospace Transportation Accessories	410
Wire, Telecommunication	Telecommunication Media	398
Wire, Telegraph	Telecommunication Media	398
Wire, Telephone	Telecommunication Media	398
Wok	Cooking Vessels	151
Wood, Kindling	Firemaking Equipment	74
Woodbin	Heating Equipment Accessories	77
Woodblock	Musical Instruments	373
Woodcut	Graphic Documents	474
Woodshed	Outbuildings	38
Work, Cut Paper	Art	455
workbasket (*use:* Basket, Needlework)	Needleworking Equipment	234
Workbench	Support Furniture	57
Workbook	Instructional Documents	475
workbox (*use:* Box, Needlework)	Needleworking Equipment	234
Worker, Butter	Food Processing Equipment	167
Worksheet	Instructional Documents	475
Workshop	Industrial Structures	36
Workshop, Home	Outbuildings	38
Worm	Armament Accessories	272
Worm, Spiral	Mining & Mineral Harvesting T&E	225
Wrap, Food	Food Preparation Equipment	163
Wrap, Gift	Party Accessories	460
wrap, plastic (*use:* Wrap, Food)	Food Preparation Equipment	163
wrap, tree (*use:* Protector, Tree Trunk)	Groundskeeping Equipment	309
Wrapper	Containers	415
wrapper (*use:* Peignoir)	Dressingwear & Nightwear	88
Wreath, Floral	Art	454
Wreath, Hair	Headwear	94
Wreath, Hairwork	Memorabilia	479
Wreath, Holiday	Holiday Objects	458
Wreath, Wedding	Wedding Objects	466

Term	Category	Page
Wrecker	Motor Vehicles	430
Wrench	Metalworking T&E	219
wrench, adjustable-end (*use:* Wrench, Crescent)	Metalworking T&E	219
Wrench, Allen	Metalworking T&E	219
Wrench, Alligator	Metalworking T&E	219
Wrench, Armament	Armament Accessories	272
Wrench, Axle Cap	Metalworking T&E	219
wrench, bed (*use:* Bedkey)	Other Household Accessories	66
Wrench, Box	Metalworking T&E	219
Wrench, Box-End	Metalworking T&E	219
Wrench, Breeching	Armament Accessories	273
Wrench, Calk	Farrier Equipment	140
Wrench, Carriage Nut	Metalworking T&E	219
Wrench, Closed End	Metalworking T&E	219
Wrench, Cock	Armament Accessories	273
Wrench, Cock and Hammer	Armament Accessories	273
Wrench, Combination	Metalworking T&E	219
Wrench, Crescent	Metalworking T&E	219
Wrench, Fire Plug	Protective Devices	345
Wrench, Front Sight	Armament Accessories	273
Wrench, Fuze	Armament Accessories	273
Wrench, Gun Carriage	Armament Accessories	273
Wrench, Impact	Metalworking T&E	219
Wrench, Jar	Food Processing Equipment	165
Wrench, Key	Metalworking T&E	219
Wrench, Locomotive	Rail Transportation Accessories	432
Wrench, Lug	Land Transportation Accessories	422
Wrench, Monkey	Metalworking T&E	219
Wrench, Muzzle	Armament Accessories	273
Wrench, Nipple	Armament Accessories	273
Wrench, Open-End	Metalworking T&E	219
Wrench, Pin	Armament Accessories	273
Wrench, Pipe	Metalworking T&E	219
wrench, rope bed (*use:* Bedkey)	Other Household Accessories	66
Wrench, Saw	Metalworking T&E	219
Wrench, Socket	Metalworking T&E	219
Wrench, Spud	Metalworking T&E	219
Wrench, Sucker Rod	Mining & Mineral Harvesting T&E	225
Wrench, T	Metalworking T&E	219
Wrench, Tap	Metalworking T&E	219
Wrench, Torque	Metalworking T&E	219
Wrench, Track	Rail Transportation Accessories	432
Wrench, Wagon	Land Transportation Accessories	422
Wrest, Saw	Metalworking T&E	216
Wringer, Clothes	Laundry Equipment	314
Wringer, Leather	Leather, Horn & Shellworking T&E	202
Wringer, Mop	Housekeeping Equipment	312
Wristband, Admission	Exchange Media	490
Wristlet	Clothing Accessories	87
Wristwatch	Timekeeping T&E	356
Writ	Government Records	470
x-ray (*use:* Radiogram)	Graphic Documents	473
Xylophone	Musical Instruments	373
Yacht	Watercraft	444
Yad	Religious Objects	465
Yard	Water Transportation Accessories	440
Yardstick	Weights & Measures T&E	358
Yarmulke	Belief Symbols	494
Yarn	Textile Manufacturing Equipment	245
Yashmak	Headwear	94
yatate (*use:* Set, Scribe)	Writing Devices	406
Yawl	Watercraft	443
Yawlboat	Watercraft	448
Yearbook	Other Documents	486
Yoke, Animal	Land Transportation Accessories	421
Yoke, Clothing	Clothing Accessories	87
Yoke, Flight	Aerospace Transportation Accessories	410
Yoke, Head	Land Transportation Accessories	421
Yoke, Human	Land Transportation Accessories	422
Yoke, Neck	Land Transportation Accessories	421
Yoke, Withers	Land Transportation Accessories	421
Yo-Yo	Toys	525
Yuloh	Water Transportation Accessories	441
Zapper, Bug	Other Household Accessories	66
Zax	Masonry & Stoneworking T&E	204
Zenometer	Navigational Equipment	351
Zipper	Needleworking Equipment	236
Zischagge	Body Armor	275
Zither	Musical Instruments	374
Zoetrope	Toys	524
Zoo, Toy	Toys	522
Zoopraxinoscope	Toys	524
Zuccheto	Status Symbols	500
Zymosismeter	Food Processing Equipment	164